SOUTH CAROLINA

A Guide to the Palmetto State

SOUTH CAROLINA

A GUIDE TO THE PALMETTO STATE

*Compiled by Workers of the Writers' Program
of the Work Projects Administration
in the State of South Carolina*

AMERICAN GUIDE SERIES

ILLUSTRATED

Sponsored by Burnet R. Maybank, Governor of South Carolina

OXFORD UNIVERSITY PRESS · NEW YORK

SOUTH CAROLINA STATE DEPARTMENT OF EDUCATION

State-wide Sponsor of the
South Carolina Writers' Project

FEDERAL WORKS AGENCY

JOHN M. CARMODY, *Administrator*

WORK PROJECTS ADMINISTRATION

HOWARD O. HUNTER, *Acting Commissioner*
FLORENCE KERR, *Assistant Commissioner*
L. M. PINCKNEY, *State Administrator*

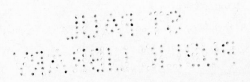

STATE OF SOUTH CAROLINA
OFFICE OF THE GOVERNOR
COLUMBIA

BURNET R. MAYBANK
GOVERNOR

THE SOUTH CAROLINA GUIDE presents a comprehensive view of the state for the first time in its long and stirring history. Herein are delineated the livelihoods, natural resources, customs, art, and history of the people from the Low Country plantations to the Indian block houses of the Up Country, from Fort Sumter to King's Mountain. Much of the information will be read for the first time by South Carolinians; and it is for them, as well as for our many visitors, that the Guide has been written. I believe the book will add to the interpretation of a singularly individual state.

Burnet R Maybank

GOVERNOR

Preface

IN preparing, *South Carolina, A Guide to the Palmetto State,* we hoped to present the subject as a well-rounded whole for two groups of people: South Carolinians who want to know more of their State and others who want to know the whys and wherefores about us. The task has been tremendous, because so many interesting facts have been discovered; and condensation has not been the least of our labors. There was the disagreement of historians as to fact, and the argument between fact and fancy. Yet, on the whole, the work has been fascinating and most informative. To get the scent of a good story and trail it for months in and out of libraries, old newspaper files, private papers, and finally to catch it by the tail has been an adventure multiplied hundreds of times.

'South Carolina is the least written about and the least understood of all the States that have played an important part in our history,' asserted a Northern historian. Through this Guide, we hope to allay some of this criticism, though we realize how briefly one small volume can cover the 400 years of activity and development. We hope the book is balanced—not too much of solemn fact, not too much of obvious tradition, not too much description, not too many dates.

Besides the members of our project, many persons whose love of South Carolina prompted them to give of their time and learning have helped toward the completion of our Guide.

Co-operation of numerous organizations has also encouraged our work and we express our thanks to Federal and State departments, civic bodies, libraries, chambers of commerce, patriotic clubs, and newspapers. Without such outside aid we should have had little confidence in our success. Grateful acknowledgment is extended to all who had a part in supplying information. In the Appendices is a list of the many specialists who assisted, and also a list of the 1940 census figures.

MABEL MONTGOMERY, *State Supervisor*
LOUISE J. DUBOSE, *Assistant State Supervisor*
SOUTH CAROLINA WRITERS' PROJECT

Contents

Part I. Past and Present

Part II. Cities and Towns

Part III. Tours

Part IV. Appendices

Illustrations

ALONG THE ROADSIDE   *Between* 436 *and* 437

All photographs credited to W. Lincoln Highton
are by courtesy of the Federal Works Agency.

Maps

General Information

Railroads: Atlantic Coast Line R.R. (ACL), Seaboard Air Line Ry. (SAL), Southern Ry. Other lines: Augusta Northern Ry., Bennettsville and Cheraw R.R. (B&C), Blue Ridge Ry., Buffalo, Union-Carolina R.R., Chesterfield & Lancaster R.R. (C&L), Carolina & Northwestern Ry., Charleston & Western Carolina Ry. (C&WC), Columbia, Newberry & Laurens R.R. (CN&L), Due West Ry., Georgia & Florida R.R., Lancaster and Chester Ry., Piedmont and Northern Ry. (electric) (P&N), Raleigh & Charleston R.R., Rockingham R.R., Ware Shoals R.R.

Bus Lines: (Interstate) Atlantic Greyhound Lines, Queen City Coach Co., Smoky Mountain Stages, Southeastern States, Greensboro-Fayetteville Bus Line, Carolina Scenic Coach Lines, Pan-American Bus Lines. (Intrastate) Carolina Motor Bus Lines, Welborn Bus Lines, Red Top Bus Lines, Eagle Bus Line, Carolina Stages.

Air Lines: Delta Airlines, daily, Charleston to Columbia to Augusta, Ga.; Eastern Airlines, daily, 2 routes: New York to New Orleans with stop at Spartanburg; New York to Miami with stop at Charleston, where connection is made with Delta Airlines. Rates and schedules in line with those in effect throughout the country. Charter service for sightseeing or travel is available at Charleston, Columbia, Spartanburg, Greenville, and Anderson.

Highways: 18 Federal highways, with connections for every part of the U.S., enter South Carolina and connect with the State highway system, which supervises 6,411 miles of hard-surfaced roads. Through routes in all directions paved. State highway patrol. Water and gasoline available in every locality. Gasoline tax, 6¢. (*For highway routes see State map.*)

Motor Vehicle Laws (*digest*): Maximum speed for passenger cars on open road, 55 m.p.h.; in populous districts, near schools, etc., 20 m.p.h.; in urban centers (except where otherwise specified by signs), residential sections, 35 m.p.h.; business sections, 25 m.p.h. No South Carolina driver's license required of nonresidents. Visitors allowed full reciprocity for 90 days, except when engaged in business or seeking employment. Minimum age limit for drivers, 14 years. Spotlights must be extinguished within 200 yds. of an approaching vehicle. Trailers must carry tail light and not exceed 8 ft. in width. Come to a full stop before passing a school bus either taking on or discharging school children. Accidents entailing injury or damage of $50 or more must be reported to State Highway Department on blanks obtainable from any patrolman, or at any filling station, city hall, police department, town hall, or courthouse. *Prohibited:* Passing on hills or curves, reckless driving, driving while under the influence of intoxicants, and blocking highways; parking so that less than 16 ft. of the highway is clear; parking without lights after dark.

Climate: Summer begins about the last of May and lasts until the middle of September. Travelers should be prepared for extremely warm weather. 90° to 100° temperatures are frequent. Fall and spring temperatures cool enough to be zestful. Winters short and mild; snow and ice the exception rather than the rule. Topcoats a necessity in winter.

Recreational Areas: Principal summer resorts at Myrtle Beach (*see Tour* 1), Charleston, Beaufort, Mountain Ranger District (*see Tour* 15), Caesars Head (*see Tour* 10); winter resorts at Camden, Aiken, Beaufort, and Summerville (*see Tour* 1). 15 State parks: Aiken, Barnwell near Blackville, Cheraw, Chester, Edisto Beach, Givhans Ferry near Summerville, Greenwood, Hunting Island off coast of St. Helena Island, Lee near Bishopville, Myrtle Beach, Oconee near Walhalla, Paris Mountain near Greenville, Poinsett near Sumter, Sesqui-Centennial near Columbia, Table Rock near Pickens; small wayside parks near Aiken, Camden, Georgetown, Greenville, Greenwood, and Walterboro. Kings Mountain Demonstration Area is north of York.

Game Laws: Nonresident hunting license $15.25, nonresident fishing license $5.25. Domestic game birds: blackbird, pheasant (grouse), dove, partridge (quail), wild turkey, wild duck, and wild goose. Destructive birds: buzzard, crow, Cooper's hawk, English sparrow, great horned owl, blue jay, loggerhead, and sharpshinned hawk. Game animals: deer, fox, mink, muskrat, opossum, otter, rabbit, raccoon, skunk, and squirrel. Game fish: jackfish or pickerel, pike, black bass, striped bass or rockfish, warmouth bass, red-belly bream, copper-faced or ball-faced bream, yellow-belly perch, sun perch, red-fin trout, flyer, crappie, rock bass, and white perch. Open season for domestic game birds and animals: Thanksgiving Day to March 1, inclusive, except that deer (buck only) may be hunted from Aug. 15 to Jan. 1, and raccoons and opossums may be hunted from Sept. 1 to March 1. Trapping, snaring, and baiting game prohibited. Birds or animals classed as destructive may be killed at any time in any way. Bag limit: wild turkey (gobblers only), 2 per day and a total of 20 per season to the hunter; deer (bucks only), 5 per season to the hunter. Fishing: Taking or catching game fish in any clear-water stream shall be only with rod and line with single bait or by casting with not more than one lure. This does not apply to fishing with ordinary cane or pole. Poison and dynamite prohibited. Gill nets and traps prohibited in some areas. The above are extracts from general State game laws, but there are exceptions and variations in every county.

Alcoholic Liquor Tax: Whisky and strong wines sold (*in packages only*) from sunrise to sunset by liquor stores licensed by the State; except on Sundays, holidays, and election days. Beer and wine sold under State license, at hotels, cafés, soda fountains, and grocery stores.

Trespassing: State laws cover trespassing in general. Few landowners object to the picking of wild flowers, but permission should be asked to cut trees or build fires on private property. A State law forbids picking, or 'gathering,' wild flowers, cultivated flowers, or shrubbery, without consent of landowners, and the penalty provided is a fine of not more than $20, or imprisonment of not more than 30 days. Today this prohibition is meant especially to preserve the springtime beauty of the State parks, most of which are conspicuously posted.

Luxury Tax: A tax of 1¢ on each 5¢, paid by customer, is levied on soft drinks and tobaccos.

Poisonous Plants, Reptiles, and Insects: Poison ivy (with its variant form, poison oak) and poison sumac are common in wooded areas. An attempt has been made to clear these plants from trails, bridle paths, and recreational areas in State parks. Poisonous snakes are rare except in thick woods and swamps, where rattlesnakes, copperheads, and water moccasins are sometimes found. There are no dangerous animals, and few insects more menacing than ordinary bees and wasps. The black widow spider is rare. First aid stations for snake bite and other accidents are maintained at most of the State parks. Tents and cabins should be screened against mosquitoes, especially during August and September.

Water: Health authorities regularly check the supplies of every corporate city, town, and village in the State, and are quick to post or cut off any polluted sources. Tests are made by State health officials quarterly, monthly, or daily, according to the size of the community. County inspectors visit rural districts and roadside tourist camps. As an added precaution, tourists are warned not to drink from open streams or pools, either running or still, nor from any well other than artesian (continuously flowing—no pump).

Accommodations: Comfortable accommodations are available the year round in hotels of the larger towns and cities. Along the coast and in the mountains are resort hotels, cottages, camps, and tourist homes, and in Camden, Aiken, Beaufort, and Summerville are excellent accommodations during the winter season. The tourist homes usually provide overnight lodging for $1 per person, and arrangements can sometimes be made for meals. Tourist camps are located on all principal highways near large towns, and specific information can be obtained from the local chamber of commerce. Inspection by health authorities is fairly well carried out. Local accommodations are noted on tours; localities in which no suitable lodgings exist are indicated.

General Service for Tourists: For additional information write to State Highway Department, State game warden, or any of the State departments at Columbia, or to chambers of commerce in the larger towns.

Calendar of Events

JANUARY

Second Tuesday	Columbia	Legislature Convenes
Throughout month	Charleston	Gardens
No fixed date	Aiken Camden	Drag Hunts, twice weekly throughout month
No fixed date	Aiken Camden	Polo Games, three times weekly through March
No fixed date	Charleston	St. Cecilia Ball
No fixed date	Sumter (Cane Savannah)	Field Trials
No fixed date	Columbia	Assembly Ball

FEBRUARY

First	Georgetown	Gardens
Twenty-second	Cameron (Golden Kernel Plantation)	Tilting Tournament
Third week	Camden	Washington Cup Races
Throughout month	Charleston	Gardens
No fixed date	Aiken Camden	Fox and Drag Hunts, twice weekly through March

MARCH

First	Charleston	Runnymede Gardens open for season
Throughout month	Charleston Georgetown	Gardens
No fixed date	Clinton	Inter-Collegiate Track Meet at Presbyterian College
No fixed date	Columbia	High School Week at University of South Carolina

APRIL

First week	Columbia	Columbia Music Festival
Last week	Columbia	Columbia Flower Show
Throughout month	Charleston Georgetown	Gardens
Thirtieth	Olar	Rivers Bridge Memorial Exercises
No fixed date	Greenville	Southern Textile Exposition (biennially—every even year)
No fixed date	Charleston	Azalea Festival
No fixed date	Columbia	Sailboat Regatta (Lake Murray)
No fixed date	Aiken Greenville Spartanburg	Garden Pilgrimages
No fixed date	Beaufort Charleston Mount Pleasant	Gardens

MAY

First week	Charleston	Schutzenfest (Shooting Festival)
Throughout month	Charleston	Gardens
No fixed date	Georgetown Sumter	Gardens
No fixed date	Charleston	Outdoor Art Exhibit

JUNE

First week	State Parks	Season Opens (closes Labor Day)
Third week	Greenville	Tennis Tournament
Fourth week	Spartanburg	Tennis Tournament
No fixed date	Columbia (Lake Murray) Beaufort Mt. Pleasant	Sailboat Regattas

JULY

Fourth	Trenton	Drill Day at Bettis Academy (Negro)
First week	Charleston	Tennis Tournament
Last week	Darlington	South Carolina Open Tennis Tournament
No fixed date	Columbia (Lake Murray) Charleston	Motorboat Regattas
No fixed date	Beaufort Columbia (Lake Murray) Charleston Mt. Pleasant	Sailboat Regattas
No fixed date	Columbia	Soap-box Derby for State Championship

AUGUST

First Tuesday	Rockville	Sailboat Regatta
First week	Mullins	Tobacco Festival
Second week	Greenville	South Carolina Singing Convention
Last week	Winnsboro (Camp Welfare)	Camp Meeting (Negro)
No fixed date	Hartsville	Carolinas' Closed Tennis Tournament
No fixed date	Columbia	City Tennis Tournament
No fixed date	Held in defending city	McIver Cup Matches (Tennis)
No fixed date	Columbia	Maharajon of Syrian-Lebanon-American Society
No fixed date	Charleston Beaufort Mt. Pleasant	Sailboat Regattas
No fixed date	Conway	Farmers Day

SEPTEMBER

Last week	St. George (Indian Fields)	Camp Meeting
No fixed date	Camden	Cotton Festival

OCTOBER

First Sunday	Columbia	River Baptism, House of Prayer (Negro)
Third week	Columbia	State Fair
Fourth week	Columbia	Palmetto State Fair (Negro)
Thursday of Fair Week	Columbia	Football game between Clemson College and the University of South Carolina
No fixed date	County Seats	County and district fairs

NOVEMBER

Day before Thanksgiving	Charleston	Cypress Gardens Open for Season
No fixed date	Columbia	Columbia-Ridgewood Open Golf Tournament

DECEMBER

Last week	Orangeburg (Rocks Plantation)	Tilting Tournament
Last week	Orangeburg (Belvidere Plantation)	Tilting Tournament
Throughout month	Charleston	Gardens

SEASONAL
(Spring)

Second Sunday after Easter	Beaufort County	Services at Sheldon Church Ruins
No fixed date	Aiken Camden	Steeplechases and Horse Shows
No fixed date	Spartanburg	Children's Chorus Concert

No fixed date	Berkeley County	Services at Strawberry Chapel
No fixed date	Columbia	Columbia Kennel Club Dog Show
No fixed date	Columbia	State Library Association
No fixed date	Charleston County	Services at Pre-Revolutionary Goose Creek Church

(Summer)

No fixed date	Spartanburg	Mid-Dixie Tennis Tournament
No fixed date	Jolly Street	Political Rally
No fixed date	Clinton	Junior Davis Cup Match (Tennis)

(Fall)

| No fixed date | Beaufort | St. Helena Island Fair (Negro) |
| No fixed date | Columbia | Flower Show |

PART I
Past and Present

Who Is the South Carolinian?

ONE has to live in South Carolina to realize the differences that, seen from the outside, become subordinated to one or two great common attributes. South Carolinians are among the rare folk in the South who have no secret envy of Virginians. They have a love for their own State which is a phalanx against all attacks of whatever order.

The average South Carolinian—assuming there is one—would not be found among the intellectuals throughout the State, nor in the larger group of comparatively uneducated adults, likewise scattered from the mountains to the sea; he would be between these two groups, and somewhat nearer the second. He is primarily a South Carolinian, and it took the World War to bring the realization that he is also a citizen of the United States.

The South Carolinian is a product of many conflicts, as well as of great unifying forces. Incongruities and contrasts abound in his environment. With some of the most beautiful gardens in the world, the State has some of the most deplorable slums; with flourishing estates owned by outside sportsmen, there are rows of dilapidated cabins where whites or Negroes live on the barest subsistence level; with great natural resources, the State has one of the lowest per capita ratings of wealth in the United States; with a variety of pleasure resorts from mountains to seacoast, there is almost a total lack of recreational facilities in the rural areas; with some of the best farm lands in the world, there are hundreds of thousands of acres so depleted that they are unfit for agriculture; with a record of some of the earliest efforts in the country for public education, both white and Negro, the State had in 1930 the highest illiteracy rate in the Nation.

Secondarily, the South Carolinian is a Low Countryman or an Up Countryman, with the native of the mid-section having characteristics of both. This classification occurs within the State and outsiders are probably unaware of it. To a certain extent the same principles that produced the Roundhead-Cavalier antagonism in England persist even now in South Carolina. In the Low Country the South Carolinian has one sort of personality, in the Up Country another, and in the middle of the State he becomes a somewhat unamalgamated combination of both. Such is the case, regardless of class or color or creed.

The Low Country inhabitant recalls his past glory with a pride that surpasses his ability to appreciate thoroughly the good things of the present. He may live in Charleston, a city that competes with the New Jerusalem in his dreams; or he may live in a drafty Georgian country house with a three-tiered piazza, hidden behind live oaks and magnolias that drip curtains of gray moss above blazing azaleas, wisteria, and camellia japonicas; or he may live in a cabin near a swamp infested by swarms of malaria-bearing mosquitoes, and look out with dull eyes over acres he must till for an absentee landlord. But wherever he is, his attitude is keyed to leisure, he thinks in terms of ease, and has a philosophical contempt for long ordered hours of daily work, week in and week out. The possession or nonpossession of material wealth is secondary to his ideas of personal value.

In this country where natural growth borders on the semitropical, and midday heat in summer is prostrating except where sea breezes creep in under the thick foliage of live oak and myrtle or between the tall trunks of longleaf pine, there seems to be no hard grinding necessity for thinking too much about money in the bank, fine clothes, and weather-tight houses. The outdoors is too free, fishing is too good, and crops grow with only part of a year's work.

The Low Countryman's social life, his habits of speech and dress, are all an outgrowth of his decades of association with the geography and history of his section. Camp meetings, surviving from ancient itinerant Methodism, and tournaments smacking of ante-bellum grandeur, are occasions for religion, sport, and social converse. The St. Cecilia balls, rigidly restricted, still attempt to preserve the old attitude of Charleston society when tradesmen were scorned and members of the upper class acted as lords and barons.

The Low Countryman speaks in a special intonation, softens his 'r's,' and slurs his words, which may be slowly drawled or fired with startling rapidity—especially the latter, if he lives in Charleston. On the sea islands, his speech changes; he will talk Gullah if he is a Negro, and if he is white there will be evidences of this unique dialect in his conversation.

From long living according to the standards of *Dieu et mon droit*, he has evolved ideas about right and wrong which do not always coincide with the law, and, during the months when cotton growing does not consume all his energies, he has time to think of his difficulties and act upon them. Nor is he unaware of the many 'spells' and 'conjures' that operate contrary to written statute. And besides all this, the Low Countryman cannot forget his leadership before the War between the States (or the Confederate War, as it is also called). Though his diet may be skimpy, his clothes old and worn, his schooling negligible, he walks with head high among the big houses, graceful churches, and tumbledown forts, with more than a bit of scorn for those whose forebears came to the State 50 or 100 years after his.

Strangely, for many years he seemed to have forgotten the pioneering spirit that established the society of his forefathers, the experimentation with crops of indigo, rice, and sea-island cotton, with tea, oranges, olives, and silkworm. But lately he has become interested in truck growing and in tobacco, in the gathering and canning of shellfish for commercial purposes, and in the conservation of his pine trees for the manufacture of pulp paper.

The Low Countryman himself, however, will not change. He will still have his afternoon nap, eat his rice, revere his ancestors, go hunting and fishing in season, and take time out from his labors to entertain his friends and guests with courtesy, ease, and graceful hospitality.

The Up Country South Carolinian, on the other hand, while possessing many qualities of the Low Countryman, will exhibit more physical energy and a greater desire to accumulate a bank account. His forebears were largely Scotch-Irish or German, who in the Old World had to struggle for existence and in the New World chose an isolated inland region. He has worked his own small farm for generations, and the few slaves he once had were of scant economic significance. For a while, he almost reached a stage of affluence; but his land was being depleted, and the price of cotton was dropping low.

Fortunately for him, the water power of the streams in the Up Country was discovered and utilized. Enterprising businessmen came in and established cotton mills, built towns around them, with schools, churches, banks, stores, and hospitals. Into the mills came the Up Country farmer who was barely making a living, and out of the mountains came the barefoot man and sunbonneted woman, to take charge of spindles and looms. The thrift and industry of the Up Countryman stood him in good stead.

He, too, is proud of his past. He remembers the battles of Cowpens and Kings Mountain, when the British hold on the Carolinas was broken, and he remembers the Indian wars when he stood as buffer between the Cherokee and the coastal settlements. The vitality of the pioneer is still in his veins—but he isn't all energy. Depending too much on corn and hog meat, he is prone to fall into the apathy produced by pellagra; and though often persuaded to change his diet and partake of the yeast supplied by the State Board of Health, he still has a yearning for his customary monotonous fare.

Like the Low Countryman, he prefers his personal standards of right and wrong to those prescribed in the courts of law, and his own opinions are much more important to him than those of legally appointed judges. In some cases, he also believes in ghosts and witches.

For social life, the Up Countryman has cities to which he may go; but often he prefers his local schoolhouse entertainments, his corn shuckings, his graveyard cleanings (*see Tour* 10), and he is quite proud of his singing associations (*see Tour* 14). His speech has not the distinction of the Low Country in either content or idiom, but Elizabethan archaisms survive in the more remote places, where 'helped' becomes 'holp' or 'holpen.' The climate of his section is less enervating in summer, and there are no large swamps with attendant malaria to sap his ambition.

For many years there was almost war between Up Country and Low Country, and it became evident that in order to have a unified State there must be some co-ordinating or compromising influence. Up Countrymen in increasing numbers demanded political rights formerly possessed only by Low Countrymen. The capital was shifted from Charleston to Columbia, a State college was established in the new capital, and suffrage was extended to include the small farmers of the Up Country. Those were the years of the introduction of the cotton gin and the expansion of cotton growing. A prominent lawyer said of the factionalism: 'In 1804, sectional jealousies were sharpened to bitterness, and there was as little unity of feeling between the upper and lower country as between any rival States of the Union.'

The centralization of political and educational interests in the middle of the State lessened the tension, until its severity lost its sharpest edges. Predominant power has passed to the Up Country, but there is an absence of the trained and cultured leadership that existed when statesmen from the plantations handled the State's destiny.

So much for the Low Countryman and Up Countryman in South Carolina. The characteristic inhabitant of the mid-section partakes of both types. He may live in a nationally known tourist center or in Columbia, or he may be hidden in the Sand Hills, where scrub oak and scrawny pines flourish, and where life has been at a low ebb for generations. He may be one of the enterprising orchardists who insist that this long stretch of desert must blossom, who set out fruit trees and vines with confidence that they will bring back their cost several times over.

This mid-sectional inhabitant is the more recent in history, and he may claim either the Up Country or the Low Country for his native heath. It is likely that he will claim the latter, for in spite of the economic advance of the Up Country, he yearns to be able to live with the ease of manner, and the ability to enjoy life without strenuous effort, that he ascribes to the Low Countryman.

Among South Carolinians, these three types recognize one another; but when differences are minimized and similarities are stressed, a composite South Carolinian may emerge. He will be an individual full of contrasts and antagonisms, yet loyal to traditions of courtesy and personal dignity to an almost fanatical degree. There is a deal of kindliness about him, too. From one end of the State to the other, he feels favored when asked for personal assistance. A neighborly spirit, derived from years when everyone was poor, from living in small communities, and from a native love of hospitality, prompts him to render services with a scorn for remuneration.

The South Carolinian has fire in his head, comfort in his middle, and a little lead in his feet. Proud of his past, often scornful of innovations, he is not willing to adapt unless thoroughly convinced that it is a good thing. Not given to the desperate pursuit of wealth, he has time for pleasure and humorous converse. His way of life is leisurely, despite his slack economic habits; and though he progresses slowly, he performs his daily task to the accompaniment of a tune. He knows his faults, at least many of them. He will discuss them and propose remedies—but woe to the outsider who reminds him of them. The faults of his State are as personal to him as a wart on his nose.

Natural Setting

SOUTH CAROLINA is roughly a triangle covering 30,989 square miles, 494 of which consist of water area. From the northwest corner a jagged man-made line, running east and southeast for 333 miles to Little River Inlet, marks the boundary between the two Carolinas; the Savannah River, with its tributaries, the Tugaloo and the Chattooga, extending southeast from the same corner for 238 miles to Tybee Sound, separates the State from Georgia; while the Atlantic shore line stretches for approximately 190 miles, between Little River Inlet and Tybee Sound.

The Blue Ridge Mountains occupy an area of about 500 square miles in the northwestern part of the State. The highest point, Sassafras Mountain (alt., 3,548 ft.), is almost on the North Carolina boundary. The South Carolina mountains are not spectacular, but their broken outline, soft blue color, and sunny exposure give them peculiar charm. Outcroppings of granite are not uncommon, and at Table Rock (*see Tour* 15) and Caesar's Head (*see Tour* 10) are vertical cliffs of gneiss. From this mountainous border the land drops successively to the Piedmont Plateau, the Sand Hills, the Coastal Plain, and sea level, over a distance of about 235 miles. The mean altitude of the State in general is estimated at 350 feet.

The chief physical feature of South Carolina, though not the most picturesque, is the fall line, which roughly bisects the State along a diagonal between the North Carolina boundary in Chesterfield County and the Georgia boundary in Aiken County. It separates two regions commonly known as the Up Country and the Low Country—regions differing in custom, history, and livelihood. The main part of the Up Country is composed of the Piedmont Plateau, with its rolling hills, ragged woods, small farms, and newly developed industries. The soil of this region is red clay, originally covered with a thin but rich layer of forest-formed humus. Much of this top soil has been washed away, and the roads, cutting through clay banks, look as if carved from scarlet cheese. These clay lands will produce good crops of corn, cotton, and vegetables if the missing humus is supplied and conserved.

In the level Low Country lie alluvial regions and much swampland where, since the State's beginning, large plantations have depended chiefly on a single crop—first indigo, then rice, and later cotton. Tobacco has recently become of considerable importance in the Low Country, as well as truck or vegetable crops. The Sand Hills along the fall line constitute the least productive agricultural land in the State, although recently peaches and grapes have been found well adapted to this intermediate region.

South Carolina is drained by three main river systems: the Pee Dee in the northeast, the Santee in the central area, and the Savannah in the southwest. Tributaries of the Pee Dee are the Little Pee Dee, the Waccamaw, and Lynches; the Santee is formed by the confluence of the Wateree and the Congaree (the latter made up of the Broad and the Saluda); and the Savannah in its upper reaches is joined by the Tugaloo, the Chattooga, and the Seneca. The Edisto River in the southeast is independent of the three main systems. The swift flow of the streams in the Up Country has led most of the State's manufacturing plants to select sites in that section. Below the fall line, these red, mud-laden rivers become wide and comparatively clear, depositing their silt on the bottom. Stained black with tannic acid from cypress and other roots, they run slowly through flat rich soils to the Atlantic Ocean. Between Georgetown and the Savannah River, along more than two thirds of the coast line, is a border of sandy barrier islands; while north of Georgetown an arc of unbroken beach extends to the North Carolina boundary. There are no large inland lakes in the State, except those formed artificially by river dams.

In climate, South Carolina ranges from temperate in the northwest to semitropical in the southeast. The lowest annual mean temperature for any station in the State is that of Caesar's Head in Greenville County, 54.9°; the highest is that of Beaufort, being 67.3°. The State as a whole has an annual mean temperature of about 63°, with normal seasonal variations. Summers are long and hot, but not as enervating as is generally supposed. Nights are cool in the Up Country, and the heat is tempered by sea breezes near the coast. April, May, and October are the pleasantest months in the Up Country, and the winter season is mild and pleasant below the fall line. Rainfall is abundant and evenly distributed throughout the year. Growing seasons range from 186 days in the mountains to 284 days along the coast.

GEOLOGIC HISTORY

More than a billion years ago, in the Archaeozoic era, schistose rock of great but unknown thickness extended along what is now the Appalachian and Piedmont Plateau region of North America. The first great upheaval of this land mass, known as the Laurentian revolution, occurred toward the end of the era to produce Appalachia—a highland that separated the Atlantic Ocean from a shallow inland sea that covered the central part of the continent. The older rocks now found in the South Carolina Up Country—the gneisses, schists, slates, and quartzites—were formed by the metamorphism, through intense heat and pressure, of the early sedimentary rocks. Into these older formations granite, diorite, diabase, and some other igneous rocks have, at different times, been intruded. In Greenville and Spartanburg Counties are found lean iron ores of the Preterozoic era, which succeeded the Archaeozoic.

During the next era, the Paleozoic, the high mountains of Appalachia were being worn down. They were steep, rugged, and gaunt, like the newer ranges of the Rockies today. Flowering plants probably did not exist until near the end of the era, and vegetation consisted mainly of huge ferns and club mosses. Aquatic vertebrates and amphibia reached their greatest development during the Devonian and Carboniferous periods, when this region was entirely above the sea— hence fossils of those periods are not found in the State. The coal, iron, and petroleum deposits of the Paleozoic era do not occur in South Carolina, though they are found in Alabama and west of the Blue Ridge. Nor is the Permian period, last of the Paleozoic, represented in the Appalachian region south of West Virginia.

Between the Paleozoic and Mesozoic eras occurred the Appalachian revolution, the second great upheaval of this land mass. The fall line was the shore of the ocean in the Mesozoic era, and from that line to the present coast are marl, limestone, and other sedimentary deposits of this era. Successive additions to the coast line were formed by sedimentary material resulting from erosion in the highlands. After the deposition of the Cretaceous sediments the coastal plain was inundated by the sea a number of times, and mantles of clay, sand, and gravel laid down. Seven such terraces, with elevations from 25 to 270 feet, rise successively along the South Carolina coast. At Charleston these beds of clay, sand, and limestone overlie the crystalline rocks to a depth of more than half a mile, but they thin out to nothing at the fall line. The South Carolina Up Country is of very ancient formation, and the Low Country comparatively recent—with little record left of the ages in between. Phosphate beds near Charleston have yielded many sharks' teeth, vertebrae of mammoths, and other fossils; and similar remains have been found around Eutawville and in the swamps of the Pee Dee near Florence. Practically no fossils have been discovered above the fall line—heat or pressure having destroyed them if they ever existed.

The Cenozoic era is represented in the lower part of the State by exposures of sedimentary rocks of the Tertiary period, mostly loose and uncompacted, and usually retaining somewhat their original horizontal positions. The movements that closed the Miocene, third epoch of the Cenozoic era, gave the Atlantic coast nearly its present outline. South Carolina entirely escaped glaciation during the Pleistocene epoch at the end of the Cenozoic era, and as a consequence it has no inland lakes or deposits of glacial debris characteristic of regions farther north.

The soils of the Piedmont Plateau are chiefly residual, having been formed by the weathering of the underlying rocks. The granites and gneisses form loams, while most of the other rocks form clay soils. Organic matter is rapidly destroyed in the warm climate, and the iron-bearing minerals become oxidized, giving the red color characteristic of the region. A few hills or small mountains are composed of rocks, such as quartzite, granite, or gneiss, that are extremely resistant to weathering, and stand up above the level of the plateau. Little Mountain, Kings Mountain, Crowder's Ridge, and Henry's Knob are the most prominent of these residual hills or monadnocks. Sugar Loaf and Horseshoe Mountains, in the Sand Hills of Chesterfield County, rouse the visitor's curiosity because they look as if they had been detached from each other by some violent explosion. Much igneous rock is scattered over the Piedmont section.

In the Sand Hills have recently been found fulgurites, long tubes of fused silica formed by the action of lightning on sand; and in the northeastern corner of the State, in Horry County, round pits in the terrain seem to give evidence of a meteoric shower at some remote time in the past.

NATURAL RESOURCES

Land: South Carolina's principal natural resource is its farm land, which in 1935 comprised 12,330,000 acres, or more than 63 per cent of the State's total land area. The value of farm land and buildings in that year was $285,516,000, and the estimated gross income from crops and livestock amounted to nearly $125,000,000.

Especially in the Up Country, where rivers flow between rolling hills now largely denuded of their original forests, erosion has taken a heavy toll of soils. A survey in 1934 revealed that of the 19,500,000 acres of land in the State, about 5,000,000 have been affected by gullying and nearly 6,000,000 by sheet erosion. Much of the eroded land includes both types, about 700,000 acres being ruined altogether for agricultural purposes. Under a program conducted by State and Federal agencies, conservation projects have been established in five areas, embracing more than 200,000 acres, where there are diversity of soil types, severity of erosion, and proximity to large groups of farmers who might take advantage of the demonstrations. Tree planting, strip cropping, and crop rotation are methods used to reclaim much of this land. Sections too steep or too badly eroded for efficient cultivation are devoted to pasturage or reforestation. The two principal soil conservation projects are the South Tiger River area in Spartanburg and Greenville Counties, and the Fishing Creek area in Chester and York Counties.

Forests: Though the forests of South Carolina have suffered severely from overexploitation, they still form one of the chief economic resources of the State, producing more than $20,000,000 in annual income through industries dependent upon their products. Of 17,000,000 acres of original forests, some 12,500,000 are wooded at the present time. To preserve the forests that remain and add to their acreage, both Federal and State governments have organized facilities in South Carolina. There are two national forests in the State, the Francis Marion and the Sumter. The first is in Charleston and Berkeley Counties, and contains 243,383 acres. The Sumter forest is in three divisions: the mountain division in Oconee and Pickens Counties; the Enoree division in Chester, Fairfield, Laurens, Newberry, and Union Counties; and the Long Cane division in Abbeville, Edgefield, Greenwood, McCormick, and Saluda Counties. The total acreage of the Sumter forest is 296,074. In addition to fire protection and supervised cutting and planting, the work in these national areas includes protection of wild life, establishment of fish hatcheries, provision for recreational facilities, and an educational program.

The South Carolina Commission of Forestry, instituted in 1927, has under its supervision and management 16 State parks, comprising more than 30,000 acres. The commission also co-operates with private land-owners in protecting and conserving their woodlands. The necessity for forest conservation in South Carolina has become more acute with the establishment in 1936 of two mills for the manufacture of paper and pulp in this State, and another just across the boundary in Savannah, Georgia. The mills at Georgetown and Charleston, representing an investment of $20,000,000 in 1938, use from 500 to 1,000 cords of pine wood a day. Unless care is taken through selective cutting and re-planting, the supply for the mills will be exhausted within a few years.

Water Power: A major factor in the establishment of pulp mills, as well as of many other industrial plants in South Carolina, has been the availability of water power. Hydroelectric plants, transmitting electric energy all over the Carolinas, now stand on sites occupied less than a century ago by small gristmills which utilized this water power in a small way. In 1939 the State had 57 public utility and private hydroelectric plants, with a combined development of 837,405 horse-power. The largest of these is the Lexington Water Power Company's plant near Columbia, completed at a cost of $23,000,000.

Many natural advantages contribute to make South Carolina one of the leading States in water power production. Two of its principal river systems rise in the near-by mountains of North Carolina and flow into the not distant ocean, with a fall of 700 feet for the course in one case and of 900 feet in the other. The Big Pee Dee, Santee, and Savannah Rivers flow through sections where they are hemmed in by comparatively high hills, which facilitate the erection of dams for storing power. Shoals have been washed out to leave a solid granite bottom, the most desirable foundation for construction work. The rivers drain an area of more than 30,000 square miles, on which there is an annual mean rainfall of 47.74 inches.

Two important projects now under way (1940) will add tremendously to the hydroelectric development in South Carolina. These are the Santee-Cooper Project, on the Santee River in Berkeley County, involving the expenditure of about $37,000,000, and the Buzzard Roost development on the Saluda River in Greenwood County, to cost nearly $3,000,000. Plans have been proposed for similar but smaller projects on Broad River between Newberry and Fairfield Counties and on the Savannah River in Edgefield County.

Minerals: Least important among the State's natural resources are its minerals, only kaolin, granite, phosphate rock, and gold being found at present in commercially important quantities. The total value of products from mines and mining of the State in 1938–9 was $2,476,378. Monuments and stone produced an output valued at $934,297.

Kaolin is found along the Savannah, Edisto, and Santee Rivers, the principal mines being in Aiken County. This clay, used as a filler for cotton goods and paper and as a coating for other materials, but chiefly for fine pottery, has long been a dependable source of wealth. Josiah Wedgwood, noted English potter, had wagonloads of the clay hauled from near Camden through the Indian country to Charleston, where it was exported to his factory in England in 1766. South Carolina is second only to Georgia in this country's kaolin production.

Granite quarries occur in 19 counties, the chief being the Palmetto near Columbia, the Weston-Brooker at Cayce, the Holston at Liberty, and the Anderson and Rion near Winnsboro. The Anderson quarry produces a blue-gray stone especially suited for monuments, and the Rion quarry a stone valuable for architectural use. The stone is of excellent texture and free from discoloration.

South Carolina phosphate was the original basis of the commercial fertilizer industry in the United States. The deposits near Charleston were discovered shortly after the War between the States, and for many years were very profitable; but mining ceased in the 1890's, after lawsuits involving State ownership and after the discovery in Florida of phosphate beds that could be worked at lower costs. At the present time new interest is being taken in the phosphate industry, and a northern concern has established at Beaufort a plant capitalized at about $1,000,000.

Recently a special survey was made of gold mines in North and South Carolina, where a considerable amount of the precious metal has been produced. Eighty-seven deposits were found in South Carolina, and the Haile mine near Camden is one of the largest in the Appalachian Range. For many years gold mining had been abandoned, but was renewed in 1934. In 1939 the value of gold produced in the State was $476,800, and it is estimated that the gold mined in South Carolina from the boom years of 1828–36 to the present amounts to more than $5,000,000.

A small tin mine, one of the few in America, was opened in 1937 in Cherokee County. There are small quantities of other ores and a few precious and semiprecious stones in the mountain section, but they do not exist in quantities sufficient to warrant commercial exploitation.

PLANT LIFE

In the narrow strip along the South Carolina coast is the subtropical growth in which are found such plants as the large palmetto, several dwarf palmettos, the American olive, the evergreen Carolina laurel cherry, several species of yucca, the evergreen holly, and the groundsel bush. Characteristic grasses along the coast are panicum, water millet, and sea oats.

Just behind this coastal strip are low sandy plains or damp flat woodlands, where magnificent live oaks, the nearly evergreen laurel and white oaks, great magnolias, hickories, gums, and pines make up the most conspicuous arboreal vegetation. In the open pine flats, and near the inlets, the dwarf white honeysuckle perfumes the air in April and May, and covers thousands of acres with snowy sheets of blossom. From May to July the sweet bay is almost as fragrant. Numerous species of pitcher plants and several other insectivorous genera are found in open flats and shore areas. From Murrell's Inlet northward grows the rare Venus's flytrap. The striking bald cypress is prevalent in swamps, both on the coast and farther inland; while the smaller pond cypress and the pond pine are found in savannahs and other poorly drained areas. On the more elevated sandy places, under the pines and oaks, are abundant dogwood, sparkleberry, American olive, and trailing arbutus. The long gray Spanish moss, so impressive to visitors, is not a moss at all, but a flowering aerial plant belonging to the pineapple family. The dense vegetation of the Low Country is prevailingly evergreen, largely due to the tangled growth of one or more species of smilax, yellow jessamine, gallberry, red bay, sweet bay, and loblolly bay. Conspicuous in the swamps are red-fruited haws, tall cottonwoods, and tupelo gums.

The Sand Hills have their own distinctive plant life, dominated by the longleaf pine, under which are such scrub growths as turkey oak, upland willow oak, and blackjack. Spring flowers are abundant and beautiful, and here and there is found one of the loveliest little plants in the State—the pyxie, also known as flowering moss and pine barren beauty.

Between the Sand Hills and the mountains, the Up Country forests contain about the same trees and flowers that are found in the Southeast generally. The magnificent white oaks and beeches attract universal admiration. Redbud, dogwood, and river plum are among the most conspicuous of the smaller flowering trees. Crabgrass and Bermuda grass are serious pests in cultivated fields, but make excellent summer pasturage.

Among the most admired flora of the Carolina mountains are the rhododendrons (three species), azaleas, and kalmias. In their spring glory the kalmias make a spectacular display, descending along the bluffs of rivers to within a few miles of the coast, as on Spring-wood plantation near Georgetown. At Kalmia Gardens in Hartsville, on the lower edge of the Sand Hills and scarcely 100 feet above sea level, is a magnificent display of kalmias in their native habitat. The Carolina hemlock occurs sparingly in the South Carolina mountains.

ANIMAL LIFE

Of chief importance among mammals found in South Carolina is the Virginia or white-tailed deer, which occurs in the coastal area in numbers seldom exceeded elsewhere. The black bear, once plentiful, is occasionally seen in swamplands of the Low Country. Others in the varied list range in size down to the shrew, tiniest mammal on the North American continent. This ferocious little beast, living mainly underground and seldom seen, will quickly kill a house mouse twice its size. The least shrew, found all over the State, is the smallest of the family. Bachman's shrew was originally identified in South Carolina by John Bachman, the collaborator of Audubon.

The wildcat or 'bobcat' still ranges the State from the mountains to the coast in the wooded regions. Opossums (two varieties) and raccoons (three varieties)—the 'possums' and 'coons' dear to the heart of the country Negro—are plentiful. One subspecies of raccoon, the Hilton Head, occurs nowhere in the world except on Hilton Head Island in Beaufort County. The gray fox and the rarer red fox are also found in various sections. There are three varieties of squirrels, the common gray, the flying squirrel, and the big fox squirrel, the latter with the striking black coat worn by occasional specimens. The cottontail rabbit abounds everywhere, and on the coast there is also the darker and heavier short-eared marsh rabbit.

Though the muskrat occurs north of the fall line and far up into the northeastern States, he perversely ignores the South Carolina Low Country. Here the coastal rice fields appear to have all the requirements of his ideal habitat, but something that is probably connected with the food supply has kept the muskrat away from this region. The Carolina otter is rare today, but not quite extinct. That highly important fur bearer, the beaver, was wiped out as early as 1840. Wolves were still plentiful at that time, but have disappeared completely. Vanished long before the 1840's were the puma (panther), elk, and bison, all common in the early days of the province. Still earlier inhabitants of South Carolina were camels and elephants, fossil remains of which have been uncovered by phosphate miners.

About a dozen varieties of rats and mice are found in the State, including both house and field or woods types. The common house mouse, a European immigrant, when isolated on one of the sandy barrier islands, becomes gradually paler and in time nearly matches the color of the sand. Other animals include the mole, bat, weasel, mink, and the woodchuck or 'groundhog.' The last named is confined to the Piedmont and the mountains.

There are six species of lizards, plus their cousin the alligator; 43 species of snakes, including the poisonous rattlesnake, copperhead, water moccasin, and coral snake; and 17 species of turtles, including the once commercially important diamondback terrapin. The prehistoric-looking salamanders, actually farther removed from the early types than their lizard relatives, number 34 species. These include the 'water dogs' or 'mud puppies,' valued as purifiers of springs. Of frogs and toads there are about 27 species.

Every few years harbor seals are reported off the South Carolina coast, although their normal range is from New Jersey to Labrador. The odd pigmy whale, a creature occurring the world over but scarce in all localities, has chosen the South Carolina coast as one of the most favored places for its rare appearances. Its relatives, the big finback, right, and sperm whales, also appear from time to time, with such others of smaller size as the bottle-nosed dolphin, the grampus, the so-called blackfish (really a whale), and the bottle-nosed and beaked whales. Sharks are numerous and of many varieties, but they do little damage. The odd little sea horse is sometimes taken in fishermen's nets offshore. Of more than 160 species of salt-water fish inhabiting the coastal waters, some 20 are valuable for food.

About 70 species of fresh-water fish found in the State include 22 edible varieties. A Federal fish hatchery has been established at Orangeburg, and another near Walhalla in Oconee County. The State maintains hatcheries at Anderson, Greer, Greenville, Spartanburg, Lancaster, Table Rock Park, Newberry, and Orangeburg.

Economically important to the State are such invertebrate fauna as shrimp, oysters, and crabs, the marketing of which represents a business of about $3,000,000 annually. The crab industry, usually monopolized by the Chesapeake region, took an active spurt in South Carolina when the northern field became partially exhausted in 1936. Clams, once valuable to the State, are now scarce, as is the much-prized stone crab.

Of the 360 species of birds that have been recorded in South Carolina, some are wanderers from the Arctic and some from the tropics, but many either visit at regular seasons or spend the entire year in the area. The coastal country is richer in bird life than the interior. This region lies along one of the great migration routes and is semitropical in character, drawing such species as the nonpareil, snake bird, brown pelican, and others associated with tropical climes. Vast armies of ducks and shore birds come annually to the barrier beaches; great colonies of black skimmers, royal terns, and brown pelicans make their teeming cities on the sandbars offshore; willets, Wilson plovers, oystercatchers, Wayne's clapper rails, and least terns frequent the inlet shores. Congregations of the lovely American egret and snowy heron gather in moss-draped cypress swamps. The Louisiana, little blue, and black-crowned night heron build their frail homes of sticks among the marshland myrtles. The old rice fields constitute a paradise for ducks; bob-whites abound in certain parts of the lowlands; and wild turkeys are still plentiful on some of the plantations. Doves, Wilson snipes, and woodcocks also are found in the State.

The favorite among songsters is doubtless the mockingbird, whose powers of melody and mimicry are unrivaled. Catbirds, orioles, warblers, thrushes, sparrows, swallows, vireos, and wrens delight many with their songs. The 'State bird' is the vivacious and cheery Carolina wren, which nests about houses and sings in mild winters straight through the cold months.

The so-called birds of prey are well represented throughout the State. Many of them are highly beneficial, and the importance of their role in keeping down injurious rodents can hardly be overestimated.

Bird refuges and sanctuaries are maintained by the Federal Government, the National Association of Audubon Societies, the Charleston Museum, and a number of private individuals. The two Federal sanctuaries are the great Cape Romain Migratory Waterfowl Refuge near McClellanville, and the sanctuary on the Savannah River near its mouth, extending partly into Georgia.

Indians

IN Colonial days the area now covered by the State of South Carolina was the home of at least 28 separate and distinct tribes of Indians, many of whom spoke radically different tongues of at least five linguistic stocks. Although the culture of these people exhibited variation, it was based primarily upon the production of food crops. Corn, beans, and pumpkins were the most important, but peaches, figs, and melons were later adopted. Next to agriculture, hunting and fishing were prominent Indian pursuits, and hunting became more so after contact with the white race.

Communal plantations and individual gardens were cultivated, a wide range of foods was prepared, some textiles were made, and there was some feather weaving, although dressed deer skins furnished material for most Indian garments. To a relative degree, basketry was advanced; stone implements were of a high order; pottery was unglazed and fragile, but well designed; dugout canoes were in general use.

Along the coast and among the Siouan tribes of the eastern section, houses were of bark; rectangular log, or mat dwellings were in use among the Cherokee and other advanced tribes. Well-fortified towns with strong palisades and a town house were almost universal. The dome-shaped town house was the council chamber, temple, and community center. Inside burned a fire, replenished ceremonially once a year.

Dancing celebrated all important occasions, the chief festival being the busk, or harvest ritual. The proverbial games were 'chunghee' and a ball game something like lacrosse. Ceremonial smoking preceded both peace and war deliberations. Common to the entire area appears to have been a ceremonial purge known as the black drink.

Intertribal warfare was almost perpetual, but related tribes were as a rule united into confederacies. Government was by the old man of the clan, not necessarily excluding the existence of a chief. A few tribes were so much under the sway of their chiefs as to be virtually under dictatorships.

Though their religion was polytheistic, a supreme deity was recognized. Shamanism and witchcraft, however, were extensively practiced. In certain respects the Indians were living in the Stone Age; in other particulars they had advanced far beyond it. No greater historical fallacy exists than that of depicting the advanced Cherokee Indian as a nomadic wanderer living in a skin tepee and wearing a Dakotah war bonnet.

Passing over the conflicting accounts of the Spanish and French, and beginning with the period of English colonization, one finds the following tribes and confederacies among the Indians in the province:

Along the coast from the Savannah River to Charleston dwelt a feeble group of minor tribes known collectively as the Cusabo. This confederacy included the St. Helena Indians, the Wimbee, Combahee, Ashepoo, Edisto, Bohicket, Stono, Wando, Etiwan, and Kiawah. Behind them a little farther up the country lived the Coosa or Kussoe, often included as Cusabo. This tribe was the first to resent white incursion and its hostility resulted in an abortive war about 1672.

The Cusabo and all the other Low Country Indians lived in constant terror of the Westo, a restless tribe of newcomers who had settled near the middle of the Savannah River area and were popularly reputed to be man-eaters. For several years this nation was signally favored by the Lords Proprietors to the great dissatisfaction of the settlers who, in 1680–2, defeated their dangerous neighbors in a war of annihilation. Only about 50 Westo survived to retire across the river into the territory of the Creek.

The defeat of these Indians was accomplished with the assistance of the Savannah, a band of immigrant Shawnee from the Cumberland. Settling on the Westobou River, to which they subsequently gave their name, they were the favored allies of the province until, about 1708, they became dissatisfied because of the cruelty and dishonesty of the traders. Despite the protests and even punitive measures adopted by the government, they left the province in large bands and removed to Pennsylvania. The Saluda, who migrated to the same region from the Saluda River about 1711, contemporaneously with a number of Savannah, were probably an independent band of that tribe.

Another Savannah River tribe was the Apalachee, 1,300 of whom were brought from Florida as free Indians by Governor Moore in 1704, following his expedition against the Spanish and their red allies. These were colonized a few miles below the present North Augusta near New Windsor. They remained in alliance with the province until the Yamasee War, the survivors retiring into Georgia at the end of the disastrous conflict.

Higher up the river lived a Yuchi band known as Hogologee or Hog Logge. Another band of Yuchi occupied territory below Augusta, and it has been suggested by Dr. John R. Swanton that the Westo themselves were still another subdivision of this tribe.

With the virtual disappearance of the Cusabo, the lower Savannah River country was thrown open to settlement by the Yamasee, a tribe that had been partly civilized by the Spaniards but had forsaken their interest for that of the English about 1684. They were loyal allies of Colonel Barnwell in the Tuscarora War of 1711, but revolted in 1715 because of gross abuses at the hands of the traders. Practically all of the other tribes joined them, and the white settlers were for a time in great danger. Upon their defeat they returned to Spanish territory but continued, for many years, to make raids upon the outlying white settlements. They have special significance for South Carolina literature through William Gilmore Simms's historical novel, *The Yemassee* —an unusual study of primitive life in the southeast.

About the headwaters of the Savannah, the Saluda, and the other rivers of the western South Carolina Piedmont, and extending inward and downward as far as the fall line and westward beyond the mountains, was the vast territory claimed by the Cherokee, that remarkable nation of Iroquoian Indians, who, for so many years, were the staunch allies of the white government. The history of their war against the colony in 1760 and their subsequent part in the American Revolution, as allies of the British, is well known. Withdrawing to northern Georgia they acquired white blood and white civilization at an early date, but actually retained a slender strip of land in South Carolina as late as 1816.

Up the coast from Charleston and along the Santee and Pee Dee Rivers and their tributaries, lived a number of Siouan tribes related to the Dakotah of the Western plains. They were less advanced than their traditional enemies, the Cherokee. This tribal group, which formed a loose confederacy headed by the Catawba Nation, included Sewee (sometimes classed as Cusabo), Santee, Sampit, Winyah, Peedee, Cheraw, Congaree, Wateree, Waxhaw, Esaw, and the Catawba tribes themselves. It perhaps included the mysterious 'Hooks and Backhooks,' who were mentioned by John Lawson as being enemies of the Santee. After the Yamasee War the remnants of the smaller Siouan tribes began migrating up the rivers and uniting with the Catawba, who, in 1743, were composed of groups speaking 20 different languages and dialects, according to Adair. Undoubtedly these people included several non-Siouan bands as well.

Following the Yamasee War, the Catawba never again forsook their alliance with the government and furnished warriors in every war in which the white people became engaged. As early as the Revolution they had become pitifully reduced in numbers, yet today they still preserve their tribal identity. Of the 200 or more in the State, only six or seven claim to be full-blooded Indian. On their tiny reservation in York County they continue to make the beautiful pottery for which they have established a deserved reputation. Though influenced to some extent by modern designs, their work is an interesting survival of an old Indian ceramic art (*see Tour 7A*).

Smallpox, war, and the cruel practice of Indian slavery reduced the aboriginal population of South Carolina almost to the vanishing point. Nevertheless, there are several small friendly groups that never deserted their original territory. These people, variously styled as Croatans, Red Bones, and Brass Ankles, are found in widely separated parts of the State, particularly in Dorchester, Colleton, Clarendon, Chesterfield, Marlboro, and Marion Counties. Similar though smaller groups exist in many other sections. The 'Turks' of Sumter County undoubtedly possess some Indian blood. Most of these mixed-blood remnants are found on the wide scrub-covered sweeps of the Sand Hill belt or in the dense swamps of the coastal rivers. They are generally small farmers who depend to a large extent upon hunting and fishing for their livelihood. Though independent and secretive, they are staunch friends once their confidence is gained.

History

WITHIN thirty years after Columbus discovered America, Spaniards were exploring the coast of what was to be South Carolina. In 1521 Cordillo and Quexos, coming from Española, or San Domingo, cruised up and down the coast touching the vague territory, Chicora, the native name for part of the present coastal North and South Carolina. Indian slaves to the number of 150 were captured and taken to San Domingo, where the governor, Don Diego, son of Columbus, ordered them released. Among the Indians was Francisco Chicorana, a charming liar who was baptized into the Catholic faith and retained as a personal servant by Vasquez de Ayllon, a superior judge of the island. Francisco's fabulous accounts of his homeland, with its strange races of men who wore tails, with its wealth and easy life, so intrigued de Ayllon that he decided to attempt settlement.

In 1526 de Ayllon gathered about 500 persons, including women, children, Dominican priests, physicians, and Negro slaves, with domestic animals and equipment necessary to successful colonization. He anchored his ships near modern Winyah Bay; and when one was lost with its cargo, he built an open boat for oars and sail, and so transported his company to the mainland. Immediately Francisco escaped and the Spaniards' troubles began. De Ayllon named his settlement San Miguel de Gualdape—Gualdape from the river near by. Disease took hold of the colonists, slaves revolted, Indians attacked, the winter was unusually severe, and de Ayllon died. Only a few months after their arrival the Spaniards, depleted by two thirds of their number, returned to San Domingo.

This was the best organized effort of the Spaniards to establish their holdings in the section, though De Soto in 1540 and Juan Pardo in 1567 explored much of the interior about the Savannah River.

Competing with the Spaniards were the French, who in 1562 briefly settled a body of Huguenots at Port Royal, close by the Spanish Santa Elena. Charlesfort or *Arx Carolina* was built under Jean Ribaut, who left 30 colonists to man the works while he returned to France for reinforcements. Mutiny followed, and a ship was built for the return

23

voyage; food gave out, and those who survived did so by eating one of their fellows. Only a few of Ribaut's men reached France.

Meanwhile, Ribaut had returned to France and René de Laudonnière set out with aid. Finding Charlesfort abandoned, he settled on St. Johns River, thereby rousing Spain to a pitch of antagonism which resulted in the establishment by 1615 of more than 20 fortified mission posts, including St. Augustine in Florida. The northernmost was San Gorges, near modern Charleston.

None of these centers endured in South Carolina, however, and it remained for the English, whose aims were commercial, to establish permanent white settlements. Charles I in 1629 granted to Sir Robert Heath 'all America from sea to sea between the 36 and 31 parallels of latitude under the name of Carolana.' But the country remained unexplored by the English until after the Restoration, when in 1663, Charles II, grateful for assistance in his cause and low in finances, chartered the same territory to eight of his loyal friends: the Earl of Clarendon, the Duke of Albemarle (George Monck), Lord Craven, Sir William Berkeley, Lord Berkeley, Lord Ashley (Anthony Ashley Cooper, later Earl of Shaftesbury), Sir George Carteret, and Sir John Colleton. They became Lords Proprietors of the province of Carolina. Charles II of England was the fourth monarch of that name to authorize settlement here; Charles V of Spain, Charles I of France, and Charles I of England had all fathered expeditions that came to nothing.

Immediately on receiving the king's grant, the Lords Proprietors began planning colonization. Captain William Hilton, sent out in 1663–4 to explore the coast, landed at Port Royal in the *Adventurer,* where he met friendly Indians who told him of Spanish friars and soldiery. Hilton Head is named for this early navigator. Three years later Captain Robert Sandford came from Barbados, an English colony in the West Indies, and landed at the same place. With him was Dr. Henry Woodward, who became so interested in the country that he remained here for several years, living among the Indians and learning their language, customs, and methods of cultivating crops. Later he joined the group who founded Charles Town. Thus he may be called the first permanent English settler in Carolina and in many respects its most useful pioneer citizen. Acting as interpreter and negotiator with the Indians, he blazed the trails for the principal trade routes and for 15 years was the chief agent in keeping for the port of Charles Town the valuable traffic in furs and pelts. He also introduced rice into the province about 1680.

Meanwhile, the Lords Proprietors, after considering various schemes for colonization, proposed to establish in Carolina an English feudal order, from which they hoped in time to gather untold wealth. In 1669 John Locke, the English philosopher, was employed to draw up plans intended to be the laws of the province. His *Fundamental Constitutions,* the 'Grand Model,' provided for three orders of nobility: barons, caciques, and landgraves, each with large landed estates. The Church of England was to be the established sect, but all faiths were to be tolerated. The territory was to be blocked off in squares of 12,000 acres, each of which was to remain exclusively a barony for a proprietor or a colony for commoners, as designated in the grant. Lord Ashley, acting for the proprietors, directed the plans for colonization, with the object of developing plantations whose produce would supply staples for European markets.

Accordingly, in March 1670, the first settlement, consisting of 148 persons, was made at Albemarle Point, on the west bank of the Ashley, 10 miles from its mouth, and named Charles Town in honor of the king. Captain Joseph West, who was in command of the ships bringing the colonists, had been directed to stop at Barbados for cotton seed and indigo seed, roots of ginger, sugar cane, vines, and olives. These, with fruits and vegetables, were to be planted at once; and periodical reports were to be made on each variety of crop. At Barbados other emigrants joined the expedition, and Colonel William Sayle, aged and infirm, was appointed governor of the province. Governor Sayle died March 4, 1670, and West was appointed his temporary successor. In his service of eight years, intermitted by proprietary appointments of less able governors, he was perhaps the most capable and efficient executive in the period before the province came under royal administration.

In February 1671, 106 more settlers arrived from Barbados, and with this addition to its numbers the Barbados group formed nearly half the total population. Its influence on the development of the plantation system in South Carolina was marked, particularly as the slave code of the province was adapted from that of the island.

Ten years after the first settlement, Charles Town was moved to Oyster Point, at the confluence of the Kiawah and the Etiwan Rivers, which in compliment to the Earl of Shaftesbury had been renamed Ashley and Cooper. In this new situation, admirable for commercial purposes, growth was rapid. The promise of representative government and religious toleration laid down in the charter and the attractions of the southern Carolina coast drew several hundred settlers from the

Mother Country and the English West Indies. These were followed by New England dissenters and French Huguenots, and by 1700 the province had an estimated population of more than 5,000.

For the first 50 years of Carolina's existence the population was confined to the 15- or 20-mile strip of coast cut by slow-moving rivers and inlets into islands or narrow peninsulas. The tides penetrated the entire area and made navigation easy for small boats. The streams were flanked by wide swamps, beyond which was a sandy expanse, well timbered and suited to both grain culture and stock raising. Timber, grain, cattle, and peltry were the chief exports from the province during the first two decades.

During this time energetic efforts were made to find a staple for European markets. Madagascar rice, introduced about 1680, proved a suitable crop for the coast. It was soon found to flourish best in the wet soil of the swamps. Slaves were introduced in increasing numbers to perform the heavy labor of clearing the margins of the smaller streams, cultivating the soil, and cleaning the grain. The yield was enormous, and the tidal watercourses formed convenient routes for transportation. The industry tended to concentrate itself within a comparatively small area readily accessible from Charles Town; and that port, already enjoying an Indian trade which by 1700 extended to the Mississippi, grew into a thriving city, the center of the political, social, and economic life of the province.

Thus was established in the tidewater region a planter class, which was to control the government for over 100 years, and a system of slave labor that in time was to wreck the commonwealth.

At first the province was dominated by the governor and grand council, but with the rise of the merchant and planter class the lower branch of the legislature, the commons house, successfully asserted itself and after 1690 became the chief political body. In 1693 the *Fundamental Constitutions* were formally abandoned, and the lower house secured the privilege of initiating legislation. Quarrels with the Lords Proprietors, who declined in ability and in interest in the province, steadily weakened the prestige of that body. The controversy centered around the question of military defense. With the Spaniards of Florida claiming the eastern territory as far north as Charles Town, the French traders along the lower Mississippi resentful of commercial invasion, the Carolina Indians watching with angry eyes the continued encroachments upon their hunting grounds, and the constant menace of pirates, the problems of defense grew ever more complex. In none of these perils did the proprietors lend aid. Considering the harm to the lucrative trade established between the province and the attacking forces, indeed, they discouraged and sometimes forbade retaliation for hostile attacks.

In 1686 Spaniards from St. Augustine, assisted by a force of Indians and Negroes, landed on Edisto Island, plundered the houses of Governor Morton and Paul Grimball, secretary of the province, murdered the brother-in-law of the governor, carried off his money, plate, and 13 slaves, and then proceeded to Port Royal, where they destroyed the Scottish settlement established by Lord Cardross. Parliament was summoned by Governor Morton, an assessment of £500 was made, two vessels were manned, and a company of 400 men was ready to sail against St. Augustine, when the new governor, James Colleton, brother of Sir John Colleton, arrived from Barbados and commanded the return of the troops, threatening with hanging any who persisted. He wished no one to interfere with the profitable trade with the Spaniards. The province never forgave this indignity.

In 1702, with the opening of Queen Anne's War, in which France and Spain were pitted against England, the American colonies along the southern frontier became involved. Governor Moore, wishing to aid the Mother Country, and remembering two former attacks by Spaniards, led an unsuccessful expedition against St. Augustine. The next year, 1703, at his own expense, the governor raised a small army and dealt a crushing blow to the Appalachian Indians as allies of the Spaniards. In 1706, while the yellow fever was raging in Charles Town, a fleet of five warships anchored off the harbor. Le Feboure, the commander, in the name of the king of France, demanded the surrender of the town, giving only one hour for reply. The governor, Sir Nathaniel Johnson, who had built a fort at Windmill Point in the harbor and made ample preparation for defense, replied: 'I do not need a minute to decide. I hold this province for Her Majesty, Queen Anne of England. I am ready to die in its defense but not to surrender it.' Colonel William Rhett was asked to take command. Mounting cannon on the decks of six small sailing vessels, he moved out to meet the warships, but the latter raised anchor and hastened away. Rhett followed and captured one of them, bringing 230 French and Spanish prisoners back to town.

Indian troubles next claimed the attention of both Carolinas. The Tuscarora, twice breaking truce with the neighboring Carolinians, were finally defeated with the aid of riflemen and friendly Indians un-

der the leadership of Colonels John Barnwell and James Moore, son
of the former governor. In 1715–16 a great uprising of the Yamasee,
resentful at encroachments upon their territory, threatened the very
existence of the province. With about 15,000 Indians on the warpath
and the prospects of others from other colonies joining them, it was
feared that all the white settlements would be blotted out. Beginning
with the slaughter of 90 settlers at Pocotaligo and 100 men at Port
Royal, the savages rushed up the coast, burning and pillaging as they
went. At the Stono River they were checked by a mounted force under
Governor Craven, while a company of riflemen went by water to Port
Royal, sailed up to Pocotaligo, and destroyed their chief town. From
the north marched a body of 400 Indians, killing as they came. Captain
Chicken met them near Charles Town with another force of riflemen
and after a long hot battle forced them to retreat. So were the Yamasee
defeated and their lands vacated, but 400 colonists had lost their lives
and the settlement had shrunk to the immediate vicinity of Charles
Town. In this struggle the proprietors were called upon for aid, but
they referred the appeal to the English Government.

In 1718 Carolina began to suffer sharply from the pirates who infested the coast. Such notables as Blackbeard, Stede Bonnet, and Richard Worley, flying the Skull and Crossbones, found in the Carolina
trade sufficient temptation for attack. Colonel William Rhett, defender
of Charles Town against the French ships in 1706, and Governor
Robert Johnson, son of Sir Nathaniel Johnson, went out after the sea
robbers. After two fierce battles Bonnet was captured, Worley and
Blackbeard were killed, while more than 60 of their crews were sentenced by Judge Nicholas Trott and later hanged on the wharf at
Charles Town.

A year later the struggles with the Spaniards, French, Indians, and
pirates had subsided, but not so the controversies with the proprietors.
These overlords refused to pay any part of the cost of the wars, raised
the quitrents to four times the former rates, and, most outrageous of
all, claimed the lands from which the settlers had expelled the Yamasee. The colonists rose in wrath, expelled the agents of the proprietors,
elected James Moore to serve as governor, and sent John Barnwell to
England to report the matter to the king and ask that Carolina be
made a royal province. During this interval South Carolina was practically self-governing for two years.

With this coup ended the burlesque of setting up in the wilds of
America an order of titled nobility who should live at ease upon the

labor of others. The social order of South Carolina was the result of the province's development, the outgrowth of circumstances and influences peculiar to the place and people. Merchants, traders, artisans, and agriculturists built up wealth in landed estates and slaves, thereby laying the foundations of the culture for which South Carolina was noted in pre-Revolutionary days.

In 1721 Sir Francis Nicholson, widely experienced in colonial affairs, was appointed by the Crown as provisional governor (1721–9) until the rights of the proprietors in lands and quitrents could be settled. In 1729 the transfer from proprietary to royal control was completed, and the next year the first attempt to define the boundary line between the two Carolinas was made, though it was not finally established until 1815. Under the new regime, the king appointed the governor and the members of the council, though the people continued to elect members of the assembly. Robert Johnson, last of the proprietary governors, was appointed the first royal governor. He at once began to devise plans for opening up the country beyond the tidewater area. A fund was provided for encouraging the immigration of white Protestants from Europe, who should be established in townships along the edge of the settled area and at strategic points farther inland. Land was laid out in 50-acre lots and granted to settlers in proportion to the size of the family and the number of slaves, allowing one share per person. Whenever 100 families should have settled in a township it was to be organized into a parish and allowed two members in the assembly.

The eight townships thus established lay above the tidewater belt and below the fall line that marked the natural division between the Coastal Plain and the Piedmont. Each township bordered a navigable stream. The middle country, as it has been called, was by nature a part of the lower country, but, lacking the transportation advantages of the tidewater and sharing the climate which was trying to the newcomer, it had no appeal at the time for the planters. By 1740 the middle country had been settled by Germans from Switzerland, Scotch-Irish from Ireland, and Welsh from what is now Delaware. Somewhat later, Germans from the Rhine Valley established themselves along the lower Saluda and Broad Rivers. After 1755 the Piedmont was assured of settlement by the great southwestern movement from the frontiers of the northern colonies, where dangers from Indian attacks and the rigors of winter led the pioneers to seek a safer retreat and more equable climate. The township plan, therefore, was of great importance in preventing a gap in the province that would have left the tidewater plantations in a perilous situation.

By the time of the Revolution the back country had nearly half of the white population of the province. It was made up of twenty or thirty thousand small farmers who with their self-sufficient way of life and their dissenter churches had little in common with the planters of the tidewater. For several decades they lived the life of pioneers. Their log houses required only a few days for construction. They spent their time in clearing new land and planting corn and other grains, always on the lookout for Indians and cattle thieves. The small farms were miles apart and work was hard; consequently social life was confined largely to church meetings and the assembly of militia companies, with an occasional log-rolling or corn-shucking. Thus began the development of the Up Country, nearly half a century after the Low Country was well established.

Nor were these pioneers free from such dangers and difficulties as had attended the earlier settlement of the lower country. Cherokee, Indian agitators from Spanish and French trading posts, cattle thieves, and general lawlessness had to be dealt with while the settlers strove to set up homes and churches in the wilderness. Governor Nicholson had sought to pacify the Cherokee with gifts and advantages in trade, but they had become dissatisfied. In 1730 Sir Alexander Cuming, in the name of King George, made a treaty with them by which they agreed to open their lands to traders and settlers.

Twenty-three years later Governor Glen found it necessary to act as peacemaker between the Cherokee and their hostile neighbors, the Creek. The Cherokee gave him a few thousand acres of land, on which he erected Fort Prince George on the Keowee River for the protection of English and Indian traders. In 1755 Old Hop, king of the Cherokee, met Governor Glen at Saluda Old Town, a point halfway between Charles Town and the Indian town Keowee, and signed a deed to the land later included in the Ninety Six District—a territory now included in ten counties of the State. On January 19, 1760, the Cherokee broke the peace and began to spread terror throughout the upper country. Many of the settlers were massacred, but, after the fields and villages of the Cherokee had been laid waste, Attakullakulla, the 'Little Carpenter,' and several other chiefs petitioned (1761) for terms of peace, which were granted by Governor Bull.

Following the defeat of the Cherokee in 1761, new settlers began to pour into the Up Country through the Waxhaws, in present Lancaster

County. A few scattered centers extended as far west as the Savannah River. Between 1765 and 1770 an outbreak of robbery, pillaging, and arson in the Up Country resulted in formation of the 'Regulators,' who, despairing of aid from Charles Town, took the law in their own hands and drove out numerous bands of offenders. Population and property had so increased that leaders in the Up Country sections felt justified in demanding a voice in the government. Patrick Calhoun and others appeared before the legislature in Charles Town and presented their claims for the same privileges granted to other taxpayers: courts of justice, roads, provision for churches and schools, and, above all, representation in the government. Soon afterward, Moses Kirkland and Patrick Calhoun took their seats as representatives from the Up Country.

While this significant development of the Piedmont was taking place, the rice plantations on the coast had been doubled in area, and indigo, a new staple in which the middle country had small share, had immensely strengthened the tidewater system.

The early promise of the merchant-planter society had been richly fulfilled. Large estates and fine commercial business provided the economic basis for a polished social life not surpassed in America. The families lived somewhat in the style of English gentlemen, many of them maintaining handsome city houses furnished with elegance and taste, as well as plantation establishments with rare gardens laid out by the best landscape artists of the day. Private schools, tutors, travel abroad, attendance at public schools and inns of court in England provided advantages for the sons of the wealthy. Provision was also made for the education of the poor, but the free school act of 1710 had never gone into operation. However, before 1710 a free school was opened in Charles Town, and in 1743 a school for Negroes.

By 1775 the estimated population of the province was 60,000 whites, half of whom were in the upper country, and 80,000 Negroes, most of whom were in the coastal belt. Trade in rice and indigo alone amounted to about £1,000,000 each year. Besides these articles, lumber, staves, tar, and cattle were sold in large quantities. About 3,000 wagons annually made the long journey from the highlands to Charles Town with wheat, corn, and peltry. Political development was marked by an unending contest with the governor and the council over the prerogatives of the Crown and by a steady growth in the commons house of ability and self-confidence, the lower house claiming all the rights and privileges of the British House of Commons. At the same time continual warfare had developed the colonists' confidence in their ability to handle arms.

The outbreak of the Revolutionary controversy found South Carolina so prosperous and so closely connected with the Mother Country by mutual interests that the situation would seem to have offered little encouragement to the agitator. Nevertheless, the long habit of self-government and the growing power of the commons house and the planter-merchant class brought about determined resistance to the various acts by which the king sought to force money out of the American colonies.

To the Stamp Act Congress, held in New York in 1765, South Carolina sent three delegates who took a prominent part in the activities of that body. Chairmen of the respective committees preparing addresses to the House of Commons and the House of Lords were Thomas Lynch, father of the Signer of the Declaration of Independence, and John Rutledge, brother of another Signer. Christopher Gadsden, the third delegate, should be remembered along with James Otis of Massachusetts and Patrick Henry of Virginia as one of the prime movers for American independence. He was opposed to asking any favor of the king and Parliament, and advocated the union of all the colonies in resisting unjust taxation. He led in opposition to the Townshend Acts (1767), by which a tax was laid on glass, wine, oil, paper, tea, and other articles. When the tax was removed from every article except tea, the merchants of Charles Town refused to buy it, even at a greatly reduced price. In 1773 they left shipments in a storehouse to mold, and on November 1, 1774, one shipload was thrown into the sea.

To the First Continental Congress at Philadelphia (1774) five delegates were sent, Henry Middleton and Edward Rutledge being added to the three who represented South Carolina at the Stamp Act Congress in New York.

In January 1775, a provincial congress met at Charles Town. A secret committee, whose members were William Henry Drayton, Arthur Middleton, Charles Cotesworth Pinckney, William Gibbes, and Edward Weyman, was appointed to make ready for any action that might be necessary for the safety of South Carolina. On Sunday, June 4, 1775, the provincial congress met again, authorized the issue of £1,000,000 in paper currency for military defense, and appointed 13 as a council of safety, with power to command all soldiers and to use all public money in the province. Henry Laurens was made president, and William Henry Drayton and Arthur Middleton, its most radical members, were ready to expel all officers representing the king in South Carolina.

In March 1776, a temporary constitution was set up under which a regular government could be established until an understanding with the Mother Country could be achieved. John Rutledge was chosen president, Henry Laurens vice president, and William Henry Drayton chief justice. It was this government that defended Charles Town against the British army and fleet on June 28, 1776, and freed the South from further attack for nearly three years. Six days later, July 4, 1776, four South Carolinians, Edward Rutledge, Thomas Heyward, Jr., Thomas Lynch, Jr., and Arthur Middleton, delegates to the Continental Congress in Philadelphia, agreed to sign the Declaration of Independence; and in due time they did so.

About this time Andrew Williamson, Andrew Pickens, and James Williams, after various contests with the Tories in the upper country, conducted a successful campaign against the Cherokee, who, siding with the British, had begun to burn and murder along the frontier. In one attack in what is now Spartanburg County they had killed Anthony Hampton, his wife, one of his sons, and a grandson. From this family, almost wiped out at that time, have sprung all the distinguished soldiers and statesmen of that name in South Carolina.

In 1780 the British renewed their attack upon Charles Town. After a siege lasting from March 12 to May 12, General Benjamin Lincoln surrendered to General Clinton. Practically all of the Continental troops in the Carolinas were captured. Three months later, the army of Gates, marching to recover South Carolina, was utterly defeated at Camden, and the British completed at leisure the process of overrunning the State. The old Loyalist feeling reasserted itself, and many who at first had embraced Whig doctrines gave allegiance to the British Government. With the majority of civil and military leaders in prison or on parole, the American cause was apparently doomed; but Governor Rutledge was indefatigable in his efforts to secure aid from Congress, and in 1781 General Nathanael Greene arrived with a body of Continentals. The most effective forces in the State, however, were the small bands of partisans under Francis Marion (the Swamp Fox), Thomas Sumter (the Gamecock), and Andrew Pickens, leaders of the lower, middle, and upper country respectively. They so harassed the British and blocked their progress through the State that the surrender of Cornwallis at Yorktown was hastened.

The tide was turned with the victory at Kings Mountain, October

7, 1780, in which not a single commander or private belonged to the Continental army. A significant stepping stone to this victory was the successful engagement with a body of Tories at Musgrove's Mill, in what is now Laurens County. Other important battles were those of Cowpens, Hobkirk's Hill, and Eutaw Springs. In December 1782, the British evacuated Charles Town, but victory had been won at fearful cost to the State. For nearly three years there had been no semblance of government; Whig and Tory fought each other in small detachments until the fury of civil war had made lynch law and plundering a habit. In all, 137 more or less significant engagements had taken place.

Historian McCrady asserted, 'of the 137 battles, actions and engagements, between the British and Tories and Indians on the one hand, and the American Whigs on the other, which took place in South Carolina during the Revolution, *one hundred and three* were fought by South Carolinians alone, in twenty others South Carolinians took part with troops from other States making in all *one hundred and twenty-three* battles in which South Carolinians fought, within the borders of their State, for the liberties of America.' In addition, 14 battles were fought in the State without South Carolina assistance, and many from this State engaged in military activities elsewhere. In no State was there more fighting or more suffering during the Revolution than in South Carolina.

Throughout the struggle the State had furnished more than its quota of men, money, and arms to the Continental Army, and two presidents, Henry Middleton and Henry Laurens, to the Continental Congress. The tradition is that Middleton supported a whole regiment at his own expense. In response to England's concession permitting the colonies to manage their own affairs as long as they remained with the Mother Country, Laurens himself indited the reply that until England acknowledged the independence of the thirteen States and removed all of her soldiers and warships, Congress would have no dealings with her. In the stupendous task of welding the thirteen States into one national government South Carolinians took an important part. The delegates elected to the Constitutional Convention at Philadelphia were John Rutledge, Henry Laurens, Charles Pinckney, Charles Cotesworth Pinckney, and Pierce Butler. Henry Laurens, however, did not serve.

The South Carolina delegates at Philadelphia bent their energies to securing a government that would protect the interests of property

From Caesars Head to Edisto

Photograph by Carl T. Julien

CAESAR'S HEAD, NEAR GREENVILLE

WILD LIFE SANCTUARY, FRANCIS MARION NATIONAL FOREST
Along The Intracoastal Waterway, Atlantic Ocean in Far Distance.

LAKE LANIER, NEAR SPARTANBURG

Photograph by Carlisle Roberts

SAND DUNES, MYRTLE BEACH

PALMETTOS ON THE COAST

Photograph by courtesy of South Carolina State Commission of Forestry

SOIL CONSERVATION, SPARTANBURG COUNTY

EFFECTS OF SOIL EROSION, UP COUNTRY

**WHITE WATER FALLS
SUMTER NATIONAL FOREST**

Photograph by Carlisle Roberts

MOUNTAIN VIEW, NEAR PICKENS

POOL IN BROOKGREEN GARDENS, NEAR GEORGETOWN

MAGNOLIA GARDENS, NEAR CHARLESTON

and that would give South Carolina a considerable voice in the government; they were thus the chief defenders of the slave interests.

Many plans of government were presented, but that of Charles Pinckney influenced the final draft of the one which was adopted as the Constitution of the United States. In the new and delicate task of forming diplomatic relations with foreign countries, it was Thomas Pinckney who filled the difficult post of minister to Britain and also that of special envoy to Spain to negotiate an important treaty.

Up Country and Low Country acted together on May 23, 1788, when South Carolina adopted the Federal Constitution. This occurred only after much pleading by the Pinckneys and others who represented the Low Country. General Sumter, who represented the sentiment of the Up Country, was bitterly antagonistic. Rawlins Lowndes, though a Low Countryman, took the same view and asked to have it carved on his tombstone that he opposed the adoption of the Federal Constitution. Efforts were now made to reconcile the interests of the two sections.

In 1786 it had been voted to move the capital to a central point in the State, though the actual removal to Columbia did not take place until 1790, and some State offices remained in Charleston until 1865. (The change of name from Charles Town had taken place in 1783—the city officials believing Charleston a less British form.) In 1800 the Santee Canal, connecting the Santee and Cooper Rivers, was completed, giving the Santee-Congaree-Wateree-Broad-Saluda system water communication with Charleston. The chartering of the South Carolina College in 1801 was also designed to remove the antagonism between the two sections. But it remained for the industrial development growing out of the invention of the cotton gin and the use of slave labor in the production of cotton to bring the sections into full harmony that continued until national politics caused discord.

In 1808 the controversy over representation of the Up Country in the legislature was settled. An amendment to the constitution provided that representation in the lower branch should be based half on taxable wealth and half on white population. This gave the Up Country control in the lower house and the Low Country control in the upper house of the legislature. Thus cotton and the extension of slavery completed the process of unifying the State into a political solidarity not found elsewhere in the South.

Hardly had this unification been effected than an economic decline, which threatened bankruptcy and partial depopulation of the State, began. As the production of cotton increased, the price fell, and with land fertility decreasing, many planters were lured away to the rich alluvial soils of the Gulf States. Meanwhile, the increase of tariff rates brought angry protests from a people who felt that they were being doubly taxed, once by the actual increase in the cost of goods, and again by interference in trade with England, the South's best customer. By 1827 there was talk of secession.

In 1811, when American commerce was being plundered by British ships, South Carolina was enraged. The State sent to Congress a brilliant young quartet—John C. Calhoun, Langdon Cheves, David R. Williams, and William Lowndes—at whose insistence, with that of other so-called War Hawks, the War of 1812 was declared. At news of the first American victory it is said that Calhoun, Lowndes, Cheves, and Henry Clay of Kentucky joined hands and danced a four-hand reel.

At this time the State favored a tariff high enough to cover the costs of the war; but as the levy increased from year to year, there was violent reaction against the Federalist attitude that for a decade had been voiced by the leaders of the State.

John C. Calhoun, himself a former Federalist, was convinced equally of the iniquity of the tariff and the danger of secession. With Daniel Webster of Massachusetts and Henry Clay of Kentucky, he was one of the 'Great Trio' to whom their respective constituencies looked for guidance. He therefore resigned the vice presidency, entered the Senate, and set himself to thwart the radical leaders of his State, at the same time endeavoring to redress their grievances. His remedy, nullification of the tariff, brought a compromise in the duties of 1833 and established him as the acknowledged leader of a notable group of Carolinians who championed States' rights. Among these were George McDuffie, member of the national house, and one of the most eloquent of Congressional orators; Senator Robert Y. Hayne, who met Daniel Webster in one of the greatest debates in American history; and James Hamilton, Jr., who had succeeded Lowndes in Congress.

Opposed to Calhoun's nullification movement was President Andrew Jackson, who ordered warships to South Carolina to enforce Federal law. Only the intervention of the compromise, before the forces reached here, prevented clash of arms. In Calhoun's own State, numerous leaders would not support the movement. Such men as Joel R. Poinsett, world-wide traveler and minister to Mexico, William Gilmore Simms, novelist, and the able lawyers, James L. Petigru, Hugh S.

Legare, John Belton O'Neall, and Benjamin F. Perry, held that while a State had full right to withdraw from the Union it had no right to nullify a law of the Federal Government.

In spite of the tariff compromise the quarrel continued. Other economic and fiscal issues embittered the relations between southern planters and New England manufacturers and financiers. The increasing violence of the campaign against slavery filled the South with anger and dread. In South Carolina the whole economic structure rested upon the plantation system with slave labor, and the State produced a group of apologists for the system who became fanatical in its defense and in their efforts to extend it into new territory.

While these leaders strove by political action to bolster up the position of the State, another scarcely less gifted group labored for the economic rehabilitation of the commonwealth, feeling that this was the true solution of its troubles. The most noted of these movements was a campaign led by David R. Williams for the diversification and improvement of agriculture. Another was to recover the declining trade of the port of Charleston by giving the State an adequate transportation system. Accordingly, the South Carolina Railroad between Charleston and Hamburg, opposite Augusta on the Savannah River, was completed in 1833. This railway of 136 miles was the longest passenger steam railroad in the world at that date. Within the next 20 years branches were constructed to other points in the State. There was yet a third group who insisted that the salvation of the State lay in manufacturing, and William Gregg, their chief, in 1846, established a cotton mill at Graniteville, Aiken County, which utilized white labor and became the model for the South.

When America declared war with Mexico in 1846, the Palmetto Regiment distinguished itself on the field under Pierce M. Butler, J. P. Dickinson, and A. H. Gladden. The palmetto flag was the first to enter the Mexican capital. Of the 1,100 volunteers who saw active service in that war, only about 300 returned.

But the State was caught in the current of the slavery controversy, and the political leaders, with an overwhelming majority in their favor, had the last word. On December 17, 1860, a convention presided over by General D. F. Jamison met in the First Baptist Church in Columbia and adjourned to Charleston, where next day it continued sessions in St. Andrew's Hall. On the 20th, the Ordinance of Secession, as prepared by Chancellor Francis Hugh Wardlaw, was unanimously adopted. By the first of February 1861, other States had followed South Carolina, and a new union, the Confederate States of America, was formed.

In the great war that followed, South Carolina, with a white population of 291,000, furnished 63,000 effective soldiers and lost 25 per cent of them in service. The part of South Carolinians in the four-year conflict is too large to be sketched here. Prominent names are those of Lieutenant Generals Wade Hampton, Richard H. Anderson, Stephen D. Lee, Daniel H. Hill, and James Longstreet, the two last appointed from other States. Five major generals and more than two score brigadier generals gave gallant service. South Carolina also furnished two members of President Davis's Cabinet, three officers on his military staff, the surgeon general, and six officers in the War Department. The most spectacular feature of the war in the State was the defense of Charleston Harbor; the most destructive was Sherman's northward march from Savannah, culminating in the burning of Columbia in February 1865. The loss of men and property, together with the depreciation of the economic structure of the State, were almost matched by the damage which came from the destruction of the plantation system.

After the fall of the Confederacy in April 1865, Governor Magrath was deposed from office and sent to a Federal prison. President Andrew Johnson, in conformity with Lincoln's previously approved plan, issued a general pardon to most of those who had taken part in the war and appointed Benjamin F. Perry of Greenville as provisional governor. As a Unionist who had opposed nullification and secession, Perry was acceptable to the North. At the same time he held the respect of the people of his own State. Immediately he called a convention of whites in Columbia during September to frame a constitution fulfilling requirements for restoration to the Union. James L. Orr of Anderson was elected governor, and in November, at its regular session, the legislature ratified the Thirteenth Amendment to the Constitution of the United States, by which slavery was prohibited.

Congress offered the Fourteenth Amendment to the Constitution, which gave Negroes the right to vote and sit on juries. South Carolina, along with the other Southern States except Tennessee, refused to ratify the amendment. The State was put under military rule, and the right of suffrage was refused to every man who had held office or borne arms under the Confederacy. Thus practically every white man was disfranchised, and the States were combined into districts under military rule. North and South Carolina became Military District No. 2, with General Sickles in command.

By sufferance of the martial authority Governor Orr remained in office until 1868, when he was deposed by act of the Federal Congress, and General Canby was appointed military governor until a reconstructed government should be established. A new constitution was framed in Columbia, the Fourteenth Amendment was ratified, Robert K. Scott of Ohio was made governor, a new legislature was elected, military rule was lifted, and South Carolina was restored to the Union. Thus began the darkest period in the State's history. The constitutional convention of 1868 was composed of 76 Negroes, only 17 of whom were taxpayers, and 48 whites, of whom 23 paid no taxes. Many of the whites were 'carpetbaggers' from the North, and a number of the Negroes could neither read nor write. This convention levied for its expense a tax of more than $2,250,000, or nearly six times the whole tax of the State in 1860.

The period from 1868 to 1874 is known as the 'Rule of the Robbers,' from the fact that within these years the public debt leaped from $5,407,306 to $20,333,901. Governor Scott (1868-72) was succeeded by Franklin J. Moses (1872-4), of South Carolina. Votes in the legislature were bought at prices varying from the cost of a man's liquor and cigars to that of a house and lot. Furniture, jewelry, clothing, and groceries were purchased with public funds, while patients in the State hospital actually suffered for food, and threats were made to turn convicts out of the penitentiary because they could not be fed.

In spite of these abuses, however, South Carolina received certain real benefits from the Reconstruction government. The code of procedure adopted by the legislature in 1870 was modeled on that of New York, and though disliked at first was soon recognized as a legal masterpiece and remains the basis for present practice. The legislature outlined an excellent plan for public schools, in the forming of which Negro members had a prominent part. The inability of the State superintendent of education to carry it out was due not merely to the ignorance of Negro school commissioners but also to a widespread misuse of funds.

By 1868 white men had begun the secret organization of the Ku Klux Klan for the purpose of controlling the Negroes and checking the operations of their white leaders (*see Tour* 16). Many acts of violence were committed, and the activities of the Klan were investigated by the United States Government. President Grant placed nine counties in the Piedmont under martial law. Hundreds of leading citizens, including lawyers, doctors, and ministers, were arrested and thrown into jail. One college president, charged with taking part in a riot that occurred without his knowledge, was arrested and lodged in five different jails before being released on a $5,000 bond. In Columbia in 1871, out of 500 men indicted 82 were sentenced. Other cases were tried in 1872; and in 1873–4 a total of 1,091 cases pending were not prosecuted.

With the election of Daniel H. Chamberlain of Massachusetts as governor (1874–6) there was for a time a prospect of better government. He openly accused the legislature of dishonesty and refused to sign the commissions of F. J. Moses and W. J. Whipper (the latter a Northern Negro of ill repute), whom the legislature had elected as circuit court judges. In the election of 1876 some of the more conservative white men considered rallying under Chamberlain, but a Democratic movement was organized with the avowed purpose of filling all State offices with Democrats. General Wade Hampton, best-loved hero of the war, was nominated for governor. In a campaign that combined skilful organization with persuasion and intimidation, Hampton was elected. Leaders assisting in the victory were Colonel A. C. Haskell, General M. C. Butler, and General M. W. Gary, organizer of the Red Shirts—an outgrowth of the 'rifle' and 'sabre' clubs that had armed themselves to put down disorder and defend white interests against the Negro militia. Bands of mounted men in red shirts patroled the grounds at political gatherings and demanded division of time between speakers of the two parties. Sometimes they exercised themselves to see that Hampton had a hearing, and sometimes they prevented opposing candidates from being heard. On the day of election they voted again and again, riding from one precinct to another as long as their horses were able to bear them.

The Chamberlain government refused to vacate office. When the general assembly met in November 1876, Federal troops were placed on guard at the State House to keep order. Two Houses of Representatives were in session: Democrats and Radicals. Members of both refused to leave the building for fear that they would be prevented from getting back in by the troops. Hampton and Chamberlain each continued to acclaim himself as governor of the State and both conducted business with their respective houses, both in the same room in the capitol. General W. H. Wallace was speaker for the Democrats and E. W. M. Mackey for the Radicals.

Hampton realized that a false step would be fatal to his cause as it would produce the riot and bloodshed that he had so faithfully tried to avoid. Outside the people were gathered, factions supporting one or other of the houses. Hampton went to the head of the steps on the north side of the State House and pleaded with the people to keep peace. For four days and nights the dual House of Representatives remained in session, divided only by the aisle down the middle of the hall, each carrying on its own duties, each refusing to yield place to the other.

In the meantime, news spread that the Hunky-Dory Club, a band of armed Negroes from Charleston, was coming to drive out the Wallace House. At once 5,000 Red Shirts from all parts of the State hurried to Columbia. It was only by Hampton's coolness and moderation that bloodshed was averted. The Wallace House withdrew but continued to hold its sessions elsewhere. The State supreme court sustained Hampton's election, but Chamberlain refused to accept the decision. Thus the dual government continued until April 1877, when the newly inaugurated President Hayes ordered the removal of Federal troops from the State. Chamberlain then yielded the office of governor to Hampton, the Radicals disbanded, and the government passed into the hands of the Democrats.

With the collapse of the Republican rule the influence of the Negro in politics rapidly declined; legislative acts made voting increasingly difficult for him, until the constitution of 1895 disfranchised the great majority. The gradual development of direct primary elections, in which by party rule the Negro was forbidden to vote, had, by 1896, reduced the general election to a mere form. In 1898–1900 only one Negro served in the house, the last to hold an important State office.

Hampton's election in 1876 re-established the leadership of what was left of the old conservative planter class, but in that campaign bitter personal differences arose between the governor's associates and several Up Country leaders. The decade following saw a resurgence of the small farmers of the Piedmont, who had by no means disappeared during the ante-bellum regime. They were rendered desperate by the poverty brought on by the war, reconstruction, and the general decline of agriculture, and were also touched by the democratic influence of the day.

In 1886 this group organized a movement with the object of securing for the farmers certain rights and privileges, among which were changes in the suffrage law and the establishment of an agricultural and mechanical college. The leader of the farmers' movement was Benjamin R. Tillman of Edgefield. In 1890 he was made governor of the State, and served until 1894, when he was elected to the United States Senate, where he remained until his death in 1918. The important pieces of legislation during Tillman's administration were provisions for agricultural and vocational education and the establishment of a State dispensary for liquor control. The State dispensary handled the sale of liquor until 1907, when the law was repealed because it was ineffective and a source of corruption. The system disappeared from the last counties with the enactment of State-wide prohibition in 1915. 'Pitchfork Ben,' colorful and radical leader, stirred up much enmity within the State, but the 'Tillman Movement' strengthened the principle and practice of democracy and rendered lasting service to the farmers and the cause of education.

By the turn of the century South Carolina had begun to be aware of itself again and to look into its problems with an eye to progress. The generation growing up after the days of reconstruction was better fitted for individual effort, and the balance of power was in the hands of farmers and industrialists in the upper section of the State. From the eight districts of pre-Revolutionary days, the State had been subdivided into 46 counties with as many units of government. The affairs of the counties are largely in the hands of the county legislative delegations, composed of State senators and representatives.

In agriculture and industry there has been an upward trend, though somewhat slow. Each decade shows the growth of manufacturing to be greater than the advance in agriculture. This is owing to numerous factors, including the development of improved transportation and water power in the Piedmont section, the decline in the proportion of Negroes to the entire population, the reduction of cotton acreage owing to inroads of the boll weevil and the crop control program of the Federal Government, and the general southward movement of the cotton textile industry. For the first time since the census of 1810 the State has more whites than Negroes in its population. With a total of 1,738,765 in 1930, the ratio was 54.3 per cent whites to 45.5 per cent Negroes. The remaining fraction of 1 per cent includes foreign-born, Indians, and all others.

During the World War, cantonments were established at Greenville, Spartanburg, and Columbia. Only Fort Jackson (formerly Camp Jackson) at Columbia remains. In 1940 it was made the home post of the Eighth and the Thirtieth Divisions. South Carolina's official roster listed about 62,000 in World War service, of whom 2,085 died. Of 78 Congressional medals awarded for distinguished service, 6 went to South Carolinians; only three States had more Congressional medalists than South Carolina, and three others as many. An indirect result of the World War was the large exodus of Negroes from the State in the early 1920's. Returned soldiers brought stories of higher wages paid elsewhere—and at home jobs were scarce and competition with white workers keener. The Negroes who emigrated were among the more enterprising and intelligent, and their leaving helped maintain the high proportion of illiteracy among those who remained.

In recent years South Carolina has moved rapidly away from its traditional isolation. The excellent highways built during the twenties and thirties, the wealth introduced by textile industries, and the new point of view brought in by various Federal agencies have all contributed to this change. South Carolinians are no longer complacent at their high illiteracy and infant mortality rates, nor at the rapid depletion of their lands. The advance in education has been marked. In 1938 there were nearly five times as many white pupils in State-supported high schools as in 1906; and during the same period the number of Negro pupils increased from none to 13,576. With its balance between agriculture and industry, South Carolina was not greatly affected by the boom of the late 1920's, nor did the subsequent depression bring suffering as desperate as in States with heavily populated urban centers.

Until recently, prohibition has been a heated issue in politics. The dispensary system of the Tillman era resulted in much bitterness, which was not removed under State and national prohibition. Bootlegging and its accompanying evils flourished. In 1934 the legislature authorized the sale of beer, and in 1935 the sale of spirituous liquors—but in packages only, and during daylight hours. After considerable controversy, sales taxes on soft drinks and tobacco were levied in 1923 and 1925, and have since been continued.

The people of South Carolina are increasingly conscious of public health problems. A State Board of Health has existed since 1879, and since 1910 it has labored especially for the decrease of diseases connected with poverty: malaria, pellagra, and hookworm. In 1915 the Bureau of Vital Statistics was established, and in 1935 the South Carolina Medical Association appointed a committee to investigate maternal mortality. The State Board of Public Welfare, established in 1920, ceased to function in 1926 when its appropriation was vetoed; but the State Planning Board was created in 1933 and legalized as a part of State government in 1938. It acts in an advisory capacity only. A

much-needed child labor law was passed in 1937 prohibiting the working of children under 16 in mines, factories, and textile establishments.

Since 1930 no development in the State has been more important
than the conservation of natural resources by the Federal Government.
Eroded lands have been terraced, new forests set out, power plants
built, and electricity supplied to rural consumers. Farm loans and rehabilitation projects have done their part in bringing new hope to those
who love and cling to the land on which they were born.

The Negro

THE first shipload of English colonists in 1670 brought three Negro slaves to South Carolina. A year later Governor John Yeamans, accompanied by fellow islanders, brought more Negroes from Barbados, and the Barbadian mode of plantation life was introduced in the new settlement of Charles Town. The *Fundamental Constitutions* (*see History*) provided for slaves, and although Locke's masterpiece was not thought to be practicable in other respects, the slave system flourished.

By 1698 rice and indigo were being cultivated. The slave population had increased to such an extent that the province, fearing insurrection, passed an act to encourage the importation of white servants, one for each ten Negroes. Little came of the plan, as the Negroes were more useful in clearing swamp land. In addition, the New England and British traders found the slave trade a source of great wealth. Before 1765 Negroes outnumbered whites, and they retained this numerical superiority until 1930 with the exception of the period *c.*1790–1810. Many came from the West Indies, but the largest number was brought directly from Africa, especially from the Gold Coast and Gambia. Certain ethnologists, recalling the preponderance of Bantu and Angola tribesmen, assert that the Gullah dialect of South Atlantic Negroes is derived from the Angola tongue.

Serious racial antagonisms did not develop in the earliest phases of slavery. In 1702 Negroes were taught at Goose Creek by the Reverend Samuel Thomas, a missionary sent from England to South Carolina by the Society for the Propagation of the Gospel in Foreign Parts. He wrote in 1703 that 'twenty slaves have learned to read,' and in his final report to the society two years later he says:

'I have here presumed to give an account of 1000 slaves belonging to our English in Carolina, many of which are well affected to Christianity so far as they know of it, and are desirous of Christian knowledge and seem to be willing to prepare themselves for it in learning to read for which they redeem their time from their labour, many of them can read in the Bible distinctly and great numbers of them were learning when I left the Province.'

The Reverend Mr. Thomas is credited with the first systematic and successful attempt to educate Negroes in America. The '1000 slaves' to whom he referred was his estimate of the Negroes in six parishes adjacent to Charles Town. Dr. Thomas was in South Carolina only a short while, returning to England for about a year, after which he came back to South Carolina and died the day following his arrival in 1705. He was succeeded by the Reverend Mr. LeJau, who was influential with prominent Carolinians, and persuaded them to have their slaves instructed. In 1712, Benjamin Dennis, an English schoolmaster, was teaching Negroes in this section, and some authorities believe that these early schools served whites, Indians, and Negroes alike. In 1741, at the suggestion of Bishop Seeker, the Society for the Propagation of the Gospel in Foreign Parts purchased two slaves, Harry and Andrew, who were educated to serve as missionaries and schoolmasters to their own people. The school opened in 1743, under the supervision of Dr. Alexander Garden, Bishop of London's Commissary for North Carolina, South Carolina, and the Bahama Islands, and rector of St. Philip's Church in Charleston; it continued until about 1764.

Though the vast majority of Negroes were employed as field hands on the plantations, a select group was trained in the domestic arts, cabinetmaking, blacksmithing, carpentry, and other crafts. Their masters frequently hired them out and received most or all of their cash wages, which sometimes amounted to as much as $1 a day. Numbers of slaves were permitted to retain part of their earnings, and some purchased their own freedom. The fact that Negro artisans outnumbered the white, and that their masters were eager to convert Negro labor into money, led first to a deep antagonism between the groups, and then to legal measures for the benefit of the white artisans.

Until the Revolutionary War the number of slaves rose consistently. Although the fears of possible revolt increased, the desire for more wealth and more slaves outweighed them. Opposition to the formal education of Negroes came early in the eighteenth century, after it was noted that the slave insurrections were usually led by Negroes of some learning.

The chief revolt of early years occurred September 9, 1739, at Stono. Spain had offered freedom to any slaves who could reach St. Augustine. In his account of the Lords of Trade, Lieutenant Governor Bull wrote:

'Many attempts of others have been discovered and prevented, notwithstanding which, on the ninth of September last at night a great number of Negroes rose in rebellion, broke open a store where they got arms, killed twenty-one white persons, and were marching the next morning in a daring manner out of the province, killing all they met and burning several houses as they passed along the road. I was returning from Granville county with four gentlemen and met these rebels at eleven o'clock in the forenoon and fortunately discerning the approaching danger had time enough to avoid it, and to give notice to the militia, who on that occasion behaved with so much expedition and bravery as by four o'clock the same day to come up with them and killed and took so many as put a stop to any further mischief at that time. Forty-four of them have been killed and executed. Some few yet remaining concealed in the woods expecting the same fate, seem desperate. If such an attempt is made in a time of peace, what might be expected if an enemy should appear upon our frontier with a design to invade us.'

Minor insurrections occurred during the next nine years, and thereafter the slave code was made more rigorous, and many privileges were withdrawn. The Barbadian code had been adapted to South Carolina, with more stringent regulations against the maltreatment of slaves and better provisions for their general care.

With the opening of the interior following the defeat of the Yamasee revolt in 1715–16, in which many Negroes bore arms for the colonists against the Indians, the transportation of slaves to the new towns and plantations began. Most of the Negroes were led afoot through the forests, except for small children and some of the women. These groups of slaves, known as coffles, would stop wherever buyers appeared, and then the band would proceed.

Slavery never became the issue for Up Country people that it was in the coastal sections, nor was there as large a proportion of Negroes to whites. By 1734, the 22,000 Negroes in the province far outnumbered the whites—some authorities assert by three to one. In 1743, four years after the Stono insurrection, a law was passed requiring men to go armed to church, in readiness for a slave uprising.

Despite the widespread fear of them, slaves were trained to bear arms. As early as 1704 the slaves were called on to render military aid in time of alarm. Seventy-three served against the Spaniards in 1742, and five years later a provision for the enlistment of slaves up to one third the enrollment of whites was written into law. During the Revolution many slaves served, and a number were freed because of their record.

Before 1800 hundreds of free Negroes were in South Carolina, most of them in Charleston. Some owned plantations and slaves, although most were artisans. In 1790 the mulattoes and others of mixed blood organized the Brown Fellowship Society to which only free brown men were eligible. The object of the Society was expressed in the preamble of the rules and regulations:

'Whereas we, Free brown men, natives of the City of Charleston, in the State of South Carolina, having taken into consideration the unhappy situation of our fellow creatures, and the distresses of our widows and orphans, for the want of a fund to relieve them in the hour of their distresses, sickness and death; and holding it an essential duty to mankind to contribute all they can towards relieving the wants and miseries, and promoting the welfare and happiness of one another, and observing the method of many other well disposed persons of the State, by entering into particular Societies for this purpose, to be effectual, we therefore, whose names are underwritten, to comply with this great duty, have freely and cheerfully entered into a society in Charleston, and State aforesaid, commencing the first of November 1790 and have voted, agreed and subscribed to the following rules for ordering and conducting the same.'

This organization continued for nearly 150 years, its name being changed in 1890 to the Century Fellowship Society. Only two or three former members are living, and the official group is no longer in existence. During its lifetime, the society educated children, supported orphans, helped widows and the needy, and sometimes purchased freedom of other Negroes. It had its own bank, church, and cemetery. The group represented by this society produced a great many leaders, among them the Reverend Samuel David Ferguson, Bishop of the Episcopal Church in Liberia, 1885–1916. The members were particularly anxious to preserve the integrity of their group and would not associate with whites or other Negroes except as necessary. The resulting antagonism, particularly between the mulattoes and the darker skinned Negroes, is illustrated in the fact that neither group was permitted to utilize the banks, churches, and schools that the other used.

In the first quarter of the eighteenth century, with the repeal of the law prohibiting interstate slave trade, the proportion of Negroes to whites once more increased. Although they did not wish to see this law repealed, certain statesmen in South Carolina knew that the slave trade was being operated illegally and believed it better to have it regulated by law than permitted to continue with no regulations. The census of 1810 noted more whites than Negroes in the State, but shortly afterward the reverse ratio was established again. Cotton had come into the Up Country and rice and sea island cotton were flourishing in the Low Country, circumstances that conduced to a large investment in slave labor. Until the outbreak of the War between the States, the purchase of slaves absorbed a great deal of money that would otherwise have gone into agricultural and industrial development.

An incipient Negro uprising was put down in Camden in 1822. The same year witnessed the Vesey insurrection in Charleston, planned and led by Denmark Vesey, a free mulatto from the West Indies, with the assistance of James Poyas and Gullah Jack. The latter, an Angola Negro, was a recognized conjurer who had deluded his brethren into believing that he could bewitch them and that the crow claws he gave to his conspirators would render them invulnerable. Four white men were also involved in the plan. The revolt was exposed by a Negro body servant; the militia was called out, and many arrests were made. One hundred and fifty cases were brought to court; Vesey and 34 of his fellows were condemned to death, and 44 others to transportation beyond the State limits. As a result of this uprising, the State passed an act forbidding manumission except through consent of the legislature. Curfew laws were more rigidly enforced and gatherings of Negroes prohibited.

The free Negroes, however, were able to make progress, and among their enterprises was the manufacture of cotton gins, begun by the Ellisons, a slaveholding family of free Negroes in Sumter County. Their business continued until a few years ago, when the last member of the family died.

The *Southern Lumberman,* a few years ago, carried an account of a South Carolina concern long under management by Negroes. The J. J. Sulton and Sons Lumber Company at Orangeburg, organized 1825, is operated by members of the fourth generation of that name, graduates of Claflin University.

In 1850 free Negroes were reported in 56 occupations in Charleston. Their work as artisans necessitated their training as apprentices, which was the principal education they received.

Among the Negroes there was little organized revolt after the Vesey episode. The issues of abolition and States' rights only remotely affected them. The abolition movement, however, received some of its most ardent support from two Charleston white women, Sarah and Angelina Grimké, daughters of a prominent judge and outspoken advocates of equalitarianism. Angelina married Theodore Dwight Weld, who was intimately connected with William Lloyd Garrison in his program.

In the Colonial and ante-bellum years, the churches were the centers of social life among the Negroes. The churches, with few exceptions, belonged to white congregations, although Negroes were sometimes allowed to organize their own and have their own pastors. As an example, what is thought to be the first Negro Baptist Church in America was organized shortly before the Revolution by Andrew Bryan in the Silver Bluff section near Aiken. Many white churches had a preponderance of Negro members, but few accommodations for them, beyond slave galleries in the rear of the large churches or certain pews in the back of the smaller ones. Negroes, however, were permitted to take communion from the same altar and at the same time with whites.

Shortly after South Carolina became dominantly Negro in population it was decided by churchmen that membership did not alter the slave's status. The Methodist Church, however, under the leadership of Bishop Asbury, was at first opposed to slavery. Asbury often spoke of the condition of Negroes, which he considered desperate and degraded. In the 1830's Bishop William Capers devoted his energies toward the religious instruction of slaves, and Dr. John L. Girardeau, of the Presbyterian Church, was threatened with attack by whites because of his interest in the slaves of Charleston.

During the War between the States, the Confederate Army claimed thousands of white men, who had to leave the women and children alone with the slaves, very often on isolated plantations. The faithfulness and industry of the Negroes during these days was a source of great comfort to the men at the front. Hundreds of slaves remained attached to their former masters after they were freed.

When Beaufort fell in 1861, the slaves were inducted into the Federal Army, or in some cases established on land formerly belonging to their owners; and numerous missionaries from the North came down to found schools and teach them. This section had the highest ratio of Negroes in the State.

Many Negroes of the Beaufort district became prominent in the State's affairs during the Reconstruction era. Robert Smalls, who had seized a Confederate vessel, the *Planter*, and turned it over to the Federals in Charleston, was elected to the United States House of Representatives, as was Thomas Miller.

Most of the trouble during this reconstruction was precipitated by Northern agitators who had more oratory than judgment. Native whites who had served in the Confederate Army were disfranchised and the lower classes of whites with the Negroes took charge of government. A number of educated Negroes, however, kept their balance. Beverly Nash, of Columbia, and Francis Cardozo, born in Charleston and widely educated, were examples. Through the legislature, largely composed of Negroes, and J. K. Jillson, of Massachusetts, a measure was introduced in 1868 that resulted in the establishment of a public school system. This movement was finally incorporated in the South Carolina Constitution of 1895, and forms the basis of the present educational program.

Numerous schools for Negroes were establish in the State during the years 1866–76, and the Claflin interests in Orangeburg provided agricultural and mechanical training for Negroes more than 20 years before similar advantages were available for whites.

By the constitution of 1895, suffrage regulations were changed and through the rule of the Democratic party, Negroes as a group were denied the right to vote—with this exception: Negroes who had voted for Wade Hampton in 1876 could vote in the Democratic primaries. With Wade Hampton's rise to power in 1876, the whites had resumed political control of the State. Hampton was a man of surprisingly tolerant doctrines, in view of the popular feeling of South Carolinians, and several Negroes were given office in his regime.

A wave of lynchings resulted in the enactment (1895) of a State law providing for the payment of a certain sum of money to families of victims of mob law, to be paid by the county in which the lynching occurred.

With the downfall of the slave system, the sharecropping system developed (see Agriculture), and increased antagonism between Negroes and whites of the lower economic levels. Such is the root of most racial conflict at the present time (1940).

Since Reconstruction days Negroes have been confined largely to menial and unskilled work in the towns and cities. Few have participated in business management or the professions, although some individuals have gone far in each. The economic readjustment after Reconstruction advanced the fortunes of Negroes in certain lines—opening new opportunities for them to gain experience in business among their own people. Although many of the well-educated and most resourceful Negroes have gone from South Carolina to other sections of the country, those who remain find their economic status improving. In agriculture, according to the 1930 census, Negroes operated 76,578 farms, comprising 3,489,252 acres, and valued at $69,829,296. They owned 18,394 farms, comprising 795,077 acres, which were valued at $14,827,788. In half of the 46 counties of the State, Negro farmers outnumbered whites.

According to the same census, there were 1,320 Negro proprietors and firm members who operated retail stores, of which the pay rolls were $180,739 and the sales $2,298,772. Grocery stores accounted for 40.2 per cent of the business. The medical, dental, legal, ministerial, and teaching professions involved 5,678 Negroes.

After the War between the States, Negroes no longer worshipped in white churches, but organized their own. In 1926 there were 2,838 Negro churches in South Carolina with a total membership of 405,614. Of these, 1,364 churches were of the Baptist denomination, with a total membership of 234,224; and 1,239 were of the Methodist denomination, with a total membership of 153,174.

South Carolina has produced some distinguished Negro leaders. Among them are Archibald Henry Grimké, lawyer and historian; Francis Henry Grimké, minister; Ernest Everett Just, internationally famous biologist and the first recipient of the Spingarn Medal, an award to Negroes for outstanding achievement; Kelly Miller, essayist and educator; Mary McLeod Bethune, educator; William Pickens, educator and an executive of the National Association for the Advancement of Colored People; Benjamin Elijah Mays, dean of the School of Religion at Howard University; Edward Brawley, minister, and his son, Benjamin G. Brawley, educator and author; Julius J. Washington, lawyer (graduated from the University of South Carolina during Reconstruction); and Robert Shaw Wilkinson, educator. The last Negro to hold a prominent civic office was Dr. William Crum, appointed Collector of the Port of Charleston in 1905–9 by Theodore Roosevelt.

Of the 14 Negroes to attend West Point between 1870 and 1936, five were South Carolinians. Two of the three Negroes sent to Annapolis during the same period also came from this State.

Negroes are affiliated with various labor unions, but their number in the organized textile industries of South Carolina has been limited. The general assembly made it unlawful in 1932 for textile manufacturers to employ operatives of different races in the same room and offer them the same accommodations; however, equal accommodations were to be provided. In 1938, the textile plants employed 3,880 Negroes—generally as cleaners, scrubbers, haulers, and in other minor capacities. Wage rates for Negroes are the same as for whites in similar capacities, the minimum being $10 and ranging to $20 per week for 40 hours.

South Carolina has the greatest proportion of illiterate Negroes in America. The annual State cost per Negro pupil in 1937-8 was $11.28, ranging from $6.28 to $18.30 per county, exclusive of the sums made available by endowments and special philanthropic funds. Enrollment in elementary and high schools was 478, 794 for an average school term of 130 days. The State cost is still very low, but since the establishment of Negro schools after the Reconstruction era and their induction into the State system, appropriations have annually increased (*see Education*).

Since 1936, under the WPA, 23,000 Negroes, formerly classified as illiterates, have been taught to read. This is an estimated 15 per cent of the Negro illiterates specified by the 1930 census. A great deal of instruction in the trades is given by the WPA, utilizing hundreds of volunteer Negro instructors.

Living conditions among Negroes and whites of the lowest economic class are not as different as is generally supposed. The lack of education, facilities for medical care, and the means of bringing people together in wholesome social activities is tragically apparent among tenant farmers and sharecroppers, Negro and white. However, the public is gradually learning that the conditions that pauperize the Negroes also impoverish the whites; lower wages for Negroes bring down the wages of white laborers; poor living conditions favor the spread of disease.

Acts of violence between the two races are less frequent than 50 years ago, although the latent antagonism can easily be brought to the danger point. In the courts the Negro sometimes meets prejudice, in addition to that which faces all the lower classes in any social order. Adherence to color lines varies throughout the State. Jim Crow customs generally prevail, but they vary from place to place, and in numerous instances are broken or ignored.

Within the race itself are clashes. The mulattoes form one group, especially along the coast, and the darker skinned another. Furthermore, the same kind of conflict obtains between rural and urban Negroes as between whites of the same groups. Probably the most serious discord among the Negroes results from occasional snobbishness on the part of those who are educated, and mistrust of the educated on the part of the illiterate or less educated.

South Carolina Negroes have migrated to other parts of the country in large numbers and for the first time since 1810 there is now a majority of whites in the State. Between 1910 and 1930 about three fourths of the number of native South Carolinians moving elsewhere were Negroes. It is asserted that this migration is a contributing cause of the continued high illiteracy rate, on the assumption that literate Negroes are able to take advantage of the greater opportunities offered to them elsewhere. Higher wages in other sections also account for much of the migration, while other factors were the depredations of the boll weevil in 1921–2, and the consequent slump in cotton production. Between 1920 and 1930 Negro farm tenancy decreased by nearly 25,000 men, although the bulk proportion of tenantry in the State rose in this period.

Recently a new factor has improved the relationships of Negroes and whites in South Carolina. A minority group of cultured Negroes, educated for the most part in other sections of the country, has been able to strike an understanding on many interracial issues with educated and socially disposed whites. Most Negroes, however, belong to the lower and impoverished group of society; where this group is in competition with a large section of the white population for the basic necessities of life, prejudice is more likely to appear. Yet there are interracial loyalties and friendships that are characteristically Southern in their nature.

Agriculture

THE ships that brought the first English settlers to Carolina in 1670 brought seeds of cotton and indigo and roots of ginger; for the Lords Proprietors were convinced that agriculture would be the chief source of profit from their new possessions. Under the direction of Joseph West, then deputy and later governor, an experimental farm was planted with the new crops. Before the year was out, cattle and 'hoggs' were also introduced and found profitable. Oranges, olives, tea, grapes, rice, and silk were all eventually tested for their commercial value.

While experiment developed, the province began to pay the proprietors with timber, furs, and skins. But, as originally planned, farm products soon became more important. The intention of the proprietors was that raw material should be exported, and manufactured articles brought in from England. This plan worked so well that by 1768 South Carolina had one fifth the total export trade of the English colonies. Many early products have since disappeared, among them olives, oranges, silk, indigo, and rice. The last two were the most valuable.

It was due chiefly to Elizabeth (more often known as Eliza), daughter of Captain Lucas, governor of Antigua, that the commercial growing of indigo was begun in South Carolina; and Moses Lindo, a Jew of Charleston, was responsible for methods of sorting and grading. Wealth began to pour into the hands of the proprietors, and, after the province was taken over by the Crown, a bounty was placed on indigo production. In 1775 a maximum of 1,170,000 pounds was reached.

Several years before 1686 Captain John Thurber sailed into Charleston harbor with a bag of Madagascar rice, which he gave to Dr. Henry Woodward, who was interested in the advance of the province. Thus began what was destined to be a flourishing enterprise. Rice was cultivated in the inland swamps and became of such importance in the eighteenth century that it was used for money, being accepted even in payment of taxes. As early as 1754 the province was exporting 104,682 barrels, in addition to supplying its own people with an abundance. Rice was later found to be less profitable than indigo; but after the Revolution and the end of commercial indigo planting, rice again took first place, largely because of the more successful tidewater cultivation by means of an elaborate system of dikes and canals. More than half of the total rice crop of the United States was produced in South Carolina, up to 1850. The last commercial planting occurred in 1926.

Cotton growing is mentioned in the first year of the settlement of Carolina, but for years it had no commercial importance. In 1747 the province exported '7 bags of cotton wool.' The long-staple type of cotton was introduced shortly after the Revolution on the islands in the Beaufort district, and immediately took the fancy of plantation owners, proving to be highly profitable. Though short staple cotton was planted for a number of years with fair success in the Up Country, it was not until after the invention of the cotton gin that prosperity in this section was comparable with that of the rice aristocracy in the Low Country.

In 1801 the legislature authorized the expenditure of $50,000 to secure use of the Whitney gin, and cotton immediately began to rise to first importance, spreading all over the State as the chief money crop. South Carolina became one of the chief cotton-producing States during the ante-bellum period, raising (along with Georgia) more than half of the American crop in 1820. Production in the State amounted to 350,000 bales in 1860.

The rise of cotton in the early nineteenth century brought significant results: the economic submergence of nonslave owners; the emigration of Quakers, Covenanters, and others opposed to slavery; the impoverishment of the soil, with a consequent departure of thousands of settlers to new lands farther west; and the development of commercial agriculture, with the tendency to neglect manufacturing and diversified farming.

After the War between the States, the price of cotton declined as its production increased. For the 20 years following 1900, cotton continued to be grown in excess of market requirements and at too great a cost of production. The tenant system with its liens on prospective crops caused debts to rise to an unbearable degree, and vast areas of land became depleted. Many Up Country farmers supplemented their income by employment in textile mills, and hundreds left their farms altogether to work for the increasingly numerous manufacturing concerns.

In spite of the discouraging situation, however, leaders continued to preach diversification and urge renovation of work lands. The Cokers, in Hartsville, are known throughout the South for their achievements with development of cottonseed. Though in 1920 a bumper crop of 1,625,000 bales was produced, by 1921 the boll weevil had reached the State and spread over the cotton fields, reducing the yield in one year by 500,000 bales. Then began a further exodus of farmers and farm employees, particularly Negroes, to other industries and other sections of the country. During this period the sea island cotton crop was ruined by the weevil, and thus another highly profitable product succumbed to changing conditions.

The disaster brought certain benefits, in spite of the poverty and consternation it caused. Farmers were compelled to diversify their crops or leave their lands idle. Experimentation with the neglected soils of the Sand Hills region resulted in the planting of orchards, vineyards, berry and asparagus farms, which have given to that section new value and profitableness. Livestock and poultry began to yield paying returns, and some of the country's best beef and dairy cattle were developed on South Carolina lands. Railroad interests were early attracted, and agricultural divisions established experimental truck, orchard, grape, and berry areas as diversification projects.

Corn has always been a staple in South Carolina. As early as 1792, exports amounted to 99,985 bushels. It was the most important agricultural product in the State in 1815 and continued so until 1850, when it was first outstripped by cotton. Since that time it has remained of secondary importance, both in acreage and money value.

About 1906, E. McIver Williamson, of Darlington, made substantial contributions to the production of corn through experimental methods of cultivation. Mr. Williamson contended that he could make more money out of corn than cotton. Features of his system are the deeper planting of seed, closer spacing in the drill, and a side application of fertilizer to increase ear production. He reached a yield of 125 bushels to the acre, which is six and a quarter times the average yield for the State. The influence of his method, adopted by some farmers, is shown in the fact that in 1905, the year he began his experiments, the State yield amounted to 10.2 bushels per acre, and five years later the average had climbed to 17.4.

Corn, it is claimed, would be a much more profitable crop if greater attention were paid to its cultivation, and this is borne out by various prize crops that have been produced in the State when special care has been taken. Captain Z. J. Drake, of Marlboro County, made a world record with 255 bushels on one acre in 1889, and in 1910 Jerry Moore, of Florence County, made the corresponding record for boys with 228.75 bushels per acre. Other outstanding yields have also occurred from time to time.

The decrease in amount and quality of corn produced was due to the fact that little cash could be secured for the crop and it was relegated to poorer land, worked in spare time, fertilized insufficiently, and the blades were stripped from the stalk for fodder before the ears were fully matured.

The War between the States marked the close of the plantation era in South Carolina. There was practically no outside sale of products during the four years of fighting, and effort was directed to the growing of supplies for the troops. Thousands of bales of cotton were burned, chiefly by the invading armies, and when the war closed little food remained for citizens and little feed for stock. In the Low Country rice was failing as a money crop; irrigation works were neglected and even destroyed; and with the freeing of slaves, labor was demoralized and the cost of production became prohibitive. Rice was finally eliminated as a commercial asset by the development of upland plats in Louisiana, Texas, and Arkansas.

For many years after the war, agriculture was more or less static. The rise of the 'share-cropping' system dates from these years, when the landowners had no money to pay for labor and the laborers had no land. The adjustment to entirely new economic standards consumed the energies formerly devoted to production.

In the dark days following the Reconstruction period, the small farmers were able to subsist under the 'lien law,' which allowed them to borrow money on the crops they were raising by giving mortgages or liens on them. Out of this grew the system of sharecropping, by which the landowners furnished land, mules or horses, and fertilizer, and the laborers agreed to work and gather the crop, profits being shared equally. Under this system many of the great plantations were broken up into small farms cultivated by sharecroppers, the more thrifty of whom soon purchased their acres.

In the early 1880's the 'fence-law' was passed, requiring the fencing of stock rather than of crops as heretofore. While this law was eminently wise and just, laying the foundation for the improvement of all kinds of stock, its immediate effect was calamitous to the small farmer whose stock had enjoyed free range. He had had meat and milk from his own animals, but they had been supported in large part by his neighbors to whose woods and unfenced pastures the stock had free entrance. To his income from a small crop of cotton he had added a few dollars by the sale of calves, pigs, mutton, hides, and wool. This food supply and supplementary income both failed. He had to turn more than ever to farming—tenant farming—for he owned little land and that generally of low fertility.

By 1880 the census showed farm occupancy in the State as follows: owners, 46,645; tenants, 47,219. By 1890 a new generation of both races had grown up, thoroughly acquainted with neighborhood customs and ways of tenancy. Then there were reported: owners, 51,428; tenants, 62,580.

Renting farm lands in the South has always been on the basis of a one-year contract, often oral, sometimes written, always easily terminated. The cotton crop about which it centers is usually gathered, sold, and the proceeds divided, according to the rent contract, by December 15. Nothing remains to be carried over into the succeeding year. When compost or stable manure was used as fertilizer for cotton, as was usually done prior to 1880, a part of its fertility remained in the soil for the second and even the third year. If the tenant furnished the compost, he knew that if he moved at the end of the year he did not get much good from it. Why should he rake leaves and straw and do the dirty laborious work of hauling manure to the fields, only to benefit the landlord? Commercial fertilizer was easier to apply, surer in its results. The cost was definitely known and could be easily apportioned between tenant and landowner. The use of such fertilizer for cotton developed to the full the evils of the tenant system.

Of all crops in the world, cotton is best suited to the conditions of tenant farming in the South. It requires much hand labor, but not of a highly skilled kind; it is grown all in one season and before the end of the year; it cannot be consumed on the farm, but must be sold for a definite price fixed by the world market. Therefore, under the tenant system, the farmers have grown cotton, and yet more cotton, limiting its acreage only by the ability of hands and fingers to pick it. And this system of yearly contract and frequent moving from farm to farm, with the use of commercial fertilizer, intended to stimulate the crop rather than to conserve the land, results in the depletion of the soil to the grievous injury of all parties, the landlord, the tenant, and the public. Commercial fertilizers contain the elements of plant food, but they do not contain, and make no claim to contain, either humus or bacteria which the soil must have to retain rainfall and continue to grow crops.

Where these elements are not furnished, as on most tenant-operated farms, the soil gradually becomes 'worn out.' Such is the condition of hundreds of thousands of acres in South Carolina today. It is an even more serious soil problem than the control of erosion. South Carolina spends more for commercial fertilizer in proportion to its area than any other State. In 1935, 614,790 tons of fertilizer were used at a cost of $12,300,000—six times as much as in 1880. It is a huge bill for poor farmers to pay year after year, for no permanent improvement in their soils.

Whether the South Carolinian likes it or not, the future of agriculture in the State depends on grass, cattle, and legumes. These are matters within the control of the South Carolina farmers themselves. In the judgment of experts they promise more lasting benefit than would easier credit for the purchase of land to enable tenants to become owners.

The 1935 Census of Agriculture reported that as of January 1, 1935, there were 5,327 farm owners; 10,615 part owners; 102,926 tenants; and 636 managers. These harvested in 1934 crops from 4,177,861 acres, an average to the farm of about 25 acres. They produced that year 18,114,237 bushels of corn, 5,057,144 bushels of sweet potatoes, and 680,880 bales of cotton (500 pounds each). In 1850, on 29,967 farms, the production was 300,901 bales (of 400 pounds each), and 16,-271,454 bushels of corn, 6,337,469 bushels of sweet potatoes, and 159,930,613 pounds of rough rice.

Considering that the population of the State is now almost three times what it was in 1850, it is evident that food crops have by no means increased in the same ratio. Tobacco and truck-produce have replaced rice as a source of income, but nothing has replaced it as a food crop. The rice eaten now in South Carolina is not home-grown.

With respect to livestock production, there has been a great decline in numbers, but a great advance in quality. The number of cattle in the State in 1850 was 777,686; of sheep, 285,551; of swine, 1,065,503. In 1935, cattle numbered 374,000, about one half the earlier figure; sheep, 12,000, one twentieth; swine, 519,000, one half. Survey after survey has shown that the tenant does not generally keep enough livestock to furnish his family adequately with either milk or meat. How can he, if his rent contract contains no provision for pasturage? All permanent conservation of the soil is dependent to a large degree upon livestock and animal manures. European and Chinese farmers learned this truth long ago.

Movements and organizations have not been lacking. In line with work begun by Joseph West, first governor of South Carolina, there was founded in Charleston on August 24, 1785, the South Carolina Society for Promoting and Improving Agriculture and Other Rural Concerns. This organization encouraged experimentation as to methods and new crops to be grown in the State. Ten years afterwards it was incorporated by the legislature as the Agricultural Society of South Carolina, and has continued in existence until today. It was to this society that John de la Howe, of French Huguenot extraction, at his death on January 2, 1797, left his plantation in Abbeville District, to be used as 'an agricultural or farm school' for poor boys and girls. It was one of the earliest such institutions in the country.

The first offshoot of this State organization was the Pendleton Farmers Society, formed in 1815. Among its members were many Charlestonians whose summer homes were in Pendleton District, and, later, John C. Calhoun and his son-in-law, Thomas G. Clemson. Records of the society show the current interest in agriculture and rural affairs. Many other such organizations were established, mainly in the middle and Low Country, including the Beech Island Agricultural Club in Aiken County, the Darlington Agricultural Society, and the Agricultural Society of Christ Church Parish. A group of these bodies combined under the United Agricultural Society of South Carolina, and, for several decades, attempted to have an agricultural professorship established at the State University. This was opposed by those who wanted a separate institution for such instruction. A few lectures on agriculture were delivered at the South Carolina College in 1866 by Joseph LeConte, but all agricultural education was interrupted by the War between the States and the ten subsequent years of Reconstruction.

The first group to organize after the war was composed of the small farm owners who, never dependent on slave labor, were not demoralized when it was withdrawn. In the midst of political disruption, the Grange was established in South Carolina in 1871, and through its efforts in persuading the farmers to take recourse to law and government for correction of their ills, materially affected the course of State government. Lien 'time prices' sometimes amounted to 100 to 200 per cent of cash values. This was changed in 1877 when interest was legalized at 7 per cent. Low-priced cotton was mainly responsible for the forfeiture of land for taxes, and because of it nearly 1,000,000 acres were taken over in 1886.

In that year the Farmers' Movement, organized and led by Benjamin

R. (Pitchfork Ben) Tillman, made a vigorous entry into politics. Up Country was once more bitterly opposed to Low Country, where small farms were in the minority. The Farmers' Alliance, coming to South Carolina in 1886, added its force to rampant Tillmanism, and by 1890 the Low Country 'Bourbons' gave way to the farmers. More concerned with local questions than national issues, Tillman and the Farmers' Movement gave little consideration to the country-wide platform of the Farmers' Alliance. However, in 1894, when Tillman was elected United States senator, he had to take part in the Alliance program. While he accepted the Free Silver issue, he opposed government ownership of utilities and loans to private individuals by the National Government.

The Farmers' Movement inspired the Clemson Agricultural and Mechanical College, opened 1893, and Winthrop College, 1894, both appealing to popular vocational education; the new State constitution of 1895; agricultural experiment stations, and club work among farm families. In 1905 the Grange died out as a South Carolina organization, but was revived in 1930, and now has between 4,000 and 5,000 members scattered over the entire State.

Club work among farm girls began in the United States when Mrs. Marie Cromer Seigler, a young schoolteacher in Aiken County, South Carolina, gathered together 47 girls and formed a tomato-canning club in 1910. Shortly before that, a corn club for boys was established in Chesterfield County by W. J. Tiller. Out of these small beginnings have grown the 4-H clubs, spreading all over the United States and into some foreign countries. In South Carolina they claim about 30,000 members, a third of whom are Negroes. Supervisors of the 4-H clubs are paid with funds provided by the State and Federal Governments.

Such State extension services, assisted by Federal grants, grew out of the Smith-Lever Act of 1914. Congressman A. Frank Lever, of this State, with Hoke Smith of Georgia, was responsible for this law, which instituted a program of education through farm and home demonstration agents throughout the counties of the various States.

South Carolina's five experiment stations, jointly operated by Clemson College and the Federal Government, are near Charleston, Florence, Columbia, Barnwell, and at Clemson College itself. At the station near Charleston attention is directed to experimentation with truck, beef cattle, and forestry; the Pee Dee station near Florence is concerned with field crops, and the chief boll weevil laboratory is located there; at the Sand Hill station near Columbia, interest centers in the development of fruits and berries, the crops most adapted to the soils of that region; at the Edisto station in Barnwell County emphasis is placed on the production of melons and asparagus; and the Clemson College station is concerned with many kinds of investigation in field crops, fruits, and livestock, and the use of fertilizer.

Clemson College has many other activities concerned with the education of farmers in the use of lands, the production and marketing of crops and livestock, and with the arousing of interest in farm problems among boys and girls of the rural schools.

There are also numerous efforts toward improved farming among Negroes. In addition to the State Agricultural and Mechanical College at Orangeburg, special farm demonstration agents and 40 odd teachers throughout the public school system give instruction and supervision to rural Negro pupils.

A few years after the War between the States, landowners in the Charleston district became interested in growing vegetables. In 1868 a cotton planter of that section went to New York to arrange for money to finance his next crop. Though he failed to get the money, he came back to Charleston enthusiastic over the broker's suggestion that he grow truck produce for the Northern markets, in which the New Yorker was willing to give financial assistance.

Truck growing began shortly afterward, and shipments were made by water from Charleston to Northern ports. After railroads had standardized their tracks and all-rail shipments of vegetables could be made, water shipments decreased. The change was also accelerated by the more rapid delivery and the refrigeration furnished by railroads. Formerly vegetables were shipped by the package, rates being based on cubic dimensions, but this plan was gradually changed to a weight basis, which was found to be more satisfactory. This change was not effected in South Carolina, however, until 1935. With cheaper freight rates, truck growing was encouraged—but the rates are not yet on a parity with those in northern and western regions. In recent years motor trucks are being used more and more in getting produce to market. Large trucks, loaded with all kinds of vegetables, are familiar sights on the highways, particularly at night. They are often headed for the wholesale market in Columbia, where they are met by buyers from other States, who use trucks to supply their local markets with South Carolina grown vegetables.

Both farms and fisheries have been stimulated by the recent discovery that South Carolina food products are unusually rich in iodine and other minerals. A food research laboratory was established at Charleston in 1928, and outside interests have been attracted, not only to truck farming, but also to the canning of shellfish and vegetables.

In the middle 1880's cotton was being produced in vast quantities and selling at only 9¢ a pound. Though farmers received small return for their efforts, they showed hardly any desire to experiment with other crops. There was one exception in what is now Florence County. Frank M. Rogers began to investigate tobacco culture with a view to adapting it to the Pee Dee section. In early days tobacco had been produced throughout the State, but other crops had supplanted it. Finding his first crop successful, Mr. Rogers increased his acreage in 1886, and secured the services of an experienced grower from North Carolina. The South Carolina Department of Agriculture became interested and offered a premium for the best sample of tobacco grown in the State. This was won by Mr. Rogers, who continued his experiments, and tried a new method of curing. One half the crop was cured on the stalk, the other half by gathering the leaves as they ripened. The second lot sold for twice as much as the first. This system was later adopted throughout the bright tobacco belt from South Carolina to Virginia.

Tobacco growing as a money crop has rapidly increased in South Carolina between the fall line and the coastal region (*see Tour 9a*). Warehouses have been built and markets opened in Lake City, Florence, Mullins, Darlington, Kingstree, and other places. Since 1900 tobacco has become one of the chief sources of income in agriculture. The 1939 crop was valued at more than $17,000,000, or 55 per cent of the combined value of cotton and cottonseed in the State for the same year.

At the present time, South Carolina, though a comparatively small State and one of the lowest in per capita wealth, is producing some of the finest farm crops in the country. Of 19,516,800 acres of land, exclusive of large cities and water, about 5,000,000 were planted and harvested in 1938. Of the remaining area, however, a large part has been so depleted that it is unfit for agriculture. Nearly 8,000,000 acres are so deeply gullied as to be practically destroyed. The soil conservation program has in charge nearly 3,000,000 acres for improvement, and other agencies have taken over large areas for parks and reforestation.

The situation is grave; but South Carolina farmers have turned their attention to better use of the land that remains suitable for cultivation, with the result that a gradual rise in production has been noted for several years. The 1939 volume was not only above the average for 1927–36, but its yield per acre for all crops combined was much higher. Prices were also generally better, the cash value of the principal crops amounting to more than $117,000,000 which was 50 per cent better than 1932. The cotton crop was estimated at 870,000 bales and the price at $49,063,000 including seed.

With the reduction in cotton and tobacco acreage beginning in 1935, there has been more than a commensurate rise in food crops and feed-stuffs. Wheat, oats, and rye have increased in volume and hundreds of acres of land have been turned into pasturage, resulting in greater income from dairy and beef cattle herds. There are now more than 100 herds of purebred beef cattle in South Carolina. Hog, sheep, and poultry raising have also received more attention.

In the report from the United States Department of Agriculture for 1939, South Carolina stood fifth in the farm value of cotton, and fourth in tobacco. In corn the State was twenty-third, and in truck crops twelfth. The State was surpassed only by California and Alabama in shipment of early Irish potatoes to northern markets, and by Mississippi and a group of States, including Texas, in second early tomatoes. It ranked next to California in early asparagus and first of all States in early fall cabbages.

The State has produced an appreciable yield of peaches, in which the 1939 value was twelfth among the peach States, realizing $1,855,000. Other substantial crops include watermelons, cantaloupes, berries, pecans, peanuts, cabbages, onions, sweet potatoes, and sugar cane. Successful innovations in the State have resulted in unusual enterprises, such as a Carneaux pigeon plant noted for rapidly maturing squabs, apiaries, bulb farms, and plant nurseries.

With expansion and diversification of agriculture arose the necessity for better marketing facilities. During 1916 asparagus growers in the southeastern part of the State formed the first co-operative association of modern times in South Carolina.

The movement grew, and in 1921 the legislature passed the Standard Co-operative Marketing Act. Under this movement, organizations have been developed for cotton, tobacco, truck crops, and fruit crops. As yet, however, the idea has not gained many adherents. The individualism of earlier times persists, much to the detriment of the farmer and of the whole system of life in the State. Leaders throughout the 46 counties, including farm agents and others, have continued to urge more co-operation for the purpose of better standards of production, both as to quantity and quality, with the eventual plan of price control in the hands of the producers. 'Agriculture can prosper in South Carolina or anywhere else,' commented a supporter of the co-operatives, 'only as business men assist the farmer in his marketing, for they must buy his wares, and he, theirs.'

Just what the future of agriculture will be is open to conjecture. The ratio of rural to urban life has dropped from 82.5 per cent and 17.5 per cent in 1920 to 78.7 per cent and 21.3 per cent in 1930, and tenancy has increased. Manufacturing has advanced so that more cotton is used in the mills of the State than the State can profitably produce. On the other hand, there is increased interest in animal industry and truck growing.

South Carolina has three rehabilitation projects conducted by the Farm Security Administration: Ashwood Plantations at Ashwood, Allendale Farms at Allendale, and Orangeburg Farms at Orangeburg. The Ashwood Project is for white farmers, the Allendale for Negro, and the Orangeburg for both. Ashwood has 11,501 acres with 160 farm units; Allendale 11,334 acres with 118 units; and Orangeburg 6,403 acres with 67 units. The purpose of the projects is stated as follows: 'To provide family-size farms for deserving tenants and other low-income rural families and give them an opportunity to achieve self-support and security. To this end a farm and home management program has been planned by the families with assistance of a farm and home management supervisor on the project. They are receiving advantages of an economic, educational, and social nature that they had previously lacked.'

Emphasis is put on home production, with garden, cow, hogs, and poultry for each family. All the projects have public school buildings, water supply, and medical facilities.

Industry and Labor

MANUFACTURING in South Carolina, which until the 1870's was largely a series of unsuccessful attempts, today produces a far greater income than agriculture, though the latter engages about three quarters of the State's population, both white and Negro. Chief among industries are textile manufacturing, hydroelectric production, cottonseed processing, and lumbering with its derivative pursuits.

From early Colonial times there were a few important local and domestic industries. From 1748 the making of 'Irish linen' in the Scotch-Irish Township of Williamsburg is recorded. Twenty years afterward, individual planters of St. David's parish, most of them Welsh from Delaware, were manufacturing cotton cloth for their establishments. At the beginning of the Revolution a planter near Charleston had 30 Negroes spinning and weaving cloth of cotton and wool at the rate of 120 yards a week. In 1777 Daniel Heyward, near Beaufort, writing to relatives, described improved machinery for his hands to use in making cotton cloth. Under supervision of skilled artisans, many plantation slaves were instructed in spinning and weaving. Such local manufacture was discouraged by the British Board of Trade, which preferred that Carolina produce raw materials for export, and purchase manufactured goods from the Mother Country. However, the interruption of commerce during the Revolutionary War gave a temporary stimulation in South Carolina to the manufacture of textile goods for home use.

By 1790 three small textile mills, operated by slave labor, had been established at Murray's Ferry, Williamsburg County; at Fishing Creek in Chester County; and near Stateburg in Sumter County. Like all the early mills, they were located at waterfalls on small creeks—the large rivers being too powerful for the local builders to manage. Jonathan Lucas, however, was harnessing the tides in 1793 for power to run his rice-husking mills. The manufacture of pottery, brick, and lumber had long been established, and in the mountainous sections of the Up Country iron furnaces were turning out implements and utensils to be peddled about in this and adjoining States. At the end of the eighteenth century, South Carolina promised to have an economy well balanced between agriculture and manufacturing.

This tendency was sharply interrupted by the invention of the cotton gin, first widely used in the State in 1802 (*see Agriculture*). Almost overnight the possibility of wealth from cotton planting was startlingly increased. In the rush for this wealth, manufacturing was neglected— and the prestige of those not belonging to the planter class declined. According to an observer of tidewater life in the early 1800's, it was 'considered disreputable to attend to business of any kind.' Many political leaders opposed manufacturing as likely to create a pro-tariff sentiment unfavorable to agricultural interests. South Carolinians were content to import their manufactured goods, and by 1810 most of the little textile mills along the creeks had disappeared.

An interesting reaction against the prevailing view occurred in Charleston in 1808, with the founding of the Carolina Homespun Company. Its organizer and president, Dr. John L. E. W. Shecut, was so enthusiastic in promoting local industries that he named one of his daughters 'Carolina Homespun.' His company was capitalized at $30,000, of which $18,000 was raised by a lottery, by permission of the State legislature. The House of Representatives in Columbia ordered its members to appear in homespun suits during the session of 1808. The company failed, however, in 1816.

The War of 1812, like the Revolutionary War nearly 40 years before it, stimulated industry within the State. At the close of the war, nationalistic sentiment was at a high pitch, and John C. Calhoun voted for a protective tariff in 1816. But this view shortly withered under the blight of a tariff that sacrificed the State to the interests of eastern manufacturers. In 1820 a mass meeting was held in Charleston to condemn protectionism. Efforts were made to boycott northern goods in retaliation for the tariff of 1824, and Congressman George McDuffie gave his broadcloth coat to a servant, declaring it a livery fit only for slaves. As the issue became more intense, South Carolina nullified the tariff laws of 1828 and 1832, while Calhoun and Hayne developed the doctrine of States' Rights. All this tended to fix South Carolina in its dependence on cotton planting, and to delay the development of industries.

David R. Williams, governor from 1814 to 1816, was one South Carolinian opposed to the idea that the State should depend on agriculture alone. In 1826 he established a cloth mill, on Cedar Creek in what is now Darlington County, employing slave labor, but the mill

shortly failed, as did two others established by New England industrialists in the Up Country about the same time. A mill built by William Bates on Rock Creek in Greenville County in 1833 was more
successful, continuing for more than 75 years; and the Pendleton factory at Autun, built in 1838, is still operating. Machinery for these
early Up Country mills had to be hauled overland from Charleston.

The most important manufacturing development before the War
between the States was that of William Gregg in the Horse Creek
Valley in Aiken County (*see Tour 6b*). In 1845 the State issued to a
Charleston company organized by Gregg a charter for the building of a
cotton mill, and two years afterward the first goods were put on the
market. Gregg was noted for his shrewd management, his paternalistic
interest in the 'poor whites,' his development of the mill village system,
and his passionate belief that manufacturing was the only solution for
South Carolina's troubles. It distressed him to see cotton hauled to
Charleston, shipped to New England, made into cloth, shipped back to
Charleston, hauled again to the interior, and sold at a great advance in
price to the farmers who raised it. Gregg opposed Negro labor in the
mills, not because he believed Negroes unfit for the work, but because
he was more concerned for the class of poor whites that the slave
system had helped to create. 'It is only necessary to build a manufacturing village of shanties in a healthy locality in any part of the state,'
wrote Gregg in the 1840's, 'to have crowds of these poor people around
you, seeking employment at half the compensation given to operatives
in the North . . . the emaciated, pale-faced children soon assume the
appearance of robust health and their tattered garments are exchanged
for those suited to a better condition.' Gregg's mill continued to operate
through the War between the States, and some of the old buildings are
still in use.

In 1850 there were 18 cotton mills in the State employing 1,019
workers; but by 1860 the number had declined to 17 mills with 891
operatives. To accuse a man publicly of owning mill stock was often
equivalent to inviting personal combat, or a libel suit. The agricultural
system and States' Rights had triumphed—but at the cost of involving
South Carolina and the rest of the Southern States in a war for which
they were not industrially prepared.

During the war years of 1861–5 the importation of goods from the
outside was cut off, and looms and spinning wheels were again set up
in private homes. Cotton mills at Columbia and elsewhere were burned
by Sherman's troops, and others had to be shut down. At the end of

the war the need of manufacturing establishments was widely recognized, but capital within the State had been largely destroyed, and investors from other States were repelled by the uncertain conditions of the Reconstruction period. Newspapers now urged the revival of manufacturing, and the white legislature of 1865 lowered the tax on factories and railroads. The 'Radical' legislature of 1870, composed largely of Negroes, exempted cotton factories from taxation for a period of four years. Existing mills were making a tempting profit, and in 1876 Henry P. Hammett opened the era of modern industrialization in the State with a new mill, the Piedmont, of 10,000 spindles. The town that resulted took its name from the mill.

After 1880 the development of the textile industry was rapid, and by 1892 there were 51 mills in South Carolina with 516,526 spindles and 12,905 looms in operation. This placed the State second only to North Carolina among the Southern States in number of spindles, and first in the number of looms. The industry had centered in the Up Country, to which outside investors were attracted by the mild climate, abundant water power, proximity to the cotton fields, and plenty of native labor already accustomed to a low standard of living. Pioneers in the industry were quick to introduce mechanical improvements. Incandescent lighting was introduced in 1881, and in 1895 electric drives and Draper automatic looms were first used in South Carolina. The Columbia Duck Mills claimed to be the first textile plant in the world to be completely equipped with electric power. By 1900 the number of mills in the State had increased to 115, with 30,201 operatives; and by 1910 to 167, with 47,028 operatives.

Progress during the next ten years was less rapid, and during the World War there was a shortage of labor. The demand for food production led many workers back to the farms and mill villages were left empty. In 1916–19, however, there was a sharp expansion, and huge post-war profits for owners led to the purchase of many South Carolina mills by northern capitalists at prices not justified by later earnings. This was the beginning of a persistent movement, still in progress, of cotton mill capital from New England to the Southern States. In 1920–2 there was a decline in the number of mills in the State from 184 to 169; but three years later the number had climbed to 220.

By 1925 South Carolina was rated as the first cotton goods producing State in the United States. In that year 5,321,264 spindles and 125,732 looms were in operation. Through the depression of the late

1920's and early 1930's the industry was not as hard hit as in some other sections; the semi-paternalistic mill village system was often beneficial to the workers during these lean years. In 1939 there were 233 mills in operation, producing $239,842,159 worth of goods and paying out $64,993,309 in wages to 89,378 workers. The figure for wages does not include the amount paid to 2,324 salaried employees. Products of the South Carolina mills today include nearly every textile in which cotton is used—cloth for wearing apparel, upholstery fabrics, window-shade cloth, bags of all sorts, asbestos cloth, tire fabrics, duck, canvas, and airplane cloth. The silk, woolen, and rayon industry attained its peak just after the World War, and about 25 mills are still engaged in manufacturing goods of this type.

Cottonseed Products: Although the crushing of cottonseed had been done experimentally in Pennsylvania as early as 1768, and as a home enterprise on Colonial plantations in various parts of the South, the first commercial venture of the sort was made by Dr. Benjamin Waring of Columbia about 1802. Another cottonseed oil mill was established by former Governor David R. Williams in 1829 in the Darlington section. The industry was long handicapped by the difficulty of persuading farmers to utilize the meal and hulls that remained after the oil was pressed out, and by a prejudice against the use of the oil as a food. By the middle of the nineteenth century the products were becoming popular, but the War between the States interrupted all progress, and for several decades production remained low. In 1880, with the general expansion of industry in South Carolina, a number of new mills were erected and in 1887 the Southern Cotton Oil Company systematically developed the product.

In the early days of cotton growing, tons of seed were destroyed every year—only enough being saved to plant the new crop. Of late years there has been a greater demand for the seed than for the fiber, and agricultural experimenters are trying to develop a cotton plant which will bear 'bald-headed' seed. The oil is now used for oleomargarine and other food products, the meal and hulls for cattle feed, and the 'linters' (short fiber taken off the hulls) for mattress-stuffing, and as an ingredient of rayon and explosives.

In 1939 there were 30 cottonseed oil mills operating in the State, with a capital investment of $2,465,100, and a product worth $7,042,-816. These mills employed 886 workers, who received wages amounting to $416,735 annually. Cottonseed in 1939 added $8,608,000 to the farm income from the cotton crop throughout the State.

Hydroelectric Production: South Carolina's interest in water power development began with the industrial boom of the 1890's when power potentialities were a necessary consideration in the selection of mill sites. Today South Carolina ranks sixth among the States in amount of water power developed.

Previous to 1900 many of the industrial plants generated their own power, and individual progress was often notable. It was not until about 1905, however, that hydroelectric power was developed in any volume in the State. Dr. Gill Wylie of Chester, and William States Lee, of the Portman Shoals plant, were the chief promoters behind the Catawba River development in 1904. Soon afterward, with J. B. Duke of North Carolina, they formed the Southern Power Company and built the first South Carolina plant of that organization at Great Falls in 1907.

As the industry ranking next to textile manufacturing in value of product, hydroelectric operations in 1939 employed 744 persons in the 41 principal electrical plants in 30 counties, the pay rolls amounting to $925,081 (exclusive of managers' salaries). The value of the product amounted to $16,198,350, and capital invested was listed at $118,-872,385. This industry has advantages over many South Carolina businesses, notably lumber, cottonseed crushing, and the raising of cotton, in that employment is available many more days per year. In the industries mentioned, employees are busy for a comparatively short time; but in the production of electrical power, plants operate every working day in the year.

In 1926 the State was rated sixth among the United States in hydroelectric power production, and in 1931, with the completion of the Dreher Shoals Dam on the Saluda River, South Carolina rose for a while to fourth place in the Nation. This dam, with the huge artificial lake formed by the impounded waters, is one of the largest earthen structures of that nature in the world. At present (1940) 838,409 horsepower are available in the State from the public concerns and the plants of the individual mills. Promises of much vaster output lie in the Santee-Cooper, Buzzard Roost, Clark's Hill, and the Lyles Ford projects, already begun or approved for early development.

Lumbering and Forest Products: The availability of lumber was one of the strongest attractions for the early colonists of South Carolina. The forests supplied a product which could at once be exported without waiting for the crop to grow, and the tall straight pines were in particular demand for ship masts. For 200 years lumber formed a great part of South Carolina's exports. Oak, gum, cypress, and pine were taken from swamps and highlands and hauled over sandy roads or floated down the slow coastal streams. Today most of the lumber shipped out of the State moves through the port of Savannah, Georgia.

Before 1850 timber was cut into boards by hand, a slow and arduous process. Two or three men could produce only a few hundred board feet in a day. Such crude methods of manufacture compelled the pioneer lumbermen to choose the soundest and straightest trees, and as a result many of the houses built long before the War between the States are still in good condition. Timber was so abundant that the 'sap wood' was often discarded, only the inner or 'heart wood' being used. Houses built of 'heart pine' will stand almost indefinitely.

About 1850 the steam-propelled circular saw came into use, and from that time the exploitation of the forests was rapid. A crew of three or four men was able to turn out ten or fifteen thousand board feet of timber in a single day. A few years after the steam sawmill was introduced, planing machines were put in the mills, and lumber could be finished for building without further hand labor. Before being planed, the rough lumber is dried, either in outdoor piles or in a heated kiln. In the past 25 years great improvements have been made in the manufacture of lumber. The larger mills haul their logs by truck or narrow-gauge railway from deep in the woods and work them into finished lumber with elaborate and high-powered machinery.

Accurate record of lumber production in the State has never been made, on account of the large number of small local mills that move rapidly from place to place as their supply of timber is exhausted. These little 'woodpecker' mills, employing less than five workers each, leave their piles of sawdust on every creek. Their methods are extremely wasteful, and as good timber becomes scarcer they strip the woods of every tree 'big enough to make a two-by-four.' Owing to the large number, small size, and scattered nature of many lumber and turpentine plants, accurate figures have not been available for their output. The 228 larger lumber and timber plants in 1939 employed 8,678 workers, and produced lumber worth $17,713,210. Naval stores produced in the State in 1939 were worth about $800,000. In 1936 a survey was made of the turpentine and naval stores industry with a view to diverting to the port of Charleston exports from neighboring Savannah.

The value of wood used for fuel in South Carolina cannot be accurately estimated; but on farms wood is used almost universally, and in small towns is generally preferred to other fuel. Even in the larger cities wagon loads of wood and kindling are peddled from house to house. There are 63 plants in the State producing furniture, coffins, tool handles, baskets, and other woodwork, and recently there has been a spectacular increase in paper pulp production. Capital invested in the last-named plants rose from $6,000,000 in 1937 to $18,270,735 in 1939; the value of their products for 1939 was $10,125,984.

The necessity of conservation to maintain these industries is now recognized, but adequate means of forest protection have only begun to be carried out (*see Natural Setting*).

LABOR

As South Carolina's industrialization progressed, labor organization developed. From the beginning, however, there were legal actions taken in behalf of the trades. The first act of the Carolina parliament to be ratified by the proprietors in England (1671) concerned wages for the artisans brought into the colony by Joseph West. With the establishment of the plantation system, and the emphasis on agriculture instead of manufacture, the few white tradesmen and artisans in the province were at a disadvantage in making a livelihood. Before 1765 Negroes outnumbered the whites in South Carolina. Masters had certain of their slaves trained as carpenters, wheelwrights, cobblers, and whatever other trades could be utilized in the plantation unit. Often these slaves were hired out and the master assumed the wages. This condition rendered the situation more acute for white artisans, and as early as 1742 a grand jury in Charleston noted that there was a 'want of a law to prevent the hiring of Negro tradesmen to the great discouragement of white workmen coming into the province.'

By 1766 a number of craftsmen had organized in Charleston, more for mutual pecuniary assistance than to secure wages and hours regulations. This group, many of whom were members of the Charles Town Mechanics' Society, developed consistent and strong opposition to English rule and commercial practices. They formed most of the Liberty party, which was led by Christopher Gadsden. A historian has remarked that this group 'furnished the backbone to the Revolutionary movement, certainly in Charleston.' It was they who met under the Liberty Tree and advocated independence in 1766. In 1794, the Mechanics' Society, outgrowing merely philanthropic design, announced itself for higher wages. The society continued to exist until 1883.

At the conclusion of the Revolution, Charleston was partially in ruins and when rebuilding was begun in 1783 the carpenters and bricklayers were accused of forming a 'combination' to force a wage of $3 a day. The workers denied the charge, but declared that the depreciated currency made higher wages essential. The South Carolina convention for ratifying the Federal Constitution once more brought up the subject of white and Negro competition. By that time, free Negroes had established themselves in trades. One speaker at the convention stated, 'cheap Negro labor was steadily undermining the white artisan class in South Carolina.' There were many debates on the subject and bills were offered, but no laws were passed. The principal reason was that owners preferred to continue hiring out their slaves and collecting the wages instead of permitting free labor, white and Negro, to become established.

From 1800 until the War between the States, labor was consolidating and becoming more vocal. A Carpenters' Society in 1809, a clerks' union in 1825, and a printers' organization in 1834 were among the groups to draw up programs. The Apprentice Library Society of Charleston, begun in 1841, was outspoken in its opposition to the employment of Negro mechanics. In 1825 a labor organ, the *Southern Free Press*, was being published in Charleston. There was much speculation as to what would happen to organized labor in what was known as the leading slave State. In 1836 the printers had organized in Columbia, and 11 years later *The Mechanics Advocate* was being published here. The printers' group was probably the most effective of the labor organizations prior to the War between the States. One of their chief complaints was concerned with the apprentice system and this is said to have provoked the strike of 1852, one of the earliest in the State, a bakers' strike having been announced in 1786. In 1860 the Charleston organization boasted 112 members, and went on record as demanding a new scale of prices for work. The time was inopportune, however, and trouble arose within the body due to Secession. Membership a year later had decreased to nine. In 1861 this group, which had been affiliated with the national organization, withdrew upon a motion of a member from the North, and formed the first labor union in the Confederacy. In 1886, after the war, the Charleston union was allowed to rejoin the national organization and assume again its old number 43.

The trades organizations, however, served only a very small part of the mass of white laborers. It was estimated that some 50,000 whites were unable to make a living in 1849. One of the first and most consistent efforts to use this unemployed white labor was made by William Gregg, in the Horse Creek Valley near Aiken, in 1847 (*see Tour 6*). Gregg was frankly paternalistic, but he did more for the 'poor whites' in the State than had ever before been attempted.

During the War between the States, the problem of labor was overshadowed by the general crisis and the surplus man power was drawn into the army; but after the war the South was economically prostrate, and with the freeing of the slaves the supply of labor greatly exceeded the demand. The Negroes were bewildered and disorganized, and the poorer whites hard pressed by the increased competition. The plantation system was broken up, and the large landowner could only survive by parceling his land out to tenants, furnishing them with seed and fertilizer, and taking a lien on the crop to protect his investment. He would naturally demand that a 'cash crop' such as cotton be planted—thus blocking the way for diversified farming, and fixing on the region a vicious agricultural system from which it has not yet escaped. The shift from slave to free labor was eventually salutary, but the growing pains were vicious. The Negroes were not accustomed to written contracts or definite agreements, and it is not surprising that with meager and uncertain wages they often broke their bargains and drifted to the cities. The reports of the Freedmen's Bureau for 1866 show that the experiment with free labor in South Carolina was at least partly successful.

The sharecropping system burdened the State more and more, until by 1890 hundreds of farms were mortgaged, crops were gathered merely to be turned over to the lien merchants, and cotton prices were the lowest in history. Eighteen per cent of the whites were illiterate. At such a time the coming of the mills to the Up Country was a godsend. In 1880 there were a few more than 2,000 employees in 14 mills; by 1900 there were more than 30,000 in the 115 mills in the State. The workers came from neighboring farms that had been eroded into gullies, turned over for mortgages, or deserted because of lack of profit; and also from the mountainous sections of this State, North Carolina, Tennessee, and Georgia. Represented among them were many formerly prosperous families ruined by the war, who had not been able to reestablish themselves. The tradition of individualism developed by farm life and habits of mountain existence has helped delay the concentration of strength necessary to accomplish political and social reforms.

In the 1890's, when 'Pitchfork Ben' Tillman rose to power (*see History*) the mill workers had begun to awaken to the fact that they had

become a different group from others in the State. 'The poor and igno-
rant felt profound disappointment at the outcome of Tillmanism, and
waited for a new agitator,' asserted a commentator. It was to be years
later that, in an evaluation of his accomplishments, it was realized
that Tillman's successful break with the 'Bourbons' gave the middle
and lower classes a real opportunity for general advance.

In the administration of John Gary Evans, who followed Tillman
as governor, the personal needs and rights of mill operatives were
legally considered. During this decade, organized labor among the textile employees attempted to enter the State from Georgia through the
mills in Horse Creek Valley. The attempt was not immediately successful, however, as the workers were suspicious of interference from
the outside and in their defensiveness lost sight of the real issue. The
South Carolina Federation of Labor was begun in 1901, but, due to
its lack of confidence in the national organization of the United Textile Workers, failed to pay its assessments, and was dismissed from
that group in 1903.

From 1903 to 1908 an experiment with immigrant labor was made
by the South Carolina Cotton Growers Association. There was some
fear that the State could not provide enough labor for its expanding
industries, and a special act was passed under Governor D. C. Heyward organizing an immigration division in connection with the State
Department of Agriculture and Industries. In 1906 the German steamship *Wittekind,* with nearly 500 workers from central Europe, docked
in Charleston on one of its two voyages to the State. These people
came to South Carolina under the supervision of E. J. Watson, Commissioner of Agriculture. During the five-year period about 2,500 persons came to the State from other sections of the country and from
abroad. Except for the importation of slaves, this was the most concentrated inflowing of labor since the founding of the colony. The results, however, were not considered worth the expense, and in 1909
the State's immigration department was abolished. Thus South Carolina has had neither the benefits nor the disadvantages of immigration
since colonial times; its population has been predominantly English,
Scotch-Irish, French, German, and Negro since the earliest pioneer
days.

Coleman L. Blease, elected governor in 1910, was thought by many
to be Tillman's successor in stirring up class and political differences.
Historian Wallace claims, 'The strength of Blease's appeal was not any
platform of measures, but his personality and viewpoint. He not only

offered no program of benefits to labor, a program which was still re-
pugnant to South Carolina individualism, but won favor by railing
against measures which labor where organized and informed demands.'
He opposed compulsory education and the sanitary inspection of factories. He gained some political support from mill owners and railroads, but incurred the condemnation of the Columbia Federation of
Trades and other bodies interested in affiliation with national labor
groups.

Under Richard I. Manning, governor from 1915 to 1919, a carefully
planned program of social welfare was carried out. Manning, definitely
of the Bourbon class and the sixth member of his family to become
governor of the State, was lacking in popular appeal, but secured the
co-operation of his legislature as Blease had never done. The American
Federation of Labor entered South Carolina while Manning was governor; the minimum age of workers was raised from 12 to 14, releasing
over 2,400 children from industrial plants; protection of mill operatives
from excessive docking was begun; and the movement for compulsory
education was furthered, though not made fully effective.

Manning acted as mediator in several clashes between labor and
capital that occurred during his term of office. The streetcar strike in
Columbia, which had tied up traffic for months, was settled by his personal mediation. A ten-week strike at the Brogden Mills in Anderson
was settled in 1915 through the governor's interposition. Though generally favorable to the workers, Manning would not support them
when he felt that public order was threatened. In 1916 prolonged
strikes in Anderson over the closed shop issue led to clashes between
strikers and local officers, and Manning called the militia to protect
constables in ejecting mill workers from the company-owned mill
village houses. At the time Manning was widely criticized by mill
owners because he failed to take a hand in the situation earlier.

When the American Federation of Labor entered South Carolina
the idea of unions was not fully acceptable even to the workers themselves. With encouragement from the more liberal newspapers, union
organizers began a campaign of education among the workers, and continued to urge labor reforms. As a result, there was slow but continuous progress in reduction of hours, increase of wages, regulation of
women's work, compulsory education, and limitation of child labor. In
1935 the State Industrial Commission was formed to administer workmen's compensation laws, and in 1936 the Department of Labor was
organized and the South Carolina Commission of Unemployment was

established. These three bodies were combined in one central State board in 1939. The age for employment in mines and factories was raised in 1937 from 14 to 16. In 1938 South Carolina was distinguished for passing the first 40-hour law for textile plants in the country, and this was enforced until the Federal Fair Labor Relations Act took effect in the fall of that year, instigating the 44-hour week.

In 1936, through Federal aid, a division of industrial hygiene was set up under the State Board of Health. A survey was made of the textile, fertilizer, clay, glass, stone, paper, tobacco, and food indus- tries for determining the dangers to which workers were exposed. Health services—medical, nursing, first aid, and sanitary—were found to be very poor, even in the large plants. Greater care, however, was taken with regard to accident hazards. It was estimated that workers were exposed to 33 materials that might cause occupational disease, the greatest danger being from the lint and high humidity of cotton mills, the dust of granite plants, and the chemicals of fertilizer and paper pulp plants. When the report was published a plan was set up for technical studies and laboratory tests. In 1937–8 such studies were carried out in 12 granite plants, and other firms had requested tests and offered their co-operation. Other laws pertaining to safety of em- ployees were concerned with building inspection (1932), and sanitary codes (1937).

Throughout the history of the textile industry, wages in South Caro- lina have been less than in the New England mills, but in this State factors other than daily labor had always to be considered. Mills were established where water and freight facilities were available. Except in rare instances this meant that houses, stores, churches, and schools had to be built along with the factories. Accommodations to operatives had to be considered as well as the flat wage. Nowadays, the lowest wage is $10 per week, with an average of $13.92. Until 1938 and the advent of the Federal Fair Labor Relations Act more than 85 per cent of the mills still observed NRA hours, but wages had advanced 20 per cent above 1933 NRA levels. In April 1937, the average textile mill weekly wage for New England was $19.30, while that for South Caro- lina was a little short of $16; the hourly wage average (part and full time) for New England was 49.2¢, that for South Carolina 40¢.

Though the mill village system (*see Tour 7*) was essential in South Carolina for the launching of the cotton mill industry, there is a defi- nite movement now toward home ownership by operatives. The mill owners claim the former system is too expensive and the workers feel themselves set off socially and economically from other groups. Assistance in the purchase of homes is often given by the owners of the mills. In 1940 the Pacific Mills in Columbia, among the largest in the country, completed negotiations for the sale of its village property. The Springs interests in Lancaster and Chester Counties are aiding their employees in buying homes and large plots of garden and farm land. Many other similar plans are under way elsewhere in South Carolina.

Most of the textile mills of the State are now unionized, and in 1938 about 3,000 employees were said to be affiliated with the American Federation of Labor and about 30,000 with the Congress of Industrial Organizations. The building and mechanical trades are also well organized, having about 3,000 members under the A. F. of L. A few Negro unions are affiliated with this group. The Longshoremen in Charleston, originally organized during the 1860's, represent the strongest unit among the Negroes. For a few years after the War between the States the phosphate industry employed large numbers of Negroes, but this business failed in the 1890's due to a high State tax and the discovery of phosphate nearer the surface in Florida. Negroes are a minor factor in the textile industry, not more than 4,000 out of a total of more than 90,000 textile workers being employed in 1938. Few, if any, work in the complicated machinery among the spindles and looms, but they are employed for hauling and cleaning cotton and for janitor work. The claim that Negroes are unfitted for textile work has never been substantiated. The whites took charge of the industry after the War between the States and by various legal and social discriminations have held it ever since.

The Nation-wide strikes in the fall of 1934 caused the greatest disruption of recent years in the textile industry. Of the 10 dissident votes (in a total ballot of nearly 600) in the national gathering in New York to propose the strike, dealing with the stretch-out system, four were from South Carolina. Spasmodic strikes took place, however, in sympathy with the national movement. At Chiquola Mill at Honea Path, rioting occurred which cost the lives of seven strikers, and troops were called out and kept in the community from September 5 to 29 (*see Tour 15b*).

The strike at Ware Shoals, at the same time, disclosed an unusual situation sometimes found in South Carolina. About 75 per cent of the workers lived on farms, some as distant as 35 miles from the industrial plants. Mill trucks transported them to and from their work each day. The remaining 25 per cent lived in the villages provided by the company. The farm element preferred to continue their work as it was, since for them it offered an income merely supplementary to that made by other members of their families on the farm. Eventually the disagreement between workers and management changed to a fight between farm and village groups, and the argument was settled only after the governor called out the militia. Upon the conclusion of the strike some of the villagers moved out in the country where they attempted to farm, but, unaccustomed to the rigors of country life, they soon forsook the fields and returned to the mills.

There were nine strikes in the textile mills of the State in 1937–8, and these were settled through provisions of the Conciliation Act. In spite of difficulties peculiar to the region and the confusion in the minds of workers over the competing claims of the A. F. of L. and the CIO, labor in South Carolina is gaining in strength and cohesiveness. The greatest advance of the 1930's, aside from beneficial legislation already mentioned, is a better understanding of the problems of labor by the general public, and a growth of confidence among the workers themselves.

Transportation

IN early colonial days there were two chief means of travel in South Carolina: tidal streams near the coast, and Indian paths in the interior. The first settlements were near the ocean, along wide rivers and creeks. Towns were built on the banks of navigable streams and planters were careful to have a river frontage and wharf. Often their boat landings were reinforced by Belgian blocks—small, evenly shaped stones that had been brought from Europe as ballast, to be replaced by cargoes of indigo, lumber, or rice.

The convenience of this river traffic partly accounts for the delay in building good roads. While citizens of other States were laying out turnpikes, the coastal gentry of South Carolina opposed the expense of a State-wide road-building program. They asserted that two thirds of all market products of the State were 'raised within five miles, and most of the other third within ten miles of a navigable stream.' Both Bishop Asbury and George Washington commented on the bad roads of South Carolina, but also mentioned the ease with which travelers got around by boat. For 100 years, plantation owners had used pirogues or 'pettiaugers'—crude boats hollowed out of cypress trees. Slaves manned the oars, and as many as 50 persons were sometimes accommodated in such craft.

Contrary to the notions of the coast, roads were badly needed in the Up Country. The aboriginal paths, which had existed long before the white men came, were hardly more than 18 inches wide. Deeply worn by moccasined feet, they afforded access to the mountains and beyond—where furs, deer, and buffalo abounded. Generally these paths, much used by early traders, followed the watersheds, and present-day highways are often continued along the same routes. There were five main Indian paths in South Carolina, located in modern terms as follows: The Creek Path, from Charleston to Augusta, Georgia; the Cherokee or Keowee Path (in its lower section known as the Broad Path) from Charleston to Columbia to Oconee County; the Catawba Path, from Charleston to Camden to Kings Mountain and into North Carolina; the Virginia Path, skirting the Blue Ridge, from Georgia through western South and North Carolina into Virginia; the Wilmington Path or King's Highway, from Charleston along the coast to North Carolina. Most of these trails were known by different names at different times.

As the frontier was pushed farther inland, 'factories' or posts for trade factors were established at points where paths crossed or where streams were forded. They were protected by forts which sheltered goods from thieves and gave refuge to isolated settlers when they were threatened by Indian raids.

Even after the Up Country was filled with settlers from Pennsylvania and Virginia there were few good roads to the coast. By 1750 there were turnpikes leading north along the eastern edge of the mountains, and it was easier to market cattle, sheep, and hogs over these than to send them across the swamps to the coast. Goods from the Up Country to Charleston had to stand much hard usage. Droves of animals were herded through the forests, in which clearings were made for overnight stops. The animals strayed away or were raided by thieves and cattle rustlers. Lumber was rafted down the rivers, and later cotton and tobacco; but until canals were built around the shoals, the expense of portage consumed most of the profits. Roads along the coast were better. Great Conestoga wagons, with hooped covers above a red body and blue wheels, rattled into Charleston from the North along the King's Highway. Each wagon was pulled by four to six horses, whose bright red harness jingled with bells.

Not until after the War of 1812 did the State as such concern itself seriously with trade and transportation. Between 1819 and 1825 duties collected on goods entering the Charleston port declined 51.7 per cent. Exports declined in similar fashion. Cotton was being produced in larger amounts, but it was moved through other markets. As Charleston went down, Savannah flourished. The South Carolina legislature decided to tap the western trade from beyond the mountains, if it could be done, and in 1817 asked John Wilson, the civil and military engineer of the State, to prepare a report on transportation facilities. 'The actual state of all the public roads is so very bad as to preclude the necessity of describing the defects of each,' asserted Wilson; 'a wagoner . . . is compelled to drive over stumps a foot high.'

After this report, plans were soon under way to build a road from Charleston to Columbia and into North Carolina by way of Saluda Gap. In 1819 the Board of Public Works was organized with Joel R. Poinsett (*see Tour* 20) as its head and Robert Mills (*see Architec-*

ture) as its chief engineer. Mills's devotion to internal improvements is commended in a letter from Thomas Jefferson: 'I hope these states [sic] will prove to the world how much more it will contribute to its happiness to lay out the contributions of the people in opening canals for communication and irrigation, making good roads, erecting public buildings for science and the arts, etc., than in slaughtering men, burning their homes, and wasting their lands. I sincerely wish you may find constant employment in this system of improvement, and derive the due reward to your merits for the useful services you may render in improving your native state.'

Mills, however, like most prominent South Carolinians of his day, was more interested in canals and inland navigation than in roads. A canal had been completed between the Santee and Cooper Rivers in 1800, but a poor route had been selected, and no great increase of trade had followed. Mills planned a system of canals between Columbia and Charleston, Hamburg and Charleston, and at various places around shoals in the Up Country. These plans were partly carried out in the construction of canals at Rocky Mount, Lands Ford, Dreher Shoals, and Columbia. The work was expensive and results disappointing—but the scheme at least resulted in the development of several boom towns, such as Cheraw.

Charlestonians were slow to give up their faith in waterways. They declared that there were no stones below the fall line for the construction of roads, and that 'the Pee Dee, the Edisto, Congaree, Wateree and the Savannah present so good a navigation, that hardly a market wagon is seen in the districts watered by these streams except those that pass through from higher regions.' Apparently Charleston was indifferent to the higher region.

But the Up Countrymen were not indifferent. They continued to clamor until in 1825 there were ten roads under construction or planned by the State supervisor of public works, Abram Blanding (1776–1839). In 1829 the road from Columbia to Charleston, a distance of 110 miles, was completed. There were eight toll gates between the cities, and it was expected that tolls would take care of interest and repairs. Roads were also built to Pendleton, Greenville, and other points in the Up Country. In the 'sickly season of summer,' white laborers were taken out of the swamplands and transferred to the Saluda Gap section. Negro slaves were sent into the swamps at $80 a year, with $60 extra for tools and equipment. Roads in the swamps were laid on a base of 'large timbers bolted down to piles . . . to prevent its rising in the highest freshets.' Malaria and bad liquor did not ease the contractor's troubles.

Traffic rules were severe, especially with regard to bridges. No slave could cross a bridge without a pass, and travelers were fined for not keeping right of center. No stops were allowed on bridges, and teams could move no faster than a walk if the spans were more than ten feet long. Tolls were made uniform in 1828. A private four-wheeled carriage drawn by four mules or horses was charged '100 cents' at the gate. A freight carrier of the same order had to pay 75¢. A foot passenger was charged 6¼¢ to cross a bridge, and animals in droves were rated at 4¢ a horse or mule, 3¢ a head for cattle, and 2¢ each for hogs, sheep, and goats.

In spite of dissatisfaction over tolls, these roads greatly increased communication between Up Country and Low Country. Wagoners from inland would make long trips to the cities, camping out along the way. Chickens, eggs, apples, chestnuts, and whisky were bartered for sugar, coffee, calico, and knickknacks. In the opposite direction would move picturesque and often sordid coffles—herds of Negroes being driven from coastal plantations to inland markets. The men walked, the women rode in wagons with their children. Sometimes the wagons were covered with chicken wire to prevent escape. At market towns buyers would inspect the group and bargain for what slaves they needed. Then the depleted coffle would move on to the next market.

Stagecoaches were quick to take advantage of the new roads. Regular service was maintained from Charleston to Columbia, and on to Yorkville (now York) and Greenville in the Up Country. The route through Cheraw, Camden, Columbia, and Edgefield practically followed the fall line. In 1828 the coach fare from Charleston to Columbia for a passenger with 25 pounds of baggage was $10, and the trip was made in 18 hours. Stagecoach travel persisted, even after the coming of railroads. In 1843 there were 19 lines operating in the State, nine of which ran daily between principal cities. Inns were established at numerous crossroads, but most stops were at private houses where the owner accommodated guests. Some of these old inns remain to the present time: The Quarter House near Charleston, the Halfway House on the Old State Road between Charleston and Columbia, the Lake House in Saluda County, and Captain Billy Young's Rock House near Greenville, among others.

The roads were little more successful than the canals, however, in capturing for Charleston any marked advance in trade. Hence the more alert Charlestonians eagerly welcomed the notion of building a rail-road. Alexander Black and William Aiken were ardent supporters, and the matter was discussed in Charleston newspapers as early as 1821. In December 1827 the State chartered a company and work was begun on the line from Charleston to Hamburg, a little town on the Savannah River, just across from Augusta, Georgia. The main purpose of the railroad was to divert cotton, lumber, and other Up Country produce from the port of Savannah to the port of Charleston.

There was considerable difficulty in securing a right of way. Colonel Barney Brown of Barnwell asserted that 'engines would run over and kill his little Negroe slaves; also that the noise of the trains, such as the blowing of whistles and the ringing of bells, would seriously dis-turb the quiet and repose of the citizens and under no circumstances would such a nuisance be tolerated by a respectable community.' It was long before trains were allowed to compete in dignity with the family coach. An old Negro calmly drove onto the track in front of an approaching locomotive, only to have his equipage overturned. When his badly shaken and indignant master asked why he had not stopped, the Negro answered in an aggrieved voice, 'I see it, suh! But I t'ink *dey* would stop when dey recognize 'twas we kerridge!' Many towns would not allow stations built except on their outer edges, and even Charleston would not sanction a locomotive within the city limits.

The South Carolina Railroad was lucky in securing Horatio Allen (1802–90) as engineer. He had worked in England and in Pennsyl-vania, where experiments in railroad building had been going on for some years. A special engine, designed by E. L. Miller of Charleston, was built by the West Point Foundry in New York. When it arrived on October 23, 1830, it was named the *Best Friend of Charleston,* and by December it was hauling passengers and freight. On Christmas day a formal opening was observed, and 140 persons were given a ride. On January 15, 1831, a notable excursion celebrated the first anniversary of the beginning of construction. The *Charleston Courier* reported: 'The first trip was performed with two pleasure cars attached, and a small carriage, fitted for the occasion, upon which was a detachment of United States troops and a field piece which had been politely granted by Major Belton for the occasion.' At each stop the cannon was fired, with cheers from passengers and astonished spectators. Dele-gations of pretty girls spread flowers on the rails as the snorting engine approached.

In less than a year, however, the *Best Friend* came to a violent

end. Annoyed at the constant hiss of escaping steam, the Negro fireman sat down on the lever controlling the safety valve until the engine
blew up and killed him. But other locomotives were soon bought, and
the line to Hamburg, 136 miles, was completed in 1833. At that time
it was the longest passenger-carrying steam railway in the world. In
1842 a branch line was completed to Columbia, and the point of junction named Branchville. Before the War between the States, other
lines had been extended to Camden, Greenwood, Greenville, and Charlotte, North Carolina. These early lines used a five-foot gauge, three
and a half inches wider than the present standard gauge. The railroad
companies were required by law to keep a man on the front of each
engine to see that the track was clear of animals. This proved so in-
convenient that the letter of the law was met by mounting on the cow-
catcher an iron model of a little Negro boy with a flag in his hand.

During the War between the States railroad property worth $1,500,-
000 was destroyed in South Carolina. On leaving Columbia, February
19, 1865, a Union officer recorded: 'There is not a rail upon any of
the roads within twenty miles of Columbia but will be twisted into
corkscrews before the sun sets, while upon two of the lines the work
of destruction will be continued perhaps to their terminus.' Little was
accomplished toward rebuilding the railroads during the Reconstruction era; but by 1880 transportation and industry were attracting
capital from South Carolinians and outside investors. The Southern
Railway ran lines through the upper Piedmont section, and took over
many small lines which had been destroyed or had failed. The Atlantic
Coast Line and the Seaboard followed a similar policy, and extended
their lines to Florida. Nowadays these major systems, with smaller
connecting lines, cover 3,620 miles throughout the State.

With the automobile came the development of modern highways. On
June 5, 1900, *The State,* a Columbia newspaper, printed the following
account: 'The first horseless carriage, a light automobile, made its appearance on the streets of Columbia yesterday. It was manipulated by
two young men who had no difficulty in doing so. Many watched the
machine with great interest. The running gear is light, but suited for
the purpose. The machine is being taken about in the interest of a
large soap manufacturing concern.'

Highway building was retarded for many years in South Carolina
by lack of State management and by the difficulty of getting people
to believe in the practicability of motor transportation. The original
system of road work that required each adult male to supply a certain

amount of labor in his district had given way to the employment of convicts. But the unit of road building was still the county. Richer counties would work their roads to the boundary line, and if the neighboring county was poor the traveler would often pass from a good road into a loblolly of mud.

After the State Highway Department was organized in 1917 this county system was gradually abandoned; and in 1929 it was voided altogether by legislative action, and a bond issue of $65,000,000 was authorized to connect all parts of the State with hard-surfaced highways. Four main Federal highways now cross the State, and the 46 county seats, as well as other points of historic and economic interest, are linked together by paved roads. Hardly a place in the State is more than six miles from an all-weather highway. Roads are built and maintained by the sale of automobile licenses ($3.50 a year for private passenger cars) and a gasoline tax of 6¢ a gallon.

It is claimed that three types of road-surfacing were originated in South Carolina: sand-clay, bituminous, and cotton fabric as a base for asphalt. The first sand-clay types were built near Columbia more than 100 years ago, and the methods forgotten. When an early twentieth-century builder originated another sand-clay formula, he was criticized for misuse of public funds. Cotton fabric roads are still in the experimental stage. The engineering of South Carolina highways has attracted wide attention. Sandbeds have been stabilized and causeways laid through dense swamps. Roads are so clearly marked that the most unobserving motorist may easily find his way about.

As good roads were built the number of motor busses rapidly increased. Seven-passenger sedans were first used between cities, but by 1925 organized lines were operating 25 vehicles. In that year the State first passed regulations to govern bus traffic. There are now three continental lines and nine local lines offering bus service in South Carolina.

The interest in water transportation has recently been revived. A few rivers have been dredged to the fall line and the Intracoastal Waterway (*see Tour* 11) has been opened for small craft along the entire coastal border of the State. A huge development under PWA of the Santee-Cooper basin will afford lakes and canals as well as water power. The old dream of cheap freight shipments by water seems on its way to fulfillment.

Air transportation is not yet highly developed, but is making rapid gains under the South Carolina Aeronautics Commission. Thirty-one fields are in operation, at the largest of which licensed pilots are trained. Government landing fields are maintained at the Charleston Navy Yard, at Parris Island near Beaufort, and at Fort Jackson near Columbia. Two commercial transport lines, connecting with national trunk lines, offer passenger service—and these two, with a third, also carry airmail and express. Service for travel or sightseeing is available at Charleston, Columbia, Spartanburg, Greenville, and Anderson. A seaplane base is located at the Navy Yard near Charleston, and that city is the southern terminal for the proposed trans-Atlantic airmail route by way of Bermuda and the Azores. The project is under development (1940).

Education

IN the earliest phase of South Carolina's educational history, illiter-acy was at a minimum and efforts were made for the instruction not only of the wealthy and influential but also of the poorer youth—the 'charity scholars,' who sometimes included Indians, 'malatas,' and Negroes, as well as whites. The facts that legal papers exhibit few marks instead of names as signatures, and that only efficient immi-grants were encouraged to settle, indicate a literate majority in the province. Later, as Negro slaves entered in large numbers, and as many new white settlers established themselves in the savage-inhabited wil-derness, the ratio of illiteracy rose rapidly. Social and political power began to be concentrated in the landed aristocracy; scant provision was made for instruction of the less fortunate whites, and almost none for the Negroes.

But during the first half-century or so of colonization, conditions were more favorable. Thomas Greatbeach is remembered for his will of November 28, 1694, wherein he provided for continuing the services of a woman tutor in his family. Sometime before 1696, Richard Mor-gan left money for the founding or endowment of a free school in the province. In 1702 the Reverend Samuel Thomas was sent from Eng-land by the Society for the Propagation of the Gospel in Foreign Parts, to take up work as a clergyman and instructor of whites and Negroes at Goose Creek. He was succeeded by the Reverend Mr. LeJau, also a teacher, who was able to persuade many influential whites to edu-cate their slaves. Benjamin Dennis, a Goose Creek schoolmaster, was teaching whites, Negroes, and Indians in 1712.

Richard Morgan's legacy was one of many that were designed to provide free schooling in the province; and to take care of such be-quests, a Free School Act was passed by the provincial assembly in 1710. Apparently this act was inoperative, as two years later a similar law was enacted to supervise fulfillment of the legacies. By an enact-ment of 1722, seven free schools were established in the province. These schools were definitely planned for children of the poorer class; the wealthy planters and merchants continued to employ private tutors and to send their children abroad to complete their education. At one time during the Colonial era, South Carolina was represented by almost half the American students at the Inns of Court in London.

The most active forces in early education were religious. The Society for the Propagation of the Gospel in Foreign Parts has already been mentioned. It was organized in England in 1701, and supported schools for whites and Negroes in the province until 1756. The Presbyterian Church, always insistent on an educated clergy, not only provided instruction in the urban centers, but attempted to extend schooling into the sparsely populated regions. Almost every minister became a schoolmaster as the frontier moved westward into the Indian lands. Plans for some of the forts, which served as refuges in times of attack, provided for a schoolroom in addition to church and living quarters.

Second to religious influence in education was that of such organizations as the St. Andrew's Society, the South Carolina Society, and the Winyah Indigo Society, which combined social purposes with securing instruction for the poor. Numerous other similar societies came into being immediately after the Revolution.

Libraries were established in South Carolina at an early period. The appropriation in 1698 of funds by the provincial assembly for the library in Charleston is the first known instance in this country of governmental aid for such a cause. The Charles Town Library Society, organized in 1748 and still operative, was the third of its kind to be formed in America.

In 1737, when the population of the province was scarcely 7,000, there were six free and charity schools in South Carolina. At that time settlement was beginning to develop in the back country. Attempts to instruct the pioneer children of this section were frequently made. The settlement of Purrysburgh, whose site is now marked only by a little cemetery near the lower Savannah River, was supplied from its beginning in 1732 until its dispersal a few years later by schoolmaster-preachers who spoke several languages and adapted their instruction to the French or German settlers. Germans in the Dutch Fork, between the Broad and Saluda Rivers, requested educational aid for their community, and in 1748 a grant of £500 was recommended by the assembly. In Prince William's Parish, a school for Negroes was opened in 1743. Meanwhile, small academies were springing up all over the province.

At the close of the Revolution, 22 schools within the 24 parishes had survived from the old regime and provided a basis for education in the new State. Most of these were classical academies in and around Charleston. Instruction of the middle and lower classes had now grown to be a serious problem, foreshadowing the widespread illiteracy of later decades. Apprenticeship in trades, with such ciphering and penmanship as were necessary, composed practically all the education available to them. Numerous societies were organized in an effort to provide educational facilities—St. David's (1777), Beaufort (1786), St. Helena (1786), Camden Orphan (1787), Upper Long Cane (1799), John's Island (1800), and others.

Important in this early period was the rise of the Up Country small-farmer element. Antagonism between the inland settlers and the stabilized aristocracy of the coast had begun before the Revolution. The removal of the capital from Charleston to Columbia in 1786 was an effort to bring the two sections of the State into more amicable relations. The selection of the new capital as a site for South Carolina College (now the University of South Carolina), when that institution was founded in 1801, also originated in a desire to unify the still somewhat antagonistic sections. An earlier educational institution that drew its students from both regions was Mount Zion Academy in Winnsboro, incorporated in 1785—simultaneously with the College of Charleston, oldest municipal college in the United States.

In 1811, after an earnest appeal by Governor Henry Middleton, and under the leadership of Stephen Elliott, the legislature provided for the establishment in each electoral district of free elementary schools equal in number to the number of representatives in the lower house from the corresponding district, with an appropriation of $300 for each school. Preference was to be given to poor children when accommodations were insufficient for all; and the subjects to be taught were reading, writing, and arithmetic.

The system of public education thus begun, which continued until the War between the States, proved fairly effective in spite of its very limited scope. Between 1811 and 1850, 720 free schools were established, and the cost of conducting the system in 1850 was $74,000. All of these schools were for white children only—Negroes were not admitted into public educational institutions until after the war. But through the efforts of private organizations, their own and others, the Negroes of the State were able to secure a modicum of educational facilities. Thomas S. Bonneau, a noted Negro teacher, conducted a successful school in Charleston from about 1803 until his death late in the 1820's.

Along with the establishment of free public schools, there was a rapid increase in the number of private academies. Perhaps the most notable of these was the one conducted at Willington by Dr. Moses Waddel. This log-cabin institution gave training to many Southerners who became prominent in nullification and secession days, including John C. Calhoun, George McDuffie, William H. Crawford, Hugh S. Legare, James L. Petigru, and Augustus B. Longstreet. Most of the private academies were eventually absorbed into the public school system.

Several denominational colleges also made their appearance during the ante-bellum period, chiefly as the result of an upheaval in the State College in the 1830's. Dr. Thomas Cooper, English scholar and free-thinking friend of Thomas Jefferson, had been secured as second president of that institution in 1821. During his term of office he published criticisms of the Bible that antagonized religious leaders throughout the South. He was tried for heresy in 1832, and though acquitted he resigned from the college presidency a year or two later. After this incident, many church people refused to let their sons attend the South Carolina College, and various denominations established their own schools. Of these, Furman (Baptist), Wofford (Methodist), Newberry (Lutheran), and Erskine (Associate Reformed Presbyterian) have been in continuous existence since that time.

Only a few tax-supported schools survived the fall of the Confederacy in 1865, and when these were thrown open to Negroes as well as whites the latter immediately withdrew. Most of the white South Carolinians educated during the Reconstruction era attended the denominational schools, which were not compelled to admit Negroes. While educational facilities for white children were thus self-limited, those for Negroes increased rapidly, owing to the activity of Northern churches, the Freedmen's Bureau, and other outside agencies, as well as of the radical State government.

The chief educational accomplishment of this period was the incorporation into the State constitution of laws that set up the basis for the public school system of recent times. The constitutional committee on education was headed by Francis L. Cardozo, a Charleston mulatto who had graduated with distinction at the University of Glasgow. J. K. Jillson, of Massachusetts, served as the first State superintendent of education.

With the resumption of political authority by native white South Carolinians in 1876, separate public schools were established for white and Negro pupils. But the new government was faced with an over-whelming indebtedness. The assessed property values of the State had been depleted 70 per cent during the war, and the subsequent decade of radical rule had bled the State of what few resources still remained. In the effects of this situation on public education, Negroes suffered more heavily than whites. Northern philanthropists continued their assistance, however, and numerous endowments were made that still are of great benefit.

Two of South Carolina's largest educational institutions had their beginnings in the decades immediately following the Reconstruction period. These were Winthrop College for women, founded 1886 at Columbia (later moved to Rock Hill), and Clemson Agricultural College, established on a land-grant basis at Clemson in 1889.

The rapid growth of South Carolina's public education system in recent decades may best be indicated by a few comparative figures. During the period from 1903 to 1939, the total school attendance increased from 288,713 to 487,610, and the number of classroom teachers employed from 5,947 to 15,043. In 1906 there were 5,704 white and no Negro pupils in State-supported high schools; the attendance in 1939 was 66,716 white and 15,030 Negro pupils. The annual school term in 1916 consisted of 137 days in white and 69 days in Negro schools; in 1939 the term comprised 175 and 141 days respectively.

Until early in the twentieth century, the public school system of the State was supported mainly by poll taxes, by a three-mill property tax, by revenues from the sale of whisky under the old dispensary system, and by special school district levies. The first direct State appropriation for public school purposes was made in 1904, and consisted of $5,000 for school libraries. In 1937 the legislature provided for a State-aided school term of eight months, with an increase of teachers' salaries, and put compulsory education laws into effect. The appropriation for public school aid in 1939 was $8,032,268, or about 26 per cent of the total revenues of $30,703,838. Average cost per pupil in average attendance for current expenses was $36.57.

Better roads and the development of pupil transportation have greatly facilitated school consolidations, thereby reducing the number of small and inadequate schools. Many rural consolidated high schools have been established, in some cases with as many as 20 teachers. Besides academic subjects, agricultural and other vocational courses are available for boys in these schools, while girls are taught home economics. Many Negro high schools are also training their pupils, both boys and girls, in practical vocations.

For many years South Carolina has had the highest illiteracy rate of all States in the Union. Although a few night schools for adolescents had previously been conducted in various localities, the first organized campaign against illiteracy among adults was begun in 1913 in the mill villages of Spartanburg County. The work was directed by a young woman of vision who volunteered her services, securing pay for the teachers from mill officials and the county board of education. In the following year, a similar campaign was instituted in a rural township of Laurens County. The results of these two experiments were so significant that in 1916 the legislature made its first appropriation for night schools; and in 1918, at the request of the State Federation of Women's Clubs, the governor appointed a commission on illiteracy. Later the legislature increased its appropriation for night schools, and authorized the creation of a division of adult education in the State Department of Education. In consequence of these and other activities, the State's illiteracy rate dropped from 18.1 per cent for all classes of population in 1920 to 14.9 per cent in 1930, giving South Carolina sixth place among the States in decrease of illiteracy for the decade. The decline among native whites was from 6.5 to 5.1 per cent, and among Negroes from 29.3 to 26.9 per cent.

In order to reach all sections and groups, three types of special schools have been developed in the campaign against illiteracy: (1) 'Lay-by' schools, organized in summer after the crops have been 'laid by' and farm workers are at leisure; (2) night schools organized in mill communities during the winter; (3) day and night schools conducted by teachers devoting their entire time to single mill villages. Classes have been taught by paid and volunteer teachers in public schools, colleges, and churches, in homes, in abandoned buildings converted into schoolhouses, in jails, and even in the fields where plowmen have stopped their mules to take a daily lesson. Pupils of every type—whites, Negroes, Indians, and mixed breeds—have enrolled in the classes. Regardless of economic or social background, they are inspired by a common ambition: to learn to read and write so that they may study their Bibles, communicate with relatives and friends, keep up with the news of the day, and be better equipped to play their part in the world about them. The eagerness and courage shown by these neglected folk have been an inspiration to all with whom they come in contact.

Two interesting by-products of the movement against illiteracy are really folk institutions—the State Pilgrimage and the Opportunity School. Out of the county and State adult school commencements has developed a great one-day spring pilgrimage, when grown-up pupils journey to Columbia from every part of the State to learn how the wheels of government turn, to worship in famous churches, and to pay homage to the history-makers who lie buried in the churchyards. The first such pilgrimage was made in 1921, when 18 counties were represented by about 100 pupils; in 1936 more than 8,000 had traveled to Columbia from every county in the State.

The Opportunity School provides vacation instruction for 'those over fourteen, who in youth did not have a chance to learn to read, write, and figure, but who long for the opportunity to study.' The first Opportunity School was held in 1921 at Tamassee, the D.A.R. mountain school, with 36 students in attendance. Since then the school has changed homes several times to accommodate an ever-growing student body. The State Agricultural and Mechanical College at Clemson now houses the annual sessions for white students. The Negro session was conducted in 1936 at Voorhees Industrial School in Denmark. In 1938 attendance at the Opportunity School at Clemson totaled 311, with representatives from every county in the State. The school is a cooperative undertaking of the State Department of Education, Clemson Agricultural College, and the Work Projects Administration. A similar vacation school for Negroes is conducted at Benedict College in Columbia.

Some counties of the State, in addition to maintaining a dual system of public education, have the added problem of providing instruction for groups of mixed blood who will not associate with Negroes but who are debarred by their color from the white schools. Separate schools, on about the same level as the Negro schools, are maintained for such groups in several counties. The Catawba Indians, as wards of the State, have a school supported by direct legislative appropriations.

Especially notable in the State educational scheme is the Parker District School in Greenville County, a cotton-mill region. Fourteen industrial communities consolidated here, and established a school system which in 1938-9 had an enrollment of 5,557 elementary and 988 high school children. A balanced academic-vocational-cultural program of instruction, conducted under the able leadership of Superintendent

History

JOHN C. CALHOUN
Detail of Portrait by G. P. A. Healy

STATE HOUSE (1851-1907), COLUMBIA

GOVERNOR'S MANSION, COLUMBIA

ERECTED
BY THE STATE OF
SOUTH CAROLINA
AND
ITS CITIZENS

GOVERNOR OF SOUTH CAROLINA
1876–1879
UNITED STATES SENATOR
1879–1891

hotograph by W. Lincoln Highton

MONUMENT TO GENERAL WADE HAMPTON BY F. W. RUCKSTUHL, COLUMBIA

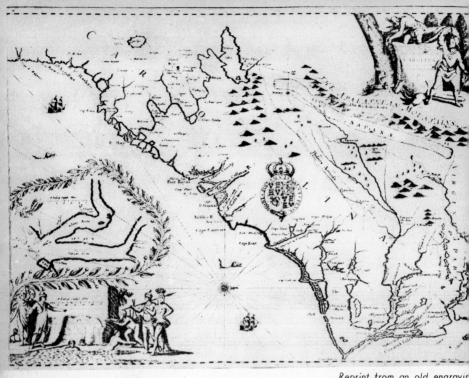

A NEW DESCRIPTION OF CAROLINA, BY ORDER OF THE LORDS PROPRIETORS (1672)

The "Best Friend," the First Locomotive built in the United States for actual service on a Railroad.

THE BEST FRIEND (1830), BUILT FOR USE IN SOUTH CAROLINA
Reproduction from the *History of the First Locomotives in America*

MORGAN SQUARE (1884), SPARTANBURG
Photograph by courtesy of the Spartanburg Chamber of Commerce

MAIN STREET, COLUMBIA, THE MORNING AFTER THE BURNING (February 17-18, 1865)

INTERIOR OF FLOATING BATTERY USED IN ATTACK ON FORT SUMTER (1863-5)
Drawing by a Confederate Officer

Photograph by Matthew W. Brady; courtesy of U. S. Army Signal Corps

RUINS OF CHARLESTON (1865)

SECESSION CONVENTION (DECEMBER 17, 1860), FIRST BAPTIST CHURCH, COLUMBIA

Reprint from a contemporary engraving

STATE LEGISLATURE (1939), COLUMBIA

Photograph by W. Lincoln Highton

L. P. Hollis, with Dr. James H. Tippett as curricular adviser, has made the Parker District widely known among American educators.

The South Carolina Textile and Industrial Institute, founded at Spartanburg by the Methodist Church, is prominent in the field of vocational education. Under the leadership of D. E. Camak and others, this institution has trained many students of high school and junior college age.

In addition to its liberal support of the public education system in general, the State maintains a number of special schools for orphans, crippled children, the deaf and blind, and other unfortunates. These include the South Carolina School for the Deaf and Blind, at Cedar Springs; the John de la Howe School for Orphans and Indigent Children, at Willington; the Industrial School for White Boys, at Florence; the Industrial School for Girls, at Columbia; and the Training School for the Feebleminded, at Clinton.

State-supported institutions for higher education include the University of South Carolina at Columbia, Clemson Agricultural College at Clemson, the Medical College of South Carolina at Charleston, the Citadel (a military college) at Charleston, and Winthrop College (for women) at Rock Hill. The State Agricultural and Mechanical College for Negroes is at Orangeburg. There are also 15 denominational four-year colleges in the State for white students, and 4 for Negroes; 4 junior colleges for whites, and 9 for Negroes.

Religion

THOUGH rewarded with the Province of Carolina for loyal support of the throne in the Cavalier-Roundhead wars, the eight British Lords Proprietors gave their dissenting religious antagonists the right of free worship in the new possessions, and the first governor they appointed was the Puritan, William Sayle. For 25 years after the settling of Charleston, Carolina was a haven for religious sufferers who, trusting in the chartered rights of the province, believed there would be no discrimination against their creeds.

Some of the ships bearing settlers were underwritten by wealthy English Jews, who themselves immigrated later. A considerable number of Huguenots found surcease here from French Catholic persecution. Covenanters and Quakers set up their forms; Congregationalists from Massachusetts, and Baptists, led by William Screven of Maine, established themselves in the interior in 1696. However, among all these elements, to which were later added German and Swiss Lutherans, the English remained dominant. A few Roman Catholics had come to the province, but they were discouraged in 1696 by political discrimination, which continued for many years afterward.

As the influx of nonconformist colonists increased, a corresponding growth in ability for leadership developed. Among dissenter governors, besides Sayle, were Joseph Morton, Thomas Smith, Joseph Blake, and John Archdale. In England the Anglican movement against dissenters was gaining strength, some of the proprietors began to fear that their powers were lessening in the New World, and an effort to abrogate the religious freedom of the provincial charter was instituted. The proprietors disagreed among themselves, however, and governing bodies in Charleston wrangled over the question of establishing a State religion.

In 1701 the Society for the Propagation of the Gospel in Foreign Parts was organized in London, and Carolina came in for its share of missionary efforts, directed toward conversion of Indians and Negroes, as well as whites, to the Anglican faith. The Reverend Alexander Garden, Bishop of London's Commissary for North Carolina, South Carolina, and the Bahama Islands, took up residence in Charleston as rector of St. Philip's. Churchmen were sent into adjacent areas and, as their influence increased, antagonism arose against all who were not of their persuasion. An unexpected result of the society's activities, and one not connected with the Establishment movement, was the beginning of Negro education in South Carolina at Goose Creek in 1702.

By 1704 political power was in the hands of the Anglicans; and, disregarding the charter, the general assembly restricted the activities of the dissenters so severely that John Ash and Joseph Boone went to England seeking redress. These two nonconformists interested Daniel Defoe, of *Robinson Crusoe* fame, in writing and broadcasting the pamphlets *Party Tyranny* and *High Church Tyranny,* describing the state of affairs in South Carolina. Their efforts were fruitless, however. In 1706 the Church of England was established as the official church in the Carolinas; and the Anglican authority, with parishes as local political units, was made supreme. Ministers of the Baptist, Lutheran, Presbyterian, and other denominations were debarred by law from performing such offices of the church as marriage, baptism, and funeral rites. After Joseph Blake's administration of 1696–1700, no governor other than one of Church of England or Episcopal faith held office until 114 years later, when David R. Williams, a Baptist, was elected.

There was immediate and continuous opposition to this union of Church and State, some of the strongest resistance coming from prominent Anglicans. Many believed that the Carolinians had experienced too much religious freedom to submit peaceably to such dictatorial authority. But it was not until 1778 that South Carolina, through its second State constitution, permitted freedom of worship to Protestant sects; and not until 1790 that all religious discriminations were annulled.

During the period of Anglican supremacy, dissenters continued to increase in the province, and not until 1730 were they outnumbered by Anglicans. By that time the social and political prestige of the State church had induced many colonists in the coastal area to change their religious affiliations. In the back country, however, nonconformists remained in large majority. Scotch-Irish Presbyterians and German Lutherans were pushing farther and farther westward into the Indian lands. Though at times they suffered because of their restricted authority, and for lack of financial aid from the government in their enterprises, they were not daunted in their efforts to establish homes and civilization in the wilderness.

Before and during the Revolutionary War, ministers in sparsely settled districts were the chief agents in spreading not only their religion but also the Whig doctrines of resistance to the Crown. 'Their centers of preaching developed into strong churches,' says an old-time writer, 'in spite of the Devil, Indians and Tories.' The Reverend William Tennant, a Presbyterian divine, was sent by the Council of Safety in 1775, with William Henry Drayton of Charleston, into the Up Country to arouse enthusiasm for the Revolutionary cause. Cornwallis is said to have remarked that he feared the prayers of the young Baptist minister, Richard Furman, more than the armies of Sumter and Marion. After the fall of Charleston in 1780, discouraged patriots gathered at old Bullock Creek Church in York County to discuss whether they should surrender to the British in what seemed a hopeless struggle. Dr. Joseph Alexander, Presbyterian minister, teacher, and physician, was fired by the challenge, and through his inspiring oratory encouraged the Americans to resist. Soon afterward came the victories of Musgrove's Mill, Kings Mountain, and Cowpens, in which members of this congregation participated.

The founders of Methodism, John and Charles Wesley, visited Carolina frequently during their stay in Georgia in 1735-6. John took ship from Charleston to England when driven from Savannah because of undeserved calumny by an irate husband. He had preached and attended services in Charleston, and remarked upon the sincerity of the churchgoers. George Whitefield, another famous English Methodist, conducted many meetings in South Carolina between 1738 and 1770.

Bishop Francis Asbury, 'the father of American Methodism,' has left a detailed account of his efforts and achievements as a circuit rider in South Carolina and elsewhere. His diary of 1785-1816 reveals his prodigious perseverance in toiling through swamps, sandbeds, and forests to preach to the irreligious, the scornful, the indifferent, as well as to an increasing number of faithful followers. The social life of the day, the Episcopal Church, and slavery were burdens on his soul which he felt divinely called upon to rebuke. 'I now leave Charleston,' he wrote, 'the seat of Satan, dissipation and folly.' And at Georgetown he noted: 'Here are the rich, the rice, and the slaves; the last is awful to me.' The new and crude Up Country troubled him also, and in Camden he 'met with a multitude of people who were desperately wicked.' But he had his brighter moods as well, often remarking upon the kindliness shown him and describing the beauty of the country that he rode through.

His services were held in log chapels, in private homes, and out of doors, with 'preaching sheds' and bush-arbors serving as shelter from the elements when no other was available. Surviving for many years from these original gatherings were numerous camp meetings throughout the State, only two of which have continued to the present. At Indian Fields in Dorchester County the camp is more than 100 years old, having been moved from an earlier site where Bishop Asbury preached. A Negro organization at Camp Welfare in Fairfield County, though developing after the War between the States, resulted from participation by Negroes in such meetings held by whites before the war. At each camp, for one or two weeks in the fall, families occupy their 'tents' in a huge circle around the 'arbor'—the old terms being retained, though nowadays the buildings are of wood. Three to five services a day attract congregations of several hundred persons of all ages; religious worship is accompanied by friendly reunions, the beginnings of courtship, and bounteous repasts cooked in iron vessels over open fires out of doors.

Soon after 1800, South Carolina felt the impulse of the Great Revival then sweeping the country. Every community and all denominations were stirred by tides of religious fervor. At the Waxhaws in Lancaster County occurred what was probably the greatest individual revival.

The slavery question was much debated in religious groups from early times until the end of the War between the States. The Quakers, among several minor sects, removed to other States because they could not support a society dependent on slave labor. In the original charter of the province, slaves were accorded an equal religious status with freemen, but their social and economic position was not thereby changed. The membership in many churches was preponderantly Negro; but, because of the small accommodations in slave galleries or specially reserved pews, the congregations were prevailingly white. Plantation owners usually provided religious instruction for their slaves, and sometimes permitted them to worship in separate churches of their own, with Negro ministers. One such church was organized at Silver Bluff on the Savannah River. Apparently dated from 'some years previous to 1778' it is said to have been the first Negro Baptist church in the United States. Andrew Bryan, a Negro minister, was active and influential here for several years. In Charleston, before the Revolution, the English Church purchased two slaves who were instructed so that they could preach to their race, and Negro schools organized from religious motives began education for that race in South Carolina.

As Abolitionist agitation increased in the political arena, church leaders took up the question in their pulpits. The Methodists were the first of the larger denominations to sever connection with the national body and form a southern group, because of differences between Northern and Southern churches over the slavery issue. Dr. (later Bishop) William Capers of South Carolina was a potent defender of the southern position when the split occurred in 1844. Other denominations waited until after the Ordinance of Secession was passed before separating from the North. In 1861, under the leadership of the Reverend Richard Fuller of South Carolina, resolutions for separation were adopted by the Baptists. The Presbyterians, headed by Drs. James H. Thornwell and Benjamin M. Palmer, both of South Carolina, formed a southern organization at Augusta, Georgia, in December 1861, Dr. Palmer being elected the first Moderator. At a session in Columbia two months earlier, the Episcopalians passed similar resolutions, but actual separation was not carried out. Among Baptists and Presbyterians, the Northern and Southern churches are still distinct; and the separate branches of the Methodist Church did not reunite until 1939.

Denominational colleges have played an important part in the religious life of South Carolina. They grew out of the 'academies' of Colonial and post-Revolutionary times, and were augmented in the 1830's when Dr. Thomas Cooper, president of the State University, fell under suspicion for his unorthodox view of the Scriptures. A further growth came during Reconstruction when white students withdrew from tax-supported institutions because Negroes had been admitted by legislative act. These private church schools, though suffering from poverty and the disorganization caused by war, were the chief means of education for whites until the public school system was again brought under white control in the 1880's.

For all South Carolina, denominationalism has special meaning. Questions of theological doctrine still have a vitality they have lost in many other parts of the country. Though antagonism among creeds is seldom evident, the recent unification of the Methodist Church stirred up the ashes of sectional controversy; and some congregations (1940) have signs in their churchyards stating that they still belong to the Methodist Episcopal Church, South.

After the World War a number of minor sects—the Sanctified Church, the Church of God, the New Lights, the Holiness Church, and others—increased and expanded rapidly. Although the more conventional denominations prevail today in South Carolina's religious life, there are many whose beliefs and forms of worship are far from conventional. Such physical manifestations as shouting, groaning, writhing, and fainting, as evidences of religious fervor, are found among various sects. Some services are conducted with the aid of tambourines and kettledrums; while only psalm-singing is permitted in others. The picturesque ceremony of river immersion is still practiced by some Baptists in rural communities. It is the custom in South Carolina to open all sorts of meetings, including conventions and political rallies, with an invocation and to close with a benediction.

South Carolina has a larger church membership in proportion to its population than any other State in the Union except Utah. In 1926, with an estimated population of 1,700,000, there was combined church membership of 873,525. The Baptist denomination, with 455,922 members, accounted for nearly half the total; the Methodist, with 285,253 members, came next; and the Lutherans, with 25,756 members, occupied third place. Roman Catholics numbered more than 9,000, and Orthodox Jews about 7,000. The church edifices of all denominations were 5,843 in number, and had a combined value of $37,109,000.

Folklore and Folkways

THE folklore of the South Carolina Up Country is predominantly English and Scotch-Irish, as is generally true throughout the Appalachian regions. More than 20 old English and Scottish ballads have been collected in South Carolina, including 'Lady Isabel and the Elf Knight,' the 'Three Ravens,' 'Lord Lovel,' and 'Barbara Allen.' Sometimes the original ballad is much changed in the local version even in title; for example, 'The Daemon Lover' is discovered as the 'House Carpenter.' In the 25 years since Cecil Sharp, the English scholar, collected ballads in the Southeast, ballad singing as a popular art has rapidly declined; but recently many amateur folklorists have set about collecting ballads and other forms of folklore. With guitars, mandolins, and harmonicas, groups gather at parties and sing 'Kindlin' Wood,' 'John Henry,' 'Bow-legged Rabbit,' and the 'Twelve Apostles.'

The Up Country has few differences in dialect from the Low Country, though there is a marked contrast between the coastal Gullah and the talk of the mountaineers. 'Hit' for 'it' is used by illiterate whites and Negroes alike, as are 'holp' for 'helped,' and 'taken' for 'took.' Such redundancies as 'tooth dentist,' 'widow woman,' and 'shower of rain' are also State-wide. Occasionally, among the Negroes in central and Low Country South Carolina, there is the pronunciation of 'w' for 'v' and 'v' for 'w,' such as 'wegetubble' for 'vegetable,' and 'vax' for 'wax.' 'Ary' and 'nary' for 'any' and 'not any,' 'favor' in the Shakespearean sense of 'resemble (in countenance),' and 'clever' as 'kind' or 'agreeable' are commonly heard from the mountains to the sea. The Up Countryman does not slur his 'r's' as the Low Countryman does, but brings them out sharply. Until very recently the speech of rural South Carolina has been remarkably free from slang; and a professor from Oxford University, touring the State in the 1930's after having visited the North, remarked in surprise, 'The people speak English, not American.' This resemblance of Carolina speech to English speech is probably as much a matter of tone as of pronunciation or diction.

From Caesars Head to Charleston, belief in spells and conjures still prevails. Farmers plant their beans carefully at the 'right time of the moon,' and the wife of a former governor is said to carry on her person a small raw potato to absorb the rheumatism from which she suffers. An old woman in the Dutch Fork can 'use' for fire. Passing her hand over a burn, she repeats a magic formula and commands the fire to leave. The cries of owls and whippoorwills are regarded as bad luck and the fire-poker must be heated red so it will burn the tongue of the bird and make him leave. Negroes mix love-potions by adding bits of their hair and nail parings to whisky, and administer the drink to the person whose love is desired. Warts are conjured away by many mysterious formulas; an ax is put under the bed of Negroes in childbirth to 'cut the pain,' and silver tea, made by boiling a handful of coins, is used to stop the flow of blood from a wound. Many 'cures' for malaria are found in the Low Country where the disease has taken its toll for decades; ague weeds of various sorts, certain kinds of spiders, and a string with 16 knots tied around the waist are some of them.

Among the many strange good luck charms in which Negroes believe is the 'black cat bone.' Here is one old woman's suggestion for obtaining it: 'Get a black cat. Mustn't have a single white hair. Put on a pot o' b'ilin' water. B'ilin' hard, throw the cat in there and b'ile him alive. B'ile him till all the meat and everything is left the bone. Mustn't kill the cat. Must b'ile him 'live. Then take pot and all to runnin' stream. Runnin' stream o' water and dump it in. And all the meat and bone and water will go with the stream—all that is, 'cep' one bone. That the lucky bone. You can work any kind o' work with that bone. Any kind o' magic. Can make a girl leave and follow you clean to the ocean.'

In the same coastal section where that old woman lives, fishing is not only a sport but an important source of livelihood and for it a ritual prevails. The fisherman believes he should never talk with an old woman before he casts off, nor let an old person handle the line before it is used. But it is lucky to talk to a young girl. Dogs must not accompany the fisherman, nor should food be eaten while fishing is under way.

Somewhat farther inland, river fishing demands special ceremony. The fisherman must spit on his bait so the fish will bite, and

> If the wind comes from the north
>   Fish bite like a horse;
> If the wind comes from the south
>   They bite like a louse;

> If the wind comes from the east
> They bite the least;
> If the wind comes from the west
> They bite the best.

Most of the games and pastimes of the State are in the English tradition. Such singing games as 'Green Gravel' and 'Here we dance, looby loo,' are played on every schoolground and even by adults at country parties. Square dances are still popular and other less common occasions when neighbors get together are 'graveyard cleanings' and 'dumb suppers.' The former, more general in the Up Country, is an annual affair at country church cemeteries when, fortified by a huge picnic dinner, the church members with their friends gather to clean up the graveyard, dig up the weeds, and prop up the sagging tombstones. Local newspapers carry announcements of the affairs. The 'dumb supper,' rarely found below the fall line, is prepared by young folk who wish to find out their future mates. Corn bread, with meal and salt in almost equal proportions, must be cooked and eaten in perfect silence. Then comes bedtime, and still no word has been spoken. If one speaks, the whole spell will be broken, but if not, the dreams that follow this salty repast will disclose the dreamer's future spouse, who will appear with a drink of water.

By far the most picturesque custom held over from Colonial times is the tilting tournament. Surviving in the Low Country chiefly near Cameron and Eutawville, the tilts have always brought together hundreds of spectators. As practiced in the old days these tournaments were elaborate tests of skill in horsemanship, and were attended by visitors from other parts of the country, including Philadelphia and New York. Each contestant, riding down the lists at full speed, endeavored to transfix with his lance a gilt ring, an inch and three quarters in diameter, suspended from a crossbar in front of the principal pavilion and the judges' stand. In the Pineville tournament of 1851, 30 knights participated. Richard Porcher rode as the Knight of Eutaw, Christopher Gaillard as the Knight of the Palmetto, Theodore Marion as the Knight of the Santee, William Ravenel as the Knight of the Chase, and Keating Palmer as the Knight of the Grove. A King-at-Arms in charge of the tournament came upon the field with a Master-of-Horse. Preceded by buglers and heralds, these two officials led the cavalcade to the grand pavilion, where the lances were lowered and slowly raised in salute. Six courses were then ridden, and after the decision of the judges the victor lowered his lance at the feet of the young lady of his choice, thus proclaiming her the Queen of

Love and Beauty. Since the War between the States, modified tournaments, stripped of much of their old-time pageantry, have been held sporadically in South Carolina and Maryland; and a revival of the tournament on elaborate scale and in accord with ante-bellum practice is a feature of the annual Azalea Festival at Charleston.

The barbecue is perennial in South Carolina and is growing in popularity. Recorded by travelers before 1700, it is one of the few surviving customs taken over from the Indians, the word itself having been brought in by the Spanish from the now extinct Taino Indians of the Bahamas. Oxen, sheep, and hogs are roasted whole or in halves over a pit filled with glowing coals, constantly renewed from piles of burning hardwood. Usually such a feast is prepared for throngs of people at a celebration, anniversary, or political meeting. Roadside stands have commercialized the process by offering an inferior grade of 'barbecue sandwich.'

No feature of South Carolina life is more striking to an outsider than the cohesiveness of families—a clannishness rooted deep in the social structure. Everybody seems related to everybody else, and these kinships are treasured to the remotest counsinhood. Family picnics, reunions, and front-porch visitings are still favorite pastimes, and the first question put to a stranger seeks to place him as to family, religion, and region of birth. Much of this family spirit grew out of the exigencies of pioneer life, and it was preserved and intensified by the hardships that followed the War between the States. Communal activities in which families join to help each other—such as harvesting, corn shucking, quilting, hog killing, and house building—are still fairly common, especially in the Up Country.

'Unquestionably the most picturesque and interesting of all the Negro strains in America is the Gullah,' says Dr. Reed Smith, noted folklorist and authority on these Negroes who live along the South Carolina coast. 'It is unique, in the real, true meaning of that much abused word.' Living close to nature, they are learned in woodcraft and the ways of animals and fish; their quaint similes and shrewd sayings apply this knowledge to their dealings with their fellows and with the outside world.

They speak a patois wholly different from the upland Negro dialects recorded by Joel Chandler Harris in North Georgia and Thomas Nelson Page in Virginia. Their language is peculiar in grammar, vocabulary, and pronunciation, and affords interesting examples of archaisms, popular etymologies, and proverbs. Among early forms that survive are 'fo' punce' and 'seb' punce' chickens, 'coz' or 'cuzn' as a form of address, 'use' for 'linger habitually about,' 'yowe' for 'ewe,' and 'frail' for 'strike' or 'beat.' Popular etymologies include 'consecrate lye' for 'concentrated lye,' 'middle blouse' for 'middy-blouse,' 'pettyaugah' for 'pirogue (a kind of boat),' 'muffledice' for 'hermaphrodite,' 'peach omelet' for 'peach marmalade,' 'curly flower' for 'cauliflower,' 'Florida lime' for 'chloride of lime,' and 'sweet religion' for 'sweet alyssum.'

Among the better-known Gullah proverbs are the following:

Ef yo' play wid puppy, ee lick yo' face (Familiarity breeds contempt).

Cut finguh f'aid ax (A burnt child dreads the fire).

Ef yo' ent hab hoss to ride, ride cow (Half a loaf is better than no bread).

Po' buckra an' dog walk one pat' (The poor man and dog walk the same path).

Mos' kill bud don't make soup (Most killed bird don't make soup).

The Gullahs sing many kinds of songs—work songs, boat songs, shout songs, and spirituals—but the spirituals, or prayer songs, outrank the others in interest and variety (*see Music*). Fortunately the Penn Normal, Industrial, and Agricultural School, which has exerted a wide influence on the Negroes of St. Helena Island, has preserved many of the spirituals, and encouraged the singers to appreciate the dignity and beauty of their art.

Painting and Sculpture

THE first permanent settlers coming to South Carolina in 1670 brought with them a number of miniatures and portraits in oil. These paintings indicate that the aristocratic colonists were not lacking in artistic taste, that an interest in the arts was taken for granted among them, and that they were able to afford the best work available in the Mother Country. For some time wealthy Carolinians traveling abroad patronized French and English artists; but soon artists began coming to the province, finding here a congenial and profitable field for their work. Within half a century after the founding of Charles Town, the city had begun to emerge as an art center of America. Mrs. Jacques Le Serrurier (the former Elizabeth Leger), who came from Picardy soon after the revocation of the Edict of Nantes (1685), was a painter of considerable ability and is believed to have painted the excellent pair of portraits of herself and her husband now privately owned in this State. The portrait of the Le Serrurier's daughter Catherine (Mrs. Henry Le Noble) is by an early unknown artist.

Before 1708 Henrietta Johnson, 'America's First Woman Artist,' was drawing portraits in pastel, and continued to work in South Carolina until her death in 1728 or 1729. Three or four pastels and 15 of her oil portraits have been identified, the earliest dated 1708. The Gibbes Art Gallery in Charleston owns one of her portraits, while others are in private collections in the State.

Before 1750 many painters from England and France had established themselves in Charleston, together with artists from New York and Philadelphia. The new arrivals often combined with their art a proficiency in various crafts, such as 'jewelry and military furnishings.' In 1735 Benjamin Roberts advertised his ability to do 'Portrait Painting, Engraving, Heraldry, and House Painting,' and in 1740 Mary Roberts asserted her competence in 'Face Painting well performed.' Benjamin Roberts made a painting of the Charleston water front, which was the basis of one by T. Mellish in 1742, the latter reproduced in an engraving. A Mr. Belzons offered to produce 'Likenesses in the most striking manner and on the most liberal terms'—£25 for the picture without the setting, and an added £2 if the setting were furnished.

The most important of these early artists was Jeremiah Theus (c.1719–74), a Swiss, who was also a painter of coaches and coats of of arms. First notice of his work appears in the *South-Carolina Gazette* of August 30, 1740, and he remained in Charleston until his death, painting portraits of many prominent families in the area. Richard Bohun Baker paid Theus £100 for a portrait in 1756, and £113 for three pictures in 1773. Baker also records that he asked Theus to criticize a portrait by Allan Ramsay (1715–84), the English court painter. About 150 portraits by Theus have been identified. The best of them are done in the formal eighteenth-century Continental manner, while others are more primitive in handling. Theus's work has been favorably compared with Copley's.

After the Revolution, the family pride that expressed itself in the commissioning of portraits did not decline; portraiture, however, was supplemented by an expansion of artistic interest that turned to historical and allegorical painting. This development was transmitted to America largely through the influence of Benjamin West, in whose London studio Washington Allston (1779–1843), South Carolina's most brilliant representative of the period, studied from 1801 to 1803. Though Allston left his native State in early youth and finally settled in Boston, he maintained contact with friends and relatives here, and his influence on South Carolina art was far reaching. His was a gracious and generous personality; he was a poet and composer of romantic tales, and his *Lectures on Art* was an important contribution to early American art criticism. From his years of study in Italy and France, Allston derived his bold application of color, which caused him to be called later the 'American Titian.' At his best in Biblical subjects, he worked on his *Belshazzar's Feast* for 25 years, finally leaving it unfinished. Jared B. Flagg, Allston's nephew and pupil, who is best known for his portraits, wrote the *Life of Washington Allston*.

Allston's most brilliant pupil, Samuel F. B. Morse (1791–1872), who won fame as an artist before he invented the telegraph, joined the coterie of Charleston artists in 1818. America's first museum had been established here in 1793, and Morse was attracted to the city, he said, because it was the center of culture in America. Like others of the period who had studied abroad, Morse scorned portraits but was compelled to paint them for a living. His *Portrait of La Fayette* is generally considered his best work, though Morse himself preferred his

Portrait of James Monroe, which hangs in the city hall at Charleston.

Thomas Coram, a native of England, was a resident of Charleston from 1769 till his death in 1811, working not only as a painter but as an engraver and die maker. He designed the official seal of the Charleston Library Society (*see Literature*) and engraved the plates for the South Carolina currency of 1779. Coram's *Christ Blessing the Little Children* hangs in the Charleston Orphan House.

John Blake White (1781–1857), a South Carolinian who studied from 1800 to 1804 under West in London, returned home to follow the style of the early Republican school in painting historical subjects. In the National Capitol are his *Battle of Fort Moultrie, Mrs. Motte Directing Marion and Lee to Burn Her Mansion to Dislodge the British, General Marion Inviting a British Officer to Dinner,* and *Sergeants Jasper and Newton Rescuing American Prisoners from the British*— all depicting scenes from South Carolina history. Engravings of the last two of the paintings mentioned were used on five- and ten-dollar bank notes by South Carolina in 1861. White's portraits of *Colonel Samuel Warren* and *John Jacob Faust* are in the State House in Columbia. Talented native artists who made their appearance in this period were T. S. Moise (1806–83), John Beaufain Irving (1825–77), Jared B. Flagg (1820–99), H. B. Bounetheau (1797–1877), miniaturist, Solomon N. Carvalho, and Robert John Curtis (1812–77), whose *Portrait of Osceola,* painted in 1838, is now in the Charleston Museum. Also painting here were Thomas Middleton (1797–1863) of Faucluse, engraver, John Wesley Jarvis (1780–1834), Henry Inman (1801–46), Benjamin Trott (1770–1839), and James Earle (1761–98), portraitist.

Thomas Sully (1783–1872), born in England, spent his youth in Charleston, and was first stimulated to paint by the Charleston artist, Charles Fraser (1782–1860), who was both his schoolmate and his instructor in the rudiments of art. Sully later lived in Richmond, New York, and Philadelphia, and his reputation as a portraitist was for a time unrivaled. A number of his works remain in South Carolina, but he is best remembered for his *Washington Crossing the Delaware,* in the Boston Museum of Fine Arts.

In the latter part of the eighteenth century, miniature painting entered upon a period of great popularity, and to this art South Carolina's contribution was distinguished. First to use the word 'miniature' in local advertisement was Louis Turtaz, whose notice appeared March 6, 1767. Abraham Delaney and Thomas Laidler inserted advertisements the following year, though none of their paintings is identified. The arrival of Henry Benbridge (1744–1812) and his wife, formerly a Miss Sage of Philadelphia, was noted in the *South-Carolina Gazette,* April 5, 1773, Mrs. Benbridge described as 'a very ingenious miniature paintress.' The Benbridges remained in Charleston for a number of years, and to them many excellent portraits and miniatures are attributed. John Wollaston (1751–69), John Grafton, who was a pupil of Sir Joshua Reynolds and who advertised his desire to paint portraits in 1774, John and Hamilton Stevenson, notice of whose drawing and painting academy appeared in 1772, and many others were then working in the city. Numerous French artists, some of them fleeing the Revolution and others the uprising in San Domingo and Haiti, settled in the State. J. B. St. Memin (1770-1852), famed for his profiles and small engravings after them, was the most distinguished. Peter Henri advertised that he would paint miniatures and offered to take back any likeness 'not bearing a pleasing resemblance to the original.' Another excellent French miniaturist was J. F. de la Vallée.

Among many miniaturists whose works remain in the State to attest their skill, Edward Green Malbone (1777–1807) and Charles Fraser (1782–1860) tower above the rest. Malbone, a self-taught New Englander, spent almost half his brief career of 12 years in Charleston. Ranked by many as America's foremost miniaturist, his rapid output of some 300 pictures shows three definite stages. He came to South Carolina with Washington Allston in 1800, and returned here after a short stay in London, where Benjamin West commended his painting. Malbone's lucid and forthright characterizations were sought by Charleston's leading families. His *Portrait of Washington Allston* is now in the Boston Museum of Fine Arts, and his *Miniature of Thomas Lowndes* is privately owned in this State.

Malbone deeply influenced Charles Fraser, the Charlestonian, of whose productions 313 miniatures and 139 oil paintings were shown in Charleston as the 'Fraser Gallery' three years before the artist's death. Most of Fraser's subjects were personal acquaintances—delineated with uncompromising honesty and power. 'His sitters are before you. . . . They are not there to be observed—they are individuals to be considered' (*Charles Fraser,* by Alice R. and Dr. Huger Smith).

In the 1830's Columbia began to attract artists, including James De Veaux (1812–44), a Charlestonian, and William H. Scarborough (1812–71), a ranking South Carolina portraitist, though a native of Tennessee. De Veaux was a protégé of Dr. Robert Gibbes, and painted more than 240 oils, including portraits of many notables at the Nullification Convention in 1832. Several of his portraits, including that of Dr. Thomas Cooper, are at the University of South Carolina. Scarborough came to the State in 1836 and worked for a time in Old Darlington District, but lived mainly in Columbia, where 110 of his portraits are now owned. He advertised in newspapers throughout the Carolinas and Georgia, and painted, as was the custom, in all three States. Critics have declared that Scarborough 'at his best is as good as Sully,' but his work is startlingly uneven. He painted rapidly, usually working on two portraits alternately, morning and evening, and often finishing both in a week. Though Scarborough seldom signed his paintings, 375 have been identified, all but 36 of them portraits. His landscapes and still life studies are comparatively unimportant. The first exhibit of his works was held in 1937 in Columbia.

Besides portraiture and historical painting, South Carolina contributed some of the earliest genre painting done in America. Mark Catesby's exquisite illustrations for the *Natural History of Carolina, Florida, and the Bahamas* (1722) were painted from life in the region. Catesby's work has been compared favorably with that of Audubon, who, about a century later, also found in South Carolina a fertile field for his famous paintings of birds. Benjamin Trott, Henry Inman (1801–46), John Wesley Jarvis (1785–1834), and Samuel Smith, artists who achieved much fame in their day, were residents of the State at various times in the second quarter of the nineteenth century.

South Carolina's first native sculptor was John S. Cogdell (1778–1847), who became proficient in the art at a time when little was known of it in the section. Beginning to paint landscapes and religious subjects for relaxation from his law practice, Cogdell was persuaded by Washington Allston to model in clay, and his career as a sculptor followed. The National Academy of Design has his *Bust of General William Moultrie;* two others are owned by the Pennsylvania Academy; and several are at the University of South Carolina. A tablet to his mother's memory, in St. Philip's Church, Charleston, showing her surrounded by her weeping sons, is by Sir Francis Chantrey.

A pioneer in American realistic sculpture was Clark Mills (1810–33), an itinerant cabinetmaker who settled in Charleston in 1835. Here Mills was employed in stucco work, and began to model in clay. He executed a number of busts and life masks according to methods originated by himself, and, having achieved some popularity, undertook a portrait bust in marble of John C. Calhoun. This proved to be such an excellent likeness that the city council of Charleston struck a medal for Mills as an expression of gratitude. John S. Preston invited him to Columbia, where he executed 10 busts, several of which are in the University of South Carolina Library. Mills was later commissioned by Congress to make an equestrian statue of Andrew Jackson. Although he had never seen either the general or an equestrian statue, Mills undertook the project and produced, after several years of labor, the Jackson Monument, Washington, which was the first equestrian statue created in America.

Hiram Powers (1805–73), noted sculptor of the *Greek Slave* (1843), and identified with the neoclassic movement in American sculpture, also made frequent visits to Columbia. Powers was an admirer of both De Veaux and Scarborough. He was a guest of the Prestons, and for their mansion (*see Columbia*) executed a marble mantel and a garden fountain, both of which have been preserved, though the fountain is now in the garden of the Boylston home in Columbia. His marble bust of Colonel W. P. Preston is at the University of South Carolina.

Little art was produced in South Carolina during the War between the States and the Reconstruction period, the unsettled conditions being unfavorable to artistic development. Some portraits were painted after 1860, when Irving worked in Columbia; but, partly owing to the introduction of photography, portraiture never regained its earlier prestige. Genre and still life painting degenerated into polite accomplishments for young ladies' schools, where china painting and the decoration of screens were also popular. Yet even during the post-war period, South Carolina produced a number of excellent artists, who reflected in the main the new realistic tendency in American art. Edward Lamson Henry (1841–1919) was noted for the accuracy of detail in his historical and genre paintings. R. F. Zogbaum (1849–1925), born in Charleston, was South Carolina's leading exponent of the newly developed art of illustration, especially of army and navy life. His *Old Ironsides* and *Lee's Surrender at Appomattox* are vividly realistic, and he painted a number of Spanish-American War scenes from personal observation. More than 40 of his pictures were exhibited at the Avery Galleries, New York, in 1895. William Fair Kline (1870–1931), a native of Columbia, was a prominent figure and mural painter.

Modern South Carolina artists, several of whom have achieved national recognition, tend to favor landscapes, local scene subjects, and character studies of native types, though portraits and miniatures are still made. Frederick Theodore Weber, born in Columbia in 1883, now lives in New York; his etchings and portraits are on display in prominent American institutions, and he is the author of the article on portrait painting in the latest issue of the Encyclopædia Britannica. A number of his pictures are in Charleston, Columbia, and Rock Hill. Anna Heyward Taylor (b.1879), also a native of Columbia, is noted for her designs and textiles, and Elizabeth O'Neill Verner of Charleston for her etchings. The latter has illustrated a number of books, including the Charleston edition of *Porgy* by DuBose Heyward, *The Carolina Low Country* by Augustine T. Smythe and others, and her own book, *Prints and Impressions of Charleston*. Alfred Hutty (b.1878), Michigan native but an adopted Charlestonian, is also a successful etcher. Perhaps the most widely known of South Carolina's contemporary artists is Alice R. Huger Smith, whose brilliant watercolors have won national recognition. Several other South Carolinians are painting portraits, miniatures, and landscapes that are being hung in public halls and educational institutions of the State as well as in private homes.

On the State House grounds in Columbia are several groups by the sculptor Frederick W. Ruckstuhl (b.1853), whose *Wade Hampton* and *John C. Calhoun* are in the National Capitol. He is noted for his monuments to the Confederacy, equestrian statues, and other historical sculpture. Nickolai Tregor, talented Russian sculptor, made busts of several Columbia citizens during the late 1930's. Frederick C. Hibbard of Chicago was commissioned by the Tillman Memorial Association to make a portrait statue of Benjamin R. Tillman for the State House park, and this work was unveiled in 1940.

The sculpture of J. Q. A. Ward (1830–1910) is represented in the *Statue of General Daniel Morgan* in Morgan Square, Spartanburg, and that of *William Gilmore Simms* in Charleston.

The Gibbes Art Gallery in Charleston, opened in 1905 with funds bequeathed for the purpose by James S. Gibbes, is the only important gallery in the State. It contains 106 canvases, including works of Theus, Henrietta Johnson, Sully, Moise, Sir Archer Shee, Gilbert Stuart, and valuable Americana. Under Robert N. S. Whitelaw, director since 1931, the gallery has arranged exhibits of the finest in European and American art. Kress's collection of Italian primitives and Mr. Guggenheim's modern exhibit (1936) excited wide interest. The Carolina Art Association (incorporated 1858), co-trustee of the gallery with the mayor of Charleston, is zealous in collecting art objects relative to the history of South Carolina. In 1934 the association exhibited more than 200 Fraser miniatures and drawings, and in the two following years brought together about 1,200 miniatures of South Carolinians painted before 1860.

The only notable private galleries in the State were lost in the Confederate era. That of the John S. Prestons was stolen when shipped from Columbia in care of a slave. The collection of Dr. Robert W. Gibbes, also in Columbia, was burned in 1865 by Sherman's men. Only two busts, one of the owner by Powers, and one of his little son, De Veaux Gibbes, by Brown, a New York sculptor, were saved and are now owned by a grandson of Doctor Gibbes.

One of the finest collections of American bronze and marble statuary in this country is at Brookgreen Gardens (*see Tour 1a*), where an open-air museum has been endowed by Mr. and Mrs. Archer M. Huntington for the people of South Carolina.

The Federal Art Project, while in operation in the State, was a stimulus to young artists in South Carolina. One unit of the project executed the murals and scenery for the renovated Dock Street Theater (*see Drama and Charleston*). Civic art centers were also established in Greenville and Beaufort. Exhibits of local artists were held, at which the average monthly attendance was 700 in Beaufort and 1,500 in Greenville. Members of the project taught art to school children and made maps, posters, and charts for the State Board of Health. They also made a number of frescoes for hospitals, and supplied illustrations for books prepared by the Federal Writers' Project.

Handicrafts

THE handicrafts that have survived in South Carolina are those which produce articles useful to the people who make them. They have not survived or been revived as hobbies or on an esthetic basis. Most important of them are pottery making, ironworking, basketry, quilting, woodworking, and rug weaving. All these have lived as applied arts, practiced for their utility value, in the home. With the growth of general interest in folk art and folk craft, a few shops devoted to them have been established, and schools now offer craft courses to promote the intelligent understanding of design and technique, with the prospective improvement of product and increased sales.

Plantation economy in its early days placed a premium on the ability to make farm implements, tools, kitchen utensils, cloth, and leatherwork, and stimulated local production of fine plaster molding, wood carving, and wrought ironwork. In Charleston, especially, the architectural ironwork surviving from early days is so excellent that it is nationally famed; but work of similar character is scattered throughout the State. Wealthy rice planters in the Low Country imported European craftsmen to ornament their buildings, and these men often established residence in the colony and taught their craft to apprentices, among whom were whites, free Negroes, and slaves.

The interiors of the larger residences built in Colonial days were finished in one or two styles: either in carved woodwork and ornamental stucco, or in paneled walls with painted ceilings. St. Philip's Church in Charleston is one of the State's finest examples of ornamental stucco treatment. When the church was renovated in 1920, the only artisan considered competent to take charge of the plasterwork in the enlarged clerestory was an ex-slave, who had repaired the ornamental plaster on previous occasions. In 1936-7, when the Dock Street Theater was renovated, he was again called upon to do the delicate handwork in plaster molding.

Fine examples of wood carving remain in many of the old homes of South Carolina as evidences of the mastery of early artisans. One of the best examples of fine wood carving is the graceful, lacelike woodwork in the 'big house' at Springfield Plantation (*see Tour 5B*) in the northern part of Berkeley County. The tools with which it was executed have been preserved. Other excellent examples, open to public inspection, are in Charleston in the Brewton-Pringle house and the Manigault house (*see Charleston*).

Charleston, like Savannah, Mobile, and New Orleans, has a rich heritage of ornamental ironwork, which conveys a vivid impression of the past. During the seventeenth and the early eighteenth centuries ironwork was of a simple, practical nature, evidence of the fact that the early settlers (preceding the moneyed aristocracy that developed from vast rice-founded fortunes) had little thought for ornamentation.

Despite the abundance of good ironwork in Charleston, little authentic data exist concerning the early Colonial smiths. Of the few records kept, in the form of personal letters and accounts, many were lost or destroyed during the War between the States, so that while tradition preserves the names of a few of the outstanding artificers and their designs, there is little documentary evidence to verify information thus secured.

Following the era of simplicity, which characterized Charleston's earliest examples of ironwork, a long middle period ensued, in which local ironwork developed a character of its own. Among the motifs were the wheel; the heart and lyre; 'S' and 'C' scrolling; and single bars. Peculiar to Charleston was the strap iron formed into 'S' and 'C' ornaments with the scrolls more curled up than those found elsewhere. A richer effect was also obtained locally by doubling the iron in a sweeping curve between the scrolls of the 'S' ornaments. The light, flowing curves seen in many of the Charleston gateways are also a local characteristic.

In addition to gates, banisters, and balcony grilles, architectural ironwork includes such articles as tie irons, thumb latches, knockers, hinge straps, lanterns, bolts, and other small pieces of hardware. Foot-scrapers, fastened into blocks of stone or iron, and weather vanes afforded opportunity for interesting treatment.

In a country not yet acquainted with mechanical mass production of commodities, silversmiths and goldsmiths enjoyed a lucrative and flourishing trade. Many craftsmen came to South Carolina early in the eighteenth century and took up residence within the State; today the best of their products are held in private collections as valued heirlooms.

Better known than any of their contemporaries were John and William Ewen, father and son, who made a number of beautiful pieces now in the possession of private families. They worked in Charleston from 1800 through 1850, and competed with such smiths as Giessandauer, Webb, and Vernon. The elder Ewen established a silverware manufactory in 1829, and created the celebrated 'Physic spoon.'

Work of the smiths consisted of designing, constructing, plating, and engraving such articles as snuffboxes, plates, goblets, candlesticks, spoons, tree urns, beakers, teapots, and sugar bowls. Among the earliest craftsmen engaged in the trade were Louis Janvier, Moreau Sarrazin, William Wright, Daniel You, and Robert Armitage.

In the Up Country, where comparatively few slaves were owned, the Negroes made most of the ironwork and farm implements, and did some weaving. It was in this section, above the fall line, that small groups of whites settled and there perpetuated the arts and crafts they had brought over from Europe. In the Dutch Fork and in the mountainous region the crafts were continued up until the present generation.

Along the coast today the basketry industry flourishes in a small way, many kinds of baskets being made by Negroes from the grass growing near the water. Sweetgrass, rush, and pine-needle baskets are well-known types. Along the Sea Level Route (*see Tour* 1) fine specimens of this craft are exhibited for sale in front of small whitewashed cabins, and in the larger cities they are available at many establishments. The baskets were peddled on the streets of Charleston until a recent ordinance prohibited the practice.

The only handicrafts art in South Carolina that has survived in its original form is the making of Catawba pottery, in York County. Indian pottery is sold at various tourist resorts and the Indians peddle it about the streets of towns near the reservation or exchange it for secondhand clothing (*see Tour* 7A).

Many articles were formerly made of clay by Negro slaves. 'Monkey jugs,' molded by Negroes near the clay deposits in Aiken County, were outstanding. One of these water jugs is in the Charleston Museum.

Pottery works are today located at Pickens (*see Tour* 15a) and near Bethune, where visitors may see clay molded on the potter's wheel.

At the tourist centers are gift shops and women's exchanges where many handmade articles can be purchased. Women throughout the State send their handiwork, knitted and crocheted goods, and quilts to be sold during the winter season.

The encouragement of handicraft by modern agencies has had notable results. The Negro schools, particularly Penn and Voorhees, have encouraged pupils in making such articles as sea island baskets, fish nets, and articles of iron and wood, both for their own use and for sale. Various State training schools, including the boys' school at Florence and the training school at Clinton (*see Tour 9c*), have given instruction in handicrafts.

The WPA has also encouraged native crafts. In equipping the buildings in State parks, the authorities called on craftsmen of the older generation for instruction in ironwork; and hinges, locks, andirons, and similar objects are all forged by hand.

Music

SOUTH CAROLINA'S marked upsurge of interest in music is evidenced by the attendance of thousands each spring at the Columbia Music Festival, the leading event of its kind in the State since 1934. The festival has become such a financial success that Hans Schwieger, formerly director of the Berlin Civic Opera, was engaged in 1939 to train and conduct a Southern Symphony—its membership augmented by professional musicians from eastern cities—and the Shandon Choral Society. The latter is one of many similar groups in the State, and out of it grew the festival, now the only one of its kind in the South, combining on its programs a professional orchestra and operatic soloists with local adult and children's choruses and a State-wide college glee club chorus. The undertaking is sponsored by the Columbia Music Festival Association, which arranges annual contests for State musicians, awarding the winners $300 in cash and a place on the following year's program.

Charleston, Greenville, and Due West all have their nonprofessional symphony orchestras, the last name sponsored by Erskine College. Every college in the State has its band and glee club; and an increasing number of communities are providing annual series of artists' concerts, these events being underwritten by colleges or civic groups. The South Carolina Federation of Music Clubs sponsors musical projects and endows scholarships for native talent thus discovered. This organization, formed in 1920 as a branch of the National Federation, has more than 6,000 adult and junior members (1939). Most South Carolina high schools have student orchestras, bands, and glee clubs, and usually support directors of music. The State Department of Education allows fractional credits for instrumental study on a basis of laboratory hours. Approximately 1,000 students compete in an annual State contest instituted in 1924 by Winthrop College, and sponsored by the music department of the college in conjunction with the South Carolina High School League.

Past or present, South Carolina's richest contribution to music has been made by its Negroes, particularly in the Gullah chants. The

Wadmalaw Singers, Negroes from a sea island, present their own strange music over radio and on tours North and South. N. G. J. Ballanta, a Negro of Sierra Leone, Africa, who was a student of music in Penn School, Beaufort County, has captured the words and music of 103 of these Gullah spirituals in his *Saint Helena Island Spirituals* (1925).

The Negroes' rendering of white people's hymns and songs has effected a transmutation of familiar airs into harmonies characteristic of the race. In these adaptations and in their original compositions, the pathos of their strange minors and the lilt of their rhythmic jig tunes have permeated all post-bellum American music. The Negro sets his life to song: whether he labors or 'pleasures himself,' whether he grieves or rejoices, his emotions are spontaneously expressed in harmonies almost impossible for the white man to reproduce.

'I can trace a popular melody in most of the boatman's chants,' wrote Fanny Kemble, the famous English actress, in 1836, of the sea island Negroes' singing. 'I often wish some great composer could hear these semi-savage performances. With a little skilful adaptation and instrumentation, barbaric chants and choruses might be evoked from them that would make the fortune of an opera.'

Her prophetic wish was realized when George Gershwin spent several months in the South Carolina coastal region, imbibing the color and feeling of Negro music before he composed the operatic score of DuBose Heyward's *Porgy and Bess* (1936).

The Society for the Preservation of Spirituals, composed of prominent white Charlestonians to whom these melodies have been familiar from childhood, has collected authentic versions of these chants and published them in book form. But the society's greatest contribution is its presentation of the spirituals in concerts over the State and on several tours in the North. On these occasions the members sit in a group, attired as ante-bellum ladies and gentlemen, and, with no accompaniment save the patting of hands and the stomping of feet, sing and sway in faithful mimicry of plantation hands. Sometimes mounting fervor impels one or more of the chorus to rise and shout, or to swing into the 'break bone' dance. Proceeds from these entertainments go to some worthy Negro cause.

Collecting ballads and folk songs has been the special concern of the Southeastern Folklore Society, which was organized in Columbia in 1933. This society's programs and its preservation of local music have been invaluable.

The development of jazz has brought to South Carolina a mushroom growth of dance bands, composed of young musicians who play both for profit and for enjoyment. Closely associated with this American departure in music are several dances that originated in this State and afterwards swept the country. The 'Charleston,' of the 1920's, assertedly began in the city of that name; the 'Big Apple' originated in Columbia in a Negro night club that occupied a former Orthodox Jewish synagogue; 'Peeling the Peach' had its origin at Myrtle Beach, a summer resort.

Singing Associations in the Up Country continue their tradition of monthly meetings for all-day singing, and still use shape-note hymn books edited by members of their own groups and filled with local compositions. At their annual singing convention, held in Greenville the second Saturday and Sunday of August, several thousand voices swell in a chorus that has peculiarly local characteristics. Until the tunes are learned, no words are used; instead, the fa-sol-la syllables are sung to their proper notes. 'Singin' Billy' (William) Walker (*see Tour* 17) was the founder of these groups. His first shape-note rural hymnal, *Southern Harmony* (1835), in which each note is represented by a geometrical symbol, swept the entire South at ante-bellum camp meetings, at which Walker, teaching and leading his songs, was a faithful attendant. His second hymnal was *Christian Harmony*.

South Carolinians have shown a love of music since earliest days. Though the aristocrats among the first settlers regarded the profession of music as somewhat beneath a 'gentleman,' they indulged in the art as a social grace and prided themselves on being its appreciative patrons. According to Eola Willis in her *Charleston Stage in the XVIII Century*, Charleston audiences in 1734–5 heard the first operas presented in America: *Flora or Hob in the Well*, by Colley Cibber, and *The Devil to Pay*, by Hill. The *South-Carolina Gazette* records a song recital in Charleston February 26, 1735, believed to be the second, if not the first, in this country. The St. Cecilia Society of Charleston, formed in 1762, was America's pioneer musical organization, though it later became entirely social. This society sponsored the Nation's first symphony orchestra, which was composed of society members and a few professionals. From their current popularity in London, concerts were early introduced, and in 1767 Charlestonians enjoyed the first open-air concert in the United States.

Agricultural prosperity, which this State enjoyed with the rest of the South following the Revolution, fattened the planters' incomes and enabled them to summon from Europe music masters who instructed young South Carolinians in voice and in the fashionable instruments, such as the harpsichord, the flute, and the 'cello. Recitals by amateurs as well as professionals became the rage.

Within little more than a decade after its founding as the new capital, musical interest was evident in Columbia. Here the city's first opera, *The Devil to Pay,* was presented August 30, 1799, and in 1807 the first commencement program of the South Carolina College (now University) featured instrumental music. The Uranian Society, one of many American organizations for the improvement of church and choral music, was active by 1816, and in 1826 the Columbia Female Academy added music to its curriculum. Musical development in several States was stimulated by the South Carolina Female Institute (Barhamville, 1828–65) in Columbia. Its most noted instructor was Torriani, and his most talented pupil was Sally McCollough of Columbia, an operatic star who married Brignoli, an Italian tenor.

Following the French Revolution and the San Dominican uprising, many refugees came to South Carolina and scattered over the State. Among them were musicians and dancing masters, whose instruction in both arts stimulated young people of talent. Operas, cantatas, and elaborate balls were frequent; local publishers of native compositions were kept busy getting out songs and airs appropriate for the mazurka, the schottische, and the minuet; in the music-filled homes throughout the State, plantation melodies mingled with the classics.

During the Confederate era little time and money were left for music as a cultural interest, but war inspired the local composition of stirring marches and patriotic songs. No extensive cultivation of the fine arts was possible until the end of Reconstruction, but in that sterile era South Carolina's greatest prima donna, Clara Louise Kellogg (1842–1916) of Sumter, attained renown in America and Europe.

A period of general recovery in the 1890's brought the opening of more women's colleges in the State, and with their establishment came a revival of music. The departments of music in the College for Women (later Chicora) and Columbia College encouraged Columbia's first music festival in 1894, though in that period the event was repeated only a few times. In co-operation with Converse College, Spartanburg held in 1895 the South Atlantic States Music Festival and continued for 35 years the elaborate undertaking that was important to cultural development in this region.

South Carolina's greatest composer is Lily Strickland (b.1887) of

Anderson, best known for her songs of the South and of the Orient, where she lived for ten years. Her 'Lindy Lou' and 'Honey Chile,' both reflecting the atmosphere of her native locale, are favorite recital and encore numbers. Another Andersonian, Reed Miller (1880–1923), was a well-known concert tenor, who was singing at the Cathedral of St. John the Divine in New York at the time of his death. His voice is preserved in many phonograph records. He married Nevada Van Der Vere, a Metropolitan Opera star. William Laurence (b.1895), Negro pianist, singer, and composer, of Charleston, uses Negro themes effectively in his compositions, among which are *Rhapsodie Africaine-Bambara* and 'Three Spirituals' for string quartette. He served for some time as Roland Hayes's accompanist. Another Negro musician of note is Edmond S. T. Jenkins (1894–1926) also of Charleston. His symphony *Charlestonia* was first played at the Kursaal D'Ostende, Belgium. South Carolina has also a long roster, both Negro and white, of less distinguished musicians—composers, singers, and instrumentalists.

Drama

SOUTH CAROLINA'S theatrical history dates from about 1730, when Anthony ('Tony') Aston was cast ashore near Charleston by shipwreck. Aston states in his journal, 'We arrived in Charles-Town full of Lice, Shame, Poverty, Nakedness, and Hunger. I turned Player and Poet and wrote one Play on the Subject of the Country.' He remained in Charleston several months before going to New York, and his appearances in South Carolina's early capital were probably the first professional dramatic productions in America of a play written in this country.

In the *South-Carolina Gazette* of January 18, 1734-5, appeared the first theatrical notice for this State: 'On Friday the 24th instant, in the Court Room will be attempted a Tragedy called "The Orphan or the Unhappy Marriage."' This performance of Otway's play featured the first American prologue. It was printed four weeks later in the *Gazette* without a signature, but was doubtless by some local poet.

The first building in America devoted wholly to the drama was Charleston's Dock Street Theater, opened February 12, 1736. Plays had been given in 1716 in a Williamsburg, Virginia, playhouse, but the building became a town hall in 1745 and was not subsequently used for theatrical purposes; New York had witnessed plays as early as 1732 'in a large room on the second floor of a building near Pearl Street'; Charleston, too, had enjoyed theatrical performances in makeshift quarters before its regular theater was built. That edifice, on Queen Street near the corner of Church Street, kept the name by which Queen Street was originally called. When the curtain fell on its first play, Farquhar's *The Recruiting Officer,* the first American epilogue was recited. It was a versified apology for the broad humor of the performance and was printed that year in the *Gentlemen's Magazine,* London, over the signature of Dr. Thomas Dale, who was associate justice of South Carolina.

Notice of the fourth presentation of *The Recruiting Officer* appeared in the *Gazette* of May 21, 1737, and listed as an additional feature

Industry and Agriculture

Photograph by Carl T. Julien

GRANITE QUARRY, WINNSBORO

Photograph by Howard R. Jacobs; courtesy of Major Henry F. Church
LAUNCHING THE GUNBOAT CHARLESTON, BUILT AT UNITED STATES NAVY YARD, CHARLESTON

POWERHOUSE UNDER CONSTRUCTION, SOUTH CAROLINA PUBLIC SERVICE AUTHORITY
THE SANTEE-COOPER HYDROELECTRIC PROJECT

HYDROELECTRIC DAM, PARR SHOALS

AMONG THE SPINDLES
GREENVILLE

Photograph by Bill King

PRINTING COTTON CLOTH, HARTSVILLE

Photograph by The Pryors

**HARDWOOD LUMBER MILL
CAYCE**

WOOD PULP MILL, GEORGETOWN

Photograph by Post; courtesy of Farm Security Administration

GOING TO CHOP COTTON, CLARENDON COUNTY

COTTON MARKET, HARTSVILLE

Photograph by courtesy of Coker Pedigreed Seed Company

TAKING TOBACCO TO MARKET

PICKING BEANS, EDISTO ISLAND

OYSTER PLANTING, BEAUFORT COUNTY

PIGEON PLANT, SUMTER

' "The Song of Mad Tom" in proper habiliments.' Eola Willis, in *The Charleston Stage in the XVIII Century* (1924), points out that 'Mad Tom's Song' must have been from *King Lear* and thus probably constituted 'the first recorded instance of the production of anything Shakespearean on this continent.'

The first known dramatic criticism of an American performance appeared in the *Gazette* following this production: '. . . there was a fuller house on this Occasion than ever had been known in this Place before. A proper Prologue and Epilogue were spoke, and the entered Apprentices and Masons' Songs sung upon the Stage, which were joined in Chorus by the Masons in the Pit, to the Satisfaction and Entertainment of the whole Audience.'

Fire damaged the first Dock Street Theater in 1740 and a second opened on the site October 7, 1754, with Lewis Hallman's Company in Rowe's *The Fair Penitent*. Weekly plays followed and in this theater occurred notable dramatic events accredited to New York and Philadelphia in Seilhamer's *History of the American Theater* (1888–91). Miss Cheer, a popular star of the period, made her American debut here April 25, 1764, in Mrs. Cibber's translation of the French of Mrs. Centlivre's *A Wonder! A Woman Keeps a Secret!* In 1766 Miss Wainwright, Miss Hallam, Mr. Wall, and Thomas Woolls made their first American appearances in drama; the same year brought to Charleston the first American productions of *The Orphan in China*, *The School for Lovers*, and *The Oracle*. Advertisements of David Douglass's Jamaican troupe at the Dock Street Theater in 1763 designated it as 'The American Company' three years before it was so announced in New York. These priority claims for South Carolina's second theater are substantiated in files of the *South-Carolina Gazette* and in the *Diary* (1754–81) of Mrs. Gabriel (Ann Ashby) Manigault.

So theater-minded were wealthy Carolinians, in their brocades and broadcloth, powdered wigs, and costly jewels, that a third and larger theater was put up (probably by Douglass) on nearly the same site. It opened in 1773 with Kelley's *A Word to the Wise* and *High Life Below the Sea*, and was described in Rivington's *New York Gazette* as 'the most commodious on the continent.' Seilhamer ranks this theater's first season as 'the most brilliant . . . of Colonial America,' and the list of its entertainments that year is one of two preserved of American theatrical showings before the Revolution. There were 118 productions, including 11 Shakespearean plays (the presentation of *Julius*

Caesar being the first in America), eight Garrick performances, and all popular operas of the day.

Clouds of the impending Revolution cast a shadow on theatrical gaiety—already the object of tirades by Dissenters in pulpit and press: 'Although there is a great Want of Money to procure the Conveniences and even the Necessaries of Life, yet large Sums are weekly laid out for Amusements, these by Persons who cannot afford it; and is a Means of promoting the frequent Robberies that are committed and of Vice and Obscenity' (*South-Carolina Gazette*, February 28, 1774).

Charleston's principal theater escaped British shells during the Revolution, only to burn in 1782. Around its ruins the Planters' Hotel was built in 1809, and remodeled in 1835 to include a theatrical auditorium. This famous old hostelry and playhouse was faithfully restored with WPA assistance and reopened November 26, 1937, as the Dock Street Theater, repeating the initial play of 1736, *The Recruiting Officer*.

The completion of Charleston's first post-Revolutionary theater, Harmony Hall, in 1786, coincided with the founding of Columbia and the transfer of the capital there. Though a blue law in 1787 banned theatrical productions for four years and classed actors as vagrants, love for the drama increased steadily in both the old and new capitals during the ante-bellum era. No regular theater was built in Columbia before the 1820's, but plays and operas were presented in stores and elsewhere. Local playwrights were numerous; 19 Charleston writers produced about 34 plays in this period. Chief among them was Isaac Harby (1788–1828), a critic as well as a playwright, who mercilessly reviewed his own works. His masterpiece, *Alberti*, a blank verse drama of Florence in 1480, reflecting the prevalent European influence, was first presented in 1818; its second performance was witnessed by President James Monroe, who was visiting in Charleston.

In 1861 the outbreak of the war succeeded, where both legislation and Dissenters had failed, in ringing down the curtain on dramatic achievement. Amateur entertainments of all kinds continued to amuse the people, but no money for professional plays was available until the 1880's. Then began the great period of road shows, and celebrated actors were again drawn to South Carolina cities.

In the twentieth century, community theater activity is adding an interesting chapter to the history of the drama in the State. The Columbia Stage Society is the pioneer South Carolina organization and the only one in the State playing in its own building—the Town Theater. In 1938 the society celebrated its 20th anniversary. Its success won national recognition when the local director was elected by the Drama League of America as regional representative for South Carolina. Throughout its existence the Town Theater has had a full-time professional director, and it also employs a business manager and a director for the Junior Stage Society, a corollary group. Plays by local authors, particularly those interpreting South Carolina traditions and history, are a stimulant to native talent; and from the Town Theater young actors have advanced to the professional stage and to directorship of other community theaters.

The Footlight Players of Charleston engaged in 1938 a full-time director for their performances in the renovated Dock Street Theater, and DuBose Heyward was appointed by the Rockefeller Foundation as resident playwright in 1939, serving till his death in June 1940. Greenville's Little Theater is directed by the head of the speech department of Furman University, and members of the group supervise plays in county communities. Anderson has a community theater. Florence formerly had its Pinewood Players; Spartanburg's Little Theater has given way to the finished performances of Converse College students. In almost every South Carolina college and high school dramatic clubs stimulate young people's interest in the drama, and occasionally departments of English offer prizes for student-written plays.

Most of the old opera houses in the State have now been pre-empted for movie theaters, and South Carolina has contributed to the screen its romantic backgrounds and eventful history. The interior of the State House was faithfully reproduced in *The Birth of a Nation,* and for greater verisimilitude later productions have been filmed within the State. Several South Carolinians are Hollywood players; Clements Ripley, a Charlestonian by adoption, is the author of *Jezebel* and other scenarios; the movie rights to *Master Skylark* by John Bennett, also of Charleston, were sold in 1937; DuBose Heyward assisted in writing the film version of *The Good Earth,* and wrote the scenario for *The Emperor Jones.*

On the legitimate stage DuBose Heyward's *Porgy* was played as *Porgy and Bess* (1936); *Brass Ankle* (1931), and *Mamba's Daughters* (1939) have also been produced; Dorothy Heyward, the author's wife, collaborated in the dramatized versions. Julia Peterkin's *Scarlet Sister Mary* has also been given a professional production. *Hilda* (1923),

The Face (1924), and other poetical dramas published in book form
by Frances Guignard Gibbes have been performed by the Columbia
Stage Society in the Town Theater, and elsewhere by professionals.
Apparently it is chiefly in talented young playwrights, many of whose
plays have been published and presented in and out of the State, that
the future of the drama in South Carolina is brightest.

Literature

THE literature produced by the Colonial writers of South Carolina derived closely from the contemporary Classical and Romantic schools of English letters. The standards and traditions of these influenced both prose and poetry: the early prose writers of Carolina followed the conventionalized formality, dignity, and balance of Dr. Johnson's school; and the poets wrote didactic and narrative verse in the heroic couplets standardized by Pope and Dryden.

From the Revolutionary War to the War between the States, the literature of Carolina was essentially political rather than esthetic. An aristocratic planter society maintained the standards of culture, and these shaped literary taste. Thus orations, essays, and editorials were more widely esteemed than poems, novels, or plays. The political papers of John C. Calhoun (1782–1850) were typical, and contained the loftiest exposition of the doctrine of States Rights. His 'A Disquisition on Government' and 'A Discourse on the Constitution and Government of the United States' epitomized the philosophy of that physiocratic society which found Nullification and Secession equitable and justifiable.

Robert Y. Hayne (1791–1839), remembered for his debate with Webster on 'The Foote Resolution,' and George McDuffie (1790–1851), whose passionate eloquence often aroused Congress, powerfully voiced the social discontent engendered in their planter society by a tariff-regulated economy. This discontent, augmented and intensified by the injection of Abolition about 1835, stimulated the editors of the Charleston *Courier* (1813–65), now the Charleston *News and Courier,* and the Charleston *Mercury* (1851–64), especially those of the latter, to embittering vehemence and invective. The *Southern Review* (1828–32), a quarterly founded by Hugh S. Legare and Stephen Elliott; the *Southern Quarterly Review* (1842–57), successfully edited by James D. B. DeBow, William Gilmore Simms, and James H. Thornwell; and *Russell's Magazine* (1857–60), edited by Paul Hamilton Hayne, were established likewise to express the political and economic philosophy of the ante-bellum South.

In the realm of esthetic literature, as distinguished from political literature, William Gilmore Simms (1806–70) was the most prolific and distinguished of the nineteenth-century writers of South Carolina. As poet, novelist, playwright, biographer, historian, essayist, and editor, with a total literary output of more than 80 volumes, he succeeded in preserving the history and traditions of his people as well as in extolling the beauty and glory of his State. *The Yemassee* (1835), a historical romance dealing with the Yamasee uprising, 1715–18, in which the Indians were first treated in a fictional manner, and *The Partisan* (1835), the first of a series of novels dealing with the Revolutionary War, have best succeeded in retaining both critical and popular esteem. (Simms's spelling of 'Yamasee' as 'Yemassee' has resulted in much confusion.) *Mellichampe* (1836), a legend of the Santee country during the Revolution, and *Katherine Walton* (1851), an account of the British occupation of Charleston, completed the trilogy begun in *The Partisan* (1835); and *The Scout* (1854), *Eutaw* (1856), *The Casique of Kiawah* (1859), and *The Wigwam and the Cabin* (1845) illustrated a maturer narrative skill.

In addition to Simms, ante-bellum South Carolina helped form the work of Augustus Baldwin Longstreet (1790–1870), author of *Georgia Scenes* (1833), whose *Master William Mitten* (1864) centered around Willington Academy, the famous preparatory school of Dr. Moses Waddel (*see Education*). Longstreet was a notable humorist with his sketches of early Southern life, and was also an educator, being president of South Carolina College and later first head of Mississippi University. Henry Junius Nott (1797–1837) was the author of the two-volume *Novelettes of a Traveler* (1834), and Susan Petigru King (1824–75) satirized the social life in which she moved in such novels as *Busy Moments of an Idle Woman* (1854), *Lily* (1855), *Sylvia's World* (1859), and *Gerald Gray's Wife* (1866).

Although Simms wrote or compiled 24 volumes of verse, poetry was but a minor phase of his work. He was the older friend and counselor of both Henry Timrod and his intimate, Paul Hamilton Hayne, and, as the guiding spirit behind the literary coterie that made Charleston famous just before the War between the States, he helped found *Russell's Magazine* in 1857. Planned as the Southern counterpart of the *North American Review*, this magazine voiced the philosophy of a large group of brilliant Southern apologists: that of Dr. Samuel Henry Dickson (1798–1872), author of many martial lyrics, and of his kinsman, Dr. John Dickson Bruns (1836–83), whose 'Our Christmas Hymn,'

'The Foe at the Gates,' and, 'O Tempora! O Mores!' were included in Simms's *War Poetry of the South* (1867); that of James Mathewes Legare (1823–59), the South Carolina poet most sympathetic in his interpretation of nature, and of William J. Grayson (1788–1863), pro-Union apologist for slavery whose 'The Hireling and the Slave' (1855) was written in excellent Popean couplets; and that of James L. Petigru and Mitchell King and of Basil L. Gildersleeve and Bishop Lynch.

Henry Timrod (1829–67), one of the most prolific contributors to *Russell's Magazine,* became the uncrowned laureate of the Confederacy. His 'Ethnogenesis,' 'Ode to the Cotton Boll,' and 'Carolina' produced a profound impression on both soldiers and civilians. And there is scarcely a more beautiful and moving lyric in American literature than his 'Ode to the Dead in Magnolia Cemetery' (1866), a part of which is:

> Sleep sweetly in your humble graves,
>   Sleep, martyrs of a fallen cause;
> Though yet no marble column craves
>   The pilgrim here to pause,
>
> In seeds of laurel in the earth
>   The blossom of your fame is blown
> And somewhere, waiting for its birth,
>   The shaft is in the stone!
>
> Stoop, angels, hither from the skies!
>   There is no holier spot of ground
> Than where defeated valor lies,
>   By mourning beauty crowned!

Paul Hamilton Hayne (1830–86) was reared by his uncle, Robert Y. Hayne. Upon his graduation from the College of Charleston in 1852, he decided to devote himself to literature, and in 1857 with W. B. Carlisle became editor of *Russell's Magazine.* During the War between the States he wrote a number of popular war lyrics. After that struggle he resumed his editorial and journalistic work, achieving a large volume of poems, much prose fiction, and many essays. His narrative verse, nature poems, and sonnets were of high order. Ludwig Lewisohn once wrote that 'Daphles' is the best American narrative poem ever written.

During this period several women writers attained both local and national recognition. Caroline Howard Gilman (1794–1888) founded and edited *The Southern Rosebud* (1832), one of the earliest weeklies in the United States devoted to young people, and then expanded it into its successor, *The Southern Rose* (1833–9). Mary Elizabeth Lee (1813–49) contributed stories and poems to *Graham's,* the *Southern*

Literary Messenger, the *Orion,* and *The Southern Rose.* Mary S. Whitaker (1820–1906), the wife of Daniel K. Whitaker, editor of the *Southern Quarterly Review,* contributed many sketches of Southern life to *Graham's, Godey's, Arthur's,* and *Sartain's* magazines. And, lastly, Louisa S. McCord (1810–79), the author of many vigorous articles on Southern political questions and the woman writer to whom Simms entrusted the review of *Uncle Tom's Cabin,* was the author of *Gaius Gracchus* (1851), a blank verse tragedy, and *My Dreams* (1848), a volume of fugitive verse.

The War between the States ruined the leisured class from which had come most of the literature of the South. The Charleston school—Petigru, Simms, Grayson, and Timrod—was broken up, and Timrod soon died of anxiety and strain. For a generation thereafter Hayne, struggling along in the pine barrens of Georgia, carried on its tradition. Pessimism and despair reigned, but George Herbert Sass (1845–1908) and Carlyle McKinley (1847–1904) sang bravely on toward a new order, and each left a volume pitched in minor key: Sass's *The Heart's Quest: A Book of Verses* (1904) and the *Poems of Carlyle McKinley* (1904).

John Bennett (b.1865) links modern South Carolina letters with this heritage of tradition, for he was a friend of Sass and McKinley. A journalist, novelist, poet, and illustrator, as well as a writer of children's stories, he is a master of magic phrases and poetic cadences, of character etching, and of sound literary structure. *Master Skylark* (1897), *The Story of Barnaby Lee* (1902), *The Treasure of Peyre Gaillard* (1906), *Madame Margot* (1921), and *The Pigtail of Ah Lee Ben Loo* (1928) are each distinguished by at least one of these characteristics.

The poetry of Archibald Rutledge (b.1883) conforms to that of the Romantic and traditional school of Simms, Timrod, and Hayne. His nature stories, however, are spontaneous, the work of a keen observer, a sympathetic artist, and a sensitive moralist. *Old Plantation Days* (1921), *Tom and I on the Old Plantation* (1918), and *Plantation Game Trails* (1921) are deservedly popular. In 1930 Rutledge was awarded the John Burroughs medal for distinguished writing in the field of nature; and in 1931, in conformity with an act of the South Carolina legislature, Governor Ibra C. Blackwood appointed him Poet Laureate of South Carolina.

Herbert Ravenel Sass (b.1884) is also a writer of vigorous and masterly stories of wild life. Published in the leading American periodicals, these have been collected in *The Way of the Wild* (1925), *Adventures in Green Places* (1926), *Grey Eagle* (1927), and *On the Wings of a Bird* (1929). He has published two historical novels: *War Drums* (1928) and *Look Back to Glory* (1933).

In the renaissance of local-color literature Ambrose E. Gonzales, DuBose Heyward, Julia Peterkin, and E. C. L. Adams have developed the South Carolina Negro as a regional type, yet one differing from that interpreted by Harris and Page. Drama, realism, and humor are characteristics of their work. Ambrose E. Gonzales (1857–1926) preserved the Gullah dialect in his incisive vignettes of the Black Border series: *The Black Border* (1922), *The Captain* (1924), *Laguerre, a Gascon of the Black Border* (1924), and *With Aesop along the Black Border* (1924). DuBose Heyward (1885–1940), poet, dramatist, and novelist, has best succeeded in popularizing this material and has added to the portrait gallery of American fiction that remarkable creation *Porgy* (1925). *Mamba's Daughters* (1929) lacked the vitality of *Porgy*, and the author turned to the historical novels inherent in Charleston. His *Angel* (1926), *Peter Ashley* (1932), and *Lost Morning* (1936) are distinguished by many beautiful descriptive passages.

Julia Peterkin, whose *Scarlet Sister Mary* won the Pulitzer Prize in 1928, has succeeded in depicting the strength, grimness, and tragedy in the Negro life around her home on Lang Syne Plantation at Fort Motte. *Green Thursday* (1924), *Black April* (1927), *Scarlet Sister Mary* (1928), and *Bright Skin* (1932) are grimly realistic, but they show an astonishing knowledge of the woof and warp of Negro life.

Dr. E. C. L. Adams is the author of *Congaree Sketches* (1927) and *Nigger to Nigger* (1928), delightful vignettes of the humorous, philosophical side of Negro life.

Elliott White Springs (b.1896), World War ace and winner of the Distinguished Flying Cross, has written many realistic yet rollicking satires on the war: *Nocturne Militaire* (1927), *Above the Bright Blue Sky* (1928), *Leave Me with a Smile* (1928), *Contact* (1930), and *The Rise and Fall of Carol Banks* (1931). He also edited *War Birds, the Diary of an Unknown Aviator* (1926).

Katherine Ball Ripley (b.1899) wrote of experiences that she and her writer husband, Clements Ripley, had on a peach farm in North Carolina in two successful books, *Sand in My Shoes* (1931) and *Sand Dollars* (1933). The latter was a collection of short stories. Her first novel, *Crowded House* (1936), deals with modern life in her home city, Charleston.

The founding of the Poetry Society of South Carolina (1920) stimulated interest in poetry. In 1922 DuBose Heyward and Hervey Allen issued their *Carolina Chansons,* and Heyward followed that with *Skylines and Horizons* (1924). They emphasized legendary, historical, and romantic material inherent in South Carolina. Their volumes were followed by two others of significance: Beatrice Ravenel's *The Arrow of Lightning* (1926) and Josephine Pinckney's *Sea-Drinking Cities* (1927). In these poets the influence of traditional forms and subject matter is lacking, and here, as well as in the novels of Heyward, Sass, and Peterkin, the literature of South Carolina converged with the national stream. Hervey Allen (b.1889), though beginning his literary work in South Carolina as a poet, has of late become widely known for his novels, *Anthony Adverse* (1933) and *Action at Aquila* (1937).

Architecture

THE architecture of South Carolina shows the influence of several distinct traditions. The first permanent settlers were English who came in 1670—some directly from England and others by way of Barbados. Fifteen years later, upon the revocation of the Edict of Nantes, a number of Huguenots took refuge in Carolina. Some of these in turn had spent a considerable time in Holland. Thus there is a basic English tradition, affected by West Indian, French, and Dutch influences. Curiously enough, the Dutch strain is more evident than the French; but the French feeling for proportion and monumental planning undoubtedly left its stamp.

For the creation of a significant architecture there must be not only taste and purpose, but also sufficient wealth and leisure. The Colonial planters found these in the exploitation of their abundant natural resources. Thanks to the lucrative Indian trade and then to commerce in rice, indigo, and cotton, the architecture of South Carolina enjoyed a long and continuous development. As Charleston was the first center from which colonization and civilization spread (with minor foci at Georgetown and Beaufort), it follows that the best pre-Revolutionary architecture in the State is to be found there.

The powder magazine of one of the city bastions, built in 1703, is the earliest dated building. The city has experienced five great fires (1700, 1740, 1778, 1838, and 1861), many hurricanes, and earthquakes in 1811 and 1886. Of the oldest dwelling houses now standing, therefore, only a few antedate 1740, especially as the earlier houses were largely of wood.

From 1740 to 1760 the houses were built with thick brick walls, generally two stories in height, the first floor being only about two feet above grade. The general effect is simple and somewhat heavy, with a balance of architectural elements rather than a rigid symmetry. Inside, the rooms are paneled full height from floor to ceiling, and the mantels are bold and plain, showing strongly the characteristics of Georgian England. Kitchens and servants' quarters form separate structures in the rear, or extend into the rear gardens in continuous bays with sweeping roof lines broken by chimney-tops and dormers. The steep roofs were bell-cast with an outward curve at the eaves, and were covered with pink or deep purple-black tile, depending on whether or not they were salt-glazed in the burning. The 'S'-shaped tiles are characteristic of English and Dutch work rather than Italian.

Practically all of these early houses fall into two general types, known as the 'single house' and the 'double house.' The single house had its gable end toward the street with the entrance in the center of one long side, the latter usually facing a side yard or carriage drive. The double house, symmetrical and almost square, had its entrance fronting the street. Its center hall plan provided kitchen and servants' quarters in the basement; parlors, dining room, and library or office on the first floor; and large drawing room and bed chambers on the second floor. Additional servants' quarters and carriage house were housed in separate outbuildings to the side or rear. The plans of these two characteristic types of houses usually included a one- or two-story piazza or gallery porch on the front or side, a feature that attained even greater popularity during the nineteenth century. With the increase of wealth from 1760 to the Revolution, these two schemes were maintained, but the houses became larger and richer in detail, while the height of the first floor was increased. This was done to insure coolness and to lift the house above possible flood from hurricane or tide.

The practice of educating the younger sons in England accounts largely for the introduction of the Georgian style, then the latest architectural fashion of England. The exteriors of the Georgian Colonial houses were adorned with finely molded classic cornices and trim; delicate wrought-iron work enriched the detail of window openings and garden gates; stately portals with graceful fanlights and paneled doors were framed with fluted pilasters and columns, and crowned with classic headings. Many of the eighteenth-century houses in Charleston were covered with stucco often painted pastel shades of pink, green, yellow, and blue, or tooled with joint lines to simulate stone.

The interior decorating reflected the Georgian mode with heavily paneled and wainscoted walls, fine mantels, cove ceilings, classic cornices and trim, and ample stairways designed with open stringers and decorative handrails. Windows above the stair landing were frequently of the traditional Palladian type. The fireplaces were often lined with imported Sadler & Delft tile. The rich decorations of the late-eighteenth-century Charleston interiors reflected the elegant manner of Chippendale.

Some examples of the better Georgian Colonial buildings still standing in Charleston are: Miles Brewton House, 27 King Street (c.1765); Horry House, 59 Meeting Street (c.1751–67); Robert Pringle House, 70 Tradd Street (1774); Colonel Robert Brewton House, 71 Church Street (1730); Charles Fraser House, 53 King Street (c.1750); Ralph Izard House, 110 Broad Street (before 1757); house at 59 Church Street (c.1740); Colonel William Washington House, 8 S. Battery (1768); Colonel John Stuart House, 106 Tradd Street (1772); Humphrey Sommers House, 128 Tradd Street (1765); house at 19 Archdale Street. The first seven of these are of brick construction, the last four of frame covered with clapboards or flush boarding. All are in excellent condition considering their age, owing chiefly to the skill of the original builders and the enduring materials from which they were constructed—kiln-baked brick and heartwood of original growth long-leaf pine.

Construction ceased during the Revolution but was resumed with the economic recovery that followed. After 1790 a new development took place in Charleston. The houses of this early Republican period show an increasing variety of plan and decorative elements in contrast to earlier structures, which were well proportioned but severely rectangular. Winding stairways and oval rooms appear, and the Adam influence is apparent in decoration. Paneling, which had occupied the full height of the four walls, was now developed full height on the fireplace wall or more often omitted entirely in favor of plain plaster wall areas lined only with a narrow chair rail and base board.

The moldings of this period were small and delicate, with much reeding and channeling. Plaster was also beginning to replace wood cornices. From about 1800 larger piazzas or open galleries, two or three tiers in height and three to ten bays long, made their appearance. This addition was unknown in England and was manifestly an importation from the West Indies, where it proved to be an architectural necessity because of climatic conditions. These piazzas were placed on the west or south sides of the houses and in many instances were added to pre-Revolutionary buildings. They constitute one of the distinctive features of Charleston architecture.

This Post-Colonial style flourished until the War between the States, although in the middle third of the century the buildings were larger in scale, and details became somewhat less delicate. In this period decorative ironwork for balustrades, stair rails, gates, fences, and balconies reached its highest development.

Some of the Post-Colonial houses are still to be seen in Charleston. The best examples are: Joseph Manigault House, 350 Meeting Street (c.1790); William Blacklock House, 14 Bull Street (c.1800); Nathaniel Russell House, 51 Meeting Street (c.1811); Henry Manigault House, 18 Meeting Street (c.1818); William Gibbes House, 64 S. Battery (before 1789); T. G. Simons House, 128 Bull Street (before 1818); Axson House, 4 Greenhill Street (c.1805); Magwood House, 39 S. Battery.

Just prior to the War between the States, architecture became grandiose and magnificent, within the traditions of academic classicism. Rigid symmetry became almost a mandate. Porticos and doorways derived from Greek architecture appeared. Ceilings became very high, and windows were extended to the floor. During the short ante-bellum period, comparatively few houses were built, but some of the better examples are the following: Joseph Aiken House, 20 Charlotte Street (1848); Charles Alston House, 21 East Battery (1838); Robert Martin House, 16 Charlotte Street (c.1840); William Roper House, 9 East Battery (c.1845); Alston House at 172 Tradd Street (c.1850); house at 87 Smith Street (c.1850); house at 178 Ashley Avenue (c.1850).

While architectural design reached its greatest development in Charleston and other coastal towns, the Low Country plantation houses were designed much in the same manner with additional dependencies common to a country estate. Plantation houses varied from extreme simplicity in the early types to the pretentious three-story houses with tiered piazzas that showed a closer kinship to the urban types, in the later works. Nearly all were carefully oriented to the site.

The typical Low Country plantation house was two-and-a-half stories in height above a full raised basement. The main house had flankers or separate wings symmetrically disposed. In the basement of the main block were housed the kitchen storage rooms, servants' hall, and plantation office. Slaves were usually quartered in rows of small houses in a remote section of the plantation or in a neighboring village. The plantation house, set in spacious, formally landscaped grounds, fronted a tree-lined avenue of approach and commanded a splendid vista of the adjoining rice fields, meadows, and distant waterways.

In the six counties adjacent to Charleston are about 100 plantation houses that deserve careful study. Hampton (1735) and Drayton Hall (1738) are among the finer examples. Most of the present owners have either restored the original houses or followed Georgian Colonial plantation styles in building on the old sites.

Of the religious edifices of lower South Carolina the basic plan was naturally that of an Anglican church. The mother church of the colony was St. Philip's, Charleston, built in 1682. A second structure was built in 1712 and burned in 1835. The third, called the Westminster Abbey of South Carolina, was erected in 1838. St. Michael's, 1752, with its Wren-like tower and portico, is therefore the oldest existing building as far as city churches are concerned, but a score of parish churches and chapels of ease (small plantation churches at a more convenient distance than the parish church) antedate it by a quarter century. St. James, Goose Creek, safeguarded during the Revolution by the Royal Arms over the chancel, has acquired a just architectural fame, but a dozen others, each with their characteristic box pews, wineglass pulpits, and slave galleries, now in varying degrees of preservation, must have ranked with it in their day of glory.

When the colony enjoyed religious freedom, other denominations constructed buildings for themselves, generally similar in style to those of the Protestant Episcopal Church. As their congregations grew or split off from the parent stem, new buildings were erected, and these varied from the original pattern. In later years, adaptations of Greek temples housed congregations of Lutheran, Jewish, and Presbyterian faith, while the Unitarians were among the earliest to adopt the Gothic in 1852, almost at the same time that the Gothic Revival edifices were being erected in New York.

In the public and semipublic buildings of Charleston the Georgian style held sway. The huge rice mills were masterpieces having the dignified and stately characteristics of Georgian Colonial architecture, yet exemplifying the adaptation of a style to fit needs not dreamed of when the style began. Taste for the massive Greek Revival spread in the 1830's and 1840's, partially destroying the pleasing unity that had marked the city's appearance.

A confused scramble of styles and machine-made novelties offered a more serious threat to traditional architecture (as witness an Arabic bank building of the mid-fifties) when the War between the States closed the scene and preserved the past by eliminating progress for half a century.

Little is known of the actual builders and architects of Charleston and the Low Country generally. Some record can usually be found in the case of public buildings; but few of those responsible for the masterpieces of domestic architecture will ever be identified. When an entire class of owners possessed the taste and knowledge of design to inspire a whole class of master craftsmen, it is impossible to say to whom credit should be given. A few, however, are known. Peter and John Horlbeck, who practiced about 1767–92, were the leading builders of the public edifices of the Colonial city of Charleston. With them belong Ezra Waite, 'Civil Architect, House Builder in General and Carver, from London,' the unknown Mr. Gibson (possibly Gibbs) who furnished the plans for St. Michael's Church, and Mr. Samuel Cardy, the 'ingenious architect' who undertook and completed the building, and who died in 1764. In the late 1700's came Gabriel Manigault (1758–1809), gentleman rice planter, who was the first Charleston architect in the more modern acceptance of the term. He prepared designs to be executed by builders, but it seems to have been his avocation as a cultured amateur and not at all a profession. These were followed by the man who became South Carolina's first nationally known architect, Robert Mills (1781–1855), designer of the Washington Monument at Washington, D. C., and a number of other works scattered throughout the country. Joseph Hyde, Frederick Wesner, Edward Brickell White (1806–82), Edward C. Jones, and Francis D. Lee carried on the tradition of architectural skill in the public buildings of Charleston and other parts of the State from 1813 until the War between the States.

Up Country architecture is less significant than that of the coast, but the influences that formed it are fully as interesting. As settlers from the Low Country moved inland they met others coming down from Pennsylvania and Virginia. There was thus a tendency to produce hybrid forms, badly carried out because of the relative isolation and lack of skilled workmen. Even when taste and money were available, little enrichment or refinement was possible. As a result, the architectural detail of Up Country houses (with the exception of mantelpieces brought from Charleston) is often clumsy and crude.

Many of the mansions are simply farmhouses elaborated by adding wings and porticos. This is particularly true of Fort Hill, the Calhoun house at Clemson, which was transformed into a mansion by various additions and the erection of three two-story porticos. The same thing is true of Sycamore Avenue, the Pickens estate outside of Pendleton, where the addition of four tall columns and a pediment, together with low flanking wings at each side, turned the farmhouse into a 'great mansion.'

Such remodeling on the part of long-established Up Country families, who desired to enlarge rather than to tear down and rebuild their homesteads, was facilitated by the fact that the then prevalent fashion in architecture was the Greek Revival, and all that was deemed necessary to convert any rectangular farmhouse into a mansion in the Grecian manner was to erect a portico with a pediment at the front, and to coerce the eaves into some semblance of a classic cornice. The houses themselves remained rather crude, but in the instances where they have been kept in repair and freshly painted, or where the long avenue of trees at the front has not been destroyed, the general effect of house and setting has great dignity.

In general, the domestic type of the Up Country consisted primarily of a simple rectangular unit, one room deep, two stories in height, with two rooms to a floor and chimneys at each end. While some brick houses are to be found, dwellings are usually of frame construction, weatherboarded. Windows and doors were framed in the most elementary manner, and interior enrichment often consisted only of a crudely carved mantelpiece. Additions were usually in the form of one-story wings, at each end of the original unit. In many cases this plan was followed even when house and wings were built at one time, although after 1825 this was true of the small house rather than of the large mansion.

A considerable number of houses were square in plan, having two rooms on each side of a wide hall that ran from front to back. With the increase of wealth during the second quarter of the nineteenth century, the new houses of the section tended to follow this four-square arrangement, which, together with an increase in size of the rooms and the larger columns of the front portico, resulted in a much more imposing dwelling than the earlier type.

Workmanship improved somewhat but still left very much to be desired. Fortunately the Greek Revival style required but the simplest decorative details, and many of the doorways of the Up Country houses after 1825 are not inferior to work done elsewhere. Framed with fluted or molded bands, with side and transom lights, these doorways set a precedent that is followed to this day. In general such doorways were squareheaded but in some instances, as in the Ravenel House (recently burned) between Clemson and Seneca, the transom light was elliptical.

In some cases decoration was confined to the doorway, the windows being framed in the simplest manner. However, in the Van Wyck house, a few miles outside of Pendleton, the windows of the first floor were treated as doors, with the large central opening flanked by side lights and having a transom light above. Framing the window was an elaborate cast-iron trellis supported on a shallow balcony. Such ornate treatment was not general, however.

At the present time most of the old houses in the Up Country are in a distressing condition. Fallen into disrepair, they are depressing sights and many have completely disappeared. Scattered through the country on what are now back roads, they are difficult to locate and when found are all too often merely disintegrating shells. Perhaps the largest number can be seen in or near Pendleton. The United Daughters of the Confederacy and the Daughters of the American Revolution have recently restored Fort Hill, the Calhoun Mansion, which is in the center of Clemson College (*see Tour* 14), and the college authorities are maintaining the grounds so that, of all the houses extant in the Up Country, Fort Hill presents the most adequate picture of the domestic architecture of that section.

In central South Carolina, examples of Colonial architecture are not as distinctive as in other parts of the State. The J. J. Seibels house (1795), 1601 Richland Street, Columbia, is one of the oldest houses in this section and follows Georgian lines. Not until well past the Revolution, during the period of the Greek Revival (1820–60), did this section reach its highest development in the work of Robert Mills. His influence is especially strong in Columbia.

Mills served as Civil and Military Engineer of South Carolina from 1820–30, and in 1836 was appointed by President Andrew Jackson as the first Federal architect and engineer. In Columbia, he designed the original building of the State Hospital (1822–8), the main building of the Columbia Theological Seminary (1823), the Maxcy Monument (1825), and probably the DeBruhl-Marshall House (1820), 1401 Laurel St.—serving in addition as consultant for a number of other structures. Several courthouses in the State are also the work of Mills; Lancaster, Conway, Kingstree, and Walterboro, still in use, all show, with minor modifications, a general design of two stories over a high basement, with single gabled portico. These buildings are of brick, some finished in gray or buff-colored stucco, sometimes coursed to imitate stone. Other ante-bellum buildings, including the courthouses in Marion and Chester, the First Baptist Church (1856) in Columbia, the University Gymnasium (1855) in Columbia, and the Edgefield County Courthouse, show the persistence of Mills's influence as late as 1860. In Camden, Mills designed Bethesda Presbyterian Church, the old courthouse, and the De Kalb Monument.

The indirect and deferred influence of his work was probably greater than the direct and immediate, for here and there are fine old buildings, some of distinct classic type and many of the persisting Georgian Colonial enriched with classic detail. Examples are the Boylston House (1822), 829 Richland Street, Columbia; Chicora College, or Ainsley Hall Place (c.1818), Columbia; Milford (c.1837), 12 miles from Manning; Coateswood, Newberry; Halcyon Grove (c.1810), Edgefield County; the Craig House, Chesterfield County; The Columns (1850–6), the Johnson House, near Florence; and Liberty Hill, 22 miles north of Camden on State 97.

In Columbia the two most interesting churches from an architectural point of view are Trinity Episcopal (1840–6) and First Presbyterian (1854). The former, modeled after York Cathedral in England, is the only church in the city with a clerestory. The Presbyterian church is noted for its adherence to the early English Gothic characterized by the vaulted ribbed ceiling.

The State capitol (*see Columbia*) is a three-story granite building of Italian Renaissance style, designed by John R. Niernsee (1823–85) of Baltimore. It was begun in 1851, shelled by Sherman's troops in 1865, and first used in 1869. Not until 1907 was it virtually completed. The clean gray walls, handsome porticos, and comparatively small dome give the building a peculiarly light and graceful effect.

With the War between the States, building largely ceased, and when it began again, poverty made a flourishing architecture impossible. There was also a Nation-wide decline in taste, and South Carolina did not escape its share of jigsaw porches and gingerbread towers. But with the turn of the century appreciation of good design was again aroused, and a few years later there was a revival of interest in Colonial and post-Revolutionary work. From this came the present-day adaptation and restoration of early masterpieces.

There is also a tendency at present to make more varied use of the building materials in which the State has always been rich. From early years the local clay has been utilized for brick and stucco—and near Sumter are found two beautiful examples of *pisé de terre:* Borough House (pre-Revolutionary) and the Church of the Holy Cross (1850) at Stateburg. Brick and brick veneer are used increasingly, and the small city of Florence boasts that it has more brick houses than any other city of comparable size in the Southeast. Granite is an important building material, especially in the upper section of the State, where numerous quarries are in operation.

An expanding program of education in South Carolina has been accompanied by the construction of a large number of schools, more than 60 per cent having been built since 1923. Few schools are architecturally important, but the Greenwood High School, designed by C. C. Wilson (1865–1933), and St. Andrews elementary school in Charleston County, the work of A. D. Benson, deserve mention as modern versions in brick and concrete of Georgian Colonial design. Winyah High School in Georgetown, built after plans by Arthur Hazard, is of brick and has a slightly projecting two-story entrance motif in concrete with a triple arcade, pilasters, and pediment, while the roof is decorated with a lantern cupola. Modern design is carried out in the elementary schools at Sullivan's Island and Fountain Inn. Various colleges throughout the State have recently added new buildings through the assistance of Federal funds. Winthrop College has just completed an auditorium (James B. Urquhart, architect), a huge brick structure with a façade of pilasters and arched openings; and a new Indiana limestone library, Henry C. Hibbes (b.1882), architect, has been constructed at the University of South Carolina.

Federal housing projects in Charleston and Columbia provide accommodation at low rental for families of small incomes. The Columbia project has provided flat-roofed three-story brick apartment buildings, with a small porch for each unit. The Charleston development offers a number of small stucco houses on the outskirts of the city.

Among larger public buildings, modern construction shows a wide variety of style. The United States Veterans' Administration Facility, locally known as the Veterans' Hospital, in Columbia, is an adaptation of late English Renaissance design. Its portico over a basement story with high arcade is reminiscent of the Greek Revival. Most of the Federal post offices built during the past decade are compact Georgian brick buildings with pedimented entrance, flat roof, and balustrated parapet. Richland County Courthouse, completed in 1936, shows the present trend toward the use of fire-resisting brick. The Beaufort County Courthouse, by J. Whitney Cunningham, is of monolithic concrete—severe in contrast with its ancient setting of palmettos and giant oaks.

Gardens

IT is the gardens, the great gardens of South Carolina, that invite and lure scores of thousands of visitors from distant places to visit the State each spring. In March and April, when flowers in the Carolina Low Country are at their peak of color, motor traffic is dense along the highways, all hotel space is occupied, tourist homes turn tourists away for want of beds to offer them, restaurants are jammed, motor service stations operate during long hours and at forced speed, and sales of all items go upward. The flower season is a harvest season, surpassing in economic value to South Carolinians any other harvests except those of major crops.

Yet, conventional historians and patriotic custodians of South Carolina's past seem generally unaware of the fact that the State now derives more substantial benefit from the garden makers of the past than from any of the men of passion—warriors, orators, and the like—whose stories fill so many pages in history books. This is not surprising. Stories of fury are easier to tell than the stories of quiet gardening; and human standards of value being what they usually are, the stories of fury are bigger stories. None the less, thousands of persons find livelihood in the Carolina Low Country today because the men and women who have lived here have done creative work in the soil—not because they worked mightily in politics and war.

But to think of the work of the gardeners as wholly economic in its effects is incorrect. That work is inspirational, also. Only the dullest person can look at great beauty and come away unaffected. Especially does this seem true when the beauty of nature is concerned. One who has spent many hours, many days in the beautiful gardens of South Carolina reports what he has seen and heard. Some persons, when they enter Magnolia, Middleton, Cypress, Belle Isle, Brookgreen, or Kalmia, can find no words to utter; they gasp, or exclaim, and sometimes their eyes overflow. Some of them say as they depart: 'We can't have anything as fine as that, but we can do something to improve that yard of ours!'

Thus do the gardeners of South Carolina continue to live in the beauty-creating and health-bringing activities that they unintentionally have inspired in others. It is encouraging to think now that the early Carolina garden makers have achieved a poetic kind of immortality they did not seek. They terraced and planted and arranged vistas for their own pleasure. Possibly they thought no noble thoughts as they did these things, and probably they had no far-projected purposes. But their gardens survive, and the influence of those gardens spreads, though the political philosophy the earlier Carolinians developed has been discarded, the social system on which they depended has been destroyed, and the war they fought has been lost. All the barbaric splendor of slavery times is gone, but the civilized and civilizing gardens built in slavery times remain.

The golden era of South Carolina's agrarian culture extended, roughly, from the Revolution to Secession. In the course of that period scores of fine estates were established along the winding Low Country rivers and creeks that flow so smoothly in and out with the tides, and scores of other estates along these rivers and lesser streams were improved. There was wealth. There was leisure. There was culture. But the golden era in South Carolina is not distinguished for literature or art, though both were produced. Often, instead of creating beauty on canvas, the Carolinians created it on a plot of earth; sometimes, instead of writing history in books, they wrote it in terraces, in lovely garden walks, and in pools that reflect the beauty of their banks and of the sky, and the swiftness of the birds that pass above them.

Writing of the men of that great era, Thomas R. Waring said: 'They looked upon life gratefully and found it good. They built good homes, planted fine gardens and cultivated an appreciation of leisure as not incompatible with enterprise and achievement. They respected scholarship, they patronized the arts, they studied statecraft, they practiced oratory, they cultivated manners, and, if they produced no notable literature nor music nor painting, they yet drew upon all these for a way of life which, perhaps, in the last analysis, is the greatest of the arts, as it is the only one whose prime objective is human happiness.' (*The Carolina Low Country,* Macmillan.)

There are several reasons why the early South Carolina planters thought of gardens as almost essential parts of country estates. Those planters were of English stock, and many of them were men of means. To South Carolina, sometimes via Barbados, they brought their English customs and appreciations. The climate, with eight or nine frost-free months each year, was perfect for rapidly developing gardens, and

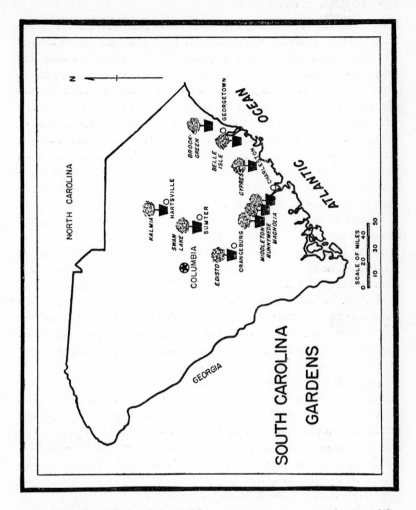

SOUTH CAROLINA GARDENS

the quickening effects of the mild temperatures were supplemented by the extraordinarily heavy rainfall that is common along the Carolina coast. In addition to these factors, the native flora was remarkable, and the streams along which the estates were built had promontories and indentations that formed natural, informal lines for gardens. At ebb tide, when there is no wind, the surfaces of those streams become enormous, curving mirrors that repeat the beauties of the shores, sometimes with enhancement due to a kind of wispiness that results from the slightest rippling.

A characteristic of several of the finest Carolina gardens is the river border on one irregular side, the forest borders elsewhere. Those beautified plots seem to have been rescued from the semitropical forests, into which, on the land sides, they blend. The plan is something like this: somewhere in the garden is open space, the heart of the garden. Around this are the plantations of flowers and of trees, arrangements of walks, formal or informal orderliness. Then there is the forest, somewhat thinned and somewhat cleared of underbrush on the fringes of the garden; and finally the natural forest with trees and immense vines growing as nature allows. There are, of course, some gardens that do not have stream and forest borders, yet such borders are somehow expected—perhaps because most of the earliest and greatest gardens had them, and several of the surviving great gardens have them.

Visitors to South Carolina think of these gardens as seasonal, and of course they are. All gardens are to some degree seasonal, reaching, in spring or in summer, their height of color and of fragrance. But the great Carolina gardens are seasonal mainly to visitors. Those that are open to the public are open only from December, or about that time, until May. To their creators, however, to their present owners, and to those who are fortunate enough to get inside after the gates have been closed, these gardens had and have perpetual charm. What E. T. H. Shaffer says in his book *Carolina Gardens* of Middleton Place is true of that garden, and essentially true of many others:

'There is here a year-'round procession of flowers. The camellias begin in late November and linger until the end of April; March and April form the spring festival of azaleas; and as they pass the gardens are filled with the delicate pinks of mountain laurel. Through the summer months there is a succession of roses, while the air is filled with the heady perfume wafted down from the towering magnolia grandiflora. And blending with these major notes are always a thousand minor flowers—heatherbell and hawthorn, lotus and iris.'

DuBose Heyward in his introduction to Mr. Shaffer's book—the most complete work on South Carolina's gardens up to the present—says this of the beauty spots that decorated the State long ago:

'No man could begin to write about gardens without discovering them to be so deeply rooted in history, so interwoven with social, economic and political mutations, that what purposed in the beginning to be a mere book of gardens would become in part the story of the land which bore them . . .

'The gardens of Carolina first came into being as an overseas projection of the English gardening that was still held by the strict confines of the Continental methods and that clung tenaciously to the small, obvious details of the Dutch . . . [But] along the Carolina coast . . . formal gardens blended from their very creation ordered lines with natural beauty, for even the most formal intentions failed to achieve the same results here amid wistful live oaks and Spanish moss, where forests were fragrant with magnolia and jessamine, as in the more sedate landscapes of northern Europe. So the English-planned gardens of Carolina grew and mellowed into gardens unlike any others in the whole world. While today one finds only the broken forest-strewn lines of those first great gardens, their peculiar spirit and charm survives in others created under their influence—Middleton, Magnolia, Belle Isle or Harrietta, and this peculiar quality followed the footsteps of the pioneer as he moved northward and westward across the state.'

Mr. Heyward is correct, 'their peculiar spirit and charm survives,' sometimes in forms so recognizable that it easily may be traced to the first great gardens, sometimes in forms and in places not so easily traced to origins. The beautiful resort towns, Aiken, Beaufort, Camden, and Summerville owe their present existence to the early Carolina beauty creators, as well as to climate. In South Carolina are numerous other villages and towns with climate equally pleasing, but they had not the luck to be touched by the hands of the beauty creators of former generations; or, if they had that good luck, intervening generations have partly or wholly effaced the evidence of it.

Cookery

THOUGH South Carolina is widely noted for good food, and pride in old recipes is traditional, unfortunately it is hard to find many dishes of local renown on the menus of public eating-places. Only in private homes and at barbecues, turtle suppers, catfish stews, and oyster roasts can one, as a rule, sample the distinctive cookery of the affluent past.

The records of early visitors to the State frequently refer to food. William Bartram, eighteenth-century botanist, told of the wild pigeons and of slaves hunting them by torchlight in the swampy sections of southeastern Carolina. Shortly after the Revolution, John F. D. Smyth, an English traveler, wrote of the wealthy widows on Edisto Island and suggested that the demise of their husbands was due partially to the rich food and drink in which they indulged. Bishop Asbury spoke appreciatively of the 'hot potatoes and gammon' served him in the home of a poor family as he went through the country in his labors for Methodism. But the bishop preached that corn should be eaten rather than drunk.

Mrs. Basil Hall, wife of an English naval officer, was entertained at the State capital on February 22, 1828. The second course of the afternoon dinner party she describes as follows: '. . . eight pies, down the side of the table, 6 dishes of glasses of syllabub and as many of jelly, besides one or two "floating islands," as they denominate what we call custard with whipped cream, and odd corners filled up by ginger and other preserves.' Mrs. Hall also records a sumptuous breakfast in a Combahee River plantation home, consisting of 'such admirably boiled rice, such hashed turkey, broiled quails and Indian corn flour, which heretofore I have thought so bad, made into cakes of every description, each one more delicious than the other.'

During the War between the States, when the blockade prevented the importation of foreign goods, the ingenuity of plantation mistresses was taxed to replace accustomed delicacies with homemade substitutes. A woman of the period thus describes these makeshifts: 'The things we ate and drank came in too for a prominent position. The first duty, after the blockade cut off supplies, was to store away what groceries and luxuries were left in as safe places as possible for sickness and in view of the return of friends. So then, our coffee was made of rye, wheat and sweet potatoes, chipped, dried and parched. Also okra seed and other substitutes too numerous to mention. It was sweetened, if at all, with sorghum or honey. For tea the leaves of blackberry vines were gathered and dried with as much care as a Chinaman manipulates his "Young Hyson" and "Oolong." For medicine we used roots and herbs, glad to make use of the red man's medicinal skill. Salt, white and pure, was obtained by digging up the earthen floors of long-used smokehouses, dripping water through it in hoppers and boiling it down.'

The culinary connoisseur may collect recipes that memoralize plantations of the flourishing era, such as Ophir, Ashley, Cooper River, Sampit, Weenee, and Awendaw breads; or those through which the names of famous cooks have been handed down for generations, as for example Selena La Bruce's rice bread, Uncle Wood's 'possum and potatoes, Aunt Sarah's persimmon beer. These recipes recall the good old times when wedding cakes were sometimes four feet high and the feasting lasted for several days.

The very names of certain dishes arouse curiosity and titillate the palate—Pompey's head, tipsy pudding, jambalaya, panygetta, bops, espetanga corn bread, okra daube, ratifia pudding, and almond florendine. Calapash (also spelled calipash, calibash, capapash, and perhaps derived from the Spanish *calabaza,* gourd) is turtle cooked in the shell, one recipe for which dates back 200 years. Served now only on State occasions, it was formerly a familiar household dish, and in the back yards of many Charleston homes turtles were kept in small 'cooter' ponds covered with wire. Calapash is only one of the many succulent turtle dishes once common in this region. The native yellow-bellied terrapin and the famous sea turtle have both been served for generations in concoctions worthy of the culinary artist.

The Low Country has a great variety of shrimp, oyster, and crab dishes. Charlestonians are partial to their tiny native shrimp, which they claim tastes best when pronounced 'swimp,' recalling the early morning cries of Negro vendors. This section of the State is also noted for its recipes based on rice—purleaus (pilaus) of innumerable kinds, hop-in-John (rice and peas), red rice, rice wine, and many breads made from rice flour. In the Pee Dee region, chicken bog, a variety of chicken pilau, is favored for midday or moonlight picnics.

From the days when beaters in the rice fields kept the big plantation house supplied with rice birds, these little creatures have been a delicacy. Ducks were once supplied in season by caretakers and foremen in the rice fields on a few hours' notice. Today, hunting for duck, wild turkey, partridge (quail), and deer attracts hundreds of out-of-State sportsmen. Though new game recipes are constantly being added to the records of families and clubs, many old ones still produce not only savory repasts but arguments as to their relative merits. Among the cherished dishes are spicy renditions of rabbit or squirrel stew, flavored with native bay leaves.

Various hunting and fishing clubs are inordinately proud of their recipes for cooking venison, quail, duck, and shad. The Otranto Club boasts of its pinebark stew, of which the Katawba Katfish Klub soup is a variant. It contains no pinebark, but is a highly seasoned concoction of fish in tomato sauce. On his visit to Florence in 1909, President Taft sampled it and pronounced it good. In the northeastern section of the State, fish fried in cornmeal and served with red horse bread (made of cornmeal and named for a variety of fish called red horse) finds especial favor.

The use of rice, universal in the Low Country, is not so characteristic of the Up Country, where hot breads and potatoes often take its place. The mountaineer has his poke 'sallet' (salad) made of tender young leaves of the pokeberry, his leather-breeches beans (dried in the pod for winter use), and such drinks as cherry brandy, plum beer, scuppernong and elderberry wine, and velvet wine from dewberries. Jelly is made from wild muscadine grapes, blackberries, and maypops.

Pie is common in both Up Country and Low, but the term has a different significance in the two locales. The Up Country pies have one or two crusts; in the Low Country no crust is used, the dish being more like a pudding. The mid-section of the State formerly had its own distinctive fare. Game and corn dishes were abundant. The Germans clung to their Old World recipes for sauerkraut, sausages, scrapple, and preserves.

Recipes that call for the use of native plants, as in frontier times, are still popular. A few of the commonest are said to have originated with the Indians. Among these, corn dishes predominate, notably succotash (dried beans and corn).

The Negro cook who is an artist in preparing food for a white family will often follow quite different methods in her own kitchen. 'White folks' vittles ain't got no suption,' she will say, meaning that they have no flavor. Though a definite line can hardly be drawn between Negro cookery and white cookery, Negroes in general relish more fat in their food, and sharper flavoring. No vegetable is prepared to their taste without a chunk of fat back or side meat—but this is a predilection shared by many white folk. Okra and tomato pilaus, catfish stews, 'possum and 'taters' (yam), and even 'coon are rated as great delicacies. Recipes ascribed to Negro origin often bear odd names that do not at all describe the contents of the dish—wildcat stew and monkey sauce, for example.

The State is rich in excellent recipes for sweets. At Christmas time, syllabub (cream, wine, and sugar whipped to a froth) is the time-honored dessert in many homes. Others adhere to the English triumph of 'plum pudding on fire,' and nearly every family treasures its own hallowed directions for making fruit cake. Peach leather and benneseed brittle are Charleston specialties in the way of confectionery. 'Long sweetenin'' cookies, molasses pudding or pie, and sweet potato pone may have originated in wartime blockade days, but they are quite as good now as when molasses had to serve for sugar. Wafers cooked on irons that are family relics, 'stickies,' and charlotte russe of various kinds—these are still served with confidence and pride.

RECIPES

Okra Pilau

Dice four slices of breakfast bacon and fry in deep pan until brown. Lift out bacon, and place in pan one chopped onion and one tablespoon chopped green pepper; then add two cups stewed tomatoes and two cups okra sliced thin. Let them cook down, stirring occasionally to prevent burning, and season with salt and pepper. Meanwhile cook two cups rice in two quarts water with one teaspoon salt; after boiling 12 minutes drain and mix with ingredients in the pan. Turn into double boiler and steam for 20 minutes. Add bacon just before serving.

Stickies

One-half pound butter
One cup sugar
Pastry enough for two pies

Roll dough thin. Cut in 12 squares (about 3½ inches). Divide the butter into 12 parts, place on each square, and pour the sugar over. Then fold corners of dough to center. Press edges closely and place in pan just allowing to touch each other. Bake in fairly hot oven.

Cracklin' Bread

Sift one quart of cornmeal and one teaspoon salt into a bowl and add sufficient boiling water to make stiff dough. Add one heaping cup cracklings (crisp bits of fresh pork from which the lard has been fried) and mix well. Mold into small cakes as for corn pone and bake until brown and crusty.

Hop-in-John

Soak one pint dried field peas (cow peas) for several hours. Boil in one quart water one hour, then add one pound salt pork and cook one hour more. Add one pint rice and boil half an hour longer. Season with salt and pepper when rice is added.

Peach Leather

Select ripe freestone peaches, peel, and remove stones. Crush through a sieve, and to four cups of pulp add one cup sugar. Bring to a boil and boil two minutes. Spread in thin layer on flat dish and dry in hot sun for three days. When mixture is thick and leathery sprinkle with powdered sugar, cut in strips and roll out as for jelly roll. Dry rolls in sun for two more days. Pack in airtight box. (This is the most famous confection of plantation days.)

Benne Brittle

Melt two cups sugar in saucepan, stirring constantly. When sugar is melted add half teaspoon each of vanilla and lemon extract. Then add two cups parched benne seed, stirring it in quickly. Pour at once on marble slab or into lightly buttered pan. Mark off in one-inch squares while still warm and break along markings.

(Benne seed, or sesame, brought from Africa according to tradition, is still grown in South Carolina.)

PART II
Cities and Towns

Aiken

Railroad Station: Park Ave. and Union St. for Southern Ry.
Bus Station: Commercial Hotel, corner Laurens St. and Richland Ave., for Atlantic Greyhound and Southeastern Stages.
Airports: North Augusta Airport, 1 m. W. on US 1; Municipal Airport, 1 m. SE. on State 78; no scheduled service at either.
Taxis: 25¢ within city, ½ m. outside limits 35¢, 1 m. 50¢.

Accommodations: 4 hotels (2 open only during tourist season Oct.–May 15).

Information Service: Chamber of Commerce, Richland Ave. and Newberry St.

Motion Picture Houses: 1.
Polo: 17 fields, including practice fields.
Riding: Flat and steeplechase courses, bridle paths.
Golf: Highland Park Course, Highland Park Road adjacent to Highland Park Hotel, 18 holes, greens fees $1.10 afternoons, $2.20 all day. Term fees (Jan.–May) men $30, ladies $25, family $60; (Apr. 15–Oct.) $15.

Annual Events: Steeplechase, hunter trials, polo, flat racing and horse shows— mainly in spring. Garden pilgrimages to certain estates in spring (consult Chamber of Commerce).

AIKEN (527 alt., 6,033 pop.), seat of Aiken County, in the west central sandhills, is known as the 'Polo Capital' of the South and is dedicated to the horse. It is a peaceful, quiet place of large estates and small cottages, of numerous parks where pines, magnolias, and oaks form an effective background for grass and flowers; of winding bridle paths and magnificently wide streets—mostly unpaved for the convenience of the horses—bordered by trees and centered by landscaped parkways.

Every winter this little town sees an influx of more nationally known personages than a place of similar size would expect to encounter in a lifetime, and at this time of the year is given over completely to the wealthy and their sports. The summer is a less ostentatious season, when the town's own inhabitants resume their normal mode of living.

Many handsome private estates and parks combine to make Aiken residents acutely garden-conscious, so that gardeners vie with each other for floral effects that reach a dazzling climax in the spring. Hardly does this beauty pass its prime, however, when the wealthy throngs that arrived such a short while before begin to dash out just as quickly, migrating to Bar Harbor, Newport, Long Island, and other favored resorts.

The stay of the wealthy is punctuated by rounds of parties, fox hunting, drag hunts (a form of fox hunting), trap shooting, and hunting. On its many well-tended polo fields men and women daily participate in this exciting sport or spend spare moments watching the United

States International Polo Team train for trophy events. Young and old meet on bridle paths and race courses, cantering or galloping on thoroughbreds—some more timid souls on animals of less fire—but in any event, on a horse.

The area around Aiken was sparsely settled before the Revolution. Reminiscent of pioneer traders, who cut notches on trees to mark their way through forests where hostile Indians lurked, is Two Notch Road. George Washington used this route on his tour in 1791 and it is still an important highway through Aiken between Augusta and Columbia. Whiskey Road, so named because of numerous whiskey bottles cast aside by Saturday night celebrants, leads to Tory Trail, a path used by Britishers passing through this country, where most of the scattered inhabitants were Tories. At Dean Swamp, in present Aiken County, patriots wreaked vengeance on the loyal king's men in a Revolutionary engagement.

At the beginning of the nineteenth century, when South Carolina farmers began to grow cotton extensively, a constant stream of wagons carried the product over the old roads through the Aiken section to Augusta on the Georgia side of the Savannah River. The consequent decrease in Charleston's trade was a prime factor in the establishment of Hamburg (*see Tour 6b*), to which the first railroad constructed for steam engines in the United States was begun from the port city in 1830. This was the Charleston-Hamburg line, later a branch of the Southern Railway. Two years were required for the completion of the tracks, and meanwhile William Aiken, father of Governor Aiken, had become president of the company. When a town site was laid out in 1834 near the western terminus of the road, it was named for him. The Nation's first passenger train and the first train carrying United States mail passed through Aiken.

Though incorporated in 1835, the new settlement made little progress until 1845, when William Gregg built a cotton mill and village in the Horse Creek Valley six miles from Aiken. The mill and village were constructed chiefly of granite, and Gregg called the place Graniteville. This mill gave impetus to the community. Later people from other sections of the country were attracted by the dry, bracing climate of the section, which has an average winter temperature of about 55°.

Aiken lay outside the battlefield area in the early days of the War between the States. Its mills provided equipment for Confederate soldiers, and troops frequently passed through on the railroad. In February 1865, Sherman ordered General H. J. Kilpatrick out from Savannah to destroy the Graniteville mills. Kilpatrick was met and defeated by General Joe Wheeler in an encounter on Aiken's principal street, down which ran the railroad track. In the midst of the fray an engineer unwittingly ran his engine almost into the fight and had to back out hurriedly to Graniteville.

In the days of 'Carpet Bag Government' after the war, two of the bloodiest race riots of the period occurred at Hamburg and Ellenton, both in Aiken County, and terror was precipitated over the entire State.

The town and county of Aiken became a hotbed of radical excitement and here in 1876 the Democrats launched the movement to re-establish white political supremacy (*see History*). Many believe that the flaming costumes of the 'Red Shirts' were first worn when the followers of Wade Hampton met at Kalmia Hill, Aiken County.

After State government was again functioning smoothly, prosperity returned to the community. Mills were reorganized, railroads rebuilt, natural resources capitalized, mines reopened, and agriculture developed by diversified crops. Aiken was the birthplace of the first girls' Tomato Club in 1910, the movement having since become Nation-wide in 4-H clubs. But the town's fame as a tourist resort surpassed all other activities.

The Charleston *News and Courier* on April 1, 1882, carried an account of the introduction of polo in Aiken. A portion of the article states:

'Gay parties of ladies and gentlemen mounted on prancing steeds dashed over the country adjoining the delightful fields of our celebrated pine woods. Sumptuous lunches were served that would have done honor to Delmonico's. The crack military company of the city, the Palmetto Rifles, entertained with dress parades, but all this paled into insignificance before the brilliant and successful introduction of James Gordon Bennett's popular national game, polo. It caused a great sensation, and completely revolutionized the city as far as amusements are concerned.'

In the early nineties, when the late Mrs. Thomas Hitchcock set the seal of her approval on Aiken, the city's prominence as a social and sporting center was assured. Mrs. Hitchcock established here a polo school for boys when her own sons were young, and when her grandsons came along she still maintained her interest in the training and practice games of future players.

Aiken, however, is not economically dependent on the tourist trade. There are six textile mills in the county, employing an average of 4,360 people. The mining and refining of kaolin were early established and today eight mines are operated. Aiken clays have been shipped to Limoges, France, to Belgium, and England for the making of fine china. The kaolin products are also shipped for use in glazing paper, in the manufacture of automobile tires and rubber goods, in the making of paints, crockery, and chalk. Granite quarries and lumber mills are also successful industries.

POINTS OF INTEREST

The BAPTIST CHURCH, Richland Ave. between Fairfield and Union Sts., was burned by Negroes in the riot of 1876 and then rebuilt. Among the graves in the adjoining cemetery is that of an unknown Union soldier who died of wounds following the skirmish of 1865. His grave is decorated along with those of Southerners' on Confederate Memorial Day.

The ASTRONOMICAL MARKER, in the garden of the E. P. Henderson home, Laurens St. and Edgefield Ave., was erected by the German Government to commemorate the successful observations made here by German astronomers, December 6, 1882, during the transit of Venus between the sun and the earth. Three expeditions in Germany had failed on account of clouds, and, because of its sunny climate, Aiken was selected for another effort to record this rare phenomenon. The astronomers remained in the city six weeks, set up a small observatory for the telescopes they had brought, and selected this site because the instruments would not be jarred by traffic.

'LET'S PRETEND' (private), Horry St. and Colleton Ave., is a rambling weatherboarded Colonial cottage with rooms on different levels. This is Aiken's literary shrine, once the home of Gouverneur Morris, who not only wrote a number of his earlier works here but had as his guests Rudyard Kipling, Richard Harding Davis, and Gilbert Parker.

ELM COURT (private), Colleton Ave. between Fairfield and Union Sts., formerly one of the homes of William Gregg, utilized as Aiken's first courthouse, was later purchased and extensively renovated by the Vanderbilts and is now owned by Mrs. Augustus Goodwin. The exterior is unusual with its battened vertical boards of yellow pine.

CHINABERRY (private), Whiskey Road between S. Boundary Ave. and Barnard Road (US 1), now the Converse home, is one of the oldest houses in Aiken. The large two-story frame structure has been thoroughly modernized. Formerly the property of the Williams family, a good deal of fighting occurred in the front yard during the skirmish of 1865. An unknown Union soldier was cared for in the house and is buried in the Baptist churchyard.

JOY COTTAGE (private), Whitney Ave. between Chesterfield St. and Fourth Ave., the winter home of Mrs. G. MacCullough Miller, daughter of the late William C. Whitney, is probably the largest residence in Aiken and like most of the earlier homes of Northern residents its exterior is of white clapboards. It is an unusually fine example of Georgian Colonial architecture.

ROSEBANK (private), Laurens St. between S. Boundary and Colleton Aves., home of the Eugene V. Grace family, one of the older homes of Northern residents in Aiken, is noted for its beautiful garden rather than its architecture.

EUSTIS PARK, between Lancaster St. and Vaucluse Road, is the largest and most recently developed of Aiken's many municipal parks, with athletic fields and playgrounds. On the edge of the park is Aiken's new COUNTY HOSPITAL, one of the best equipped smaller hospitals in the South.

KALMIA HILL, W. edge of town between US 1 and Vaucluse Road, a suburban development, was named for the home of William Gregg. Once the center of the ante-bellum summer colony from Charleston, the old home was the scene of an early rally in the Red Shirt Campaign,

1876, and is reputedly the site where the Red Shirt insignia originated. Only part of the brick cellar remains.

HITCHCOCK WOODS, SW. border of town, an area of nearly 20 square miles, where no automobile may enter save in case of fire, is the site of picturesque drag hunts. The drag hunt has been known in Aiken for many years, but it was not until 1916 that this sport became truly 'smart.' Hounds were brought from the North and club uniforms of green coat with yellow collar were adopted.

Drag hunting is a sport that has everything pertaining to a fox hunt, except the fox. It may include the presence of internationally famed huntsmen, thoroughbred horses, pedigreed dogs, and even a tea room in the woods—but no fox. A bag of anise seed is dragged over a laid-out course, and the hounds, just as excited as in a true fox hunt, follow this scent. The drag lines consist of lanes cut through the woods, with rail fences providing barriers to horse and rider. These barriers in some cases are very high and spills are not infrequent. The racing idea is uppermost at all times and some of the drags are ridden at a terrific speed. A rider must keep with the hunt for the honor of the drag and his own stable.

Gentler events are the children's drags each Saturday, when the incipient sportsmen and sportswomen of the two boarding schools turn out. Older riders who prefer an easier pace join these drags.

POINTS OF INTEREST IN ENVIRONS

Edgewood, 1.5 *m.;* Irvin Court, 2.3 *m.;* Cemetery Hill, 2.5 *m.;* Granite-ville, 4.8 *m.;* Aiken State Park, 12.8 *m.;* Hamburg, 16 *m.* (*see Tour 6b*). Sand Bar Ferry, 20 *m.;* Beech Island, 29.3 *m.;* Silver Bluff, 40.5 *m.* (*see Tour 19b*).

✳✳✳

Anderson

Railroad Stations: 120 N. Main St. for Blue Ridge Ry.; 106 W. Market St. for Charleston and Western Carolina Ry.; 116 Murray St. for Piedmont & Northern Ry. (electric).
Bus Station: 31 W. Whitner St. for Atlantic Greyhound, Red Top Bus, and Carolina Motor Lines, Carolina, Great Eastern, and Smoky Mountain Stages.
Airport: Municipal, 3 m. W. on SC 81; charter service only; taxi 75¢.
Taxis: 15¢ within city limits.

Accommodations: 3 hotels; boarding houses.

Information Service: Chamber of Commerce, 316–320 N. Main St.

Radio Station: WAIM (1200 kc.).
Motion Picture Houses: 3.
Swimming: Electric City Country Club, 2 m. on W. Market St. Ext., nonmembers 35¢–50¢; Keys' Spring and Lake, 2 m. on W. Market St. Ext., 15¢–25¢; Geddings Lake, 3 m. W. on SC 18.
Golf: Electric City Golf Club, 2 m. on W. Market St. Ext., 18 holes, greens fee 50¢ Mon.–Fri., 75¢ Sat. and Sun.
Tennis: NYA courts, N. Fant School, N. Fant St. between Marshall Ave. and Calhoun St.; W. Market St. School, corner W. Market and Tower Sts.; Anderson College, Boulevard between Fourth and Calhoun St. Ext.; Anderson Country Club, Market St. just outside western city limits; NYA courts, North Anderson, N. Main St. between Anderson St. and North Ave.

Annual Events: Anderson County Fair, 1 m. E. on US 29, Oct.

ANDERSON (754 alt., 14,383 pop.), in the foothills of the Blue Ridge Mountains in northwest South Carolina, is primarily an industrial city, and the seat of an important agricultural county. Covering red clay hills on the watershed of the Savannah River, and rimmed almost entirely by nine textile mill villages, physical Anderson revolves about its terra-cotta courthouse in a landscaped park centering the public square. The business district is a congested area around the square and on the streets leading into it. In Anderson's residential areas, shaded by old oaks and hickories, comfortable modern homes with no pretensions to period styles are interspersed with occasional ante-bellum dwellings.

The population of Anderson, 72 per cent white, is composed mostly of descendants of Scotch-Irish settlers from Virginia and Pennsylvania, augmented by Low Country families who sought the hill country for summer comfort and remained permanently.

The close kinship between the city's industrial activity and the agricultural interests of the well-populated rural districts is evident in the county fair each fall when ten counties, five of them in Georgia, combine in staging an outstanding Up Country event. Exhibits of cotton, grains, stock feed, fruit, and vegetables mingle with textile, electrical, and mechanical displays.

Anderson County is part of the old Cherokee Indian lands, deeded to the State in 1777. A few pioneers had settled in the region prior to that date, but after the treaty made the district safe for white people, settlers poured in rapidly. By 1790 the Cherokee territory, covering 8 per cent of South Carolina, had more than 10 per cent of the State's free population. In 1789 the present counties of Anderson, Pickens, and Oconee became Pendleton District, with the courthouse in Pendleton.

In 1826 Anderson County was created out of the district and for the courthouse a central location was selected on the 'General's Road,' the highway used by General Andrew Pickens in traveling from Abbeville County to his home, 'Tamassee,' in Oconee County. This old road is Anderson's Main Street. Town and county were named in honor of General Robert Anderson, Revolutionary soldier, who in 1801 had founded a river port called Andersonville (*see Tour 7*) about 12 miles from Anderson. Destructive freshets and the transfer of interest to the county seat made of Andersonville only a memory.

With a trading area extending over South Carolina's Piedmont section and into Georgia, manufacturing enterprises in Anderson developed rapidly, along with cultural influences, such as reading and debating societies, singing schools, academies, and churches. The area was noted for its fine race horses, Hambletonians and Arabians among them, and there was much horse racing on courses in town and county. Few mules were imported here before 1840.

During the War between the States, Anderson County furnished 5,000 Confederate soldiers and became an ammunition-manufacturing center. Not in the path of invasion, it was the haven of many refugees with their possessions. Only two minor skirmishes were fought in the county.

A highlight in the city's history occurred September 2, 1876, when General Wade Hampton delivered here, before an enthusiastic crowd of approximately 6,000, the first of 40 speeches in the exciting campaign that resulted in his election as governor. With bands playing and banners flying, a long line of cheering Democratic club representatives marched in procession. Mounted rifle club members, wearing brand new 'Red Shirt' uniforms, swelled the parade. To them the tall figure of Hampton on the bedecked platform was a symbol of liberation.

During the Reconstruction period, when feeling ran high in the community, Anderson produced a remarkable character, Manse Jolly, whose exploits on his horse, 'Ironsides,' are still vividly remembered. Jolly became involved (justifiably, some say) with Federal military authorities soon after being mustered out of the Confederate army. Tradition records that a Union officer sent two mounted Negroes to Jolly's farm to apprehend him, but neither ever returned. When Jolly was later observed plowing their horses, it was deemed wiser to send four Negroes; these also failed to return. A whole company of Federal troopers next attempted to capture Jolly as he was attending church, but he leaped into the pulpit, and thence out of the window. The following day he walked boldly into Anderson, brandished a pistol at the colonel of the regiment, and demanded the return of his horse, which he had left behind on his hurried exit. The frightened colonel is said to have granted Jolly not only his horse, but unconditional amnesty as well. He soon got into more trouble, however, fled to Texas, bought a ranch, married, and made a belated attempt to settle down. His career soon ended, however, when he was drowned attempting to ford a river.

Anderson was incorporated in 1882. In 1897 a hydroelectric plant, believed to be one of the first in the United States for the transmission of power for public use over a distance of several miles, was built at Portman Shoals on the Seneca River, nine miles from town. The city has made extensive progress in electrical projects since that time.

Anderson's textile mills, employing 5,185 people with an annual pay roll of $3,283,400, manufacture all types of cotton cloth. In addition widely diversified commodities are produced: brooms, horse collars, mattresses, brick and tile, cottonseed products, fertilizer, meal, flour, metal shingles, eyeglasses, monuments, and lumber.

POINTS OF INTEREST

'THE OLD REFORMER,' a Revolutionary cannon used first by the British and later by the Americans, stands on the plaza in front of the courthouse, Main and Whitner Sts. Luke Hanks, a reputed relative of Abraham Lincoln, brought it to Anderson in 1814 from Star Fort near Ninety Six (see Tour 8). When the British evacuated the fort, Americans adopted the gun they had left behind. The iron carriage went into plowshares in the Confederate era. When the Ordinance of Secession was signed in 1860, the old cannon boomed, acquiring its name when fired in 1876 to celebrate Hampton's election and the end of Reconstruction. For many years a pillory stood near by for the punishment of petty criminals.

ARLINGTON (private), 765 E. Whitner St., a two-and-a-half-story white frame house with portico and pediment, is set well back from the street in extensive grounds, with flower gardens at the rear. The fluted Corinthian columns are of cement over brick, and yellowed with age. One-story porches on each side of the portico have flat roofs and balustrades. On the main roof is a cupola with domed top. The house was built by slave labor in 1859 for James L. Orr, governor of South Carolina, 1865–8, who was deposed when the government was taken over by Federal military authorities. In 1872 President Grant appointed Orr Minister to Russia, where he died. His body was brought home and buried in the Anderson First Presbyterian churchyard.

The FIRST BAPTIST CHURCH, E. end of Church St., is designed in the Romanesque style with red brick walls and stone trim. Erected 1853, the church was remodeled in 1882. The congregation, numbering

2,100 (1938) and one of the largest in the State, was organized in a bush arbor. Their first church edifice, Mt. Tabor, was built of logs in 1821.

The SITE OF THE CONFEDERATE TREASURY, 1032 S. Main St., is now occupied by the modern W. W. Sullivan home (*private*). In 1864 a branch of the treasury was moved here from Columbia and notes and bonds were signed by four young Richmond women. Yankee raiders destroyed the plates and dies in 1865. The old building had formerly been occupied by the Johnson Female University and the section is still called University Hill. After the war the seminary became the Patrick Military Institute; the building was later used as a hospital. A son-in-law of Colonel John Patrick, head of the military school, bought the property and built the present house.

In SILVERBROOK CEMETERY, E. of White St., S. of Cemetery Road, at the southeastern city limits, is a large grove of edible bamboo, which sometimes grows two feet in 24 hours. It overshadows a chain of lily pools connected by rustic bridges over a trickling brook. Samuel M. Wilkes, believed to be the first Andersonian to die in the War between the States, lies buried here. Before the city bought the property in 1898, it was a picnic ground and a picnic was in progress here, May 1, 1865, when a Union raid on Anderson resulted in a post-war skirmish.

ANDERSON JUNIOR COLLEGE, Boulevard between Fourth St. and Calhoun St. Ext., a Baptist institution for girls, has a 32-acre, tree-shaded campus with five white-columned red brick buildings connected by covered passageways.

The school has had a continuous history since 1848. Then known as Johnson Female Seminary, it was adopted by the Saluda Baptist Association and later called Johnson Female University. In the late 1880's it became first coeducational, then a school for boys. In 1910 the property of the college was given by Anderson citizens to the Baptists of the State and two years later the present institution came into existence. It was made a junior college in 1929, and is now a member of the American Association of Junior Colleges.

POINTS OF INTEREST IN ENVIRONS

Cedar Spring Lake, 2 *m.;* Starr, 9 *m.;* Andersonville, 12 *m.* (*see Tour* 7). Boscobel Plantation, 11.3 *m.;* Pendleton, 13.2 *m.;* Woodburn Plantation, 13.3 *m.;* Old Stone Church, 16.1 *m.;* Hopewell, General Andrew Pickens's Home, 17.9 *m.;* Mt. Pelier Plantation, 18.5 *m.;* Stump House Mountain Tunnel, 42.8 *m.;* Oconee State Park, 48.5 *m.* (*see Tour* 19a). Clemson College and Fort Hill, Calhoun's mansion, 18 *m.* (*see Tour* 14).

Beaufort

Railroad Station: W. end Depot St. for Charleston & Western Carolina Ry.
Bus Station: Bay St. between West and Charles Sts. for Greyhound Lines.
Airport: Ladies Island (4.9 m.), landing field; no scheduled service.
Piers: Bay St. between Scott and West Sts. for Beaufort-Savannah Steamship Lines, fare to Savannah $1, 3 round-trips weekly; between Carteret and Charles Sts., piers for travelers using Intracoastal Waterway.
Taxis: 35¢ within city limits.

Accommodations: 3 hotels; tourist homes.

Information Service: Chamber of Commerce, or City Manager, City Hall, SW. corner Carteret and Craven Sts.

Motion Picture Houses: 1.
Swimming: Burckmyer's Beach, Ladies Island.
Golf: Colony Gardens, Ladies Island, 6 m. E., 9 holes, greens fee 50¢.
Tennis: W. end Boundary St.
Hunting: Club membership not essential; local owners of dogs and preserves act as guides for reasonable fee; nonresident license $15.25. Seasons: deer, Sept. 1–Jan. 1; doves, Sept. 15–Nov. 15, Dec. 15–Jan. 15; quail, Thanksgiving Day–Mar. 1.
Fishing: Boats for rent with or without guides; surf bass fishing on Atlantic side of outlying islands; cobia can also be caught in vicinity of Beaufort.

Annual Events: Sailboat Regatta, three days during middle of July. St. Helena Island Annual Fair, in fall, under auspices of Penn School.

> For further information regarding this city consult *Beaufort and the Sea Islands,* another of the American Guide Series, sponsored and published in 1938 by the Clover Club of Beaufort.

BEAUFORT (21 alt., 2,776 pop., pronounced Bewfort), seat of Beaufort County and second oldest town in the State, is a seacoast town on Port Royal Island, one of the 65 islands that make up the county. It is the center of large truck-farming interests, to which, along with the shrimping and oystering industries and the year-round tourist trade, it owes its livelihood.

Beaufort, for all its turbulent history of wars and hurricanes, preserves its Old-World charm and tranquillity. Almost inaccessible until the advent of good roads—being 22 miles off the main highways of travel—the march of progress has touched it lightly and in appearance it is today very much as it was a century and a half ago.

Handsome old houses, wearing the patina of time, seem to brood over their memories—a prideful brooding because they have resisted and outlasted invasion. Designed primarily for coolness, with high basements and spacious verandas, they are set in old-fashioned gardens where yellow jessamine, moss, and wisteria intermingle; where oleanders, camellias, and evergreens grow riotously. Architecture presents a combination of the Classical Revival and an adaptation of the smaller plantation house, with here and there a touch of semitropical Spanish and the more formal Georgian. Peculiar to the Low Country are the houses of 'tabby,' a composition made of crushed oyster shells.

Seldom is the day that the sun does not shine on Beaufort, and flowers are always in bloom. Scarlet poinsettias are framed against tabby walls; an avenue of palmettos lines Boundary Street. Great spreading live oaks, festooned with Spanish moss, weave shifting patterns on the narrow, crooked streets; these still bear their original names, although in some cases their former oyster-shell whiteness has surrendered to progress and modern cement. Beneath the trees a carpet of lush grass slopes down to ancient sea walls, and through green vistas gleams the gray-green tidal river, with little fleets of sailboats in the bay beyond.

The town serenely accepts the fact that traffic is held up by a small Negro boy solemnly urging along a fat, lazy ox; or that its masculine contingent gathers in the late afternoon on the 'settin' ' plank, nailed across the row of posts in a vacant lot in the very heart of its business street. The whistle of the one daily train is heard only faintly, for Beaufort's citizens had the foresight to build their railroad station a mile away, to avoid smoke and noise. Even rooster-crowing and unnecessary tooting of automobile horns have been banned by authorities.

Though the town is about equally divided between whites and Negroes, there are about two-and-a-half times as many Negroes as whites in the county. The races live in friendly harmony, each recognizing and observing social distinctions. The whitewashed cabins, in which most of the Negroes live, are not in any segregated district but interspersed among the white peoples' homes. The blue doors and shutters are to keep the 'ha'nts' out, but the custom may have originated 150 years ago, when the Negroes were given the residue of indigo left in iron dye vats and used it to decorate their homes. Negroes, like whites, make a living catching and canning shrimp and oysters and in truck farming, and still raise enough rice for their own consumption. Since the War between the States, Beaufort Negroes have been the focus of numerous social and educational campaigns sponsored by Northern white people, notably at Penn School (see Tour 5B). In spite of these efforts, however, strange folklore and folk customs persist; the last articles used by the deceased are placed on his grave and never disturbed for fear of 'plat-eye.' With grave ornaments ranging from whisky bottles to alarm clocks, cemeteries present an odd appearance.

A town without monuments—it does not need them—Beaufort is itself a monument to endurance. Its history dates from 1521, when Spanish rovers first saw the wide expanse of harbor and called it Punta de Santa Elena, which survives today in St. Helena Island and Sound. Jean Ribaut called it Port Royal when he came with his Frenchmen in 1562 to make the first Protestant settlement in North America. Two years later the Spaniards returned to remain for a decade, and in 1670 William Sayle brought the first English colony to South Carolina, remained for a short time in Port Royal, and moved on to settle Charles Town. A Scotch colony under Lord Cardross came in 1684 and existed two years before being destroyed by the Spaniards.

Thus all the early attempts at colonization ended in disaster. When the town of Beaufort was laid out in 1710, and named for Henry, Duke of Beaufort, a Lord Proprietor, seasoned planters came from Barbados and other colonies, along with tradesmen and adventurers.

The town was practically wiped out by the Yamasee Indians in 1715 and conquered by the British in the Revolution. Though Beaufort was frightened by English gunboats in 1812, they did not attack, because the port was too strongly fortified. In spite of all the fighting that has taken place in the community, however, 'the war' in Beaufort's vocabulary is the War between the States. An unusually wealthy area in 1861, the village and the surrounding sea islands fell November 7 of that year into the hands of a strong Federal fleet which attacked the two strongholds, Hilton Head and Fort Beauregard.

Nearly all of the men having volunteered for service in Confederate defense, their unprotected families fled when aliens took possession, leaving only one white man in the town—a newcomer from the North. Their beautifully furnished homes, their crops, and their many slaves were abandoned, and Beaufort was occupied by Union soldiers. When their property was confiscated by the United States Government, few old families were able to get back their homes. Some of them were set aside for military and naval properties; other plantations were sold to Negroes in small tracts; Negroes acquired possession of certain Beaufort homes, in which their descendants are still living. A tragically changed community, Beaufort was overrun from 1865 to 1876 by carpetbaggers, ex-slaves, and scalawags. Lashed by the terrible hurricane of 1893, when its phosphate mines were ruined, and sadly ravaged by the storm of 1940, Beaufort still endures, courageous and intact.

Naval stores, indigo, rice, long staple cotton, phosphate mining, truck farming, fishing, and of recent years tourists, have in succession contributed periods of remarkable affluence between the eras of war and terror. During the last half-century practically one third of the taxable land of Beaufort County has been withdrawn from cultivation through sales as hunting preserves to wealthy Northern sportsmen, some of them nationally known. Their handsome estates lie along the rivers and creeks, occupying in most instances the sites of the original old plantation homes.

Truck farming has declined to some extent, owing to market conditions, but canning factories, which have sprung up all over the county to take care of surplus vegetables and seafoods, furnish employment seasonally to both races. Parris Island, the Marine training station 7.6 miles away, also affords employment to many carpenters, painters, and other workers.

POINTS OF INTEREST

There is no pleasanter way of browsing around the little town than on foot, but the streets are also adapted to automobiles. Unfortunately for the visitor, all the old homes are private.

The NATIONAL CEMETERY, Boundary St. at the NW. (only landward) entrance to the town, contains the graves of 12,000 Union soldiers who died or were killed in the South from 1861–5, besides those of a small group of Confederates. The home of the keeper is in the cemetery.

BELLAMY INN, Boundary and Carteret Sts., of white frame, with the typical plantation piazzas and with dormer windows on the top floor, stands as an unpretentious survivor of the past. The rear entrance has fluted pilasters and flat pediment with dentils and cornice.

The DE TREVILLE HOUSE, corner Carteret and Green Sts., a buff frame dwelling, was in use in the early 1800's. The double six-columned piazza, with flat roof, rests on an arcaded brick foundation and is surmounted by three dormer windows.

The OLD BARNWELL HOUSE, NW. corner Carteret and Washington Sts., of shabby gray tabby, has a narrow pedimented portico, a curved single flight of entrance steps, and T-shaped plan, with projecting wings at the side. There are small windows in the high basement story. The house was built by Elizabeth Barnwell Gough soon after 1773. Her daughter married James Smith, who was a grandson of Colonel William Rhett. In 1830 some of the Smith children assumed the name of Rhett in order to perpetuate it. One of them was Robert Barnwell Rhett, ardent Secessionist.

The OLD BEAUFORT COLLEGE BUILDING, Carteret St. between Washington and Duke Sts., of gray stuccoed brick, is used as a grammar school. The front pedimented portico, with gable roof and rather coarse detail, has columns with large curved, bell-shaped capitals. The central part was erected in 1852, but the wings were added when the county bought the building for a school. It first accommodated the college, which was incorporated in 1795 and existed until the Federal Government took over the building and leased it to the Freedmen's Bureau. There is still a Board of Trustees of Beaufort College, who handle funds of the old institution.

The BEAUFORT LIBRARY BUILDING (*open 4–6 weekdays; also* 10–12 A.M. *Wed.,* 8–10 P.M. *Fri.*) NW. corner Craven and Carteret Sts., built in 1918, was donated by the Carnegie Foundation. The entrance to the red brick edifice of modified Georgian Colonial design has a broken pediment with freestanding columns. Three dormers break the roof line. The library society, organized in 1802, had that year some 2,000 volumes. When Beaufort was captured in 1861, agents of the United States Treasury shipped the books to New York, where many were auctioned off, until their further sale was prevented by Chief Justice Chase, then Secretary of the Treasury. 'We do not war on libraries,' he wrote, explaining that the books had been removed only for safe-keeping, to be returned to Beaufort 'whenever the authority of the Union should be re-established in South Carolina.' Most of the volumes dealt with scientific and historical subjects, and were destroyed by fire in 1868 in the Smithsonian Institution in Washington, where they had been sent from New York. The United States Senate passed a bill in April 1940, appropriating $10,000 to pay Beaufort for the books.

The present Township Library, supported by a small tax, numbers about 7,000 books. The new collection was begun in 1902 and continued until 1916 by the Clover Club Circulating Library.

The BEAUFORT ARSENAL (*open 8-6:30 weekdays*), NE. corner Craven and Scott Sts., built in 1795 and rebuilt in 1852 on the site of the first courthouse, is a long rectangular building of brick and tabby. Its Spanish appearance is enhanced by a row of palmetto trees that parallels the surrounding wall, with its massive arched gateway, battlements, and two brass trophy guns captured from the British in 1779. These guns were seized by Union soldiers at the fall of Fort Walker in 1861 and returned to Beaufort after 1880.

The old Beaufort Coast Artillery, organized in 1776 as the fifth military company recognized in the United States, had its headquarters here. The Artillery has served in every American war since the Revolution. During the Spanish-American War the company was divided into two units, one at Parris Island and the other at Fort Fremont on St. Helena Island.

The WATERHOUSE HOME, NW. corner Bay and New Sts., is a white frame Greek Revival structure built in 1856 by Louis Sams. The two-story piazza, with superimposed colonnades of Doric and Ionic columns, has a long flight of marble steps leading to its first floor. The small house at the rear, with overhanging cornice, was the kitchen in ante-bellum days. There was no drinking water on the property then, and little Negroes formed a continuous procession as they brought water for the household from a well a quarter of a mile distant.

The GOLD EAGLE TAVERN, New St. between Bay and Port Republic Sts., with buff-colored tabby walls, is two-and-a-half stories in height and follows a rambling plan. The original part was built in 1795 and was once the home of Chancellor Henry William DeSaussure, Director of the Mint in 1795 when the first Gold Eagles were coined, which explains its name. There were originally the customary piazzas and dormers in the gable roof. A modern addition to the house, overlooking the water and resembling a large silo with a conical roof, was designed by the late Kate Gleason, who remodeled other Beaufort homes. Here artists and others of the winter colony gather, with bridal pairs seeking an ideal retreat.

The OLDEST HOUSE IN BEAUFORT, SW. corner New and Port Republic Sts., is a story-and-a-half white frame cottage that is believed to have stood here since the Yamasee Indian era. The structure measures about 25 by 40 feet and has a high brick foundation; clustered brick chimneys rise above the gable roof with its small projecting dormers. An enclosed exterior stair well is unusual. The rear elevation, on Port Republic Street, has small openings in the foundation, said to have been used as portholes during Indian raids, with the inside ledges holding ammunition. The mantels and cupboards are said to resemble those of the House of the Seven Gables. The building was once known as the 'Temple of the Sun' and used as a Masonic Hall.

The JOHNSON HOUSE, also known as the PORTER DANNER HOUSE, East St. between Craven and North Sts., a buff-gray stuccoed ante-bellum edifice, set in a garden of luxurious shrubs and trees, overlooks the water front. It has a two-story portico over a high arcaded basement and octagonal columns with simplified caps and bases. The second-floor balcony is balustraded and the flat parapeted roof has arched drip molds.

The OAKS, Short St. between King and Prince Sts., is a typical Beaufort plantation house. The two-story piazzas extend across the front and both ends, with six octagonal columns on each floor, and the roof is surmounted by a square-windowed cupola. Built in 1856 by Colonel Paul Hamilton, the house was among those deserted by the family in 1861. They returned in a mule-drawn wagon in September 1865, and resumed their residence only because Mrs. Hamilton's brother rented it for them; former owners could not rent their own property.

When the house was auctioned in November, Colonel Hamilton declared that he would bid to $1,000,000 to save his home from the possibility of becoming a normal school for Negroes. The property was knocked down to the colonel with payment to be made within three days, this period allowing for a boat trip to Charleston to secure funds. On the second day, however, the colonel's little son ran home with the news that the house would be sold at sunset. Mr. George Holmes, a Northern merchant, led other indignant citizens in hastily raising the money before sunset, and the house was bought in the name of Colonel Hamilton. Describing the incident, the colonel's daughter, Mary S. Hamilton, wrote: 'I had said that I would never shake hands with a Yankee, but that night across the counter I offered mine in thanks to Mr. Holmes.'

The CROFUT HOUSE, Short St. between Prince and Duke Sts., built in the late 1850's by Dr. Barnwell Sams, is of brick in variegated colors with a flat roof ornamented by a brick parapet. The two-story portico, also topped with a flat roof and balustrade, instead of the customary pediment, has four lugubrious columns.

The FRIPP HOUSE, Short St. between Prince and Duke Sts., an ante-bellum residence built by Edgar Fripp, has a story of how it was restored to its owner, James Fripp, brother of the builder, that illustrates how the hearts even of strangers were touched by Beaufort's tragic situation after the war. Like many others, the house was being sold for taxes and its owner returned from the war just in time to watch the sale with bitter tears because he could not buy his own home. A Frenchman had been living there and it was he who bid in the place, kissed Fripp on both cheeks, presented him with the deed, and slipped away, never to return.

The TABBY RUINS, NE. corner Hamilton and Duke Sts., are the remains of a mansion built in 1820 and owned by Thomas Talbird. It was burned in 1907 and its blackened walls are now covered with ivy and almost hidden by undergrowth.

CHAPLIN COURT, NE. corner Washington and New Sts., a yellow frame two-story house over a high brick basement, built in ante-bellum days and remodeled in 1931, has a rather bizarre feature in its external stairway leading to the second floor. The builder was John Chaplin, eight of whose 22 children were Confederate soldiers.

ST. HELENA EPISCOPAL CHURCH (*open daily*), Church St. between North and King Sts., of brick, stuccoed and coursed to resemble masonry, was built in 1724 for a parish organized in 1712. The building has been twice enlarged, and its tottering steeple, which is said to have been 118 feet high, was removed in 1866. A substitute square frame tower has served for many years since then. Plans were under way in 1940 for a more appropriate spire, for which one parishioner subscribed $10,000. The fanlighted entrance is flanked by pilasters and arched windows, and two side entrances, supported by smooth white Doric columns, lead to large interior galleries around the rear and sides. A semicircular apse with domed ceiling contains the altar and chancel. The silver communion plate, given by Captain John Bull in memory of his wife who was carried off by the Yamasee Indians in the uprising of 1715, is still owned by the church. Tombstones from the surrounding burial ground served as operating tables when St. Helena's was used during the War between the States as a hospital.

The shady graveyard holds among its many old tombs that of John Barnwell, who came here from Ireland in 1701 and won the sobriquet of 'Tuscarora Jack' for his successful leadership of a campaign in North Carolina to subdue Tuscarora Indian uprisings. In addition to being a distinguished Indian fighter, he was chosen as a diplomatic representative to present the cause of the colonists in England when South Carolina revolted in 1719 against the Lords Proprietors. Lieutenant General R. H. Anderson, C.S.A., is also buried here.

The BAPTIST CHURCH, Charles St. between King and Prince Sts., was built in 1844 and designed in the Classical Revival style with columns and enclosed portico. Its rectangular plan is typical of Baptist churches. The stucco is coursed to simulate masonry and the pediment, containing a circular window, is surmounted by a massive square bell tower. A Sunday school building near by is patterned after the church. Julia Baker, Beaufort poet and author of *Mizpah,* is buried in the churchyard, among gravestones dated in the first years of the 1800's.

The church was organized in 1780. The congregation split in 1811, and the withdrawing membership built the Tabernacle Church on Craven Street. A reunion was shortly afterward effected and the Tabernacle Church used for evening services. The slave membership here numbered 3,317 in 1857, with only 182 white members. The building served as a hospital during the War between the States.

The EDMUND RHETT HOUSE, NE. corner Church and Craven Sts., built after the Revolution by Milton Maxcy and remodeled by Edmund Rhett before 1861, is a cream-colored two-story structure of frame over an arcaded basement, with fine iron grills in the arches. The two-deck piazza has an interesting treatment of superimposed orders, fluted Corinthian columns surmounting Ionic columns on the first floor. The house is distinctly Greek Revival in conception and treatment, with modifications characteristic of plantation homes. Here Barnwell Rhett is said to have drawn up a draft of the Ordinance of Secession.

The LA FAYETTE BUILDING, NW. corner Bay and Scott Sts., is an unpainted frame Greek Revival house with two stories over a high basement. La Fayette spoke from the piazza, in 1825, when he was a guest of the Verdiers, whose descendants have owned the house continuously since it was built in the late 1700's by John Mark Verdier. The taste and refinement of the builder are revealed in a rear Palladian window at the turn of the stairs, and in the paneled walls and ceiling molds. The narrow front portico has a pediment and Roman Doric columns, with Ionic pilasters.

The ELLIOTT HOME, Bay St., middle house between Charles and New Castle Sts., of white frame, has a large double piazza across the front, with columns and balustrade; a small dormer window surmounts the flat piazza roof. This house was moved from William Trescot's plantation on Barnwell Island (now Big Island) and occupies the site of a former county courthouse. It is one of two homes on the bay brought by boat from neighboring islands.

SEA ISLAND HOTEL, E. corner Bay and New Castle Sts., built about 1820 by George Mosse Stoney, has received additions and extensions that include colonnaded piazzas around three sides of the raised-basement house, added in 1872, and supported by square stuccoed brick piers. Particularly notable are the entrance details, with elliptical fanlights and side lights.

The ANCHORAGE, occupying a triangle formed by Bay, New Castle, and Craven Sts., finished in gray stucco, has an imposing Classical Revival façade with six Corinthian columns surmounted by a balustraded flat roof and recessed pediment which contains an elliptical-headed window. A local characteristic is the broad flight of entrance steps and arcaded high basement story. The design is enriched by a corbelled cornice. William Elliott built the house presumably before the Revolution, since his dwelling in Beaufort is mentioned in his will of 1778. Twice have retired admirals of the United States Navy owned the property, and the enlarging and stuccoing of the building have left it little like the original.

The TABBY MANSE, E. corner of Bay and Harrington Sts., built by Thomas Fuller soon after 1786, is a two-story hip-roofed house over a high basement and is constructed of tabby with buff-colored stucco. The two-story portico, with slender columns and flared steps, provides a pleasing feature of the symmetrical façade. Set well back from the street, its trees and shrubbery form a charming approach.

The LEE HOUSE, W. corner Bay and Harrington Sts., a white frame structure with clapboard construction, has two-story piazzas extending around both ends, interior chimneys, and a hip roof. A transom and side lights enhance the entrance. The house is believed to be a pre-Revolutionary Jenkins plantation home formerly on St. Helena Island, and to have been moved to Beaufort after it became Rhett property.

The McLEOD HOUSE, W. corner Bay and Wilmington Sts., amid dogwood, japonicas, and oaks, behind a white picket fence, presents an imposing front. Six tall Doric columns run through two stories and form breaks in the two-deck piazza. The parapet above has a pierced balustrade of unique design and the hip roof on the main part of the house has a low pitch. A stairway at the side leads to the piazza.

During Federal occupation this house was a Union hospital and afterwards the headquarters and residence for the special agent of the U. S. Treasury Department. In 1865 it was Major Blair's headquarters, and later was used again as a hospital.

The BEAUFORT COUNTY COURTHOUSE, Bay St. between Monson and Bladen Sts., of monolithic concrete in severely chaste design, is a surprisingly modern note in the midst of Beaufort's older architecture and aged oaks. The tall second-floor windows are set in recessed panels and the projecting entrance porches are enhanced with fluted pilaster panels and, like the building, have flat roofs. Remodeling in 1936 was accomplished with local and Federal Government funds. In summer open-air concerts are given by the Parris Island Marine Band on a stand opposite the courthouse.

POINTS OF INTEREST IN ENVIRONS

Port Royal, 3.6 *m.;* The Retreat, 5.4 *m.;* Parris Island, 7.6 *m.;* Sheldon Church, 15.5 *m.;* Tomotley Plantation, 16.5 *m.;* Pocotaligo, 17.7 *m.* (*see Tour 5c*). Ladies Island, 0.5 *m.;* St. Helena Island, 5 *m.;* Hunting Island State Park, 16.4 *m.;* Penn Normal, Industrial, and Agricultural (Negro) School, 7.5 *m.* (*see Tour 5C*).

Camden

Railroad Stations: 0.5 m. W. on US 1, for Seaboard Air Line Ry.; DeKalb St. E. of Mill St., for Southern Ry.
Bus Station: Corner of DeKalb and Lyttleton Sts., for Atlantic Greyhound and Stokes Bus Lines.
Airport: 2.5 m. NE. on US 1; taxi fare 50¢; no scheduled service.
Taxis: 25¢ within city limits.

Accommodations: 5 hotels; numerous boarding houses.

Information Service: Chamber of Commerce, Crocker Bldg., NW. corner DeKalb and Broad Sts.

Motion Picture Houses: 2.
Polo: No. 1 Field, N. of Kirkwood Hotel, between Greene St. and Seaboard Air Line Ry. tracks; new field 1 m. SW. on DeKalb St. (US 1) within city limits.
Golf: Kirkwood Hotel course, 18 holes, N. of No. 1 Polo Field, grass greens; greens fees vary with season.
Horseback: Kirkwood Hotel Riding Academy at hotel, Greene St. W. of Broad St.; Floyd Stables, No. 1 Polo Field, for polo ponies. Numerous individuals board and stable horses.
Football: Municipal Field, Fair Grounds, bounded by Bull, Fair, Meeting, and Mill Sts., day and night games.
Baseball: Fair Grounds, adjacent to Football Field; Grammar School Field, Fair and Laurens Sts.
Recreation Field: Grammar School field, Fair and Laurens Sts.

Annual Events: Fox and drag hunts 3 times weekly, Jan., Feb., and March; polo, regular games every Sun., polo fields, Dec., Jan., March, and Apr.; hunter trials, horse shows, and related events during tourist season; Washington Birthday Races, Steeplechasing, and Flat races, Springdale Course, Feb. 22; Community Barbecue, May; Cotton Festival, Sept.; Christmas Festival, mid-Dec.

CAMDEN (222 alt., 5,183 pop.), seat of Kershaw County and one of the oldest inland towns in the State, lies in the heart of the sandhill, long-leaf pine section near the Wateree River. Camden's fame as a winter resort substantiates the saying of J. F. D. Smyth, an Englishman traveling in America soon after the Revolution: 'Here all the inclemency of the weather is in summer.' The annual mean temperature is 62.8°, winter temperature 47.5°, and there is an average of 267 days of sunshine a year.

Surrounded by battlefields and containing battlefields within its corporate limits, Camden, a thriving trade and industrial center, retains its flavor of age. At the southern end of Main Street, the broad business thoroughfare, dignified public buildings and old homes under spreading elms remain from the day when this was the center of town; modern growth has spread northward. During the lucrative tourist season, when visitors flock to join the inhabitants in their time-honored enthusiasm for all equestrian sports, the charm of the Old South is paradoxically combined with sporting Long Island. But in spite of its fashionable crowd, its polo games, its races, and its hunts, Camden retains its individuality.

Some of the finest homes, set back in extensive grounds, are almost hidden by the generous plantings in their beautifully planned old gardens. Architecture ranges from typical plantation houses to modern bungalows. Reminiscent of Charleston design are some tall, narrow houses, with entrances leading directly from the sidewalk into secluded side piazzas. Majestic pines along the quiet streets and in the six parks heighten the sylvan atmosphere. In Camden there is room to breathe, and the air is redolent of clean pine woods.

The settlement here began in 1733-4, when a few English families settled along the Wateree River. They were joined in 1750-1 by Irish Quakers, who called their scattered colony Friends' Neck. Concentration came in 1758 with the establishment of Joseph Kershaw's store, and the settlement became known as Pine Tree Hill. By 1760 Kershaw was milling 'Carolina flour,' operating saw and gristmills, indigo works, a tobacco warehouse, and a distillery. Camden's name was selected in 1768 to honor Charles Pratt, Earl of Camden, Colonial Rights champion, and the community was incorporated in 1791.

As early as 1756 Camden's 'porcelain earth' was shipped to British potters. Recognizing superior material, Josiah Wedgwood expressed fear at the possible establishment of Camden potteries. Richard Champion, maker of famous Bristol Ware, attracted by the clay, settled in Camden in 1782, but never established a pottery. Today this clay is used as ordinary earth in highway construction.

Following the fall of Charles Town, Cornwallis entered Camden, June 1, 1780, and made it the principal British garrison in the State. For a year its streets were bloody with the execution of American prisoners. Fourteen Revolutionary battles were waged in the vicinity. The most important was the Battle of Camden, August 16, 1780, called America's most disastrous defeat, resulting in the ignominious routing of General Gates by Lord Rawdon, and the mortal wounding of General DeKalb.

General Nathanael Greene, who had superseded General Gates in command December 1780, advanced on Camden and arrived in its vicinity on April 19, 1781. With only about 1,500 men he did not feel strong enough to attack the fortifications and withdrew to Hobkirk Hill, where on April 25 Lord Rawdon, with slightly less than 1,000 men, took him partly by surprise and drove him from the field. Casualties were about equal—American 271; British 258. Through chinks in the stockade jail, Andrew Jackson, 13-year-old future President, imprisoned by the British, watched the fight. After militia raids had captured British posts and almost destroyed communication between Camden and Charles Town, Rawdon burned, then evacuated Camden in May 1781.

After the Revolution, people of wealth and culture established estates along the wide streets laid out through fragrant pine woods. Washington was fittingly entertained in one mansion in 1791; La Fayette was royally welcomed in another in 1825.

A series of disastrous fires, beginning in 1812, and a malaria epidemic in 1816 were factors in the gradual abandonment of the original low site. Hilly Kirkwood, a village laid out in 1818 as a summer resort and named for Captain Robert Kirkwood, whose Delaware troops fought on Camden battlefields, has become the fashionable district.

Six Confederate generals were born in Camden, again war-torn in the years 1861–5. An important railroad terminus, it became a Confederate storehouse, hospital, and haven of refuge, until burned by Sherman, February 24, 1865.

In Reconstruction days Camden statesmen were leaders. Kershaw County claims commencement of the 'Straightout' movement April 4, 1876. 'Straightouts' favored an all-Democratic ticket; Conservatives advocated some Republican nominees to preserve peace. The 'Straightouts' swept the State, electing Hampton as governor.

For nearly a century Camden, noted for its duels, was the mecca for gentlemen seeking instruction in the code of honor, until the Cash-Shannon duel in 1880 caused the adoption of the antidueling law still retained in the State constitution.

Development of the city as a winter resort began in the 1880's and is steadily progressing. Many visitors have become permanent residents, writers and artists finding congeniality among talented natives, and reveling in the fairyland that spring makes of surrounding peach orchards and the flame of blackjack oaks in fall.

Two textile mills, one cottonseed oil plant, an iron and brass foundry, a veneer plant, and three lumber mills flourish in Camden, and it is also the market-place for a considerable agricultural and garden produce area. The city instituted an annual three-day Cotton Festival in 1938. With cotton displayed in bales and in decorative effects, the September event begins on a Sunday with home-comings in all local churches. During the festival the town is ruled by an honorary farmer mayor and six farmer councilmen. Features of the week are amusing contests, a parade of floats, the crowning of a beauty queen, and a carnival street dance. Another recent accomplishment is the fine recreation area at the Fair Grounds, with a seating capacity of 5,000 at the football field, and a baseball field adjoining, with grandstand seating 3,500 and a well-equipped field house. Here the Syracuse club of the International League trains every March and April.

POINTS OF INTEREST

The LA FAYETTE CEDAR, Broad St. between DeKalb and La Fayette Sts., near the new courthouse, is the sole survivor of a group planted to ornament the grounds of the new home of Congressman John Carter, built in 1824. There La Fayette was entertained March 8, 1825, when he came by invitation of Camden Masons to lay the De

Kalb monument cornerstone. In La Fayette's honor Camden's best plate and mahogany were sent to Carter's. Of a set of china specially made a few pieces remain. Carter's house, known as La Fayette Hall, burned in 1903.

IVY LODGE (*open*), 1205 Broad St., a three-story Charleston-style house built about 1780, has a brick and stucco first story, frame second and third stories, with wide beaded siding. The street entrance to the piazza has freestanding columns, pediment, and fanlight. This was once the home of Dr. Simon Baruch, Surgeon in the Army of Northern Virginia, who moved from Camden to New York in 1881. He performed the first recorded successful operation for the removal of a perforated appendix, and was given credit by the New York Academy of Science for the development of appendectomy. Camden's hospital is his memorial, given by his son, Bernard M. Baruch.

GREENLEAF VILLA, 1307 Broad St., built by Samuel Flake in 1803 and resembling the Charleston house of 1780–1830, is set in elaborately landscaped old gardens enclosed by a wisteria-covered wall. The piazza entrance, with pilasters supporting a Classic entablature, opens directly on the sidewalk and the two-story piazzas have columns, balustrades, and a flat roof. After 1826 the house was the home of Doctor Lee, General Lee's cousin, who used it as a Confederate hospital. Fired by Union soldiers in 1865, it was saved by Mrs. Lee, who directed a bucket brigade of servants and neighbors.

The DICKINSON MONUMENT, Monument Square, corner Laurens and Broad Sts., an Italian marble shaft surmounted by a helmet and laurel wreath, was erected in 1856 to honor James Polk Dickinson, Mexican War hero and Colonel of the Palmetto Regiment, who died from wounds received August 1847 at Churubusco.

The KIRKWOOD HOTEL, Greene St. W. of Broad St. in Camden Heights, Camden's finest tourist hotel, is a large wooden edifice, its central part the old Kennedy mansion, with the original portico, columns, and cornice intact. Surrounded by golf courses, it rises on the battlefield of Hobkirk Hill. Close by, at the corner of Broad and Greene Streets, a brick wall protects the crumbling brick that marks British soldiers' graves.

HOBKIRK INN, Lyttleton St. facing Greene St., set back on shady grounds, is one of Camden's oldest hostelries, opened in the 1880's and since remodeled. Its central part, with columns and balustrade of Colonial type on a one-story piazza, was originally 'Pine Flat,' home of Colonel William Shannon, killed in the State's last legal duel, July 5, 1880. The site, part of the battlefield of Hobkirk Hill, was granted Thomas Hobkirk in 1769. As late as 1900, Revolutionary relics were unearthed here and bullets were found embedded in the old trees.

PANTHEON TO CONFEDERATE GENERALS, Kershaw Square, on Chesnut St. between Lyttleton and Fair Sts., is a vine-covered pergola supported by six concrete columns with bronze tablets in honor of Camden's Confederate generals: Cantey, Chesnut, Deas, Kennedy, Kershaw, and Villepigue. The base for the columns forms a pool centered by a fountain. Surrounding are four old cannon; two, bearing the French fleur-de-lis, were reputedly captured at Louisburg, Nova Scotia.

COURT INN, Mill St. at E. end of Laurens St., surrounded by old gardens famous in the State, is a rambling two-story frame house. Now much altered, it was built in 1830 for Mrs. John C. McRae and called Upton Court, but was soon bought by Richard Lloyd Champion for his daughter, Mrs. J. M. DeSaussure, whose husband named it Lausanne after his ancestral home in Switzerland. A Peale portrait of Washington, now in the Corcoran Gallery of Art, Washington, hung at Lausanne, where La Fayette admired it in 1825 and where it later narrowly escaped destruction by Sherman's men.

To Lausanne clings the legend of the 'Grey Lady,' ghost of Eloise DeSaussure, who pined away in a French convent, where her Roman Catholic father confined her because she loved a Huguenot. A gentle soul, she nevertheless pronounced a curse on her parent, who committed suicide when his wife died soon after his daughter. The 'Grey Lady' first appeared to Eloise's brothers in Europe the night before the Huguenot massacre in 1572. Disguised as a monk, one escaped to America. When tragedy forbodes, the 'Grey Lady' still appears at Lausanne.

As young people gathered here to dance in April 1865, news of Lee's surrender arrived and Major DeSaussure's daughter lit the gas with Confederate paper money.

Lausanne was bought by Mrs. Roger Griswold (Caroline Jumelle) Perkins in 1884. A pioneer in Camden's development as a winter resort, she named her home Court Inn and accommodated tourists therein.

The METHODIST CHURCH, Lyttleton St. between Laurens and DeKalb Sts., is of stuccoed brick with stone quoins on the corners, and Norman style stained-glass windows with heavy mullions. The main entrance is arched and set in a bell tower, the principal feature of the building. An interior tablet honors Samuel Mathis (1769–1825), 'first white male born in Camden,' who, although a Quaker, fought in the Revolution. Built in 1879, the church occupies lands given in 1851 by members who also gave three slaves for the parson's use. Camden Methodists held their first services in 1787 in private homes and built their first church between 1800 and 1804.

A MARBLE HORSE TROUGH, Hampton Park, NE. corner De-Kalb and Lyttleton Sts., now flower-filled, was erected by Camden school children and the National Humane Society to Howard Kirkland, C.S.A., for carrying water to suffering foes under hostile guns at Fredericksburg in 1862. He fell at Chickamauga, aged 20.

Revolutionary cannon thundered welcome to General Wade Hampton at his Red Shirt campaign meeting here in 1876.

BETHESDA PRESBYTERIAN CHURCH, DeKalb St. between Broad and Lyttleton Sts., was designed in 1820 by Robert Mills. The charm and dignity of this red brick church, with circular-headed windows and gable roof, reflect the taste of its architect, a leading American proponent of the Greek Revival. Mills, in his *Statistics of South Carolina* (1826), says the building has 'a portico of four Doric columns in front and a neat spire in the rear, containing a bell . . . the floor and pews rise as they recede from the pulpit, giving every advantage to the audience, both in seeing and hearing.' The pulpit, with twin steps, stands between two front doors, the main entrance being at the rear; the pews are gated. Originally there were five rear porches. On lands bequeathed by Joseph Kershaw, the Presbyterians had Camden's first church about 1771. The first building was destroyed during the Revolution.

The DE KALB MONUMENT, Broad St. between Lyttleton and Market Sts., a squat obelisk on a square base, was designed by Robert Mills and dedicated in 1825 by La Fayette, whom Baron DeKalb accompanied to America in 1777. Born John Kalb, a German peasant of Alsace, the soldier joined the French army, added the 'de' to his name and assumed the title of baron to insure promotion, then dependent in France on social rank. DeKalb, in command of the American Army in the South until replaced by Gates, fresh from his triumph at Saratoga, fell at the Battle of Camden.

The INDIAN WEATHERVANE, City Hall tower, corner Broad and Rutledge Sts., the gilded iron figure of an Indian, honors King Haigler, a Catawba chief, friend and benefactor of Camden Quakers in 1753. He fought with the Americans against the Cherokee in 1759, and was killed from ambush by the Shawnee in 1765. The weathervane, made by J. B. Mathieu, and the four-faced city clock beneath it were placed in 1826 on the old market steeple and later moved twice. The town bell was cast in 1824 by John Willbank of Philadelphia, and formerly sounded the nine o'clock curfew for slaves.

The OLD POWDER MAGAZINE, Church St. between Rutledge and York Sts., has 22-inch brick walls, strengthened with iron bolts running through and fastened outside with S-bolts, and the original lock and hinges on its old door. Tin now covers the roof. The interior wall is inscribed: 'James Langley, Builder, June 13/59.' The magazine was probably built for storing State militia ammunition for use in slave uprisings. In 1816 the plot for a contemplated revolt was revealed by a slave to his master, Colonel Chesnut. The loyal Negro was purchased by a legislative appropriation in 1817 and granted his freedom, with $50 annually for life. When the town adopted the building, the old ammunition was dumped at Magazine Hill.

The OLD COURTHOUSE, now the Masonic Hall, Broad St. between King and Bull Sts., designed by Robert Mills and erected in 1826, is a two-story buff-colored stuccoed brick building with corner pilasters, Classic frieze, gable roof, and pedimented portico. A broad flight of steps with iron handrail leads to the second-floor balcony in the portico. The four Greek Doric columns were substituted in 1847 for the original six sandstone Ionic columns of the portico, capitals of the latter being used as carriage blocks. This is Camden's third courthouse.

In the first, built in 1771 and burned by Tories in 1779, a 'Little Declaration of Independence' was drawn up, November 5, 1774.

As late as 1881 cows, grazing on streets, sought nightly refuge in the courthouse basement.

The FAIR GROUNDS, Mill St. between Bull and Meeting Sts., accommodated Camden's first fair in 1775. To the rear stood Kershaw's store, built in 1758, and his mansion, which was built in 1780, used as British headquarters 1780–1, and afterwards called Cornwallis House. From the second-story windows American prisoners were hanged on beams. Later a State storehouse for Confederate supplies, the edifice was burned by Sherman's men in 1865.

Near by is MAGAZINE HILL, originally Pine Tree Hill, its later name arising from a Revolutionary magazine used as a State storehouse and fortified with earthworks. The British converted it into a redoubt and partially destroyed it upon evacuation. Greene later demolished it to prevent recapture. All that remains is a heap of broken brick on a star-shaped mound, surrounded by a ditch that was once a deep moat.

The QUAKER CEMETERY, between Wyly and Campbell, Wateree and Meeting Sts., was established in 1759 on land granted by Samuel Wyly, Quaker leader, after the Meeting House was built, and has been enlarged to include all denominations. The grounds were laid out in ante-bellum years by Crammond, a Scotch landscape gardener who designed most of Camden's loveliest gardens. Quaker graves are marked only by arching brick, because they considered monuments ostentatious.

Around an inconspicuous stone, engraved for 'Agnes of Glasgow,' who died in 1780, aged 20, hangs one of Camden's memorable legends. Cornwallis himself is said to have attended the funeral and ordered the monument for the girl, who is reputed either to have followed her lover across seas, arriving just before or just after his death, and later to have become merely a camp follower, or to have been Cornwallis's mistress. Illness and death soon overtook her in Camden.

POINTS OF INTEREST IN ENVIRONS

Mulberry Plantation, 2.5 *m.;* Site of Battle of Camden, 6.9 *m.;* Haile Gold Mine, 23 *m.;* Ingram Home, 26.2 *m.* (*see Tour* 4). Forest Tree Nursery, 2.3 *m.;* Indian Mound, 3.2 *m.;* Sesqui-Centennial State Park, 21.6 *m.;* Sugar Loaf and Horseshoe Mountains, 38.1 *m.* (*see Tour* 6a).

Charleston

Railroad Stations: Union Station, Columbus and Bay Sts., for Southern Ry. and Atlantic Coast Line R.R.; Grove St. and Rutledge Ave., for Seaboard Air Line Ry.
Bus Station: 85–91 Society St. for Greyhound and East Coast Stages. 99 St. Philip St. for Gray Line (local tours).
Airport: Municipal Airport, 10 m. N., W. of US 52, for Eastern Airlines and Delta; taxi $1, time 30 min.; Seaplane Base, Ashley River, W. of Yacht Basin; Coast Guard Plane Base, S. of Navy Yard on Cooper River.
Busses: Fare 5¢.
Taxis: 10¢ upward, according to number of passengers and distance.
Piers: On Ashley River—Municipal Yacht Basin, W. end of Calhoun St.; US Lighthouse Depot, W. end Tradd St.; steamer to Fort Sumter, S. end of King St. On Cooper—16 piers, from Carolina Yacht Club, 50 E. Bay St., to Columbus St. Wharves, including Clyde-Mallory, E. end Queen St.; steamer to Mount Pleasant, E. end Cumberland St.; Union Pier, E. end Pinckney St.; US Customhouse, SE. corner East Bay and Market Sts.; Charleston Shipbuilding & Dry Dock Co., 106 Concord St.
Traffic Regulations: Turns may be made in either direction at intersections of all streets except where traffic officers or lights direct otherwise; watch street signs for parking limitations and one-way streets; chief one-way street (N. to S.) King St., between Calhoun and Broad, and its tributaries.

Accommodations: 9 hotels; rates higher during winter and early spring.

Information Service: Chamber of Commerce, 50 Broad St.; Francis Marion Hotel, NW. corner King and Calhoun Sts.; American Automobile Ass'n (AAA), Charleston Hotel, 198 Meeting St., with branch office at Fort Sumter Hotel, corner King St. and Murray Boulevard.

Theaters and Motion Picture Houses: Dock Street Theater, SW. corner Church and Queen Sts.; 8 motion picture houses.
Athletic Field: Johnson Hagood Stadium, W. end Congress St.
Swimming: Municipal pool, George St., between Meeting and Anson Sts.; Folly Beach, 2 m. W. on US 17, 8.8 m. S. on Folly Beach road; Sullivan's Island, 4.9 m. E. on US 17, 3.1 m. S. on State 703; Isle of Palms, 4.9 m. E. on US 17, 9.6 m. S. on State 703. Bus service to all beaches; to Folly Island, June 1 through Labor Day only.
Golf: Municipal Golf Club, US 17 and Folly Beach road right on Riverland Terrace turn-off, L. on Johns Island road; greens fee 50¢, caddy 50¢, $1 for 18 holes including caddy.
Riding: St. Andrew's Parish, 3 m. W. on US 17, 7 m. NW. on State 61 (R).

Annual Events: Artists' Street Exhibit, in early spring. Azalea Festival, depending on date of Easter; tilting tournament, street callers' contests, parades, dances, pageants. Schutzenfest, by Carolina Rifle Club, 1st week in May. Annual Regatta, under the auspices of the Carolina Yacht Club, early summer. Charleston Kennel Club Dog Show, Oct.; Charleston Agricultural and Industrial Fair, late Oct. or Nov., Johnson Hagood Stadium, Congress St., between Parkwood St. and Citadel Ave. Horse shows at intervals.

CHARLESTON (9 alt., 62,265 pop.), on a narrow peninsula extending into a broad bay, with the Atlantic Ocean about three miles distant, is almost detached from the State in which it has always been the chief city. 'Charleston is the place where the Ashley and Cooper Rivers meet to form the Atlantic Ocean,' is the traditional geography lesson of a Charleston child—a lesson as significant as it is descriptive.

From the height of 152 feet on the double-spanned Cooper River bridge, a view of the city below discloses ancient and lovely homes facing southward, trade depots on the two river fronts, between which run three railroad lines and a double-lane highway to connect 'The City' with the interior. Along narrow crooked streets, a few still cobble-stoned, rise block after block of two- and three-story buildings, topped by old-fashioned chimney pots. Three church spires, soaring above the others, and two modern skyscrapers break the low skyline. Southward lies the old city, and northwest is 'The Neck,' as the strip from Calhoun Street to the crook in the Ashley River was originally called. Scarified now by railroads, and congested with phosphate plants, oil refineries, and other industrial establishments, with their accompanying laborers' homes and garish eating places, 'The Neck' has its traditions of former suburban plantation homes, and of Indian, British, and Federal attacks.

King Street, the principal thoroughfare, follows the old King's Highway through the entire length of the city, its upper stretch a region of odd little shops operated by proprietors representing the 2 per cent foreign population. Meeting Street, the companion mercantile artery, parallels King through Charleston, joining it north of the limits in a national highway. The southern extremities of both thoroughfares are lined with distinguished residences and begin at South Battery.

In Charleston, it is important to live 'below Broad Street,' and outsiders believe that to live on, or to claim relationship with one who lives 'on the Battery,' is a Charlestonian's prime distinction. Here the Ashley and Cooper Rivers meet to form the water front noted even in Europe for its beauty, and called since the War of 1812 'The Battery.' The high east seawall was built before 1820 of ballast rocks from trading vessels, replacing a barrier of palmetto logs swept away in 1804; between 1848 and 1852 the south wall was added. An oyster-shell beach that tipped the peninsula gave way in 1830 to White Point Gardens, now sharing the more familiar name of this locality. Since the first seaside boardwalk in the United States was only rough boards atop the log barrier, this has been Charleston's fashionable promenade.

Above the driveways, sentineled by swishing palmettos, the railed sidewalks along both East and South Battery are still a favorite place to stroll, to pause and look out over the landlocked harbor at Castle Pinckney, Fort Sumter, and the site of old Fort Johnson on James Island—which have all helped to defend the seaport against invasion. As a grim reminder, a man-of-war rides the waves beside a masted schooner; saucy little sailboats glide between. Under the live-oaks in the landscaped gardens, Charleston children, guarded by white-turbaned Negro 'maumas,' play among monuments and guns that recall the city's war-torn history of more than 250 years. Near this peaceful park in 1718, 49 pirates swung from the gallows in one month; 22 ghastly figures, including the notorious Stede Bonnet's, dangled there one day. This was the visible proof that Colonel William Rhett and Governor Robert Johnson had rid the coast of these persistent buccaneers. A modern tourist hotel towers over the Battery—evidence that its visitors are of economic importance to Charleston.

The westward marshlands of the Ashley have been reclaimed in the twentieth century for a fashionable residential section. Along South Battery old houses, with lawns formerly stretching to the seawall, now find themselves separated from the water by a block of modern homes. Murray Boulevard, an extension of the sea drive, forms a continuous avenue of palmettos, with a landscaped parkway between traffic lanes.

Charleston architecturally retains its eighteenth-century aspect, showing the character of the best English work of the time, with certain later concessions to the subtropical climate, chiefly the gallery, or piazza, and the high basement, forming a full story on the ground level. Many tall old dwellings, with steep slate roofs, are of stuccoed brick. Most of them, locally known as 'single houses,' are built flush with the sidewalk, turning their shoulders to the street to insure the occupants that privacy that is as sacred to the Charlestonian's soul as his ancestors or his rice. Their paneled and transomed outer portals, cut through a curtain wall, lead into a long open piazza at one side. The piazzas, with from one to three superimposed galleries, usually face south to catch the breeze. Long ago a visitor to the city gave an apt description: 'Houses stand sidewaies backward into their yard and only endwaies, with their gables toward the Street.' 'Double houses,' of the symmetrical center hall type, face the street.

Wrought-iron gateways in high brick walls give inviting glimpses of old gardens, sleeping in the sun. Almost the year round Charleston is a city of flowers. In the mild winter the green lawns of 'Charleston (sea island) grass' are bordered with pansies and daffodils, camellia-japonicas burst into bloom, sweet olives and the tiny golden fluff-balls of opopanax trees scent the soft air. Tourists throng the city in spring when wisteria, roses, feathery tamarisk, and magnolias join the riot of azaleas. Summer brings a profusion of oleanders, the lavender racemes of spikenard trees, crape myrtles, and altheas; the branches of celestial fig trees curve over the walls and drop their lush fruit on the sidewalks.

Owing to losses suffered during the Confederate era, some old residences have fallen into the hands of outsiders, though many are still owned by the descendants of the builders; and some have lapsed into disrepair. The salvaging efforts of the Society for the Preservation of Old Dwellings have borne visible fruit during the past decade, but the old period of plenitude has never returned. Numerous antique shops, sometimes operated by 'the quality,' indicate the compromise that Charleston has been forced to make with formerly abhorred 'trade.' It is said that the city was spared a golden-oak period because its residents, lacking money to buy the popular atrocities of the nineties, necessarily clung to their rosewood and mahogany.

In spite of its latter-day commercial traits, the city exhibits an old-fashioned courtesy even in its casual contacts with visitors, but the real Charleston is seldom touched or discovered by the stranger. There are few commercial places of entertainment and social life is centered in the homes of the people to a degree rarely found in America today.

The city is honeycombed by fascinating alleys that have now been reclaimed and are eagerly sought by white residents, though formerly they were occupied by Negroes, who compose 46 per cent of the population and live in scattered areas, many of them in upper Charleston. The Negroes earn a livelihood on the city's outskirts as small truck farmers, plantation hands, sawmill or fertilizer plant workers. Those near the salt rivers supplement their small earnings by fishing. Along streets no longer fashionable, clothes lines flap above abandoned gardens, and several Negro families are crowded into some tumble-down big houses, spilling their progeny out on the sidewalk. Few old dwellings occupied by the wealthier white families are without their servants' quarters in the rear. Many of these are now renovated for occupancy by white people with a love of the unusual; others are still used by the many domestics who have served Charlestonians in successive generations.

There are also many well-educated, prosperous Negroes in various professions and businesses. None of these was more respected by both races than the Reverend Daniel J. Jenkins, who founded the Jenkins Orphanage for destitute Negro children in 1891 and for a time personally supported it. The upkeep proved so expensive that the founder organized his more musical inmates into a band, which has become a permanent feature, and its street concerts, at which collections are taken up, invariably draw a delighted crowd. The smaller Negro boys, tooting their horns and wearing brass-buttoned uniforms, are supplemented by a quartette in evening regalia. The band makes annual tours of the United States and has made several to Canada and Europe. Since 1928 the Duke Endowment has contributed annually to the orphanage.

Of all the many slaves in ante-bellum Charleston, the Gullah Negroes spoke the most peculiar jargon, which through the years has passed from 'mauma' to white child, to stamp itself on the language of Charleston. It is fitting, however, that the speech of the city, like the atmosphere, should be just a little different. 'Charleston accent' is famous throughout the South. Though the native Charlestonian takes his time to think and to live, he talks with inconsistent rapidity. 'Garden' here is characteristically 'gyarden,' and 'car,' 'cyar,' while the 'a' of Charleston is fully as distinctive as that of Harvard. The genuine Gullah speech is easily discernible in the chants of street criers.

In the early morning Charlestonians are awakened by the rhythmic, melodious calling of Negro vendors hawking their wares. Shrimp tastes a little different, a little better, when bought from a dusky peddler who calls, as he passes the doorway—

Ro-ro swimp
Ro-ro swimp
Roro-ro-ro-ro-swimp
Come and git yo ro-ro swimp.

From the previous night's fishing of the 'mosquito fleet,' owned by Negroes, the vendors hawk their catch through the streets, singing an old song—

Porgy walk
Porgy talk
Porgy eat wid knife and fawk;
Porgie-e-e-e.

(Porgy is a small fish.)

The vegetable peddlers and the flower sellers also call, in Gullah cadence, from early morning until sundown. Negro children offer boiled peanuts for sale, or vary their proffered wares with insistent offers to dance 'the Susy-Q, the Charleston, the Black Bottom,' or to sing a 'church song,' all for a 'pinny.'

The street-criers' contest is a feature of the nine-day Azalea Festival in spring, Charleston's biggest annual event. This opens with a gorgeous parade of floats, some carrying the queens who represent every county in the State. On the closing night, prior to the grand ball, the festival queen is selected from the galaxy of beauties and crowned by the mayor for a year's reign over the old city, which even after nearly 300 years is South Carolina's social capital.

Charles Town, as it was originally called, was settled in 1670 by English pioneers who established themselves on Albemarle Point, westward across the Ashley River from the present location. Oyster Point was higher and better adapted for defense, and was selected for the site of the 'great port towne' laid out in 1672 by instructions of Lord Ashley-Cooper, one of the Lords Proprietors. The colony, increased meantime by settlers from Barbados, England, and Virginia, moved across the river in 1680 and Charles Town became a 'City State.' For many years its history was the history of South Carolina. It was the center from which colonizations radiated and the capital of the province until 1786, when Columbia was founded for that purpose.

The elaborately graded society planned by the Lords Proprietors (see History) proved too complicated for a new colony; but through wars, earthquakes, and depressions, remnants of the system have survived in distinctive cliques. Descendants of extensive landholders or prominent statesmen among early settlers cling to the family pride that neither misfortune nor modern invention has been able to shake. In Charleston what one is is important, but equally or more important—so it is said— is what one's ancestors have been and how much land they have held.

Provision crops, naval stores, and the Indian trade gave the colony its start; rice and later indigo brought it wealth, and Charleston became a flourishing urban center for opulent planters, who maintained 'country seats' on Low Country rivers.

The influx of French Huguenots and of French Catholics from Acadia in the seventeenth century gave the city a cosmopolitan atmosphere, which was increased in the eighteenth by the arrival of Scots and South Germans; the nineteenth century brought further immigrations of North Germans and Irish. A writer of this last period described Charleston as 'owned by the Germans, ruled by the Irish, and enjoyed by the Negroes.' The different creeds represented added breadth as well as variety to spiritual and intellectual life. Social ideas remained English, and an English gentry, recruited from planters, successful merchants, and tradesmen, grew up in the colony, achieving in three generations distinguished standards of education and political leadership. A public library, the first in the colonies, in 1698 (succeeded after its decline by the present Charleston Library Society in 1748), a free school in 1710, a theater in 1735, a group of professional men nationally and internationally known, and the practice by the wealthy of sending their sons to England or the Continent for training were the more obvious signs of this development.

About 1730 the first newspaper, the *South Carolina Weekly Journal,* was founded by Eleazer Phillips, Jr., and lasted six months. The *South-Carolina Gazette,* with Thomas Whitmarsh as editor and printer, first appeared January 8, 1731–2, and for over half a century its tiny sheets were spicy with gossip that interspersed news of the world. Whitmarsh died of 'strangers' (yellow) fever' in 1735, and the following year Benjamin Franklin sent Lewis Timothy, one of his printers, to take charge. In 1738 Timothy was succeeded by his widow; later her son, Peter Timothy, assumed the editorship until 1775. The paper was then suspended for two years and revived by Peter's son, Benjamin Franklin Timothy, as the *Gazette of the State of South Carolina,* continuing under that name and management until 1792. Its successor in 1803 was the *Courier,* antecedent of Charleston's present morning paper, the *News and Courier.*

An intimate tie-up with the Old World was evidenced in the correspondence of local scientists with famous European colleagues. Audubon considered Charleston his second home, where Dr. John Bachman was his collaborator. Agassiz spent two years here; Bartram collaborated with Chalmers of Charleston, and was an admirer of Catesby, an English scientist who formerly lived three years in the city. Dr. Alexander Garden, a Scottish physician for whom the gardenia was named, corresponded with Linnaeus. Arthur Hugh Clough, the English poet, spent his boyhood in Charleston, where his father was a cotton broker. André Michaux was called upon to lay out gardens, and the uncle of Rousseau is credited with planning the fortifications of 1736. Rousseau wrote that his uncle, Bernard, 'superintended the planning of the city of Charles Town, the plan of which he had designed,' but Rousseau evidently confused fortifications and city plans.

Because of their affiliation with the Mother Country and its traditions, many leading Charlestonians found it difficult to sever their British allegiance at the onset of the Revolution, but the first Provincial Congress of South Carolina, meeting at Charleston in 1775, secured strict loyalty to the American cause from most citizens. Christopher Gadsden,

John Rutledge, Henry and John Laurens, and other local leaders were active in the affairs of the new Nation (*see History*).

A British attack upon Charlestown, June 28, 1776, was repulsed by William Moultrie's brilliant defense of the palmetto fort on Sullivan's Island, but in 1780 the city fell into the hands of the British and was held for two-and-a-half years. The relationship of Charlestonians and the enemy was not, however, that of conqueror and conquered. Even in these circumstances Charlestown remembered its manners, and treated the British with courtesy, if not cordiality. Not until December 1782, after General Greene and the partisan leaders had cleared the rest of the State, was Charlestown evacuated by the enemy. The next year the city's name was changed from Charles Town to Charleston.

The Revolution aroused a vigorous democratic spirit among the mechanics of Charleston and the small farmers of the interior. In consequence, the planters, lawyers, and merchants, who had governed the province and the State, now found their control threatened. An incident in this contest was the removal of the capital to Columbia. Fear of these democrats, and the need of a stronger government to protect trade and invested money caused Charleston leaders to join heartily in the movement for a new Federal constitution, and years after the rest of the State had gone over to Jefferson's party, the city remained stiffly Federalist.

Charleston's prosperity increased during the great plantation era of post-Revolutionary years. J. F. D. Smyth, an Englishman traveling through the country then, wrote that 'for size, and beauty and trade (Charleston) may be considered one of the first cities in British America, and one in which the conveniences of luxury are most to be met with.' The city became noted in Europe and America as 'a flourishing capital of wealth and ease.' By 1791, Charleston gentlemen had two golf clubs, one of which is believed to have been organized four or five years earlier.

The embargo on trade accompanying the War of 1812 was a temporary setback, but when developing transportation deflected commerce to Savannah, Charleston launched the bold experiment of that pioneer among early steam roads, the South Carolina Railroad, built to the Savannah River opposite Augusta during the years 1830–3. Coincident with the beginning of the road was the establishment of the world's first department store in a mammoth building, now razed, at the corner of King and Market Streets.

The Southern fight for political power, however, was a losing one, and Charleston, welcoming the convention that passed the Ordinance of Secession, entered enthusiastically into the War between the States. The long siege of the city abounded with dramatic incidents: the defense of Fort Sumter; blockade running, of which this port was the Confederate center; submarine warfare, here first introduced by Confederates in 1863. After Sherman had demolished Columbia, in February 1865, the city was evacuated. Sherman had intimated his intention of destroying Charleston, but later plans turned him in another direction. Federal forces had bombarded the city heavily, however; public buildings and homes, particularly in the lower section, were badly damaged. Charleston was left poverty-stricken, its economic and social life utterly disrupted. There followed the long, hard struggle for recovery, a fight that succeeded without sacrificing the best of the old regime.

One of the most destructive events in Charleston's history was the earthquake of 1886, with damage to real estate estimated at between five and six million dollars. After the cataclysm, weakened buildings were strengthened with tie rods running between floors from wall to wall, still visible in surviving brick structures.

September 20, 1938, two tornadoes struck the city, killing 29, injuring many more, and wreaking property damage of more than $2,000,000. Though some of the most historic buildings and sites were damaged, none of the most notable were demolished. Again, in August 1940, the city was swept by a hurricane and the lower section flooded, but no important buildings were destroyed.

The important shipping trade, disrupted by war, returned but slowly. The bars in the harbor had no channel of the depth required by modern ships until 1880, when work was begun on the construction of jetties by Federal appropriation. One jetty extends from Sullivan's Island and the other from Morris Island, closing all channels but one, and causing an increased flow with a consequently increased depth in the remaining channel. With an inside depth ranging from 27 to 50 feet, the harbor can accommodate the largest battleships and has an anchorage for hundreds of vessels.

The water front of the Cooper River has fine dock facilities, controlled by the Port Utilities Commission of the City of Charleston. There are a few privately owned docks. The Columbus Street wharves have large docking and warehouse facilities. The port terminals above North Charleston, constructed during the World War for an army base, are used by a pulp and paper company.

The new international seaplane base, constructed with the aid of WPA funds, is near the mouth of the Ashley River. Charleston is listed as an alternate for transoceanic planes by the United States Post-Office Department. Due to favorable year-round conditions, Yankee and Pan-American Clippers used the base in the severe winter of 1940, when high winds and severe cold made landing at New York or Baltimore hazardous.

Charleston in 1938 had an estimated population of 88,176. Besides trade in timber, fruit, vegetables, and seafoods, it has 16 large fertilizer factories, one of the largest cigar factories in the country—manufacturing its own boxes—asbestos and rubber, paint and oil, cotton bagging factories, and other varied industries.

A low-rent housing project, developed in 1939 by the Charleston Housing Authority with Federal aid, is appropriately called Mills Manor, after Robert Mills, first Federal architect, a native of Charleston in 1781, though the site of his birthplace has never been determined. The area includes the old Marine Hospital, designed by Mills, and the gaunt and castlelike old jail, built 1783–1800, for which Mills later designed the rear octagonal extension. The hospital, opened in 1833 to succeed the first refuge for disabled seamen, used as early as 1802, was once the battleground in the old city's fight against yellow fever. Mills Manor includes parts of blocks in the section between Smith Street, west, and upper Logan, east; between Queen Street, south, to Magazine and continuing almost to Beaufain Street, north. On the site of such gruesome reminders of the past as the workhouse with its pillory and stocks, Potter's Field, and the poorhouse, a group of modern, sanitary homes rises today.

The best way to see the old section of the city is on foot. The narrow streets, some marked for one-way traffic, make sightseeing from a motor-car difficult. Moreover, the small alleys and lanes leading to secluded courts are rewarding to those who have the curiosity to poke about for local color and the unusual.

A peculiarly distinctive service to tourists is rendered by several Charleston ladies as guides to points of interest both in the city and among the many Low Country plantations near by. Charges are $2 to $3 per hour, depending upon whether the guest or the guide furnishes transportation. The 'lady guides' have no formal organization, but arrangements can be made through the Chamber of Commerce, the Historical Commission of Charleston, or the hotels.

POINTS OF INTEREST

1. ST. MICHAEL'S EPISCOPAL CHURCH (*open* 9–5 *daily*) 78 Meeting St., was begun in 1752 and, though its plan has been credited to a Mr. Gibson, the architect's name may have been properly James Gibbs, designer of St. Martin's-in-the-Fields, London, after which St. Michael's is patterned. White stucco-covered brick walls are adorned with Doric pilasters, and an octagonal tower, crowned by a steeple, rises 168 feet above the Doric portico on the front, a total of 182 feet from the ground. The tower holds a four-faced clock that has marked Charleston's time since 1764, and chimes that have crossed the ocean five times, that have pealed in triumph and in tragedy, their mellow tones still sounding the hours and ringing out familiar hymns on Sundays and special days. The bells, brought originally from England in 1764, were seized during the Revolution by the British, carried back to England in 1784, and eventually returned to Charleston, thus achieving three trips. In 1862 they were shipped to Columbia for safekeeping from Federal shells and stored in a shed on the State House grounds, where in 1865 they were partially destroyed in the burning of Columbia. The fragments were returned to England in 1866 and the chimes recast in the original molds by the successors of their makers. Their return to Charleston in 1867 made the fifth crossing.

The interior is impressive with rich mahogany-paneled choir railings and gated pews, a semicircular chancel with fluted Corinthian pilasters, painted domed ceiling, and octagonal pulpit, topped with a canopied sounding board. The windows are shaded by characteristic dark green louvered shutters, which spread in a graceful fan in the arched head of the window and fold back in long narrow panels, over the sash below. The white plaster ceiling is adorned with a classic fret band and modillioned cornice of unusually large scale.

St. Michael's is the first offspring of Charleston's mother church, St. Philip's, and occupies the site on which the original St. Philip's was built in 1681–2. The parish was divided in 1751 and the lower half named St. Michael's. Here both George Washington and La Fayette had reserved pews on their visits to Charleston, and here one of the first vested boys' choirs in this country was formed. Among mural tablets is one to Charles Cotesworth Pinckney, signer of the Constitution, whose grave is just behind the building in the churchyard.

An exceptionally fine wrought-iron gate leads from Broad Street into the graveyard. In the southwest corner the grave of Mary Layton is marked with the headboard of a cypress bedstead, which has withstood the elements for over a century. Two of many famous South Carolinians buried here are Robert Y. Hayne, nullification statesman, and James Louis Petigru, leading Unionist of South Carolina and considered the State's ablest lawyer of the day. A copy of his widely quoted epitaph was requested by Woodrow Wilson at the Peace Conference in France. Part of it reads:

> Unawed by Opinion,
> Unseduced by Flattery:
> Undismayed by Disaster,
> He confronted Life with antique Courage:
> And Death with Christian Hope:
> In the great Civil War
> He withstood his People for his Country:
> But his People did homage to the Man
> Who held his Conscience higher than their Praise:
> And his Country
> Heaped her Honours upon the Grave of the Patriot,
> To whom, living,
> His own righteous Self-Respect sufficed
> Alike for Motive and Reward.

2. SOUTH CAROLINA SOCIETY HALL (*open* 10–7:30 *weekdays;* 10:30–2 *and* 5–7 *Sun. during winter;* 10–5 *weekdays,* 10:30–2 *and* 5–6 *Sun. in summer*), 72 Meeting St., is a stately building erected in 1804 as a charity school and meeting place for one of the oldest benevolent societies in the United States. The society, founded in 1737 by French Protestants, was known as the 'Two-Bit Club,' because of the sum contributed at each meeting by each member. The building was designed by Gabriel Manigault (1752–1809), Charleston's first native architect and cited as the most gifted one of his period, though he had no professional training. The two-story portico, added in 1825 after a design by Frederick Wesner, is a notable example of the Greek Revival. The superimposed colonnades and fine classic pediment are carried to the curb, and two flights of steps have wrought-iron scroll banisters and lamp posts on their landings.

3. The HORRY HOUSE (pronounced O-ree) (*private*), 59 Meeting St., also known as the Governor Branford House, is a three-story brick 'double house' built between 1751 and 1767. Typical of its period is the first floor level, raised little above the street. A second-story gallery, extending over the sidewalk, is a later addition. There are graceful interior arches, massive doors, carved paneling and mantels with elaborate cornices and molding in the dignified second-story drawing room.

4. The (FIRST) SCOTCH PRESBYTERIAN CHURCH (*open 10–5 daily*), 53 Meeting St., is a massive stuccoed building, with twin towers rising above a columned portico. The fine auditorium contains many mural tablets, and in the adjoining churchyard some famous Charlestonians are buried. The building was erected in 1814, but the congregation dates from 1731, when Scottish families withdrew from the original Presbyterian body and bought this site. Land titles stipulated that the property should be used only for a Presbyterian church retaining the Church of Scotland form of government.

5. The NATHANIEL RUSSELL HOUSE (*private*), 51 Meeting St., built about 1811, is a splendid example of Post-Colonial architecture. The rectangular three-story mansion, with its full three-story octagonal bay at one side, is constructed of brick with white stone and wood trim. Especially notable are the transomed entrance portal with its elliptical fanlight and the wrought-iron balcony at the second-story windows, bearing the monogram of the original owner. The flat roof is enclosed by a balustraded parapet characteristic of the period. The interior, decorated in the Adam style, is planned with an oval drawing room and a graceful spiral stairway.

6. The FIRST BAPTIST CHURCH (*open 8:30–12, 1–5 daily, except Thurs.*), 61 Church St., is a stately little building with trim Doric portico topped with triglyphed entablature and pediment showing the first traces of the Greek Revival beginning to appear about 1820, when it was designed by Robert Mills (*see Architecture and Columbia*).

This congregation was the first Baptist organization in the South

---

KEY FOR CHARLESTON MAP

1. St. Michael's Episcopal Church   2. South Carolina Society Hall   3. Horry House   4. (First) Scotch Presbyterian Church   5. Nathaniel Russell House   6. First Baptist Church   7. Jacob Motte House   8. Robert Brewton House   9. Colonel Charles Brewton House   10. Heyward-Washington House   11. Cabbage Row   12. Petigru Law Office   13. Old Exchange   14. Old Carolina Coffee House   15. Vanderhorst Row   16. Missroon House   17. Colonel William Washington House   18. Josiah Smith House   19. John Edwards House   20. Huger House   21. William Bull House   22. Miles Brewton (Pringle) House   23. Stuart House   24. Sword Gates   25. Sass Iron Gates   26. Wood and Iron Gates   27. William Gibbes House   28. H. A. Middleton House   29. William Drayton (or Manigault) House   30. Samuel Axson House   31. Alston House   32. Chisolm Rice Mill   33. City Hall   34. Fireproof Building   35. Hibernian Hall   36. Gibbes Art Gallery   37. Circular Congregational Church   38. Old Powder Magazine   39. St. Philip's Episcopal Church   40. Pirate House   41. Huguenot (French Protestant)

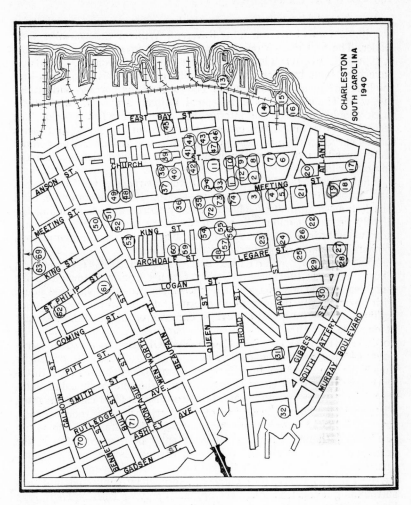

CHARLESTON
SOUTH CAROLINA
1940

Church 42. Planters Hotel and the Dock Street Theater 43. Pink House 44. Slave Market 45. Firemarker 46. Scottish Rite Tablet 47. Chamber of Commerce 48. Market Hall (Confederate Museum) 49. Charleston Hotel 50. Beth Elohim Synagogue 51. St. Mary's Catholic Church 52. Washington Light Infantry Armory and Museum of War Relics 53. Charleston Library Society 54. Quaker Churchyard 55. Oldest Drugstore 56. Izard House 57. John Rutledge House 58. Cathedral of St. John 59. Unitarian Church 60. St. John's Lutheran Church 61. Glebe House 62. College of Charleston 63. Marion Square 64. Joseph Manigault House and Lodge 65. Chapel of the Charleston Orphan House 66. Medical College of the State of South Carolina 67. Porter Military Academy 68. Hampton Park 69. Citadel 70. Charleston Museum 71. William Blacklock House 72. Daniel Blake Tenements 73. County Courthouse 74. Old Jewish Orphanage and was founded about 1683, partly by sectarians who had left inhospitable New England. The Reverend William Screven was their leader. The first church on this site was built in 1699.

7. The JACOB MOTTE HOUSE (*private*), 69 Church St., believed to have been built by Richard Capers between 1745 and 1750, was long the home of Jacob Motte, 'Public Treasurer of the Colony' and father-in-law of Thomas Lynch and General William Moultrie. Originally a brick 'double house,' the interior has been somewhat altered. The second-floor drawing room extends the width of the house and has a mantel carved with 'a procession of Bacchus and Ariadne.' The pointed arched windows of the outbuildings were a popular detail when the house was built.

8. The ROBERT BREWTON HOUSE (*private*), 71 Church St., built prior to 1733, is the earliest accurately dated example of a Charleston 'single house.' The three-story stuccoed brick building has slightly projecting quoins, key-blocks over the windows, and a second-story wrought-iron balcony. Its corbeled brick cornices and high-pitched roof are distinctly local characteristics of its era.

9. The COLONEL CHARLES BREWTON HOUSE (*private*), 73 Church St., was the house given by Colonel Charles Brewton to his daughter, Mrs. Thomas Dale, in 1733. It is a two-story stuccoed house with an unusually delicate iron balcony at the second story, a simple pedimented doorway, and a carriage entrance opening off the sidewalk at one side.

10. The HEYWARD-WASHINGTON HOUSE (*open 10–2 weekdays; 9–6 during Mar. and Apr.; adm. 50¢*), 87 Church St., owned by the Charleston Museum, built in 1730 of small English brick, is a three-story residence of an early Georgian type. The fine pedimented doorway is a restoration. When Washington visited Charleston in 1791, Thomas Heyward, Jr., a Signer of the Declaration of Independence, turned his house over to the President and his suite. The rooms, all furnished with museum pieces, have recently been redecorated in the original colors. The old brick kitchen, carriage house, and servants' quarters are in the rear, with a small formal garden beyond.

11. CABBAGE ROW, 91 Church St., formed by connected buildings surrounding a court, is where the original Porgy of DuBose Heyward's book of that name lived. In the book, however, the locale was called 'Catfish Row' and placed on East Bay St.

12. The PETIGRU LAW OFFICE (*private*), 8 St. Michael's Alley, renovated in 1910 for a private residence, is a Greek Revival style two-story building that was the office of James Louis Petigru until his death in 1863.

13. The OLD EXCHANGE (*open 10–2, 3–5 weekdays Nov. 1–May 1, adm. 25¢; Sun. and in summer by appointment*), E. Bay St. at end of Broad St., occupying the site of the Court of Guards in 1680, was begun about 1767 as an exchange and customhouse, and finished in 1771. It is a good example of English Georgian architecture erected in the colonies. While for the most part in its original state, it has had some

unfortunate alterations: land reclamation has removed it from its water-front setting, a narrow street, built over the reclaimed land, causing the sacrifice of a stately east portico that was the main entrance, and making the secondary façade, originally the rear, the principal approach. Other losses are the monumental urns that once graced the attic para-pet, and the cupola, twice constructed and twice destroyed, which com-pleted the composition. The central section of the E. Bay front, flanked by Palladian windows and crowned with a classic pediment, is pierced in the lower level by three rusticated doorways with Ionic pilasters above them. The interior has similar pilasters. Windows are of London crown glass, decorations of Portland stone, and the roof of Welsh Carnarvon slate—all utilized with painstaking care and fine workman-ship. The architects were John and Peter Horlbeck, who practiced about 1767–92.

In the Court of Guards, Stede Bonnet, the pirate, was imprisoned in 1718. The present building held the tea stored in 1774 to prevent its sale with the English tax. After the capture of Charleston in 1780 British troops were quartered here, but failed to discover 10,000 pounds of powder which had been hidden by General Moultrie in a secret room in the basement. During British occupation of the city, 61 Americans were imprisoned here. Among them was Colonel Isaac Hayne (*see Tour* 1), hanged by the British as an example to other patriots who, after giving paroles, felt that conditions justified them in resuming arms. In 1791 Washington stood on the steps here to witness the parade given in his honor; the ball and Governor's dinner which crowned the occasion were held in the Exchange Hall.

The Federal Government purchased the building in 1818 for a cus-tomhouse and post office. It escaped demolition, but was badly damaged during the Federal bombardment. In 1913 it was granted to the D.A.R. as a museum and has among many relics an original Gilbert Stuart portrait of Washington.

14. The OLD CAROLINA COFFEE HOUSE, 120 E. Bay St., now a liquor shop, was a pre-Revolutionary meeting place for citizens who indulged in political and social gossip over their coffee cups. On early maps the name is also given as Old French Coffee Shop and as Harris Tavern, but it cannot be determined if the present building is the original structure.

15. VANDERHORST ROW (*private*), 78 E. Bay St., a three-story Georgian building erected in 1800 by Arnoldus Vanderhorst, governor of South Carolina 1794–6, is believed to have been the first apartment house in America. After being used many years as a warehouse, it has recently been restored to its original purpose, with three apartments of three floors each. The façade is divided into three sections, each three bays in width. The slightly projecting central section is topped with an eave pediment. Especially notable are the scrolled keystones of con-trasting stone above the narrow many-paned windows. In the eave pedi-ment is a large sentinel window.

16. The MISSROON HOUSE, now OMAR TEMPLE OF THE AN-
CIENT ORDER OF THE MYSTIC SHRINE (*open* 11:30–5 *week-
days*), 40 E. Battery, at the end of the sea wall, retains in its southern
two thirds the Missroon House, built 1789–95. Its foundations are those
of old Granville Bastion, one of the chief fortifications of defense in
1704, which occupied a considerable area on the southeastern boundary
of the city as designed in 1680. The greater portion of the building
was constructed in 1925.

17. The COLONEL WILLIAM WASHINGTON HOUSE (*private*),
8 S. Battery, is a handsome frame residence built by Thomas Savage
about 1769 and bought by Colonel Washington after the Revolution.
The exterior is finished in white-painted beaded clapboards; the windows of the first story are crowned with Georgian pediments, and the
paneled entrance portals, flanked by louvered shutters, lead into a two-
story gallery porch at the left side. The interior is furnished in the
early nineteenth-century manner.

18. The JOSIAH SMITH HOUSE (*private*), 7 Meeting St., frame,
with broad hip roof capped by an octagonal cupola, was built about
1800 for a great-grandson of one of the original landgraves. The circular entrance portico on the east end, with twin stairway and delicate
iron rail, was later supplemented by the double piazza on the south,
designed in the Doric order of the Greek Revival.

19. The JOHN EDWARDS HOUSE (*private*), 15 Meeting St., built
in 1770, has two stories over a brick basement. The exterior is finished
with gray-painted cypress boards, cut and beveled to simulate rusticated
stone. The rounded piazza is a variation of the usual Charleston theme.
The square flat-roofed entrance portico, supported by Ionic columns,
is approached by a broad, two-way flight of steps, protected by a curved
iron railing. During the British occupation in the Revolution, the house
was Admiral Arbuthnot's headquarters.

20. The HUGER HOUSE (pronounced U-gee) (*private*), 34 Meeting
St., built about 1760, is an immense stucco-covered structure with three-
story piazzas later added. It was the home of Lord William Campbell,
last of the royal governors, whose wife was Sarah Izard. In 1775, after
a hostile demonstration in front of his house, Campbell fled by boat
through a creek at the rear of his garden to H.M.S. *Tamar*, and carried
with him the Great Seal of the province.

21. The WILLIAM BULL HOUSE (*private*), 35 Meeting St., a three-
story mansion with two-story side galleries and entrance steps on the
sidewalk, was built by William Bull, first lieutenant governor of the
province, who died in 1755. The stone-covered façade has tan and
brown wood trim. Especially notable is the paneled wood door, topped
with a pediment supported on acanthus leaf brackets. At the outbreak
of the Revolution, William Bull, son of the builder, himself lieutenant
governor under Lord Campbell, lived in the house.

22. The MILES BREWTON (PRINGLE) HOUSE (*open* 10–1 *and*
3–5 *Wed., adm.* $1), 27 King St., built about 1765, is probably the
best-preserved and most elegant example of a Charleston Georgian resi-

dence. A handsome iron fence with double gate encloses the small flag-stoned front court, which gives way to large gardens in the rear. The coach house, with pointed arch windows and Gothic Revival battle-ments along the gable ends, is on the north side. This is a typical 'dou-ble house,' square with overhanging eaves and a classic cornice, and has a fan-transomed doorway, stately two-story front portico, and hip roof. The portico, with Doric and Ionic columns, is surmounted by a pedi-ment containing a delicate oval window. Within is a broad staircase of two flights, with a landing beside a Palladian window, and a magnificent crystal chandelier with tall glass chimneys hanging from the elaborate cove ceiling of the drawing room on the second floor. Nearly all of the characteristic furnishings have traditions associated with them—a frag-ment of Axminster carpet is the remnant of a large one cut up by invading troops to make saddle cloths in 1865; chairs came from the sale of the belongings of Louis Philippe; and a Sir Joshua Reynolds portrait of Miles Brewton, with a sword mark through it, is a reminder that the house was the headquarters of Sir Henry Clinton during the British occupation. Lord Rawdon and Lord Cornwallis also adopted the house for their residence in the city.

23. The STUART HOUSE (*private*), 106 Tradd St., was built about 1772 by Colonel John Stuart, who was sent here from Scotland in 1763 as commissioner of Indian affairs. The white three-story frame edifice is topped with a hip roof and a captain's walk. The three-bay façade is finished in flush boarding. The arched entrance with its fluted Corinthian columns and pediment leads into a long hallway on one side. The shuttered windows at the first and second stories are flanked with dog-ear trim and crowned with bracketed pediment in the Georgian manner. A double-deck porch and a two-story wing with octagonal bay have been added at the left and rear, overlooking a beautiful walled garden. The drawing room on the second floor, with its notable paneling, is reproduced in miniature at the Charleston Museum. A part of the orig-inal paneling is now in the Minneapolis Museum of Art.

Colonel Stuart remained loyal to his king, fled this country, and his property was confiscated. Tradition records that General Francis Marion once leaped from a window here to escape a too convivial drinking bout.

24. The SWORD GATES, at the entrance to the Simonton house, 32 Legare St., date from 1815–20 and form one of Charleston's most beau-tifully executed examples of wrought-iron, with elaborate scrolls and a central motif designed with two spears, the points of which join at the center of a broadsword to form a cross. The gates, set in a high brick wall, offer glimpses of an old garden and magnolia-bordered walk in front of the house, of which the north hip-portion, of brick, dates from about 1776; the south sections, of wood, were added in 1850–60–80.

25. The SASS IRON GATES, entrance of 23 Legare St., the home of Herbert Ravenel Sass, author, are among the most delicate examples of wrought-iron workmanship in a city of famous gateways. The central motif resembles a conventional daisy.

26. The WOOD AND IRON GATES, entrance of 14 Legare St., are a skillful combination of cypress and iron in scroll work. Tall coach gates stand between high brick pillars with smaller gates on each side. The 'G' and the 'E' in the tracery were placed here when George Edwards owned the three-story brick house in the early eighteenth century. Topping the gateposts are white marble ornaments from Italy, resembling pineapples—but believed to represent the edible fruit of an Italian pine tree, which, in Italy, are Yuletide symbols of peace, good will, and hospitality.

27. The WILLIAM GIBBES HOUSE (*private*), 64 S. Battery, a three-story clapboarded cypress residence above a basement with arched entrances and windows and a central eave pediment supported on scrolled brackets, was built before 1789 and redecorated in the Adam manner in 1794. Double flights of steps with wrought-iron rails ascend to the main floor. The graceful interior stairway, of unusual design, has carved banisters. A brick wall encloses one of Charleston's loveliest gardens, where the old seawall is utilized as a terrace.

28. The H. A. MIDDLETON HOUSE (*private*), 68 S. Battery, a vine-covered, stuccoed residence with lovely gardens and pool, was built prior to the Revolution by William Gibbes and later became the home of Henry Augustus Middleton. The wrought-iron balcony at the second story is especially notable. In the handsome drawing room, second story, is a beautifully carved high mantel.

29. The WILLIAM DRAYTON (or MANIGAULT) HOUSE (*private*), 6 Gibbes St., was built in 1820 and is typical of the more pretentious frame dwellings of the prosperous post-Revolutionary era. Its two stories rise above a stuccoed basement and wide two-story piazzas follow the curve of the house. Doorways, interior arched paneling, molding, and wainscoting are contemporary details. A carved parlor mantel is supported by columns topped with busts.

30. The SAMUEL AXSON HOUSE (*private*), 4 Greenhill St., a two-story wooden house, was built in 1805 by Samuel Axson, one of the master carpenter-builders of his day, for his own home. At that time the Ashley River extended to within less than 50 feet of the house, which typifies the medium-sized residence of the time.

31. The ALSTON HOUSE (*private*), 172 Tradd St., exemplifies the classic type with freestanding two-story portico dating about 1850–60. It represents the popular idea of the Southern Colonial mansion, but is in reality a comparatively rare type in this State, the style developed just before the Confederate era. Interior doors are three-and-a-half inches thick.

32. The CHISOLM RICE MILL, Murray Blvd. and Tradd St., on the Ashley River, a massive three-story white stucco building adorned with classic pilasters, is used by the Sixth District, U. S. Bureau of Lighthouses. Built in 1830, partially burned in 1859, restored and used until 1900, all but one wing demolished in 1916, the structure was later rebuilt.

33. The CITY HALL (*Council Chamber containing works of art open 9–6 Mon.–Fri., 9–1 Sat.*), NE. corner Broad and Meeting Sts., designed by Gabriel Manigault and built about 1802 as a branch of the Bank of the United States, was bought by the city in 1818. The picture gallery, second floor front, was acquired through the local custom of commissioning artists to paint portraits of famous visitors. John Trumbull's valuable *Portrait of George Washington,* made during the President's triumphal tour of 1791, shows him without wig or false teeth and is accepted as one of the best likenesses of his later years. Other notable items are the Charles Fraser *Miniature of La Fayette,* a *Portrait of James Monroe* by S. F. B. Morse, and a Vanderlyn *Portrait of President Andrew Jackson* in uniform after the Battle of New Orleans. Paintings in the mayor's office include an early picture of the city's volunteer fire company in full uniform.

The building, on the site of the market of Colonial days, is set in Washington Square or City Hall Park. Near the west gate the statue of William Pitt, who denounced the stamp tax in the British House of Commons, was carved by John Wilton of England and erected July 5, 1770. Other monuments in the park are the shaft honoring the three companies of the Washington Light Infantry that fought for the Confederacy, the bust of Henry Timrod, and a monument to General P. G. T. Beauregard, who commanded Charleston's defense 1861–5.

34. The FIREPROOF BUILDING, SE. corner Chalmers and Meeting Sts., in Washington Square, designed by Robert Mills, and built in 1826 for the purpose of housing local records safely, is believed to be the first building of fireproof construction in the United States. Besides being a repository for county files, it houses some county offices.

35. The HIBERNIAN HALL (*open 10–7:30 weekdays, 10:30–2 and 5–7 Sun. in summer; 10–5 weekdays, 10:30–2 and 5–6 Sun. in winter*), 105 Meeting St., a classic two-story building, dedicated in 1841, was the first semipublic structure of pure Greek type in the city. It has a front colonnade of Ionic columns surmounted by a pediment. The entrance leads into a large stair hall, centered by an open rotunda covered by a dome with coffered panels, supported by superimposed columns of the three Greek orders. Each floor contains a large hall.

This is the home of the Hibernian Society, founded March 17, 1801, by eight Irishmen who had recently arrived in the State. The society is nonsectarian and nonpolitical and for years the presidents have been selected, by unwritten law, alternately from Roman Catholic and Protestant members.

Annual events of long standing held here are the society's St. Patrick's Day banquet and the New Year's Day dinner, at which 'Hop-in-John' is a traditional dish. This mixture of rice, black-eyed peas, and bacon is as dear to Charlestonians as porridge to the Scot.

The hall is most distinguished, however, as the scene of St. Cecilia Society Balls. This society, formed in 1762 for amateur musical concerts, has always been the city's most exclusive organization, and its musicales gave way some years after its founding to a series of annual balls. Members and guests are selected according to rigid rules and to attend a St. Cecilia ball is an honor as greatly coveted in South Carolina as to be presented at court.

36. GIBBES ART GALLERY (*open* 10–5 *weekdays,* 3–6 *Sun., free*), 135 Meeting St., was built in 1905 with funds given to the city by James S. Gibbes and is managed by the Carolina Art Association, which was founded in 1858. The field is the fine and applied arts, with particular emphasis on South Carolina portraiture. The Gallery has about 106 canvases and over 100 miniatures (*see Painting*) and has held many temporary exhibitions in the fine and industrial arts of all periods.

37. CIRCULAR CONGREGATIONAL CHURCH (*open* 9–6 *daily, except June, July, and August,* 2–6), 138 Meeting St., a massive brick structure of Romanesque design with a circular auditorium and lofty curved ceiling, was built in 1891. The church was founded in the 1680's by Calvinists of several countries and known first as Church of Dissenters, later as White Meeting House, explaining the name of Meeting Street. The first building on the site was erected before 1695; the present structure replaces a former circular church dedicated in 1806. The growing congregation mothered in 1730 the Scotch Presbyterian Church, in 1785 the Unitarian Church. The templelike chapel in the churchyard, an interesting example of the Classical Revival style, with its Doric portico and two-way flight of steps, was built after 1861 and houses the Sunday school. The cemetery contains some of Charleston's oldest graves, one of them that of David Ramsay, M.D. (1749–1815), historian.

38. The OLD POWDER MAGAZINE (*open* 9:30–1, 2:30–5 *weekdays, Nov.* 1 *to first Tues. in June*), 23 Cumberland St., was built in 1703 within the city's original fortifications near the northwest bastion. The low square building of stuccoed brick has a steep hip roof, covered with red tile and cut on each side by two large gables. The building is used as a museum by the Colonial Dames. A tall iron picket fence encloses the tiny garden and lawn.

39. ST. PHILIP'S EPISCOPAL CHURCH (*open* 8–6 *daily*), Church St. between Cumberland and Queen Sts., is a late Georgian edifice planned by Joseph Hyde and erected 1835–8. The lofty octagonal steeple, later designed by Edward Brickell White and one of the city's landmarks, formerly held a mariner's light and was a target during Federal bombardment. The three Doric porticos, flanking the bays of the tower, lead to an elaborate interior with Corinthian columns, vaulted ceilings, box pews, side galleries, and elaborate plaster ornamentation in the Roman manner. In 1920 the formerly elliptical sanctuary, with coffered domed ceiling, was made semicircular, giving a monumental character to the east end of the building, the third owned by St. Philip's, which was the first Anglican parish organized south of Virginia. The first rector, the Reverend Atkin Williamson, was also the first Anglican minister in the State, and in his day enjoyed high living. His credibility as a witness was questioned in court because in 1682, while confusing spirits with spirituality, he had christened a young bear.

Church Street cuts through the graveyard, leaving one section across from the church. Among those buried in the two plots are Edward Rutledge, a Signer of the Declaration of Independence; Rawlins Lowndes, president of South Carolina, 1778–9; John C. Calhoun, Vice President of the United States, twice United States senator and Cabinet officer; Colonel William Rhett, captor of the pirates; Christopher Gadsden, Revolutionary leader, whose grave is unmarked by his own request; and other distinguished South Carolinians. One is said to be that of Charles Pinckney, author of the Pinckney draft and signer of the Federal Constitution, who was four times governor of South Carolina, but no stone marks his grave and its whereabouts are uncertain.

The GATEWAY WALK starts at the east wall of the churchyard along Philadelphia Street; extends across Church Street, through the Circular Church grounds; across Meeting Street and through a garden developed by a club on the north side of the Gibbes Art Gallery, around the building of the Charleston Library Society; across King Street through a passage to the gateway of the Unitarian Church and into the graveyard of St. John's Lutheran Church.

40. The PIRATE HOUSE, 145 Church St., operated as an antique and gift shop and tea room, was described by Julian Street in *American Adventures* as 'a perfect example of the rude architecture of a French village, stucco walls, tinted and chipped, red tile roof and all.' The entrance door frames, the roof with its outward curving eaves, and the dormers were remodeled in the decade 1920–30. The house is believed to have been erected by French Huguenots, but the legend told tourists, that it was used as headquarters by early-eighteenth-century pirates who harassed the Carolina coast, is apparently a modern myth entirely unconfirmed by historical research.

41. The HUGUENOT (FRENCH PROTESTANT) CHURCH (*open 10–1, 3–5 daily*), SE. corner Church and Queen Sts., Gothic type, remodeled in 1845 on the walls of its predecessor, burned in 1797, is the third on the site. The congregation was founded in 1680 by Huguenot refugees and is said to be the only church in America using the Calvinistic Huguenot liturgy. Until recently the service was conducted in French on certain Sundays, but now English is always used. The interior walls are lined with small white marble tablets, memorials by Huguenot descendants to their ancestors.

42. The PLANTERS HOTEL and the DOCK STREET THEATER, SW. corner of Church and Queen Sts., are Federal Emergency Relief Administration restorations of two famous buildings of the past. The Dock Street Theater, first building in America designed solely for theatrical purposes (*see Drama*) opened in 1736 with *The Recruiting Officer* by George Farquhar. The Planters Hotel, built around the ruins of the theater soon after 1809, was for over 50 years a social center famous for its food, and Planter's Punch is said to have originated here. The carefully reconstructed building, though not intended for use as a hotel, recalls much of the spirit of the old hostelry. Reproduced here is the small courtyard, the favorite rendezvous of the rice planters and

plantation owners while their wives watched the Charleston street scene from the little wrought-iron balcony, reconstructed on the second floor; here also are the small auditoriums and studios, with the courtyard providing an entrance to the theater. Its restoration recaptures the charm of the original, duplicating the gallery, the 13 boxes, each accommodating eight persons, and the pit, with the backs and arm rests added to make the old-style benches comfortable. The walls are paneled in natural-finish cypress and the electric candle fixtures imitate the lighting in theaters of the days of Charles II. The old playhouse was reopened November 26, 1937, repeating the initial play. Leased by the city to the Carolina Art Association, associated with the Charleston Footlight Players, it is used for the performances of the latter and rented to other organizations.

43. The PINK HOUSE (*private*), 17 Chalmers St., is a three-story brick, gambrel roof Revolutionary house with one room on each floor. The interior, a restoration, carefully carries out local architectural tradition.

44. The SLAVE MARKET, 6–8 Chalmers St., is the erroneous name for an enclosure which existed somewhere on Chalmers Street where slaves were impounded pending sale. The slave market itself was located on the Vendue Range, now occupied by Clyde Line steamship wharves. The name Vendue was derived from the French *vendre*, to sell. Typical sweetmeats sold here are made from old recipes, and include 'peach leather,' 'benne brittle,' made with benne (sesame) seed— called 'goodwill seed' by Negroes—'monkey-meat' (cocoanut) cakes, and 'ground-nut' (peanut) cakes. The last two are not cakes at all, but round patties of candy.

45. The FIREMARK, 7 State St., fastened on the wall in the gabled pediment above the second story, is one of few remaining from hundreds first used in this country in the early part of the eighteenth century, after a London custom originating in 1666. These marks showed that the building was insured and by what company, and were a guarantee that the company represented would reward any brigade or individuals extinguishing a blaze.

46. The SCOTTISH RITE TABLET, 46 Broad St., on the Citizens and Southern Bank, marks the birthplace of the Scottish Rite in 1801 and the chartering of Solomon's Lodge No. 1 in 1735, the first order of the Ancient Free Masons in the United States. Before the tavern was razed, the room in which the organizations were founded was reconstructed in the Scottish Rite Cathedral, corner Wentworth and Smith Streets.

47. CHAMBER OF COMMERCE, 50 Broad St., organized in 1773, is believed to be the oldest city commercial organization in the United States and the second oldest commercial body of any kind in this country. The building was erected in 1784, the worn marble steps attesting its antiquity. The Bank of South Carolina was located here until 1833; from then until 1914 the Charleston Library Society occupied the building.

48. MARKET HALL (CONFEDERATE MUSEUM) (*temporarily closed on account of damages to building in* 1938), Meeting St. facing Market St., is a Roman Doric style two-story stuccoed edifice, designed in 1840 by Joseph Hyde. The decorations include a frieze of bulls' heads. Two flights of stone steps lead to the lofty portico; on the first landing is one of the first rifled cannon made in the United States and constructed of Swedish iron from one of the first locomotives of the South Carolina Railroad. Behind the building is the second city market, the center of the wreckage in the tornado of 1938. Charles Cotesworth Pinckney and others deeded the site to the city in 1788. In 1903 the Daughters of the Confederacy leased the market building to exhibit rare Confederate relics.

49. CHARLESTON HOTEL, 198 Meeting St., built in 1839, is an immense white stuccoed building with a columned portico, which shared importance with the Planters Hotel in the latter's heyday. Thackeray, charmed by the city in 1852, made illustrations of the life he found, including an amusing pencil sketch of the Charleston Hotel lobby. During his visit he attended a Negro ball, where he was served spruce beer, but in writing of the event he neglected to include the recipe.

50. The BETH ELOHIM SYNAGOGUE (*open* 9–12 *daily*), 74 Hasell St., designed by David Lopez and built in 1840, is one of the city's most accurate Doric examples of the Greek Revival; its fine proportions and Hellenic details are reminiscent of the Parthenon. The entrance portico fronts a beautifully landscaped lawn enclosed by an iron picket fence with a delicately wrought gate. In the first synagogue, erected here in 1792, Reform Judaism had its origin in America in 1824, when the Reformed Society of Israelites was founded. The first Jewish congregation in Charleston was organized in 1750.

51. ST. MARY'S CATHOLIC CHURCH (*open* 7–6 *daily*), 79 Hasell St., is a brick edifice erected in 1838. This congregation was the nucleus of the mother parish of the Roman Catholic Church in the Carolinas, having been organized in 1794.

52. The WASHINGTON LIGHT INFANTRY ARMORY AND MUSEUM OF WAR RELICS (*open; hours vary*), 240 King St., is headquarters for the company that was organized in 1807 and has taken part in all American wars since then. Among its museum relics are a likeness of George Washington, woven on silk in France, a storm flag of the Confederate cruiser *Shenandoah,* pikes used by John Brown's raiders, and the 'famous Eutaw flag.' This square of embroidered crimson silk was ripped from the back of an armchair in her plantation home by Jane Elliott (later Mrs. Washington) and presented to Colonel William Washington in 1780 for his cavalry colors. The flag was borne at the Battle of Cowpens and at Eutaw Springs, September 8, 1781, and later presented by Mrs. Washington to the Washington Light Infantry.

53. CHARLESTON LIBRARY SOCIETY (*open* 8:45–7 *weekdays*), 184 King St., occupying a modern building, is the third oldest library in this country, organized in 1748 by 17 young Charleston gentlemen.

This private enterprise has 67,500 volumes, many of them exceedingly rare, and a file of newspapers, beginning with 1732, which is one of the most valuable pre-Revolutionary collections in America.

54. The QUAKER CHURCHYARD, 138 King St., dates from 1694, when John Archdale gave the site from the Archdale tract on which the Quaker Meeting House was built. Only two slabs and two white stone markers inlaid on the old approach to the church entrance now remain, the building having been blown up in July 1837 to stop a fire. Though rebuilt, it burned again in the great fire of 1861.

55. The OLDEST DRUGSTORE, 125 King St. (originally 111 King St.), has a sign on front of building designating it as America's oldest drugstore business. Its career antedates 1781, when Dr. Andrew Turnbull bought the business and began dispensing his own remedies. In 1920 Mr. Huchting, present owner, gave much of the old equipment for the Apothecary's Hall in the Charleston Museum, where it has been reset for public display. The original building occupied by the drugstore, at 111 King Street, probably antedates 1725.

56. The IZARD HOUSE (*private*), 110 Broad St., was erected before 1757 for Ralph Izard, planter and Revolutionary statesman, who devoted his fortune and energies to the American cause. Like most of its contemporaries, the house has three stories, thick stuccoed brick walls, corbeled cornices, and high hip roof. The balcony is in the center and the entrance door to the left, a lack of symmetry characteristic of the period. Unlike later houses, the first floor is raised only a few steps above the sidewalk. The interior walls are paneled and moldings are bold with comparatively little carved ornament.

57. The JOHN RUTLEDGE HOUSE (*private*), 116 Broad St., now much altered, was built about 1760 as the home of John Rutledge, Chief Justice of the United States for a brief period, president of the State of South Carolina, 1776–8, and later governor. Because of his military and political authority during the Revolution he was known as 'Dictator Rutledge.' The cast- and wrought-iron balconies and gates, by Christopher Werner, the parquet floors, the stately second-story ballroom, and crystal chandelier are noteworthy.

58. CATHEDRAL OF ST. JOHN (Roman Catholic) (*open 7–7 daily*), corner Broad and Legare Sts., a brownstone structure of Neo-Gothic type, was begun in 1888, on the site of the former Vauxhall gardens, which had been replaced by the Cathedral of St. Finbar in 1820. The central entrance is through a single front tower which suggests English Gothic. There are fine stained-glass windows and a pipe organ.

59. The UNITARIAN CHURCH (*open 9–5 daily*), 6 Archdale St., was erected in 1772 and partly reconstructed in 1852 from plans of Francis D. Lee, who gave it a Gothic cast. Behind the ribbed and vaulted plaster ceiling are the rafters and trusses usually found in early Charleston churches. A marble shaft and a Harvard room memorialize the Reverend Samuel Gilman, D.D., author of 'Fair Harvard' (1836), who was pastor here 1819–57.

60. ST. JOHN'S LUTHERAN CHURCH (*open* 10–1, 2:30–5:30 *daily during tourist season, closed Thurs. other seasons*), corner Archdale and Clifford Sts., was built in 1815 after the Robert Adam tradition, but has been changed so often that it now resembles no special style. The heavily pedimented steeple is noteworthy; and the fine wrought-iron gates, forming a screen between the columns of the portico —which were designed and executed in 1823 by craftsmen members of the congregation—are among the city's masterpieces. Of equal merit are the gate and fence around the churchyard, which form part of the Gateway Walk. The congregation was founded in 1757; Dr. John Bachman, Audubon's collaborator, and pastor when the present, second building was dedicated in 1818, is buried beneath the pulpit.

61. The GLEBE HOUSE (*private*), 6 Glebe St., a brick structure, was once the rectory of St. Philip's Church and stands on former glebe lands. Here the Reverend Robert Smith conducted the Parsonage Academy, which in 1770 formed the nucleus of the first classes of the College of Charleston, with Mr. Smith as first president.

62. The COLLEGE OF CHARLESTON, between Glebe, George, St. Philip, and Green Sts., founded in 1770, chartered in 1785, opened in 1790, a municipal college since 1837, is the oldest municipal college in America; it has been coeducational since 1918. The college is one of the units in the local school system that enables a resident student to gain an education free of charge, from the kindergarten through college. In 1939 it received a $10,000 endowment from Bernard M. Baruch.

The college having occupied the same site for 146 years, its buildings represent nearly every period of American architecture. The main block is a composite group: nothing remains of the Revolutionary barracks originally used for classrooms; the central building was designed by William Strickland (1828); the Ionic portico and the two wings, added in 1850–1 by Colonel Edward Brickell White, were destroyed by the earthquake in 1886 and restored later.

The extension at the extreme western end was designed by Albert Simons and Samuel Lapham in 1930. Buildings of conspicuous merit are the gate lodge (erected in 1850–1 by Colonel White in the strictest form of the Classic Revival with adornments of the Tuscan order) and the college library, which contains 20,000 books and pamphlets, many of them valuable.

63. MARION SQUARE, Calhoun, between Meeting and King Sts., resembles a Spanish plaza; it is also known as Old Citadel Square from the northern line of buildings, designed by Frederick Wesner and erected in 1822 as an arsenal, later accommodating the military college. To the south stands a monument to John C. Calhoun; a shaft honoring General Wade Hampton is eastward; near the center is a fence-enclosed section of the old tabby wall which served as the northern boundary of Charles Town as designed in 1680, when Calhoun Street was Boundary Street.

64. The JOSEPH MANIGAULT HOUSE AND LODGE (*open* 10–5 *weekdays during tourist season; 10–5 Mon., Wed., and Sat. other*

months; adm. 25¢. Temporarily closed for repairs, 1940), 350 Meeting St., designed 1790–7 by Gabriel Manigault, displays the architectural preference of the day for the Adam influence and shows a less rigid adherence to the Georgian-Colonial. Its two-story circular portico at the left side is obviously a later addition, greatly inferior in detail to the front portico. The house, recently deeded to the Charleston Museum, has regained its gardens through the gift of an oil company, which previously had a filling station on the southwest corner.

65. The CHAPEL OF THE CHARLESTON ORPHAN HOUSE (*open 9–6 weekdays; Sun. Services 4, 4:30, or 5 according to season*), Vanderhost St. between King and St. Philip Sts., was erected in 1802 on design of Gabriel Manigault and remodeled in 1855 on plans of Jones and Lee, architects. The interior is distinguished for its late Georgian character. The orphanage itself was built 1792–4.

66. MEDICAL COLLEGE OF THE STATE OF SOUTH CAROLINA, NE. corner Calhoun and Lucas Sts., the oldest medical school in the South and coeducational since 1931, occupies a site donated by the city in 1914. The main three-story brick building was then erected by Charleston citizens at a cost of $75,000 and presented to the State. Opposite is Roper Hospital, in co-operation with which since 1919 the School of Nursing has been operated.

Soon after the Revolution, the Medical Society of South Carolina was organized in Charleston; in 1821 Dr. Samuel Henry Dickson proposed that it found a medical college. The institution opened in 1824 at the corner of Queen and Franklin Streets, with 6 professors and about 30 students. After administrative difficulties and schisms, the divergent elements united in 1839 and the college became in ante-bellum days one of the leading medical schools of this country. Louis Agassiz taught here 1851–3.

The institution closed in the Confederate era to be reopened in 1865, sadly depleted in every way, and underwent a struggle for existence during Reconstruction. After 1878 attempts were made to include it in the State University, but not until 1913, during the administration of Governor Coleman L. Blease, did it become a State institution in fact as well as in name.

At the centennial celebration in 1924 a tablet, presented by the class of 1900, was unveiled in the main building to honor Dr. Francis Le Jau Parker, professor of anatomy 1865–1913, dean 1891–1906. He was one of many outstanding physicians who have served on the faculty.

Among noted graduates have been: Dr. Eli Geddings, a member of the first class (1825), sought as teacher by four leading medical colleges in the United States; Dr. R. W. Gibbes, Confederate Surgeon General of South Carolina (*see Columbia*); Dr. J. Marion Sims, internationally known gynecologist (*see Columbia*); Dr. St. Julien Ravenel, who discovered the economic value of phosphate deposits near Charleston, that lime could be made from marl, and was the inventor of the *Little David,* Confederate torpedo boat; Dr. Robert A. Kinloch, first in the world to perform a laparotomy for a gunshot wound; and

Dr. Francis L. Parker, first in the world to suture a divided nerve.

Besides the Schools of Medicine and Nursing, the college has the School of Pharmacy, first operated 1881–3 and permanently established in 1893.

67. PORTER MILITARY ACADEMY, Ashley Ave. between Doughty and Bee Sts., occupies a group of weathered buildings set in a shady campus enclosed by a brick wall. This is a preparatory school founded for orphans and children of widowed mothers in 1867, and later granted a 99-year lease by the United States Government. In 1886 the academy was named for its founder, the Reverend A. Toomer Porter.

68. HAMPTON PARK, main entrance W. end Cleveland St., occupies part of the 250-acre grounds of the Interstate and West Indian Exposition of 1901–2, including the sunken garden and the rose-bordered walk then established. Winding drives lead through shady landscaped lawns, and there are a menagerie, ball park, and pavilions. This property, the Revolutionary estate of John Gibbes and later the Rhett farm, was acquired by the city from the Library Society. Exposition grounds also included the farm of Captain Frederick W. Wagener, president of the company, who leased his property for the undertaking without restriction for three years. President Theodore Roosevelt was the guest of honor April 9, 1901. The exposition, participated in by 31 States and territories, brought favorable publicity to the city and resulted in its securing the American Cigar Factory, the Oyster Cannery, and the direct line of the United Fruit Company between Charleston and West Indian ports.

69. The CITADEL, the Military College of South Carolina, Murray Driveway and Citadel Ave., has a campus of some 200 acres adjoining Hampton Park on the Ashley River opposite the site of 'Old Town.' Founded in 1842, the college moved in 1922 into its present gray stuccoed buildings, the first group costing more than $1,000,000. The paved parade quadrangle, of 6,100 square yards, is surrounded by barracks with tiers of arches on the galleries of three floors, architecturally an adaptation of the Spanish-Moorish.

The name is derived from the institution's origin in one of the State's two fortresses for use in slave uprisings: The Citadel on Marion Square, Charleston, and the Arsenal (now Governor's Mansion), Columbia. By suggestion of Governor Peter Richardson, the garrisons of enlisted men at both strongholds were replaced by youths who should simultaneously act as guards and receive military and practical training. Thus the two schools became the South Carolina Military Academy in 1861. A detachment of Citadel cadets stationed on Morris Island under Major P. F. Stevens, Superintendent, fired the first shot of the War between the States January 9, 1861, at the Union relief vessel, *Star of the West*, approaching Fort Sumter. Arsenal cadets, under Captain J. P. Thomas, Superintendent, fired the last shot of the war by any organized Confederate troops east of the Mississippi May 9, 1865, on Stoneman's Raiders near Williamston, S. C. The *Star of the West* medal, an oaken star made from a piece of the vessel of that name and presented years ago by Dr. B. H. Teague, alumnus, is annually awarded the best-drilled cadet at the Citadel.

From 1865 the old Citadel buildings were occupied by Federal troops, the United States retaining control until 1881. After the State regained possession, the institution reopened in 1882, adopting its present name in 1910. For a 'Greater Citadel,' the city of Charleston donated the new site in 1919. Legislative appropriations, gifts, and subscriptions by alumni made the new buildings possible. Approximately 1,000 cadets are enrolled and receive full military training, with courses leading to regular academic degrees.

70. CHARLESTON MUSEUM (*open* 10–5 *daily*, 3–5 *Sun.; free*), Rutledge Ave. between Calhoun and Bennett Sts., oldest in the United States, occupies the Thompson Auditorium, built in 1899. The museum, founded by the Charles Town Library Society in 1773, was revived by trustees of the College of Charleston in 1852 and housed in the college building. After several transfers and reorganizations, the museum was established here in 1907, and incorporated under its present name in 1915. It has, from the beginning, used a logical order in the arrangement of its acquisitions, has endeavored to build up a collection representative of local culture, and, in acquiring such material as fine wainscoting, has scrupulously refrained from removing material from buildings otherwise intact.

The galleries are devoted almost entirely to South Carolina culture. In the north gallery are keys, locks, and hinges of the eighteenth century, primitive agricultural and cooking implements, illustrations of stages of the silk industry, a cypress canoe built in 1830, a keeled plantation barge, a brick press, an old gristmill, and a rice fan for cleaning rice by hand, as well as other valuable relics of early plantation days. Here also is an extensive exhibition of South Carolina woods, stones, and fossils, and a very unusual group of fresh- and salt-water shells from all parts of the world.

In the east and south galleries are collections tracing the history of local fire insurance and fire fighting, a collection of beautiful silver by local silversmiths (supplemented at times by loan exhibits), of dresses and other garments of earlier days, of elaborately designed bed quilts, an array of bath pans, bathtubs, and primitive shower baths of plantation days. One of the prized possessions is the 'Apothecary's Hall,' a greater part of one of the oldest drugstores in America. The proportions and fittings of the original shop of 1780 have been preserved, even part of the cornice and wainscoting, with complete equipment. Also in the east gallery are models of typical local architecture and paneling and woodwork of several rooms from old houses which have been torn down. One is from Elmgrove Plantation, Christ Church Parish, built about 1735, another is the drawing room from a dwelling of about 1764. In the galleries and halls are various models showing local topography and scenes from local history. The first floor is devoted to natural history, and every effort has been made to have it complete for the State.

The ambitious educational program includes lectures and gallery talks to visiting school classes, story hours for children, handwork classes, and contributions of museum extension exhibits to schoolrooms as visual material for classroom work.

71. The WILLIAM BLACKLOCK HOUSE (*private*), 18 Bull St., is an impressive Post-Colonial mansion erected about 1800. It is almost square in plan, constructed of brick, and has a pedimented central pavilion with large fan-shaped window in the upper gable. The graceful elliptical arched doorway has fine leaded tracery in the fan transom and side lights. The entrance stoop, raised above a columned basement entrance, is approached by a broad two-way flight of steps. Several of the outbuildings of this former 'suburban' plantation still stand at the rear.

72. The DANIEL BLAKE TENEMENTS (*private*), 2–4 Courthouse Square, is a three-story brick building erected by Daniel Blake in 1762, when high basements were being introduced to raise first floors for greater coolness and safety from storm-flooding. The grace of the iron balcony railing, the handcarved mantels, and interior paneling are exceptional. Separate dwellings have been made of the old brick kitchen and carriage house. Originally granted to Joseph Blake, Lord Proprietor and governor of South Carolina 1694–5, 1696–1700, the property passed to the Kittle family early in the nineteenth century and was willed by Emma Kittle to St. Michael's Church, never to be sold.

73. The COUNTY COURTHOUSE, NW. corner of Meeting and Broad Sts., was designed by Judge William Drayton and built about 1800 on the site of the State House, which was burned in 1788. In the offices of the probate judge and clerk of court are records from the days of the Lords Proprietors.

74. The OLD JEWISH ORPHANAGE, 88 Broad St. opposite Courthouse, was established by the Hebrew Orphan Society in 1802. Annual appropriations were made and children were not housed within the orphanage, but boarded out in private homes, where they could have family atmosphere and training until 1860, when it was decided to experiment with maintaining residence within the walls. After the war, the original and more parental execution of the trust was resumed and is still continued. The building was purchased by the Society; it was probably erected shortly before the Revolution and remodeled possibly about 1795.

OTHER POINTS OF INTEREST

IN HARBOR

Fort Sumter, Castle Pinckney, Morris Island Lighthouse (*see Tour* 11). Sullivan's Island, Fort Moultrie, Isle of Palms, Site of Fort Johnson on James Island (*see Tour* 1b).

IN ENVIRONS

Site of Old Town, 7.1 *m.;* Magnolia Gardens, 11.9 *m.;* Runnymede Plantation, 12.4 *m.;* Middleton Place Gardens, 15.4 *m.;* Summerville, 25.9 *m.;* Edisto State Park, 35.2 *m.* (*see Tour* 1c). Navy Yard, 6.5 *m.;* The Oaks (Gardens), 19.3 *m.;* Cypress Gardens, 28.3 *m.* (*see Tour* 2b).

Columbia

Railroad Stations: Union Station, S. Main St. between Wheat and Rice Sts. for Southern Ry. and Atlantic Coast Line R.R.; Gervais and Lincoln Sts. for Seaboard Air Line Ry.; 630 Gervais St. for Columbia, Newberry & Laurens Ry.
Bus Station: 1224 Blanding St. for Atlantic Greyhound, Carolina Motor, Pan-American, Eagle, and Stokes Lines; Carolina Scenic Coach Co.
Airport: Municipal, S. end of Edisto Ave. for Delta Air Lines.
Taxis: Fare 25–50¢ within city limits, depending upon number of passengers.
City Busses: Fare 7¢, or 5 tokens for 25¢.

Accommodations: 10 hotels.

Information Service: Chamber of Commerce, DeSoto Hotel, 1108 Lady St.; AAA, Jefferson Hotel, 1801 Main St.; S. C. Auto Assn., 1235 Washington St.

Radio Stations: WIS (560 kc.); WCOS (1370 kc.).
Theaters and Motion Picture Houses: Town Theater, 1012 Sumter St., local productions; Columbia Township Auditorium, 1703 Taylor St., dances, concerts, boxing, wrestling, carnivals; 5 motion picture houses; 1 for Negroes.
Football: U. of S. C. Stadium, Fair Grounds, Bluff Road, just S. of city limits; Melton Field, U. of S. C. campus, Green St. between Sumter and Bull Sts.
Baseball: Dreyfus Field (night games), Olympia Mill Village, S. of city on Assembly St. Extension; Pacific Mill Ball Park, SW. of Heyward St. just beyond city limits.
Swimming: Lakeview, 3 m. E. of city limits on Forest Drive; Twin Lakes, 5 m. E. on US 76, N. of Leesburg Road; St. Peter's Roman Catholic Parochial School, 1500 block of Assembly St., adm. 10¢.
Golf: Fort Jackson, 6 m. E. on US 76, 18 holes, greens fee, 50¢; Glenwood, E. of city limits on Glenwood Road between Forest Drive and Trenholm Road, 9 holes, greens fee, 50¢; Trenholm Road Golf Course, 1 m. E. of city limits on Trenholm Road, 9 holes, greens fee, 50¢, caddy charges extra; Ridgewood Country Club, 2 m. N. of city limits and 2 blks. W. US 21, 18 holes, greens fee $1.50, caddy charges extra; Forest Drive Country Club, 5 m. E. of city over Forest Drive, 18 holes, greens fee $1.50, caddy charges extra.
Tennis: Valley Park, one block E. of Harden, between Green St. and Santee Ave.; Earlwood Park, N. Main St. at city limits.
Fishing and Boating: Lake Murray, 15 m. NW. on US 76, or US 1 from Lexington and State 6.

Annual Events: S. C. legislature convenes 2nd Tues. in Jan., session continues indefinitely; Columbia Music Festival, usually 1st week of Apr.; American Kennel Club Dog Show, Township Auditorium, spring; State-wide Soap-Box Derby for boys, July; City Tennis Tournament, for men and women, Aug.; South Carolina State Fair, 3rd week of Oct.; Thurs. of Fair Week, annual football game between U. of S. C. and Clemson; Palmetto State Fair (Negroes) last week of Oct.; Columbia-Ridgewood Open Golf Tournament, held at Ridgewood Club, near Thanksgiving.

COLUMBIA (312 alt., 51,581 pop.), the capital of South Carolina, on an undulating plateau east of the confluence of the Broad and Saluda Rivers, forming the Congaree, is almost exactly in the center of the State. Wide, shady streets mark the two-mile checkerboard square of the original plat, but the city has swelled irregularly over twice that area. The more modern residential areas are southeast; Eau Claire to the north, mill villages to the south, and West Columbia are separately incorporated.

From all approaching highways, the green-domed State House stands out significantly. As it dominates the skyline, so politics dominates Columbia. The legislature meets the second Tuesday in January, and local tradition runs that the Japanese magnolias on the capitol grounds bloom when the assembly convenes and the *Magnolia grandiflora* blossoms in the late spring before it adjourns. When the solons are in town, hotels are jammed, and the buzz of politics in lobbies and cafés, as well as in the State House, ends only when the sword of State in the senate and the mace in the house are put away, the palmetto flag of the State is hauled down from the State House, and the lawmakers at last go home.

Northward and southward from the State House stretches Main Street, the principal business thoroughfare, its broad span ablaze at night with neon signs, the flood-lighted capitol dome looming above. Streams of government workers, State and Federal, increase the street crowds, and scarcely a day passes without bringing to the capital one, often two, conventions, white or Negro. Mingling with civilians and lending a military aspect are the throngs of khaki-clad soldiers from Fort Jackson, on the edge of town, and the boys in white or blue uniforms from the Naval ROTC at the State University.

Excepting the State House, no structure on Main Street antedates 'The Burning' by Sherman, in 1865. His name is still anathema to Columbians. Each old house left standing in residential sections has a story of how it escaped the invader's torch. Recalling the typical Charleston residence, some stand sideways to the street; others, designed with delicate ironwork and columns over high arched basements, indicate the influence of Robert Mills, who lived here from 1820 to 1830. A characteristic architectural type, fast disappearing, is the 'Columbia cottage,' of a story and a half, usually with a dormer and slender square columns, and a first floor portico over a raised brick basement that is really another story. Columbia's chief beauty, however, is not in architecture but in its atmosphere of space and its fine old trees, three rows of oaks, elms, or hackberries shading some 150-foot wide avenues. Giant camellias, century-old magnolias, and sweet olives, perfuming the air, remain from former extensive gardens; roses and wisteria climb over fences and drape piazzas; azaleas and roses add their springtime color; a profusion of mimosa trees are fragrantly lovely in summer.

Between Main Street and the river lies a dismal section around the jails and penitentiary, where unpaved streets and alleys thread between rows of weather-beaten 'shotgun' houses—two or three rooms strung along one side of a narrow hall. Here live whites and Negroes of the poorer classes. Columbia's one-third Negro population is elsewhere grouped in more closely segregated areas. Waverly, a community of substantial brick and frame houses in the neighborhood of Allen and Benedict, Negro colleges, is the most prosperous. It is occupied by business and professional people who operate their own retail concerns and a tourist camp. The city has two Negro insurance companies. A Negro bank remained solvent during the depression, but unfortunately had placed its deposits in a local national bank, which closed.

The coeducational University of South Carolina, with more than 2,000 students, and the numerous other educational institutions give the city an academic air; their faculties add to a cultural and social life of dignified traditions. The Columbia Music Festival annually engages artists of national repute and tickets are usually sold out a year in advance; since 1918 the Columbia Stage Society has supported a successful Town Theater; a downtown bookstore serves coffee informally each morning to customers who drop in for intellectual discussions. With all its cultural atmosphere, the capital retains the characteristics of a big village. Since there are few opulent citizens, wealth is by no means an entrée to Columbia's informal but lively social life. The Assembly, with rigidly restricted membership, is the oldest dance organization, having served since 1889 to introduce debutantes at its annual balls. Tourists and seasonal sports' visitors contribute to gaiety; racing interests are important both to recreation and business. Some of this country's most famous race horses have been trained at Buxton Stables (see Tour 6) at the Fair Grounds.

A big event in Columbia's calendar is the State Fair, instituted in 1856, and by no means relegated solely to agriculturists. Family reunions are the order of the day and social events crowd the schedule. On 'Big Thursday' thousands fill the football stadium when two traditional rivals, the State University and Clemson College, meet on the gridiron. The governor of the State, with great ceremony, changes his box from one side to the other during the intermission between halves.

The Palmetto State Fair for Negroes follows on the same grounds the next week, when the Negro population of South Carolina enthusiastically gathers to view its own exhibits. Negro domestics make this occasion so complete a holiday that local white restaurants are crowded.

The effort to give consideration to the accomplishments of both races and all classes illustrates the theory of fair-mindedness that led to the founding of Columbia as the capital in 1786. The city had its origin in a political compromise designed to unify the antagonistic sections of the State. The small farmers of the Up Country were contending with the wealthier Low Country planters for fair representation. Removing the seat of government from Charleston was a concession that presaged the political ascendancy of Up Countrymen in subsequent decades.

Southward across the Congaree, Granby was already a flourishing trade center, its site having been early selected for a central trading 'factory,' with a fort near by erected and garrisoned by 1718. But the site was low and swampy. Stateburg, General Thomas Sumter's town in the 'High Hills of the Santee,' Camden, Orangeburg, and other places were advocated as the capital. After acrimonious debate, Colonel Thomas Taylor's plantation, 'The Plains,' and parts of the surrounding farms near Friday's Ferry were selected. When Columbia had been laid out, with wide streets designed to prevent the spread of epidemics, Colonel Taylor reputedly remarked: 'They spoiled a damned fine plantation to make a damned poor town.'

In 1790, after stage lines from Charleston to Columbia were well established, the first horse races and a ball brought the people of the State together when the legislature first convened in the unfinished State House. The following year George Washington was entertained there. In his journal he described Columbia as 'an uncleared wood with very few houses in it.'

Gradually the big city blocks were sold in four lots each. Before 1795, churches, a newspaper, and an academy were established. A tobacco warehouse was opened in 1797 and by 1800 commerce was well under way; boats plied the rivers to Charleston and barges were poled down from the Up Country. After the cotton gin was introduced in 1801, cotton planting and slavery spread in the Piedmont, and Columbia's business boomed. By 1805, when the town was incorporated, three factories were manufacturing gins; grist and sawmills, a tannery, cottonseed and castor oil presses, a brickyard, a paper mill, a rope walk, and iron and metal foundries were all in operation. In a little brick building on Colonel Taylor's plantation, cotton goods were manufactured for and by slaves in 1809; a few years later Edward and John Fisher established there a small cotton factory, using slave labor. Thus began the textile industry that is still Columbia's economic backbone. Cotton Town, in northwest Columbia, was a beehive where factors and farmers met. Above it was Butcher Town, where cattle were slaughtered.

In the young capital the mingling of Low Country dandies and sturdy Up Country Scotch-Irishmen was often far from peaceful. There were heated arguments in the State House, fisticuffs and brawls on the streets, and more gentlemanly duels in secluded spots. Realizing that sectional prejudice could best be overcome by education and by friendships between the youths from all parts of the State, thoughtful statesmen advocated the establishment of a State college in Columbia. Accordingly, in 1801, the South Carolina College (now University) was chartered.

In the decade from 1820 to 1830 Columbia's population increased to 3,310; the first steamboat, the *City of Columbia,* came up the rivers from Charleston; horsecars ran from Cotton Town to the canal wharves at the foot of Gervais Street; the Congaree, Saluda, and Broad Rivers were bridged; Barhamville, a female academy of high cultural and scholastic standing, the Columbia (Presbyterian) Theological Seminary, and the State Asylum were established. In 1842 a great celebration greeted the arrival of the *Robert Y. Hayne,* the engine bringing the first train from Charleston to Columbia. Lines to other points soon followed and river traffic, so recently a triumph, was doomed.

With the turbulent 1830's came the fight against high tariffs and the State House rang with oratory that affected national history. During Nullification and States' rights conventions Columbia's streets almost became battlefields. The line between Up Countryman and Low Countryman faded as practically every citizen became either Secessionist or bitterly antagonistic Unionist. Feeling between the two parties rose steadily, reaching fever heat by 1860.

When the legislature convened that year, Secessionists swarmed into the capital. From balconies and public halls speeches resounded; societies meeting for routine purposes became Secession hotbeds; a military company was organized by State college students; one businessman was tarred and feathered for Union sentiments.

In contrast to prevailing excitement was the solemnity of a meeting in the First Baptist Church, December 17, 1860. With their womenfolk tensely looking on, dignified men drew up the Ordinance of Secession, to sever South Carolina's connection with the Union. An epidemic of smallpox in Columbia caused the convention's removal to Charleston, where the document was signed December 20. When this news reached Columbia, bonfires flared, cannon roared, bells pealed, and military companies paraded.

A few months later feeling culminated in war. Almost every student in the State college, defying faculty authority, enlisted. Columbia women, led by Miss Isabella Martin, established in 1861 the world's first 'Wayside Hospital,' which cared for more than 1,000 soldiers the first year. A central relief association was soon formed in the capital; manufactories for arms and a Confederate mint were set up, women doing the work of men. Though social life remained courageously gay, the chief form of entertainment was benefit bazaars—one in 1865 netting $350,000 in Confederate currency. Led by Henry Timrod, Columbians crystallized in editorials, poems, and songs the emotions of the times.

The capital, believed safe from invasion, became a city of refuge rather than of defense. Nearly all the banks in the State and practically all the wealth were concentrated here; refugees doubled the population. Private homes opened their doors; everybody shared what he had; but food, clothing, and shelter became a problem. Old men and sixteen-year-old lads having joined the army, only 500 men remained in Columbia, besides Hampton's 800 cavalrymen.

Such was the situation February 16, 1865, when Sherman and his 40,000 troops began without warning to shell the city from across the Congaree River. As the army marched upon Columbia they were met by Mayor Goodwyn, who surrendered the capital at what is now Fifth Street and River Drive, a granite slab marking the spot. Sherman took up his headquarters in Colonel Blanton Duncan's new home, 1615 Gervais Street, promising that order would prevail and courtesy be shown. The next night, however, Columbia was in flames: 84 blocks, or 366 acres, with 1,386 buildings were destroyed. Besides the unfinished new State House, only the home of the French consul, protected by the French flag, remained standing on Main Street. Significant of a spirit fire could not quench was *The Phoenix*, a newspaper that literally rose from the ashes (March 21, 1865), with William Gilmore Simms as its distinguished editor.

South Carolina was the last State to succeed in re-establishing its native white government after Reconstruction. Throughout that grim period, Columbia, as the capital, bore the brunt. Government was in the hands of 'Carpet-baggers' (Northerners whose worldly goods were supposedly brought South in carpet-bags), 'Scalawags' (Southerners turned Republican), and Negroes, newly freed and intoxicated by sudden and unaccustomed power. City officials issued $850,000 worth of bonds from which Columbia derived no improvements but on which interest amounting to $2,500,000 had been paid by 1939. A 'Black and Tan' legislature spent State funds riotously on such absurdities as gold spittoons, their own coffins, and the like, leaving almost nothing for legitimate expenses. The city narrowly escaped being at the mercy of criminals, when prison officials threatened to turn them out of the penitentiary because no appropriation was made for their upkeep. The Ku Klux Klan sought to terrorize the Negroes by playing on their superstitions. Its membership including mediocre as well as leading white citizens, the Klan's activities resulted in a series of trials held in Columbia; hundreds of prominent men were involved. Radical Republican rule continued until 1876, when with the aid of the Red Shirts, an organization of white Democrats, General Wade Hampton was elected governor. Where the Klan had failed, the Red Shirts succeeded in restoring native white supremacy.

The post-election contest that followed attracted national attention. The Radicals insisted that Chamberlain was elected, and for weeks both men claimed the governorship. In the State House the Democratic, or Wallace House of Representatives, on the right side of the aisle, held forth in simultaneous oratory with the Republican, or Mackey House, on the left. Judge T. J. Mackey, Democrat, uncle of Republican Speaker Mackey, addressed the house: 'We see here two bodies assembled, each claiming to be lawful—each claiming to be the child of our mother State, but it is manifest from the difference in complexion that one of them must be illegitimate.'

Bloodshed between the Hunky-Dory clubs, armed coastal Negroes, and the Red Shirts, who swarmed into the capital ready to fight, seemed imminent. Hampton, with his usual tact and moderation, withdrew his faction from the State House to Carolina Hall. This little building on the courthouse grounds was the first erected after the burning of Columbia—constructed of brick collected from the ashes. It served for some years as courthouse and for county offices. When the second story was burned in the late seventies, the remainder was moved to the rear of the courthouse, where it is now a garage.

Before the election contest was settled, both governors went to

Washington, where President Hayes suggested to Hampton that the gubernatorial race be run over. Hampton reputedly consented on condition that Hayes would likewise submit to a second election. Remembering how narrowly he had defeated Tilden, Hayes declined, and shortly afterward Washington recognized Hampton's authority. Wild with enthusiasm, Columbia staged the greatest celebration in all its riotous career. Northern newspapermen, congregated in South Carolina's capital, recorded in metropolitan journals that seldom had anything in the United States equaled it.

At the end of the Reconstruction era, educational institutions, disrupted by war, were reopened; new ones were founded; textile industries expanded, and many new businesses were established.

The stormy administration of Governor Benjamin R. Tillman in the 1890's and his State dispensary system of handling liquor precipitated riots in the State. So opposed to 'Pitchfork Ben' were some of the elite that the State Ball, a brilliant annual function held in the State House from 1870 intermittently until the World War, was given elsewhere during his term of office. *The State*, Columbia's morning newspaper, founded in 1891 by N. G., Ambrose, and W. E. Gonzales, fought the Tillman faction so openly that resultant bitterness culminated in 1903 in the fatal shooting of N. G. Gonzales, editor, by Tillman's nephew, James H. Tillman, then lieutenant governor, on Gervais Street in front of the State House.

An asset of immense importance to Columbia's economic and social life is Fort Jackson, where approximately 40,000 men and officers are accommodated (1940). Established during the First World War as Camp Jackson and permanently maintained by the Federal Government since, it was made a regular army post in 1940 and more than $4,000,000 appropriated to equip it for training and occupation. The Fort is headquarters for the Eighth, one of the nine streamlined divisions of the United States Army, and the Thirtieth; the combined pay roll amounts to $1,000,000 monthly. Three squadrons of the Air Corps have also been assigned to Columbia, to train at Owens Municipal Field.

Between 1910 and 1930 the city's population doubled and in 1939 was estimated at 65,000. The percentage of foreign born is small, but a local American-Syrian Society numbers nearly 200 and annually sponsors a State-wide convention of Syrians.

The Negro population has produced several outstanding figures. The Reverend Charles Jaggers, a gray-haired ex-slave, affectionately known as 'Uncle Jaggers,' preached for 79 years from one text, 'Let this mind be in you which was also in Christ Jesus.' Through personal solicitations among whites and Negroes, he founded and maintained the Jaggers Old Folks' Home for Negroes. When he died in 1924, all business houses, by proclamation of the mayor, were closed during the funeral, which the governor and many officials attended. Another ex-slave, Celia Saxon, Reconstruction-era graduate of the University of South Carolina, was for 55 years a public school teacher. Local newspapers widely memorialized her on her death in 1935, and a Negro school is named for her. Dr. Mathilda Evans, a graduate of the Woman's Medical College of Philadelphia, was the first woman of her race to found a hospital, which was in Columbia a few years.

Textile manufacture has progressed with the city's growth, assuring financial stability. Olympia mill has an extensive village of substantial frame houses on shady streets; the Columbia Duck Mill, established in 1895, is reputedly the first electrically driven cotton mill in the United States; the Sumner Company, Inc., makes cloth from human hair. Among other industries are printing and engraving, fertilizer plants, cottonseed oil mills, and mattress factories.

As regional headquarters for the Farm Credit Administration, with its several branches, as State headquarters for the Work Projects Administration, the Home Owners' Loan Corporation, the Federal Housing Administration, the Farm Security Administration of Rural Rehabilitation, and the Civilian Conservation Corps, besides numerous State institutions, Columbia attracts a transient and stable population that has caused the conversion of many old homes into apartments and the rapid erection of countless new apartments and houses. In government the capital had its origin; government has made its fiery history, and government remains the force propelling the city forward in prosperity and eminence.

POINTS OF INTEREST

1. The STATE HOUSE (*open 7–6 weekdays, Sun. by appointment*), Gervais St. between Assembly and Sumter Sts., and extending to Senate St., a three-story, gray granite building of Italian Renaissance design, its hilltop park shaded by fine old trees and studded with monuments that portray South Carolina's history, has been for 75 years the center of the State's political life. Despite the substitution of the incongruous dome for the rectangular tower designed by its Viennese architect, John R. Niernsee, the State House ranks as one of the Nation's handsomest capitols.

Begun in 1851, when the first capitol proved inadequate, its foundations were unsatisfactory. Niernsee, a resident of Baltimore, was consulted in 1854, found the work defective, and at a cost of $75,000 tore out the faulty walls and started again. Appointed architect in 1854, he moved to Columbia and construction thereafter progressed satisfactorily until war halted work. Most of the granite, excavated largely by slave labor, was hauled by wagon from Granby quarry, until a three-mile railroad was specially constructed in 1857.

Bronze stars on its south and west façades mark scars made by Sherman's shells, and heat from the flames of the old State House caused the flaking of the new building's western walls. Even Sherman spared further demolition of the unfinished structure because he admired it as a 'beautiful work of art,' according to the published journal of Brevet Major George Ward Nichols, his aide-de-camp. However, the destruction by Sherman's men of finished marble, granite, wrought-iron work, and construction machinery on the grounds, with the burning of the architect's plans in the old building, represented an estimated loss of $700,000.

The structure was roofed and first used in 1869. Niernsee's death in 1885 was followed by a succession of architects and his plans were not fully carried out. Not until 1907 was the State House brought to its present state (not yet fully completed) at an approximate cost of $3,000,000. The building is 300 feet long, 150 feet wide, and 180 feet high from ground to top of dome.

The second-floor entrances, north and south, their porticos supported by 12 immense fluted Corinthian columns, are approached by monumental granite stairs. On the first landing of the north, or front, entrance, stands a life-sized bronze statue of George Washington, a duplicate of the Houdon statue at Richmond, Virginia, cast by W. J. Hubbard; the staff was broken by Sherman's men. On each side of the doorway bas-relief plaques bear likenesses of Robert Y. Hayne and George McDuffie, South Carolina statesmen of nullification days.

Inside the lobby, a niche, right of the front entrance, holds a life-sized statue of John C. Calhoun, South Carolina's greatest statesman, who served as Vice President, two terms as United States senator, and twice as a Cabinet member. The plaster figure is the model used by F. W. Ruckstuhl for the marble statue of Calhoun in Statuary Hall in the National Capitol. Adorning the lobby's marble walls are numerous other statues, busts, and commemorative plaques to distinguished South Carolinians, both men and women.

The senate chamber, in the east wing, is dominated by an oil portrait of Calhoun over the rostrum, with smaller paintings of other notables around the walls. When the senate is in session the sword of State hangs on the front of the rostrum. Made by a Charleston swordsmith in 1704, it resembles the medieval two-handed flamberge type of sword, with a silver hilt and long steel blade with waved edges. It is believed to have been in constant use since its purchase in 1704 for about $129.

The house of representatives, in the west wing, displays above the speaker's desk during legislative sessions the American flag, the State flag, and the Confederate flag; a special rack on the desk holds the gold-burnished silver mace, emblem of authority of the house. When the house files into the senate chamber, and upon state occasions, the mace is borne at the head of the procession. Made in London in 1756 by Magdalen Feline, purchased by the 'Commons House of Assembly of the province of South Carolina' for about $450, and bearing the royal arms of Great Britain, the House of Hanover, and the arms of the province of South Carolina, besides other insignia, it is reputedly the only pre-Revolutionary mace in use in the United States. In Revolutionary days it disappeared from the old State House in Charleston, was found in the vault of the Bank of the United States at Philadelphia, and restored to the State in 1819 by Langdon Cheves, a South Carolinian who that year became president of the bank.

Architecture

ROBERT MILLS (1781-1855)
Native South Carolinian and First Federal Architect
Medallion by Bela Janowsky, sculptor

OLD COURTHOUSE (1826), CAMDEN; Designed by Robert Mills

Photograph by Walter Connolly

THE FIREPROOF BUILDING (1826) CHARLESTON
Designed by Robert Mills, it is believed to be the first building of fireproof construction in the United States

Photograph by W. Lincoln Highton

BETHESDA PRESBYTERIAN CHURCH (1820), CAMDEN; Designed by Robert Mills

THE MILLS BUILDING (1828)
SOUTH CAROLINA STATE
HOSPITAL, COLUMBIA
Designed by Robert Mills

Photograph by courtesy of Anderson Chamber of Commerce
FORT HILL (c. 1803), THE HOME OF JOHN C. CALHOUN, CLEMSON COLLEGE, NEAR ANDERSON

HAMPTON (1735), NEAR McCLELLANVILLE

BOROUGH HOUSE (1754), STATEBURG

DRAWING ROOM, MILES BREWTON (Pringle) HOUSE (c. 1765), CHARLESTON

STAIRWAY
JOSEPH MANIGAULT HOUSE (1790-97)
CHARLESTON
Designed by Gabriel Manigault

Photograph by W. Lincoln Highton

DOCK STREET THEATRE (1735-36), INTERIOR, CHARLESTON; (Restored by WPA 1937)
Photograph by courtesy of Federal Works Agency

Photograph by W. Lincoln Highton

DOORWAY, COLONEL JOHN STUART HOUSE (c.1772), CHARLESTON

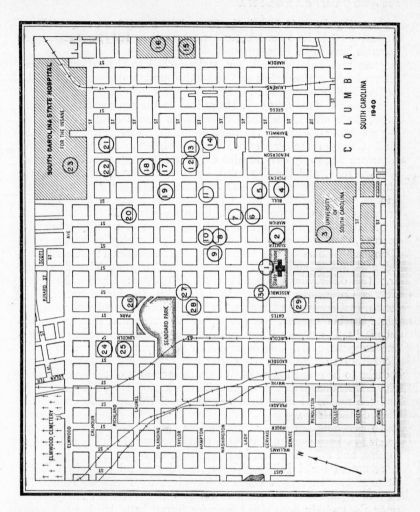

1. State House 2. Trinity Episcopal Church 3. University of South Carolina
4. Guignard House 5. La Fayette House 6. Kinard House 7. First Presbyterian
Church 8. Richland County Library 9. Richland County Courthouse 10. First
Baptist Church 11. Shaw House 12. Fisher-Bachman House 13. Woodrow
Wilson Museum 14. Chestnut Cottage 15. Allen University 16. Benedict College 17. Old Columbia Theological Seminary 18. Old Chicora College 19. Crawford-Clarkson House 20. DeBruhl-Marshall House 21. Taylor Burying Ground
22. Seibels House 23. South Carolina State Hospital 24. Boylston House
25. Governor's Mansion 26. Laurel Hill 27. Memorial Drinking Fountain
28. Ursuline Convent 29. Old Slave Market 30. Columbia Curb Market

Centering the main floor is the STATE LIBRARY (*open 9–5 weekdays*). Begun in 1800, its 25,000 books were burned in 1865; about 110,000 volumes have since been amassed.

From each side of the lobby, stairs ascend to the gallery, its wall centered by a stained-glass seal of South Carolina, designed in 1776 by Arthur Middleton and W. H. Drayton, and symbolizing the Battle of Fort Moultrie (*see History*). Doors lead to the senate and house galleries, State offices, and the CONFEDERATE RELIC ROOM (*open 9–12, 3–5 weekdays*). Dating from the Revolution, its mementos include the famous flag of the Palmetto Regiment of South Carolina, the first American flag to fly over Mexico City after its capture in the Mexican War of 1846, and the flag taken by Sherman in 1865 from the old State House. The last of these flags Sherman later gave to Andrew Sabine, whose daughter, Mrs. C. H. Mead of Beckley, West Virginia, presented it to Governor Olin D. Johnston in 1936.

From the lobby to the first floor two flights of wrought-iron stairs descend, with bronze plaques on the landing of each. One honors South Carolina's Signers of the Declaration of Independence: Edward Rutledge, Arthur Middleton, Thomas Heyward, Jr., and Thomas Lynch, Jr.; the other, the signers of the Constitution: Charles Pinckney, Charles Cotesworth Pinckney, John Rutledge, and Pierce Butler. With formal east and west entrances, the ground level, floored with pink and white marble squares, has groined brick arches and massive granite monoliths. It contains office suites of the governor, secretary of state, and supreme court. On the wall near the courtroom entrance is the Constitution shrine, surmounted by two bronze eagles and concealing a cache to be opened in 1988. Within are accounts of the sesquicentennial celebration of South Carolina's Ratification Day, May 25, 1938, and the names of more than 20,000 school children who contributed towards the shrine.

To accommodate other State offices, one five-story building was erected in 1927 south of the State House, corner of Senate and Sumter Streets, and adjoining it another was built in 1939.

Scenes of social brilliance have rivaled political gatherings in the State House. In 1909 a luncheon was given for President Taft in the hall of representatives, when ladies looked down from the galleries upon the lavishly decorated scene; for formal balls, hardwood flooring has often been laid over the marble. On the steps of the north portico, several governors have been inaugurated; William Jennings Bryan in 1900 addressed thousands; Schumann-Heink led community singing in World War days; Major General Leonard Wood in 1917, General Pershing in 1920, and President Roosevelt in 1938 greeted South Carolinians. Two World War guns, captured from the Germans, flank the north plaza.

Guarding the portico, west, is a life-sized iron PALMETTO TREE, a monument to the famous Palmetto Regiment of South Carolina in the Mexican War (*see History*). Designed by Christopher Werner of Charleston, and scarcely distinguishable from a living tree, its pedestal bears plates engraved with the names of about 450 regiment members who died in the service; only some 300 of the 1,200 members survived. Sherman's men destroyed the original plates; they were replaced by Matt Heffler, whose father helped cast the monument. Broken into bits by a freak tornado of February 1939, the statue has been restored.

North of the Palmetto Tree, and facing east, stands the bronze STATUE OF BENJAMIN RYAN TILLMAN, which was designed by Frederick C. Hibbard and unveiled in 1940.

The Confederate era is perpetuated by three monuments. Directly north of the State House is the MONUMENT TO THE CONFEDERATE DEAD, a tall white marble shaft surmounted by a figure in Confederate uniform, carved by Nicoli, Italian sculptor. The inscription, by William Henry Trescot, is a stirring summary of Southern ideals. That on the south side reads:

Let the Stranger,
Who May in Future Times
Read This Inscription,
Recognize That These Were Men
Whom Power Could not Corrupt,
Whom Death Could not Terrify,
Whom Defeat Could not Dishonor,
And Let Their Virtues Plead
For Just Judgment
Of the Cause in Which They Perished.
Let the South Carolinians
Of Another Generation
Remember
That the State Taught Them
How to Live and How to Die.
And that From Her Broken Fortunes
She Has Preserved for Her Children
The Priceless Treasure of Their Memories,
Teaching All Whom May Claim
The Same Birthright
That Truth, Courage and Patriotism
Endure Forever.

Eastward is the bronze equestrian STATUE OF GENERAL WADE HAMPTON, by F. W. Ruckstuhl. Facing Gervais Street, north, is a small-bore cannon from the U.S.S. *Maine.* Ruckstuhl's bronze group, a MONUMENT TO THE WOMEN OF THE CONFEDERACY, has an impressive inscription by W. E. Gonzales.

Facing Sumter Street, east, the MONUMENT TO SOUTH CAROLINA PARTISANS, a Scotch granite shaft, topped with a bronze figure, carries on its base bas-relief medallions of South Carolina's Revolutionary leaders: Sumter, Marion, and Pickens. Ruckstuhl was the sculptor. South of the monument is an osage orange tree brought from the D.A.R. Continental Hall at Washington, one of the cuttings given each of the Thirteen Original States to be planted on capitol grounds. Near by a little dogwood tree is marked in memory of Robert E. Lee.

On the southeast corner, in a niche approached by curving steps, is the BRONZE BUST OF J. MARION SIMS, by Edmond Quin. Doctor Sims, one of the State's great physicians, is known as the 'Father of Gynecology.'

In the 1840's Robert E. Russell planted on the eastern section of the grounds a botanical garden, from which seedlings still survive. Shading the Sims monument an overhanging spikenard tree is heavy with lavender blossoms in spring. The last old Chinese Paulownia recently died, leaving numerous progeny. The leaves of gingko trees spread an autumn shower of gold medallions on the lawns. South of the building, parallel with the east line of Main Street, which formerly bisected the park, stands a Pride of India tree, the last of those originally bordering Columbia streets. Colonel Abram Blanding, an early leading citizen, replaced them with oaks in 1805.

On the southwest corner of the grounds, enclosed by an iron fence, is the GRAVE OF CAPTAIN S. LUNSFORD, a Virginian who served in the Revolution under 'Lighthorse Harry' Lee and died in Columbia in 1799. Until the burial of Huey Long in Louisiana's capitol park in 1936, this was the only grave in the United States on State House property.

Just west of the present building, a granite marker indicates the SITE OF THE FIRST STATE HOUSE in Columbia. A wide frame structure, with a columned portico on the main floor above a brick basement, it was designed by James Hoban, afterwards appointed by President Washington architect for the White House and other Federal buildings. A branch of the Bank of the State of South Carolina, at Charleston, was established in 1812 in the basement. There the banquet honoring La Fayette was probably held in 1825. Daniel Webster, Henry Clay, and ex-President Polk were entertained, and many other elaborate social functions held. In the old State House, John C. Calhoun, Robert Y. Hayne, and George McDuffie stirred assemblies with the oratory that later electrified Washington.

2. TRINITY EPISCOPAL CHURCH, 1100 Sumter St., buff-plastered English Gothic style with arched oak doors, capped by twin towers, each supporting eight pinnacles, was designed by Edward Brickell White in 1840. Transepts added in 1861–2 have not marred its beautiful symmetry. Most of the stained-glass windows, including the rose windows, are originals from Munich, and were gifts from the Preston family, who also gave the marble baptismal font, by Hiram Powers. The church was organized in 1813, with a frame building erected the next year. Under a live oak in the shady, flower-filled churchyard adjoining are buried five governors of South Carolina, two Revolutionary officers, three Confederate generals, Henry Timrod, the poet, Dr. Thomas Cooper, and other eminent persons.

3. The UNIVERSITY OF SOUTH CAROLINA, Sumter St. between Pendleton and Divine Sts., and extending to Pickens and Main Sts., has a rolling campus of 47 acres, intersected by city streets. The elm-shaded quadrangle, formally patterned after English universities, is surrounded by a brick wall, erected in 1835. The line of aged buildings

bordering the quadrangle, completed in 1848, presents a balanced grouping and harmony of design—gray-painted brick walls and the austere simplicity of early Republican architecture. Breaking the gray note are the massive red brick library building and the double faculty residence opposite, with its two flights of stone steps leading to fanlighted front doors on the second floor. Robert Mills and Edward Clark were architects of the two oldest dormitories, Rutledge College in 1805 and DeSaussure College in 1807, and Mills's influence is evident in the other early structures. Brick walks traverse the quadrangle and on encircling drives the original lamp posts are still in use. Two-story brick houses built as slave quarters and outdoor kitchens remain behind four early faculty residences. Centering the landscaped lawn is the monument to Dr. Jonathan Maxcy, the university's first president, designed by Mills and erected in 1827 by the Clariosophic Literary Society. The Italian marble obelisk on a square base is topped with a gilded ball in wrought-iron framework.

Behind the quadrangle, Gibbes's Green, so called from old Gibbes property adjoining, is bordered along Pickens and Green Streets by memorial trees, a bronze tablet at the base of each bearing the name of a student who died in World War service.

With two professors and nine students, the university opened in Rutledge College in 1805 and is the oldest educational institution in this country entirely supported by State funds. Never having received an endowment, it has nevertheless played a vital part in State history and influenced the entire South. Here in 1820 the second separate chair of geology in the United States was established; in 1840 the study of political economy was first seriously introduced in this country by Dr. Thomas H. Cooper, becoming in 1855 a separate professorship under Francis Lieber; and in 1840 the first separate library building at any school in the Nation was erected.

The first president, Doctor Maxcy (1805-20), a pulpit orator, stressed public speaking. Such orators as George McDuffie, U. S. senator and governor, W. C. Preston, U. S. senator, and James Henley Thornwell, educator and divine, were trained at the university.

Cooper and Lieber profoundly influenced South Carolina history. To the teachings of the former, an Englishman, South Carolina's stand on nullification and States' rights is frequently attributed. Professor in 1819, he became president in 1820, and in 1827 he declared, 'It is time to calculate the value of the Union'—a remark that reverberated as treason in Northern newspapers. Wanted by Jefferson as president of the University of Virginia, the brilliant Cooper's unorthodoxy was objectionable to Virginia clergy. To offset his agnosticism, several denominational colleges were established in the South. That parents feared Cooper's influence on their sons is shown in the decrease of the student body. 'From Dr. Henry's report to the board, November 26, 1834,' writes Dr. E. L. Green, in his *History of the University of South Carolina*, 'the substance of which has been preserved by Dr. LaBorde, we learn that only twenty students had been left in the

college; at no period during the year had the number exceeded 52.'
Though acquitted in a heresy trial, Cooper resigned in 1835 by request
of the board. The three presidents following him, Robert Woodward
Barnwell (1835–41), William C. Preston (1845–50), and the Reverend
James Henley Thornwell, D.D. (1851–5), did much to regain the
people's confidence; but repercussions of accusations hurled at the university during Cooper's administration are still felt.

Lieber, German liberal, professor from 1835 to 1856, was as passionate a Unionist as Cooper was Secessionist. Many of the State's
leading Union men were his pupils: James L. Petigru, Governors Wade
Hampton III, J. H. Hammond, and John L. Manning; Hugh S. Legare,
U. S. Attorney General, William C. Preston, and C. G. Memminger,
secretary-treasurer of the Confederacy. Affectionately dubbed 'Old
Bruin' by college boys, Lieber wrote here his best-known political
science works.

Other distinguished ante-bellum professors included Dr. Robert W.
Gibbes, scientist, writer, and publisher; Dr. William Ellet, who made
the first daguerreotype in America, and fired the first gun with gun
cotton; Lewis R. Gibbes, scientist; William Capers and Stephen Elliott,
both afterwards bishops; John and Joseph LeConte, eminent scientists; Edward Hooker, whose diary has furnished data for early-nine-
teenth-century South Carolina history; Maximilian LaBorde and William J. Rivers, historians; Augustus B. Longstreet, author of *Georgia
Scenes*. Louis Agassiz was a visiting lecturer. Many university graduates have served as college presidents and statesmen in this and other
States.

Federal and Confederate wounded were quartered in the dormitories
(1862–5) under the yellow flag, thus saving the buildings from Sherman's conflagration. Homeless citizens crowded into the southern side
of the quadrangle after 'The Burning' and remained there with Union
soldiers in 1866, when the institution opened in the northern dormitories as the University of South Carolina. Though the school of law
had been recommended by the first president and law lectures given
by Doctor Cooper, the law school was formally established in 1867.
A school of medicine, opened the same year, continued until 1873.

The Reconstruction constitution of 1868 authorized the admission of
Negroes, but the tenure of some white professors and students staved
off the occurrence until 1873, when white faculty and students immediately left. In the four years of Negro admission only 23 degrees were
conferred. Governor Hampton closed the institution in 1877; it was
reopened in 1880 as the College of Agriculture and Mechanic Arts
and for some years seesawed between college and university. The German Club, first college dance organization in the United States, was
organized in 1882.

Coeducation was established in 1893. After 1906, when the charter
of the university was again granted, the rocky path of the historic institution was smoothed for continuous growth. Bachelors' and Masters'
degrees are offered in the various departments.

The WORLD WAR MEMORIAL (*open 9–5 weekdays, 9–1 Sat.*), SE. corner Pendleton and Sumter Sts., is a two-story Carolina granite building of Neoclassic design with Indiana limestone trim. Designed by Lafaye and Lafaye of Columbia, it was built in 1935. The first floor foyer opens into the trophy hall, with archives open to research. Offices of the secretary of the State Historical Commission are at the rear. Marble stairs ascend to the memorial hall. Its central shrine, with pink Tennessee marble walls and a white marble altar, is carved with the State seal, flanked with flags, and inscribed to 'The Soldiers of South Carolina.'

The LIBRARY (*open 8:30 A.M.–10:30 P.M. weekdays, 3–6 Sun.*), NW. corner of the quadrangle, is a three-story structure with four immense Doric columns forming a front portico and a vine-clad bay in the rear accommodating the main stairway. Ivy on the walls is from cuttings brought by Lieber from Kenilworth Castle, England. Showing Mills's influence, the design was submitted by faculty members, the architect unknown. Fireproof wings were added in 1927. From the wide hall of the first floor stairs ascend and doors open on the reading room and stacks. From these rooms spiral staircases wind up to the main library and continue to balconies on the third floor. Around the walls of the principal library room, where the senate met, 1865–8, arched alcoves with supporting buttresses are trimmed with fluted panels and Corinthian capitals. Adorning the walls of this room and the hall are portraits and busts of ancient scholars, professors, trustees, and alumni of the university. Most notable is the marble bust of W. C. Preston, by Hiram Powers.

In the west wing, second floor, is the museum, in which is the armchair, or 'quasi-throne,' used by South Carolina proprietary governors at Charleston, 1670–1719. The third floor, west wing, contains a valuable collection of South Caroliniana. The library has about 125,000 volumes; some 25,000 are in special departmental libraries. Among the priceless books is the elephant folio edition (1827–38) of Audubon's *The Birds of America*. The board of trustees announced in 1940, the centennial of the building of the library, that after the completion of the new one, the old library will be devoted to South Carolina books and manuscripts.

HARPER COLLEGE, centering the north quadrangle line, has on its third floor the Euphradian Literary Society Hall, containing valuable portraits of distinguished members. The Euphradian and Clariosophic Societies were organized in 1806. Harper College, named for Chancellor William Harper, the university's first matriculate, was built in 1848 and occupies the original site of Commons Hall, the scene of many historic riots. Four rooms in the central portion were used by a Federal garrison as a military prison.

DESAUSSURE COLLEGE, NE. end of quadrangle, was used by Union and Confederate troops successively as a hospital. Originally called 'North,' the name honors Chancellor H. W. DeSaussure, first Director of the Mint, who was instrumental in founding the university and one of its first trustees.

Rear of DeSaussure, facing Pendleton St., is the OFFICE OF THE UNIVERSITY NEWS SERVICE, a small, buff, stuccoed structure erected in 1858 as the observatory and greatly damaged in the War between the States.

Facing the quadrangle is the new LIBRARY, designed by Henry C. Hibbs and completed in 1940 at a cost of $657,000 appropriated by the State government and PWA and constructed by WPA. Built of Indiana limestone, darkened by chemicals, the wide building has two main stories and a basement, with three stories in the north and south wings, and a fourth story under the central dome. Main entrances are east and west under porticos with tall Doric columns, and basement entrances, north and south, are beneath similar porticos. The immense fireproof structure is visible on streets approaching from all sides, presenting an imposing appearance. The interior is entirely modern, with book stacks, a periodical room, reserve reading room, offices for the staff, quarters for the library school, a faculty room, and seminars.

Immediately in front of the library formerly stood the president's house, built in 1807 and torn down as unsafe in 1940. In the Post-Colonial mansion Daniel Webster was entertained by William C. Preston, president of the institution in 1847; and from its portico President Taft addressed students in 1909. The house became a Confederate officers' hospital in 1865, and behind it were buried the Confederate and Union soldiers who died on the campus, their remains later removed to Elmwood Cemetery. From 1873 to 1877 the Negro Normal School was housed in the dwelling. After Reconstruction it was again the president's residence, and from 1922 to 1938 was used as the Administration Building.

Facing Green Street, SW. corner of Gibbes's Green, is the MELTON OBSERVATORY (*open* 7–9 P.M. *Mon. and Wed.*), a gray structure suggestive of a Greek shrine. The dome, reached by a winding stair, contains a Bausch and Lomb telescope, one of the largest in the South. The observatory was the gift of Edwin G. Seibels, alumnus, in honor of William Davis Melton, university president 1922–6.

In the oldest building, RUTLEDGE COLLEGE, SE. end of the quadrangle, the library was originally housed and literary societies first met in the central first-floor chapel. The old bell hangs in its cupola. Long known as 'South,' the building is named for John Rutledge, Revolutionary statesman. Burned and rebuilt on original lines in 1855, it accommodated Union staff headquarters in 1865 and the house of representatives, 1865–8.

On the first floor of LEGARE COLLEGE, center of south quadrangle line, is the Clariosophic Literary Society Hall, with portraits of noted members. Built in 1848, it is named for Hugh S. Legare, class of 1814. The offices of the commandant of Confederate troops, the provost marshal's office, the Columbia post office, and an extra legislative session in 1865 were in this building.

The cream-colored, stuccoed GYMNASIUM, centering Sumter St. at Green St., resembles a Mills building and rises two stories above a basement, a broad sweep of steps leading to the columned portico on the main floor. Designed by Jacob Graves in 1855 as a chapel, the faulty acoustics prevented its use for that purpose and caused the legislature to vacate it after one day's session in 1865. From 1862–5 this was a hospital; in 1870 the basement became an armory, and the influenza epidemic of 1918 caused the building's second use as a hospital.

Behind the Gymnasium is the tile and concrete SWIMMING POOL in a well-equipped building erected in 1939, partly with WPA funds.

4. The GUIGNARD HOUSE (*private*), 1527 Senate St., is a two-story white frame dwelling with green shutters and a street level entrance to the basement, over which is a little sloping roof. The original portion of the house was reputedly built soon after Columbia's founding by John Gabriel Guignard or his brother-in-law, General Peter Horry. It was saved from burning in 1865 by the ingenuity of the slave cook, Dilcie. She voluntarily went to meet Sherman after the tenants had sought refuge elsewhere, offered hospitality and 'de bes' cookin' in Columbia.' Union officers established headquarters here and, as Dilcie predicted, presented her on their departure with the house and its contents, which she guarded for her 'white folks.'

5. The LA FAYETTE HOUSE, 1409 Gervais St., operated as a boarding house, is a two-story gray frame building of Post-Colonial style, with piazzas on both floors. It was built by Isaac Randolph in 1820. On the sidewalk in front is a granite marker stating that La Fayette and his party were entertained here March 11–14, 1825.

6. The KINARD HOUSE (*private*), 1400 Lady St., a two-story brown frame structure, is often erroneously described as the old courthouse at Granby, seat of Saxe Gotha District, old Lexington County, but is more correctly believed to have been a former Guignard residence built at uncertain date. Major John Niernsee, State House architect, bought the property in 1858 and resided here till 1874, greatly improving the interior. The materials of the old Granby courthouse, bought by the First Presbyterian Church, may have been used in their first manse, which once stood on the northwest corner of Lady and Marion Streets. The house, with a slate roof and iron grillwork around its one-story portico, bears on its front door the heel prints made by Sherman's soldiers in their unsuccessful efforts to kick it in. The interior walls are coursed to simulate masonry.

7. The FIRST PRESBYTERIAN CHURCH, NE. corner Marion and Lady Sts., a vine-covered Gothic Revival edifice of reddish brown, stucco-covered brick, has a tall spire that is one of Columbia's most distinctive architectural features. Built in 1853, damaged by cyclone in 1875, and remodeled in 1925, its original grace has not been impaired. Robert Mills was an elder here 1822–30. The adjoining churchyard, covering half a block, was Columbia's first cemetery, established in 1797 and bought by the Presbyterians in 1813 for their first church. Among eminent people buried here are Dr. D. E. Dunlap, the first

pastor (installed 1795), Henry William DeSaussure, first Director of the Mint, Ann Pamela Cuningham, and Woodrow Wilson's parents, Dr. and Mrs. Joseph R. Wilson.

8. The RICHLAND COUNTY LIBRARY (*open 9–9 weekdays*), NE. corner Washington and Sumter Sts., a two-story red brick building set flush with the sidewalk, is the old home of President Wilson's uncle, Dr. James Woodrow, who operated here the Presbyterian Publishing Company. Richland County has matched the Rosenwald Fund in maintenance of the library since 1930. A book truck serves the county weekdays. Volumes number more than 64,000, with a monthly circulation of 43,500.

9. The RICHLAND COUNTY COURTHOUSE (*open 9–5:30 weekdays, 9–1 Sat.*), NW. corner Sumter and Washington Sts., is a red brick structure of modified Georgian style with Indiana limestone trim, built in 1936. In the front foyer a bronze chest imbedded in the floor is marked: 'Sesqui-Centennial Cache To Be Opened in 1986.'

10. The FIRST BAPTIST CHURCH, Hampton St., between Marion and Sumter Sts., is a dignified brown brick building somewhat resembling early New England churches, with no steeple or bell, square double front door and arched windows. The wide entrance porch has four brick columns, their bases formed by encircling flanges of lighter-hued handmade brick, with a bell-shaped cross section. Indicating the influence of Mills's architecture, the church was erected in 1856, the second edifice for a congregation organized in 1809. The site of the first structure is now occupied by a modern Sunday school building. Determined to destroy the church where the 'Rebel Convention' met to draw up the Ordinance of Secession, Sherman's soldiers are supposed to have been deliberately misdirected by the Negro sexton to the old frame church, erected in 1811, which they burned instead.

11. The SHAW HOUSE (*private*), 1502 Hampton St., is a two-story white frame house with green shutters, a flat roof with wrought-iron grill work railing, and columned porticos on front and sides. Built by Henry Davis about 1850, it was saved from Sherman's torch by the Italian flag, hoisted by its resident, Alexander Herbemont, Italian consul. After the State House was destroyed, Governor Orr had his offices here. In the basement, Henry Timrod (1829–67), unofficially the poet laureate of the Confederacy, worked for 24 hours at a time as governor's clerk, his only occupation when the burning of Columbia reduced him to want.

The poet's career was frustrated by poverty, ill health, and war. His first volume of poems appeared in 1860, to be favorably reviewed North and South, but war hindered its sale; he enlisted in the Confederate Army in 1862, to be discharged on account of tuberculosis. A native of Charleston, he came to Columbia in 1864 as part owner and assistant editor of *The South Carolinian,* which shared the capital's conflagration. With his wife, his mother, and his widowed sister's family dependent on him, his attempts to found a girls' school here were unsuccessful. Timrod's spirit, however, never flagged. In a post-war letter to Paul Hamilton Hayne, his friend and brother poet, he wrote: 'We have eaten two silver pitchers, one or two dozen forks, several sofas, innumerable chairs, and a huge bedstead.'

12. The FISHER-BACHMAN HOUSE (*private*), 1615 Hampton St., a two-story white frame house with green shutters, set on a shady lawn surrounded by an iron fence, is one of Columbia's most attractive dwellings. Dr. Edward Fisher built the original structure soon after 1801. The delicate iron grillwork around its flat roof and long Corinthian front portico, the carved wood medallions under the cornices, and arched decorations over doors and windows were designed by Dr. John Bachman and his daughter when the house was much enlarged in the 1840's, in preparation for the latter's wedding. Interior remodeling included arched panels, sliding on chains, between the hall and two front drawing rooms. At the time of the marriage, a panel stuck, and Dr. Peter Shand, Episcopal rector, performed the ceremony peering over the top at the bridal couple on the other side.

13. The WOODROW WILSON MUSEUM (*open 9–6 daily, free*), 1705 Hampton St., a two-story white frame house, was Wilson's boyhood home from 1871 to 1875, and was designed by his mother, Mrs. Joseph R. Wilson, who personally supervised its construction. On the lawn, surrounded by a green wooden fence, four magnolia trees and a giant sweet olive remain from Mrs. Wilson's garden. Among Wilson mementos displayed is the bed in which the President was born. Bought by the State in 1929, the museum was placed under the custody of the South Carolina Historical Commission and the American Legion of South Carolina; a small sum is annually appropriated for its upkeep.

14. The CHESTNUT COTTAGE (*private*), 1718 Hampton St., a story-and-a-half white frame house with green shutters and a central dormer with an arched window, is an example of the 'Columbia cottage.' Its small portico has octagonal columns and an ironwork balustrade. Jefferson Davis was entertained here in 1864 by General James Chestnut, Jr. Mrs. (Mary Boykin) Chestnut, in *A Diary from Dixie*, describes the event: 'Mr. Davis sat out on our piazza . . . Some little boys strolling by called out, "Come here and look; there is a man on Mrs. Chestnut's porch who looks just like Jeff Davis on the postage stamps." People began to gather at once on the street. The President then went in . . . Colonel McLean came to inform us that a great crowd had gathered and they were coming to ask the President to speak to them . . . An immense crowd it was—men, women, and children . . . The President's hand was nearly shaken off.'

15. ALLEN UNIVERSITY (Negro), SE. corner Taylor and Harden Sts., consists of several two- and three-story red brick buildings, its campus surrounded by a brick wall. Owned and controlled by the A.M.E. Church of South Carolina, Allen was founded at Cokesbury and moved here in 1880. With an enrollment of over 300, it confers degrees in arts, science, and theology, and is officially recognized as a leading Negro college. In addition to regular equipment, there is a printing plant and an employment bureau for students.

16. BENEDICT COLLEGE (Negro), NE. corner Taylor and Harden Sts., occupies a group of three- and four-story brick buildings on a shady 20-acre campus enclosed by a white picket fence. The square chapel has a cupola containing the college bell. Founded in 1870 by the Baptist Home Mission Society, it gives courses in religion and education and confers degrees in arts, science, and theology. It also offers a pre-medical course and is rated a Class A Senior College by the State department of education. The average enrollment is 332.

17. The OLD COLUMBIA THEOLOGICAL SEMINARY (Presbyterian), Blanding St. between Henderson and Pickens Sts. and extending to Taylor St., now owned and occupied by the Columbia Bible College, has spacious grounds shaded by tall trees for its three red brick buildings with white stone trim. An iron fence with brick gate posts surrounds it. The Greek Revival central building was designed by Robert Mills for Ainsley Hall immediately after the latter sold his residence, now Old Chicora College, to General Hampton in 1823. With a mansard roof, its two stories rest upon a high gray stone basement with arched entrances, and from the portico four Doric columns reach to the gabled pediment. Seminary trustees bought the property in 1829 from Mrs. Hall, and used it continuously until the institution was moved in 1927 to Decatur, Georgia. Near Henderson Street originally stood a brick carriage house, later converted into the chapel where President Wilson, whose father taught at the seminary, worshipped as a boy, and where in 1886 Winthrop College was founded. The building was moved in 1937 to Winthrop's campus in Rock Hill.

Among the seminary's most distinguished professors were Dr. George Howe, historian, professor 1831–81, Dr. B. M. Palmer, Dr. J. H. Thornwell, Dr. J. L. Girardeau, Dr. Joseph R. Wilson, and Dr. James Woodrow. About Doctor Woodrow in the 1880's raged the evolution controversy that shook the Presbyterian Church to its foundations, temporarily closed the seminary, and in 1886 forced Woodrow's resignation. He was elected president of the University of South Carolina in 1891, having previously served on this faculty while holding his seminary professorship.

18. OLD CHICORA COLLEGE (*open*), Blanding St., between Henderson and Pickens Sts. and extending to Laurel St., occupied by Federal and State governmental agencies, was formerly the Hall-Hampton-Preston mansion. Built about 1818 by Ainsley Hall, the two-story gray-stuccoed edifice of Post-Colonial design is almost hidden by evergreens. Sometimes attributed to Robert Mills, it has a front portico with Doric columns and a fanlight in the cornice over the portico. Broad iron steps extend from the ends of the piazza into the garden. A graceful circular stairway with mahogany rails leads from the wide hall to the second story; a white marble mantel in the east drawing room was designed by Hiram Powers, friend and protégé of the Prestons. Columbia's first incandescent gaslights were installed here by Hall, an early merchant and cotton factor.

Surrounding the property is a wisteria-covered brick wall, with an iron fence on a low wall across the front. Magnolias, japonicas, and sweet olives grow to enormous size; paths are bordered by giant box-wood hedges. Sadly neglected now, the gardens were once famous as among the finest in the State. The property was bought in 1823 by General Wade Hampton I; and the design of the gardens is credited to Mrs. Hampton and to her daughter, Mrs. John S. Preston, who inherited the home. General John A. Logan established his Union headquarters here in 1865, and intended to burn it on his departure, but the house was saved by persuasion of the Ursuline Sisters, who temporarily used it as a refuge when their convent was burned, and from 1887 to 1890 as a convent. Franklin J. Moses, governor 1872–4, bought it for his Reconstruction administration. Purchased by the Presbyterian Synod in 1890 for its College for Women, the place became Chicora College from 1915 to 1930. The Columbia Art Asso-ciation is now (1940) planning to convert the place into a museum.

19. The CRAWFORD-CLARKSON HOUSE (*private*), 1502 Bland-ing St., a two-story yellow frame house over a raised red brick base-ment, has a flat copper roof. Tall green-shuttered windows lead out on a long western balcony with grilled railing; second floor piazzas have delicate ironwork rails. The first-story portico is approached by iron steps and flanked by slender, square, metal-framed columns with glass on each face. The hollow glass columns, originally designed for illumi-nation with tall candles, are now lighted by electricity. John A. Craw-ford built the house about 1837; still owned by his descendants, the stately interior is little changed. Hand-stenciled wallpaper has with-stood time and fire, and upon it hangs a Scarborough portrait of the builder. Though he secured a guard to protect his home from burning in 1865, a mahogany secretary bears two scars made by bayonet thrusts of Sherman's soldiers.

20. The DeBRUHL-MARSHALL HOUSE (*private*), 1401 Laurel St., commonly attributed to Mills, is a two-story red brick mansion, Greek Revival style, with white stone trim and green shutters. Under the portico, with its massive Doric columns, are the arched basement entrances characteristic of Mills. Built in 1820 by Jesse DeBruhl, political leader, it was later owned by Colonel J. Q. Marshall, also prominent in State affairs. Colonel James Johnstone, C.S.A., is believed to have used the house as headquarters prior to 1865. Mrs. John S. Wiley, DeBruhl's widow, persuaded Sherman's soldiers to extinguish flames they had set to the house.

21. The TAYLOR BURYING GROUND, NW. corner Richland and Barnwell Sts., no longer in use, is surrounded by an old red brick wall with iron gates. The old Taylor home once stood near by. In a tangle of bushes and weeds are several raised marble tombs and new granite headstones. One grave is that of Colonel Thomas Taylor. Among other members of the family buried here is the colonel's son, John, Colum-bia's first mayor in 1806, governor of South Carolina 1826–8, and later congressman and United States senator.

22. The SEIBELS HOUSE (*private*), 1601 Richland St., a two-story building with Georgian lines, somewhat resembles Mt. Vernon. It was built by A. M. Hale, the figures 1796, carved on an interior beam, indicating the date of erection. The first story is of brick with white shutters, the second of white clapboards with green shutters. Three dormers and a doorway with square fluted Doric columns are on each side. Supported by slender white columns, piazzas extend on three sides and a colonnade leads to a brick kitchen in the rear.

23. The SOUTH CAROLINA STATE HOSPITAL (*open by permission*), entrance on Bull St. at Elmwood Ave., is set in a park with tall trees and many flowers, a high brick wall enclosing the original grounds, locally called the 'campus.' The MILLS BUILDING (R), named for its architect and erected in 1828, is the Nation's oldest edifice continuously in use as a mental hospital. Greek Revival style, the three-story red brick structure has a two-story portico with Doric columns, a windowed cupola painted white, and a red roof. Around arched basement entrances, curved stairs lead to the portico. The door and windows are arched and long symmetrical wings are set at oblique angles to the central pavilion. Other buildings architecturally harmonize with the oldest and have decorative grillwork instead of the conventional window bars. The Dix Cottage perpetuates the name of Dorothea Dix, who visited the hospital in 1852 and 1859 and raised a benefit fund. The institution's farms extend northward, and the plant, including property at State Park, has 2,707 acres.

The hospital, founded in 1821, has national repute. Pellagra was first recognized and treated here, under Dr. J. W. Babcock, superintendent 1891–1914. In 1931 the United States Public Health Service established here a division of Field Investigation of Malaria, the central depot in this country for dissemination of curative material in malarial therapy for paresis. An extensive laboratory was added in 1937.

24. The BOYLSTON HOUSE (*private*), 829 Richland St., is one of Columbia's finest examples of Greek Revival architecture. The three-story yellow frame house with green shutters, surrounded by an iron fence and hedge, and set in densely planted gardens that extend a block to the rear, was built in 1822 by John Caldwell, merchant, cotton factor, and railroad magnate. A marble fountain, now broken, designed by Hiram Powers for the Preston garden, was bought and moved here in 1931.

25. The GOVERNOR'S MANSION (*private*), entrance Richland St., between Lincoln and Gadsden Sts., is a simple Post-Colonial white-stuccoed two-story building, with green paneled shutters. The landscaped grounds, shaded by tall trees, are enclosed by a cast-iron fence on a low plastered wall. The house was built in 1855 as officers' barracks of the Arsenal Academy, and was the only part of the school to escape 'The Burning.' Here, December 5, 1938, President Roosevelt was the guest of Governor Olin D. Johnston at breakfast, the menu consisting entirely of South Carolina dishes.

26. LAUREL HILL (*private*), NW. corner Laurel and Assembly Sts., a three-story white Georgian mansion with tall white chimneys topped by green chimney pots and set on a hilltop, is a distinguished land-mark from a distance, though the 23-room mansion with columns in front is almost hidden from close view by the brick wall enclosing its evergreen garden. One of two cork oaks now in Columbia was re-putedly grown here from seed from the Royal Botanical Gardens, Kew, London.

Designed in 1897 by the firm of Brite and Bacon of New York, and requiring two years' work for elaborate interior carved paneling, the house occupies the site of Governor John Taylor's home. Captain and Mrs. Basil Hall of England, traveling in the South in 1828, were enter-tained by the Taylors. In her *Aristocratic Journey* Mrs. Hall records the menu of the first course as follows: 'Ham, turkeys (roast and boiled), chickens, roast ducks, corned beef, and fish, together with various dishes of sweet potatoes, Irish potatoes, cabbage, rice, and beets.'

27. The MEMORIAL DRINKING FOUNTAIN, at the end of the central parkway in Assembly St. at the intersection with Taylor St., one of similar watering places for horses and dogs on each highway entering Columbia, was erected in 1925 by Mrs. A. D. Porcher in memory of her setters, Dick and Fan, and bronze tablets on the white marble fountain are so inscribed. On the side toward the intersection is a curved trough for horses; protected from traffic, at the back, is a low trough for dogs.

28. The URSULINE CONVENT, 1505 Assembly St., is a red brick building erected in 1891; it adjoins St. Peter's Roman Catholic Church. As the Academy of the Immaculate Conception it was established in 1852 by the Sisters of Mercy. They were succeeded by the Ursuline Nuns, who came to Columbia from Black Rock, Ireland, in 1858. After the first building, corner Main and Blanding Streets, was burned in 1865, the convent occupied several others before its present quarters were built. The curriculum includes a high school for girls and parochial school for girls and boys.

29. The OLD SLAVE MARKET (*private*), SW. corner Senate and Assembly Sts., includes the ante-bellum residence of Samuel Mercer Logan, 1016 Senate Street, who operated the market, and in the rear a small square red brick building with high barred windows, where slaves were confined at night until sold in the street. The court and driveway are paved in odd design with irregular slabs of granite and marble, the work having been done by slaves.

30. The COLUMBIA CURB MARKET occupies a series of fireproof sheds, with canvas awnings, in the middle of Assembly St. between Lady and Pendleton Sts. The 160 market stalls display a large assortment of produce ranging from lightwood or 'kindlin' ' fagots and little bundles of sassafras roots in season through every type of vege-table and fruit within trucking distance, to gaily colored and scented flowers fresh from the hinterlands. In the open-sided stalls mingle the

diluted odors of onions and wild azaleas, peanuts and apples, oranges and cabbages. Chickens cluck in wooden crates, stall owners sell out their wares as housewives fill their baskets with the various commodities, and traffic honks and rumbles past on both sides of the long narrow sheds.

Assembly Street stores catch the spirit of the mart and line their curb with smelly tow bags, the tops rolled down to show fuzzy cotton-seed, six-foot conical fish traps of woven oak splits, farming tools, and dozens of seasonal oddments. Occasionally, late in the day, a guitar-playing Negro singer strolls through the market section, collecting coins in a cup.

The southern block of the market, between Senate and Pendleton Streets, is the box, basket, and crate wholesale center, where loaded trucks await a buyer for their entire lot. Trucks with Florida licenses pull off the tail gate to display red mesh bags filled with oranges, grapefruit, tangerines, and lemons. Virginia trucks open baskets of shiny red apples packed in purple paper. South Carolina trucks are filled with ruffled green globes of cabbages, or any one of many other vegetables or fruits in season. Truckers from distant States swap entire loads of truck to carry back to their respective homes.

Many proprietors spend the night watching over their produce. Men, women, and sometimes children, white and Negro, pull out cots and blankets or stretch out on counters to sleep till six, when business begins again.

POINTS OF INTEREST IN ENVIRONS

Kendall Farm, 2.6 *m.;* Cayce House, 3 *m.;* Lutheran Seminary, 3 *m.;* Columbia College, 3.5 *m.* (*see Tour 5*). Buxton Stables, Fair Grounds, 2 *m.;* Sesqui-Centennial State Park, 10.7 *m.;* Sand Hill Experiment Station, 14.8 *m.* (*see Tour 6a*). Millwood, 4.3 *m.;* Veterans' Hospital, 4.8 *m.;* Fort Jackson, 4.8 *m.;* Stateburg, 32.1 *m.;* Poinsett State Park, 43.9 *m.* (*see Tour 9b*). Lake Murray, 14.1 *m.* (*see Tour 9c*).

Florence

Railroad Stations: Between northern extremities of Gaillard and Dixon Sts. for Atlantic Coast Line R. R., main line; SE. corner of W. Darlington and N. Irby Sts. for Seaboard Air Line Ry.
Bus Station: Union Bus Station, 242 W. Evans St., for Atlantic Greyhound, Stokes Bus, Greensboro-Fayetteville Bus, and Pee Dee Coach Lines, Southeastern Stages, Queen City Coach Co.
Airport: Municipal, 2 m. E. on US 301, 0.5 m. S. on Air Port Road. Pee Dee Flying Service field, privately owned, 1.5 m. E. on US 301, 0.5 m. S. on Air Port Road.
Taxis: 10¢ and upward.

Accommodations: 3 hotels, tourist houses.

Information Service: Board of Trade, City Hall, 123–7 W. Evans St.

Radio Station: WOLS (1200 kc.).
Motion Picture Houses: 2.
Swimming: Municipal Pool, open 7 A.M.–11 P.M., June–Sept., adm. 10¢, City Park, southern end of S. McQueen St.
Tennis; Soft Ball: City Park, S. McQueen St.
Golf: Florence Country Club, 2 m. W. on US 76; 9 holes; greens fee, $1.

Annual Event: Pee Dee Fair, held in fall.

FLORENCE (136 alt., 14,774 pop.), seat of Florence County, in the eastern part of the State, 65 miles from the coast, is the largest railroad transfer point in South Carolina and consequently a shipping center for the various industrial plants in the city and the rich agricultural products of the surrounding country. At the intersection of five paved highways, geographically half way between New York and Miami, the city has become an important stopping place for tourists.

The business district differs from the shopping areas in hundreds of other small cities in the Southeast only by its atmosphere of busy activity, for Florence is the trade center of several surrounding counties. One six-story structure soars ambitiously above the buildings on Evans Street, the retail thoroughfare, which has a crook in its course where an old brick yard stood in early days beside a frog pond.

Street numbers are listed north and south from Evans Street, east and west from Dargan Street. West Florence is the popular residence section, in which extensive lawns, flower gardens, and well-kept streets shaded by oaks make an attractive setting for an unusual number of brick dwellings, though back streets have the usual number of drab little houses, generally unpainted and overcrowded, for the lower classes of both races. In East Florence are the small homes owned by the hundreds of railroad shop workers, who compose a good proportion of the inhabitants.

The city's population is almost entirely American, composed of the descendants of Scotch-Irish, Huguenot, English, and a scattering of Scottish settlers of the region, with 48 per cent Negro. Most of the Negroes live in the northern and eastern sections of town, with the better homes in the latter area. Florence Negroes make a notable contribution to the South Carolina Tuberculosis Association with a 'community sing' each Christmas, when the offering taken yields a substantial sum. The railroad shops employ only 10 per cent Negro labor, domestic and agricultural pursuits absorbing the greatest number.

Hunting and fishing are the major outdoor sports of Florence citizens, and five local clubs own their own game preserves. Fish stews on the banks of streams and lakes are part of the birthright of all—men and women, whites and Negroes, young and old. Remarkable fish tales are told, which none believe but all enjoy.

The city is in the heart of the tobacco section and the Tobacco Jubilee is an important event of the Pee Dee Fair in Florence each fall. Jubilee queens are chosen from the towns roundabout and ride in a parade of gaily decorated floats.

Florence has no site of Revolutionary War fame to lend it glamor, though the surrounding swamps were favorite hiding places for Francis Marion's men. In early times the territory was covered by plantations and timberlands owned by sober, industrious churchgoers. Toward the southeast the Scotch-Irish Presbyterians settled in 1732, and northwest the Welsh Baptists came in 1736. The present site of the city is nearly bisected by the boundary line on old plats between the plantation of Miss Susannah Connell of the Ebenezer Baptist congregation and that of Thomas McCall of the Hopewell Presbyterian Church.

Florence, revolving economically around its railroad shops, owes its existence to the eccentricity of Colonel Eli Gregg who, in the 1850's, owned the largest store at Mars Bluff, seven miles eastward. Due to his prejudice against railroad workmen, Colonel Gregg refused to allow a depot in his neighborhood, and consequently the Wilmington and Manchester Railroad was forced to locate its station some distance away in an uninhabited forest of virgin pines. First called 'Wilds' for a distinguished jurist in the vicinity, this point became in 1853–4 the junction for the Wilmington and Manchester and the Northwestern Railroads. A third line, the Cheraw and Darlington, entered and established shops in 1859. The name was then changed to Florence in honor of the baby daughter of General William Harllee, head of the Wilmington and Manchester Line, who was largely instrumental in the young town's progress. Florence boomed ahead while Mars Bluff, left to its traditions, today is merely a flag station.

In Florence's early days the depot was also the post office; church services were held in one end of an old railroad eating house; children played hide-and-seek behind the barrels of turpentine and the bales of cotton piled on freight platforms. In 1860 a small hotel was erected where passengers on the one daily train could stop for meals and a night's lodging. A few other straggling buildings served as quarters for railroad operatives and homes for the families that had moved in. A school and a Presbyterian church were soon established, to be followed by a Baptist, and later by a Methodist and an Episcopal church.

During the War between the States, Florence rose to importance: first as a shipping center and point of embarkation for troops, next as a hospital town, and finally as a prison. Three miles south of the city a 'prison pen' was built for some 8,000 Federal prisoners. Before the stockade was completed the incoming streams of prisoners were herded into an improvised camp in the middle of the village. Florence was ill equipped to feed them and sanitary conditions resulted in a typhoid fever epidemic. There was a daily procession of wagons, piled high with bodies, often 100 at a time, hauling the dead out of town. Since coffins could not be supplied fast enough, the corpses were wrapped in blankets and buried. The Union dead lie in a National Cemetery near Florence (*see Tour 2a*).

Just before the close of the war, news was received that a detachment of Sherman's cavalry was approaching from Cheraw to free the prisoners, who were hastily escorted to North Carolina. Having been guarded only by old men and boys many had already escaped, and when the Union troops arrived, March 5, 1865, none remained. Confederate cavalrymen under Wheeler and Colcock, awaiting orders in Florence, rushed their horses off the already loaded boxcars, quickly mounted, and, after a skirmish behind Gamble's Hotel, chased the Yankees back towards Darlington.

When the war ended, there were only about 200 people in Florence, but in 1868 the Northeastern Railroad established temporary shops here, bringing a boost to enterprise that has continued to the present. When the town applied for a charter in 1871, the population was 700. This was in the Reconstruction period, locally called the 'ringed, striped, and streaked' era, when two of the four local officials were Negroes. The third ward was known for many years afterwards as the 'Black Ward' because its alderman was a Negro.

The Atlantic Coast Line Railroad established shops in Florence in 1871 and began taking over the lines already running. These shops have developed into the largest operated by that railroad in the State and have insured the growth and prosperity of Florence.

The organization of Florence County, in 1888–9, meant the lopping off of prosperous parts of five other counties, and was accomplished only after warm debate that lasted through 12 years of agitation.

In the eighties, when cotton dropped to 9¢ a pound, the challenge to farming resulted in varied experimentation, and Florence County became and has remained a leader in tobacco growing. The production of corn and cattle were also found remunerative, and the county has raised the only two world-record dairy cows in the South. About 1905 the United States established near Florence one of its five experiment stations for the production of drug plants and spices usually imported from other countries—Cannabis Indica (Indian hemp), digitalis (fox-glove), and paprika. Only paprika in an American form (not Hungarian, as originally) continues in appreciable quantities. About 15 carloads of peppers are shipped annually, making South Carolina second to Louisiana in the production of that commodity. Florence is also headquarters for the Carolina Co-operative Association, through which many cars and truck loads of pecans, sweet and Irish potatoes, poultry, and peaches are shipped annually.

In addition to its railroad and agricultural interests, Florence has numerous industrial plants: one of the largest furniture factories in the State, one of the most extensive bakeries in the Carolinas, the only plow factory in South Carolina, the Palmetto Nurseries, one of the largest florists' concerns in the State, and others. The annual pay roll of all industries exceeds $790,000, of which $500,000 comes from the railroad shops.

POINTS OF INTEREST

McLEOD INFIRMARY, 111–21 W. Cheves St., consists of a group of brick hospital buildings, centered by a seven-story red brick structure with concrete entrance motif and roof parapet designed in the modern manner. Completed in 1936 and sharing the Duke Endowment Fund, it is classed among the finest single hospital units in the South.

TIMROD SCHOOLHOUSE (*open by permission; inquire at the Board of Trade*), City Park, between Coit and McQueen Sts., southern city limits, is a small one-room white frame building with green shutters and gable roof, in which Henry Timrod (1829–67), poet laureate of the Confederacy, taught school in 1859. The school originally stood about four miles east of the city. Near by stands a small obelisk erected to Timrod's memory by his friends and inscribed with the poet's own lines: 'The poet to the whole wide world belongs,' 'All human thoughts and human passions wait upon the genuine bard,' and

> So in thy thoughts,
> Though clothed in sweeter rhymes,
> Thy life shall bear its flowers
> In future times.

The FLORENCE PUBLIC LIBRARY (*open 9–1, 3–6 weekdays; except July and August, 9–1, 6–9 Mon.–Fri.; 9–1, 3–6 Sat.*), 319 S. Irby St., is a red brick building of modified Georgian design set in landscaped grounds. A broad flight of brick steps approaches the entrance, which projects slightly and contains a double doorway with side lights surmounted by a large semicircular window. Fanlighted windows range symmetrically over a high basement story. The building, which contains an auditorium with seating capacity of 300, a dining room, assembly room, and kitchen, is an important community center. The library is owned and maintained by the city, and its 35,000 volumes include the collection of rare South Caroliniana amassed by the late Senator S. A. Graham of Williamsburg County. Italian cypress trees on each side of the building were brought from the Villa d'Este near Rome.

A MUSEUM (*no regular hours*) temporarily housed in the library, contains among other items a collection of peace and war emblems used by the Indians of the Carolinas and Virginia, a donation from the Valentine Museum of Virginia. There are also big game heads from America, Africa, and Germany, Egyptian vases of great antiquity, and ivory carvings from China.

PROPELLERS OF THE PEE DEE CRUISER, in the library grounds, are mounted on stone bases. The Pee Dee Cruiser was a Confederate gunboat constructed on the Pee Dee River and sunk by its crew to avoid capture. In 1934 the propellers were salvaged from the scuttled man-of-war and brought to their present location.

The FARM WOMEN'S COMMUNITY MARKET (*open 6–12 Tues. and Thurs.; 6–2 Sat.*), Courthouse grounds, 120 N. Irby St. between Evans and Front Sts., is a brick building with 65 stalls where farm women, under the direction of the Home Demonstration Agent, sell farm produce, homemade edibles, and handwork. The building has refrigeration facilities for perishable goods and a small cannery which utilizes the surplus. Annual sales amount to around $17,000.

The RE-ICING PLANT (*open day and night*), A. C. L. R. R. freight yard, E. Day St., is one of three such plants between Florida and New York established for the refrigerating of perishable produce. The best time to visit the plant is afternoon and evening in late spring, when Georgia peaches are being shipped.

POINTS OF INTEREST IN ENVIRONS

South Carolina Industrial School, 0.8 *m.;* National Cemetery, 1 *m.;* Pee Dee Experiment Station, 1.6 *m.;* Lake City Tobacco and Truck Market, 22.4 *m.* (*see Tour 2a*). The Columns, 14.8 *m.;* Coker College and Sonoco Products Company, Hartsville, 23 *m.;* Kalmia Gardens, 25 *m.;* Lee State Park, 38 *m.* (*see Tour 3a*).

Greenville

Railroad Stations: End of W. Washington St. for Southern Ry.; 317 W. Washington St. for Piedmont and Northern Ry. (electric); SE. corner of Falls St. and E. McBee Ave. for Charleston and Western Carolina Ry.
Bus Station: 105 W. Washington St. for Atlantic Greyhound, Eagle Bus, Red Top, and Welborne Bus Lines.
Airport: 3.5 m. E. of city on US 276; no scheduled service.
Taxis: 25¢ within city limits.

Accommodations: 5 hotels.

Information Service: Chamber of Commerce, 2nd floor Chamber of Commerce Bldg., 135 S. Main St.

Radio Station: WFBC (1300 kc.).
Motion Picture Houses: 9.
Concert Halls: Textile Hall, 322 W. Washington St.; Greenville Woman's College Auditorium, College St.
Golf: Greenville Country Club, 3 m. S. on US 25, 18 holes, greens fees 50¢ weekdays, 80¢ Sundays; Greenville Golf Course, Dreamland Lake, 3.5 m. N. on US 25, 9 holes, greens fee, 40¢.
Swimming: Paris Mountain State Park, 5 m. NE. of city; Wood's Lake, 3 m. E. near Airport; Lakeside, 3 m. SW., off US 29; Dreamland Lake, 3.5 m. N. on US 25; Greenville Country Club Pool, 3 m. S. on US 25.
Tennis: Cleveland Park, Washington Road, 2 courts; City Park, N. Main St. and E. Park Avenue, 2 courts; corner Leach and Douthit Sts., 2 courts; corner Pendleton and Calhoun Sts., 1 court; Furman University, University Ridge; Greenville Woman's College, College St.

Annual Events: Garden Pilgrimages, spring, sponsored by Greenville garden clubs; Southern Textile Exposition, biennially, spring; S. C. Singing Conv., 2nd Sat. and Sun. in Aug., at Textile Hall; Greenville County Fair, October.

GREENVILLE (966 alt., 29,154 pop.), the city limits of which are a circle with a radius of a mile and a quarter, stands on hills just below the falls of Reedy River, which runs through the heart of the city. The seat and center of a rich industrial county of the Piedmont, South Carolina's busiest and most densely populated section, it is the third largest city in the State, with the population of textile mill villages in the contiguous area more than that within the city limits (*see Tour 7*). The green beauty of the city is remarkable in a manufacturing center. The numerous parks and shady residential streets, bordered by many handsome homes in spreading lawns and gardens, make Greenville seem almost like one large park. Accessibility to the mountain country of North Carolina has made it a tourist center from earliest days. Range after range of the Blue Ridge Mountains is visible against the horizon from high buildings and hillcrests within the town.

Winding streets, following old woods paths and roads, cross and recross Reedy River. Bordering the twisting stream in some sections are cool sylvan retreats, contrasting with the bare unlovely scenes in the commercial area. The central business district spreads over several streets and its skyscrapers and hotels look down upon lower store buildings. Surrounding the city are its big mills, each the center of a village composed of the small, generally uniform houses for employees. Most of the villages are attractively landscaped, and have their own government, churches, and recreation centers.

Second only to the hum of textile industries is the religious life of Greenville, a city of many churches. Furman University and the Greenville Woman's College, both Baptist institutions, are assets to cultural and social life. Directed by a Furman professor, a Little Theater group is active in Greenville.

Inhabitants are mostly the descendants of Scotch-Irish settlers augmented by Low Country families, particularly from Charleston, drawn to Greenville because of the climate and visions of textile fortunes. Negroes, composing about 10 per cent of the population, have developed activities and interests that contribute not only to their own welfare but to the general good of the community. Among these are Mayberry Park, an area of 16 acres, and the Phillis Wheatley community center.

Greenville County is part of the old Cherokee lands, deeded to South Carolina in 1777. The Indians remained in their mountain fastnesses for 20 years after signing their grant, however, and not many white people ventured into the beautiful Cherokee country before the Revolution.

The first white settler in present Greenville County was Richard Pearis, an Irishman, who came from Virginia about 1765 as a trader, and not even the pirates of old Charles Town were more daring fortune hunters than he. He married a Cherokee woman and so ingratiated himself with the tribe that tradition records their repeated gifts to him of land that finally covered a tract 10 miles square. On part of this lordly estate now stands the city of Greenville and Paris Mountain, its name a corruption of Pearis. The enterprising settler called his acres 'Great Plains.' He built a home, a mill, storehouses, and a trading post, and lived the life of a prince. He served with the British forces in the French and Indian War and had the distinction of being the first Britisher to enter Fort Duquesne.

When the Revolution began, Pearis's allegiance was sought by both sides. It is said that he had promised his help to the Americans, but, disappointed at the military rank offered him, turned to the king's party. Held prisoner in Charles Town nine months, he became on his release a captain of the loyalist militia and attained the rank of colonel after performing several daring exploits. While he was in prison (1776) his plantation was captured and destroyed by Colonel John Thomas's Spartan regiment, on the grounds that it was a Cherokee and Tory stronghold. Ironically enough, after the fall of Charles Town, May 1780, Colonel Pearis received the 'submissions' or surrenders of General

Andrew Pickens and, possibly, of Colonel Thomas. After the Revolution Pearis settled in the Bahama Islands on a grant from the British Government.

Greenville County was established in 1784. Its name is variously said to honor General Nathanael Greene of Revolutionary fame, to attest the flourishing verdure of the section, or to recall Isaac Green, an early settler. Most evidence points to the last inference.

Lemuel J. Alston, a brother of Governor Joseph Alston, the husband of the beautiful and ill-fated Theodosia Burr (*see Tour 1*), came to the county in 1788. He bought 400 acres, 'a portion of the former plantation of Richard Pearis, and including his mill seat,' and there in 1797 laid out a village called Pleasantburg. Alston built a stately mansion in his little town, sure that settlers would soon be attracted, not only because of the proximity to the mountains, but because of the dawning possibilities for planting cotton and building mills.

Edward Hooker, who visited Pleasantburg in 1806, gives this picture: 'We . . . arrived at Col. Alston's home, which is the most beautiful I have seen in South Carolina. The mansion is on a commanding eminence which he calls Prospect Hill. From the village six hundred yards distant, there is a spacious avenue formed by two handsome rows of sycamore trees.'

In 1816 Alston sold his holdings to Vardry McBee. Born in Spartanburg County in 1775, McBee was called 'The Father of Greenville.' He leased the Alston house to Edmund Waddell for a hotel and summer resort until 1835, when he made it his own home, famous for hospitality until his death in 1864 at the age of 89. McBee's gifts included lands for the first four churches and the first academies. A constructive thinker, he recognized the potential sources of wealth in the county's climate and water power, and erected on the Reedy River one of the earliest cotton mills. He was instrumental in removing Furman University from Edgefield to Greenville in 1851, and in securing for Greenville in 1853 its first railroad, the Columbia and Greenville, later serving as its president.

Pleasantburg flourished as a resort, connected even in its early days by what were then considered good roads leading toward western North Carolina and Tennessee, and toward Charleston and Augusta. The falls of the Reedy River were soon utilized to furnish power for iron works, corn, and cotton mills. Robert Mills commended the community in 1825 for its beautiful site, its two well-kept taverns, and its new courthouse. 'So much wealth, intelligence and leisure are collected annually at the village,' said Mills, that he could not but 'anticipate a favorable result to the interior of South Carolina.' Pleasantburg then had 500 inhabitants.

In 1831 a progressive fever seized the town and its placid existence as a summer resort was disrupted by restless activity; stores, mills, and foundries sprang up. Citizens now wished their courthouse town to bear the county name. Accordingly, in 1831, little Pleasantburg vanished in the incorporation of Greenville and future industrialism was foreshadowed in the stir that replaced quietude. A busy factory, the predecessor of modern Camperdown Mills, usurped the young people's favorite swimming hole, opposite the site of Pearis's old mill. With the arrival of the railroad in 1853, Greenville's growth was assured.

In the years preceding the War between the States, the community was a hot-bed of Union sentiment with Benjamin F. Perry, respected throughout the State, as the leading spirit. When war broke out, no battles were fought in the vicinity and the city did not lie in Sherman's path. Wayside hospitals were established and women labored to comfort and supply the needs of war-weary Confederate soldiers. The mountainous area surrounding Greenville was overrun by deserters. In organized bands they preyed so persistently on the property of citizens that Major A. D. Ashmore requested a cannon to destroy one of their blockhouses in the 'Dark Corner' (*see Tour* 12). In June 1865, President Andrew Johnson appointed Perry provisional governor of South Carolina. James L. Orr of Anderson County succeeded him the following November.

Greenville's manufacturing enterprises, crippled by war, revived upon its cessation, and the present city limits were established in 1869. The Charlotte and Atlanta Air Line, now the Southern Railway, was completed to Greenville in 1874, and about the same time the modern textile industry had its real start.

The State Teachers' Association was organized here in 1881 by a leading citizen, Hugh S. Thompson, elected State superintendent of education on the Hampton ticket in 1876. The organization now includes practically every teacher in the State and has been a strong factor in the uplift of South Carolina public school education.

The first woman to serve as a mill president in South Carolina, and possibly in the United States, is Mrs. Mary Putnam Gridley. Her grandfather, George Putnam, bequeathed her in 1889 the old mill at Batesville, Greenville County, which had been established soon after 1816 by William Bates of Rhode Island. For 25 years Mrs. Gridley successfully operated the plant.

The site of Camp Sevier, five miles northeast of the city on US 29, presents a strange contrast now to its hum of activity during the World War. An important training camp for the Thirtieth Division, its concrete roads are now weed grown; Southern Railway tracks traverse its area; and huge trailer trucks use warehouses here as a loading station.

A mountain lake formed by impounded waters at the head of the Saluda River furnishes Greenville's municipal water supply. The Saluda plant is a notable achievement. The county's 37 textile plants, manufacturing bedspreads, men's, women's, and children's garments, handkerchiefs, rayon underwear, hosiery, sewing thread and other such articles, in 1937 had a pay roll of $13,661,569 exclusive of managers' salaries. Other factories produce such diverse commodities as brick and tile, patent medicines, compounds and chemicals, fertilizers, flour, feed and grist, confections, bakery products, paints, meat products, and foundry and machine products.

POINTS OF INTEREST

FURMAN UNIVERSITY, one block S. of S. Main St. on University Ridge, has an extensive campus dotted with red brick buildings and shaded by native oaks, hickories, and maples, supplemented by evergreens.

The university has had a migratory history. First proposed in 1821 by Dr. Richard Furman, who that year was a leader in organizing the South Carolina Baptist Convention, it was founded in 1826 at Edgefield and named Furman Academy and Theological Institution. With the academic department dropped, the seminary was moved in 1828 to the 'High Hills of Santee.' A classical and English department was again added in 1836, when the school was moved to near Winnsboro, Fairfield County, and called 'The Furman Institution.' Though the classical and English department was discontinued in 1840, the 'Theological Seminary' continued in growth. Dr. James C. Furman, son of the founder, became senior professor and administrator in 1844, when the name was changed to the 'Furman Theological Seminary.' As Furman University the institution was moved to its present site in 1851, with Dr. James C. Furman as its first president. In 1859 the theological department was transferred to Louisville, Kentucky, as the Southern (Baptist) Theological Seminary.

Furman has an enrollment (1940) of more than 500. Students of Greenville Woman's College are admitted to junior and senior classes and bachelor's and master's degrees for both institutions are awarded by Furman. An endowment from the James B. Duke Trust Fund in 1926 amounted to $2,000,000, and was in addition to a smaller outright Duke bequest and several other endowments from Greenville people.

The oldest building on the campus is FURMAN HALL (1851), an ivy-covered Italian Renaissance building of brick and stucco, with a semi-detached bell tower or campanile. An open loggia at the top, with pyramidal roof, contains the bell; variety is added by narrow and circular windows.

The CARNEGIE LIBRARY (*open* 8–1, 2–6, 7–10, *Mon.–Fri.; 8–5 Sat.*), erected in 1907, a red brick building with gray stone trim, harmonizes with the older buildings. It was endowed by several Greenville citizens as a memorial to Richard Biggs Quick, class of 1920.

The ARBORETUM, on the S. bank of Reedy River 300 ft. from S. Main St., bordering and merging into Furman University campus, is a five-acre tract planted with flora native to the Piedmont.

MUNICIPAL STADIUM, adjoining Furman University campus, has a seating capacity of 20,000 and was completed in 1936 at a cost of more than $100,000. The site was donated by the university, and grants and loans from the FERA made construction possible. Outdoor events sponsored by the university, the city, and civic organizations are held here.

TEXTILE HALL, 322 W. Washington St., a large brick structure accommodating 5,000 people, is taxed to capacity biennially when visitors from every part of the United States and foreign countries flock to the Southern Textile Exposition, the only national institution of the kind. Exhibits include products, machinery, and tools of textile and allied industries. Equipped with a large stage, the building is used as a theater, to accommodate conventions, the Southern Textile Basketball Tournaments, and the South Carolina Singing Convention in August attended by about 10,000 people (*see Music*).

GREENVILLE PUBLIC LIBRARY (*open 9–9 weekdays, 3–6 P.M. Sun.*), corner of College and Laurens Sts., temporarily housed in a former garage, contains 58,538 volumes, specializing in books on textile industries. It is noted for a system of county-wide distribution. Windowed vans, revealing the contents of shelves, carry volumes to 213 distributing points.

GREENVILLE WOMAN'S COLLEGE, College St. three blocks west of N. Main St., occupies extensive lawns with old trees shading red brick buildings of Georgian Colonial architecture. The earliest was erected in 1855, but the institution has had a continuous history since 1821, when it was opened as the Greenville Academy for Girls on land donated by Vardry McBee. A companion school for boys was concurrently founded, its site now occupied by the MARY C. JUDSON LIBRARY, named to honor a principal who served from 1874 to 1920. The building became a hospital during the War between the States.

Both academies were bought in 1854 by South Carolina Baptists, and the girls' school became Greenville Female College under the control of Furman University. Separately chartered in 1909, its present name was adopted in 1933 when it became an associated part of Furman. The same president and trustees serve both institutions. In addition to the usual classical degrees, the 450 students are offered home economics courses and diplomas in nursing may be obtained with a bachelor's degree after a five-year course conducted in co-operation with the Greenville General Hospital.

CLEVELAND PARK, Washington Road E. of Ridgeland Ave., comprises 126 acres and is equipped with tennis courts, swimming pools, baseball diamonds, bridle paths, and other recreational features. It is the largest unit of parks and playgrounds to share in funds received from the 1924 city bond issue of $110,000, which provided for activities of the park and tree commission, created more than 25 years ago.

CITY PARK, N. Main St. and E. Park Ave., in the heart of the city, is Greenville's oldest park. Within its 30 acres are swings, slides, and other playground facilities, a baseball diamond, a bandstand, and a zoo.

CHRIST EPISCOPAL CHURCH, N. Church St. near E. Coffee St., is of red brick with black slate roof. The bell tower, surmounted by a tall steeple, the fenestration in Victorian Gothic style, and the corner buttresses are all characteristic of Episcopal church architecture. Some historians credit its design to Joel R. Poinsett. President Millard Fillmore attended the laying of the cornerstone, May 2, 1852.

A CEDAR OF LEBANON, on a vacant lot between 303 and 307 Crescent Ave., was reputedly brought as a seedling from Palestine by Judge Baylis Earle more than a century ago. The landscaped grounds of the stately Earle home opposite formerly included a large surrounding area.

The FIRST BAPTIST CHURCH, McBee Ave. facing Richardson St., is a stuccoed brick structure, the front façade dominated by a pedimented Ionic portico approached by a broad flight of steps. Pilasters relieve the severity of the side façade. The steeple is reminiscent of the smaller English Renaissance churches. Built in 1858, it replaces the first building (1826) on the site given in 1821 by Vardry McBee.

ST. MARY'S PARISH SCHOOL, a Roman Catholic coeducational institution, 101 Hampton Ave., is a modern two-story red brick building, symmetrically laid out, with concrete basement story and flat roof. A central tower, which projects slightly, is neo-Gothic with arched entrance, buttresses, and parapet. At the rear of the school, an auditorium, Gallivan Hall, contains a basketball floor. Its name honors a generous Greenville benefactor. Adjoining the school, a convent, containing a small chapel, houses the teachers, Sisters of Our Lady of Mercy.

The school opened modestly in a rented house in 1900 under the patronage of the Sacred Heart and was taught by Ursuline nuns from Columbia. Within a year a larger building was purchased and by 1923 the school had substantial additions. A movement to secure fitting quarters for the growing institution was launched in 1928 and in spite of the comparatively small number of parishioners the present buildings were dedicated in 1930, having been erected at a cost of $116,000. The enrollment is approximately 135.

The VICTOR-MONAGHAN MILL, Smyth and Ravenel Sts., produces fancy dress cloths. The grounds, planted with rose beds and surrounded by fences covered with rambler roses, present an attractive appearance.

POINTS OF INTEREST IN ENVIRONS

Shriners' Hospital, 3.4 *m.;* Site of Camp Sevier, 5 *m.* (*see Tour* 7). Paris Mountain State Park, 5.7 *m.;* Municipal Waterworks Plant, 28.1 *m.;* Caesars Head, 32 *m.* (*see Tour* 10). Parker District School, 3.3 *m.* (*see Tour* 14). Table Rock, 33 *m.* (*see Tour* 15a).

Greenwood

Railroad Stations: Union Station, in the center of the public square, for Southern Ry. and Charleston & Western Carolina Ry. Terminal on Maxwell Ave., for Seaboard Air Line Ry. and Piedmont and Northern Ry. (electric).
Bus Station: 115 Maxwell Ave., for Atlantic Greyhound, Carolina Scenic Coaches, Eagle Bus Lines, Carolina Motor Lines, and Smoky Mountain Stages.
Airport: 2.7 m. W. from center of city; taxi fare 50¢; no scheduled service.
Taxis: 25¢ within city limits.

Accommodations: 2 hotels.

Information Service: Chamber of Commerce, City Hall, 509 Main St.; also hotels.

Motion Picture Houses: 5.
Athletic Field: Fair Grounds, Phoenix St. between Millwee and Harvey Sts.
Football: Fair Grounds.
Baseball: Fair Grounds.
Golf: Municipal Links, Grace St. Extension, NW. about 2 m. from center of public square; 9 holes, no greens fee. Greenwood Country Club, on State 7; 9 holes, greens fee, $1, 50¢ for invited guests.
Swimming: Thompson's, 6 m. NE. on old Laurens Hwy.; Gaddy's Lake, 1 m. NW. on Dixie Hwy.
Tennis: High School campus, S. Main St. between Millwee and Fair Sts.; Lander College, Stanley Ave. between Durst Ave. and Crews St.; municipal courts, Oak St. between Monument and Main Sts.

GREENWOOD (671 alt., 11,020 pop.), seat of the county by that name and a textile, manufacturing, and railroad center for western South Carolina, occupies a cluster of hills between the Saluda and Savannah Rivers. With five railroads and nine highways radiating in every direction, it is an important distributing point and one of the few South Carolina towns with the city manager form of government, which it adopted in 1939.

The business district is built around a square, with a railroad station placed uncompromisingly in the center. But Greenwood owes much to its railroads and, instead of allowing the shifting and tooting of trains to become an esthetic offense, has set about lessening the effect of this intrusion by planting willow oaks to overhang the tracks, and building its prettiest houses along broad streets on each side. The monuments to the Confederate and World War dead have been placed near the station. Near by is the successful community market, operated by the County Council of Farm Women. Two tall buildings, one each side of the tracks, rise above the skyline.

Greenwood avoids the aspect of the usual industrial town by its clean, shady streets, well-kept parks, and private flower gardens, in which native granite has been attractively utilized for walls and gateways. The town has grown without a city plan and streets curve around blocks of irregular length. Bordering the limits are neat mill villages, one with all brick houses for its employees presenting a home-like atmosphere.

The city's growth has occurred largely in the last 25 years, but the county was originally a part of old Ninety Six District (*see Tour 8a*), and the community has the background of Indian and Revolutionary history. The first settlers on the wooded ridge that is now Greenwood County are believed to have been John Blake and Thomas Weir, Irishmen, in 1802. The name, however, dates from 1823–4, when Judge John McGehee built his log cabin on a tract of 600 acres of forest land on the main road from Abbeville to Old Cambridge and his wife named the plantation Green Wood. When the McGehees sold the tract in 1829–30 to J. Y. Jones, he parceled it off in 'lots' of from 10 to 20 acres. The success of the town's first real estate promoter is tradition-ally attributed partly to mosquitoes at Old Cambridge, these pests inclining settlers there to seek the higher site as a summer resort.

The first general store opened on the 'Cold Saturday' of the winter of 1833, as the freakishly bitter day has become known in weather annals of the State. Mrs. Mary Miller, daughter of the store's promoter, recorded in a letter: 'Chickens and birds fell dead from their roosts, cows ran bellowing through the streets'; but she failed to state what effect the freeze had on the gala occasion of the store opening.

Although the residents called their settlement Green Wood, the first post office, established August 24, 1837, was Woodville. And Woodville it remained until July 6, 1850, when the Post Office Department finally conformed to local custom, making the name one word, Greenwood, for convenience.

Before 1840, the little community had two academies, one for boys and one for girls, and for a time both were successful. Lack of trans-portation practically isolated the village, however, and with no means of shipping agricultural products, its success seemed hopeless.

It was a gladsome day in 1852, therefore, when the Greenville and Columbia railroad (now part of the Southern Railway) reached Green-wood. The settlement, clustering about 'the chapel,' where all denomi-nations worshipped, shifted to the area around the new depot. Green-wood was incorporated in 1857.

The outbreak of the war in 1861 concentrated all energies on supply-ing the Confederate Army and Greenwood claims the State's first 'Ladies' Soldiers' Aid Society,' organized at Mt. Moriah Baptist Church, now in Greenwood County, July 4, 1861. Reconstruction brought riots and tragedy to the community, but in the ensuing peaceful years cotton production spread, textile manufacturing followed, and more railroad facilities were added.

Before 1882 Greenwood traffic could not reach Augusta, the nearest river port, except by the round-about journey through Columbia; that year, when the population was only about 1,300, the village made a heroic effort and achieved a railroad to the Georgia city. Leading citizens organized themselves and secured a charter. They hired convicts and built a stockade, though funds were so slight that even the workmen's food supplies had to be bought on the installment plan. Raising money for the laying of the tracks, a mile at a time, took tireless boosting and persuasive oratory; but the job was done. Though there was only an old boxcar for a station, cotton poured over the new line and Greenwood proudly watched itself grow. Other railroads realized the convenience of the little center, and pushed their way in.

In 1897 Greenwood was made the county seat of the new county created from parts of Edgefield and Abbeville Counties. Interest in education was revived. Lander College, one of the State's denominational institutions, was moved here in 1904. The Bailey Military Academy for Boys, once a part of the South Carolina Coeducational Institute of Edgefield, was transferred here in 1914 and became known throughout the State and beyond before it was destroyed by fire in 1936. This was one of the many disastrous fires in the town's up and down career.

Greenwood's unusual interest in publicly owned power projects is largely responsible for the Buzzard Roost hydroelectric development on the Saluda River, a project which has attracted national attention. The city also maintains a municipal system of power distribution, supplying electrical current liberally and at small cost to householders, and it has one of the two remaining individually owned telephone systems in the State.

There are five cotton mills within the city and its suburbs, and others in the county that turn out a variety of prints, shade cloths, surgical gauze, and sheeting. Greenwood also has a large cottonseed oil mill, lumber plants, a garment factory, foundries, machine shops, a meat-packing plant, a flour mill, and the only cheese factory in the State. In addition to its industries, the county seat is the shipping center for the rich farm lands surrounding it and yielding cotton, corn, truck, grain, and fruits.

POINTS OF INTEREST

CARNEGIE PUBLIC LIBRARY (*open 9:30–5:30 Mon.–Sat.; 7–9 P.M. Tues.*), 520 Monument St., of buff-colored brick with main floor and basement, contains more than 10,000 volumes. Through the efforts of the Greenwood County Council of Farm Women and the financial assistance of the county, a system of county-wide distribution of books has recently been inaugurated.

GREENWOOD COTTON MILL, Maxwell Ave. occupying several blocks between Hill and Mathis Sts. in E. Greenwood, is the largest of the four cotton mills in Greenwood. Visitors are not encouraged as a rule, but special permission for a guide to conduct an inspection tour may be had from the mill offices.

CONNIE MAXWELL ORPHANAGE (*open weekdays*), Maxwell Ave. at western city limits, owned and operated by the Baptist State Convention, is a village in itself. Its seven red brick buildings, Georgian

Colonial in style, are two stories in height with white porticos and columns; numerous cottages are scattered over the lawns and farms. Recreational facilities include a tennis court. Since its founding in 1880, Greenwood citizens have contributed several buildings, and the orphanage is now one of the largest in the State. More than 300 children are cared for in the cottages.

LANDER COLLEGE, Stanley Ave. between Durst Ave. and Crews St., owned by the Upper South Carolina Methodist Conference, has the second largest enrollment of any women's college in the State, with a student body of more than 500. On a campus covering several blocks, the red brick buildings have arch-headed windows and red hip roofs. The ADMINISTRATION BUILDING is three stories high, with bell tower. Dr. Samuel Lander founded the institution in Williamston in 1873 as the Williamston Female College. He was a pioneer in the 'one study method,' which created interest over many States and continued at Lander until about 20 years ago. When the institution was moved to Greenwood, its name was changed to honor the founder. Besides the usual degrees, domestic science courses and commercial diplomas are offered. Lander was one of several South Carolina colleges to receive in 1939 a $10,000 endowment from Bernard M. Baruch.

BREWER NORMAL INSTITUTE, for Negroes, E. Cambridge St. between Hospital and University Sts., is a three-story building, the first two stories of red brick, the third of frame painted brown. The campus covers 20 acres. Building and campus were deeded to the city by the American Missionary Society of New York in 1935. The Brewer Hospital adjoins the grounds.

The KRAFT-PHENIX CHEESE CORPORATION PLANT, Reynolds St. (US 221) NE. city limits, is South Carolina's only cheese factory. Six persons are employed, with total wages, including managers' salaries, amounting to $14,805, and its annual output averages $47,000. Inspection tours may be arranged at the office, though visitors are not encouraged.

POINTS OF INTEREST IN ENVIRONS

Ninety Six, 8.8 *m.;* Greenwood State Park, 10.8 *m.;* Site of Star Fort, 11.2 *m.;* Buzzard Roost hydroelectric development, 16 *m.* (*see Tour 8a*). Bordeaux, 33 *m.* (*see Tour 19A*). Long Cane Massacre Site, 30 *m.* (*see Tour 19b*).

Rock Hill

Railroad Stations: Railroad Ave. between Ebenezer and White Sts., for Southern Ry.
Bus Station: 129 Caldwell St., for Greyhound Line, Carolina Stage Line, and Smoky Mountain Stages.
Taxis: Fare 20¢ for 1 or 2 passengers, 10¢ for each additional passenger within city limits.

Accommodations: 2 hotels.

Information Service: Chamber of Commerce, 148½ Main St.

Motion Picture Houses: 3.
Tennis: Confederate Park, Confederate Ave. between Pickens and Jasper Sts.; Winthrop College campus, Oakland Ave. between Stewart and Lancaster Aves.
Golf: Municipal Country Club, 3 m. S. on US 21, 9 holes; greens fee 30¢; caddy fee, 30¢ for 9 holes, 50¢ for 18 holes.
Swimming: Confederate Park pool, Confederate Ave. between Pickens and Jasper Sts.

Annual Events: High School State Music Contest, at Winthrop College in spring; York County Fair, Oct.

ROCK HILL (680 alt., 11,322 pop.), near the Catawba River in the north-central part of the State, is a college town where cultural and industrial interests are well balanced. Among its street crowds are mill executives and employees, farmers, and hundreds of girls in navy blue, students of Winthrop, the South Carolina College for Women.

Railroad tracks run through the middle of the town, and the Memorial Bridge viaduct, honoring the military dead, connects the business district with the north residential section. While the houses are not outstanding architecturally, many along the wide, tree-bordered thoroughfares are distinguished for their lawns and gardens. Homes of the better educated and more prosperous Negroes are on the southern outskirts, with the usual fringe of cabins and 'shot-gun' houses where the poorer classes of both races live. From the Indian reservation near by, the last remnant of Catawba Indians, locally called 'The Nation,' peddle their pottery along the streets.

Rock Hill derives its name from a small flinty hill in the vicinity, and in 1852 was merely a depot on the new Charlotte-Columbia Railroad, now a division of the Southern Railway. For two years there was not a building near the depot. Gradually country stores, grog shops, and railroad buildings began to appear. By 1861 the village was still nothing more than a sprawling country crossroads, a center for shipping local products, chiefly cotton. Wagons, bearing bales of cotton for Northern mills, came in from miles around. Farmers met in the stores and grog shops to discuss crops and politics. Indians lolled about the counters, selling their wares and buying whisky with the proceeds.

During the War between the States Rock Hill became a point of transfer for Confederate troops and military supplies. Only one slight skirmish occurred in the village, when a detachment of Stoneman's cavalry came down from Charlotte to destroy bridges and railroads, and one resident was killed. The Reconstruction era was a time of terror, when this section became a hotbed of Ku Klux activities. The county's first klan was organized in 1868 at York, 14 miles away, and most of the white people in the community became members. Bases for *The Clansman, The Traitor,* and other novels by Thomas Dixon were found hereabouts.

Rock Hill was incorporated in 1870 and its growth came with the spread of cotton mills in the Up Country. In 1880 the Rock Hill cotton factory, now the Cutter Manufacturing Company, was begun by Captain A. E. Hutchison. From farms with depleted fertility, where cotton was gradually decreasing in price, workers came seeking jobs in the mills. During the next 15 years new mills caused rapid growth in Rock Hill and a movement to secure the State College for Women was launched. A farsighted real estate company turned fields into building lots and laid out streets. One energetic Rock Hillian, visiting in California when Oakland was developed by a real estate auction, returned to organize a similar enterprise. From his efforts rose the upper part of the town with broad, shaded streets, its principal thoroughfare named Oakland Avenue for the California town after which it was patterned. Several hundred acres of this tract were offered for the State normal college, one enthusiast even giving his home place; but other towns, equally anxious to secure the institution, matched this generosity. Then Rock Hill, with scarcely 3,000 citizens, floated a $60,000 bond issue, and so clinched the deal. In 1895 Winthrop College was transferred to Rock Hill from Columbia, where it had been founded in 1886. A close relationship, marked by mutual co-operation, exists between town and college.

Contemporaneous with Rock Hill's factory expansion was the development of hydroelectric power. One of the State's earliest plants was built in 1904 a few miles northward on the Catawba River, and near by Dr. Gill Wylie, W. S. Lee, and J. B. Duke began the construction that resulted in wealth and prestige both for themselves and their communities (*see Industry*).

Textile mills in the town represent an investment of $8,821,625 and employ 3,555 people with a pay roll of $3,268,900. There are 132,580 spindles and 2,237 looms manufacturing a wide variety of cotton goods.

Rock Hill also has commercial truck- and body-building plants, cottonseed oil mills, a factory with a daily output of 30,000 coat hangers, a small mill that manufactures women's full-fashioned hosiery, and one of the largest printing and finishing plants in the South—the Rock Hill Printing and Finishing Company, which differs from most Southern mills in having no mill village and thus requiring employees to make their own living arrangements. Visitors are not as a rule en-couraged at the plants, but arrangements for an inspection tour are possible through the Rock Hill Chamber of Commerce.

POINTS OF INTEREST

WINTHROP COLLEGE, Oakland Ave. between Stewart and Lan-caster Aves., the South Carolina College for Women, occupies a campus of 80 acres, shaded by oak, pecan, and chinquapin trees. Paved walks traverse the well-kept lawns, dotted with red brick buildings. The DINING HALL, seating 2,000, is designed in the manner of the dining hall at Christ College, Cambridge, England. Recent additions are the HOME ECONOMICS BUILDING, AUDITORIUM, and CONSERVATORY OF MUSIC. The auditorium seats 3,500; behind it is an amphitheater where Sunday vespers and dramatic performances are held in spring and fall.

In the one-story brick CHAPEL, the smallest building on the campus, the institution was founded in 1886 in Columbia by David Bancroft Johnson, superintendent of Columbia city schools, as a training school for teachers. His remains now rest within the building. Erected about 1823 as a carriage house for the home designed by Robert Mills for Ainsley Hall, it had been converted into a chapel when the residence became the Columbia (Presbyterian) Theological Seminary (*see Columbia*) and was a gift to Winthrop from the Southern Presbyterian Church. The structure was torn down, moved, and reconstructed here in 1937. Dedication services at the shrine were attended by thousands of Winthrop alumnae.

In 1891, Dr. Johnson and Governor B. R. Tillman secured State aid for the school. Its name then became Winthrop Normal and In-dustrial College, honoring Robert C. Winthrop of the Peabody Foun-dation, who had helped support the institution from the beginning. The title was later shortened to its present form. Moved to Rock Hill in 1895, Winthrop's curriculum was expanded to a four-year course. That year there were 335 students and 31 faculty members; now (1940) the student body numbers more than 1,400 with 123 faculty members. The institution's phenomenal growth and individual character are fruits of the vision and labors of Dr. Johnson, affectionately known to the students as 'Debe,' who was president from 1886 until his death in 1928.

Winthrop offers courses in 16 departments, including education, commercial science, home economics, physical education, and music. All four-year courses lead to bachelors' degrees. WINTHROP TRAINING SCHOOL, built in 1912, and architecturally patterned after Westminster Abbey, affords practice teaching from kindergarten through high school grades. A MODEL HOME is operated by senior home economics students.

In co-operation with Clemson College and the United States Depart-ment of Agriculture, the Extension Department of Winthrop carries on research and extension work in home economics. The State Home

Demonstration Agent and staff have offices on the campus and direct the activities of county agents.

When Winthrop was established in Rock Hill the LIBRARY consisted of two small bookcases of nondescript volumes and a few magazines in a small room of the administration building. In 1896 the library was designated as a Federal depository for Government publications; Carnegie aid was secured in 1905, and the present building, completed in 1907, now contains 45,000 volumes and has four large reading rooms in which 800 students can be accommodated.

The 360-acre college farm, a mile from the campus, provides the college with dairy products, poultry, eggs, and vegetables. Winthrop's entire plant is valued at approximately $3,250,000.

CONFEDERATE PARK, covering 12 acres on Confederate Ave. between Pickens and Jackson Sts., is one of two municipal parks. It was acquired by the city in 1924 and named for a monument to the Confederate dead. This monument has since been removed to Laurelwood Cemetery. A swimming pool, tennis courts, and a dance pavilion for public use are under the supervision of a commissioner of playgrounds.

The CITY LIBRARY (*open 9–6 weekdays; 7–9 P.M. Tues. and Thurs.*), SE. corner Oakland Ave. and St. John's Court, municipally owned, occupies a modern red brick building with stone trim, flat slate roof, parapet, and concrete cornice. Formerly the post office, the building was sold by the Federal Government to the Rock Hill School District for $100, moved to its present site, and remodeled at a cost of about $26,000. The library has about 10,000 volumes and an unusually well-equipped children's reading room.

The WHITE HOUSE (*private*), SE. corner White St. and Elizabeth Lane, believed to be the oldest house in town, is designed in the Southern Plantation style. The big square frame dwelling has two-story piazzas with small columns. There are many small outbuildings used by slaves in ante-bellum days. Built 1841–2, it was formerly the plantation home of the White family, but is now surrounded by paved streets and smaller houses. The old kitchen in the yard was erected about 1832.

The ORATORY, Charlotte Ave. facing Aiken Ave., a Roman Catholic school for underprivileged boys, consists of one large frame and one red brick building in grounds that include a recreation area and farm, tended by lay brothers. Faber Hall accommodates 50 boys, and Newman Hall contains high school classrooms and living quarters for the ecclesiastics. There are four fathers, 16 scholastics, and three brothers. Supported by missions, retreats, and supply work in Northern States, as well as donations from benefactors, the home was founded in 1934 by Father Ernest Musial, of the Leipzig Congregation, in the small rectory adjacent to the Church of St. Anne. He was assisted by the Franciscan Sisters, who also have charge of Rock Hill's only hospital, St. Philip's Mercy Hospital, and the Foundling Home for Babies.

The Congregation of the Oratory was founded in Rome by St. Philip Neri in the sixteenth century and one of its most famous members was Cardinal Newman.

POINTS OF INTEREST IN ENVIRONS

Ebenezer Church, 3 *m.;* Indian Reservation, 11.6 *m.;* Landsford Canal, 20 *m.;* Andrew Jackson's Birthplace, 27.5 *m.;* Great Falls, 28.7 *m.* (*see Tour* 7A); King's Mountain National Military Park, 36 *m.* (*see Tour* 16).

Spartanburg

Railroad Stations: Magnolia St. at Cannon St. for Southern Ry., Charleston & Western Carolina Ry., and Carolina, Clinchfield and Ohio Ry.; 142-4 N. Spring St. for Piedmont and Northern Ry. (electric).
Bus Station: N.E. cor. N. Liberty and Dunbar Sts., for Atlantic Greyhound Line and Carolina Scenic Coach Co.
City Busses: Fare 10¢; 4 for 25¢.
Airport: Spartanburg Memorial Airport, 2.5 m. S. of city on US 221, R. on Airport Rd. 0.5 m., for Eastern Air Lines.
Taxis: 25¢ within city limits.

Accommodations: 7 hotels; boarding houses.

Information Service: Chamber of Commerce, Cleveland Hotel, 178 W. Main St., American Automobile Association, Hotel Franklin, 185 E. Main St.

Radio Station: WSPA (920 kc.).
Motion Picture Houses: 4 for whites; 1 for Negroes.
Athletics: Snyder Field, Wofford College campus, E. Cleveland St.; Cleveland Playground athletic field, Chapel St. between Pearl St. and Fremont Ave.; Pine St. Playground athletic field, Pine and Poplar Sts. (football during season).
Baseball: Duncan Park, 3 m. S. of city on US 176.
Swimming: Cleveland Park pool; YMCA pool, 231 E. Main St.; Rainbow Lake, 12 m. N. of city on US 221.
Golf: Shoresbrook Golf Club, 5 m. W. of city on US 29; 18 holes, greens fee, 50¢.
Shooting: Spartanburg Gun Club, 3 m. S. of city on US 221, R. on Airport Rd. 0.5 m.
Tennis: Cleveland Park, between the lake and Mattoon Ave., three courts; Happy Hollow, Glendolyn Ave. between S. Fairview and Connecticut Aves., one court; Wofford College, N. Church St.; Converse College, E. Main St. between St. John St. and Mountainview Ave.; Church of the Advent, 137 Advent St.

Annual Events: Children's Chorus Concert, Converse College Auditorium, E. Main St., spring; Garden Pilgrimage, auspices of the Spartanburg Garden Club Council, April; Spartanburg County Fair, Fair Grounds, 1.5 m. NW. of center of city on Bishop St., Oct.; Mid-Dixie Tennis Tournament, Park Hills Tennis Club, Fairforest Rd. in Park Hills, midsummer.

SPARTANBURG (875 alt., 28,723 pop.), seat of Spartanburg County in the northwestern section of the State, and in the foothills of the Blue Ridge Mountains, is not so much a city as it is the civic center of a county highly developed agriculturally and industrially. Served by 12 paved highways, 7 railroads, and an air mail route, radiating outward like the spokes of a wheel, the city, with circular limits, is the hub of traffic for a densely populated area of considerable extent. Its streets are always crowded, especially on Fridays and Saturdays, when the 41 textile plants in the county are closed and thousands of mill workers flock to town. On Saturdays, farmers and farm hands, teachers and pupils swell the crowd.

For all of its activity, Spartanburg has not entirely outgrown the aspect of a bustling village. The business district, where tall buildings, handsome stores, and modern hotels hobnob with shabby little old structures, occupies several blocks on narrow streets converging at Morgan Square. In the entire city, blocks are of irregular length and, without civic plan, streets have evolved from twisting woodland paths and lanes.

In residential sections, however, tree-shaded streets are lined with handsome homes in spreading lawns and gardens. A few restricted suburban areas are marked by modern landscaping and architecture, the newest being Woodburn Hills in the southeast section. Two textile mills within the city limits occupy trim villages. Spartanburg has no distinctive slum district but shanties sprawl over hilly unpaved streets on the western fringe of the city and encroach here and there upon the town.

Among the city's many churches is one built in one day by a zealous Methodist congregation. Two of the State's leading colleges add to the cultural atmosphere: Wofford, a Methodist institution for men, and Converse, an independent college for women. Spartanburg has a considerable number of wealthy citizens and social life is unusually formal for this section.

The whole city unites in its enthusiasm for tennis and some of the State's champion players are Spartans. The Mid-Dixie Tournament has been held in Spartanburg every summer since 1933 and draws players from throughout the southeastern States. Visitors are entertained in local homes and the tournament is a gala event in the sports and social calendars.

The population is largely Scotch-Irish, with a very small percentage foreign born. A Greek colony, numbering about 125, worships in a Greek Orthodox Church served by a Greek priest, and endeavors to perpetuate in the children the language and culture of Greece. The proportion of whites to Negroes is three to one. Spartanburg has three grammar schools, one high school, and four municipal playgrounds for Negroes, who are engaged almost wholly in domestic and agricultural labor and do not work in the mills.

The county and city derive their name from the Spartan Regiment, a body of South Carolina militia which was formed in this area in 1776 and served with distinction throughout the Revolution. Its most noteworthy engagement was at Cowpens, January 17, 1781, in what was one of the decisive battles of the war (see Tour 17). Citizens of the county are still called Spartans.

Spartanburg County was created out of old Ninety Six District in 1785, but there were settlements in its area as early as 1761, some of them cultured and thriving from their beginnings. Early settlers arrived overland from Pennsylvania and Virginia, and overseas— through Charleston—from Scotland and Ireland. They soon began to raise cattle and grain. Cotton followed after the invention of the gin. The main industry for the first half century, however, was iron manufacturing. Pre-eminence in this line caused the section to be known as 'The Old Iron District.' South Carolina's first iron works were erected in 1773 within five miles of Spartanburg. Farming implements, household utensils, and weapons made here were peddled by wagon train over rutted roads throughout the Carolinas, Georgia, and Tennessee.

The site and name of the new county seat were selected in 1785, when Thomas Williamson gave two acres of virgin forest on his plantation for the purpose. In 1787 the courthouse was begun on what is now Morgan Square. But the settlement that struggled into existence was known only as 'the courthouse village' of Spartanburg District until the town's incorporation in 1831. The only advantage of the site was its central location. It commanded no established trading path or waterway. Thus the ingenuity and courage of Spartans was immediately challenged to provide means of transportation and reduce the prohibitive cost of getting their produce to Charleston, the favorite market.

Extensions from the old Buncombe and Blackstock Roads were soon made and wagon trains plied to and from Columbia, Charleston, and Augusta. These roads, however, were never satisfactory and at times were impassable. Some determined Spartan farmers rolled their tobacco to market in hogsheads, but even so they could not avoid tolls at river crossings. In 1792 legislative statutes prescribed a scale of fees, the lowest for foot passengers and for each head of cattle ferried or swum over streams. Toll bridges in later years absorbed even more profits.

Isolation and transportation problems did not prevent the establishment of two cotton mills on the Tiger River in Spartanburg County in 1816. Like grist mills, they were at first operated by barter and trade.

In the three or four decades following Spartanburg's incorporation in 1831, some of the finest homes now standing were erected. In 1859, amid wild excitement, the first train puffed into town. From the hinterlands, thousands congregated near the station to see the iron horse that had triumphed over bad roads and heralded easy communication and certain prosperity. In great open trenches 8,000 pounds of meat were barbecued to feed the crowd. Trestle tables were heaped with other succulent dishes. Speeches were made, toasts drunk, and everybody was elated.

The railroad lent impetus to grain raising, besides providing an outlet for the shipment of cotton goods. But enthusiasm over increased commerce was checked one year later by war fever, when the State's secession in 1860 precipitated the War between the States. Something of a boom resulted in Spartanburg. Every plant in the county worked overtime to supply provisions, cotton and wool yarns, corn and wheat, arms and tools for the Confederate forces. Even a manufactory for wooden shoe soles was established during the latter part of the war.

Following the war, adjustment to the changed economic order was not as difficult for Spartans as for Low Country people, since the former did not own slaves in such large numbers and had not become so dependent on Negro labor. However, financial embarrassment followed the loyalty that had invested capital in Confederate bonds, and overworked machinery was badly worn. But Spartans still had their streams, their roadbeds, and their pluck. Hardly were they back from the war when they began holding railroad meetings, planning to secure capital for their mills, and reorganizing agricultural societies. Recovery was swift and steady. The carpetbagger and scalawag never acquired much power locally, and after 1868 white Democratic leadership was firmly established. In 1873 the 'Air Line' railroad to Charlotte (now part of the Southern Railway) marked a definite upturn. Between 1878 and 1882, two miles in the business district were paved and 29 buildings erected.

In 1881, with the active and enthusiastic co-operation of the Washington Light Infantry of Charleston, the Centennial Celebration in Spartanburg of the Battle of Cowpens was a gala event that signalized a reunited country. All of the Thirteen Original States, Tennessee, and the Federal Government shared in the program and in the erection of a monument to General Daniel Morgan, commander at Cowpens. The monument was placed in the old 'Public Square,' since called Morgan Square.

A decade later the population had more than doubled, textile mills had greatly increased throughout the county, and 114 miles of railroad were in operation. With the development of iron and coal elsewhere and the depletion of timber fuel, the iron industry declined, but this loss was more than offset by the advance of other industries, particularly textile manufacturing and the successful diversification of farming.

Spartanburg profited by war for the second time in 1917, when it became nationally important as the site of Camp Wadsworth, which covered more than 2,000 acres on the city's outskirts and was at one time the largest cantonment in the United States. Trained there for overseas service was the famous Twenty-Seventh Division, comprising the National Guard units of New York State, the Sixth Division, and the Pioneer or 'Rainbow' Division. The soldiers numbered one-and-a-half times the population of Spartanburg and there was, besides, a constant stream of visitors and sightseers, taxing the city's capacity for entertainment to the limit, but resulting in enormous prosperity. The camp site reverted to Spartanburg in May 1919 and part of its area is a memorial park, where the original flagpole still stands. Some of the cantonment buildings are now used as residences.

In Spartanburg County 41 textile plants employ around 15,000 workers, with an approximate pay roll of $11,694,443, exclusive of officials' salaries. The mills operate more than 966,000 spindles and 25,000 looms and consume annually 950,000 bales of cotton. Although most of the mill villages are in the immediate environs of Spartanburg's small corporate limits, they are separately incorporated. The result in census ratings is somewhat equivocal, since citizens of the villages are classified as rural population. With a total population of 116,323,

Spartanburg County reports the highest rural population of any in South Carolina even though thousands live in the textile communities contiguous to Spartanburg's municipal boundaries.

Cultural development has kept pace with industrial growth; the city has long been a recognized musical center; local groups and college dramatic departments have encouraged talent that has progressed to professional success.

POINTS OF INTEREST

MORGAN SQUARE, at the triangular intersection of Main and Magnolia Sts., is the center of Spartanburg's business district. First known as the 'Public Square,' it was created in 1787 and has evolved from a pasture with a spring and a tiny frame courthouse, through the stage of public well and drinking troughs, hitching posts, whipping post, and pillory. Three courthouses have occupied this site, the last having been removed in 1892.

Here stands the statue of General Daniel Morgan, erected in 1881. Sculptured by J. Q. A. Ward, the nine-foot bronze figure, in the costume of a Revolutionary rifleman, tops a massive granite shaft 21 feet high. The surrounding paved area, formerly a park, has reviewing stands for civic celebrations.

WOFFORD COLLEGE, 429–509 N. Church St., occupies a hilltop campus of 65 acres, shaded by pines, oaks, and elms. Red brick buildings and faculty residences are connected by winding paved walks and driveways. The hip-roofed ADMINISTRATION BUILDING, containing the chapel, is a buff-colored stuccoed brick structure of three stories. Its pedimented portico has square Corinthian columns and is flanked by twin square towers with louvers and pyramidal roofs. This was the first building erected after the college was founded in 1850, when a local Methodist minister, the Reverend Benjamin Wofford, bequeathed $100,000 for 'the founding of a college in my native district.' At that time his was the largest bequest ever made for education in the South. Other Spartanburg citizens donated the campus. The most imposing buildings are the JOHN B. CLEVELAND SCIENCE HALL, the WHITEFORD SMITH MEMORIAL LIBRARY, and the JAMES H. CARLISLE MEMORIAL HALL. Buildings that were formerly the Wofford Fitting School have been converted into dormitories and professors' homes.

On the campus is a simple granite MONUMENT over the graves of the founder and his wife. Doctor Wofford's Latin inscription is the same as that of Sir Christopher Wren. A translation reads: 'If you would see his monument, look about you.'

The college, controlled by the Methodist Church of South Carolina, is a charter member of the Southern Association of Colleges and Secondary Schools and of the American Association of Colleges.

Dr. James H. Carlisle, president of Wofford for 54 years, was probably the institution's outstanding figure. During his tenure of office he became noted throughout the South for the force and originality of his educational methods and his success in character building. Doctor Carlisle was a signer of the Ordinance of Secession (1860).

CONVERSE COLLEGE, E. Main St. between St. John St. and N. Fairview Ave., a nonsectarian institution for women, is on a rolling campus landscaped with evergreens and flower beds well placed among the natural growth of oaks and hickories. Curving driveways lead to red brick, vine-clad buildings, which follow no specific architectural style. Centering the main group is the ADMINISTRATION BUILDING with its arcaded central loggia and bell tower with conical roof. Connected by an enclosed passageway is the AUDITORIUM, which has a seating capacity of about 2,000. Among detached buildings is the SCIENCE HALL (*open by permission from president's office*), in which is the Henry W. Ravenel collection of pressed Carolina plants, a botanical treasure. On the back campus are tennis courts, a horse paddock, nine-hole golf course, the VICTOR MONTGOMERY GARDENS, and the 'FOREST OF ARDEN,' an artistic amphitheater where outdoor festivities are held, notably the crowning of the May Queen.

Near the main entrance is a MONUMENT TO THE FOUNDER, D. E. Converse, a pioneer textile magnate who came to Spartanburg from Massachusetts in 1856. In order that his only daughter might receive her education at home and because he believed that 'the well-being of any country depends on the culture of the women,' he made liberal donations in his lifetime and bequeathed one third of his estate of $600,000 to the founding of the institution in 1889. From its beginning, Converse College has combined the best features of the old-fashioned finishing school with high scholastic standing, and now holds membership in eight outstanding educational associations. The institution has been of great cultural importance to the State, particularly in the fields of creative arts (*see Music*). Among its distinguished graduates are Julia Peterkin, author; Lily Strickland, composer; and Blondelle Malone, artist.

Affectionately revered by Converse students and alumnae is the dean, Miss Mary Gee, who was a graduate in the first class (1892) and has served her Alma Mater continuously since.

KENNEDY FREE LIBRARY (*open 9-5, Mon.-Sat.*), corner Magnolia and Library Sts., a memorial to Dr. Lionel Chalmers Kennedy, beloved Spartanburg physician, is set in landscaped grounds with magnolia and pomegranate trees at each side. The ivy-covered one-story red brick building has an arcaded portico and windows with semicircular heads. Containing 22,000 volumes and including a small but valuable collection of rare and out-of-print South Caroliniana, it was founded in 1883 by Doctor Kennedy's widow, who gave the site for the first building. It was completed in 1885. The present lot was donated by the city and the building was erected with aid from Andrew Carnegie. A museum displays Confederate and Revolutionary war relics and a group of dolls dressed in the costumes of many nations.

OFFICES OF THE SOIL CONSERVATION SERVICE (U. S. Dept. of Agriculture), NE. corner St. John and N. Church Sts., which serves seven southeastern States, occupy an entire floor in the Montgomery Building, a yellow brick skyscraper. Headquarters for the South Tiger Project occupy all of the former post office building, corner Walnut and N. Church Sts. (*Visitors may obtain directions for inspecting these areas by inquiring at either office.*)

The COURTHOUSE, Magnolia St. N. of Morgan Square facing Walnut St., is a three-story red brick edifice with a squat arcaded entrance loggia, arched and bull's-eye windows, and a multi-gable roof. The architecture is typical of the banality of the 1880's. Although this is Spartanburg's fourth courthouse, it is the first on this site. On monthly sales days a portion of the grounds known as the 'bone-yard' is thronged with rural inhabitants and mountaineers who swap horses, mules, cows, pigs, knives, handiwork, and farm produce. Saturdays also bring many gatherings, when whole families make the grounds their headquarters for the day. They build fires, fry bacon, boil coffee, and exchange gossip. Preachers of strange cults, surrounded by curious or sympathetic hearers, sway with religious ecstasy, their fervor undiminished by the barking of dogs and the crying of babies.

MAGNOLIA CEMETERY, Magnolia St. adjoining the Union Station, was donated to the city in 1885 by Jesse Cleveland and is no longer in use. It contains the monument to Dr. James H. Carlisle, former president of Wofford College, one to the donor, and that to 'Singin' Billy' Walker (*see Music*). The last is an upright marble tombstone with the following inscription: 'Christian Harmony. In memory of Wm. Walker, A.S.H. Died Sept. 24th 1875 in the 67th year of his age. He was a devoted Husband and kind Father, a consistent Baptist 47 years, taught music 47 years. The Author of 4 Books of sacred music. He rests from his labors. He died in the triumph of faith. Sing praises unto the Lord.' The letters, 'A.S.H.,' stand for 'Author Southern Harmony,' Walker reputedly having said that he would rather have these letters after his name than be President of the United States.

POINTS OF INTEREST IN ENVIRONS

Textile Institute, junior industrial college, 3.9 *m.* (*see Tour 7*). South Carolina School for the Deaf and Blind, 4.6 *m.;* Glenn Springs, 13 *m.* (*see Tour 12a*). Governor Gist Mansion, 29.5 *m.* (*see Tour 12b*). Kings Mountain National Military Park, 37 *m.* (*see Tour 16*). Musgrove's mill, Revolutionary War battlefield, 30 *m.* (*see Tour 17*). Cowpens Revolutionary War battlefield, 18.9 *m.* (*see Tour 18*).

Sumter

Railroad Stations: Harvin St. and Railroad Ave. for Atlantic Coast Line R.R.; Green St. for Seaboard Air Line Ry.
Bus Station: 106 N. Main St. for Atlantic Greyhound Line.
Taxis: 25¢ within city limits.
Traffic Regulations: Left turns on green lights except Main and Liberty Sts.

Accommodations: 2 hotels.

Information Service: Board of Trade, 128 N. Main St.

Motion Picture Houses: 3.
Swimming: YMCA pool, NW. corner Sumter and Liberty Sts.; Pocalla Springs, 3.9 m. S. on US 15.
Golf: Sunset Country Club, 1 m. SW. city limits, 9 holes, greens fee 60¢ unless permit is obtained from Board of Trade.
Tennis: Memorial Park, W. Hampton Ave. and Park St., free; Boys' High School, Haynesworth St.
Football: Football stadium, Fair Grounds, western extremity of W. Liberty St. just outside limits.
Baseball: Municipal Park, corner N. Church and Pine Sts.

Annual Events: Gamecock Field Trials, run at Cane Savannah, Jan.; Sumter County Fair, W. Liberty St. grounds, Oct.

SUMTER (169 alt., 11,780 pop.), in the central part of South Carolina, is the seat and market center of Sumter County, one of the State's leading agricultural and lumber areas. What textiles are to Greenville, furniture and woodworking are to Sumter. City markets also provide outlets for widely diversified crops, livestock, and poultry supplied by the large rural population.

Main Street, the chief business artery, divides the city north and south; Liberty Street, its companion thoroughfare, is the east and west line. The business district, on several blocks of these two streets in the central area, has practically no vacant stores, and its neat appearance and careful traffic regulations are notable. In spite of its narrow streets, Sumter is one of 21 United States cities in the 10,000 to 25,000 population group in which no fatal automobile accident has occurred for several years.

Along highways leading into town from the north are many of the most attractive homes, churches, and the magnolia-surrounded courthouse. Sumter has not sacrificed its fine trees to paving; their branches interlace across residential streets where comfortable homes, architecturally undistinguished, are set in well-kept grounds. The only town in the State to employ a civic landscape architect, Sumter is proud of its well-designed parks and gardens, large and small. Springtime garden tours are arranged by a women's club and strangers are often granted permission to visit private beauty spots. Southeast of the railroad tracks is the industrial section, where streets, reminiscent of horse and buggy days, are barely wide enough for two cars to pass. Interspersed among the furniture factories, with their huge stacks of lumber adjacent, an occasional shabby old residence indicates that this was once a fashionable neighborhood. Negroes, who compose about 40 per cent of the population and live in scattered areas throughout the city, earn a livelihood largely in these plants. One of Sumter's parks is devoted to Negroes, and just outside of the city is Morris College, a Negro coeducational institution.

Sumter is exceptional in its proportion of Jewish citizens, especially those of Spanish descent. They maintain a synagogue and have always been prominent in business, government, arts, and letters. Also unusual for its size is Sumter's Roman Catholic element, with a distinguished record of contribution to cultural life.

Sportsmen are plentiful here. Though game abounds in the near-by Wateree River swamp, local enthusiasts do not confine their excursions to neighboring territory, and think nothing of driving 75 miles each way for a day's sport.

October brings the rural and urban population together at the Sumter County Fair, a noncommercial project sponsored by the American Legion assisted by the county farm agent and 4-H clubs. The week's most unusual event is the tilting tournament, and another high light is a football game between two State colleges.

The city, a straggling settlement by 1785, was first called Sumterville after General Thomas Sumter, the 'Gamecock' of the Revolution, whose home was near by (see Tour 9b). In 1798 the village was selected for the courthouse of old Sumter District, which included Claremont, Clarendon, and Salem Counties. Court was at first held in the home of John Gayle and the records were kept in Claremont courthouse, which burned in 1801. Sumterville was laid out in 1800 and drew a cultured citizenry from surrounding plantations. In 1809 they established a public library, still in existence. With no access to waterway or railroad, development was slow, but William Gilmore Simms, in his geography of 1843, noted that 'Sumterville has a handsome courthouse and jail, two churches, an academy, a public library, a weekly newspaper.' The old courthouse, much altered, is now the National Bank of South Carolina, 20 N. Main Street. The Camden branch of the South Carolina Railroad extended into the town in 1843, to be followed by other railroads and a system of highways, bringing steady growth, and in 1845 Sumter was incorporated.

During the War between the States only minor skirmishes occurred in the vicinity, but the city proudly remembers that a Sumter boy, George E. Haynesworth, then a Citadel cadet, fired the first shot of the war, January 9, 1861, at the Star of the West, Federal relief boat on its way to Fort Sumter in Charleston harbor. Another Sumter citizen, General Richard H. ('Fighting Dick') Anderson, was the State's ranking Confederate officer. A third, the Reverend John Leighton Wilson, D.D., a pioneer missionary to Africa, author, and naturalist noted as the discoverer of the gorilla, probably accomplished more than any other individual in abolishing the slave traffic. In 1840 he was offered, but refused, the governorship of Liberia. One of the greatest orators in Wade Hampton's 1876 campaign was General E. W. Moise, distinguished Sumter lawyer, who was elected State adjutant general on the Hampton ticket.

Since Reconstruction days the city has progressed steadily and without backset, maintaining always its reputation as a cultural center. In the era of road shows, the old opera house was crowded when leading theatrical performances came regularly to town. Sumter was the birthplace of South Carolina's most illustrious prima donna, Clara Louise Kellogg (1842–1916), and has produced other musicians and writers. The portraits and etchings of Elizabeth White, native artist, have received wide recognition.

In 1912 Sumter was first in the United States to adopt the commission-city-manager form of government. It has established a reputation for honesty in civic government and for co-operation in the solution of urban-rural problems. Sumter annually ships $100,000 worth of hogs and large quantities of sweet potatoes. In 1938 the city deeded 103 acres adjoining the limits to the State Forestry Commission for conservation purposes, and this area is now a forest tree nursery.

In 1939 a site in the suburbs was selected by the Crippled Children's Society of South Carolina for their State home. The same year Sears, Roebuck and Company located here one of their four furniture factories. Sumter's industrial pay roll now (1940) amounts to approximately $50,000 per week, with seasonal variation. The city has four of the largest industries of their kind in the world—the Palmetto Pigeon Plant, shipping over 100,000 squabs annually; the Brooklyn Cooperage Company, using ten acres of trees daily for making barrels; the Williams Veneer Company, makers of garment hangers; and the Williams Furniture Corporation, shipping solid carloads of bedroom furniture. Its 26 industrial plants include also a textile mill, a hosiery mill, a canning factory, three bedspread factories, and a brickyard manufacturing Airedale brick.

With five highways converging within its limits, Sumter profits from tourists. As dusk approaches, white-coated Negro porters extoll with gleaming smiles the comforts of their respective hostelries and eagerly assist transient arrivals with their luggage.

POINTS OF INTEREST

BLAND TOWN GARDEN (*open*), Hampton Ave. and Purdy St., is one of two beauty spots privately developed for public enjoyment by a civic-minded townsman, H. C. Bland. The garden, with a central lawn, is bordered with a profusion of evergreens and flowers. Mr. Bland's other gift is Swan Lake Garden (*see Tour 9a*).

MEMORIAL PARK, Hampton Ave. between Park and Salem Aves., of more than six acres, was bought in 1920 by 25 citizens and presented to the city as a memorial to Sumter's white soldiers in the World War. In the corner stands a granite slab with a bronze plate appropriately engraved. Beautifully planted and arranged by the civic landscape architect in charge of streets and parks, it was the first unit in the park system that now includes 155 acres. There are tennis courts, a wading pool, and playground apparatus; weekly band concerts in a vine-covered pergola enliven summer evenings.

The SUMTER HIGH SCHOOL, Haynesworth St. between Purdy St. and Mood Ave., a two-story brick structure enlarged in 1939 at a cost of $240,000, now covers more than a block. Only boys were pupils here from 1908 to 1939, and the school was a pioneer in establishing military training. Old army rifles, some dating from the Confederate period, are kept in the attic armory and used during recess for drilling. Officered by high school seniors, smaller boys stagger under their long muskets. At commencement a medal is awarded the best-drilled student, climaxing a competitive drill conducted by former World War officers.

The EDMUNDS MONUMENT, 215 Calhoun St., is a granite rectangular slab on the grounds of the Junior High School, which was the Girls' High School from 1908 to 1939. The granite shaft, with a bronze plaque bearing the raised likeness of Dr. S. H. Edmunds (1870–1935), superintendent of Sumter schools 1895–1935, was erected by the citizens of Sumter as a tribute to this distinguished educator. During his 40 years as superintendent the public school enrollment increased from approximately 600 to 3,898, with 92 teachers; school property increased in value from about $12,000 to $417,950; and the Sumter school system and methods became famous in the State.

The POLLY PRENTISS FACTORY, N. Main St. between Pine and northern city limits, has brick showrooms in landscaped grounds, with the adjoining factory of wood and galvanized iron. This depression-born industry started on a small scale with Sumter County women working in their homes to make candlewick bedspreads, bathmats, aprons, and maids' caps. Now between 600 and 700 white workers, mostly women, are employed at the factory, and hundreds of visitors stop to see the display of samples in the showrooms.

CROSSWELL ORPHANAGE, Crosswell Drive E. of N. Main St. near northern city limits, has four one-story brick buildings in a 20-acre campus. It was founded with funds bequeathed by J. K. Crosswell, a Sumter businessman. Each unit houses 16 boys or girls and additional buildings will be erected as need arises.

The HAMPTON OAK, 429 N. Main St., stands on the grounds of the house that was formerly the home of Richard I. Manning, governor of South Carolina 1915–19. The tree sheltered the garlanded platform where General Wade Hampton, surrounded by his Red Shirts (*see Columbia*), spoke in 1876. A draped figure, bound with chains, preceded him, and just as he reached the stand the funereal regalia dropped away to reveal a young woman in white, 'South Carolina' emblazoned on her golden crown. The crowd went wild and this meaningful tableau provoked the Sumter Democrats' battle cry, 'Hampton or Hell!'

OLD ST. JOSEPH'S ACADEMY, 206 E. Liberty St., a large white frame building with piazzas extending the length of its two stories, was built in 1867 to house the academy established in 1864 by the Sisters of Our Lady of Mercy, who now conduct a kindergarten in the building. The Sisters live in a two-storied columned residence at 125 E. Liberty Street, which is the former home of Neill O'Donnell, by whom it was willed to St. Anne's Catholic Church for its present use.

Adjoining the old academy building is St. Anne's Church, designed by the Right Reverend Monseigneur Charles D. Wood and built in 1911 for a congregation organized in 1838, its first parish located north of Sumter township.

POINTS OF INTEREST IN ENVIRONS

Swan Lake Garden, 1.3 *m.* (*see Tour 9a*). Palmetto Pigeon Plant, 2 *m.;* Stateburg, 12 *m.;* Poinsett State Park, 22.8 *m.;* Milford, 26.9 *m.* (*see Tour 9b*). Morris College, 1 *m.;* U. S. Resettlement Project (Ashwood Plantation) 13.1 *m.;* Lee State Park, 26.2 *m.* (*see Tour 3a*).

PART III
Tours

Tour 1

(Wilmington, N. C.)—Georgetown—Charleston—Walterboro—(Savannah, Ga.); US 17. North Carolina Line to Georgia Line, 231.1 *m*.

Roadbed concrete-paved with sections of asphalt.
Intracoastal Waterway parallels entire route.
Atlantic Coast Line R.R. and Seaboard Air Line Ry. parallel route between Charleston and Savannah.
Accommodations available at resorts in season; hotels and tourist homes in larger towns.

US 17 hugs the curving coast line of South Carolina, varying in altitude from about 9 to 15 feet, and generally follows the former King's Highway, which developed from an old Indian path. Bishop Francis Asbury traversed this route (1785–1816), when he strove to introduce Methodism into this predominantly Anglican region. The zeal of his missionary spirit rose above the hardships he endured on the rough trail through the lonely swamps and savannas. He thus recorded his impressions: 'What blanks are in this country—how much worse are the rice plantations! If a man-of-war is a "floating hell" these are standing ones; wicked masters, overseers, and Negroes—cursing, drinking—no Sabbaths; no sermons.'

Mason Locke Weems, preacher, biographer, fiddler, and pioneer book agent, peddled his wares along this road to aristocrats and tavern loafers alike, and gathered material for his own lurid and moralizing tracts.

April 26, 1791, George Washington's lumbering entourage entered the State and followed the King's Highway on the first presidential tour. He wrote:

It may as well in this as in any other place, be observed, that the country from Wilmington through which the Road passes, is, except in very small spots, much the same as what has already been described; that is to say, sand & pine barrens —with very few inhabitants—we were indeed informed that at some distance from the Road on both sides the land was of a better quality, & thicker settled, but this could only be on the Rivers & larger waters—for a perfect sameness seems to run through all the rest of the country—on these—especially the swamps and low lands on the Rivers, the Soil is very rich; and productive when reclaimed; but to do this is both laborious and expensive.

This is country reminiscent of ancient Indian towns, of venturesome Spaniards and Frenchmen, who sought to settle and claim Carolina in the sixteenth century. It is the region of Colonial baronies, of antebellum plantation grandeur; it is scarred with sites of Revolutionary battles and of the debacle of the War between the States and Reconstruction years. Markers tell of incidents in history, and indicate side roads to estates of once prosperous rice and indigo planters, properties now usually owned by Northern sportsmen. Each place has its story— Indian raids, pirates, romantic ladies, 'the most beautiful gardens in the world,' the stabling of horses in old churches, the burning of homes, the quiet that came after the storm, and the downfall of the economic system on which plantation life was based. Here is the romance that awakens the nostalgia of the Southerner for the country that was his— the life of beauty, ease, culture, and chivalry that has passed.

Section a. NORTH CAROLINA LINE to GEORGETOWN, 58 m. US 17.

Following the arc of the shoreline around Long Bay, US 17, one-half mile from the ocean, gives frequent glimpses of the sea. Dipping seaward among windblown clumps of myrtle, veering landward through groves of tall pines, the road progresses past one coastal resort after another and proceeds along the salt marshes to Charleston.

US 17 crosses the NORTH CAROLINA LINE, 0 *m.*, about 46 miles south of Wilmington, North Carolina.

Once an important shipping point for rice, naval stores, and lumber, LITTLE RIVER, 2 *m.* (10 alt., 2,219 pop.), was facetiously known as 'Yankee Town' because of its numerous North Carolina settlers. Just east of the settlement is the wide salt stream for which it was named. Huge oaks furnish shade for picnic dinners; boats may be chartered for ocean and river fishing, or for cruises down the Intracoastal Waterway (*see Tour 11a*).

At NIXON'S CROSSROADS, 5 *m.*, is the junction with State 9 (*see Tour 21a*).

At 5.4 *m.* is the junction with a dirt road.

Left on this road 1 *m.* to a fork.
1. Left here 5.5 *m.* to the SITE OF FORT RANDALL, a Confederate stronghold captured by Federal forces in 1864, which is on a privately owned estate, bordered by waters once a rendezvous for pirates; a fortune in booty is supposedly concealed on these shores.

2. Right from the fork 3 *m.* to CHERRY GROVE BEACH, a growing summer resort with good fishing.

At 7.5 *m.* on US 17 is the junction with a dirt road.

Left here 0.5 *m.* to OCEAN DRIVE BEACH, a small resort.

At 10.3 *m.* on US 17 is the junction with a narrow sandy road.

Left here 0.5 *m.* to ATLANTIC BEACH, a small summer resort for Negroes.

At 19.1 *m.* is a junction with a hard-surfaced road.

Left here 2 *m.* to WASHINGTON PARK, a popular race track during the summer months. Trotting and harness races are featured on the half-mile course; the grandstand seats 2,500, and five stables provide accommodations for more than 200 horses.

Named for its thick growth of myrtles, MYRTLE BEACH, 23.2 m., is South Carolina's largest seashore resort. With the Gulf Stream only about 40 miles seaward and sand dunes landward lending protection, the climate is equable throughout the year and the town has evolved from a summer colony into a year-round pleasure place. The northern end has attractive, substantial houses in sodded lawns and bright gardens; the southern end, clustering around the pavilion, the village, stores, and the various concessions, is a miniature Coney Island.

Within two miles of the town, in an area of less than 10 acres, more than 100 species of plants have been officially catalogued. The yaupon, or cassine holly, growing here in profusion, furnished the Indian with his ceremonial drink; near Charleston tea is still made from this plant. These evergreen shrubs are laden in winter with scarlet, waxy berries that attract cardinals and mockingbirds when other food is scarce. Candle wax was formerly made from myrtle berries.

At Myrtle Beach is the junction with US 501 (*see Tour 13*).

MYRTLE BEACH STATE PARK, 26.6 m. (*free camp grounds on highway; bathing suits for rent; cabins, at nominal fee, should be reserved in advance through State Commission of Forestry*), has 321 acres of beach, sand dunes, and longleaf pine forest. It is one of the most popular parks in the State.

MURRELLS INLET, 35.1 m. (210 pop.), is the center of a settlement spreading along the marshes. According to local legend, Captain Murrell, a pirate, often took shelter here. The fishing is unusually good, and one has only to wade into the shallow water to pick up oysters, crabs, and clams. Shrimp abound in season and the salt marshes teem with mussels and terrapin. Soft-shelled crabs may be obtained, and in the more remote sections, the choice stone crab is found. Local menus offer these sea foods and fish at low prices. Night fishing for flounder, which are gigged from row boats provided with lightwood torches, furnishes a source of cash for many of the natives and an interesting, if uncomfortable, sport for visitors. Clam diggers move in slow and patient lines in the creeks at low tide, bobbing under water like ducks to pick up clams buried in the soft mud. Trucks carry oysters and fish to market, and clams are shipped north in winter. In early spring, shad, taken in the Waccamaw River, are sold for fancy prices both on local and out-of-State markets, and the shipment of salt mullet is economically important. Some residents knit comfortable cord hammocks; others build and sell small but seaworthy cypress boats.

This vicinity has a large proportion of jet-black Gullah Negroes, who supplement their sea-food diet with products of their gardens. A typical boast made by one of them is: 'I know uh man who hab ground so *berry* rich, wen 'e plant corn de corn grow so high dey hab t' build ladder 500 yahd high t' brek out de year. An' wen she get t' tosselin'—well, wen she *did* ready t' shoot out—all de angel in Heaben, an' de sun, an' de moon, an' de star hab t' move. Dey hab t' back up out de way; an' t'ree day aftuh she grow up, dey hab de word from Heaben dat all de Missy angel eatin' roastin' years!'

The SUNNYSIDE HOUSE (L), 35.2 *m.*, home of Mott Allston, was built in the 1860's. In front of the house a physician, shortly after 1900, shot his beautiful wife on the lonely, mist-hung beach at sunset, saying that he mistook her for a ghost.

Right from Murrells Inlet post office on a rough sand-clay road to a fork, 1.4 *m.;* L. to another fork at 0.6 *m.*

1. Right here 0.5 *m.* to WACHESAW PLANTATION. Graves here have yielded 13 Indian skeletons and other relics.

2. Left at the fork 1 *m.* to a public landing where Negroes from Sandy Island (*see Tour* 11a) still trade sacks of hand-threshed rice for potatoes and groceries. Julia Peterkin pictured these Sandy Islanders in her novel *Black April.*

At 36.9 *m.* is the junction with a sandy road.

Right here 1 *m.* to the MURRELLS INLET MUSEUM (*adm.* 10¢ *and* 25¢), which contains many souvenirs.

Parts of four former rice plantations were combined by Archer M. Huntington to form BROOKGREEN GARDENS (R), 40.1 *m.* (*open* 9–5:30), an unusual open-air museum. The 4,000-acre tract was incorporated in 1932 for 'the preservation of the flora and fauna of the Southeast and to exhibit objects of art.' The museum is operated by seven trustees under a $1,000,000 fund established by Mr. Huntington.

Old Brookgreen plantation was the birthplace of Washington Allston in 1779 and Julia Peterkin used it as the 'Blue Brook' plantation of *Scarlet Sister Mary,* a Pulitzer prize novel.

A narrow concrete road leads through a dense pine forest into the gardens, where the zoo houses deer, bears, wildcats, mink, and other specimens of wild life indigenous to the region. Left of the zoo the road curves past the statue, *Youth Taming the Wild,* by Anna Hyatt Huntington, which shows a lad holding a plunging horse by a crude halter. Past the pool, the road runs through a gateway, guarded by two disdainful stone dogs, to the entrance of the formal garden, which contains about 40 acres. Cement walks in gigantic butterfly design lead past more than 300 pieces of statuary. In contrast with the white of the marbles is the rich green of the oaks. Squirrels frolic in the trees, and except in the heavy heat of noon the garden is filled with the song of birds. A bronze *Diana of the Chase,* by Mrs. Huntington, stands on tiptoe in a pool of water lilies; within the garden, tense bronze *Furies* kneel on the lawn and a proud white *Apollo* stands in a circle of hedge; under a moss-draped oak, Mario Morbel's *Night* reclines in marble whiteness against black-green boxwood; *Dawn* stands against the curving wall, and a laughing naiad steals a ride on the back of a huge green turtle; *The Youthful Ben Franklin,* a bundle under his arms, seems about to step out briskly from his rose-covered niche; *Narcissus* smiles at his reflection in a flower-bordered pool, and Saint Gaudens' *Puritan* stands stiff and uncomfortable; in a corner is Percy

Bryant Baker's delicate *L'Après-midi d'un Faune;* an old Indian watches his boy speed an arrow to the god of light, in *The Sun Vow.* Beside Brookgreen's entrance gates is a marked dirt road.

Left here 0.5 *m.* to the old ALSTON CEMETERY, enclosed by an ancient brick wall in the heart of the forest. Long inaccessible, the plot has been planted with azaleas, the road built, and a caretaker appointed by the Huntingtons. The site is part of The Oaks, former plantation of Joseph Alston, governor of South Carolina, 1812–14, who married Theodosia Burr in 1801. From The Oaks in 1812 she went to Georgetown and sailed for New York on the schooner *Patriot* to visit her father, Aaron Burr. The ship was lost at sea. On the tombstone of Governor Alston and his little son is an inscription that tells Theodosia's story.

At 44.3 *m.* is the junction with a dirt road and State 711.

1. Right here on the dirt road 0.5 *m.* to ALL SAINTS' CHAPEL, in a parish established in 1767. The present stuccoed building, erected in 1916, is a reconstruction of the original destroyed by fire. It follows the rectangular lines of the Greek temple, with a Doric portico having fluted columns and triglyphed frieze. On the sides are square-headed windows between pilasters.

2. Left here on State 711 0.5 *m.* to PAWLEY'S ISLAND, oldest of the resorts between North Carolina and Georgetown. Behind beach cottages and old summer homes rise high sand dunes, whose landward slopes are covered with thick mats of myrtle, palmetto, yucca, and tamarisk. The dress of vacationists, mostly perennial visitors, astonishes newcomers. Bare feet are the rule even for bank presidents; girls dance at the pavilion in sweeping evening gowns—but without any shoes or stockings; others wear slacks and beach pajamas, and their escorts, invariably barefooted, are clad in white ducks and sleeveless shirts. A persistent legend at Pawley's concerns the 'Gray Man,' who heralds the approach of every storm. Tradition records that in 1893 a gray-clad man appeared at the door of the Lachicottes, a family of French descent long associated with this region, and begged for bread. Accepting this as a warning from the traditional apparition, they left immediately for the mainland. Their flight was followed by one of the severest storms in South Carolina history. Vacationists claim the 'Gray Man' still visits the beach, but they nevertheless rely on the Coast Guard's modern warning system.

HOBCAW BARONY (L), 53.9 *m.,* owned by Bernard M. Baruch, was a grant to John, Lord Carteret, one of the Lords Proprietors.

As it curves across the LAFAYETTE DRAWBRIDGE, 55 *m.,* the route diverges from the original King's Highway, which ran straight down the coast and across the mouth of the bay by ferry. At Dover, the northern terminus of the old ferry line, is the graveyard for travelers who died of fever as they waited, days at a time, for the waves to become quiet enough to cross.

GEORGETOWN, 58 *m.* (14 alt., 5,082 pop.), seat of Georgetown County, lies at the head of Winyah Bay, the confluence of the Waccamaw, the Big Pee Dee, the Sampit, and the Black Rivers. It was established in 1735, named for the Prince of Wales (later George II of England), and laid out in large, uniform squares on a tract donated by the Reverend William Screven. Most of the settlers were English, and the town flourished as a port, shipping rice and indigo to the West Indies and to Great Britain. Though these staple crops have long since been supplanted by others, Georgetown has remained a distinct influence in the development of coastal South Carolina. The principal retail artery, Front Street, parallels the Sampit River, and boats from plantations still dock at the wharves behind the stores. The rich timberlands surrounding the town have long made it a leader along the Atlantic seaboard in lumber production. Logging trails and railroads, now weed-grown, radiate from the town. The SOUTHERN KRAFT CORPORATION WOOD PULP MILL, Hawkins St., on US 17, on the southeastern outskirts of town, is one of the largest of its kind, furnishing employment to more than 1,000 people. Its coming has revivified the community, which holds its nose and discounts the price of prosperity—the repellent odor that a land breeze sweeps from the plant over the town.

Georgetown's broad streets lead to many pre-Revolutionary structures. The rectangular CHURCH OF PRINCE GEORGE, WINYAH, Protestant Episcopal, corner Highmarket and Broad Sts., belongs to a parish founded in 1721; the building was erected 1742-6, partly with funds from a three-year tax on imported liquors. Of red brick, it terminates in a semicircular apse. The large fanlighted windows have white stone lintels and sills. Brick pilasters and corner quoins ornament the exterior. An entrance tower, added in 1820, has an arcaded octagonal belfry above the clock and is surmounted by a cupola with a large cross. Tradition asserts that the British stabled their horses in the building during the Revolution.

The MASONIC TEMPLE, corner Prince and Screven Sts., erected in 1735 as a bank, has walls of stuccoed brick, painted white to resemble stone, and is crowned by a flat roof and parapet.

The cornerstone of the white stuccoed brick GEORGETOWN COUNTY COURTHOUSE, diagonally opposite the Masonic Temple, was laid with Masonic rites in 1824. This building, if not designed by Robert Mills, shows his influence. The familiar Classical Revival design, with gable roof, pedimented and balustraded portico, has been modified in the basement story, which is heavily rusticated. Twin stairways, leading to the portico, have entrance arches.

The MARKET BUILDING, Front and Screven Sts., was erected in 1841 and used as the slave market. The mellowed red brick walls of the two-story structure are broken by windows with white stone lintels and sills. The clock tower, its old timepiece still marking the hours, is topped with an open balustraded belfry surmounted by a pagoda-like sway roof and weather vane.

When George Washington visited the town in 1791 he is said to have stayed in the PYATT HOUSE, Front St. between Wood and King Sts. This two-and-a-half-story white-painted brick dwelling facing the river has a six-columned piazza reached by a double flight of brick steps, tall chimneys, and curved bays.

The two-story red brick WINYAH INDIGO SOCIETY HALL, corner Prince and Cannon Sts., was built in 1857. It has a pedimented portico with white stuccoed Corinthian columns on piers. The large hall upstairs is used for social functions.

The Convivial Club, organized in 1740, was the forerunner of the

Winyah Indigo Society which received a royal charter in 1758. It is still in existence as a social club, though its former aim was to provide funds for education of poor children. Dues were paid in indigo. The society became educational in purpose in 1753. According to a local historian, approbation of the cause followed a toast which concluded: 'It has been wisely ordained that light should have no color, water no taste, and air no odor; so, indeed, knowledge should be equally pure and without admixture of creed or cant. I move, therefore, that the surplus funds in the Treasury be devoted to the establishment of an Independent Charity School for the Poor.' All members rose to their feet, drank the toast, 'the glasses were each turned down without soiling the linen, and the Winyah Indigo Society was established.'

Washington was entertained at lunch by the Society when he stopped in Georgetown.

Federals took over the hall when they invested the town in the War between the States and appropriated the most valuable part of an extensive library, including copies of Audubon's ornithology. The remaining volumes are still in the possession of the organization.

In Georgetown are junctions with US 521 (*see Tour* 4) and US 701 (*see Tour* 20).

Section b. GEORGETOWN to CHARLESTON, 61.3 m. US 17.

In these coastal swamps, Bartram found the rare gordonia and Venus's-flytrap, which still grow in secluded localities. Audubon, delighted with the wild life on his way to Charleston, wrote of 'traveling through the woods already rendered delightfully fragrant by the clusters of yellow jessamin that bordered them.' In April, the woods are lacy with the white bloom of dogwood; a little later the sweet bay, then the magnolia, fill the air with fragrance. Moss-hung cypress trees border roadside lagoons, where water lilies and blue water hyacinths float. The white egret has its nesting place on secluded islands, and other rare fowl find refuge in protected spots.

As night comes to the swamps there is a feeling of eeriness; the traveler recalls the 'ha'nts' and 'plat-eye,' as he sees the jack-o'-lantern and hears bull alligators bellow to the accompaniment of owls. The moon shines through the torn walls of little chapels-of-ease and the fox scampers beneath stairways of deserted mansions.

Along the route are Negro shacks, many of them with ladders instead of stairs leading to the loft, where children usually sleep. The roofs are punctured with 'dog houses,' or typical Low Country dormers. Doors and window shutters are often painted blue to keep away spirits. At houses and wayside stands near Charleston, baskets are offered for sale. These are substantially woven of grass by a process handed down from generation to generation of Negroes.

At 4.5 *m.* is the junction with a dirt road.

Left here 2.8 *m.* to a sandy road; R. through an almost sunless forest 0.5 *m.* to BELLE ISLE GARDENS (*open March* 1–*May* 1, $1). Here in a setting of sloping lawns and giant live oaks on the banks of Winyah Bay, the flames of tree-high japonicas and azaleas of every shade are reflected in a fresh-water lake. The gardens, on a 5,000-acre estate, are part of Winyah Barony, first granted to Landgrave Robert Daniell in 1711, but associated with the Horry (pronounced O-ree) family. The place was inherited by General Peter Horry, who named it Belle Isle. The white frame mansion (*private*) with one-story wings was built in 1829 by a Dr. Mendenhall in Newberry County; in the 1930's it was reconstructed here.

Partly screened by moss and a heavy growth of magnolias are the RUINS OF BATTERY WHITE, a Confederate fort. Iron cannon, with '1864' cut deep into their breeches, point to the sky. Out in the water is the rusted boiler top of the Federal supply ship, *Harvest Moon,* which was sunk by a Confederate mine.

At 13.1 *m.* on US 17 is the junction with a sandy road.

Right here 0.6 *m.* to deserted HOPSEWEE, a white frame house standing gaunt in the somber company of giant oaks and a garden overrun with weeds. Here, in 1749, was born Thomas Lynch, Jr., a Signer of the Declaration of Independence. Broad double piazzas and square columns identify the faded building with the pre-Revolutionary period. The rooms, with finely molded mantels and wainscot, open on a central hall.

At 16 *m.* on US 17 is the junction with an almost imperceptible dirt road.

Right on this road 0.4 *m.* to FAIRFIELD PLANTATION, once Tarleton's temporary Revolutionary headquarters. The oldest part of the white frame 'big house' was built about 1730 by the Lynches. In 1758 it passed to the Jacob Mottes, who enlarged and remodeled the dwelling; in one chimney is scratched, 'Jan. 27, 1766, Compleated.' The house, on a high brick basement, has a hip roof and a small portico facing the river.

Here lived Thomas Pinckney (1750–1828), brother of Charles Cotesworth Pinckney (*see Tour 11c*), and aide to Admiral D'Estaing and Generals Lincoln and Gates. Wounded in the Battle of Camden in 1780, he was captured and held until the end of the Revolution. He was governor of the State, 1787–9, and the first United States minister to England, 1792–4. In Spain, on a special mission, 1795, he negotiated a treaty that secured for this country the free navigation of the Mississippi for three years. From 1797 to 1801 he was a member of Congress, and was made a major general in the War of 1812. He served as the second president of the South Carolina Society of the Cincinnati, 1806–26, and succeeded his brother, General Charles Cotesworth Pinckney, as president general on the latter's death in 1826. His wife was Elizabeth Motte, whose father owned Fairfield.

At 17 *m.* on US 17 is the junction with a cross road at a filling station.

1. Left here 0.8 *m.* to the junction with a dirt road; L. 1.6 *m.* to HARRIETTA, a two-story frame house, built in 1797 by the second Mrs. Daniel Huger Horry for her daughter, Harriot, Mrs. Frederick Rutledge. The structure was long unoccupied before 1858, when its stately interior, with carved moldings and mantels, was completed. When the house was remodeled in the twentieth century, a false door was added between the two entrances under the garden portico to eliminate the confusing effect of the traditional 'twin' portal. The house and gardens are among the most notable in the Low Country.

2. Right from US 17 1 *m.* to the junction with a barely perceptible woods road; R. 1 *m.* to a field 200 yards from Bowman or PEACHTREE PLANTATION (*guide necessary*). Overlooking a tarn of the Santee River, this crumbling, neutral brown brick structure was occupied during the Revolution by Thomas Lynch, father of the Signer of the Declaration of Independence.

At 1.5 *m.* on the main side road is the old King's Highway.

Left here 2.2 *m.* to the red brick ST. JAMES (SANTEE) EPISCOPAL CHURCH, built *c.*1768, the fourth oldest in St. James Parish. Its plan is unusual in that the portico and apse are on the sides instead of the ends; the old gated pews face the pulpit from three directions. Its fanlighted windows and entrances, however, are typically Georgian. The pedimented portico has columns of curved brick. The St. James congregation was organized by the Huguenots, but later joined the Church of England. At the occasional services here the pre-Revolutionary pulpit Bible and prayer book are used.

At 1.9 *m.* on the main side road is a dirt road; R. here 0.4 *m.* to HAMPTON PLANTATION, the home of Archibald Rutledge, poet laureate of South Carolina. A small box at the gate mutely solicits contributions for the continuation of the restoration of one of South Carolina's finest houses. The house was begun by Noë Serré about 1735 and passed in 1757 to his son-in-law, Daniel Huger Horry. Horry added to the six-room structure by squaring the second story; this and several other additions have not spoiled the appearance of the two-and-a-half-story white frame mansion which has a hip roof and small dormers. The smooth white columns of the large Roman Doric pedimented portico are of solid pine; rosettes, panels, and flutings adorn its frieze, and the pediment contains a circular window. In the east wing a ballroom has a carved mantel above a wide fireplace lined with old Dutch tiles. In 1791 Hampton was the home of Mrs. Daniel Horry II, whose mother, Eliza Lucas Pinckney (*see below*), was there when Washington was a guest. Washington was so charmed with the great Mrs. Pinckney that he asked to serve as a pallbearer at her funeral in Philadelphia in 1793. In front of the Hampton house stands the 'Washington Oak.'

At 5.7 *m.* on the main side road is another dirt road; R. on this road 0.8 *m.* to the DANIEL HUGER (pronounced U-gee) MONUMENT, erected in 1820. Huger, born in Turenne in 1651, was among the Huguenots who settled in South Carolina after the revocation of the Edict of Nantes in 1685. The monument is on the site of his plantation, Waterhorn, where he was buried in 1711.

At 22.8 *m.* on US 17 is the junction with State 179.

Left here 0.5 *m.* to McCLELLANVILLE (600 pop.), a village started in the early 1850's as a summer settlement. Several oyster canneries in and around the village operate spasmodically.

CHRIST CHURCH (L), 48 *m.*, has a register dating back to 1694. Two of the former structures were destroyed by fire; the third was badly damaged by use as a stable during the War between the States. The present building, completed in 1874, is of brick stuccoed and coursed to simulate masonry, has stained-glass windows in a small apse and fanlighted windows and entrance. Its hip roof is topped with an octagonal cupola placed directly over the center of the building.

MOUNT PLEASANT, 56.4 *m.* (25 alt., 1,415 pop.), originated as a summer resort for the island planters. A quiet, pleasantly situated town, it attracts numerous vacationists.

The symmetrical white frame HIBBEN HOUSE, 111 Hibben St., was headquarters for General Moultrie and other Continental officers on parole in 1780-1. The Georgian structure has a façade with lofty portico, square columns, and a flat roof; a small balcony projects above the entrance. Andrew Hibben operated the first direct ferry from Hadrell's Point in 1770 and may have built the house soon after; or it may have been previously built by Jacob Motte.

The MOUNT PLEASANT PRESBYTERIAN CHURCH, corner Hibben and Church Sts., is a white rectangular clapboarded structure with pedimented and columned portico. It was a Chapel of Ease under Wappetaw Church of Christ Parish. A number of the Wappetaw Episcopalians drifted away, and, about 1838, organized a Presbyterian congregation at Mount Pleasant. After the War between the States the church property was divided; the Episcopalians retained the parish church, and the Presbyterians were given the Wappetaw Chapel of Ease. The extent of the plantations, the hazardous early roads, and the great distance that separated plantation families from their churches complicated regular church attendance until these small chapels of ease were erected and used for all except special services.

ST. ANDREW'S EPISCOPAL CHURCH, corner Whilden and Venning Sts., a brown frame structure with modified Gothic details, has pointed windows, a small wooden portico, a gable red tin roof, and a small square apse. St. Andrew's was erected in Christ Church Parish about 1856-7. The first building (1833-5), which replaced the Wappetaw Chapel of Ease, claimed by Presbyterians, adjoins the present church and is now a Masonic lodge.

The rectangular, stuccoed MOUNT PLEASANT BAPTIST CHURCH, corner Pitt and King Sts., formerly the Berkeley County Courthouse, has modified Italian Renaissance details. Above the heavily coursed first story are pedimented second-story windows, separated in pairs by Corinthian pilasters below a bold projecting cornice. Behind the church is a WAR OF 1812 MONUMENT, one of the few in the South.

Left from Mount Pleasant 3 m. on State 703 to SULLIVAN'S ISLAND, an ante-bellum seashore resort and location of the U. S. Coast Artillery Station. The township of Sullivan's Island, at both ends of the island, has many substantial old houses with high basements and latticed piazzas, surrounded by oleanders of many colors. Centering the island is FORT MOULTRIE RESERVATION, headquarters of the 8th Infantry, and a small maintenance detachment of coast artillery. Numerous batteries, strategically placed for coast defense, are named for South Carolina patriots—Thomson, Gadsden, Butler, and Jasper.

FORT MOULTRIE (R) 3.7 m., now a museum (free), was occupied by Major Anderson in January 1861 before he evacuated to Fort Sumter (see Tour 11b). In front of the fort is the GRAVE OF OSCEOLA, Seminole chief, captured, in spite of his flag of truce, during the Florida Seminole War of 1835, and imprisoned in a dungeon within the walls, where he died in 1838. Near the grave is a memorial to the Patapsco, inscribed with 66 names of the crew of the Federal ship, which was torpedoed in Charleston Harbor by Confederates. Edgar Allan Poe, a soldier here in 1828, wrote his poem 'Israfel' on the island, and later utilized the local setting for his story 'The Gold Bug.'

The first Fort Moultrie, the site of which is now about 100 yards out in the harbor, was an incomplete fort of sand and palmetto logs, when, June 28, 1776, the Carolinians defended Charles Town against 11 armed British vessels. From a distance of 400 yards the fleet's cannon began pounding the little fort at 10 o'clock that morning, but the balls were harmlessly imbedded in the spongy palmetto logs. From their shelter Colonel William Moultrie's men turned their guns on the two most powerful ships—the Experiment, and the flagship Bristol. Aboard the latter, 100 men were lost; the masts were shot to pieces; Sir William Campbell, fleeing Royal governor, received the wound from which he died; and Sir Peter Parker, commander of the fleet, was wounded twice, and compelled to retire when his pants were burned off. In the severe crossfire, the fort's blue flag was shot down. Over the wall leaped Sergeant William Jasper, who recovered the flag, tied it to a stick, and planted it in the side of the fort nearest the enemy. Three of the British ships swung westward to attack the unfinished

Charleston

MELLOWED BY TIME
Etching by Elizabeth O'Neil Verner ©

ST. MICHAEL'S
EPISCOPAL CHURCH
(1752)

Photograph by W. Lincoln Highton

SOUTH CAROLINA SOCIETY HALL (1804: Portico added in 1825)

Photograph by Walter Connolly

Photograph by W. Lincoln Highton

ST. PHILIP'S CHURCH (1835-8)

EAST, OR HIGH BATTERY

Photographs by W. Lincoln Highton

THE COMMODORE INGRAM HOUSE
also known as the Henry Manigault House (1818)

HEYWARD-WASHINGTON HOUSE (1730)
AND PORGY'S INN

CHARLES BREWTON HOUSE (BUILT BEFORE 1733)

Photograph by Walter Connolly

Photograph by W. Lincoln Highton

PIRATE HOUSE AS SEEN THROUGH GATES OF ST. PHILIP'S

LOWER KING STREET

Photograph by Carlisle Roberts

INNER COURTYARD

Photograph by Carlisle Roberts

WATER FRONT

CHARLESTON FROM THE AIR

MAIN BUILDING (1828), COLLEGE OF CHARLESTON
The Oldest Municipal College in America

MAIN BUILDING (1922), THE CITADEL (FOUNDED 1842)

section of the fort and went aground. Two were eventually floated and retired from action; the third, the *Actaeon,* remained fast. On the northeast shore of the island, 3,000 British under Sir Henry Clinton and Lord Cornwallis were held back by the 780 men of Colonel William Thomson. Shortage of powder at the fort saved the British ships; additional ammunition did not arrive from Charles Town until late in the afternoon. The battle was over at 9:30 o'clock. An hour and a half later the British fleet had returned to its anchorage at Morris Island, with a loss of 200 men. At the fort 12 were killed and 25 wounded. The next morning the grounded *Actaeon* was set afire by her captain and abandoned, her colors flying, her guns loaded. A party of Carolinians under Lieutenant Jacob Milligan boarded the ship, fired three of her guns at the British fleet, brought off her colors and ship's bell and left only a few minutes before the ship exploded. A few days after the departure of the British, word was received that the Declaration of Independence had been signed. The fort was named Moultrie for its commander, and a white palmetto added to the State's flag.

The THOMSON MEMORIAL BRIDGE, 7.7 *m.* on State 703, connecting Sullivan's Island and the Isle of Palms, honors Colonel William Thomson, a Revolutionary officer. The ISLE OF PALMS, 8 *m.* (25 year-round pop.), has a broad, smooth, seven-mile beach, attracting many summer vacationists to its palmetto-bordered shore.

The COOPER RIVER BRIDGE, 57.5 *m.* (*toll: car and driver 50¢, passengers 15¢ each; week-end round trip for car and all passengers 75¢*), completed in 1929 at a cost of $4,700,000, is 10,000 feet long and 150 feet above the water. From its crest it is possible to see the WANDO and COOPER RIVERS (R), and between them DANIELL'S ISLAND, site of the plantation of Robert Daniell, governor of South Carolina 1716–17. On HOG ISLAND (L), a stretch of marsh and highland adjacent to Mount Pleasant, Jonathan Lucas once built a windmill while experimenting with rice cultivation on his plantation.

In CHARLESTON, 61.3 *m.* (9 alt., 62,265 pop.) (*see Charleston*), is the junction with US 52 (*see Tour 2b*).

Section c. CHARLESTON to GEORGIA LINE, 111.8 *m. US* 17.

South of CHARLESTON, 0 *m.,* the road moves inland, passing over the marshes, and through shadowy tunnels of moss-curtained live oaks. Later, it runs between tall pines and crosses tangled swamps, where on still nights can be heard a hound baying on the trail of a 'coon or 'possum, and the plaintive call of the whippoorwill.

On the outskirts of Charleston, US 17 crosses the ASHLEY RIVER BRIDGE, 1.9 *m.,* an electrically operated bascule draw, completed in 1926 as a memorial to Charleston World War soldiers. Palmettos and oleanders line the causeway.

At 2.7 *m.* is the junction with Folly Beach Road.

Left here 1.5 *m.* to WAPPOO HEIGHTS, a wooded suburban development. The McLEOD HOUSE (L), 2.4 *m.,* with stately portico and a live oak avenue, was a hospital during the War between the States, and was later used by the Freedmen's Bureau, established to aid former slaves.

At 2.5 *m.* on the Folly Beach Road is the Wappoo Hall Road; R. here 1.3 *m.* to the MUNICIPAL GOLF COURSE (*greens fee 50¢*).

On Wappoo Creek in this vicinity was the plantation where Elizabeth Lucas (1723–93), more often called Eliza, successfully cultivated indigo in 1742. Though not the first person in the province to plant the crop, she is cited as the founder of an industry that brought millions to South Carolina. The daughter of Lieutenant Colonel George Lucas of the British Army, who was stationed at Antigua in the West Indies, Eliza, a girl of 16, was left in charge of her invalid mother and three plantations. Along with the usual crops, she experimented with indigo, ginger, cotton, lucerne, and cassava seeds that her father sent her from Antigua. After several unsuccessful attempts, she was notably successful with indigo. In 1744 she married Chief Justice Charles Pinckney, who was then 45, and later became the mother of Charles Cotesworth and Thomas Pinckney, both prominent in State history. In her widowhood Eliza Pinckney settled at Belmont, her husband's semi-urban plantation on the Charleston 'Neck,' where she experimented with the culture of silk.

The main part of FENWICK HALL, 4.1 m. on Wappoo Hall Road, was built in 1730 by the seventh John Fenwick. Twenty years later, his heir Edward added two-story brick flankers to the sides, one a coach house and stable for coach horses, the other a stable for the string of thoroughbreds that Fenwick made the most celebrated of their time in the province. Today the coach house is a garage; the opposite flanker is no longer standing. The shingle roof is surmounted with a balustrade. The fanlighted entrance, altered during restoration, has a pediment supported by paired Doric columns. Ghosts in the house are said to be those of a handsome English groom and the daughter of the house who eloped but were brought back and the girl imprisoned in a room overlooking the courtyard where her lover was hanged.

Cacti, some of the rare night blooming variety, grow about 25 feet high in the garden here. Fenwick Hall faces Johns Island Road along which the British surprised and routed the Continentals in a night attack.

At 8.1 m. on the Wappoo Hall Road is a dirt road; R. here 0.3 m. to the 1,000-year-old ANGEL OAK (adm. 5¢ and 10¢), in an enclosure on a site once owned by the Angel family. The limbs of this tree spread over 14,560 square feet and its circumference is 21 feet.

On the Folly Beach Road at 4.5 m. is a hard surfaced road; L. here 1.7 m. to the gates of the AGRICULTURAL SOCIETY PLOT, which memorialize Samuel Gaillard Stoney, president for many years of the Agricultural Society of South Carolina (see Agriculture).

Here is the junction with the King's Highway.

Left on the King's Highway 5.4 m. to the UNITED STATES QUARANTINE STATION and the RUINS OF FORT JOHNSON. The latter, Charleston's oldest fortification, built in 1704–8, was a fully garrisoned British post in 1765, but was nevertheless quietly occupied one night by a group of Charlestonians, who trained all its guns on a British war sloop anchored alongside with a cargo of despised tax stamps. Next morning the Charlestonians invited the commander into the fort, showed him their preparations, and threatened to sink his ship unless he returned to England with the stamps. Bewildered, he accepted the ultimatum and sailed. The flag used by the Carolinians on this occasion, a blue field with three white crescents, was the first used by any American colony. Here, September 15, 1775, Moultrie first hoisted his blue banner. The colors of this first 'flag of liberty' raised in the United States are retained in the present South Carolina flag.

The TOLLGATE (20¢ per person round trip), 8.2 m. on Folly Beach Road, heads a long causeway. Tiny palmetto-crowned islands dot the marsh, changing in color and form with the tides.

FOLLY ISLAND, 8.8 m., is a popular resort on a ten-mile beach. On the eastern end of the island is a US radio station. Off the southern end of Folly, low tides reveal the ruins of an old fort, last used in the War between the States. In 1862 the stronghold was dismantled and its equipment placed aboard the *Planter* for shipment to another Confederate fort. But during the night, Robert Smalls, one of the slave crew, navigated the ship into the hands of the Federal forces. This exploit won for him during Reconstruction a seat in Congress, and his sudden fortune enabled him to buy the home of his former owner.

At 3.6 m. on US 17 is the junction with State 61.

Right on this road, along the tidal Ashley River, through old St. Andrew's Parish, where avenues lead to Ashley River estates, which had entrances from both land and river.

At 1.9 *m.* is a dirt road; R. here 1.6 *m.* to the SITE OF OLD TOWN. The Cassique of the Kiawah tribe persuaded the English colonists to select this spot for their first settlement in Carolina. Occupied in 1670, it was called Albemarle Point. Within a year Governor William Sayle had built his 'mansion house' and set aside four acres as a churchyard. Southeast of the settlement Joseph West, agent for the Lords Proprietors and commander-in-chief of the first ships to arrive, established the first 'experimental farm' in South Carolina, planting cotton, indigo, ginger root, and other crops. Late in 1670 he reported that cattle brought from Virginia were doing well and the corn was flourishing. The farm afterward became Hillsborough Plantation and is now the site of a Negro settlement known as Maryville. In 1680 the colony moved across the Ashley and established the walled city that is now Charleston.

ST. ANDREW'S PARISH CHURCH (R), 5.6 *m.* on State 61, completed as a cruciform in 1733, was burned in 1763 and rebuilt by popular subscription—a white painted brick structure, with red roof and green blinds. The church, like many others, formerly served as a financial yardstick for its parishioners—the front pews renting higher than the rear ones.

DRAYTON HALL (R), 8.2 *m.*, an immense two-story brick house, built about 1738 by John Drayton, stands on a high basement; a double flight of steps lead to the pedimented, double-deck entrance portico, which is partly recessed. The only Ashley River home not vandalized by Yankees in 1865, it was saved because a Confederate officer learned of the enemy approach and transferred a number of slaves, ill with smallpox, into the house. This is still a Drayton home and the furnishings carry on its traditions of splendor.

Adjoining Drayton Hall are MAGNOLIA GARDENS (R), 8.9 m. (*open Jan. 1– May 1; adm.* $2), owned since the early eighteenth century by the Drayton family. The 25-acre gardens, developed by the Reverend John Grimké Drayton in 1830, were pronounced by John Galsworthy 'the most beautiful gardens in the world,' and Baedeker ranked them as one of three 'double star' sites in America. Centering the labyrinth of azalea-bordered paths on the banks of the curving Ashley, the third frame dwelling rises on the original foundations. The first mansion was burned by the British during the Revolution; the second was razed by Sherman's army in 1865. In this garden oriental exotics bloom among the rich flora of the Carolina coast. The amazingly tall azaleas, ranging from coolest white through warmer shades of lavender and coral, to a bonfire blaze of scarlet, contrast with the green of lawns under the cypress trees and live oaks, soberly garlanded in gray moss. The dark waters of a lake, crossed by a wooden foot bridge, reflect the camellia japonicas and the wisteria. The garden has also specimens of California redwood, Chinese yew, Spanish and French cypress.

On RUNNYMEDE PLANTATION (R), 9.4 *m.* (*open Mar.–April; adm.* $1), a royal grant in 1705 to John Cattell, camellias, roses, jessamine, dogwood, and wisteria are reflected in the winding Ashley River and black lagoons, and blaze against the dark forest background. The garden's several hundred acres include ALPHABET AVENUE, composed of trees whose names begin with the letters of the alphabet, arranged in consecutive order. The 'K' tree, a koelreuteria, was imported from the Orient.

What is said to be the first landscaped garden in America was designed in 1740 at MIDDLETON PLACE (R), 12.4 *m.* (*open Feb.–May; adm.* $2), when Henry Middleton, who later became temporary president of the first Continental Congress, imported an English landscape artist to plan the setting for the brick Tudor house built by his father-in-law, John Williams, in 1738. The mansion was enlarged in 1755. The left flanker and three-story central unit were burnt by Federal troops in 1865, but with the use of old brick the right flanker was restored in the 1930's, roughly along the original eighteenth-century lines, with stepped and curvilinear gable ends. In front of the house and to the left, the gardens rise from the river in sweeping terraces, at the foot of which are the paired Butterfly Lakes. The chief charm of Middleton Place is its eighteenth-century elegance and the dignity of its landscaping. For 10 years 100 slaves labored to complete the 45-acre garden and 16-acre lawn. Camellia japonicas, some 20- to 30-feet high, form pleached avenues and bloom red, white, and pink from late winter through early spring; a succession of pools reflects the rich color. Chinese azaleas, the gingko, mimosa, varnish, and spice trees, besides other exotics, grow in this 'botanical paradise of native American flora.' Among the trees, MIDDLETON OAK, on the river's edge, is monarch. Estimated as 900 years old, its mossy limb-spread is 144 feet, and its trunk 37 feet in circumference. Arthur Middleton, son of Henry, added to the gardens. A Signer of the Declaration of Independence, he is buried in the brick mausoleum in the gardens.

On State 61, at 19.7 m. is a dirt road; R. here 2.2 m. to a narrow lane; R. on this lane 0.2 m. to OLD FORT DORCHESTER, of tabby-topped brick, marking the site of the old town of Dorchester. Settled and named in 1696 by a colony from Dorchester, Massachusetts, the town lasted some 50 years and once numbered 1,000 inhabitants. Materials from all the buildings except the fort and church were carried away for other construction when the settlement was abandoned.

A winter resort with great natural beauty, SUMMERVILLE, 22.9 m. (2,570 pop.), has an ordinance forbidding the cutting of a pine, even on private property. Its streets ramble in curves through the trees, and the lavish bloom of azaleas, camellias, and wisteria glow against the dark background of pines. Small boys, holding up signs marked 'Guide,' besiege the motorist. Set in wide grounds are many houses of architectural charm. Two blocks from the business section is the AZALEA PARK AND BIRD SANCTUARY. More than 800 specimens of native plants grow in the park, and in winter thousands of migratory birds join the feathered year-round residents.

At Summerville is the junction with US 78 (see Tour 15b).

Right from Summerville 1.5 m. on State 64 to PINEHURST TEA FARM (open on certain days Mar.–April), planted in 1890 by Dr. Charles U. Shepard for experimentation in commercial tea growing. The plants still remain as hedges and ornamental shrubs. In 1900 Dr. Shepard founded a mission school for the Dorchester County brass ankle children, of supposedly mixed racial stock. There are two theories for the peculiar name: one that they wore a brass anklet as a mark of caste, the other that in the days of slavery, they were chained at night. They are a people apart, not mingling in either white or Negro society.

On US 17, 8.7 m., is a FEDERAL REGIONAL PLANT BREEDING STATION. The road curves past truck and dairy farms, and the countryside is dotted with small Negro shacks enclosed by 'tiger fences' of staggered split rails. A roadside marker, 12.6 m., indicates the grave of Colonel William Washington, kinsman of the first President.

In RANTOWLES, 14.9 m. (30 pop.), a scattered village of small farms, is the junction with a paved road, an alternate route.

Left here 6.8 m. to State 165; L. here 1.5 m. to MEGGETT (1,050 pop.), known as the 'Cabbage Patch.' The community is headquarters for a truck association, and has a stock exchange in direct communication with Wall Street. Sizable fortunes have been made and lost on the price fluctuations of the prosaic cabbage.

In ADAM'S RUN, 13.5 m. (500 pop.), an old summer resort on the paved alternate route, is the junction with State 174.

1. Left here to BARRELVILLE, 2.8 m. (15 pop.), where containers are manufactured for the truck grown at Meggett. Just beyond the Dawhoo River is WHOOPING ISLAND, 6.2 m., where travelers used to whoop to attract the ferryman.

LITTLE EDISTO ISLAND, 6.8 m., is dotted with a few truck farms and surrounded by stretches of marsh.

EDISTO ISLAND, 9 *m.*, a quiet resort and fishing point, was, until recently, a semi-isolated community because of the difficulty of constructing an all-weather road over the marshes. It is the home of a large Negro population, who gain a living mainly by fishing, and a smaller number of whites who are descended for the most part from old plantation families. When South Carolina was deliberating whether or not to sign the Ordinance of Secession, the Edisto Island delegate jumped to his feet and declared that, irrespective of what the State did, Edisto Island would secede from the Union.

At 10.8 *m.* is the junction with Brick House Avenue; L. here 1.7 *m.* to the RUINS OF BRICK HOUSE. In a grove of live oak and pine is the brick shell of the handsome plantation house erected on the property of Paul Hamilton between 1720 and 1730. The loopholes in the basement were designed for musketry, as the structure was built when Indian raids were still frequent and before the buffer colony of Georgia was settled.

The EDISTO ISLAND PRESBYTERIAN CHURCH (L), 12.7 *m.*, a white post-Colonial building, was erected in 1831.

On State 174 at 13.4 *m.* is the Steamboat Landing Road; L. here 0.4 *m.* to the SANCTIFY NEGRO CHURCH (L), where a black priestess directs primitive religious rites at which Negroes work themselves to an unbelievable emotional pitch.

TRINITY PROTESTANT EPISCOPAL CHURCH (R), 14.6 *m.* on State 174, whose congregation was organized in the 1700's, is a modern building; the first was destroyed by fire in 1930.

At 15.6 *m.* is the junction with Peter's Point Plantation Road; R. here 4.1 *m.* to PETER'S POINT PLANTATION, a typical ante-bellum plantation home, owned for many generations by the Mikell family. Here, where St. Pierre's Creek flows into the South Edisto River, Spanish Jesuit priests conducted an Indian mission school before the country was settled by the English.

Here is the junction with a dirt road.

Left on this road 0.4 *m.* to HAMILTON'S HILL, scene of ante-bellum horse races. Negroes say that the hill is inhabited by a variety of ghosts, including a ten-foot cat that explodes, plat-eyes in the guise of three-legged hogs, two-headed cows, boo-daddies, boo-hags, and drolls. Drolls are spirits of infants who died a painful death, and who can be heard crying in the swamps in the hour before 'fus' dawn.'

EDISTO BEACH, 20.3 *m.* on State 174 (*bait, boats, and guides available for fishing expeditions*), is the summer headquarters of the island, with about 100 cottages, a store, filling station, and a community clubhouse.

In the 800-acre EDISTO STATE PARK (*public camp grounds; bathing suits for rent; boats for hire; no fishing equipment available*) is a mile and a half of splendid beach. The State Commission of Forestry is experimenting with tabby (*see Beaufort*) for use in constructing the various park buildings.

2. Right from Adam's Run on State 174 2.7 *m.* to the junction with the main route.

At 26.8 *m.* on US 17 is the southern junction with the alternate route.

Along here the highway runs through a green tunnel of interlaced oaks and cypress boughs. The gray moss, hanging in a sunlight mist, changes from silvery gray to gray-green or a gentle purple. At the JACKSONBORO BRIDGE, 31.6 *m.*, arching over the black Edisto River, boats may be rented for cruising or fishing.

The State legislature met in 1781 at JACKSONBORO, 32.3 *m.* (75 pop.), when Charleston was in the hands of the British.

In Jacksonboro is the junction with State 32 (*see below*).

At 34.2 *m.* is the junction with a dirt road.

Right on this road 1.2 *m.* to the ISAAC HAYNE MONUMENT honoring the Revolutionary colonel hanged in Charleston by the British.

WALTERBORO, 48.4 *m.* (80 alt., 2,592 pop.), seat of Colleton County, is a tourist town and the trade-center in fertile country. It was settled early in the eighteenth century by rice planters. The town's natural beauty, pleasant climate, and excellent hunting and fishing have made it a popular winter resort. Walterboro was first named Ireland Creek; two citizens, one named Walter and the other Smith, each insisted that the town be named for him. They ended the dispute by a tree-felling contest in which Smith was vanquished. The WALTERBORO LIBRARY (*open Tues., Wed., Fri.* 3–5; *Sat.* 10–12), 127 Wichman St., containing 3,900 volumes, was built in 1820 when the Walterboro Library Society was founded. The little white frame building has a gable roof and a fanlighted entrance flanked by pedimented windows.

The COLLETON COUNTY COURTHOUSE, corner Hampton and Jeffries Sts., said to have been designed by Robert Mills, was considerably altered in 1939 by a coating of stucco and enlarged by the addition of two large wings. The original portico, with its four plain unfluted Greek Doric columns, rests on a high arcaded basement and is flanked by curved stairs. Here in 1828 the first public Nullification meeting in the State was held. KLEIN'S DRUG STORE, 121 Washington St., established in 1845, is operated by what is believed to be the oldest firm in the State with its original name. The OLD BELL, at Bethel Presbyterian Church, 26 Church St., was moved from the Bethel Church near Jacksonboro. The LUCAS RESIDENCE, Washington St., with 21 rooms, is constructed of white frame on a high brick foundation. The piazza roof is supported by six square tapering columns.

In Walterboro is the junction with US 15 (*see Tour 3b*).

At 49.5 *m.* is the junction with State 303.

Left here 7.7 *m.* to RITTER (30 pop.); L. from Ritter on a dirt road 1.2 *m.* to BEECH HILL (L), one of the few Low Country estates still occupied and cultivated by the family who owned it in the early 1800's. A stately avenue of palmettos leads to the old house, which was visited nine times by Sherman's raiders, but escaped destruction largely through the unruffled serenity with which the owner's wife met every threat of eviction.

Opposite Beech Hill is the long private road leading to BONNIE DOONE, part of a royal land grant of 1722; by the avenue is (R) an ante-bellum rice field. The original house, reduced to ruins by Sherman's men, has been replaced.

At 13.5 *m.* on State 303 is the junction with State 32.

1. Left on State 32 2.1 *m.* to a junction with the Airy Hall Road; R. 0.5 *m.* to POCO SABO PLANTATION (L), part of the vast barony on Ashepoo River granted Edmund Bellinger, the first landgrave of his name. Enclosed by a high brick wall is a stone erected to the memory of the fourth Edmund (1743–1801), his wife, and seven children. The old house has given way to a long, narrow, white plantation dwelling with many chimneys.

Near the ASHEPOO RIVER, 4.1 *m.* on State 32, the deserted town of Edmundsbury was laid out in 1740 on a tract of 600 acres, part of the Bellinger Barony, and called after Edmund Bellinger. A Chapel of Ease to the church of St. Bartholomew's Parish, created in 1706, was begun here in 1753.

At Jacksonboro, 10 *m.*, State 32 joins US 17, the main route.

2. Right on State 32 2.6 *m.* to a dirt road; R. here 5.2 *m.* to WHITE HALL (L), one of the finest of the Low Country plantations. The house is owned by C. L. Lawrence, who designed the motor of Lindbergh's *Spirit of St. Louis*.

On State 32 at 3.9 *m.* is another dirt road; L. here 3 *m.* to the gates of

LONG BROW PLANTATION. One mile from the gate stands the rambling white farmhouse, an enlargement of the original structure.

On LAUREL SPRING PLANTATION (L), 4.2 *m*. on State 32, Theodore Ravenel, South Carolina's last commercial rice planter, gathered his final crop in 1927. Backwater rice fields still exist about half way between Laurel Spring and OAKLAND. Both plantations are owned by the same person and both are part of the original grant to the Lowndes family. The eighteenth-century dwelling is a large square cypress structure with mahogany stairway and carved mantels and moldings. It was reputedly the only house on the Combahee River spared, with its old outbuildings, on Sherman's march to the sea. From Oakland, a curving road leads to a white brick lodge, built in the shape of a 'Z,' on a wide lawn among camellia japonicas and azaleas. By the lodge is (R) the TOMB OF DOCTOR JAMES LYNAH, a Revolutionary surgeon.

The drawbridge, 6 *m*. on State 32, crosses the COMBAHEE RIVER, which the Spaniards are said to have called the River Jordan in 1525. In ante-bellum days, planters, crossing the river in their flat boats, drank a toast to 'God's Country' in Combahee water. Old rice fields, now used to entice ducks, are on each side of the causeway and an old rice mill chimney is visible (R) on Cypress Plantation. Near the Combahee the town of RADNOR was laid out in 1734 by William Bull, and its site unsuccessfully advocated in 1763 as a port of entry.

In GARDEN'S CORNER, 12 *m*., is the junction with US 21 (*see Tour 5c*).

South of Walterboro US 17 proceeds through a flat region marked by swampy landscapes with an occasional truck farm.

At 65.5 *m*. is the junction with US 21 (*see Tour 5b*), which unites with US 17 between here and Pocotaligo.

In YEMASSEE, 68 *m*. (12 alt., 589 pop.), is the junction with State 28 (*see Tour 19c*). To enjoy the good hunting in the surrounding forests numerous Northerners maintain winter residences near by.

POCOTALIGO, 72.6 *m*. (317 pop.), traces its history back through Indian massacres and several wars to the earliest settlement of the section.

Here is the southern junction with US 21 (*see Tour 5b*).

COOSAWHATCHIE, 78.6 *m*. (3,498 pop.), 'The Refuge of the Coosaw' (Indian tribe), is the site of a Revolutionary battle in which half of the Continentals engaged were killed.

RIDGELAND, 85.9 *m*. (705 pop.), seat of Jasper County, has been the scene of numerous marriages, because of its proximity for Georgians and the leniency of South Carolina marriage license laws. The turpentine-yielding pines hereabout are the basis for a lumber industry; stock raising and farming are other means of livelihood, and unemployment is rare.

Right from Ridgeland on State 128 to the tiny village of GILLISONVILLE, 10 *m*. In the 1860's every building except the Baptist Church and a residence was burned by Sherman's army. The church was used by the Federals as headquarters and one of the silver communion plates is marked: 'War of 1861 & 2 & 3 & 4. Feb. 7, 1865. This done by a Yankee soldier.'

At 87.3 *m*. is the junction with a dirt road.

Left here 1.5 *m*. to a fork; L. 4.3 *m*. to another dirt road; R. 0.1 *m*. to the gates of a pasture in which is the THOMAS HEYWARD TOMB, marking the grave of a Signer of the Declaration of Independence.

OKETEE CLUB (R), 90 *m.*, is a 42,000-acre hunting preserve owned by a group of Northern sportsmen.

The sawmill industry furnishes a livelihood for most of the residents at HARDEEVILLE, 100.9 *m.* (278 pop.). Here are junctions with State 5 and State 46 (*see Tour 5A*).

South of 105.6 *m.* the route passes through a part of the SAVAN-NAH RIVER WILD LIFE REFUGE. Purchase began in 1927 and now there are more than 9,000 acres in this State and Georgia. On the coastal migratory paths of various kinds of birds, it is a point of biannual concentration. Tens of thousands of teal, wood duck, and other fowl winter here each year, attracted by the many old rice fields with which the reservation abounds.

US 17 crosses the GEORGIA STATE LINE at 111.8 *m.*, 10 miles north of Savannah, Georgia.

Tour 2

(Wadesboro, N. C.)—Cheraw—Florence—Kingstree—Moncks Corner —Charleston; US 52. North Carolina Line to Charleston, 158.8 *m.*

Roadbed concrete-paved with one short section of asphalt.
Atlantic Coast Line R.R. parallels route.
Abundant accommodations; hotels in larger towns.

US 52 traverses the Pine Belt uplands, through peach orchards and vineyards, until rolling hills give way to tobacco fields and long straight rows of vegetables. These crops, with cotton, punctuate the farmers' year with three cash periods. Moving toward Charleston, the route slices through dense Low Country swamps associated with the indigo and rice planting eras, when Carolina gentlemen lived on baronies along the tidal rivers.

Section a. NORTH CAROLINA LINE to KINGSTREE, 86.8 m.
US 52.

In this section, forests still yield their substance for profit, and their game for sport; streams and lakes lure anglers, as they did nearly 50 years before the Revolution, when Dissenters came to the uplands for freedom.

US 52 crosses the NORTH CAROLINA LINE, 0 *m.*, about 13 miles south of Wadesboro, North Carolina.

In CHERAW, 9.6 *m.* (145 alt., 3,575 pop.) (*see Tour 6a*), are junctions with US 1 (*see Tour 6a*) and State 9 (*see Tour 21a*).

At 12.6 *m.* is the southern junction with US 1 (*see Tour 6a*).

CASH'S DEPOT, 15.6 *m.*, was named for the family of E. B. C. Cash, Confederate colonel and a participant in the Cash-Shannon duel (*see Tour 3a*).

SOCIETY HILL, 22.6 *m.* (161 alt., 573 pop.) (*see Tour 3a*), is at the junction with US 15 (*see Tour 3a*), which unites with US 52 for 2 miles.

Built around its courthouse square, DARLINGTON, 39.5 *m.* (175 alt., 5,556 pop.), seat of Darlington County, was settled in 1798 and incorporated in 1835. Streets are shady with magnificent Darlington oaks—South Carolina name for the Laurel Oak. South of the square, the highway bisects a prosperous Negro section which trails off into an area of shanties around the veneer plant, called by its Negro employees the 'canary plant.' Northward lies 'factory hill,' for Darlington boasts a textile mill and a chair factory as well as tobacco and cotton markets. The community entertains the State Open Tennis Tournament every summer.

A constable and two citizens were killed and others wounded in the 'Darlington War' of 1894, an outbreak aroused by Governor B. R. Tillman's liquor regulations, particularly by his order permitting private homes to be searched without warrant for concealed liquor. The day after the fatalities, Darlingtonians fired on a train bringing in constables, and scoured the countryside for others. Tillman ordered the militia to Darlington and Florence Counties. Many companies refused to obey, and were dishonorably discharged. Among these was the Charleston company, whose members declined to surrender their arms, defending their action in Federal court against 'one B. R. Tillman, styling himself Governor of South Carolina.' Tillman finally collected more docile troops, but the Darlington Guards had restored peace before they arrived.

WILLIAMSON PARK, with entrances on Spring and Cashua Sts., is a large crescent-shaped tract bordering Swift Creek on the northern edge of town, where familiar garden shrubs have been planted along with native flowering trees. With Swift Creek bordering its rolling terrain, LEMON PARK, on St. John's high school grounds, Park St., between Main and St. John's Sts., has a handsome natural amphitheater.

In Darlington is a junction with State 151 (*see Tour 3a*).

Left from Darlington on Cashua St. to the DARLINGTON COUNTRY CLUB (R), 1 *m.* (*no admission fee for guests accompanied by members*), with facilities for golf, tennis, and water sports. Here a favorite picnic dish is 'chicken bog'— chicken and rice, usually cooked over an open fire in a big iron kettle.

The PEE DEE EXPERIMENT STATION, 47.5 *m.*, comprises 200 acres, with a substation of 159 additional acres, and makes experiments with major crops growing hereabouts.

At FLORENCE, 49.1 *m.* (136 alt., 14,774 pop.) (*see Florence*), is the junction with US 76 (*see Tour 9a*).

At 49.9 *m.* is the junction with Cherokee Road, unpaved.

Left on this road to the SOUTH CAROLINA INDUSTRIAL SCHOOL (R), 0.4 *m.* The white boy inmates do their own work and grow most of their food. Established in 1865, the UNITED STATES NATIONAL MILITARY CEMETERY (L), 0.7 *m.,* was the burial ground for Union soldiers dying at a prison camp near by (*see Florence*). Under grave No. 2480 lies Florena Budwin, who, disguised in Union uniform, had fought with the troops. Florence women, horrified that a woman was among the soldiers with only men's clothing, sent her feminine attire. She served as a nurse to sick prisoners for about a year before she died. At 0.9 *m.* is the junction with a sandy road; R. on this road, 0.7 *m.* to the PRISON STOCKADE, 110 acres surrounded by earthworks, where 16,000 Northerners were imprisoned by Confederates.

At 51.1 *m.* is a junction with State 51 (*see Tour 20*).

At EFFINGHAM, 58.1 *m.* (106 alt., 200 pop.), named in honor of one of the Lords Proprietors, is the junction with US 301.

Right on this road to the villages of OLANTA, 14 *m.* (433 pop.), and TURBEVILLE, 20 *m.* (210 pop.), two of the largest settlements in this area of farms, with tobacco growing up to the road.

In this vicinity is Pudding Swamp, named, according to local tradition, for a Negro who appeared at every farmhouse roundabout at hog killing time, in hopes of getting some liver pudding. About 1750 a trail across this and other swamps was blazed from Kingstree to Camden.

William Henry Mouzon (1741–1807), member of a Huguenot family that left Charles Town to move north of the Santee River, was one of the four captains under whom Marion's first battalion was formed in 1780. Mouzon's home, the only one in the neighborhood to suffer, was burned by Tarleton, August 6, 1780, because the captain, of French descent, still spoke the language and was a local leader in the Revolution. In 1775 Henry Mouzon, Sr., made a remarkably accurate map of the Carolinas. Later his son and namesake submitted a route for the Santee Canal, and engineers believe that had not Colonel Senf's professional jealousy prevented his following Mouzon's route, the canal might have been successful.

At MANNING, 38 *m.* (95 alt., 1,884 pop.) (*see Tour 4*), is the junction with US 521 (*see Tour 4*).

Fields of cotton and tobacco, forests of tall pines, and dense swamps lie along the straight, level route.

At SUMMERTON, 49 *m.* (138 alt., 812 pop.) (*see Tour 3b*), is the junction with US 15 (*see Tour 3b*).

Deriving its name from Lake Swamp, a near-by lagoon of Lynches River, LAKE CITY, 71.5 *m.* (74 alt., 1,942 pop.), is allowed no restful summers. Its most active season occurs in the hottest months. Strawberries and English peas begin the surge of activity about April 10–15. In May, sweating teamsters and truckers come to town from miles around, line up two by two, have their vegetables graded, and enter the municipal market shed. All day and into the night, the raucous auctioneer calls for bids, and produce dealers from the North and East are ready with cash. A levy of 2¢ per package, split between producer and buyer, finances the sales. In 1938 more than 500 carloads of beans were shipped, besides an unestimated amount dispatched by motor truck. After snap beans come squash, potatoes, cucumbers, and lima beans. The season closes in mid-July, giving a brief breathing spell before August brings tobacco auctions to Lake City.

At 77.8 *m.* is the junction with a dirt road.

1. Left on this road to INDIANTOWN PRESBYTERIAN CHURCH, 14 *m.*, a white frame edifice with a broad portico. This is the third building for the congregation, organized 1750–60. The first was destroyed in 1780, when the British Major Wemyss desolated Williamsburg County. Early records indicate the conflict between piety and conviviality; members were expelled for dancing, horse racing, gambling, fighting, intoxication, and Sabbath breaking. During the Confederate era, a tolerant pastor played his fiddle for the youth of his congregation to dance off the depression of war.

2. Right on the dirt road 6 *m.* to the junction with a dirt road; L. here 1 *m.* to the junction with another dirt road; R. here 0.5 *m.* to SPRINGBANK PLANTATION AND GARDENS (*open by arrangement*), approached over sweeping lawns by an avenue of magnolia and holly trees. The two-story cypress house, with paneled interior, built in 1783 by James Burgess, has been enlarged and altered, with tall columns added on the front portico. The old corncrib forms one of two low wings. A water garden has been formed by damming Springbank Creek.

The oldest inland settlement in South Carolina, KINGSTREE, 86.8 *m.* (54 alt., 2,392 pop.), seat of Williamsburg County, dates from 1732 when 'poor Calvinists' from Ireland sailed up Black River to build their clay shelters around the 'King's Tree,' a white pine on the banks of Black River near the present Kingstree Bridge. An early explorer had marked the tree with an arrow, as white pines farther north were marked for masts in His Majesty's ships. Thereafter all royal grants issued hereabouts reserved white pines for the king. Modern Kingstree has protected its old trees by curving the sidewalks around those not in line.

Williamsburg Township, in which the 'King's Tree' grew, was named by its settlers for William III, the Presbyterian king. Few Williamsburgers held public office before the Revolution, for appointments then required allegiance to the Church of England, and these Covenanters made few bows to Episcopacy. Plentiful game and fish made living easy, and descendants of the Scotch-Irish and Huguenot settlers are still inveterate hunters and anglers, prizing catalpas as 'bait trees,' for their burden of caterpillars. Though fish fries and fish stews are popular community picnics, the favorite way to raise money for church or civic cause is by advertising a 'hot supper.' The public gladly pays for a plate heaped with viands that are samples of the most expert housewives' pet recipes. Early traditions and names are perpetuated by white 'indwellers,' whose brogue is unmistakable. Soft-voiced Negroes, living on 'Buzzard's Roost' and 'Frog Level,' skirted by the highway, flock to the stores 'big Satdy' afternoons, in their gaudy best.

Kingstree, like Lake City, sells its bountiful truck by the auction method in its 1939 market building. It also has a furniture factory, a veneer plant, and a sand refinery. Important economically is the winter colony of Northern sportsmen, who have leased lands, renovated old homes, built lodges, and employ local men as superintendents. The greatest stimulation, however, comes with the tobacco season, when stores remain open far into the night to catch the farmers' cash.

At the head of what is now Academy Street, Major Wemyss was met in August 1780 by Major John James. Before the outnumbered Williamsburg Battalion could take cover, 30 men had been killed. The others drove the British before them into Georgetown County.

The COUNTY COURTHOUSE, Main St. between Academy and Jail Sts., designed by Robert Mills in 1823, is a two-story, buff-colored building with paired steps to its portico, which has fanlighted pediment; the detail of the frieze is also worth attention. The surrounding park was a parade ground for the Craven County regiment when the town was surveyed in 1737. Here, during riotous Reconstruction days, the leader of Negro aggression was S. A. Swails, mulatto lawyer of Philadelphia, made a colonel by General E. E. Potter, whose raiders ravaged this section.

At Kingstree is the junction with US 521 (*see Tour* 4), which unites with US 52 for 3 miles.

Left from Kingstree on State 175 to WILLIAMSBURG PRESBYTERIAN CEMETERY (L), 0.2 *m.*, where in 1736 the congregation organized the first Presbyterian body in the 'back country.' The church was moved to Kingstree in 1890. Here, in 1737, the first person buried was John Witherspoon, descendant of Robert the Bruce and of John Knox, patriarch of the first two colonies of settlers, many of them his descendants. Here, in 1749, were buried 80 pioneers of the hundreds who died during the 'Great Mortality,' probably caused by influenza; famine had followed prolonged drought and men trekked to North Carolina for food. Mary Ervin Scott, says tradition, pounded cattail roots into flour to feed her starving children, and others profited by her ingenuity. Here, in 1780, the men of Williamsburg, paroled after the fall of Charleston, were goaded by British taunts into organizing under Major James four companies that became the nucleus of 'Marion's men.'

Section b.   KINGSTREE to CHARLESTON, 72 m.   US 52.

South of KINGSTREE, 0 *m.*, US 52 cuts through several miles of Black River Swamp, with white beaches contrasting with the dark waters of roadside lagoons, and leads through fields dotted with unpainted Negro cabins. Black smoke of fat pine fires pours from clay chimneys, sometimes from a perilously attached length of stovepipe. At dusk, open doors afford glimpses of the blaze that, never quenched winter or summer, furnishes light, heat, and a means of cooking.

At 3 *m.* is the western junction with US 52 (*see Tour* 4).

At 15 *m.* is the junction with State 261, paved.

Left on this road 0.5 *m.* to LONGLANDS, a flash of white clapboard at the head of a live oak avenue. This two-story lodge of the Eugene DuPonts, was formerly the home of Senator S. A. Graham.

The Santee Swamp, 15.2 *m.*, formerly a barrier separating this section from the rest of the State, was crossed only by widely separated ferries until the completion in 1923 of the five-mile causeway and drawbridge—an important link in the Quebec-Miami highway. At the bridge was Murray's Ferry, guarded by the British after they captured

Charleston, and was taken August 23, 1780, by General Marion. Early Huguenot settlers were driven out of the Santee Valley by floods; on the north side of the river, zigzag 'line banks,' once separating fields, attest former habitation, but the swamp has long since been reclaimed by semitropical growth. In the flooded forests, tulip trees spread their fanlike leaves; wild turkeys, deer, bears, and wildcats challenge the hunter. Poised on slim pink legs, herons rise and drift away in snowy clouds.

At 19.8 *m.* is the junction with State 45 (*see Tour 5B*).

In the 244,228-acre Francis Marion National Forest, through which the route leads, wild life has long found refuge. Deer are so plentiful that they are sometimes shot as pests devouring young crops.

At 21.2 *m.* is the junction with a dirt road.

Left on this road 3.2 *m.* to the PALMETTO SNAKE FARM, where the Canadian proprietor raises mainly snakes and alligators, catching about 1,200 annually in the swamps. His busiest season is fall, when all his reptiles are hatched. Their principal diet is rats, frogs, and raw meat; from September to March they eat nothing. Reptiles and birds are profitably shipped for scientific, educational, and breeding purposes.

A pretty old village, with attractive homes of mill executives bordering the highway, ST. STEPHENS, 24 *m.* (75 alt., 910 pop.), prospers through its lumber interests. On the frontier in the Yamasee War of 1715, an entire garrison was massacred at a near-by fortification. ST. STEPHEN'S EPISCOPAL CHURCH (L), a well-preserved little red brick edifice, was built 1767–9 as St. Stephen's Parish Church. The high gambrel roof with its curvilinear gable ends resulted from the architects' ambition to pattern the ceiling after St. Michael's (*see Charleston*). Paneled side portals have fanlight transoms; white-shuttered arched windows are set between brick pilasters. Francis Villepontoux and A. Howard, traditionally credited as architects, cut their names in the masonry.

Left from St. Stephens on State 45 to the junction with State 179, 14 *m.*; L. 4 *m.* to the junction with State 511; L. on State 511 to LENUD'S FERRY, 1.5 *m.*, the only ferry now linking State highways. Here French Acadians settled, transported by government expense from Charleston, where 1,200 had huddled after the British had scattered their colony along the Atlantic seaboard in 1755. Efforts to disperse these homeless Catholics were partly 'to avoid danger of any infectious distemper breaking out among them,' but many died of yellow fever; others gradually left the State. Henry Laurens adopted two of the orphans, the Lanneaus—progenitors of Dr. Basil Lanneau Gildersleeve (1831–1924), a native of Charleston, first professor selected for Johns Hopkins University, and one of America's greatest philologists.

Beginning as a Cooper River Ferry, BONNEAU, 31.8 *m.* (58 alt., 118 pop.), took its name from the Huguenot forebears of Mrs. John C. Calhoun (*see Tour 14*).

At Bonneau is the junction with an unpaved side road.

Left on this road, its exact location undetermined, is HELL HOLE SWAMP, an area of indefinite extent, its whereabouts always designated as 'just a piece down the road.' During prohibition days, when South Carolina was actively advertising the iodine content of its vegetables, the Hell Hole brand of 'liquid corn' was notorious with its waggish slogan: 'Not a Goiter in a Gallon.'

At 37.4 *m.* is the junction with State 402 (*see Tour 2A*).

The abandoned SANTEE CANAL, 38.3 *m.*, 22 miles long, was an outcome of the depression of 1770, which was caused by the decreasing importance of indigo and the coming success of rice and cotton. Partly to bring the commerce of the interior to Charleston, partly to benefit by the wages of their slaves, the gentry petitioned Commons House for the canal. In 1786 the Santee Canal Company was chartered, with General William Moultrie as president and John Rutledge as vice president and assistant to Colonel Senf, chief engineer. The canal, begun in 1792 and completed in 1800, cost the State $650,000, but the slaves' wages assumed by masters put money in circulation. As a commercial venture, the canal was crippled by the railroad from Charleston to Columbia in 1842, and doomed by the Camden branch in 1848.

Since then the desire to unite the Santee and Cooper Rivers has never wholly died. It needed a greater depression, however, 150 years later, to launch the present mammoth scheme of a hydroelectric project harnessing the two streams. Begun in 1939, the completed project will submerge many old plantations under two great lakes, and necessitate rerouting several highways. The plan also includes a 145-mile navigation channel between Columbia and Charleston.

At 39.8 *m.* is the junction with a dirt road.

Left on this road 1.5 *m.* to STONY LANDING PLANTATION, where, in 1863, under the direction of the scientist-owner, Dr. St. Julien Ravenel, the *Little David,* Confederate torpedo boat, was built secretly. In one of the first recorded torpedo attacks, *Little David,* with Lieutenant Glassel in command, made a brave but futile attempt to blow up *Ironsides,* Goliath of the Federal blockade. Thirty-seven Confederate volunteers, knowing there was no possibility of survival, perished in the first submarine activities in Charleston Harbor.

A straggling village, unusual in lacking a Confederate monument and in having its courthouse away from its few stores, MONCKS CORNER, 40.2 *m.* (55 alt., 623 pop.), seat of Berkeley County, has moved a mile from its Colonial site. There, Monck's store, in the 'corner' formed by the roads from Charleston to Murray's Ferry and to the Congarees, gave rise to the name. Citizens of Moncks Corner, long an isolated community, are sometimes a law unto themselves. During the depression of the 1930's, several depositors broke into a closed bank and took their personal deposits. Opened in 1933, the handsome brick BERKELEY COUNTY HOSPITAL is among pines in attractive grounds at the western end of the principal street. A nonprofit organization with an endowment from the Duke family, its plant cost $130,000.

At Moncks Corner is the junction with State 6 (*see Tour 5B*).

The two-story white clapboarded house at GIPPY (L), 41.5 *m.,* was built in 1821 by John White. Green-shuttered, with a pedimented Doric portico, it has been recently remodeled. Originally part of Fairlawn Barony, granted Sir John Colleton, a Lord Proprietor, Gippy is

named for an old slave. It has a fine pecan orchard, sheep, Guernsey
herd, and dairies.

At 41.9 *m.* is the junction with a dirt road.

Left on this road 0.9 *m.* to LEWISFIELD, where Keating Simons in 1774 built
the big square plantation house, designed for coolness, with two-and-a-half
frame stories over one of brick. It also has a wide piazza. The property, first
called Little Landing, was sold from Fairlawn Barony to Sedgewick Lewis,
whose daughter married Keating Simons, later a brigade major under Marion.
Lewisfield was often frequented by the British, and Lord Cornwallis was a
coldly if courteously received guest. One Keating Simons after another for
many generations owned the place. When it once passed to owners whom
Negro hands disdained, they vowed 'Mas' Keatin's ghos'' filled the chimney
to make the fire smoke, unless 'the quality' were being entertained.

At 42.8 *m.* is the junction with a lane.

Left on this lane 0.3 *m.* to EXETER, with an H-shaped brick house believed
to have been built in 1726 by Hugh Butler. Later alterations included the
removal of the two front wings, the addition of a piazza, and the connection
of the rear wings by a stairhall. Brickwork and stucco trim formerly white
have been painted red.

At 43.3 *m.* is the junction with a private road.

Left on this road to MULBERRY CASTLE, 1 *m.*, a low, two-story Jacobean
style brick house built in 1714 by Thomas Broughton, governor 1735–7, who
is said to have patterned it after Seaton, Broughton manor house in England.
The hip-on-gable roof of the main house has five dormers, front and rear.
The four small tower rooms, topped with bell-shaped cupolas and wrought-
iron weather vanes that give the house a medieval aspect, may explain the
title 'castle.' During the Yamasee War, however, it was a fortified stronghold.
Later, British cavalrymen adopted it as headquarters. The site, on a bluff
overlooking the Cooper River, was named for a mulberry tree growing here
when settlers found Indians cultivating this land; a branch laden with berries
is carved in the pediment of the small entrance porch. Renovated, and with
gardens once more well cared for, Mulberry retains its character as one of
the finest houses in the State.

At 45.9 *m.* is the junction with a dirt road.

Left on this road 2 *m.* to WAPPAOOLA HUNTING CLUB, where the old part of
the cypress house was erected in 1806 by the Reverend Milward Pogson, rector
of Goose Creek Church. He reputedly built his dwelling around the frame
of a barn moved from Charleston. The brick-floored piazza has heavy columns.

At 47.8 *m.* is the junction with State 520, paved.

Left on this road is a junction with a dirt road, 1.3 *m.;* L. on this road 4.5
m. to THE BLUFF, a low rambling story-and-a-half frame house now a hunting club. It was built about 1790 by Major Isaac Child Harleston.
State 520 runs between the whitewashed cabins of the descendants of plantation slaves; blue-painted doors and shutters are to keep out evil spirits. Grinning
little pickaninnies offer 'bokays' of wild flowers for sale, and will dance or
sing for a penny.
From the inky waters of CYPRESS GARDENS (*open day after Thanksgiving to
May* 1; *adm.* $2), 4.1 *m.,* on State 520, rise ghost-like trees hung with moss
in shimmering gray and lavender. The great trees and bright-hued azaleas mir-
rored in the lake produce an effect of unreal loveliness. The gardens were first
opened to the public in 1930. Benjamin R. Kittredge, their owner, redeemed

an abandoned rice reservoir, clearing the growth of a century, forming islands, connecting them with paths, and planting myriads of bulbs and azaleas. Visitors can stroll or ride in rolling chairs along miles of blossomy paths, or float over the black waters in gaily painted little boats, paddled by Low Country Negroes.

The gardens are part of Dean Hall Plantation, established before 1725 by Sir John Nisbett of Dean, Scotland. William A. Carson bought the property in 1821 and built the house of brick made at Medway Plantation. Above a brick arcade, with access to the flag-stoned basement, a piazza encircles the main floor.

At 51.3 *m.* is the junction with a dirt road.

Left on this road 2.1 *m.* to MEDWAY, built in 1686 by Jean d'Arsens, Seigneur de Wernhaut. Using handmade brick, d'Arsens erected a typical one-story stuccoed Dutch house with stepped gables, its entrance leading into the principal room. Additions have included a second story and wings, but the original design has been preserved. A double avenue of live oaks leads to the vine-covered house. D'Arsens's widow married the first Landgrave Thomas Smith, governor 1693–4, whose grave is here. Smith acquired wealth through his wife, but her resting place near by is unmarked.

Marl along the Cooper River banks made brick making profitable; 'Carolina Grey' was the trade name for the Medway product, used in constructing Fort Sumter. On adjoining Parnassus Plantation, Zachariah Villepontoux made brick used in St. Michael's Church, Charleston.

At 54.1 *m.* is the junction with State 31 (*see Tour 5b*).
At 54.2 *m.* is the junction with a dirt road.

Left on this road 1.5 *m.* to THE OAKS (*open 9–6 March and April; adm. $1*). The nineteenth-century white brick house, built by Edwin Parsons and since remodeled in the Georgian style, is approached through a splendid live oak avenue. Behind it are sunken gardens, with a formal rose garden at the side. Azalea-bordered paths approach a lake in a grove of ancient live oaks. The Oaks was in 1679 the estate of Edward Middleton, progenitor of a distinguished South Carolina family.

GOOSE CREEK CHURCH (*see caretaker*), 2 *m.*, is a little pink stuccoed brick edifice with a Jerkin-head roof in a walled graveyard overhung by live oaks. Built 1711–19 as the parish church of St. James, it is said to have escaped destruction in the Revolution because of British Royal arms still above the chancel. Here also is the hatchment of the Izards, a distinguished family of the old parish.

Goose Creek is architecturally one of the finest churches in this area. The severity of the exterior is relieved by graceful arched windows with the heads of tiny cherubs carved in the key-blocks, a wide pedimented portal, and a smaller doorway in the center of the north façade. The corners are accented with quoins. The interior, with its wide slave gallery above the entrance, paneled box pews, and flagstone floor, is characteristic of the period. Especially notable is the graceful wine-glass pulpit with canopied sounding board, curving stairway and protecting chancel rail, all finished in natural wood in contrast to the all-white interior. On either side of the pulpit fluted Corinthian pilasters rise in support of elaborate entablature and broken-scroll pediments, their surfaces painted in imitation of marble. Framed by the pediments is the polychrome seal of Great Britain cast in bold relief.

Both sides of GOOSE CREEK, 55.1 *m.*, were settled prior to 1680 by wealthy Barbadian planters known as the 'Goose Creek Men.'
At 56.1 *m.* is the junction with US 78 (*see Tour 15b*).
At 56.8 *m.* is the junction with a dirt road.

Left on this road 3 *m.* to YEAMANS' HALL, since 1927 a country club. Around the handsome white brick clubhouse are a group of corporation-owned cottages and private houses. The grounds, extending to Cooper River, have landings for member-owned yachts and other craft, and an 18-hole golf course. The property long known as 'Goose Creek,' granted 1674 to Lady Margaret after the death of her husband, Sir John Yeamans, Landgrave, passed to Thomas Smith, second landgrave of that name, who, with his Dutch wife, Anna Cornelie Myddagh, is buried on the grounds.

At 65.5 *m.* is the junction with a paved road.

Left on this road 0.3 *m.* to the UNITED STATES NAVY YARD, the only one on the Atlantic Coast south of Norfolk, Virginia. It provides repairs and docking to all classes of vessels except battleships and large aircraft carriers. Moored to a yard pier is the U.S.S. *Hartford.* Launched in Boston in 1858, it became Admiral David G. Farragut's flagship. Through a maze of mines in Mobile Bay, he directed it with the command, 'Damn the torpedoes!' After serving as a station ship at Annapolis, the *Hartford* eventually found port in Charleston. Here President Franklin D. Roosevelt saw its rotting hulk in 1938, with the result that a $100,000 Federal appropriation assured its restoration. The Navy Yard occupies parts of two old plantations on 'The Neck.' The Marshlands house, built in 1810 by John Ball, is an officers' residence. Only the stone steps of the Turnbull mansion which stood on the Retreat, a plantation granted to Thomas Hart in 1672, have been utilized in the present structure, also an officers' house.

The OLD SIX MILE HOUSE, 67 *m.*, known for the past 50 years as the Four Mile House, has two frame stories above one of stuccoed brick, with paired flights of steps leading to the high front porch. It was one of a series of stagecoach taverns designated by their distance from the center of Charleston. Travelers stopping here were robbed or mysteriously disappeared. John Fisher the landlord, and his wife, Lavinia, were convicted of murder in 1820, after the discovery of skeletons in the tavern cellar. An irate mob, gathered to see the couple hanged, was shocked by Lavinia's rebellious outcries and her obdurate unrepentance. She screamed, as she stood on the gallows: 'If you have a message you want to send to hell, give it to me; I'll carry it!'

At 70.8 *m.* is the junction with a paved road.

Left on this road 0.1 *m.* to MAGNOLIA CEMETERY, established in 1850 when churchyards in Charleston grew overcrowded. With other neighboring cemeteries, it belonged to Magnolia Umbra, part of the plantation granted Joseph Pendarvis in 1672. Among notable South Carolinians buried here lies Hugh Swinton Legare (1797–1843). He was Attorney General for the United States (1841–3) and acting Secretary of State upon the resignation of Daniel Webster (1843). Just inside the grounds is a Confederate plot where Memorial Day exercises are held annually on May 10; they include the reading of Timrod's ode, *Magnolia Cemetery,* composed for the first exercises in 1866.

CHARLESTON, 72 *m.* (9 alt., 62,265 pop.) (*see Charleston*), is at the junction with US 17 (*see Tour 1b*).

Tour 2A

Junction with US 52—St. Thomas Church; 26.9 *m.*, State 402, State 511.

Roadbed unpaved.
No accommodations.

Estates along the banks of tidal streams in this region were established when the water route to Charles Town was the most practical. Hereabouts 11 Revolutionary engagements occurred, and many buildings were desolated by the British; others suffered in the 1860's. Most of the old plantations are now owned by Northerners, who are accepted by the displaced descendants of original owners because their wealth has restored order and beauty. Lands are conspicuously posted against trespass, and the traveler gets only tantalizing glimpses of mansions at the end of long green avenues.

State 402 branches east from US 52, 0 *m.*, about 3 miles north of Moncks Corner (*see Tour 2b*).

The RUINS OF BIGGIN CHURCH, 0.7 *m.*, built in 1756 to replace the first St. John's Parish Church, were once a garrisoned supply post of the British, who burned the interior in July 1781 as they were forced to evacuate. Rebuilt after the Revolution, the church was destroyed by a forest fire. The communion service, with its gilded silver chalice brought by Huguenots from La Rochelle, buried during the Confederate era at Comingtee Plantation, was never rediscovered. In the tangled growth around the crumbling walls, a marble vault covers the remains of Sir John Colleton III, great-grandson of the Lord Proprietor.

At WADBOO BRIDGE, 2.1 *m.*, three Revolutionary encounters occurred: January 24, 1781; July 16, 1781; and August 29, 1782. The third was General Marion's last battle; under the cedar avenue to the former Mansion House on near-by Wadboo Barony, he bade farewell to his troops. Wadboo Barony, granted in 1685 to James Colleton, adjoined Fairlawn, the barony of his father.

At Wadboo Bridge, on the east side, is the junction with Cooper River Road, unpaved.

Right on this road 5.7 *m.* to the entrance (R) of MEPKIN (*open on request*), formerly the estate of Henry Laurens (1724–92), president (1777–8) of the Continental Congress. Only the handsome gates and mile-long avenue of live oaks remain of pre-Revolutionary Mepkin. The present house, of modern design, is on the site of the Laurens dwelling, overlooking the river. Henry Laurens, one of the wealthiest merchants in the United States in 1762, later turned to rice and indigo planting. He was an officer in the Cherokee War; president of the Provincial Council of Safety, 1775–6; and vice president of the State of South Carolina, 1776–8. Elected a delegate to the Constitutional Convention of 1786, he was prevented by illness from signing the document. On his way to Holland in 1780, he was captured by the British and confined in the Tower of London until exchanged 18 months later for Lord Cornwallis. Previously offered pardon on condition of allegiance to the crown, he said: 'I will never subscribe to my own infamy and to the dishonor of my children.' In 1782, Laurens was one of four delegates to the Peace Conference in Paris.

'Tower' Laurens, as he was locally called after his imprisonment, stipulated in his will that his body be cremated. This is said to be the first cremation in the United States. He feared being buried alive, because his infant daughter had narrowly escaped such a fate. Having been ill with smallpox in a closely shuttered room, she was pronounced dead; but placed near an open window to be prepared for burial she revived, living to become the wife of Dr. David Ramsay, the historian.

In the Mepkin burial plot is the CENOTAPH OF JOHN LAURENS, distinguished young soldier and diplomat. With the Revolutionary cause at a critical stage and Washington himself despairing, young Laurens (son of Henry Laurens) was chosen to solicit aid from France. At a social function, disregarding court etiquette, he offered Louis XVI a document describing conditions in America, and requested further audience. The monarch frowned his disapproval, but a minister accepted the paper. Within 24 hours, the interview was granted; money and men were promised. As a member of Washington's staff, Laurens was given a lieutenant-colonelcy. He declined the promotion, explaining that having witnessed ill feeling in disputes over rank in the army, he held peace too dear to risk its disturbance. Congress, however, sustained his promotion. When Laurens was killed at the age of 28, Washington said: 'He had no fault that I could discover—unless it were an intrepidity bordering on rashness.'

James Child, an English settler, laid out a township in 1707 at the SITE OF CHILDSBURY, 7.1 m. *Little Mistress Chicken,* by Jennie Haskell Rose, is based on the life of the school that survived here until 1754. The little girl heroine of the book was tied by her schoolmaster to a tombstone in Strawberry Chapel yard for punishment, and remained alone all night. The tale recounts the event with the subsequent search and discovery of the child and the dismissal of the teacher. At Strawberry Ferry, near by, Colonel Wade Hampton captured 50 British soldiers and burned their four vessels loaded with army supplies.

Directly in front of River Road, which veers right, are the entrance gates to RICE HOPE PLANTATION, 7.2 m., first owned by Dr. William Read, Deputy Surgeon-General in the Revolutionary War. One of his descendants, on his summer vacation, received from his overseer at Rice Hope a letter that read: 'The banks are broke. The corn are out. The niggers are run away, and I are yours.' The place has been restored; a house was built in the early 1900's.

In the brick house built by Elias Ball in 1738 at COMINGTEE, adjoining Rice Hope on the south, Henry Laurens and 'the beautiful Eleanor Ball' were married in 1750. Much altered early in the twentieth century, the dwelling still has handsome interior woodwork. Deserted rice banks have been restored and the grounds are well ordered. Granted to Captain John Coming, mate of one of the first three ships bringing settlers to South Carolina in 1670, 'Coming's T' derived its name from the shape of the river at this site. Mrs. Coming left the estate to a Ball nephew, and Balls possessed it for well over 200 years.

STRAWBERRY CHAPEL (R), 7.5 m. on River Road, erected in 1725 as the Parochial Chapel of Ease at Childsbury, is a low stone building among huge overhanging live oaks. In the early years funeral parties were poled up the Cooper River to Strawberry Landing, where a small brick pit with an arched roof gave temporary shelter to coffins in stormy weather. The chapel's interior, unchanged and slightly dank, has the conventional simplicity of the times. Hundreds gather here each spring for a memorial service, on a date announced in local newspapers.

At 12.8 *m.* on State 402 is the junction with a dirt road.

Right on this road 0.2 *m.* to LIMERICK PLANTATION, established by Michael Mahon, 1707. It later passed to Daniel Huger, Huguenot immigrant of 1685, who sired a long line of statesmen and soldiers. The big cypress house has 14 fireplaces. In front of the barn, believed to have been built before 1707, rice was threshed by hand on the hard clay. Limerick passed to the Balls in 1764 and remained theirs for 150 years.

At 13 *m.* is a junction with State 511, which the route follows southward.

At 14.6 *m.* is the junction with a dirt road.

Right on this road 0.2 *m.* to the SITE OF SILK HOPE, in 1699 the home of Sir Nathaniel Johnson (governor 1702–10), who shipped samples of silk made here to Europe. The remains of a wall surrounding his grave lacks bricks said to have been stolen for building illicit stills. In 1706 Governor Johnson, notified that French and Spanish vessels were dangerously near, hurried from Silk Hope into yellow-fever-stricken Charles Town. Called upon to surrender the city, he met the demand by blindfolding the enemy envoy and leading him on a tour of the city's fortifications, removing the bandage at strategic points to show the strength of the garrisons. Unknown to the messenger, the same troops rushed from place to place, taking up their position before the governor and his war guest arrived. The messenger returned to his superior officer, reported the large number of soldiers he thought he had seen, and the enemy fleet quickly sailed away.

At QUINBY BRIDGE, 16.1 *m.*, 'Light Horse Harry' Lee's Legion was overwhelmed by the British under Colonel Coates in the summer of 1781. The Red Coats having loosed the flooring of the bridge, horses of Lee's cavalry leaped the gaps, charging into the fire of a cannon, their retreat cut off; their only means of escape was to cut their way through with sabers. The British entrenched themselves in John Ashby's brick house on Quinby Barony, where Sumter, Marion, and Lee gave up the desperate effort to rout them only when ammunition failed. Bones of the hastily buried dead are still occasionally unearthed here, and ghost riders, galloping across the bridge, are still heard by the Negroes.

At 17.9 *m.* is the junction with a shady dirt road.

Right on this road 0.5 *m.* to POMPION (pronounced Punkin) HILL CHAPEL. This little slate-roofed brick temple, replacing in 1767 the cypress edifice built in 1703, accommodated what was possibly the first Episcopal organization in the province outside of Charles Town. In 1747 this became a Chapel of Ease to St. Thomas and St. Denis Parishes. No longer in use, it is still in excellent condition. The brick and tile floor is laid in a herring-bone pattern. The high brown pews at the chancel end were for slaves; the white pews under the carved cedar pulpit, on a board floor one step above the brick, were for masters. Zachariah Villepontoux's initials, carved in north and south side doors, indicate that he may have been both architect and builder.

Facing the river, on the shady dirt road, is MIDDLEBURG PLANTATION, 1.2 *m.* Here is what is believed to be the oldest wooden house in the State. Completed before 1699 by Benjamin Simons, it has been continuously owned by his descendants. One room deep, it resembles the Charleston 'single house,' nonexistent elsewhere north of the Antilles. First floor interior walls, redecorated about 1800, are finished with wide boards. A panel, plastered on the brick chimney above a mantel, reduces fire hazard, and possibly explains Middleburg's endurance. Camellia japonicas form tunneled walks in the formal garden.

St. Thomas Church (R), 26.9 *m.*, was erected in 1819 to replace one completed in 1708 and destroyed by fire. The structure, of brick faced with stucco, is small; the large fanlighted entrance, flanked by pilasters, is surrounded by a coffered arch; the windows have semicircular heads. The church has a Negro gallery, and the small apse holds both chancel and vestry.

✹✹✹

Tour 3

(Fayetteville, N. C.)—Bennettsville—Hartsville—Sumter—Walterboro; US 15. North Carolina Line to Walterboro, 161.7 *m.*

Roadbed concrete paved, with two short sections of asphalt.
Atlantic Coast Line R.R. parallels route between McColl and Bennettsville, between Pocotaligo and Savannah; Seaboard Air Line Ry. between Hartsville and Sumter.
Frequent accommodations; hotels in towns.

US 15 cuts through the sand hills into the fertile soils of the Pee Dee River basin. Here manufacturing, though not extensive, was an early development because of abundant raw material, plentiful labor, and river transportation. The people dislike being classed as Up Countrymen, but admit that the Low Country does not claim them.

The population has a majority of Negroes, who supply most of the labor for farming and lumbering; a few work in industrial plants. Their cabins, generally unpainted, have clean-swept front yards, with beds of verbena and cosmos, and nearly always one or two big Cape jessamine (gardenia) bushes, dark green in winter and starred in summer with fragrant white blooms.

Section a. NORTH CAROLINA LINE to SUMTER, 81 m. US 15.

On both sides of the highway, many acres formerly devoted to cotton are planted with corn, tobacco, or vegetables. The horizon is rimmed beyond the fields with pines and hardwood growths.

US 15 crosses the NORTH CAROLINA LINE, 0 *m.*, 50 miles south of Fayetteville, North Carolina.

McCOLL, 1.3 *m.* (185 alt., 1,657 pop.), was first a cotton depot on a railroad. A second road, increasing freight facilities, was an inducement in the establishing of four cotton mills, whose executives once paid the highest income tax in the State.

BENNETTSVILLE, 10.6 *m.* (151 alt., 3,557 pop.), seat of Marlboro County, stretches along a shady main street. The town is in the upper part of the old Welsh Neck section, settled by Baptists from Delaware, whose chief center was Society Hill (*see below*). Marlboro was one of the State's wealthiest counties. It is a traditional jest that in the good old days farm land here was sold by the pound, not the acre, and cotton stalks were so tall that little Negroes had to climb them to find out when the bolls were ready for picking. Corn was a good crop, too. In 1889 Zachariah J. Drake topped the world's record with 255 bushels of shelled corn from one acre—winning the *American Agriculturist* prize. Nowadays, a yarn and tire fabric mill, an oil mill, a vegetable cannery, a fertilizer plant, and lumber mill utilize the resources of the land.

GREENGATE GARDEN (*open by permission*), Jennings St. two blocks west of the square, is especially noted for its irises.

At Bennettsville is the junction with State 9 (*see Tour 21a*).

Left from Bennettsville on State 38 to BLENHEIM, 8 *m.*, where during the Revolution, Tristram Thomas, with a battery of wooden guns constructed on a deep bend of the river, captured 100 Tories and a boatload of supplies.

A tract of worthless swampland called the PEE DEE SWAMP ACRES, 24 *m.*, was traded to Baron Poelnitz for a 23-acre New York City estate granted him for bravery as an officer under Washington. The Polish nobleman had formerly been a chancellor in the Court of Frederick the Great. His grave is under an oak, designated in his will, which also stipulated that hot irons be applied to his feet after death as a precaution against his being buried alive.

In LATTA, 29 *m.* (1,166 pop.) (*see Tour 13*), is the junction with US 501 (*see Tour 13*).

The white-porticoed WELSH NECK BAPTIST CHURCH (L) at the south end of the bridge over Big Pee Dee River, 22.1 *m.* on US 15, 150 feet from the road, was completed in 1939, the fifth building for a congregation organized in 1738.

A village of a few dozen old homes strung along the highway, SOCIETY HILL, 24.6 *m.* (192 alt., 573 pop.), has produced a governor and many judges, churchmen, and educators. It was the core of the Welsh Neck settlement, a tract of 176,840 acres on both sides of the Big Pee Dee River, granted by George II to Baptists from Delaware, who came here about 1736. They sought to forestall discord by discouraging settlers of other faiths, and theirs remains the most stable Baptist community in South Carolina. In 1777 they founded a society for 'educating the youth of all Christian denominations being Protestants,' and named it Saint David's Society, for the patron saint of Wales.

A small frame building (L) in the center of the town is the SOCIETY HILL LIBRARY (*closed*). Established in 1825 and containing more than 2,000 volumes, but no poetry or scientific works and no fiction except the novels of Dickens, Scott, and William Gilmore Simms, it exerted a strong influence on the community. The first president of the library board was David Rogerson Williams (1776–1830), governor of the State 1814–16, brigadier general in the War of 1812, and a pioneer in scientific experiments. He extracted oil from cottonseed, illuminated his big plantation house with gas distilled from 'lightwood,' made cotton cloth and rope, erected dykes along the river to protect his lands from freshets, and prior to 1809 was the first in the South to introduce and breed mules for farm work. General Williams's election to the governorship came as a great surprise to him. Tradition maintains that the State legislature elected him without his knowledge. The messenger, bearing news of the event, found him holding the reins of a wagon team on the side of a road he was having repaired. Adjoining the library is SAINT DAVID'S ACADEMY, now an elementary and high school.

JAPONICA HALL (*open by permission*) is typical of Society Hill homes. The two-story brick house is in oak-shaded grounds with fine camellia japonicas.

In Society Hill is the junction with US 52 (*see Tour 2a*), which unites with US 15 between this point and 26.6 *m.*

Its principal oak-shaded streets lined with gardens, HARTSVILLE, 41.9 *m.* (5,067 pop.), is one of the most prosperous towns in the State. Named for Thomas Edward Hart, on whose plantation the community developed, it is chiefly associated with the Coker family, distinguished in South Carolina and united through marriage with the Harts. Here, in 1866, Major James Lide Coker, a Harvard graduate, opened a store; he established one business after another, constructed a ten-mile railroad connecting with the Atlantic Coast Line, and founded and endowed Coker College. Major Coker was severely wounded in the War between the States. Returning home he found his farms ruined, but immediately went to work 'with a crutch in one hand and a hoe in the other.'

Many members of the Coker family have been agricultural experts and economists who have continuously contributed to local prosperity. David R. Coker (1870–1938) is known wherever cotton is grown for his successful breeding of seed to produce longer staple. Other crops of South Carolina also engrossed his attention, and were improved through his efforts. The Sonoco Products Company, manufacturing paper cones and specialties for cotton, rayon, and silk textile mills, has executive offices and its main plant here. The Carolina Fiber Mill, on Carolina Mill Hill, is surrounded by the small dwellings of Negroes, many of whom work in the plant.

On a landscaped campus is COKER COLLEGE, E. end of College St., a Baptist institution, occupying a group of red brick buildings of modified Georgian Colonial design. Originating in 1894 as the Welsh Neck High School, the school was made a liberal arts college for women in 1908, and has some 300 students. The college also owns land and a clubhouse at near-by Prestwood Lake.

1. Right from Hartsville on State 151 2 *m.* to bluffs overlooking Black Creek, where KALMIA GARDENS (*free*) are being developed by Mrs. David R. Coker as an arboretum for Coker College. The 60-acre tract represents an almost complete cross-section of South Carolina terrain and contains 700 varieties of trees and shrubs native to the Atlantic seaboard. As the name implies, the native *kalmia latifolia* (mountain laurel) predominates. Other plants have been skillfully arranged about the three small lakes in the heart of this

forest garden. Close to the live oaks and yaupons of the coast grow the mountain rhododendron, galax, and laurel; the swamp lily consorts with the prickly pear. Masses of pink laurel spread over the steep bluffs; a turn in the path discloses the black water, cypresses, and azaleas of the Low Country. Irises of every hue add their pastel loveliness, and camellia japonicas of many varieties bloom in winter.

At McBEE, 14 *m.* (473 alt., 500 pop.) (*see Tour 6a*), is the junction with US 1 (*see Tour 6a*).

At JEFFERSON, 30 *m.* on State 151 (449 pop.), is a junction with a dirt road; L. here to a junction with another dirt road, 2 *m.;* R. here 2 *m.* to Little Fork Creek and the abandoned BREWER GOLD MINE. Formerly worked on a large scale, the mine produced more than $1,000,000 in gold.

At PAGELAND, 38 *m.* on State 151 (707 pop.) (*see Tour 21a*), is the junction with State 9 (*see Tour 21a*).

State 151 crosses the North Carolina Line, 41 *m.*, about 15 miles south of Monroe, North Carolina.

2. Left from Hartsville on State 151 to COKER'S PEDIGREED SEED FARM, 1 *m.*, where scientific experiments are made in adapting and advancing seed and plants for South Carolina farmers. Partly through these activities the average length of South Carolina cotton fiber has increased one-eighth of an inch through use of pure bred seed, resulting in an advance of about $10 per bale for cotton. Visitors from other States and countries frequently call here to learn methods and new developments.

At DARLINGTON, 14 *m.* (175 alt., 5,556 pop.) (*see Tour 2a*), is the junction with US 52 (*see Tour 2a*).

At 56.8 *m.* on US 15 is the junction with a dirt road.

Left on this road 2 *m.* to LEE STATE PARK, 2,109 acres of a former State forest on the banks of Lynches River, whose clay was prized by the Indians for making pottery.

Near the bridge over Lynches River, 57.9 *m.*, the last duel in South Carolina was fought in 1880 at Shannon Hill. Colonel William S. Shannon of Camden and Colonel E. B. C. Cash of Cheraw met at DuBose's Bridge, neutral territory. Colonel Shannon was mortally wounded, and his death resulted in a State law against dueling. Before South Carolina officials take office they must still swear they have not engaged in a duel since January 1, 1881, and that they will not engage in dueling during their term of office.

Once called Singleton's Crossroads, BISHOPVILLE, 59.8 *m.* (224 alt., 2,249 pop.), seat of Lee County, was named about 1825 for Dr. Jacques Bishop. Lee County boasts two distinguished native sons, T. G. McLeod (governor 1923–7), and E. D. ('Cotton Ed') Smith, United States senator since 1909. Smith, who has served in the United States Senate longer than any other South Carolinian to date, has probably won more attention for South Carolina than any other political figure since 'Pitchfork Ben' Tillman.

On Ashwood Plantation a tract of 700 acres is embraced in a RESETTLEMENT PROJECT, 67.9 *m.* New homes on 35-acre plots are occupied under the rehabilitation program (*see Agriculture*).

Established for Negroes in 1908 by the Baptist Educational and Missionary Convention, MORRIS COLLEGE (R), 80 *m.*, is coeducational, with nearly 500 students. On the campus are brick classroom, administrative, and dormitory buildings, and an athletic field.

In SUMTER, 81 *m.* (168 alt., 11,780 pop.) (*see Sumter*), are the junctions with US 76 (*see Tour 9a*) and US 521 (*see Tour 4*).

Section b. SUMTER to WALTERBORO 80.7 m. US 15.

South of SUMTER, 0 *m.*, an occasional manor, far back from the highway at the head of an avenue, stands as a reminder of an era when plantation dwellers assembled for stately balls and were entertained for weeks at a time. Simpler dwellings, however, often stand in the midst of cultivated fields, approached from the highway by a rutty lane without trees, locally called a 'plain avenue.'

With tourist cabins and a swimming pool of cold artesian water, POCALLA SPRINGS, 3.9 *m.*, a popular hot-weather resort, contracted its name from the Indian 'pocataligo.'

The placid, shady old village of SUMMERTON, 23.9 *m.* (138 alt., 812 pop.), was crowded with refugees from Charleston in the Confederate era. Tourist homes have increased its prosperity.

At Summerton is the junction with US 301 (*see Tour 2a*).

CEDAR GROVE PLANTATION, 28.2 *m.*, on both sides of the highway, extends to the Santee River. The almost impenetrable swamp, 32.5 *m.*, is crossed at its lowest part by an earth fill, where signs (R) indicate a woodland road passable by auto but better covered on foot.

Right on this trail to SCOTT'S LAKE, 0.5 *m.* The trail leads around the lake through virgin timber and dense undergrowth. Here rises the vast bulk of an INDIAN MOUND (R), 1 *m.*, 50 feet high and 800 feet in circumference. Legend recounts that it is under the curse of an Indian girl deserted by her lover. Atop the mound is the SITE OF FORT WATSON, a British Revolutionary post. In 1780 General Francis Marion decided to capture the fort. Bombardment was out of the question, for the Americans were without artillery, but Colonel Maham, one of Marion's officers, proposed building a log tower higher than Fort Watson. Hidden by the trees, men hewed logs and the tower was erected in a single night. At dawn a shower of lead poured down into the enemy enclosure, effecting a quick victory. The scheme was used several times in later Revolutionary encounters.

At 36.1 *m.* on US 15 is the junction with State 6 (*see Tour 5B*).

At 45.1 *m.* on US 15 is the junction with State 31 (*see Tour 5B*).

ROSINVILLE, 54.6 *m.*, is at a junction with US 178 (*see Tour 15b*).

At 57.2 *m.* is the junction with a dirt road.

Right on this road 0.4 *m.* to INDIAN FIELDS METHODIST CAMPGROUNDS, a tract of 15 acres, the site since 1838 of South Carolina's largest camp meeting, organized about 1800. The central unpainted frame 'arbor' accommodates 1,200 worshippers, who occupy during the meetings a circle of rough board huts, replacing the former log 'tents.' Within the circle at intervals are water pumps and fire stands—the latter almost six feet high and topped with a sheet of metal, upon which pine knots are set blazing after dark. Hundreds of Methodists annually gather here for a week's revival ending the first Sunday of October. Three or four sermons are preached on weekdays, with four or five on Sundays, and the benediction is not pronounced until the close of the final service.

Pursuing its quiet existence as a trading center, ST. GEORGE, 60 *m.* (102 alt., 1,639 pop.), seat of Dorchester County, is little changed since it was settled in 1788. Its name is an abbreviated form of St. George's Parish, in which the community began.

Though Dorchester County was made up from parts of Colleton and Berkeley in 1897, its name and settlement go back to about 1697. As in the beginning, agriculture, lumbering, and cattle raising are still the chief sources of livelihood for whites and Negroes. Until recent years, the 'Death Scroll' notified Dorchester folk of a funeral, as was done elsewhere in many places of the State. In ornate Spencerian chirography the facts were inscribed on a sheet of note paper ornamented with streamers of black ribbon, and the notice was sent through the community.

In St. George is the junction with US 78 (*see Tour 6b*).

At 70 *m.* is the junction with State 65. A wayside park occupies the NW. angle of this intersection.

WALTERBORO, 80.7 *m.* (80 alt., 2,592 pop.), is at the junction with US 17 (*see Tour 1c*).

✢✢✢

Tour 4

(Charlotte, N. C.)—Lancaster—Sumter—Kingstree—Georgetown; US 521. North Carolina Line to Georgetown, 174 *m.*

Roadbed concrete-paved with section of asphalt between Sumter and Andrews. Southern Ry. parallels route between Lancaster and Camden, Northwestern R.R. of South Carolina between Camden and Sumter, Atlantic Coast Line between Andrews and Georgetown.
Accommodations of all kinds; hotels chiefly in large towns.

Stretching diagonally across the State between hilly farm lands and swampy bottoms, this route affords an index to the development of South Carolina, disclosing many factors that have influenced the minds and habits of the people. Streams take their way coastward to merge with sluggish tidal rivers, and the fresh atmosphere of the uplands changes to the miasmic air of the swamps. Among red hills at the northern end of the route settled the first whites of the Up Country; near Georgetown, at the other end, the Spaniards planted their fleeting colony in 1521. Scotch-Irish farmers in the Piedmont, with their Calvinistic theology, left a permanent stamp on South Carolina culture. The coastal area still reveals a greater elasticity of mind and the tradition of a slave labor aristocracy.

US 521 crosses the NORTH CAROLINA LINE, 0 *m.*, about 16 miles south of Charlotte, North Carolina.

The early stagecoach inn, CHANEY TAVERN (L), 8.5 *m.*, an unpainted one-story frame structure, was operated in the first half of the nineteenth century by Milt Chaney, whose crimes become bloodier with every telling. He is said to have been responsible for the disappearance of many guests, but it was not until a skeleton was unearthed near the tavern that he was sentenced to the gallows. Chaney is also supposed to have marketed the same slave many times. By agreement the slave would run away from each new master and return to be sold again.

OSCEOLA, 9 *m.* (85 pop.), is named for the Seminole chief who so bitterly opposed white invasion of Florida (*see Tour 1b*).

At 15 *m.* is the junction with a dirt road.

Left on this road 0.4 *m.* to the reputed and disputed BIRTHPLACE OF ANDREW JACKSON. This favorite son's nativity has caused great argument; but South Carolina can point to a letter in which Jackson says he was born on the James Crawford Plantation 'about one mile from the Carolina road-crossing of Waxhaw creek.' Crawford's plantation home, according to Mills's map of 1825, was near the five-foot granite monument here, which quotes Jackson's reference to the place of his birth. Visitors who may have seen a similar site just across the North Carolina Line are reminded by local historians that even had Jackson been born there he would still be a South Carolinian, as the site was South Carolina territory at the time of his birth.

Andrew Jackson (1767–1845) is often portrayed as a red-necked, high-tempered frontiersman, but he gained an early reputation for square dealing, and had a large and devoted following. From early childhood the rugged disposition that earned him the nickname 'Old Hickory' was apparent. When he was still in knee breeches, he was captured while visiting an older brother at a battle near Camden, and a British officer tried to force upon him the role of bootblack. The boots remained unpolished, but the young Jackson received a saber lashing whose scars stayed with him for life. In the embryo State of Tennessee Jackson served as a jurist, and later volunteered his services and those of a troop of experienced fighting men in the War of 1812. His strategy in the Battle of New Orleans made him nationally popular and opened his way to the presidency he held from 1829 to 1837. South Carolina, threatening Nullification during his double term, was not as anxious then as now to claim Jackson as its own; the President sent armed vessels to Charleston to enforce the tariff law, and war was averted only by Clay's compromise bill that called for a gradual tariff reduction.

At 16.7 *m.* on US 521 is the junction with a narrow dirt road.

Right on this road 1.4 *m.* to a fork; L. here 1.6 *m.* to the white frame WAXHAW PRESBYTERIAN CHURCH, with gable roof and a louvered transom above the entrance. It is the latest of several that replaced the log building erected about 1755. The church was a center of community life for the Scotch-Irish settlement in the Waxhaws. Among the immigrants, who came from North Ireland by way of Charles Town and down from Pennsylvania over the Carolina Pike, were Jacksons, Crawfords, McCalls, Pickenses, and Dunlaps. These men brought their books, mostly of a religious nature, and raised log schools and churches among their cabins. Many of these patriots, a hell-fire preaching lot, are buried in the cemetery here, their graves marked by weather-beaten, triangular stones, with carved inscriptions that refer to birthplaces in the Old Country. Within a brick-walled enclosure are DAVIE and RICHARDSON GRAVES; a headstone bears the arms of the latter family. A marble slab here recites the career of General William Richardson Davie (1756–1820), Revolutionary soldier, statesman, delegate to the Constitutional Convention from North Carolina, later governor of that State, founder of the University of North Carolina, and ambassador to France. In 1805 Davie retired to Tivoli, his plantation near here, and served as the first president of the South Carolina Agricultural Society. A medallioned headstone bears the profile of the Reverend William Richardson, pastor of the Waxhaw Church from 1759 to 1771. Richardson was found dead in a kneeling position, with a bridle around his neck; village talk buzzed, and about a year later the widow, married to a Mr. Dunlap, was subjected to a gruesome test. The community gathered at the grave, the corpse was exhumed, and she was made to touch the forehead in the belief that blood would flow if the murderer's hand were placed on the victim's body.

Near the Davie plot a granite monument marks the GRAVE OF ANDREW JACKSON, SR., who, tradition says, was lost between his deathbed and the grave. On a cold winter evening of 1767 his coffin was placed on a sled and dragged from one house to another, after the custom of Irish wakes. The rites lasted for two days, with neighbors joining the entourage and fervor increasing with the consumption of whisky. The drink-inspired mourners reached the cemetery to find they had no corpse; the coffin had been raked off the sled by low-hanging limbs at Sugar Creek. The body was retrieved and buried in the flare of smoking lightwood torches by a sobered group who still felt an awe of witches and black magic.

LANCASTER, 23 m. (600 alt., 3,545 pop.), seat of Lancaster County, is a sunny little town bordered by several mill villages whose combined population almost equals that of Lancaster proper, though mill officials have encouraged decentralization and hope to establish employees in brick homes on small farm plots. Almost legendary among the mill folk are the antics in which Elliott White Springs, former World War flying ace and author, indulged when he returned from overseas. Planes were still a rare sight in this section when Springs performed stunts above the textile plants of his father, whom he later succeeded as mill president.

Lancaster's history has been tinged with many religious vagaries, including legal recognition of witchcraft, and the Waxhaw Revival. Early in the nineteenth century a poor girl of Lancaster testified that Barbara Powers had converted her into a horse and had ridden her so incessantly that her health had suffered. The case was thrown out of court. At about the same time the Waxhaw Revival, offshoot of the Nation-wide Great Revival, threw many of the county's staid Presbyterians into trances and ecstatic shouting.

The buff-painted brick LANCASTER COURTHOUSE, NW. corner of Dunlap and Main Sts., was built in 1823. Designed by Mills, the structure is typical of many that he planned. A four-columned portico with fanlighted pediment rests on a high base with an arched lower entrance, and is approached by a twin flight of steps. The unfluted columns are of plaster-covered brick. Square-headed windows on the front are in arched surface panels.

The stuccoed LANCASTER JAIL, a block behind the courthouse, was designed by Mills and erected in 1823. Deeply recessed windows, heavy string courses, and huge stone quoins give the building a massive dignity.

In the old Presbyterian churchyard, W. Gay St., is the IRVIN CLINTON MONUMENT, erected to Clinton by Isom, one of his former slaves,

who became a bishop in the African Methodist Episcopal Church.
Isom is buried on the outskirts of town.

In Lancaster is the junction with State 9 (*see Tour 21a*).

Fields of cotton and corn spread on both sides of the highway between Lancaster and HEATH SPRINGS, 33 *m.* (687 alt., 520 pop.).
B. D. Heath laid out the town of Heath's Spring, but in 1910 its name
was changed to Heath Springs, honoring Colonel Leroy Springs, Heath's
business partner.

> Right from Heath Springs on a dirt road 0.7 *m.* to STEVENS SPRINGS FISH
> HATCHERY, from whose pools several thousand young bream are distributed
> annually.
>
> At 1.8 *m.* is the junction with another dirt road; L. here 2.4 *m.* to the SITE
> OF THE BATTLE OF HANGING ROCK. Five days after Colonel William Davie de-
> feated three Tory companies on August 1, 1780, within sight of a British post
> here, he was joined by General Sumter for a major assault against Major
> John Garden's post command of 500, more than 200 of whom were killed,
> wounded, or captured. The American loss was about half that of the British.
> The large stone from which the battle takes its name is upstream (R) from
> the bridge that crosses Hanging Rock Creek at this point.

At the INGRAM HOUSE (R), 35.8 *m.* (*visited by arrangement*),
George Washington spent a night while on his southern tour of 1791.
Washington's return trip through South Carolina roughly followed the
course of US 1 and US 521, by way of Columbia, Camden, and Lancaster. In 1865 Sherman's staff used the building.

KERSHAW, 41 *m.* (500 alt., 1,120 pop.), was named for Colonel
Joseph Kershaw, a soldier in the Revolutionary War.

> Left from Kershaw on State 265 to the junction with a dirt road, 2.5 *m.;*
> R. here 0.6 *m.* to the HAILE GOLD MINE. Since its discovery in 1828 this deposit
> has been sporadically worked, most successfully during 1888–1908 with the use
> of a chlorination process. Another method has been used since mining was
> revived in 1934. Wide open pits extend into the hills where the quartz is
> quarried and hauled to machines that crush it to a fine powder. After treat-
> ment with a chemical solution the gold is separated and made into bars, or
> 'pigs,' and sent to the Treasury in Washington. About 150 men are employed;
> skilled workers receive $1 an hour. Between 1922 and 1936 South Carolina
> produced 274 ounces of fine gold, valued at $9,600, but in 1938 production had
> a value of $399,500, and in 1939 of $476,800.

DeKALB, 51.5 *m.* (410 alt., 26 pop.), was named for Baron Johann
DeKalb (*see Camden*), German champion of American freedom.

At 57.5 *m.* is the junction with a dirt road.

> Right on this road 2.4 *m.* to the SITE OF THE BATTLE OF CAMDEN, in which
> Gates's American command was routed by the British and DeKalb fell mortally
> wounded August 16, 1780. It is told that DeKalb arose from his grave here,
> stalked to Camden, and buried himself under the monument that was erected
> to his memory. When Washington visited Camden he rode out to this site and
> later reconstructed the battle in his diary.

At 59.9 *m.* on US 521 is the junction with State 97.

> Right on State 97 about 300 yards to SPRINGFIELD RACE TRACK. Thousands
> of sportsmen come here each year, particularly for the Washington's Birthday
> and Carolina Cup Races, the latter usually held on a Saturday between March

14 and April 1. State laws that prohibit pari-mutuel betting fail to curb wagers between individuals, who name their own odds.

Through LIBERTY HILL, 16 m. (250 pop.), in February 1865, a part of Sherman's army swarmed in a procession led by the beautiful Marie Boozer of Columbia in an open carriage escorted by jubilant officers. A dubious symbol of Yankee victory, she drew down upon herself the wrath of the citizens.

Marie and her mother lived in Columbia, where they entertained lavishly in an attempt to get into 'society.' Popular with Union officers, she married one of them in North Carolina. In her travels she associated with Cora Pearl, Louis Napoleon's friend, and later her name was linked with a scandal concerning Russian jewels. Later she became the wife of Count Pourtales, a member of the French Embassy in Washington, whose relatives thereupon had him sent to the legation in China. There Marie married a Japanese nobleman, who, because of her infidelities, it is asserted, had her beheaded.

At 31 m. is the junction with State 5 (see Tour 7A).

At 52 m. is the junction with US 21 (see Tour 5a), 2 miles south of CHESTER (see Tour 5a).

CAMDEN, 62 m. (22 alt., 5,183 pop.) (see Camden), is at the junction with US 1 (see Tour 6a).

South of Camden the countryside changes. The flat sand hills are gradually being planted with peach orchards, vineyards, and berry patches. Beyond this long-neglected area lie fertile flatlands, bordering on swamps.

Just south of Pine Tree Creek is two-and-a-half-story MULBERRY PLANTATION (R), 64.5 m., approached through a grove of oaks and laurels. The plain brick and stone structure, with broad piazza and a ground-floor basement, was built in 1820 by Colonel James Chestnut, assertedly on designs by Mills. The slate roof of the severely plain house is broken by four dormers. Son of the builder was James Chestnut (1815–85), United States senator (1852–8) and a member of the military staff of President Jefferson Davis.

Southeast of REMBERT, 75 m. (220 alt., 200 pop.), where Bishop Asbury's opposition to slavery did not restrain local enthusiasm for his Methodist doctrines, the highway runs through red hills, rare in this part of the State. Loblolly pines of nursery stock grow in uniform rows at intervals along the road. The Wateree Valley sweeps R. across to the High Hills of the Santee where Tories and Patriots fought.

In and around DALZELL, 85 m. (80 pop.), live a colony of several hundred 'Turks,' all said to be descendants of two pirates, a Turk and a Frenchman, who joined the Revolution as scouts under General Sumter. Their dark complexion and wary habits have left them an ambiguous group, farming their land in isolation. They refuse to associate with Negroes, and, despite prevailingly Caucasian features, are ignored by the whites.

At 90 m. is the junction with US 76 (see Tour 9b), which unites briefly southward with US 521.

In SUMTER, 93 m. (169 alt., 11,780 pop.) (see Sumter), are the junctions with US 76 (see Tour 9a) and US 15 (see Tour 3a), which unites with US 521 to a junction at 95 m.

The founder of ALCOLU, 109 m. (117 alt., 326 pop.), D. W. Alderman, named the settlement with parts of his family names, combining

Alderman, Coleman, and Lula, though some assert the word was formed of syllables of Alderman Lumber Company.

MANNING, 113 *m.* (95 alt., 1,884 pop.), seat of Clarendon County, is an old country town with old country ways. Along Brooks Street, the main thoroughfare, large neat houses and tourist homes with wide lawns extend to the single block below the courthouse that accommodates most of the little stores and shops. As is customary in many South Carolina towns, on cold winter days professional dignitaries find time to mingle with tradesmen over a glowing stove in the back of a drugstore or barber shop. A number of the older homes show the need of paint and repair, a reminder of what the boll weevil did to this trade center of farmers. Today the town draws some income from lumbering, canning, and dairying.

Manning was named for Richard I. Manning, second of six South Carolina governors, all related. Five of them came from Clarendon County—the sixth from Sumter. They were: James Burchell Richardson, 1802–4; Richard Irvine Manning, 1824–6; John Peter Richardson, 1840–2; John Laurence Manning, 1852–4; John Peter Richardson, 1886–90; Richard I. Manning, 1915–19. The Richardsons were father, son, and grandson; the Mannings, father, son, and grandson, were nephews of the first Governor Richardson. The grandmother of the last-named Manning was probably more intimately related to more State governors than any other woman in America. Mrs. Elizabeth Peyre Richardson Manning was niece, wife, sister, mother, aunt, and grandmother of the governors above respectively in the order named.

Clarendon County was named for Edward, Earl of Clarendon, one of the Lords Proprietors.

At Manning is the junction with US 301 (*see Tour 2a*).

At 124.6 *m.* is the junction with a dirt road.

Left on this road 1.2 *m.* to the white frame BREWINGTON PRESBYTERIAN CHURCH, with three-columned portico and gable roof. The picket banister around its small porch was built to keep out stray cattle. The church was erected soon after 1812, when its congregation numbered only five. Records list the trial of members, generally slaves charged with drunkenness. Adjoining the church, gray moss dips low above a cemetery, whose tilted headstones are inscribed with the names of Plowden, Montgomery, Mills, and Durant— prominent families in this vicinity.

Surrounded by a heavy growth of trees, BREWINGTON LAKE, 1.7 *m.*, attracts picnickers and fishermen.

At 129 *m.* is the junction with US 52 (*see Tour 2a*), which unites briefly with US 521.

KINGSTREE, 132 *m.* (54 alt., 2,392 pop.) (*see Tour 2a*), is at the junction with US 52 (*see Tour 2a*).

Along the swamp causeways south of Kingstree, the rural fisherman, of any age, sex, or color, dawdles along the highway, pole over his shoulder, trying to sight a strategic spot in the black waters. Fishing in these slow moving rivers is more a passion than an art, and judges have been known to speed up court procedure so that they and their confreres could reach their favorite haunts while the moon was 'right.'

Traces of breastworks still remain at the SITE OF LOWER BRIDGE BATTLE, 138 *m.*, the last Revolutionary engagement in which General Marion was on the defense. Near here in the Ox Swamp neighborhood, General Tarleton is reputed to have said that the Devil himself could not catch 'this Swamp Fox.'

ANDREWS, 155 *m.* (36 alt., 1,712 pop.), first called Rosemary, was named for the lumber mill owner who made the settlement a boom town. The empty roundhouse and network of rusty railroad tracks are reminders of that brief prosperity. Until coastal pulp mills revived lumbering, Andrews was largely a market town for farmers.

GEORGETOWN, 174 *m.* (14 alt., 5,082 pop.) (*see Tour 1a*), is at the junction with US 17 (*see Tour 1a*) and US 701 (*see Tour 20*).

✦✦

Tour 5

(Charlotte, N. C.)—Chester—Columbia—Orangeburg—Pocotaligo— Gardens Corner—Beaufort—Port Royal; US 21, State 281. North Carolina Line to Port Royal, 227.9 *m.*

Roadbed concrete-paved, with one section of asphalt between Branchville and junction with US 17.
Southern Ry. parallels route between Charlotte and Columbia, and between St. Matthews and Branchville; Charleston and Western Carolina R.R. parallels route between Yemassee and Beaufort.
Accommodations at intervals; hotels only in cities and larger towns.

US 21 is one of the busiest highways in South Carolina. Motor trucks laden with goods or cotton from the Up Country pass loads of produce from Low Country truck farms; limousines encounter rattletrap jalopies. Toward the coast are wide flat plantations across which ran South Carolina's first railroad (*see Transportation*).

Section a. NORTH CAROLINA LINE to COLUMBIA, 96.8 *m.*
US 21.

Little remains of the original vegetation but blackjack oaks. Other trees were cut and burned to make way for the farmer, who worked his corn between Indian fights, and drove his cattle and turkeys across the country to coastal markets. The cotton gin interrupted this free life and cotton production became a passion. Slaves were brought into the section and greedy cultivation soon exhausted the land. But railroads soon followed, and mills a little later. When textile plants began operation in the 1880's, cotton was selling for less than the cost of production, and farmers flocked to the mills for the cash they could not make on their land. 'There wasn't no difference then between mill folks and anybody else,' said an octogenarian who had lived through the transition from farm to factory. 'When my children went into the mills we didn't know the village schools and the machinery would make 'em different—them and their children.'

US 21 crosses the NORTH CAROLINA LINE, 0 *m.*, 13 miles south of Charlotte, North Carolina.

A new system for textile mill villages is established at FORT MILL, 2 *m.* (640 alt., 2,112 pop.), with its three plants of the Springs mills. Brick houses surrounded by several acres of tillable land may be purchased by employees through monthly payments. The highway twists and turns through the paved streets of the town, compelling drivers to slow down to avoid collision with trains and houses. A sign declares confidently, 'You can't go wrong on Fort Mill sheets.' The two main roads intersect at a small park, with monuments to the Confederate soldiers and women of the Confederacy and, less usual, two memorials to Catawba Indians and faithful Negro slaves, erected by John McKee Spratt and Samuel White. The former was descended from Thomas Spratt, first white settler in the Catawba Nation, who was adopted into the tribe under the name Kanawha (Ind., friendly brother).

The route crosses the CATAWBA RIVER, 10 *m.*, known lower in the State as the Wateree. Indian tradition asserts that prior to white settlement a treaty between warring Cherokee and Catawba declared the area between the Broad and Catawba Rivers neutral territory where both tribes might hunt in peace.

In ROCK HILL, 14.7 *m.* (690 alt., 11,322 pop.) (*see Rock Hill*), is a junction with State 5 (*see Tour 7a*).

Seat of Chester County, CHESTER, 34.1 *m.* (487 alt., 5,628 pop.), is one of three South Carolina towns (the others are York and Lancaster) named by settlers who came from Pennsylvania soon after 1755. A placid town built around a brick-paved square, it is rimmed on the northeast by textile mills. In 1904, Dr. Gill Wylie, a native of Chester who became a prominent New York physician, helped to launch the hydroelectric development that brought many mills to the section. Farming persists, however, with an increased interest in cattle raising, though cotton is still the main crop.

The T-shaped CHESTER COURTHOUSE (R), York St., one block north of the square, was erected in 1850 on the site of the old structure built 1795. The two-story gray stuccoed brick building is entered through a six-column pedimented portico that rests on an arcaded basement; windows have corniced headings supported on consoles. A memorial stone in front of the courthouse was erected by Chester gentiles to Jack Simons, a childless Jew who loved children.

In 1807, Aaron Burr while under arrest for treason, here broke away from his guards, climbed on a big rock, and harangued a curious crowd before he was recaptured.

In Chester are junctions with State 9 (*see Tour 21b*) and State 97 (*see Tour 4*).

South of Chester, the highway and railroad lines follow the Ridge, watershed of the Broad River system (R) and the Wateree (L). Negroes and a few whites crowd the little crossroad stores on Saturday afternoons; but most of them pile into trucks and wagon beds for an all-day trip to Chester or Winnsboro. On Saturday nights home-going mule-wagons are a traffic hazard; often bearing no lights, they loom out of the dusk in front of speeding cars. Sometimes, however, they carry a lightwood torch, a smoking lantern, or a burning rag stuck in a pop bottle filled with kerosene.

WOODWARD, 46.6 *m.* (578 alt., 135 pop.), named as a railroad stop for a family of old coastal settlers, was first called Youngsville. Here is told the far-fetched story of General Pakenham, British officer, who fell at New Orleans in 1814. His body was embalmed in a barrel of rum for shipment home. By some mistake it came to Youngsville, and remaining heavy after continual tapping, was broken open, revealing the general's body. Prohibition still has strong support in the area.

Two granite columns (R), 59.8 *m.*, form the entrance to FORTUNE PARK and commemorate a Negro slave who attended La Fayette during the Revolution.

Opposite the park is the junction with State 22 (*see Tour 7A*).

One of the older, and consequently one of the prouder Up Country towns, WINNSBORO, 60.7 *m.* (545 alt., 2,344 pop.), seat of Fairfield County, settled about 1755, was incorporated in 1785 and named for Colonel Richard Winn, Revolutionary officer and early town father. The first settlers came from the coastal States between Pennsylvania and North Carolina, but to their number was added a group of Low Country 'quality' seeking a more healthful climate and broader cotton lands. In 1780, when British troops occupied the settlement, Cornwallis's supposed comment on the outlying 'fair fields' gave the county its name. General Sherman burned part of Winnsboro after his demolition of Columbia in February 1865. In spite of raids by enemy generals and the boll weevil, however, Winnsboro maintains its agricultural standing and attracts the mercantile business of the county.

A Confederate monument at the intersection of Congress and Washington Streets marks the dividing line between the residential and business sections. A two-story red brick building (L) houses the police station and municipal offices. Its tower supports the town clock, made before the War between the States and hauled here from Charleston in an ox-cart. This huge timepiece was once mortgaged to a citizen who lent money to the town, which, when unable to pay, presented the clock to its creditor. Having no use for it, he returned it to the city fathers.

Mount Zion High School, in two large red brick buildings accommodating nearly 600 pupils, occupies the SITE OF MOUNT ZION INSTITUTE, chartered 1777. Forced to close during the Revolution, it reopened with a college charter in 1785, and was attended by many pupils from other States. Sherman burned the building after occupying it as headquarters.

FAIRFIELD INN (R), a big frame house, reputed to have been Cornwallis's headquarters, is now patronized by mill officials.

Though incorporated in the town, the WINNSBORO MILL VILLAGE exists as a separate entity. Attractive cottages of varied design, equipped with electricity and plumbing, are surrounded by lawns and shrubbery. Rented for about 27¢ per room monthly, the houses are maintained by the U. S. Rubber Company, which employs 1,600 people in the manufacture of cord for automobile tires. The YMCA community house (R), accommodating religious, social, and labor meetings, is a two-story brick building of a neo-Georgian type, with Mount Vernon porch, steep gable roof, and dormers. Beyond the mills, out of sight of the highway, unkempt houses in the older part of the village are gradually being deserted as occupants move into the newer section.

ROCKTON, 61.8 *m.*, a group of stores centered about a small station, is an important shipping point for Winnsboro blue granite, quarried near by and hauled over a spur track.

A drawing of ANVIL ROCK (R), 62.7 *m.*, a large granite monolith about 100 feet off the highway, appears in Lyman C. Draper's *King's Mountain and Its Heroes*.

Enclosed by a rough wall, WOODWARD CEMETERY (R), 63.8 *m.*, contains many old granite tombstones, hand-hewn and joined with small iron clamps. The tallest shaft honors Thomas Woodward, 'The Regulator' (*see Tour 8b*), revered ancestor of many county families, killed May 17, 1779, while pursuing a band of Indian and Tory marauders.

Skirting the edge of RIDGEWAY, 74.2 *m.* (624 alt., 404 pop.), the highway avoids the narrow streets and the railroad cut that splits open the little farm village. Chicken farms are helping to restore the agricultural loss caused by erosion and the boll weevil.

BLYTHEWOOD, 76.8 *m.* (504 alt., 112 pop.), sheltering more reminiscences than citizens, was Doko (Ind., watering place) until postal authorities changed its name. It has been a watering station for locomotives since the railway was built, and one family has remained continuously in charge through the days of a slave-operated pump, a mule-power engine, and the mechanical pump of the present. This neighborhood fathered J. Gordon Coogler, printer for Columbia's daily, *The State*, who gained notice with extraordinary rhymes and surprising metaphors. His house bore a legend, 'Poems written while you wait.' This humorless, conscientious versifier first printed his lines at his own expense, but gradually they caught the public fancy and were reviewed in New York and London papers, his name becoming so well known that 'cooglerism' came to mean a solemn absurdity. The printer-poet's most frequently quoted couplet is:

> Alas, for the South! her books have grown fewer,
> She never was much given to literature.

At 84.9 *m.* is the junction with a dirt road.

Left on this road 0.1 *m.* to the Negro Unit of the SOUTH CAROLINA STATE HOSPITAL. Ten brick buildings house about 2,000 patients; cottages accommodate physicians and attendants. Patients cultivate the surrounding farm.

STATE PARK SANITARIUM, adjoining on the northwest, has beds for more than 300 tuberculosis patients in the 25 buildings scattered over attractive grounds. Campbell Hall is a preventorium for children under 13.

Near by is the unmarked site of LIGHTWOOD KNOT SPRING, early summer resort for Columbians, and muster grounds for Confederate soldiers. Here a duel occurred about 1833 between two South Carolina College students, Roach and Adams, both under 21 and close friends. The challenge followed an altercation over a plate of fish at the college mess. Adams was killed; Roach, deeply remorseful, died from alcoholism in 1836.

At EAU CLAIRE, 92.7 *m.* (2,915 pop.), is COLUMBIA COLLEGE (L), with brick administration and dormitory buildings, surrounded by a campus of 36 acres. A Methodist liberal arts institution with an enrollment of 400 girls, it was chartered in 1854 as the Columbia Female College. By 1865 it had about 200 students, but had to close until 1873. The present plant was begun in 1905, destroyed by fire in 1909, and immediately rebuilt.

The LUTHERAN SEMINARY (R), with two granite buildings and three professors' homes, was founded in 1830 and established on this, its third location, in 1911 on a campus given by the city of Columbia. The institution is closely connected with the history of Lutheranism in the South. Early Lutherans of the State were all Germans, and services were conducted in German until about 1815. This retarded the growth of Lutheranism after the speaking of English became general. The few Lutheran ministers in South Carolina and Georgia organized a South Carolina synod in 1824, one of the first objectives being the training of English-speaking pastors.

At Eau Claire is the junction with State 215 (*see Tour* 18), which unites with US 21 between this point and Columbia.

IN COLUMBIA, 96.8 *m.* (312 alt., 51,581 pop.) (*see Columbia*), are junctions with US 1 (*see Tour* 6*a*), US 76 (*see Tour* 9*b*), and State 215 (*see Tour* 18).

Section *b.*   COLUMBIA *to* POCOTALIGO, 109.8 *m.*   US 21.

This section of the tour crosses the Sand Hills, at their best in spring when lupines bloom and the scent of pine and crabapple drifts across the road. Among the blackjack oaks and scrawny pines white sand pits make bald patches where sand is obtained for concrete and glass. Southward, the flatlands afford some of the best farming soils in the State.

Westward from COLUMBIA, 0 *m.*, US 1 (*see Tour* 6*b*) unites with US 21 between this point and 2.4 *m.* (*see Tour* 6*b*).

At 5.4 *m.* is the junction with State 5 (*see Tour* 5*A*), which unites with US 21 between this point and 9.2 *m.*

SANDY RUN CHURCH (L), 17.9 *m.*, is a little white clapboarded structure housing a Lutheran congregation organized in 1765. In the iron-fenced cemetery the rough granite stone marking the GRAVE OF CHRISTIAN THEUS recalls a strange story. Theus, brother of Jeremiah

Theus, Charleston painter, was an itinerant Lutheran pastor for nearly 50 years. At his death he was buried about 10 miles north of Sandy Run, but the remains were transferred here a few years ago. Pastor Theus is credited with uncovering the Weber heresy, which existed about 1756–61 under the leadership of Jacob Weber and John George Schmidt, Swiss-German settlers. A pastor visited their isolated community hardly twice a year, but they began to conduct their own services, and their creed quickly degenerated from orthodox Lutheranism. Three of the leaders claimed to be the Holy Trinity, and declared that the wife of one was the Virgin Mary. In their religious rites they fell into trances; they sanctioned nudity and marital confusion. Christian Theus reported to Charles Town the 'abominable wantonness' and blasphemy he had discovered. Later he fell into the hands of the heretics. They were unable to decide whether to hang or drown him, and meanwhile he escaped. Dissension followed. A quarrel led 'God' to chain 'Peter' in an underground cave. Failing to starve in the expected time, he was beaten to death at Weber's command. After another murder in February 1761, the authorities intervened. Weber was executed, his wife freed. Before its suppression the cult spread to other sections of the State, and to North Carolina, Virginia, and Maryland.

In the vicinity of Big Beaver Creek, 25.6 *m.*, picnics were formerly held near the GRAVE OF GENERAL HAIGUE. This early settler went to Charleston to find a wife, taking his waiting man. Prosperity being reckoned by the number of slaves, the prospective bride's maidservant asked Haigue's valet how many slaves his master owned. 'Me and forty mo',' was the answer. When the wedding party arrived at the country home, only one slave was visible. 'Where all de forty slaves you been braggin' 'bout?' asked the maidservant. 'I ain' said nothin' 'bout no forty slaves. I said me and Forty Mo'—dat nigger yonder, he name' "Forty Mo'." '

At 33.1 *m.* is the junction with State 6 (*see Tour 5B*).

At 37.1 *m.* is the junction with the Robert E. Lee Highway, or State 31.

Left on State 31, persistently called the Old State Road. Much of the old roadbed, laid under the direction of Joel R. Poinsett (*see Tour 20*), has been utilized in hard surfacing. Sand and logs formed causeways through the dense Four Hole and Great Cypress Swamps, when the first road was completed early in the nineteenth century from Charleston through Columbia to Buncombe County, North Carolina. Upstate it was known as Buncombe Road. Along here it is almost arrow-straight to Charleston. Isolation preserved old ways of living. German farmers followed the pattern of old world peasant villages; seven to ten low farm buildings, often surrounded by a fence, are grouped close together. Great trees almost hide the little structures; an occasional well sweep pokes through the foliage. Even today it is not uncommon to see a skinned tree set up in the ancient manner to draw well water in the yard of a new brick bungalow.

At METTS CROSSROADS, 3.7 *m.*, a marker tells of the Tory murder of John Adam Treutlen (1726–82). Austrian-born, he took refuge in South Carolina when driven out of Savannah, following British occupation in 1778. He had been Georgia's first governor under the State constitution, 1777.

The big square frame two-story BATES HOUSE (R), 16.3 *m.*, was built about

1835 by Dr. W. T. C. Bates. Its front piazza, supported by fluted columns, is approached by a straight flight of steps. Immense double doors with a gracefully curving fanlight lead into the wide hall. Ceilings of hall and living room are corniced; the latter having a carved mantel.

The rambling old frame structure (R), 20.5 *m.*, was the famous HALFWAY HOUSE when the State Road was the chief thoroughfare between Charleston and Columbia. Frequently mentioned in old diaries, it afforded overnight accommodations for legislators, businessmen, and other travelers.

At 26.7 *m.* is the junction with US 15 (*see Tour 3b*).

HOLLY HILL, 32 *m.* (106 alt., 702 pop.), stimulated to new life by the Santee-Cooper development (*see Tour 2b*), is a truck-farming capital. In 1938, 22 cars of peas (500 bushels to the car) were loaded, with about three times that quantity shipped by motor truck. In addition, there were 50 carloads of sweet potatoes, with about 10 per cent more in trucks. Hogs and cattle with truck farming are now supplanting cotton.

At 64.7 *m.* is the junction with US 52 (*see Tour 2b*).

The flourishing countryside indicates the prosperity of ORANGEBURG, 46.9 *m.* (264 alt., 8,776 pop.), seat of Orangeburg County. East Russell Street leads to the business section and the center of the city. The landscaped Memorial Plaza, corner Russell and Broughton Streets, has an illuminated fountain and several monuments. Of the latter, the metal figure of an old-time fireman is the most diverting. Honoring the local volunteer brigade, one of the earliest in South Carolina, it also marks the site of the first engine house.

Orangeburg, settled in the 1730's, and named for William, Prince of Orange, became the head of old Amelia Township. Low Country gentry followed Swiss and German farmers, setting up plantations with slave labor. At the intersection of two Indian paths, the community was an early trade center and the scene of both Whig and Tory Revolutionary victories. Good soils and stable population of thrifty stock, able to adapt their farming to changed conditions, have contributed to lasting prosperity. Orangeburg County reputedly once produced more cotton than any other county in the world; even after the ravages of the boll weevil, it remains one of the 20 principal agricultural counties in the United States.

Two seasons bring visitors into town. When Edisto Gardens bloom in spring, hundreds visit the acres of sward that blaze with azaleas under tall moss-hung cypresses. The park, on the former city dump-heap, is edged by the North Edisto River. In the fall Orangeburg offers the county fair, second in size and attendance only to the State Fair in Columbia.

In the angle formed by College Ave. and E. Russell St. are two Negro schools. CLAFLIN UNIVERSITY, founded by Northern philanthropists in 1872 and under the Methodist Episcopal denomination since 1878, furnished agricultural training to Negroes of the State almost 20 years before such training was provided for whites. The STATE AGRICULTURAL AND MECHANICAL COLLEGE, coeducational, was established in 1896. Its enrollment of 700 to 800 students is generally doubled at summer sessions by teachers from small Negro schools. The 40 buildings are on a campus, partly farmed, extending beyond the city limits. Many graduates of both institutions are employed as home economic and farm agents.

The LUTHERAN CHURCH, corner Amelia and Green Sts., which Sherman used as a smallpox hospital, is a white frame structure with arched windows. The central tower, with a fanlighted entrance, is surmounted with a belfry and shingled spire.

The PRESBYTERIAN CHURCH, corner Windsor and Amelia Sts., a rectangular white clapboarded building, was erected in 1858, by a congregation organized in 1835. Above a six-column Doric portico with triglyph frieze and a pediment rises a shingled belfry topped with spire and cross. The interior has been redecorated and the old slave gallery reduced in size. The first communion service was stolen by Northern soldiers in 1865 when the basement served as their stable.

In Orangeburg is the junction with US 178 (*see Tour 15b*), which unites with US 21 for 2 miles.

1. Left from Orangeburg on State 4 to the DONALD BRUCE HOUSE (L), 3.3 *m.*, on Middlepen Plantation. Surrounded by a brick wall with massive arched gateway and by shaded gardens, the old two-story white frame structure has green shutters and double piazza. In the two front rooms are carved frame mantels and high paneled wainscoting. This house was Revolutionary headquarters for both Governor John Rutledge and Lord Rawdon, and was later temporary headquarters for Union officers.

2. Right from Orangeburg on State 4, 1.2 *m.*, is the junction with the Cannon's Bridge Road; L. on this road 5.6 *m.* to the COUNTY FISH HATCHERY, one of the largest in the State. Seven pools are lighted at night to attract insects. The landscaped grounds, covering approximately 150 acres, are used for public recreation.

BRANCHVILLE, 63.1 *m.* (125 alt., 1,689 pop.), owes its existence and name to the first branch railroad in the State (*see Transportation*). It was the point from which a connecting line to Columbia was begun in 1840 and completed in 1842, when the *Robert Y. Hayne*, wood-burning engine, made the first run. Only a few old houses remain—where nowadays orders for fried chicken, telegraphed ahead, are filled for passengers on the Charleston-Columbia trains.

In Branchville is the junction with US 78 (*see Tour 6b*).

US 21 crosses the EDISTO RIVER, 68.5 *m.*, one of the tidal streams in this nearly sea-level country, where abandoned rice fields, attractive to waterfowl, are owned or leased by hunters.

At 89.7 *m.* is the junction with State 63, unpaved.

Right on this road past several bridges across the Big and Little Salkehatchie Rivers and swamps to the DOWMAN CYPRESS, 8.8 *m.*, about 500 yards from the causeway (L) past the second bridge. The tree is inaccessible and its bronze marker invisible from the road. Estimated as at least 3,000 years old, it was named in 1914 for the operator of the most extensive cypress cuttings in the Nation at that time.

At 102.7 *m.* is the junction with US 17 (*see Tour 1c*), which unites southward with US 21 for 7.1 miles.

YEMASSEE, 106.2 *m.* (12 alt., 589 pop.), is at the junction with State 28 (*see Tour 19c*).

POCOTALIGO, 109.8 *m.* (317 pop.), is at the southern junction with US 17 (*see Tour 1c*).

Section c. POCOTALIGO to PORT ROYAL, 21.3 *m.* US 21, State 281.

US 21 branches east from US 17 at POCOTALIGO, 0 *m.* Out of the tidal river swamps the route enters a truck growing area. Tomatoes, lettuce, melons, and okra are shipped North by rail and motor truck, and through the inland waterway.

At 1.8 *m.* is the junction with a dirt road.

Right here 2 *m.* to STONEY CREEK PRESBYTERIAN CEMETERY, where a church was built in 1743. The Reverend William Hutson, an Englishman trained as a lawyer, came to Charles Town in 1740. He joined a band of strolling players in their performances at the Dock Street Theater; but he was converted by the Reverend George Whitefield, and went to Savannah to teach in an orphanage. When Stoney Creek Church was organized as the Independent Church of Indian Land, he became its first pastor. The church records note that the Reverend James Bulloch Dunwody, pastor, and cousin to the mother of Theodore Roosevelt, officiated at her marriage in Georgia. Some of the ancestors of President Theodore Roosevelt and Mrs. Franklin D. Roosevelt came from South Carolina. A later pastor was the Reverend Edward Axson; his daughter, Ellen, who became the wife of President Woodrow Wilson, lived here as a child. After Sherman burned the church in 1865, the congregation moved to McPhersonville.

At 4.8 *m.* on US 21 is the junction with a dirt road.

Left on this road to the brick RUINS OF SHELDON CHURCH (R), 2.6 *m.*, another reminder of Sherman's visit. An eerie place in moonlight, the surrounding groves draped with swaying moss, it is scarcely less ghostly in the sun, when lizards scurry off among the graves. Annually on the second Sunday after Easter, prominent churchmen conduct well-attended services from the battered altar. The first building was erected 1745–57 on glebe lands donated by Elizabeth, widow of Landgrave Edmund Bellinger. Members of the Bull family were on the building commission, and from Sheldon Hall, their country place in England, came the name of the church, though to ecclesiasts it was Prince William's Parish Church. On one of the graves here the family arms are carved. Bulls were both Tories and Whigs. One served the State ably as lieutenant-governor for many years prior to the Revolution. During that war, the British burned Sheldon Hall and Sheldon Church. The second building was reduced to ruins by Sherman.

TOMOTLEY PLANTATION (L), 3.6 *m.* (*visitors allowed to circle avenue*), was once part of Tomotley Barony, a tract of 13,000 acres granted to Captain Edmund Bellinger, who was made landgrave in 1698.

GARDENS CORNER, 5.1 *m.*, a crossroads named for Colonel Benjamin Garden, a former landowner here, is sometimes erroneously said to be named for Dr. Alexander Garden, who also lived near by. Dr. Garden was a popular Scottish physician and a distinguished naturalist, for whom the gardenia was named.

Here is the junction with State 32 (*see Tour 1c*).

LOBECO, 9 *m.*, combining the first syllables in the names of packing plant owners, is an important shipping point for locally grown truck. Packing sheds with rough posts accommodate many Negro workers during the season. The tomato crop is the only one requiring outside labor. Sowed in hotbeds from December to January, the plants are transferred to the open field in mid-March.

About May 20 the tomatoes are ready to pick, and Negro packers, who have followed the crop from Florida, begin to arrive. Workers, singing and laughing as they pick the fruit, are careful to select those that will ripen by the time they reach market. One group picks, another rushes the filled boxes to trucks that haul them to packing sheds, where the tomatoes are graded. Some hands grade, others hammer together the lugs, or crates. Each tomato is wrapped in tissue paper and placed in the lug. Filled, it passes to the nailer, who, with a few skilled strokes, hammers on the lid, and the tomatoes are ready for shipment. Little singing is heard here, for the work is hard and fast. Most of the crop is shipped by truck, but toward the end of the season refrigerated cars are used. The peak is reached by the middle of July; tomatoes are ripening farther up the coast. Almost overnight, the packers are gone as suddenly as they arrived. They are paid 5¢ a lug, the most expert filling 250 to 300 a day. The fields are still scarlet, and local pickers continue to work; the ripe tomatoes are sold to canneries, of which there are several at Beaufort and one at Lobeco.

Among many streams threading the tidal marshes nearer the coast is WHALE BRANCH, 9.7 *m.*, where a whale that came up during high water was unable to escape when the tide fell.

Beyond the branch the country grows more tropical. Palmettos, gray moss, and wide sweeps of marsh grass grow between the fields. When the tide is out, the shining black mud flats give off their distinctive odor; at high tide the pools suggest pale ocher mirrors framed by marsh grass. Such scenes have enticed many artists and writers to Beaufort County.

At 13.2 *m.* is the junction with Grays Hill Road.

Right here 2.1 *m.* to the CORNING ESTATE, including two old plantations, Laurel Bay and Woodward. Remains of the tabby plantation house still stand at Woodward, with its avenue of oaks and magnolias. Laurel Bay's avenue of live oaks is 85 feet wide and 150 yards long. On the estate is the grave of Paul Hamilton (1762–1816), South Carolina governor and Secretary of the Navy under President Madison.

At 14.1 *m.* is the junction with a dirt road.

Right here 1.4 *m.* to BEAUFORT COUNTY TRAINING SCHOOL, an industrial school for Negroes, established in 1901 through the efforts of a Northern woman living in Beaufort. The school, incorporated into the county system in 1918, has about 330 pupils.

At BURTON, 15.7 *m.*, is the junction with State 280, asphalt-paved.

Right here 2.7 *m.* to the junction with a dirt road; L. here through woods to THE RETREAT, 0.7 *m.* The little pre-Revolutionary two-story tabby house, with handcarved panels and wainscoting, dormer windows and a low piazza, crumbled to ruin under vine-tangled palmettos, yaupon, and oaks until its recent restoration. Lizards and snakes basked among fallen timbers and piles of broken tabby. It has its own lurid tradition. Before the Revolution a well-mannered

Frenchman named DeLagaye established himself here. Nobody ever learned whence he came, nor why. In 1776, two of his slaves murdered him. One was caught, hanged, and decapitated. The head, set high on a pole, served for two generations as a warning, and gave the neighborhood the name of Nigger Head, by which it is known today. No heirs could be found, and the property was escheated and sold at public auction to Stephen Bull. He regretted his purchase and sold it to John Barnwell, whose descendants still operate the plantation.

PARRIS ISLAND (*open Sun. and holidays 8 A.M. to 5 P.M.; Wed. and Sat. noon to 5 P.M.; or by special arrangement with Post Adjutant*), 5.6 *m.*, United States Naval Station, was named for Colonel Alexander Parris, public treasurer of South Carolina prior to 1733. From 3,500 to 4,000 marines are trained here annually. Federals used the island as a ship coaling base during the 1860's, and it was made a Naval Station in 1876. In 1915 the entire property, except the 200 acres of the original post, was purchased and turned over to the Marine Corps. About 60,000 recruits were trained here for World War service. Spaniards came to the island in the 1520's, and Franciscans and Jesuits strove for a century to establish missions among Indians; but their civil rulers loved the gold of Peru more than the souls of red men. A band of French Huguenots arrived in 1562, led by Jean Ribaut, a naval officer under Admiral Coligny, French Protestant leader. Charlesfort, honoring Charles IX, was built of earth and logs before Ribaut returned to France for reinforcements, leaving Captain Albert, a stern disciplinarian, in charge of the 26 settlers. Food grew short; Albert hanged one man, and left another, La Chere, to starve on an island. The remaining men mutinied, killed Albert, and rescued La Chere. Believing themselves deserted, they built a boat and set out for France. The craft leaked and the men were starving. La Chere proposed that one of their number be killed for food. When lots were cast, he was the victim. An English ship eventually picked up the survivors and returned them to France. The Huguenots, on a subsequent voyage, veered off their course, reached Florida and began what afterwards became St. Augustine. The Spaniards, alarmed at French aggression, established mission posts up the coast nearly to Charles Town.

At 6 *m.* is the junction with a side road; L. here to MARINE POST, 1.3 *m.*, with its rifle and pistol ranges, naval radio station, hospital, golf course, tennis court, and athletic fields.

At 8.1 *m.* is the junction with a dirt road; R. here to CHARLESFORT MONUMENT, 1.8 *m.*, dedicated March 27, 1926, on the alleged site of Ribaut's French post, where excavations in 1917 uncovered cedar foundations, either from Charlesfort or from Fort San Marcos, built by the Spaniards in 1577.

In BEAUFORT, 17.7 *m.* (21 alt., 2,776 pop.) (*see Beaufort*), is the junction with State 285 (*see Tour 5C*).

South of Beaufort the main route follows State 281, locally known as the Port Royal or Ribaut Road.

The MATHER SCHOOL for Negro girls, 19.1 *m.*, founded 1868 by Mrs. Rachel Crane Mather, of Boston, consists of groups of two- and three-story white frame buildings with green trim, scattered over several acres of land. One red brick building has a gable roof with dormers. Revenue for the operation of the school comes partly from the sale of old clothes shipped from the North. Operated since 1882 by the Women's Baptist Home Missionary Society, its curriculum extends from the fifth grade through two college years, offering courses in domestic science, nursing, and teaching. About 100 pupils attend.

At 19.8 *m.* is the junction with a marked dirt road.

Left on this road 0.5 *m.* to the SITE OF FORT LYTTLETON, erected in 1758 against Indian and Spanish incursion, and named for Governor William Henry

Lyttleton, State leader during Indian upheavals. Here also is the SITE OF STUART TOWN, where in 1684, Lord Cardross, Scottish Presbyterian, attempted to settle a small group of Covenanters. Indians and slaves, inspired by Spaniards, massacred the colonists, 1686. During the World War a large shipyard operated here.

PORT ROYAL, 21.3 m. (353 pop.), has one of the rare names surviving from early French attempts at settlement. The English considered settling here in 1670, but the colonists voted to proceed to Albemarle, the first site of Charles Town. Activity has again sprung up on this flat island, since the building of the Parris Island Bridge in 1939. Little frame houses look out from the live oaks over Port Royal harbor, of which Ribaut in 1562 wrote in his report to Admiral Coligny: 'One of the greatest and fairest havens in the world, where without danger all the ships in the world might be harbored.' It is the deepest natural harbor south of Chesapeake Bay, with an average depth of 5 fathoms for nearly 27 miles. The population of the village, mostly civilian employees on Parris Island, is augmented from July to November by Portuguese and Italian fishermen, who follow the shrimping season up the coast from Florida.

About the middle of August the shrimp season reaches its peak. Battered little sailing smacks with auxiliary engines, well-iced, and manned by two or three fishermen, sail out from the harbor in the early morning. About a mile offshore, large weighted nets are thrown overboard, trawled along the bottom for a few minutes, then hauled in and the shrimp dumped into the ice in the hold. Fifty bushels make a good day's haul, and usually two or three days at sea are required to fill the boat. Along the docks, in sheds leased by owners of the fleet, the shrimp are unloaded onto long tables. Chattering Negro women fall to work 'picking' or beheading, washing and chilling the shrimp before packing them in barrels of ice for shipment. A factory for the processing of crab meat adds its aroma to Port Royal air, and furnishes employment to local Negroes.

These industries indicate a new trend in Port Royal business. Formerly lumber and cotton were shipped; during the 1870's railroad coaches were built; between 1870 and 1890 the harbor was alive with vessels from many countries, awaiting their cargoes of phosphate. This last industry may be revived; in 1939 a small quantity of phosphate was dredged from river bottoms and shipped through the inland waterway.

In Port Royal Sound is CAT ISLAND, where in the early 1930's, warm climate, sea breezes, and the beauty of subtropical vegetation attracted a nudist colony from the North. For a while it flourished on publicity that sprang from the petitions of outraged citizens to the governor, but interest lagged, and the venture was finally dropped by its promoter.

Tour 5A

West Columbia—Hardeeville—Bluffton; 149.7 *m.*, State 5, State 46.

Roadbed concrete-paved with sections of asphalt.
Seaboard Air Line parallels route between West Columbia and Estill; Southern Ry. between Estill and Hardeeville.
Limited accommodations.

Between Columbia and Hardeeville little towns are strung like beads along the railroad; the highway parallels the tracks for almost the entire route. From scrubby sand hills the road emerges into wide gray fields. Grains, vegetables, melons, tobacco, pecan orchards, pastures, and pine forests have nearly edged King Cotton off his throne in this section. Chief buildings in the little towns and at flag stops between are the large packing houses, where, in season, refrigerator cars and motor trucks wait to receive produce for distant markets.

In the swamplands nearer the coast, ditches of clear dark water flow between the railroad and highway, to drain the 'causeys' (causeways) on which the roads are stabilized. In the spring, wild iris and purple thistle struggle for bloom. Later on, masses of golden growth catch the attention; but on closer inspection the gold turns to a sickly green as the apparent lily is found to be a flycatcher, pitcher plant, side-saddle flower, or jack-in-the-pulpit—all local names for the *Sarracenia flava*, of which Mark Catesby (*c*.1680–1749), English naturalist, gives the following description:

> The leaves of this Plant are tubulous and ribbed, arising from a knotty fibrous root to the height of about three feet; they are small at the root, widening gradually to the mouth of the tube; which, in young leaves, are closed, but open by degrees, as the leaf increaseth; and, when near its full growth, arches over the mouth of the tube, in form of a friar's cowl. This cowl expands itself till the leaf is at full bigness, having its inside of a greenish yellow, veined with purple, yet retaining somewhat the position it first had, by hanging over the mouth of the tube, which otherwise would be filled with rain and fall by the weight of the water; it being of a thin substance, and of a yellowish green color.

The flower of the plant is inconspicuous and rises from a stem parallel with the leaf. Its roots were used in the difficult days of the Confederacy for medicine, as a 'tonic for the digestive organs.'

For many years the land roundabout was covered with thick woodlands, but of late, hundreds of acres have been burned over. As the highway nears the sea, the air is odorous with sweet myrtle and, at low tide, with the pluffy mud of the salt marshes.

State 5 branches south from US 1–US 21 in WEST COLUMBIA,

0 *m.* (*see Tour 6b*), at 1.3 miles west of Columbia (*see Columbia*).

CAYCE, 1 *m.* (1,267 pop.), named for a local family, prospers from a lumber mill, granite quarry, and surrounding fields of cotton and corn. The CAYCE HOUSE, on the southeastern edge of town, built 1765 as a trading post, was alternately a British and American stronghold. Lord Rawdon lost it, as did the American Generals Sumter and 'Light Horse Harry' Lee; finally, General Nathanael Greene captured and held it. The gaunt black hewn-pine two-story house, with large chimneys at each gable end, the lower hall from front to back and upper hall from side to side, would nowadays inspire little confidence as a garrison.

Immediately south of Cayce a graveyard and a marker indicate the SITE OF GRANBY, once known as The Congarees. Here an Indian trading factory was built in 1718. By 1754 Granby was an important river depot and the seat of old Lexington District. With the development of Columbia, Granby declined.

At 5.2 *m.* is the junction with US 21 (*see Tour 5b*), which unites with State 5 to a southern junction (*see Tour 5b*) at 9 *m.*

The name SWANSEA, 21.6 *m.* (717 pop.), is said to be a corruption of *zwanzig* (German, twenty), the town being about 20 miles from Columbia. The steep hills hereabouts, over which the highway curves like a scenic railway, are unusual for this part of the State where the land, theoretically, slopes consistently toward the coast.

At NORTH, 30.5 *m.* (755 pop.), is the junction with US 178 (*see Tour 15b*).

NORWAY, 42.4 *m.* (494 pop.), and DENMARK, 51.6 *m.* (250 alt., 1,713 pop.) (*see Tour 6b*), were named, apparently at random, by railway officials.

At Denmark is the junction with US 78 (*see Tour 6b*).

The waters and swamps in this section drain into the Salkehatchie (Saltketcher) Rivers. The Big and Little Salkehatchie form the Combahee (Cumbee) and empty into St. Helena Sound. The bream, flat fish, sturgeon, and perch of these streams have lured fishermen for decades. In the swamps are wild deer and turkey, and the sedges hide doves and quail. Wildcats, 'coons, alligators, and an occasional black bear leave their tracks on the fresh earth that smells of ancient vegetable mold. Thick vegetation has preserved the animals from extermination.

SYCAMORE, 73.7 *m.* (149 pop.), was named for the sycamore or plane tree that grows abundantly in the woodlands and marshes of this section.

Left from Sycamore on an asphalt road, State 641, 9.2 *m.* to RIVERS' BRIDGE MEMORIAL GROUNDS, where since 1876 has been held an annual celebration of the battle of February 4, 1865.

At the main crossing of the river, 1,200 Confederates of South Carolina, Georgia, and Tennessee, under the command of Major General McLaws, held 22,000 men of Sherman's army in check for two days to give Confederate forces in other sections a chance to mass their strength, and families in the line of invasion time to conceal their possessions. In the spring of 1876 the bodies of the

Confederate slain, interred along the battle site, were exhumed and reburied here in a single grave. A landscaped park accommodates the thousands of visitors who attend the yearly memorial exercises and barbecue. In the RIVERS' BRIDGE MUSEUM, a small brick building, are relics pertaining to the battle and the period.

At FAIRFAX, 79.5 *m.* (136 alt., 1,376 pop.) (*see Tour* 19c), is the junction with State 28 (*see Tour* 19c).

At DUKES, 81.5 *m.* (10 pop.), is the junction with State 361, dirt.

Left on this road to OAK GROVE, 1.2 *m.,* where hunters are entertained in winter and house parties held in summer. Built in 1852, it was a stagecoach stop for a few years; then Sherman took it for headquarters in March 1865, on his way from Savannah to Columbia. Twenty-two thousand of his troops camped in the surrounding fields. Negroes in the neighborhood maintain they can see spirits of the soldiers wandering among the big oak trees on moonlight nights. After many years of disrepair, the house and grounds were restored in 1934.

GIFFORD, 86.3 *m.* (85 pop.), is the home of a seed industry conducted by Edward H. Hanna, who, turning from cotton growing when the boll weevil came, created a country-wide demand for the California peas, Kansas alfalfa, Texas oats, Tennessee corn, white Dutch clover, Sudan grass, Russian sunflowers, Jerusalem artichokes, and other seeds cultivated by him.

Around LURAY, 89.4 *m.* (188 pop.), and ESTILL, 93.7 *m.* (115 alt., 1,412 pop.), a good part of the State's crop of peanuts and strawberries is grown. Land near Estill has produced from 1,000 to 1,100 pounds of tobacco to the acre. A large lumber mill is here. Tennis courts, golf courses, and a gun club furnish recreation for the neighborhood. An AMARYLLIS GARDEN (*open*), begun as a hobby by its owner, covers several acres and has developed into a paying business, with many varieties of lilies.

The DAVIS SWIMMING POOL (*20¢ and 25¢*), with its pavilion and picnic grounds (R), has many visitors who bring their lunch baskets. The pool is supplied by a deep artesian well with a flow of 22,000 gallons an hour, and an even all-year temperature of 78°.

At GARNETT, 108.2 *m.* (50 pop.), is the junction with a dirt road.

Right on this road 7 *m.* to PARACHUCLA LANDING, in Colonial times an Indian ford across the Savannah River, later used by traders in approaching the Creek lands westward, and then as a loading point for cotton hauled here over the old Orangeburg Road. The name is a corruption of Apalachee, a tribe of Indians defeated in the Yamasee War of 1715 and afterward united with the Creek. A few miles south of here is a bluff named Tuckassa King, apparently for Chief Tuckassa of the Apalachee.

ROBERTVILLE, 111 *m.* (30 pop.), was named for the family of Henry Martyn Robert (1837–1923), a celebrated military engineer, who would have been more popular hereabouts had he not been a Union soldier. He was the author of *Rules of Order,* a widely known handbook on parliamentary procedure.

The woodlands here are largely the property of the W. M. Ritter Lumber Company, whose headquarters are at 113.1 *m.* (R). Unusual for these parts is the camp, fenced, landscaped, and with neat cottages for its employees. Water and lights are furnished free. Millions of feet of lumber, hardwood as well as pine, are stacked up in the drying yards on the roadside.

TILLMAN, 121.3 *m.* (398 pop.), is named for Governor B. R. ('Pitchfork Ben') Tillman (*see Tour 8b*).

At 132.4 *m.* is the junction with a dirt road.

Right on this road 2.5 *m.* to the PURRYSBURGH CEMETERY, the site of a town established here in 1732 by Jean Pierre Purry, a Swiss who was inspired by rumor to print broadsides advertising the glories of Carolina, and who, under the English king's bounty, persuaded several hundred German-Swiss colonists to settle here. In a few years, malaria had killed them or driven them to other sections. Purry's methods are described in Rousseau's *Confessions*.

At HARDEEVILLE, 134.2 *m.* (278 pop.), is the junction with US 17 (*see Tour 1c*). Here the main route becomes State 46.

PRITCHARDVILLE, 143.7 *m.* (50 pop.), is said to have been settled by an Ohioan who asked for a ticket to Levys, Georgia, but received one to Levys, South Carolina. Liking the section, he stayed instead of continuing to Georgia.

At 144.6 *m.* is the junction with a dirt road.

Right here 2 *m.* to the RUINS OF PALMETTO PLANTATION HOUSE, in a 14-acre garden with box-bordered walks. Recently bought by a company operating a pulp mill, the property is being reforested and will also be a game preserve.

At 149.5 *m.* on State 46 is the junction with a narrow dirt road.

Right on this road, which becomes a tunnel through myrtle, yaupon, young oaks, azaleas, and palmettos, to the SECESSION OAK, 0.5 *m.*, under whose vast limbs Daniel Hamilton is said to have made the first secession speech in this section.

A summer resort for inland rice planters in ante-bellum years, BLUFFTON, 149.7 *m.* (520 pop.), on State 46, is popular with writers and artists. Here the poet Henry Timrod taught school in the 1860's, and here the botanist Dr. Joseph Mellichamp is buried. A plant called deer tongue was formerly gathered here and shipped North for the manufacture of scents. During the War between the States Bluffton was almost destroyed by bombardment from a Federal gunboat. A detachment of Confederates arrived in time to save the small Gothic Revival EPISCOPAL CHURCH from destruction by fire.

1. Left from Bluffton on the Brighton Beach Road, 2 *m.*, to BRIGHTON BEACH, a small secluded summer resort. The cottages are all privately owned, but some may be rented.

2. Left from Bluffton on a white shell road to the junction with a woods road, 4.9 *m.*; R. here 1.1 *m.* to KIRK'S FOLLY, the name locally given to Rose Hill, the two-and-a-half-story, frame plantation house built by Dr. John Kirk. The entrance leads into a circular hall with winding stairway. Construction of the elaborate dwelling was stopped by the outbreak of war in 1861, and glass for a huge cupola was stored in an upper room. The place has recently been renovated as a clubhouse.

Tour 5B

Junction with US 21—St. Matthews—Junction with US 15—Eutaw Springs—Pinopolis—Moncks Corner; 51 *m.*, State 6.

Roadbed concrete-paved with sections of asphalt; unpaved between junctions with US 15 and Pinopolis.
No accommodations.

Along this route lie good farm lands, now being turned from cotton to other crops, and cut-over woodland, used for pasturage or planted with slash pines. The lower section, long called the Santee River Road, traverses St. John's Parish, Berkeley, settled after the Revolution by Huguenots driven from earlier homes in lower St. James's by Santee freshets and the decline of indigo. Now, more than 150 years later, their descendants are again threatened by flooding—this time from the upper lake basin of the Santee-Cooper Project.

State 6 branches southeast from US 21 (*see Tour 5b*), 0 *m.*, about 16 miles northeast of Orangeburg (*see Tour 5b*).

Live oaks heavy with moss line the sandy streets of ST. MATTHEWS, 2.9 *m.* (70 alt., 1,750 pop.), except in the main section, dominated by cotton warehouses. This old town, seat of Calhoun County, is beginning to recover from the destruction of its Sea Island cotton by the boll weevil. The Wannamaker family, long interested in the improvement of cottonseed, have lately encouraged the revival of the once-important Sea Island strain. This variety is now so rare that it may be planted under the Agricultural Adjustment Act without acreage allotment. The boll is soft and easily bored, but experiments are under way to develop a weevil-resistant type. St. Matthews, taking its name from an early parish, was first the site of a trading post on the Cherokee Path; the Palatine Germans arrived in 1730–40, clearing small patches for cattle enclosures and food crops. By the onset of the Revolution many large plantations had been established. Sea Island cotton came in shortly afterward, followed by the short staple crop that has since been the chief agricultural interest. After the boll weevil's advent, in 1920, decreased production was accompanied by decreased population; many farms were sold for taxes. A few inhabitants had had the foresight to plant pecan groves, or to raise cattle, hogs, and truck crops, all of which are now profitable. With the coming of pulp mills in the coastal section, pine trees were planted on cut-over acres. Nearly 200,000 little pines, obtained from State nurseries, were set out in 1938. Agricultural misfortune has not lessened the ability of St. Matthews' residents to enjoy life. Here are some of the best bird dogs in the State, and hunters who appreciate them. Deer and wild turkeys abound in the Wateree Swamp; fox hunting and fishing are time-honored occupations.

Left from St. Matthews on State 26 to a junction with State 267, 7.4 *m.;* L. here 2.5 *m.* to FORT MOTTE (125 alt., 464 pop.), a hamlet that grew up around the Revolutionary post. During the Battle of Fort Motte, British officers, protecting a large store of powder, were quartered in Mrs. Rebecca Motte's house. She and her family were compelled to occupy a servant's house on the estate. When the Americans approached she brought out some fire arrows given to her brother by a sea captain, urging her compatriots to destroy her home rather than permit the British to remain there. The Red Coats, realizing their danger, surrendered, and both Whigs and Tories scrambled up on the roof to jerk out the flaming darts before the fire could reach the powder.

On State 26 is LANG SYNE (L), 8.9 *m.,* home of Julia Peterkin, author of Negro stories and Pulitzer Prize winner. It was formerly the home of another South Carolina writer, Mrs. Louisa Cheves McCord.

The white frame house has a fine entrance with elliptical fanlight. The simple portico has four square columns and a fanlighted pediment. The gable roof is of green tile.

At 21.9 *m.* on State 6 is the junction with a dirt road.

Right here 0.5 *m.* to three LIMESTONE CAVERNS. Formed by subterranean streams, the caverns are believed to connect. Their low passageways make them difficult of access and they have not been extensively penetrated.

At 25 *m.* is a junction with US 15 (*see Tour 3b*).

At 37.4 *m.* on State 6 is the junction with a dirt road.

Left on this road to EUTAW PLANTATION, 0.6 *m.,* where the story-and-a-half clapboarded house above an arched brick foundation, built in 1808 by William Sinkler, is still owned by his descendants. Three dormers break the low-pitched roof line; wings added in 1820 and 1838 open on an encircling piazza raised on an arcaded basement. The placing of entrance steps to one side is character-istic of the Santee houses. The rooms, with handsome woodwork, are beauti-fully proportioned. Under the live oaks near the house stands a small lodge, built as a doctor's office, with pedimented portico and round wooden columns. The Eutaw Sinklers are noted horsemen and among the trophies in the house are an old costume, silver hunting cups, and a silver pitcher won in the Pine-ville races in 1839. Tilting tournaments at the Christmas season and the St. John's races in the spring are held here annually. Eutaw, like its neighbors, suffered during the era when it was the headquarters of General Hartzell's Union troops.

Cedar trees, characteristic of this lime soil, dogwoods, and live oaks cluster in EUTAW SPRINGS BATTLEFIELD PARK, 37.9 *m.,* where a granite boulder commemorates the battle, September 8, 1781. At the foot of a steep declivity, clear cold-water springs bubble up, forming a lake, colored green by the limestone bottom. General Nathanael Greene marshaled regular troops with militia under Marion and Pickens, to attack the British under Colonel Stewart. Greene hoped to prevent British forces from joining Cornwallis until Washington, aided by La Fayette, could complete his northern coup. Both sides claimed the vic-tory. The ragged, almost nude Colonials used their blankets for waist cloths and put moss under their belts and powder horn straps to keep the leather from cutting their flesh.

Left through the gates at Eutaw Springs on a woodland road to BELVIDERE PLANTATION, 1 *m.*, where in 1810 James Sinkler built his frame house with its twin entrance portals and high brick foundation on the site of one which had been burned. Overlooking some 30 acres of lawn and live oak grove, the big house, with its whitewashed slave quarters, old chapel for slaves, and outdoor kitchen with mortised joists, iron firedogs, and crane, presents a picture of ante-bellum prosperity. The bell that called the slaves to work and to 'nooning' still hangs near the garden gate. In the garden is a tangled Cherokee rose vine with enormous trunk and a sundial, measuring its second century, inscribed:

> Suns rise and shadows fall,
> Love reigns eternal over all.

On State 6 by the park is the junction with State 45.

Left on this road 2.2 *m.* to the junction with an avenue bordered with black walnut trees; R. on this avenue to WALNUT GROVE PLANTATION (*open by permission*), 0.6 *m.*, where James Gaillard built his ten-roomed two-story house of hand-hewn cypress about 1820. Of typical design, it has a wide piazza, double entrance, and elaborate interior woodwork.

At 2.8 *m.* on State 45 is the junction with a dirt road; L. on this road 1.3 *m.* to POND BLUFF, first granted to Francis Fludd in 1758, and acquired by General Francis Marion in 1773. After Marion's house burned in 1816, the present structure was erected, with dormers breaking the sloping roof and double front parlors opening on the piazza that looks out on the grass knoll with its cedar grove. The well proportioned rooms have some of the original furniture, and on the wall hangs a transcript of the childless Marion's will. He devised his place to a nephew who was to take the Marion name, but the document was improperly witnessed and Mrs. Marion bequeathed Pond Bluff to Keating Simons, whose descendants still own it. This is the site of an old Indian village; an Indian burial urn found here was given the Heye Indian Foundation of New York.

Marion (1732–95), the 'Swamp Fox,' was a small, swarthy Huguenot born at Chachan Plantation, Berkeley County. As a lieutenant in the Cherokee War, he learned the guerrilla tactics that disrupted British morale and helped turn defeat into victory after Charleston and Camden fell in 1780, and South Carolina was considered a conquered province. A romantic hero, his exploits, grown legendary with the years, live in William Cullen Bryant's 'Song of Marion's Men.' Devotedly followed by ragged boys, old men, and experienced fighters, Marion struck suddenly at British wagon trains, then disappeared to hidden bases, in swamps whose byways were unknown to the British. His men, without funds or uniforms, often with no ammunition but the bullets their womenfolk made by melting pewter, slept in the woods, ate whatever they could find or forage, and went home between encounters. Marion's wily strategy, and his unsurpassed system of espionage, made him the chief scourge of the British in lower South Carolina. When he was nearing 50, Marion married Mary Videau, his 47-year-old cousin, and settled at Pond Bluff. Tradition says that the general, unconquerable in battle, cowered before his wife's shrewish temper and adopted the precaution of pitching his hat through a window before entering the house. If the hat were batted out with a broomstick, he rode off to await a more propitious time.

At 4.5 *m.* on State 45 is the junction with a narrow dirt road; R. here 0.1 *m.* to THE ROCKS PLANTATION (R) where Peter Gaillard in 1797 raised a cotton crop that presaged his own and South Carolina's affluence. Noted as the first South Carolinian to grow cotton successfully, Gaillard, his indigo trade ruined in the Revolution and his first plantation near St. Stephens swept away by Santee floods, chose this safer land, naming it for the many limestone rocks that promised fertile soil. By 1803 he could afford to begin construction of his cypress house; slave artisans and white carpenters, cheered by rations of rum, completed the two-story edifice on its brick foundation in 1805. Notches in the piazza railing, serving as a rude sundial, are reputedly a souvenir of Gaillard's addiction to whittling.

At The Rocks entrance gates is the junction with a dirt road; L. here 0.1 *m.* to the junction with a wooded road. L. here 0.8 *m.* to SPRINGFIELD PLANTATION (*open Tues., Thurs., and Sun., 3 to 6 P.M.; adm. 50¢*). The big green two-story house of cypress, with its exterior and interior hand-carved moldings, was begun by Joseph Palmer in 1817. Above the double parlor mantels, carved panels with medallions and gauge work extend to the high ceiling. Treasured in the house are the carving tools used by the artisans.

At 0.7 *m.* on the wooded road is a junction with a dirt road; L. here 0.5 *m.* to MOUNT PLEASANT and LOCH DHU (R), adjoining plantations established on lands granted in 1741 to William Kirk, Scottish immigrant. The old Mount Pleasant house, burned about 1886, was soon followed by another, a two-story frame dwelling atop a green-swarded knoll with a live oak grove overlooking an artificial lake. In the old-fashioned garden near the lake is a camellia japonica believed to date from the early nineteenth century and measuring 70 inches in circumference at the base of the trunk. The house at Loch Dhu, 0.5 *m.* southeast of Mount Pleasant, was built in 1816.

At 12.3 *m.* on State 45 is the junction with a dirt road; L. on this road 1 *m.* to the GRAVE OF FRANCIS MARION on the former Belle Isle Plantation. Here Marion lived 15 years with his brother who, in 1758, built the house that is now a crumbling ruin. The granite monument stands within a wrought-iron fence in a grove of moss-hung crape myrtles.

PINEVILLE, 17.3 *m.* on State 45 (81 alt., 100 pop.), once a popular race track town, was settled about 1794. Near by are traces of an Indian mound and of an old quarry where Colonel Christian Senf (*see Tour 7A*) selected marl used in the construction of the Santee Canal (*see Tour 2b*).

At 20 *m.* is the junction with US 52 (*see Tour 2b*).

At 40.7 *m.* on State 6 is the junction with a dirt road.

Left on this road 2 *m.* to NORTH HAMPTON, once the home of General William Moultrie. The original house, built about 1716, was demolished by the British; a second, burned in 1846, was rebuilt. Moultrie (1730–1805), the son of Dr. Hugh Moultrie, a Scottish physician, at the age of 19 married an heiress, Elizabeth Damaris St. Julien, and became a planter. Like others of his family he had held office under the crown, but at the outbreak of war he took the American side, though his brother remained a loyalist. As colonel of the second South Carolina regiment, he commanded Fort Johnson in September 1775, and in June 1776, Fort Moultrie (*see Tour 1b*). After the Battle of Fort Moultrie he was captured in the surrender of Charleston, and imprisoned for two years; later he was made a major general. He served in the Provincial Congress 1775-6, and as governor 1785-7 and 1792-4. In 1779 he married his second wife, Hannah Motte Lynch, daughter of Jacob Motte and widow of Thomas Lynch. In 1783 he became first president of the Cincinnati Society of South Carolina. His *Memoirs of the Revolution* were published in 1805.

PINOPOLIS, 46.5 *m.* (88 alt., 210 pop.), was established as a summer retreat among the pines by owners of South Carolina's oldest plantations. Its repose has recently been shaken by construction of the huge powerhouse rising (1940) by the old Santee Canal (*see Tour 2b*). The town will be a terminus of the 7- or 8-mile-long dam that will divert Santee River into an immense lake for the Santee-Cooper hydro-electric project. Here the water will flow through a controlled outlet into the Cooper River. In the powerhouse, 300 feet long and 160 feet wide, huge generators and turbines will convert the water into electric power. One hundred and ninety-six thousand cubic yards of concrete will go into the construction of the house and lock; 3,700,000 cubic yards of earth will be used to make the dam.

In Pinopolis is one of the two Negro Reformed Episcopal churches in the State.

MONCKS CORNER, 51 m. (55 alt., 623 pop.) (see Tour 2b), is at the junction with US 52 (see Tour 2b).

✿✿

Tour 5C

Beaufort—Ladies Island—Frogmore—St. Helena Island—Frogmore; 33.2 m., State 285 and unmarked county road; Loop Tour.

Roadbed asphalt-paved to Frogmore; remainder improved.

As early as 1525 Spaniards explored the sea islands that make up Beaufort County, and French, English, and Scottish attempts to claim them followed. The section, though unusually beautiful, is not thickly populated. Along the route are remnants of plantations evacuated by Carolinians when Yankees plundered the area, little Negro cabins in flat gray fields, old forts, and the first Southern school opened for ex-slaves by Northern philanthropists.

State 285 branches east from US 21 at the end of Carteret Street in BEAUFORT, 0 m. (21 alt., 2,776 pop.) (see Beaufort).

LADIES ISLAND, 0.5 m., was claimed by the Spanish on Our Lady's Day in 1525 and the English retained the name in translation. Completion of the bridge in 1927 established overland connection between the island and the mainland.

At 1.9 m. is the junction with a dirt road.

Right here 1.8 m. to BURCKMYER'S BEACH, a resort given to Beaufort in the early 1900's by the trustees of old Beaufort College (see Beaufort).

At 2.9 m. is the junction with a dirt road at a country store.

Left here 0.3 m. to a shell road. Left 0.2 m. to LADIES ISLAND OYSTER FACTORY, where a few vegetables and many oysters are packed for shipment to Northern and Eastern markets. Oysters were appreciated here before the coming of white men, as piles of shells left by the Indians attest. These were once used in constructing Beaufort County's glistening white roadbeds; factories now grind the shells for chicken feed or sell them for fertilizer. Oyster beds, scattered for miles along the shore, are leased by the State to canning companies and are subject to governmental inspection. Gathered from company boats with a 'grab' or hook, the oysters are paid for by the bushel, 200 bushels usually being brought in at a time. At the factories Negro women, hands bandaged against sharp shells, remove the oysters after steaming. Carefully sorted, they are washed and put into cans of salt brine, for sealing, processing, labeling, and shipping.

At *2.2 m.* on the main side road is the junction with another dirt road; L. *2 m.* to CUTHBERT POINT, a two-and-a-half-story white frame clubhouse. Erected in 1931 among oaks and camellias, it faces a broad stretch of salt river, and the town of Beaufort is visible in the distance. A double-deck piazza flanks three sides of the house; at the rear is an enclosed swimming pool. The original plantation house near by, a one-story frame on a high basement, has a hip roof, flared entrance steps, and square columns on its brick-piered piazza.

The bridge and causeway, 5 *m.*, is the only overland entrance to ST. HELENA ISLAND (pronounced S'int Hellena), largest of Beaufort County's 65 islands—18 miles long and 4 to 6 wide. Catholic Dons under Quexos gave the name Punta de Santa Elena to the island; the English stretched it to include the sound, island, and parish. Planters here became wealthy soon after Indians were subdued in 1715–18. In 1815, hearing of Napoleon's exile and fearing that their calm was to be disturbed, they wrote protests to the British Government, unaware that another St. Helena island existed.

When indigo failed as a commercial crop after the Revolution, long-fibered sea island cotton, introduced from the Bahamas, replaced it as a source of wealth. French silk mills often bought a crop before it was planted. This cotton was bagged, not baled like other varieties. A planter's wife reported that cotton profits were 'mostly expended in the purchase of Negroes, and nothing is so much coveted as the pleasure of possessing many slaves.' Thus, slaves enormously outnumbered whites. When the latter, threatened by Union ships in 1861, hurriedly left the island with only the barest of personal possessions, thousands of Negroes remained, falling heir to the properties their white owners never saw again.

Behind the Union lines, Negroes forced an unexpected problem on the United States Government. Edward L. Pierce, a Boston lawyer, was selected by the Treasury Department to inspect the conquered territory and organize agencies to care for the Negroes. He conceived a plan fostering land ownership. Northern benevolent societies assisted with the work. The county was flooded with white teachers and missionaries sent to instruct the former slaves. Results were not immediately encouraging.

The island today is inhabited by a few whites and about 6,000 Negroes, descendants of the freedmen to whom the Federal Government sold tracts of land on the plantations where they had worked. Deeds to practically all Negro-owned lands in Beaufort County are still registered in the names of these ex-slaves; their children and grandchildren pay taxes in the names of the forefathers long since dead; their cabins are generally constructed from material of old slave quarters or 'big houses.'

The farm animals or 'critters' roam the countryside, foraging as they can. Most of them have no shelter, but a few are kept in 'critter houses' of poles and palmetto leaves. At planting time they are tied by one leg to a stake. Plows are drawn by the ox or the marsh tacky (said to be

African for 'horse'). These wiry little horses of St. Helena are believed by some to have deteriorated from fine plantation stock, by others to have been introduced by the Spanish. They live mainly on marsh grass, running wild over the islands between seasons of work. Two-wheeled carts, pulled by tackies or oxen, are still the means of conveyance, but a few automobiles have come in with the completion of bridges. Roads are very narrow, and it is a matter of everyday courtesy for one vehicle to pull aside to let the other pass. A long bow, a quick smile, and a friendly greeting are characteristic of a 'mannussuble' or well-mannered Negro, even though he has never seen the person he meets.

Many studies have been made of the customs of these isolated St. Helena Negroes, of purer African blood and tradition than any other Negro group in America. Very few outsiders have settled here, and there has been no intermixture with whites. The area has depended entirely upon natural excess of births over deaths for its increase. The Negroes speak a queer jargon, practically unintelligible to strangers. Called 'Gullah,' it is an intermingling of simplified English, archaic English, and a few African expressions. Characteristic of the speech is the use of 'he' for he, she, or it; 'um' for it, her, him, or them; nouns and adjectives as verbs, as 'pleasuring' oneself. The island folk are also noted for their music, particularly spirituals. Contrary to popular belief, these are generally sung in unison. The spirituals are constantly changing, and now show many traces of contact with white people. Superstitions still have a vital part in the folkways of these Negroes—with belief in healing rites, conjures, and ghostly visitation.

FROGMORE, 7.2 *m.*, a crossroads group of stores, named for a neighboring plantation, is 'The Corner.' Island roads are bad, but if visits are desired to the two Sams family seats, a tabby chapel, and a cemetery, permission may be obtained at 'The Corner' where the caretaker lives.

At the first store is the junction with a dirt road.

Left on this road to DAWTAW or Datha, 1.4 *m.*, named for a giant Indian chief who roamed the coast lands.

INDIAN HILL (L), 8.7 *m.*, said to be a burial mound, is called 'a mountain' by the Negroes, few of whom have been out of the flat island country. Tradition preserves the account of an old Indian chief's funeral here. The sachem's body was strapped to his favorite horse. The tribe danced around in funeral rites, each member throwing a handful of sand upon the figures until both were entombed and the 'mountain' raised.

The winding road is deeply rutted in sand and crosses numerous tidal rivulets. In summer the wild phlox spreads a varicolored carpet over uncultivated fields, and the aroma of sweet myrtle is brought in by the ocean breezes. The little schoolhouse in the fork of the roads, 14.4 *m.*, one of the landmarks of St. Helena, serves as a point of reference in reaching other sites.

Left from the fork on the main side road is a junction with a dirt road, 1 *m.*; R. on this road, crossing Harbor River and Johnson Creek to HUNTING

ISLAND STATE PARK, 1 *m.* A 5,000-acre tract is being developed with land and water recreational facilities for whites and Negroes. A wild life sanctuary is maintained, and a section of the island is leased for private vacation cottages.

In a wide lawn on the main side road is COFFIN POINT, 1.7 *m.*, with its yellow frame house of two-and-a-half stories on a high basement. It faces the water front, and the land approach is at the rear of the house. A two-deck six-column piazza is reached by a double flight of steps. Variations in the usual design probably indicate additions to the original building. The small dormers with exquisite detail probably belong to the pre-Revolutionary structure. The unoccupied Coffin place was purchased by one of the first Northerners buying property in this section after 1865. Annually it receives a coat of 'Colonial yellow' paint, in accord with the will of the owner to whose estate it still belongs. Right of the avenue approaching the house is a Negro cemetery, one of many hereabouts. There are a few low marble stones, but more conspicuous are possessions of the deceased—medicine bottles, lamps, razors, spectacles, and even a mustache cup. Penalty for 't'iefing' (stealing) any of these articles is pursuit by the dread 'plat-eye,' which may be a fiery eye or some sort of animal that never vanishes until vengeance is achieved.

COFFIN POINT EGG BANK, 2 *m.*, reached from Coffin Point by water ($1 *for Negro guide and boat*), is on an island of 10 acres, where the eggs and young of sea birds cover the ground in May and June. The colony often contains as many as 15 varieties, whose calls are deafening as they darken the sky in fluttering crowds.

FROGMORE PLANTATION (L), 19.5 *m.*, belonged to William John Grayson, ante-bellum writer (*see Literature*). The white frame house has a two-story piazza supported by six columns and is surrounded by a large grove of pines, oaks, native magnolias, and other trees.

The white frame FRIPP PLANTATION HOUSE (L), 20.4 *m.*, built shortly before the War between the States, is one of the finest Georgian Colonial houses in the Beaufort region. Characteristic plantation features are the piazza and projecting stair well. The entrance, with elliptical fanlight and side lights, leads to an interior having elaborately carved ceiling molds, panels, and niches, a curved stairway, and a central hall containing an arch and pilasters.

On the Barnes property, 25.4 *m.*, is FORT FREMONT (*open by arrangement*), built with massive concrete bastions and gun-emplacements during the Spanish-American War. Bats rustle through unused subterranean passages, and snakes glide out into the light.

At the Barnes property is the junction with a dirt road (R) which becomes the main route.

The tabby RUINS OF OLD WHITE CHURCH, 31.6 *m.*, shine stark and white. Erected years before the Revolution as a Chapel of Ease of St. Helena Parish, for the convenience of plantation owners situated too far from Beaufort to attend the church there. It was destroyed by a forest fire after 1865.

The first school opened for Southern Negroes by Northerners was the PENN NORMAL, INDUSTRIAL, AND AGRICULTURAL SCHOOL, 32.4 *m.* Founded in 1862, soon after the Federals took the island, it was operated for more than 40 years by Laura Towne and Ellen Murray of Philadelphia. Privately endowed, the school provides training in agriculture, homemaking, and hygiene. It sponsored the first South Carolina agricultural co-operative agency, and its influence among island

Negroes increases with the years. Probably the most widely known of South Carolina Negro schools, Penn has been the model for four institutions in South Africa. The plant consists of the workshop, the South Carolina State Teachers' Home, a dormitory, and other buildings. The workshop, where tanning, basketry, carpentry, shoe repairing, and wheelwright craftsmanship are taught, is of white concrete with red tile roof and dormers. A small Doric portico is in front.

At 33.2 *m.* is Frogmore (*see above*), 7.2 miles east of Beaufort.

Tour 6

(Rockingham, N. C.)—Cheraw—Camden—Columbia—Aiken—(Augusta, Ga.); US 1. North Carolina Line to Georgia Line, 171.3 *m.*

Seaboard Air Line Ry. parallels route between Cheraw and Columbia, Southern Ry. between Columbia and Batesburg.
Roadbed concrete-paved.
Tourist accommodations at short intervals; hotels in cities.

US 1, the Jefferson Davis Highway, follows the fall line across the middle of South Carolina. Tufts of wiry grass, low bushes, shortleaf pine and blackjack oaks grow along deep sandy ridges. For years this poverty-stricken strip was relieved only by the presence of the State capital and a few resort towns; now much of the land is planted with orchards, berry farms, and vineyards. Most noticeable along the highway are acres of low peach trees in curving rows—fragrant and pink in spring, crowded in summer with pickers and their baskets. At roadside stands peaches, berries, and grapes are sold in season.

Section a. *NORTH CAROLINA LINE to COLUMBIA, 97.8 m.*
US 1.

This section of the route traverses an area where small Colonial resorts harbored Low Country plantation families during the summer months, and Revolutionary forces fought running battles through neighboring forests. The lands, once considered almost worthless, now benefit from State and Federal experimentation in agriculture.

US 1 crosses the NORTH CAROLINA LINE, 0 *m.*, about 12 miles southwest of Rockingham, North Carolina.

At 7.6 *m.* is the junction with State 9 (*see Tour 21a*), which unites briefly with US 1.

CHERAW, 9.5 *m.* (145 alt., 3,775 pop.), settled *c.*1752 by Welsh folk from Pennsylvania, shows the influence of these home-loving people. The number of trees, in four rows along some of the broad streets, is explained as the result of an old town law that required anyone seen intoxicated in town to bring and plant a tree from the woods. The uniformity of size and spacing suggests that some settlers anticipated occasions of frailty and planted their quota in advance.

When by the Act of 1768 South Carolina was divided into seven judicial districts, this area became the District of the Old Cheraws. South Carolina's claim as to the origin of 'lynch law' is recounted here. The judge advocate at courts-martial for the forces commanded by Revolutionary General Nathanael Greene, camped near by, was Colonel Charles Lynch of Virginia—whose arbitrary judgments gave his name a sinister significance.

In 1819 Cheraw's population was only 35, but by 1823 it had 250 houses and more than 800 inhabitants. Between these dates, the Big Pee Dee River had been opened for traffic, largely owing to the efforts of General D. R. Williams (*see Tour* 3), and team boats, pole boats, and steamboats brought to Cheraw produce from both Carolinas. Captain Moses Rogers, who in 1819 made the first transatlantic crossing using steam power in the sailing packet *Savannah,* lived here after his ship had burned, and commanded a steamer plying the river between Cheraw and Georgetown. In 1820 he built his own steamer, the *Great Pee Dee,* but on its maiden voyage he contracted yellow fever and died aboard ship. He was buried in St. David's Episcopal churchyard.

ST. DAVID'S EPISCOPAL CHURCH, First and Church Sts., built 1770–3 and named for the patron saint of Wales, is a small frame edifice. In its square tower are three arched windows, one above the other, each set below a balustraded deck. During the Revolution the British used the church as a smallpox hospital; 50 who died here are buried in one grave in the shady yard. The cemetery contains the graves of James H. Thornwell (1812–62), Presbyterian theologian and president of the State university, and of Bishop Alexander Gregg (1819–93). The Confederate monument was erected in 1867.

About 1824, local Baptists and Presbyterians both wanted to hold services in St. David's. One Sunday, with the Baptists in possession, Presbyterians loaded and fired an old Revolutionary cannon. Consternation ensued; the Baptist preacher hurriedly dismissed his congregation and fled. Later, Episcopalians occupied the building, and the Presbyterian preacher responsible for the cannon episode wrote ruefully: 'While the lion and the unicorn were fighting for the crown, up came the puppy dog and knocked them both down.'

OLD MARKET HALL, Market and Second Sts., built in 1836 as the town hall, is now the city court. Two stories high, the lower of stuccoed brick, the upper of frame covered with white clapboards, the building is topped with a square cupola supporting a flagpole. A second-story piazza supported by four columns juts out over the sidewalk, sheltering the leisurely occupants of benches and chairs.

In the square two-story McKay House, southwest corner Kershaw and Third Sts., La Fayette was entertained in 1825. Built in 1820, it has a flat balustraded roof. The entrance portico, with octagonal posts, has a modillioned cornice and a flat roof that forms a balustraded second-story porch. The entrance doorway, with elliptical fanlight and ornamental architrave, is repeated on the second floor. A side portico is identical with the one on the front except for its round, tapered posts.

The Hartsell House, 143 McIver Ave., a two-story white frame dwelling with wide six-columned piazza, was built about 1780 of hand-hewn timber; it contains a fine collection of old furniture and china. General Sherman used the house in 1865.

In Cheraw are junctions with State 9 (*see Tour 21a*) and with US 52 (*see Tour 2a*), which unites southward with US 1 to a western junction (*see Tour 2a*) at 11.8 *m.*

The 700-acre CHERAW STATE PARK (L), 13 *m.*, has a ten-acre lake.

PATRICK, 22.8 *m.* (223 alt., 250 pop.), has three naval stores plants, from which tar, rosin, and turpentine are shipped.

At 27.4 *m.* is the junction with an improved dirt road.

Right here 3 *m.* to a dirt road; R. here 0.5 *m.* to another dirt road; R. here 1.3 *m.* to high timber-covered sand hills called Sugar Loaf Mountain (R), and, behind it, Horseshoe Mountain, the former looking as though it had been scooped out of the latter. Center of the Sand Hill Development Project, a game, fish, and forest preserve of nearly 100,000 acres, Sugar Loaf's summit offers a wide view of the area.

A shipping point in a fruit-growing district, McBEE, 37 *m.* (473 alt., 500 pop.), came into existence in 1900 when a barbecue was held and lots sold at auction. Efforts of the Seaboard Air Line to stimulate the production of crops that would increase freight turned cotton and corn farmers of this section to the cultivation of fruit. Fine quality grapes from local vineyards are sold almost exclusively to North Carolina wine makers.

In McBee is a junction with State 151 (*see Tour 3a*).

In CAMDEN, 65.5 *m.* (22 alt., 5,183 pop.) (*see Camden*), is the junction with US 521 (*see Tour 4*).

At 67.2 *m.* is the junction with a dirt road.

Right here 0.5 *m.* to a gate; beyond the gate 0.5 *m.* (*accessible only on foot*) to an Indian Mound, about 30 feet high and 160 feet in circumference, overgrown with low bushes. Indian artifacts and several old European coins have been discovered during excavations.

The Forest Tree Nursery (L), 67.3 *m.*, first of the State commission of forestry's experimental reforestation plots, was established in 1930.

From the basin of the Wateree, US 1 climbs to a high ridge of the Sand Hills. George Washington traveled between Camden and Columbia in May 1791, and from his lumbering coach looked out on 'the most miserable pine barren' he had ever seen. Stretching to the horizon are sandy troughs and crests, dunes of an ancient beach, overgrown with scrubby blackjacks and pines, scattered with ponds fed by springs or wet weather streams. Unpainted shacks crouch in the hollows for protection against the winds that drive sand through every crevice. Here live the Sand Hillers, who lead a precarious existence and are often victims of pellagra.

A few of these families have straggly peach orchards, and in summer they gather the fruit, often green and wormy, to haul it in mule wagons or Model T's to the Columbia Curb Market. Sometimes the Sand Hill women find it pays better to take the blossoms to market; one of them said she made $3 on her blossoms, and that was more than her peaches would have brought for the season. In winter, kindling wood is brought to the Curb Market dealers, or hawked along the streets. To the Sand Hillers is attributed a song, each verse ending dolefully: 'I'm selling kindling wood to get along.'

Established in 1926, the SAND HILL EXPERIMENT STATION (R), 83 m., under supervision of Clemson College, seeks through research and practical experimentation to improve the productivity of these lands.

SESQUI-CENTENNIAL STATE PARK, 87.1 m., named to commemorate the 150th anniversary (1936) of the founding of Columbia, contains a lake surrounded by pines.

At 93.2 m. is the junction with a dirt road.

Right on this road 1 m. to a large wholesale MULE MARKET, which sells six to eight thousand mules a year. Much of the stock is brought from Midwestern States.

At 95.6 m. on US 1 is the junction with a dirt road.

Right on this road 0.2 m. to the junction with another dirt road; L. 0.2 m. to the KENDALL FARM, where the owner breeds waterfowl that bring him top honors in national shows. Within the wired-off area, three ponds reflect flowers and the traffic of swans and geese; pheasants, wild turkeys, and chickens of many varieties have their own yards; brown native deer and white English fallow deer run free in a wooded tract. The one-story white frame building at the far end of The Farm, now a pleasure lodge, was formerly the office of Dr. Elias Marks, founder in 1828 of the South Carolina Female Institute. The neighborhood was named Barhamville for Jane Barham, Marks's first wife, and the college was familiarly known by that name. Existing until 1865, Barhamville maintained a high classical standard and enrolled as many as 200 students from Southern States. Its music department produced Sallie McCullough, a well-known opera singer of her day. Among the school's best-known pupils were Martha ('Mittie') Bulloch, who became the mother of Theodore Roosevelt, and Ann Pamela Cuningham (see Tour 17). In 1869 fire destroyed the entire plant with the exception of Dr. Marks's office.

The highway is edged by an almost unbroken line of residences.

In COLUMBIA, 97.8 m. (312 alt., 51,581 pop.) (see Columbia), are the junctions with US 76 (see Tour 9b), US 21 (see Tour 5b), and State 215 (see Tour 18).

Left from Columbia on Lower Main Street, which becomes State 48, to the entrance (R) of BUXTON BROTHERS' STABLES, 1.5 m. (visitors not allowed in *railed-off areas).* Here have been trained some of the world's most famous horses: Sun Beau, winner of more than $370,000; Seabiscuit, greatest money maker of all time; Bold Venture, winner of the Kentucky Derby and the Preakness in 1936; Cavalcade, winner of the Kentucky Derby in 1934; Pompoon, winner of the Belmont Futurity in 1937; Columbiana, named for the South Carolina capital, winner of the Widener Handicap in 1937; Kayak II, winner of the Santa Anita Handicap in 1939; and Stagehand, winner of the Santa Anita Handicap and Derby in 1938. The property is part of the fair grounds, leased from the State Fair Association, and its low frame stalls, offices, storehouses, and quarters for employees are painted brick red trimmed with white. Early spring brings bustling activity to the farm. Seven days a week each horse is put through his routine and nothing but illness or a rare spell of bitter weather can upset this program. An easy pace is set for early workouts; but later in the season the horses are 'breezed' around the track, counterclockwise, and urged to better their previous speeds. Sticking to the inside rail, jockeys bend low over the straining necks of their mounts, whispering or shouting words of encouragement. As each horse streaks by the post a trainer glances at his stop-watch.

The day's training period, beginning at sunrise, may last until 10:30 or 11. After midday, when most employees' chores are done, the shadeless farm assumes a quiet and peaceful aspect. The horses are left alone—except for feeding and watering, or inspection by a trainer or superintendent. Trainers and jockeys find their chief recreation in track and polo events at Aiken and Camden. Two noticeable characteristics of the training farm are its cleanliness and the presence of numerous pets—dogs and cats of nondescript breed that supposedly exert a soothing influence on the high-strung horses.

Section b. COLUMBIA to GEORGIA LINE, 75 m. US 1.

Between COLUMBIA, 0 *m.*, and the Savannah River, the highway skirts the upper edge of the Sand Hills. Barren lands give place to forests and fields planted with a variety of crops; sedate old towns and communities have made room for manufactories.

The Gervais Street Bridge, under which the Broad and Saluda Rivers from the north meet to form the Congaree flowing south, connects Columbia with WEST COLUMBIA, 1.3 *m.* (243 alt., 1,772 pop.), known until 1938 as New Brookland. Columbia mill workers live here. Few streets are paved except at the center of town. One- and two-story clapboarded houses in small yards are shaded by old oak trees. The entire population is white, the last lone Negro having died in 1936. Many palmists and crystal-gazers living here draw trade from Columbia.

In West Columbia is a junction with State 5 (*see Tour 5A*).

At 2.4 *m.* is the junction with US 21 (*see Tour 5b*).

From the site of GREEN HILL TOURIST CAMP, 2.7 *m.*, Sherman's batteries shelled Columbia on February 16, 1865.

LEXINGTON, 12.1 *m.* (359 alt., 1,152 pop.), seat of Lexington County, confines its business district to several blocks along the highway; old homes and bright new bungalows spread on each side. Lexington County's population is made up of thrifty farm owners, descendants of German settlers. Produce from this section finds ready purchase on the Columbia Curb Market.

In Lexington is a junction with State 6 (*see Tour 9c*).

Between LEESVILLE, 28.5 *m.* (1,540 pop.), and BATESBURG,

30.9 *m.* (660 alt., 2,839 pop.), is a joint public school. The towns have practically grown together. Both have coffin factories, and since the development of peach and asparagus culture, both have plants manufacturing boxes and crates.

In Batesburg is the junction with US 178 (*see Tour 15b*).

AIKEN, 58.7 *m.* (527 alt., 6,033 pop.) (*see Aiken*).

Left from Aiken on US 78 to MONTMORENCI, 6.4 *m.* (150 pop.), which, like most small towns roundabout, depends largely on the surrounding acres of asparagus for its livelihood. Bare in spring but for the stubby shoots poking through sandy soil, the fields are later spread with feathery 'grass.' About March 20, Negro workers begin gathering the crop, bending over long rows to cut the stalks beneath the surface. Shipment is made by truck and growers usually sell through co-operative marketing associations, that at Montmorenci being the largest in the State. South Carolina's crop was not introduced commercially until about 1900.

At 8.5 *m.* on US 78 is the junction with an improved dirt road; L. on this road 4.3 *m.* to the 100-acre AIKEN STATE PARK, spread along the banks of the South Edisto River.

WILLISTON, 22.5 *m.* on US 78 (1,024 pop.), headquarters for another asparagus-marketing association, has crate and box factories, necessary adjuncts to the increasing production of truck crops. The EDISTO EXPERIMENT STATION, 28 *m.*, was established by the State in 1937 to promote the production of watermelons, cantaloupes, cucumbers, and asparagus.

BLACKVILLE, 32 *m.* (296 alt., 1,284 pop.), named for Alexander Black, early railroad executive, ships cantaloupes, watermelons, and cucumbers in large quantities. During the 'cuke' season, beginning about May 20, the town council employs an auctioneer to conduct daily sales, generally starting at 10 in the morning and frequently lasting until 6. At the auction, growers may accept or refuse the offered prices. Buyers are generally local produce merchants, though there are often purchasers from markets out of the State.

In the line of Sherman's march to Columbia in 1865, Blackville shared the general devastation. During Reconstruction the town served sporadically as county seat, but so unsettled were the times that the sheriff in advertising sales announced they would be held 'at the courthouse,' hesitating to say in advance where the courthouse would be.

Right from Blackville on State 3 3 *m.* to BARNWELL STATE PARK (R), a tract of 250 acres with a little lake.

BARNWELL, 9.6 *m.* on State 3 (1,834 pop.), seat of Barnwell County, is a town of quiet dignity. Taken over by Sherman's men and consigned to the flames, it was given fitting valedictory. When General Kilpatrick invited the Barnwell ladies to dance, they took the invitation as a command. Proud and unsmiling, they went through the figures while their homes burned. The present courthouse serves as an unofficial social center. Townspeople meet there; on the portico under double wrought-iron stairways, nursemaids gather with their charges, their voices mingling with the click of typewriters from the open windows. In the courthouse yard is a sundial, its square face turned southward instead of skyward; it was presented to the town in 1828 by a wealthy eccentric. Barnwell was the center of mid-country plantation life and still has some handsome old houses. When the South Carolina railroad was first proposed, a line was surveyed through Barnwell, but slave owners refused to grant right-of-way for fear the trains would kill their young slaves and turkeys. They also contended that the noise of the steam engine would disturb the inhabitants of the neighborhood.

The community's most distinguished contribution to the Confederacy was General Johnson Hagood, who as governor from 1880 to 1882 gave the State one of the most tranquil administrations of its lively history. Asked if he wished to be called 'General' or 'Governor,' Hagood said, 'Call me General.

I fought for that and begged for the other.' In Reconstruction days the five Barnwell County legislators were Negroes; among them was Simon Coker, killed in the Ellenton Riot (*see Tour 19c*).

At 40.7 *m.* on US 78 is the junction with a dirt road; L. on this road 1 *m.* to VOORHEES INDUSTRIAL AND NORMAL SCHOOL FOR NEGROES, supported by the Episcopal Church but founded in 1897 by a Negro school teacher, Elizabeth Wright. From the six or seven day-students who paid 10¢ a week to attend classes on her back porch the enrollment has grown to more than 600 boys and girls with a faculty of 30. Officials of the school assert that no graduate has ever been on relief.

DENMARK, 41.1 *m.* (250 alt., 1,713 pop.), has the exchange for the main lines of both the American Telegraph and Telephone Company and the Southern Bell Company, which employs a large force of operators. Ticker-tape quotations, trans-radio broadcasts, Associated Press and United Press news, connections for radio network, both NBC and CBS systems, and radio photos from anywhere south of Denmark going north, or vice versa, pass over the telephone lines here.

At Denmark also is the office of a utilities company that distributes hydroelectric and steam-electric power to that section of the State, and is connected with the superpower system of the southeast at a point near Augusta. Three main lines come into Denmark—from Columbia, St. George, and Charleston. At Denmark is the junction with State 5 (*see Tour 5A*).

The business section of BAMBERG, 48 *m.* (163 alt., 2,450 pop.), seat of Bamberg County, lines the one main street; the rest of the town has grown lopsidedly to the northeast and surrounds CARLISLE FITTING SCHOOL, a military preparatory institution. Uniformed cadets crowd the drugstores on free afternoons. Bamberg County watermelons, waxed for preservation, are shipped to Europe. Another profitable venture in diversified farming is the auction of livestock, which benefits the entire section. Sales in 1938 amounted to $250,000.

Right from Bamberg 7.3 *m.* on State 36 to a dirt road; R. here 0.9 *m.* to CLEAR POND, by which, according to an unsupported tradition, the first submarine was built by a planter, Dr. F. F. Carroll. Clear Pond, almost circular, is the larger of two lakes, which together are called Crystal Pond and cover several hundred acres, their sandy bottoms visible at great depth. Surrounded by oaks, pines, and cypress, Clear Pond is a favorite place for picnicking and fishing, and formerly swimming, though alligators now have an uncontested monopoly in that sport.

WOODLANDS (R), 52 *m.* on US 78, in a dense grove of mossy oaks, was the ante-bellum home of William Gilmore Simms. Only the study in the yard (*open*) and one wing of the house escaped burning in 1865 by stragglers following Sherman's army. The 10,000-volume library went up in flames with the dwelling and outbuildings. An upper story was added to the wing and the building is now rented as a hunting lodge. Born in Charleston in 1806, Simms was the moving spirit of a group that included William Cullen Bryant, Paul H. Hayne, and Henry Timrod. He wrote poetry, biography, geography, history, short stories, articles, novels, plays, political speeches, and orations without number. After the war he lived here for several years, but died at Charleston in 1870. He wrote as his epitaph: 'Here lies one who, after a reasonably long life, distinguished by unceasing labor, has left all his better works undone.'

BRANCHVILLE, 62 *m.* (125 alt., 1,689 pop.) (*see Tour 5b*), is at the junction with US 21 (*see Tour 5b*).

ST. GEORGE, 77 *m.* (102 alt., 1,639 pop.) (*see Tour 3b*), is at the junction with US 15 (*see Tour 3b*).

At 91 *m.* is a junction with US 178 (*see Tour 15b*), at a point 14 miles northwest of Summerville (*see Tour 1c*).

At 60 *m.* on US 1 is the junction with a dirt road.

Cities and Towns

Photograph by W. Lincoln Highton

MAIN STREET, LOOKING NORTH FROM STATE HOUSE, COLUMBIA

PENDLETON FARMERS' SOCIETY HALL (1826), PENDLETON

LIBRARY (1840), UNIVERSITY OF SOUTH CAROLINA

JAIL (1823), LANCASTER; Designed by Robert Mills

CLINTON MASONIC LODGE (1810), MARION

OLD MARKET HALL (1836), CHERAW

Photograph by courtesy of Sargeant Studios

PARADE AT FORT JACKSON, COLUMBIA

SENIOR PLATOON, CLEMSON COLLEGE, NEAR ANDERSON

Photograph by Robert Hufford; courtesy of Clemson College

Photograph by Carlisle Roberts

BEAUFORT ARSENAL (REBUILT 1852), BEAUFORT

JUNIOR-SENIOR DAISY CHAIN AT COMMENCEMENT, WINTHROP COLLEGE, ROCK HILL

FURMAN HALL (1851),
FURMAN UNIVERSITY, GREENVILLE

STATE AGRICULTURAL AND MECHANICAL
COLLEGE FOR NEGROES, ORANGEBURG

Photograph by W. Lincoln Highton

TEXTILE MILL VILLAGE, WINNSBORO

PYATT HOUSE (PRIOR TO 1791), GEORGETOWN

Photograph by Walter Connolly

MORGAN SQUARE, SPARTANBURG

CURB MARKET, COLUMBIA

Right on this road 1 *m.* to IRVIN COURT, a one-story frame house built before the War between the States by Chancellor Carroll and restored with Greek Revival additions by the present owner. The house was one of the first occupied by Aiken's early tourists, Charlestonians who annually fled the malaria of coastal summers.

A little log cabin (R), 60.2 *m.*, marks the entrance to EDGEWOOD. Built by Governor Andrew Pickens in 1831, it was also the home of his son, Governor Francis W. Pickens. The white frame house was erected at Edgefield and in 1928 was taken down for the 20-mile journey to this place. An old-fashioned garden surrounds it.

At 61.6 *m.* is the junction with a sandy road, the William Gregg Highway.

Right on this road 2.6 *m.* to GRANITEVILLE (215 alt., 2,560 pop.), where William Gregg, father of southern cotton manufacturing, in 1845 established a textile mill. Numbers of the old mill houses and one of the granite mill buildings are still in use. In the mill yard is a monument to Gregg, who came to Columbia in 1824 from what is now West Virginia, and within ten years built up a substantial fortune as watchmaker and silversmith. Later he moved to Edgefield where he became interested in a small struggling 'cotton factory,' Vaucluse, which, with his brother-in-law, he bought and put on a paying basis. In 1843 Gregg moved to Charleston as a silversmith in the firm of Hayden and Gregg, but retained his interest in cotton manufacturing. He believed that plants should not only begin with adequate capital and be self-sustaining, but have a surplus over current needs. Charleston capitalists became interested in his plan and he secured $300,000 to build the Graniteville mill, which continued to operate through the War between the States. Gregg, who traveled extensively in New England and Europe, wrote articles for the *Charleston Courier* on textile manufacturing, which were collected and published in pamphlet form.

Gregg, opposed to slave labor in the mills, pioneered in the employment of 'poor whites,' of whom there were some 50,000 in the State unable to support themselves. He successfully established a system of compulsory education long before the State attempted it; and his ideas on the prohibition of liquor are still in force. Today, if intoxicants are bought or sold on certain town plats, the area may revert to the mill company. Among the operatives are some whose families have been employed here for generations.

BATH, 68.5 *m.* (1,250 pop.), has textile mills and several kaolin refining plants.

At 69.2 *m.* is the junction with a dirt road.

Left on this road 1.5 *m.* to a KAOLIN MINE. Two granite millstones near by were once used to grind clay for manufacture. A wide strip extending from above Aiken to the Savannah River is one of the largest and purest sedimentary clay deposits in the country. Beds 5 to 45 feet deep contain an enormous quantity of high-grade kaolin and other clays. As early as 1765 this clay was shipped to European potters. About 30 mines and 7 refining plants are now in operation, employing more than 1,200 workers.

HAMBURG (L), 73.5 *m.*, today a mere dot on the map, was for a short time important as the terminal station of the Charleston-Hamburg Line, the longest passenger steam-railroad in the world at its completion in 1833. The town never quite fulfilled its purpose as a shipping point to divert trade from Savannah to the port of Charleston. In 1821 the State granted a $50,000 loan without interest, and $25,000 on the personal security of Henry Schultz, founder and promoter of the proposed town, which was to be mortgaged; but even this financial encouragement failed to maintain Hamburg's prosperity. In 1848 it was the center of slave trade, banned in Georgia. Factors in that State had only to cross the river into South Carolina to conduct their business.

About 1846 the word *gyascutus* was here introduced into regional language. It is said that a group of Virginia soldiers returning from the Mexican War had struggled as far as Hamburg with no funds, but a wealth of imagination. Here they advertised the exhibit of a fierce gyascutus, captured in the wilds of Mississippi and never shown before. Curious spectators paid $1 at the box office and gathered before a heavily curtained stage. Expectant silence was broken with a shriek: 'The gyascutus done broke loose! The gyascutus done broke loose!' The frightened crowd fled and the soldiers with their chimerical ally and the Hamburgers' money, beat a victorious retreat.

In the days when the value of bank notes was questionable, script from the old Hamburg Bank was readily accepted. The Hamburg Riot of 1876 was one of a chain of events resulting in the 'Red Shirt' organization and the restoration of white political supremacy in the State (*see History*).

The JEFFERSON DAVIS BRIDGE crosses the SAVANNAH RIVER, 73.5 *m.*, and the GEORGIA LINE, about 1 mile east of Augusta, Georgia.

✠✠✠

Tour 7

(Gastonia, N. C.)—Blacksburg—Spartanburg—Greenville—Anderson —(Athens, Ga.); US 29. North Carolina Line to Georgia Line, 116 *m.*

Roadbed concrete-paved.
Southern Ry. parallels route between North Carolina Line and Williamston.
Accommodations of all kinds available at short intervals; hotels in cities.

US 29 traverses South Carolina's most highly industrial area, where cotton mill villages seem to overlap each other. The mill village is not a civil or political unit, but merely a community of workers living in houses owned by a mill company. Such communities are sometimes within the limits of an incorporated town, sometimes in the country— but they are not themselves incorporated. They may consist of sordid shacks, all alike—or of well-designed brick cottages with lawns and shade trees. But good or bad, they cluster around the mill on which they depend for existence. Isolated mill villages were once common in the State, but are seldom found today except in a few mountain sections. A more usual position is on the edge of a large town where marketing facilities are good, but taxes lower than within the city. There are also towns composed exclusively of groups of mill villages. The superintendent of the mill is in charge of the village around it. He can hire and fire, receive tenants and turn them out. But he generally exercises his power with discretion, knowing that if he antagonizes employees he will get little co-operation. Houses rent for 25¢ to 50¢ a room weekly, lights and water are usually furnished by the company, and the more progressive mills provide gymnasiums, playgrounds, kindergartens, and other recreational facilities. Participation in these is voluntary, as mill workers resent interference with their private lives. Many older people regard all amusements not connected with church work as sinful, and permit themselves nothing more exciting than attendance at revivals and 'singing conventions.' When the mills are closed, workers are usually allowed to remain in their houses rent free; and even during strikes this is often the case. Interest in politics is keen, and mill workers vote freely when they feel able to pay the poll tax—though women often refrain from voting because 'it isn't a woman's place.'

Mill owners declare almost unanimously that the village system is a matter of necessity and not of profit. It is estimated that South Carolina mills have more than $18,000,000 invested in villages, with an annual upkeep cost of $1,500,000. Mill workers are often a wandering lot, or fresh from the mountains, with no capital or savings. The mill village provides a house and a place to work, with wages that seem large to tenant farmers who have had practically no cash income. The average weekly wage in 1938–9 was $13.92. The county furnishes police protection, with a local magistrate in charge, but the mill sometimes employs a special policeman called 'the outside man.' Each village has a fire crew with the master mechanic of the mill in charge of equipment. Children under 16 may not legally work in the mills, and the State's compulsory education laws are better enforced in mill villages than in the rural districts. In 1938 South Carolina passed a 40-hour-week law, but it was soon set aside for the national limit of 44 hours. When times are good, the machinery roars day and night, with three eight-hour shifts, and four hours on Saturday.

At 5:30 in the morning the mill whistle rouses the sleeping village. Women hastily cook breakfast—grits, coffee, fatback, puffy biscuits, and sometimes eggs. Overalled men sit down to the table with their womenfolk, who wear cotton dresses and rayon stockings, and have permanent waves. A few minutes later, at three warning blasts of the whistle, hundreds of men and women from 16 to 50—but most of them from 20 to 35—hurry to their places in the mill. The buzzing of spindles and clattering of looms, so deafening to the visitor, do not disturb the accustomed ear; nor do workers seem to mind the heavy close air. Some mill hands develop an affection for their machines. 'I shore love it,' said one man of his loom. 'This same one has belonged to me for 25 years or more. But I'm scared of it just the same—it'll bite me if I don't watch out.'

Bales of cotton are brought from the warehouse to the bale-breaker, which splits open the 500-pound bundle of lint. The cotton is sucked through a vacuum tube to the picker-room, where trash that escaped the gin is removed. Then it goes through the lapper and slubber, which form it into bands, first broad, then narrow. These are seized by the carder with its hundreds of little teeth that shape the lint into loose rolls, ready to be twisted by the spindles into tight, strong thread. Some of the thread is wound on bobbins for the woof, or cross-thread of the cloth. Young workers grab the full bobbins from the machines, and replace them with empty ones. In the slasher room the warp, or lengthwise thread, is dipped in starch and wound on drums. After the warp dries, the drums are attached to looms in the weaving room. The bobbins dart back and forth between the alternating threads of the warp, and the cloth is woven. The whole process is merely an intricate mechanization of the age-old craft of spinning and weaving. Negroes are employed about the warehouses, power plants, and grounds, but seldom operate machines. Women generally work the spindles and men the looms. The finished cloth is inspected by girls, and sent to the baling machines, where it is wrapped for sale. It is usually bleached and printed at another mill.

There are many pauses in the eight-hour shift, during which workers go out for a cold drink or a cigarette, some of the older women dip snuff and gossip, the young folks make dates, and the men discuss lodge affairs, politics, or 'the union.' When the noon whistle blows, everybody swarms home to dinner—fried meat, bread, coffee, fresh or canned vegetables—eaten to the blaring of a radio. The workers are in the mill again from 1 to 4 o'clock; the second shift then takes charge if business is good. Farm and factory are closely related in South Carolina, and the spirit of independence traditional on the farm is often retained in the mill village. But a vague boundary line has grown up. The mill worker, obedient to whistles and machines and economic authority, feels himself different. Once begun, the mill life is hard to escape. Marriages are early and large families the rule. A man needs children to support him when his eyes are too dim and his hands too stiff to tend the machines.

US 29 crosses the NORTH CAROLINA LINE, 0 *m.*, about 16 miles southwest of Gastonia, North Carolina.

When pioneer Stark established his trading post in ante-bellum years on the site that is now BLACKSBURG, 5.9 *m.* (766 alt., 1,500 pop.), it was called Stark's Folly, for the vicinity was desolate and the land appeared worthless. But Stark was a good salesman, and had soon persuaded numerous white neighbors to stake the surrounding acres. In 1886 a railroad company ran one of its lines by the post, bringing a boom to the scattered settlement that has developed into the flourishing little town of today. From ARROW HEAD FIELD have been gathered numerous artifacts of the Cherokee.

In Blacksburg is the junction with State 5 (see Tour 7A).

South of Blacksburg the Blue Ridge foothills merge with the Piedmont plateau, where busy little mill villages are separated by rolling farm lands and orchards.

GAFFNEY, 15 m. (799 alt., 6,827 pop.), seat of Cherokee County, is a textile manufacturing town and marketing center for farmers. On 'Sales Monday' the town resembles an Eastern bazaar; people gather from the surrounding countryside to trade eggs, butter, and livestock for brogans, coffee, and snuff. Held the first Monday in each month, the occasion was known for years as 'swap day,' 'trade day,' or 'bone yard day.' Like poor Jack in the old fairy story, some farmers bring a cow to the market and go home with things less useful than a handful of beans.

Previously called Gaffney's Old Field, the town was named for an Irishman, Michael Gaffney, who settled here in 1804. Hardly had the first little frame shacks been grouped around the crossroads, than promoters took over Limestone Springs, which they ballyhooed as the South's Saratoga. It was the heyday of mineral therapeutic treatment and plantation owners in the Low Country, plagued every summer by malaria, which they called 'country fever' and believed was caused by 'miasmas,' flocked here to drink the water. A $75,000 hotel was built in 1835, and the town assumed the characteristics of a gay resort. Wealthy patients paid through the nose for the sumptuousness to which they were accustomed at home; the corks of champagne bottles popped at night and race tracks were crowded in the afternoon. The town also became noted for its tilting tournaments, cockfights, and gander pullings, the last a cruel sport in which a plucked and greased gander was suspended in mid-air and exposed to competing horsemen who tried to snatch off its head while riding past at a hard gallop.

LIMESTONE COLLEGE, N. Limestone St., the State's oldest institution for the higher education of women, was founded in 1845 as a Baptist seminary. It now has about 500 students and is fully accredited.

On the landscaped campus are the library and the gymnasium, also eight brick buildings containing dormitories, classrooms, and two auditoriums. Cooper dormitory, the former Limestone Hotel, was built in 1836. The long narrow three-story building, with front piazzas across the central part of each floor, contains more than 100 rooms. Dr. Thomas Curtis, of Charleston, and his son William bought the old hotel in 1845 for the $10,000 mortgage due to the State Bank. It was remodeled in 1936–7.

A monument on the Carnegie Library lawn, N. Limestone St., marks the second GRAVE OF COLONEL JAMES WILLIAMS, who was killed at the Battle of Kings Mountain (see Tour 16) and buried in the Buffalo section of Cherokee County. In 1915, his dust was reinterred here. The monument's two howitzers, mounted on a granite foundation, are Con-

federate artillery captured in 1863 by Stevenson's Division, at Philadelphia, Tennessee.

In Gaffney is the junction with State 11 (*see Tour* 18).

Near THICKETTY, 21.5 *m.* (620 alt., 27 pop.), a name derived
from the area's dense vegetation, General Morgan and Colonel William
Washington camped their united forces at 'Gentleman Thompson's,'
on the eve of the Battle of Cowpens (*see Tour* 18).

On THICKETTY MOUNTAIN (R), in view from the road, are the
deserted iron mines that were factors in the early development of the
section and in the origin of its name, Old Iron District. Here the ore
was smelted and transported by wooden tramway to Glendale, to be
manufactured into nails, pots, pans, and other utensils that were peddled in covered wagons through the Carolinas and Tennessee. During
the War between the States, production was pushed to capacity, and
the machinery soon wore out. Scarcity of labor and money in the Reconstruction era caused abandonment of the enterprises.

COWPENS, 27.7 *m.* (1,115 pop.), was named for the cow pens of
Tory cattleman Hanna. In the State's early days when cattle raising
was lucrative, the pens were maintained commercially for the convenience of herdsmen driving their stock to Low Country markets. For
a reasonable fee drovers were allowed to pen their cattle in such enclosures along the way and break their tedious journey with a night's
sleep.

Rugged, steep CLIFTON, 30.2 *m.* (756 alt., 2,380 pop.), a settlement in three sections, lies on both sides of the highway. Each section
centers about a textile mill, Clifton One, Two, and Three, all part of
the Converse system. Winding roads lead through the neat villages,
past old-fashioned whitewashed cottages. A feature of the Clifton mills
is a terraced warehouse of stone, on a hillside; on each story a door
opens on a railroad track. The track is built so that the switching
engine can zigzag backward and forward, loading from each level in
turn.

Passing through here in 1795, Bishop Asbury commented, 'The
country improves in cultivation, wickedness, mills, and stills.' Five
years later, he held a meeting in the neighborhood and remarked that
he thought most of his congregation had come to look at his wig.

Across HURRICANE SHOALS, 31.6 *m.*, near the bridge span over the
Pacolet River, Jane Thomas swam her horse in July 1780 to warn
the Patriot camp at Cedar Spring of an impending Tory attack. Her
son, the commanding officer, was enabled to prepare a counteroffensive
that resulted in victory.

Down this valley in 1903 the Pacolet River roared in one of the
State's most devastating floods, which swept over villages and mills,
drowning more than 50 people.

CONVERSE, 32.2 *m.* (713 alt., 1,025 pop.), was named for Dexter
E. Converse (1828-99), a Vermonter who became interested in cotton
manufacturing in the South, served in the Confederate Army as a
private, and later founded Converse College.

In SPARTANBURG, 36.7 *m.* (875 alt., 28,723 pop.) (*see Spartanburg*), are the junctions with US 176 (*see Tour 12a*), US 221 (*see Tour 17*), and State 9 (*see Tour 21b*).

At 38.1 *m.* is the junction with a brick road.

Right on this road to the junction with a dirt road, 0.4 *m.;* L. on this road 1.1 *m.* to the TEXTILE INDUSTRIAL INSTITUTE, founded in 1911 by the Reverend D. E. Camak. The school, directed by the Board of Missions of the Methodist Church, is coeducational, has an enrollment of approximately 300, and is an accredited junior college. Fifteen cotton mills in the surrounding area co-operate with the school by providing part-time employment for its students while one permits the use of its plant for demonstration purposes. Besides its industrial course, the school offers a general cultural course that many students elect. Fifteen per cent of the ministers of the Upper South Carolina Conference of the Methodist Church have attended the school. One of its graduates, Olin D. Johnston, became governor of the State in 1935. Many others are public school teachers, especially in the industrial centers.

Between Spartanburg and Greenville, US 29, a double-lane concrete highway, carries more traffic than any other in the State. Industrial communities lie close together. Southwest of Spartanburg the route, with distant mountain views, follows a fairly straight line.

A drive on Ridge Road in LYMAN, 48.4 *m.* (850 alt., 1,765 pop.), reminds visitors of New England. Here live most of the Pacific Mills executives and office employees, many of whom came from Rhode Island. The former Spartan Academy, now Lyman Inn on Ridge Road, was attended by many of the older men in the community; the old administration building is the home of a Pacific Mills executive.

At 49 *m.* is the junction with unimproved Woods Fort Road.

Right on Woods Fort Road through a wood-lot Demonstration Area of the Soil Conservation Service to a junction with a dirt road, 3 *m.;* L. here 0.5 *m.* to the SITE OF THE HAMPTON MASSACRE. Anthony Hampton, a flax breaker, was the first of his name to arrive in South Carolina. In 1774 he brought from Virginia his wife, Betty, his daughter, Mrs. James Harrison, his sons, Wade, Preston, Edward, Henry, Richard, and one other, and his son-in-law, James Harrison. When efforts were made just before the outbreak of the Revolution to enlist Cherokee sympathies on the American side, Edward and Preston were sent as emissaries to the Indians. They found a British agent, Cameron, inciting Cherokee against the Patriots. He imprisoned the Hamptons and gave their horses and arms to the Indians. A few days later Anthony Hampton, unaware of hostilities, was killed by a Cherokee chief to whom he extended his hand in greeting. Mrs. Hampton, one son, and an infant grandson were also murdered. Other members of the family were absent, except a grandson, John Bynum, whom a chief took captive and held for many years. The house was burned. In a later battle led by Colonel Andrew Williamson against the Cherokee, Captain Henry Hampton killed an Indian wearing the coat of his dead brother. Five of Anthony's sons became officers in the Revolution. Edward was killed by a scout, 'Bloody Bill' Cuningham. Near the old Hampton spring are picnic grounds and a swimming pool.

The SITE OF WOODS FORT, 8.6 *m.*, is almost on the 'Old Boundary Line' separating Cherokee territory from that ceded to Governor Glen in 1755. The fort was used as a place of refuge from Indians. Tradition says that a Mrs. Thompson who was scalped in an Indian attack escaped to the fort and recovered.

GREER, 54.2 *m.* (1,000 alt., 2,419 pop.), a mill village that grew up on an old cotton patch, lies largely north. In 1873 the Richmond and Danville Railroad established a flag station on the land of Manning Greer, and progressive farmers in the neighborhood used it to ship their products. Development of a village was slow, however, until industrialists selected this as a site for a factory. The young people on the farms, who had seen their fathers hard-hit through lean cotton years, deserted the plow for the security of small but regular pay checks. The revolution grew, and today life in the community centers around its three textile mills. A consolidated school has 1,200 students.

TAYLORS, 58.7 *m.* (900 alt., 1,500 pop.), was formerly Chick Springs, a summer resort. It is being developed as a residential suburb of Greenville because of the wooded hillsides around the springs. The two plants of the Southern Bleachery, a concern finishing goods made elsewhere, employ most of the local working population.

The SITE OF CAMP SEVIER is at 64 *m.;* the place was named for John Sevier (1745–1815), a colonel in the Battle of Kings Mountain and the first governor of Tennessee. It was a training center during the World War, and soldiers from South Carolina, Georgia, and Tennessee made up the camp's Thirtieth Division, which took part in the breaking of the Hindenburg Line. Some of the cantonment buildings have been converted into warehouses; private homes have been erected on part of the grounds.

The SHRINER'S HOSPITAL (R), 64.3 *m.,* for crippled children, set on a slope covered by sweeping lawns, is a three-story red brick building with white pedimented portico and sun porches. Construction of the building was made possible by a gift from a Greenville citizen who was not a Mason. The hospital has established a high reputation for corrective surgery. Between this point and Greenville the highway is bordered by small cotton farms, most of them with unpainted dwellings, dusty and neglected.

In GREENVILLE, 69 *m.* (966 alt., 29,154 pop.) (*see Greenville*), are the junctions with US 25 (*see Tour 8a*), US 276 (*see Tour 10*), and State 13 (*see Tour 14*).

At PIEDMONT, 80.1 *m.* (819 alt., 1,374 pop.), the mill company has a museum of Indian relics, curios, and coins.

PELZER, 86 *m.* (850 alt., 3,315 pop.), one of the first Up Country textile towns to be developed by Low Country capital, was named for Francis J. Pelzer, who, with Ellison A. Smyth, both of Charleston, established the Pelzer Manufacturing Company in 1881.

Before the War between the States, WILLIAMSTON, 88.2 *m.* (817 alt., 2,235 pop.), was a fashionable health resort around a mineral spring. The town is named for West Allen Williams, the wealthy planter who owned this land. Williamston Female College, a Methodist school, was founded here in 1871 by Dr. Samuel Lander; it later became Lander College (*see Greenwood*).

In ANDERSON, 102 *m.* (754 alt., 14,383 pop.) (*see Anderson*), are the junctions with US 178 (*see Tour 15a*) and State 28 (*see Tour 19a*).

At 103 *m.* is the junction with State 80, asphalt-paved and formerly called the Dobbin's Bridge Road.

Right here to KEY'S SPRING LAKE (L), 1.2 *m.*, an attractive swimming pond. CEDAR SPRINGS LAKE (L), 2.1 *m.*, is in reality two fish ponds, where half a day's angling costs only a small fee.
At 8.5 *m.* is the junction with a dirt road; L. here 1.5 *m.* to the SITE OF ANDERSONVILLE, laid out by General Robert Anderson, at the junction of the Seneca and Tugaloo Rivers. Destroyed by flood in 1852, the town, once the chief Piedmont port for the pole boats that transported freight on the Savannah River, was never rebuilt. Around the prosperous commercial center were cotton mills, a wool factory, fashionable hotels, and private houses.

US 29 crosses the GEORGIA LINE, 116 *m.*, about 49 miles east of Athens, Georgia.

﹆﹆﹆﹆﹆﹆﹆﹆﹆﹆﹆﹆﹆﹆﹆﹆﹆﹆﹆﹆﹆﹆﹆﹆﹆﹆﹆﹆﹆﹆﹆﹆﹆﹆﹆﹆﹆﹆﹆

Tour 7A

Blacksburg—York—Rock Hill—Great Falls—Winnsboro; 88.6 *m.*, State 5, State 22.

Roadbed partly concrete-paved, partly asphalt-paved.
Southern Ry. parallels route between Blacksburg and Rock Hill.
Accommodations only in larger towns.

A list of the little communities along the upper sections of the road —Smyrna, Sharon, Ebenezer, and many others—reads like part of a Bible concordance. Formerly there was much activity around the Presbyterian meeting houses that gave name to the settlements. Just prior to 1800, several congregations burst into argument as to whether psalms or hymns should be used in their services; as a result, the supporters of David became Associate Reformed Presbyterians, and the followers of Isaac Watts continued as plain Presbyterians. Farming is the chief activity, though in some towns there are large mills.

State 5 branches east from BLACKSBURG, 0 *m.* (766 alt., 1,500 pop.) (*see Tour 7*), at a junction with US 29 (*see Tour 7*).

At SMYRNA, 8.3 *m.* (117 pop.), gold was formerly extracted by the 'shaft' method from the Bar Kat and Terry mines, but now they are operated only irregularly. Recently a tin mine, idle since 1899, was reopened by a corporation composed largely of local people.

HICKORY GROVE, 11.9 *m.* (318 pop.), is an old-fashioned settlement dependent on farming for a livelihood. The proximity of the Magnolia Gold Mine, no longer worked, has ceased to be exciting.

SHARON, 18.5 *m.* (324 pop.), grew up around a church of the same name. The congregation split off from Bullock's Creek Church near by, when the controversy over psalms was raging.

At YORK, 25.4 *m.* (720 alt., 2,826 pop.) (*see Tour* 16), is the junction with US 321 (*see Tour* 16).

The little village of EBENEZER, 37.9 *m.* (250 pop.), is connected with Rock Hill by an unbroken stretch of houses. EBENEZER CHURCH, of red brick with a gable roof and two battlemented corner towers, has a two-column entrance portico. The building, constructed in the 1890's, is the third for this Associate Reformed Presbyterian congregation, organized about 1785. Under its auspices an academy was conducted until the Rock Hill High School in 1891 absorbed the higher classes, leaving a grammar school here. Church and school were the center of a community which flourished until the 1850's. The Charlotte-Columbia railroad, attempting to lay tracks through the section, met with opposition from conservative farmers, and established the depot at Rock Hill —whereupon Rock Hill grew and Ebenezer declined.

A winding trail behind the church leads to a granite boulder bearing a depression the size and shape of a moccasined footprint. What sentimentalist would deny that an Indian girl, prevented by her irate father from running away with her white lover, had strength to stamp her foot on the rock, leaving an eternal sign of love to encourage Sunday strollers? The lover, recognizing her footprint, placed therein a few beads—token of his affection. Finding the beads, she waited; he returned—playing his violin. Tribesmen, following her, fled in terror from the mysterious sounds of his fiddling, and the lovers departed to find happiness in the land of romantic legend.

In ROCK HILL, 40.9 *m.* (690 alt., 11,322 pop.) (*see Rock Hill*), is the junction with US 21 (*see Tour* 5a).

At Leslie, 47.6 *m.*, is the junction with a gravel road.

Left here 3.5 *m.* to a dirt road; R. 1.1 *m.* to another dirt road; L. 0.3 *m.* to the CATAWBA INDIAN RESERVATION, known locally as the Nation. Here, on 652 acres of poor soil, the only Indian wards of the State live in 34 small frame houses, sometimes three families to a house. Of the 216 remaining Catawba, few are pure blooded; only former Chief Sam Blue and two others speak the Catawba language; the customs of their forefathers have been almost completely abandoned. Pottery making is the only ancient skill to survive: with primitive instruments the women mold pitchers, flower jars, bowls, and pipes in traditional forms of turtles and ducks. A few men find occupation in mills and garages in Rock Hill, some fish and hunt, others attempt to raise corn on the scant bottom lands—the only arable part of the reservation. One lone mule labors in the corn fields, other cultivation being by hand. Anemic vegetable gardens, scrawny chickens, and bony-rumped cows contribute their part to the nourishment of these once-rugged warriors. Mormon missionaries, who built a chapel in 1928, have received grateful co-operation from Chief Blue. Following the ideals of former chieftains, he insists upon sobriety and an ordered life in accord with Mormon doctrine. A two-teacher school, supported from the annual State allotment of $3 for each Indian, was established by Chief Blue, who has never learned to read or write. He has achieved an unprecedented recognition: the Rock Hill High School now admits Indian pupils— though no transportation is provided for the intervening nine miles. In late years the Catawba have numerically increased. The former steady decline can be ironically traced in part to their loyalty to their 'white brothers': they supported them in all wars, and furnished troops to the Confederacy. In return, the whites have expropriated the lands of the Indians, in spite of George Washington's promise of protection.

At 57 *m.* on State 5 is the junction with a dirt road.

Left here 3 *m.* to another dirt road; R. here 1 *m.* to LANDSFORD TOLLHOUSE AND CANAL, both of field stone. The tract, including an aboriginal ford, was granted to Thomas Land in 1754, and thus the place derived its name. Fort Taylor, a protection against hostile Indians, stood here in early days. As part of the inland navigation system from the Up Country to Charleston, a series of Catawba canals was begun in 1819 and was completed in 1823. Landsford Canal, the highest in the system, was built in 1823 by Engineer Leckie. The masonry is still strong and secure, though tall trees have grown in the bed of the canal, and with the years the river has changed its course. From an arched stone span the roar of the shoals is audible through the forest.

At FORT LAWN, 59.5 *m.*, is the junction with State 9 (*see Tour 21b*).

The road, gashed into the red soil of the rolling country, winds down to the valley of the Catawba River, to turn east on wide farming land.

At the SITE OF THE BATTLE OF FISHING CREEK, 64.5 *m.*, Sumter suffered one of his few defeats, August 18, 1780. Tarleton surprised the Gamecock's men, who had stacked arms after a tiring march. Sumter barely escaped capture, and became obsessed with the determination to avenge his reversal. After a series of skirmishes, he completely broke up the British camp at Rocky Mount.

Since the early part of the nineteenth century, GREAT FALLS, 69.6 *m.* (3,649 pop.), has been an important power center, and in 1849 had a cotton mill. Today three plants in the vicinity derive their power from the Catawba River, and generate electricity for about 150 towns and cities. The first cotton mill here opened with slave labor, and was destroyed in the War between the States; other early mills were abandoned or swept away by high waters. Today large factories make print cloth fabrics, fine lawns, shirtings, rayon, and silk-filled goods.

East of town, on a river island, are the RUINS OF FORT DEARBORN (properly Mount Dearborn) outlined by a weed-grown base of stone and logs. In 1794–5 a congressional committee recommended the erection of two arsenals in the Southern and Middle Atlantic States. In the hope of procuring an institution for South Carolina, General Sumter, who owned these lands, sold 523 acres to the Government in 1802, deeding them to 'Thomas Jefferson and his successors in the presidency.' The following year Eli Whitney and Colonel Senf, appointed to select a suitable site, accepted the deed; work was begun at once. The arsenal, named for Secretary of War Henry Dearborn, became a military post in 1812.

South of Great Falls the route follows State 22.

In the gardens of ROCKY MOUNT, 72.4 *m.*, is the unmarked GRAVE OF COLONEL JOHN CHRISTIAN SENF, one of South Carolina's most noted engineers. As a Hessian officer he fought under Burgoyne and was captured at Saratoga. Henry Laurens, learning of Senf's talents, secured his allegiance and later his service as chief engineer of the State. Senf died in 1806, aged 53, after planning and constructing numerous canals.

At 76.5 *m.* is the junction with a dirt road.

Left here 1.5 *m.* to another dirt road; L. here to CAMP WELFARE, 2.5 *m.*, owned by the African Methodist Episcopal Church. The organization, an outgrowth from a 'brush-arbor' camp meeting in the time of Bishop Asbury's fervid preaching (1785–1816), was set up shortly after 1865 when Negroes withdrew from white churches. They had previously attended white camp meetings, of which Indian Fields (*see Tour 3b*) is the only South Carolina survival. The 'arbor,' a roof supported by uprights, shelters several hundred worshippers, who wander in and out among the rough pine benches during the several daily services the last week in August. This week is in 'lay-by time,' which begins after cotton and corn have grown too thick for further cultivation, and lasts until harvest season. Surrounding the arbor is a flint-strewn oak grove, in which a circle of tents was first replaced by log cabins, then by board shacks, now blackened with age. Negroes travel many miles to the camp meeting, a number even returning from Northern States in big new cars—which do not seem ill at ease among the mule teams, lopsided buggies, and creaky Model T's of their stay-at-home brethren. Out-door cooking in spiders and iron pots is as much a pastime as a necessity, and courtship is stimulated by religious fervor.

At WINNSBORO, 88.6 *m.* (545 alt., 2,344 pop.) (*see Tour 5a*), is the junction with US 21 (*see Tour 5a*).

Tour 8

(Hendersonville, N. C.)—Greenville—Greenwood—Edgefield—(Augusta, Ga.); US 25. North Carolina Line to Georgia Line, 138.4 *m.*

Roadbed concrete-paved.
Georgia and Florida R.R. parallels route between Greenwood and Augusta.
Hotels and tourist homes in larger towns; few tourist camps.

US 25 unwinds in a blue haze from the Blue Ridge Mountains and cuts diagonally across the Piedmont to the Savannah River. Part of the roadbed coincides with the State Road begun under the supervision of Joel R. Poinsett (*see Tour 20*) in 1818–20 and called the Buncombe or Augusta Road in its upper stretches. White pines, spruce, and hemlock tower above the hardwoods of the mountain forests; rhododendron and mountain laurel bloom in spring; vineyards cling to terraced hillsides; and gnarled apple and peach orchards yield blossom and fruit in season. As the tour proceeds, the cottages of mountaineers, perched on steep inclines or snug in secluded valleys, give way to larger farm-houses standing in cottonfields on the red clay hills.

Section a. NORTH CAROLINA LINE *to* GREENWOOD, *82.4 m.*
US 25.

The upper part of the route passes through a sparsely inhabited region of tilted cornfields on rocky hillsides, and then among textile mills, large and small, that have changed trading corners and summer resorts into scenes of industry.

US 25 crosses the NORTH CAROLINA LINE, 0 *m.*, 11 miles south of Hendersonville, North Carolina.

The rock walls of POINSETT'S SPRING (R), 1.3 *m.*, 200 yards from the highway, were constructed by Poinsett about 1821.

The HILL BILLY SHOP, 3 *m.*, sells pottery made in both Carolinas, hooked rugs fashioned on the premises by mountain girls, and furniture and smaller inlaid objects manufactured by local craftsmen, who draw upon surrounding forests for more than 100 varieties of wood. People hereabout supplement their small cash resources by gathering winter-green or teaberry leaves to be shipped into North Carolina for flavoring a chewing gum made there.

The immense waterwheel of BALLENGER MILL (L), 7 *m.*, shakes the vine-covered building with measured rhythm.

At 7.6 *m.* is the junction with a dirt road.

Left on this road 1.8 *m.* to POINSETT BRIDGE, a massive stone culvert with pointed arch of rough wedge-shaped blocks whose construction was supervised by Poinsett in 1820. Of all bridges built under his direction, this is the best preserved. The keystone bears the date of construction.

At 22.1 *m.* on US 25 is the junction with a dirt road.

Left on this road 8 *m.* to GLASSY MOUNTAIN, so named because of its sheer rock face, which rises 1,000 feet from base to summit. During the World War, soldiers from Camp Wadsworth used the cliff as a backstop for their firing range. Columbus Hale, traveling in his carriage from Charleston to these mountains in 1805, described his impressions: 'The sun just rising gilded the world . . . and the reflection on the Glassy Mountain was beyond any description . . . Farms and settlements of different extent carpeted numberless acres, and although not pleasant to the eye of the lower countryman in their mode of erecting houses, being mostly built of logs, still there might be per-ceived a neatness within, which destroyed other impressions.' The mountain stands in an area known as the Dark Corner because of its isolation and the primitive ways of its inhabitants. As late as 1936, 22 pupils of Glassy Rock Mountain grammar school saw their first motion picture, radio, and barber shop when they took a trip to Travelers Rest.

At TRAVELERS REST, 22.3 *m.* (322 pop.) (*see Tour* 10), is the junction with US 276 (*see Tour* 10), which unites with US 25 for 8 miles (*see Tour* 10).

South of Travelers Rest the highway straightens out along a ridge where increased speed is hampered by slow-moving wagons, usually loaded with lumber or stove wood and driven by mountain farmers.

Cotton grows up to the corporate limits of closely grouped mill villages, and many inhabitants have left their farms to work in the mills. West Greenville has advantages of its adjacent city but is not incorporated in Greenville. Along the road are 'piccolo joints,' where city and mill village youths gather for dancing.

In GREENVILLE, 30.4 *m.* (966 alt., 29,154 pop.) (*see Greenville*), are the junctions with US 276 (*see Tour 10*), State 13 (*see Tour 14*), and US 29 (*see Tour 7*).

South of Greenville the highway is lined with the handsome houses and well-kept grounds of a fashionable suburban section that extends to the GREENVILLE COUNTRY CLUB (L), 33.4 *m.* (*greens fee, $2 weekdays, $3 others*). Here are a golf course, tennis courts, and a concrete swimming pool.

At 47.9 *m.* is the junction with a dirt road (*see Tour 10*).

At PRINCETON, 57.4 *m.* (183 pop.), an old settlement with a large consolidated school, is the junction with US 76 (*see Tour 9c*).

The road coasts down a steep incline to cross the red Saluda River, on the banks of which is WARE SHOALS, 65.1 *m.* (3,502 pop.), a mill community whose hands live mostly on farms within a radius of 35 miles; most of them are picked up at dawn by company busses. Thus, as in the days of the spinning wheel and the family loom, farm women convert the cotton they helped raise into thread and cloth.

Built about 1835, the frame VANCE GODBOLD HOUSE, 72.2 *m.*, is a typical rectangular farm dwelling.

At 73.6 *m.* is the junction with an asphalt road, State 246.

Left on this road 0.9 *m.* to COKESBURY (117 pop.), once a center of Methodist education. In the three-story frame building (R), with small square tower and four square columns supporting a pediment, was conducted the Masonic Female Collegiate Institute (1854–76) and the Cokesbury Conference School (1876–1911). In 1918 the building was bought by Greenwood County for a public school, and is now used for that purpose. Among distinguished alumni of the Conference School and its predecessor, the Dougherty Manual Training School for Boys (founded in 1836 and conducted in a building no longer standing), are Ellison Capers (1837–1908), bishop in the Episcopal Church and brigadier general in the Confederate army; Holland N. McTyeire (1824–89), Methodist bishop and founder of Vanderbilt University; and J. D. B. DeBow (1820–67), founder of *DeBow's Review*.

At 74.4 *m.* is the junction with US 178 (*see Tour 15b*), which unites with US 25 for 13 miles.

In GREENWOOD, 82.4 *m.* (671 alt., 11,020 pop.) (*see Greenwood*), are the junctions with State 7 (*see Tour 17*) and State 10 (*see Tour 19b*).

Left from Greenwood on State 22, paved, to NINETY SIX, 8.8 *m.* (570 alt., 1,381 pop.), which sprawls out on both sides of a railroad. Though it has moved two miles from its first site, this is the oldest white community in the Up Country and began around the trading post established about 1730 by Captain John Francis at the convergence of Indian paths, now country roads. Legend says that Cateechee (*see Tour 19a*) rode to the post from Keowee to warn her white lover, Francis's son, Allen, of an impending Indian raid; and that One Mile Creek, Six Mile Branch, Twelve Mile Creek, and Ninety Six represent various stopping points in her journey. Actually the numerical names were given by traders erroneously calculating the mileage from Keowee. When the railroad reached this point in 1855, the inhabitants moved to this site to meet it. South of the business district, downhill, is Kate Fowler Branch, named for a colonial lady with amorous inclinations and a preference for the Tory uniform. The lapse of 157 years has not hushed the scandalous tales about Kate, who is said to be buried somewhere on the banks of the branch.

Right from Ninety Six on a hard-surfaced road 2.1 m. to the SITE OF OLD NINETY SIX, or Cambridge. Here the first courthouse in the Up Country was authorized in 1769 and built immediately afterward. Here the first South Carolina bloodshed of the Revolution occurred when 562 patriots under Colonel Andrew Williamson, outnumbered two to one, defeated Colonel Robinson's force in November 1775. When three colleges were chartered by the State in 1785, the one at Ninety Six was named for England's Cambridge University, which ambitious sponsors planned to emulate. Two years later the town took the name of the college. Aided by the Friendly Cambridge Society and directed by a distinguished group of men organized as the Cambridge Association, the Cambridge Academy was active for 38 years. Its most noted pupil was Dr. Moses Waddel (*see Tour 19A*). Left here on a cinder road 0.3 m. to the SITE OF STAR FORT, near which on May 12, 1781, General Nathanael Greene camped with his American force to begin a 37-day siege of the star-shaped redoubt, principal defense of the stockaded town. It had been seized by the British under command of Lieutenant Colonel J. H. Cruger. Lacking artillery, Greene diverted the enemy's creek-water supply and planned to tunnel beneath the fort and do what damage he could with explosives. While Cruger's men began digging a well, Greene's men burrowed toward Star Fort with pick-ax and shovel, the project directed by Thaddeus Kosciusko, the Polish engineer, who was quartermaster general of the Southern Army. The approach of Lord Rawdon's troops forced Greene to retire and abandon the tunnel, traces of which remain. Relics unearthed here from time to time include cannonballs, powder horns, tomahawks, caisson wheels, and small British cannon.

Associated with this vicinity is the story of Emily Geiger, whose existence is violently disputed, despite the tablet erected to her in the State House at Columbia. Tradition says that when Greene called for a courier to deliver a message to General Sumter in Wateree Swamp, across country so overrun with Tories that no man could expect to get through, Emily Geiger volunteered; and when Greene protested the danger involved, she insisted the mission would be an easy one for her. The general finally gave in. On her second day out, Emily was intercepted by Rawdon's scouts and locked in a room alone. While waiting search by an old Tory matron, the girl hurriedly memorized the message and swallowed the paper. Released when no damaging evidence was discovered, she completed her journey and delivered the message verbally.

In this neighborhood lived James Adair, eighteenth-century trader and author, who is thought to have come from northern Ireland. Adair's *History of the American Indians* (London, 1775) attempted to prove that the Indians were descended from the lost tribes of Israel; his detailed observations have made the book valuable to ethnologists and students of eighteenth-century literature.

GREENWOOD STATE PARK (*camping facilities; accommodations for whites and Negroes*), 10.8 m. on State 22, spreads among the red hills bordering the Saluda River.

The BUZZARD ROOST POWER PROJECT, 16.1 m., now (1940) under construction for Greenwood County by the PWA, with a dam 2,000 feet long and 82 feet high, will provide cheap power for this section. A 200-mile shoreline borders the 12,000-acre lake, which backs up for a distance of 20 miles. Fish hatcheries and rearing pools on all tributaries entering the reservoir insure a stock of fish.

At 24 m. is the junction with a dirt road; R. on this road 2.2 m. to the SITE OF SALUDA OLD TOWN, where Governor James Glen met Old Hop, Cherokee chief, in 1755. In response to the governor's summons to come to Charleston, then State capital, Old Hop had sent word that he was growing old and could no longer walk so far. Glen interpreted the reply as the chief's sardonic refusal to go to the white man's town for negotiations. When he subsequently humored Old Hop's pride by meeting him in Saluda Old Town, his tact was rewarded by a deed to the Ninety Six District, whose area covered ten of the present counties.

At 37 *m.* is NEWBERRY (502 alt., 7,298 pop.) (*see Tour 9c*), and at 38 *m.* is the junction with US 76 (*see Tour 9c*).

Section b.   GREENWOOD to GEORGIA LINE, 56 m.   US 25.

Between GREENWOOD, 0 *m.*, and Trenton, US 25 roughly parallels the Savannah River for about 40 miles, then turns sharply toward Augusta. The topography changes gradually, like melting butter, from the irregular hills of the Piedmont to the rolling countryside of lower lands. Before and after the War between the States, political leaders of South Carolina established country estates in this section, and the route passes rural settlements that bristled with arms and defiance during the Reconstruction era.

At 5 *m.* is the junction with US 178 (*see Tour 15b*).

Near the diminutive village of KIRKSEY, 11.6 *m.*, occurred the Phoenix Riot during the general election of November 8, 1898. Investigation of a Republican ballot box brought death to a young Democratic leader and precipitated an armed riot that drew half a hundred white men from four counties. The bodies of four Negroes, toll of one clash, were piled in the rain in front of Rehobeth Church near by. More were killed the next day. Afterward the resolutions of a mass meeting expressed regret 'that deluded Negroes have to suffer the penalties for misdeeds committed as a result of the influence of white men whose greed and selfishness have led them to act the part of enemies to both the white and colored people.' Two of the Republican leaders involved, fleeing to Columbia, were arrested and confined for their own safety in the State penitentiary.

South of Kirksey the highway traverses an undefined area known as the Hard Labor District, extending west to within a few miles of State 10. The land, always poor, was given to some five or six hundred Germans who were stranded in England about 1764 when a promoter, Colonel John Henry Christian de Stumple, broke his promise to take them to America. French immigrants entered the Long Cane section at about the same time.

Plagued by horse thieves, cutthroats, and cattle rustlers, colonists at Hard Labor, Long Cane, and other Up Country sections petitioned Charleston for a government, and particularly requested that courts with local jurisdiction be established for trial of criminals. Although the coastal authorities were glad to see these back districts settled, they were not interested in extending to the newcomers political representation or court protection. Ignored by the provincial government, determined back countrymen organized themselves into groups, established their own code of laws, and became known as the Regulators. Though many farmers refused to join, believing government protection imminent, the movement grew. The stern tactics of these groups, similar to those of western vigilantes, stirred the authorities to such an extent that the governor ordered a Colonel Schovil—whose name is spelled in various ways—to take a body of men into the section and settle the matter. The selection of this arbitrator was a mistake. Later described by General William Moultrie as 'an illiterate, stupid, noisy blockhead,' Schovil joined the renegades, became their leader, furnished them with arms, and promised each follower £20 a month and a bottle of rum each day. This spurred the Regulators to more formidable organization and six or seven hundred gathered to fight their freshly armed foes. Derisively, they referred to all followers of the colonel as 'Schovilites.' For many years afterward the term was generally applied to desperadoes by people of the Up Country. Shortly after the Schovil incident, the government divided the State into seven judicial circuits, and the Regulators voluntarily disbanded.

At 21 m. is the junction with State 43 (see Tour 19b).

At 25.2 m. is the junction with a dirt road.

Right on this road 0.2 m. to BLOCKER HOUSE, built in 1775 and almost hidden by old magnolias, cedars, and shrubs in the garden. With four large outside chimneys, the two-story house is covered with wide flush boarding and has two doors opening on the front piazza. Because he sent his son John back to the Fatherland to persuade emigrants to settle on Carolina lands granted him by the king, Blocker became known as 'The Colonizer.' In a pasture behind the house is the family cemetery.

The white frame two-story house of CEDAR GROVE, 26 m., was built in 1805 by James Blocker. It has small front balconies on both floors, a fan-transomed portal, and carved cornice. The parlor, containing handblocked wallpaper imported from Paris, has a hand-carved mantel and molding.

The central part of the house of WILDWOOD (L), 28.6 m., back in a large oak grove, was built about 1820 by George Landrum, whose small law office near the highway is now a store. In the 1840's ells were added to the rambling, one-story white frame structure by the Hollingsworths, descendants of Thomas Sellers, to whom this estate was granted in 1788. Slave quarters are back of the house.

In appearance as placid as if it had never sired a politician, EDGE-FIELD, 31.6 m. (350 alt., 2,132 pop.), seat of Edgefield County, boasts that its 'population is a wholesome and old Carolina blend.' Its hub is an open landscaped square with a Confederate monument in the center. Here on Saturday afternoons the farmers gather, mostly for talk, though at cotton-selling time their cash brings new life to the business section. There is a mill on the southeast boundary, but the county is largely agricultural. In the residential sections, paved tree-lined streets run between old houses, usually square, two-story affairs set in shady yards. The impression of peace that could never have been broken by anything more stirring than housewives' arguments across back-yard fences belies the community's reputation as a source of constant upheaval when ante-bellum riots and hangings agitated the State. Such turmoil is recalled today in acrid reminiscences of older folk—at filling stations and cotton gins, at family reunions and on court days—wherever politically minded citizens chance to meet. After politics, neighborhood talk is concerned with gardening, for the sparkling color of many large gardens beneath old oaks makes the town especially beautiful in spring.

Ideas and opinions here are those of folk who live as individuals not dependent on group action. This independent spirit has prevailed since the eighteenth century, when Edgefield was a courthouse district extending north to the Cherokee lands; and though improved roads have brought an increasing flow of visitors through the county's fields of cotton and corn, local attitudes have been little altered. The inhabitants have put their blood and brawn into these fields and will not be easily persuaded that theirs is not the better way of life. Since 1835 this sentiment has been reflected by the *Edgefield Advertiser*, oldest South Carolina newspaper in continuous circulation, which has done much toward molding local thought and opinion.

In the political hotbed of Edgefield District, nine State governors, five lieutenant governors, and numerous other leaders have launched their political careers, and some of South Carolina's most illustrious citizens have been residents here. Among them are the Reverend John Lake (b.1870), founder of a leper colony on Tia Kam Island in the China Sea; Dr. Albert Henry Newman (b.1852), Baptist historian, author, and professor; Colonel Pierce M. Butler (1798–1847), who commanded the Palmetto Regiment in the Mexican War and was governor of the State, 1836–8; and many others.

A romantic story, persistently told and often denied, concerns the daughter of Francis W. Pickens. Clad in a flowing crimson gown, she is said to have rallied 1,500 men under the Red Shirt banner and to have ridden at the head of a triumphant parade in the Hampton campaign of 1876 (*see Columbia*). Her full name was Andrea Dorothea Olga Liva Lucy Holcombe Douschka Francesca Pickens, with Dugas added after her marriage. She was born in St. Petersburg during her father's term as American minister to Russia and the czar and czarina were her godparents. To her family names the czar added 'Olga' for a Russian river, and the czarina, 'Douschka' (Rus., little darling). By the last title she was affectionately known and her grave in Willowbrook Cemetery is marked simply 'Douschka.'

In the D.A.R. TOMPKINS MEMORIAL LIBRARY, NE. corner of town square, are the library and papers of John R. Abney, who served as a colonel on Wade Hampton's staff, and later a member of the New York bar. The valuable collection is largely composed of volumes acquired by Abney during his years of travel and study in this country and abroad.

HALCYON GROVE, Buncombe Hill Road, at the intersection with Academy Branch and Lover's Lane, was built about 1810 by Andrew Pickens (1779–1838), who lived here while serving the State as governor, 1816–18. The frame structure has a two-story flat-roofed piazza with lattice columns. The interior is notable for its hand-carved mantels, wainscoting, and staircase. Pickens bequeathed Halcyon Grove to his son, Francis (1805–69), who followed in the path of his father and became South Carolina's first Confederate governor, 1860–2.

The large two-and-a-half-story WARDLAW PLACE, Buncombe Hill Road at the intersection with Cedar Springs Road, was built in 1834 by William Prothro and later owned by Chancellor Francis Hugh Wardlaw, who drafted the South Carolina Ordinance of Secession. The white frame building has a modified Corinthian portico without pediment. A projecting balcony is above the front entrance, which has a handsome fanlight.

In WILLOWBROOK CEMETERY, Church St., is the Brooks family plot, which contains the graves of Colonel Whitfield Brooks, a soldier of the War of 1812, his wife, Mary Parsons Carroll, who at the outbreak of the War between the States furnished the equipment for the company to which her sons belonged, and their son, Preston (*see below*). Also buried here is Edmund Bacon, the Ned Brace of Longstreet's *Georgia Scenes*.

On the public school grounds, Church St., is the SITE OF EDGEFIELD ACADEMY, from which developed Furman University (*see Greenville*).

Left from Edgefield on the unimproved Center Springs Road to the SITE OF THE BROOKS HOUSE, 5 *m.*, birthplace of Preston S. Brooks (1819–57), U. S. congressman who caned Charles Sumner, Senator from Massachusetts, on the morning of May 22, 1856, thereby precipitating a sectional dispute that was credited with widening the rift of misunderstanding between the North and the South. Senator Sumner had previously made an antislavery speech that contained offensive remarks about the State of South Carolina, and one of her senators, A. P. Butler. Among the members of the House who heard Sumner's attack was young Brooks, a relative of Butler's. Brooks was 36 years old at the time, about six feet tall, and of robust physique. He had served with credit as a captain in the Palmetto Regiment during the Mexican War, and had won particular favor as a debater. After brooding for several days over the speech, Brooks appeared in the Senate chamber after the Senate had adjourned, waited until a few women left the room, and addressed himself to the Massachusetts senator in curiously restrained and courteous tones: 'Mr. Sumner, I have read your speech twice, with great care and with as much impartiality as I am capable of, and I feel it my duty to say to you that you have published a libel on my State, and uttered a slander upon a relative who is aged and absent, and I am come to punish you.' And punish him he did. Before the attack could be stopped, Sumner had been struck unconscious with a gutta-percha cane. News of the assault set the North on fire, but throughout the South it was approved and even applauded. The majority report of the Senate investigation committee recommended that Brooks be expelled; the minority insisted that the Senate had no power to examine or punish the conduct of a member of the House. Newspapers of the North and South took heated issue. Thus a personal dispute was magnified to the proportions of a sectional quarrel. Resigning after a defiant speech, Brooks was kissed and hugged by Southern women as he walked from the Capitol. Admirers presented him with numerous canes, some of them goldheaded. In his district he was re-elected by a unanimous vote.

In 1852 the highway between Edgefield and Augusta was a fine plank road. Tolls ranged from 1¢ to 5¢ a mile, according to the number of horses.

In the pasture (L), 32.5 *m.*, is BECKY'S POOL, in which Becky Cotton deposited the bodies of her first three husbands, whom she had murdered. The name of Becky Cotton is notorious in local history. Cotton was the name of her third husband, for whose murder she was brought to trial in 1806. Though evidence of her guilt was overwhelming, her beauty was too much for judge and jury. She was acquitted and one of the jurymen became her fourth husband. When Mason Locke Weems was peddling books in this country, he heard the story and immediately seized on it as the basis for one of his moral pamphlets, *The Devil in Petticoats or God's Revenge Against Husband Killing*. As he told the story: 'Mrs. Cotton came off clear—nay, more than clear—she came off the conqueror. For as she stood at the bar in tears, with cheeks like rosebuds wet with morning dew and rolling her eyes of living sapphires, pleading for pity, their subtle glamor seized with ravishment the admiring bar—the stern features of justice were all relaxed, and both judge and jury hanging forward from their seats breathless, were heard to exclaim, "Heaven! What a Charming creature!"' Becky was born about 1780. She killed her first husband by running a mattress needle through his heart; she poisoned her second; and she split the head of her third with an ax. She herself was eventually killed by a brother.

Large two-story DARBY, 35.1 *m.*, home of Milledge Luke Bonham, South Carolina governor (1862–4), was erected shortly after 1847, when the first family home, built 1795, was torn down. The frame structure has a piazza extending around the front and sides.

PINE HOUSE (L), 36.6 *m.*, formerly known as Piney Woods House, is at the intersection with State 19, which turns sharply here. This two-story structure was built in 1849, probably by J. R. Weaver. It has a large pedimented portico with six fluted Doric columns, sheltering a balcony above a front entrance, which is flanked by floor-length windows. Opposite the Pine House is the SITE OF PINEY WOODS TAVERN, where Washington spent a night on his tour of 1791. The tavern was so named because of the pine woodlands in which it stood.

1. Left on the upper section of State 19 to TRENTON, 1.5 *m.* (620 alt., 369 pop.), where Benjamin R. Tillman (1847–1918), son of Benjamin Ryan and Sophia Hancock Tillman, owned a country home. In front of a two-story frame house, set back in a large grove, is a sign: 'Trenton, home of Senator Benjamin R. Tillman. In 1900 he introduced here the commercial growing of asparagus.' But 'Pitchfork Ben' Tillman, governor (1890–4), and United States senator (1894–1918), is remembered for much more than his commercial growing of asparagus. To his fiery championship of the small farmer is due the overthrow of the aristocratic regime that had existed in the State from the early days of Low Country wealth and supremacy. He was largely instrumental in founding the State normal and technical colleges, Winthrop and Clemson. In his stormy stump speeches he dubbed the latter a school for 'the horny handed sons of toil.' While governor, Tillman almost precipitated war in South Carolina by his State liquor dispensaries. He was the idol of the masses and anathema to the classes, bitterly opposed by the majority of South Carolina newspapers, which were largely under conservative control. The seventh son of a widowed mother, Ben grew up as her mainstay on the farm, helping in the management of her slaves. At the age of 17 he left school to enlist in the Confederate Army, but the loss of an eye kept him out of active service. In 1868

he married Sallie Stark of Georgia, by whom he had seven children, and continued farming on land his mother gave him. Tillman participated in the Ellenton and Hamburg riots in Reconstruction days and in protest against Radical rule heatedly advocated 'Straight Out' measures regarded dubiously by the more conservative Hampton and his followers. After 1876 he became active in county politics and soon drew State-wide support by his forceful oratory and his well-written, revolutionary newspaper articles. But not until 1890, when he was a gubernatorial candidate, did he burst upon State politics with a fury that was pyrotechnical in effect. Owing largely to his efforts, the State constitution of 1895, disenfranchizing Negroes, was adopted. Despite considerable opposition, his political career was so firmly established after two consecutive terms as governor that he defeated the aristocratic Butler for the Senate, practically controlled South Carolina politics until 1902, and continued powerful in the United States Senate until his death.

2. Left on the lower section of State 19 to BETTIS ACADEMY (L), 4 *m.*, an industrial and agricultural school for Negroes. On the grounds of the school is held one of the strangest Fourth of July celebrations in the Nation. In the gray light of early dawn, Negro drill teams from far and near converge and by midday the spot is packed with a seething mass, numbering upward of 15,000. Participants, shouldering wooden guns, adjust their paces to the primitive rhythm of tom-toms. In a routine unknown to any army sergeant, contestants shuffle their feet, gyrate their bodies and swing their make-believe rifles in unison, responding to such shouted commands as, 'Right shoulder arms, di, de, do!' A standard bearer leads the marches, which, after a half-hour or so give way to dances. A gala spirit prevails throughout the day, and the crowd is good natured and on the whole orderly. Venders compete with one another in selling fish, ice cream, photographs, souvenirs, and other articles, their persuasive sales cries rising from brush stalls temporarily arranged in a long lane. Notable is the amazing variety of dress. The grandeur of a drill team is limited only by the ingenuity of its members in using to advantage whatever bright bit of clothing they may be able to rustle up for the event. Costumes vary from discarded Army and Navy outfits to plain overalls and blue denim; and the impressiveness of cast-off evening attire overshadows such simple regalia as freshly starched white shirts and trousers. The origin of these annual rites is a mystery—even to the Negroes themselves; but they are known to have centered at Bettis for more than half a century. Early South Carolina newspapers carry accounts of similar ante-bellum celebrations in the towns of Charleston, Columbia, and Greenville.

It is said that along this Edgefield-Aiken route, once part of Whiskey Road, was sung a ditty by a notorious old reprobate as he returned from Saturday night sprees:

> Barnwell District, Aiken Town;
> O Lord in mercy do look down!
> The land is poor, the people too;
> If they don't steal, what will they do?

Vegetation changes as the highway crosses the Sand Hill section. Scrub oaks and pines replace the larger trees of the Piedmont, and land becomes less rolling.

Most of the working people of NORTH AUGUSTA, 54.2 *m.* (2,003 pop.), hold jobs in Augusta, Georgia.

At 56 *m.* US 25 crosses the SAVANNAH RIVER and the GEORGIA LINE, at a point 1 mile north of Augusta, Georgia.

Tour 9

(Wilmington, N. C.)—Mullins—Marion—Florence—Sumter—Columbia—Clinton—Laurens—Princeton; US 76. North Carolina Line to Princeton, 224 *m.*

Roadbed concrete-paved; detours sometimes necessary during rare floods in Pee Dee Swamps.
Atlantic Coast Line R.R. parallels route between Nichols and Columbia; Columbia, Newberry, and Laurens R.R. between Columbia and Laurens.
Hotels and tourist homes in larger towns; few tourist camps.

US 76 draws a wavering east-west line across the fall line between the upper coastal plain and the Piedmont, passing through some of the richest agricultural lands in the State. Wide level fields of cotton and corn are bordered by distant woods. In spring the dark green of the pines is varied by lighter tones of oak, sycamore, and dogwood, and the soft red of maple buds which begin to show as early as January. Tobacco spreads over countless acres; river swamps and forests offer excellent hunting and fishing; Up Country towns are edged with textile mills.

Section a. NORTH CAROLINA LINE to SUMTER, 88 m. US 76.

Tobacco dominates this section. Fields of it, changing in appearance with the seasons, spread widely along the highway; near by are curing barns, drab little log structures sealed with cement or clay.

The long and tedious evolution of tobacco from seed-packet to warehouse floor entails constant and expert care. Though it is late summer before the crop can be hauled to market, preparation begins in winter when wood for curing fires is chopped and piled near idle barns. January and February show long narrow seed beds protected by white cheesecloth. These are always close to a forest, in moist unused soil to avoid the bacteria that thrive in old beds. In the bright cool weather of early spring, workers drop the plants in furrows, set them firmly, and pack moist sand about the roots. A water wagon brings up the rear. Through the summer months, the plants are given constant and expert care—they are fertilized, 'suckered,' and searched for worms. Sometimes an entire field must be sprayed with insecticide, which leaves a dusty white that resembles early morning frost. With the latter part of June 'green tobacco season' begins, to last about five weeks. Plants have already ripened, and in the best fields have grown to shoulder height.

'Puttin' in time' is heralded by mounting excitement. The farmer,

366

his family, some of his neighbors, and a crew of hired hands have plenty to do. Under a blistering sun only the hardiest men can work between rows, stripping leaves from the stalks, the system originating in South Carolina (*see Agriculture*). Boys big enough to handle mules move the leaves from field to barn on primitive 'drags.' There is even greater activity in the low shed around the barn, where men, women, and children busy themselves all day. Even the tiniest child can 'hand' tobacco—pass it on, several leaves at a time, to an elder who strings it on a stick. With little lost motion, the filled sticks are moved into the barn and hung between ladderlike tiers until all the tobacco has been 'cropped.' Within the next day or so the farmer's debt to his neighbor is repaid when most of his family troop over to work on the adjoining farm. The farmer himself stays home to 'fire up the barn.' Huge stacks of wood decrease rapidly as the curing fires burn day and night. For almost a week temperature within the barn is kept constantly at a temperature only a degree or two below 110. Through an opening near the roof the upper tiers of tobacco are inspected from time to time. Modern invention has offered the improvement of oil heaters with a promise of more even temperatures, but the average farmer still puts his faith in wood.

When the fire is at last allowed to go out and the tobacco removed to the shed, men and women skilled in grading gather to sort the leaves, now dried to the color of dirty gold. Only experienced eyes can distinguish the almost innumerable grades. One company lists more than 100 classifications for South Carolina bright leaf tobacco. Before grading is completed, the tobacco markets open. Day and night, early and late, on highways, byways, and sandy roads, the annual pilgrimage begins: tobacco-laden vehicles of every size, shape, and description form endless processions converging at the warehouse doors. Pee Dee highways in August and September are not easily forgotten by travelers.

Inside the warehouse, white and Negro hands quickly transfer the tobacco from truck to square, shallow baskets. Spread in uniform fanlike layers, the leaves can be piled waist-high without toppling. Miles of these baskets, tagged for identification, line the floors of long warehouses. Between them the auctioneer moves, never stopping, his monotonous chant rising above warehouse noise. To the buyers who follow him, a sniff, touch, or glance determines which tobacco they will purchase for their companies, and their secret bidding signals come quickly —the twitch of a toothpick, the wink of an eye, the dip of a cigar. With amazing efficiency they accomplish in hours what looks as if it would take days. Bookmen keep pace with the little parade to figure each sale; assistants rush their bills to a screened-in office where checks are written and handed through the window to waiting farmers. Negroes follow the bookmen, moving the marketed tobacco to company trucks that rumble away to stemmery or packing house.

US 76 crosses the NORTH CAROLINA LINE, 0 *m.*, at a point 17 miles west of Wilmington, North Carolina, and traverses a series of bridges over the Lumber River and Swamp.

At 7 *m.* is the junction with State 9 (*see Tour 21a*), which unites with US 76 to a junction at 9 *m.*

The largest tobacco market in the State, MULLINS, 16 *m.* on US 76 (97 alt., 3,158 pop.), changes in late summer from a lackadaisical little town to a bustling metropolis. Practically everybody in town does a year's work in three months. With 'long gold' exchanged for 'long green,' debts from the last nine months are paid, landowners and tenants settle up, and merchants are busy from daylight till dark selling clothes and supplies for the winter.

Nights are almost as busy as days, with trucks, trailers, 'pick-ups,' and wagons roaring and rattling into town. While the farmers' tobacco is being unloaded, their wives and children window shop, the men gossip and settle national problems, and take naps on their piles of tobacco.

After the last sale of the year has been made and the less important money crop, cotton, disposed of, farmers and merchants, with the aid of many lawyers, fix up terms of credit for the next nine months and settle down to another year of farming, dickering, hunting and fishing. Recreation is found on the Little Pee Dee River where the more prosperous citizens own fishing camps.

On the outskirts of Mullins, Negro homes are constantly being pushed farther out as the town grows, its population still equally divided between white and black. Negro life centers in numerous lodges, societies, religious organizations, and 'Satdy' night trips to town. To prevent the cutting scrapes and icepick stabbings that formerly attended these occasions, the town council adopted a curfew, and the ten o'clock bell clears the streets of Negroes.

Left from Mullins on South Park Street, which becomes a dirt road, to the DEAD LINE, approximately 5 *m.*, an undefined boundary about which gruesome stories have been told. It is said men of Horry County, none of whom had owned slaves, established this limit during Reconstruction when freedmen were running riot; Negroes who ventured beyond it were killed. Whether or not the story is true, many Negroes today avoid the neighborhood.

The highway between Mullins and Marion passes at 19 *m.* through a dense unsurveyed wood, SISTER BAY, from which wildcats and alligators sometimes emerge.

Placid and conservative MARION, 25 *m.* (68 alt., 4,921 pop.), seat of Marion County, still lives up to the description given it in 1865 by a correspondent of *The Nation:* 'a very quiet, pretty little village full of trees and gardens and light elegant houses, made of brick and iron, seems strangely out of place.' Elm trees line the streets and the Public Square, and flower gardens are planted around new homes. A pioneer in civic beauty, Marion shows the result of expert landscape planning in its public areas. The Civic League organized in 1895 had successful businessmen for its first two presidents. The older part of the town is fringed by bare industrial properties where the aroma of ancient tea olives yields to that of newly sawed pine lumber and cottonseed meal. Among the industrial plants that fringe the town are a large lumber mill, a veneer and brick plant, an oil mill, and an iron works to which machinery is brought for repairs.

In Indian times a trading post stood where the Public Square is now. Marion, called Gilesboro for Colonel Hugh Giles, began as a courthouse town in 1800; during the 1830's it followed the county in honoring General Francis Marion, the 'Swamp Fox' of the Revolution. The absence of major disturbances in Indian, Revolutionary, and Confederate eras, and bountiful natural resources have combined to produce the stable life of Marion today. An amusing paradox is the building of the jail on Liberty Street.

Social life is centered in the church and school. The men, however, escape for one night each week to their fishing clubs, small shacks on the Little Pee Dee River and near-by lakes. Bream and mollies are made into 'pine-bark stew,' and tall tales recounted around the bonfire. So devoted to the institution are Marion men that many who have moved away return regularly for the suppers. On rare and special occasions women are invited to these masculine gatherings.

The Public Square, divided into four parks by the intersection of Main and Godbold Streets, was donated by Thomas Godbold, about 1800. Once the hitching place for farmers of the county, it is now a tree-shaded landscaped park of four acres, and for long years has been the scene of fiery political 'speakings.' On its southwest corner is the MARION COURTHOUSE, 1853–4, a gray stuccoed building with high basement story, similar in style to public buildings designed by Robert Mills. A four-column pedimented portico, approached on each side by a curved wrought-iron stairway, rests on plastered brick piers. This is the third courthouse to serve Marion County since its creation in 1798. The MARION PUBLIC LIBRARY, SE. corner of the square, first tax-supported library in South Carolina, contains approximately 9,000 volumes. Among its curios is the royal grant to James Godbold in 1769 of the tract of 409 acres on which the town was built. The library organization was begun about 1826 and formally incorporated in 1898. The present red brick one-story structure with a two column pedimented portico replaces one that burned in 1929.

MARION HIGH SCHOOL, N. Main St. between Railroad Ave. and Elizabeth St., a modern red brick building, has a spacious campus with an open-air theater toward the back. Robert Mills, in his *Statistics*, speaks of an academy here in 1814; it was merged into the present school system in 1887.

The landscaped grounds of the METHODIST CHURCH, E. Godbold St., occupying an entire block between Oak and Pine Sts., is one of the most beautiful spots in Marion, and has been described in national magazines. When winter pruning is announced in local newspapers, garden enthusiasts from surrounding counties flock in to obtain cuttings.

In the CLINTON MASONIC LODGE BUILDING, E. Godbold St. between

Court and Pine Sts., many of Marion's older citizens began their education. Erected in 1810, the building has a high basement of brick and second story of frame, with the gable roof projecting to form a pedimented portico, its four unfluted Doric columns supported by square stuccoed red brick piers. It was saved from threatening flames of the Reconstruction period by Yankee soldiers who were Masons; the basement was used as a schoolroom until a graded school was built in 1887.

The DURHAM HOUSE, E. Dozier St. between Main and Pine Sts., a two-story frame residence erected in 1804 by Thomas Godbold and remodeled in 1870, is the oldest house in town.

In Rose Hill Cemetery is the GRAVE OF VICTOR BLUE (1865–1928), rear admiral in the United States Navy and a distinguished hero of the Spanish-American War. He successfully completed two highly difficult scouting expeditions behind the Spanish lines and subsequently was cited for 'extraordinary heroism.' Blue spent his boyhood in Marion where he lived on his father's plantation 'Bluefields.'

On the western edge of town is the CAMP LUMBER COMPANY PLANT, one of the largest in the State. It employs about 300 men and has an annual pay roll of $150,000. The mills, kilns and drying yards, with frame houses and a commissary for employees compose the community.

Marion is at the junction with US 501 (*see Tour 13*).

PEE DEE, 33 *m.* (623 alt., 31 pop.), a railroad junction, bears the tribal name of Indians who lived in this territory. Variously spelled Pee Dee, Peedee, and occasionally Pedee, the name is sometimes erroneously attributed to Patrick Daly, an Irish adventurer, who in his peregrinations left his initials upon many trees. Between Pee Dee and the bridge, the route parallels Big Pee Dee River, crossing a number of small streams and depressions where the forbidding gloom of dense foliage is enlivened in spring with flowering trees and shrubs.

At MARS BLUFF, 35 *m.*, Regulators (*see Tour 8b*) of the section engaged in armed combat with British militia in August 1768.

At 37.2 *m.* is the junction with a dirt road.

Right here 4 *m.* to the sycamore-shaded avenue of THE COLUMNS (R), a massive Greek Revival white frame two-story structure surrounded on three sides by 22 free-standing stuccoed columns. Windows are square headed and the entrance has side lights and transom. Built 1850–60 by Dr. William R. Johnson, The Columns was used as a model for the principal setting of *Carolina*, a motion picture based on the *House of Connolly* by Paul Green. In the search for an old 'typical southern home' surrounded by tobacco fields, the picture company selected this house, and constructed a replica of it in Hollywood.

At FLORENCE, 48 *m.* (136 alt., 14,774 pop.) (*see Florence*), is the junction with US 52 (*see Tour 2a*).

TIMMONSVILLE, 59 *m.* (147 alt., 1,919 pop.), has markets for both cotton and tobacco. Warehouses, which are scenes of frenzied activity during market season, stand bare and silent the rest of the year. The town is the birthplace and home of Melvin Purvis, one of the G-men who ran down Dillinger. Pecan groves and acres of pepper plants are sandwiched between tobacco fields. On broad pastures of lespedeza and carpet grass some of the State's finest cattle graze. A farmer of this section raised two cows that won world championships in butterfat production.

Known during Revolutionary days as Willow Grove, LYNCHBURG, 69 *m.* (150 alt., 512 pop.), is now a business center for surrounding farms. Here under cover of a thick growth of willows and the log walls of a rum shop, General Marion's army defeated British troops in 1781. MAYESVILLE, 78 *m.* (145 alt., 649 pop.), is the birthplace of Mary McLeod Bethune, Director of the Division of Negro Affairs in the National Youth Administration and rated one of the 50 greatest women in America. Born of ex-slave parents in 1875, she worked as teacher and missionary in South Carolina for many years. In 1904 she established the Daytona-Cookman Collegiate Institute at Daytona Beach, Florida, with 'five girls, a small cabin, $1.50, and a million dollars' worth of faith.' Today the plant, comprising 15 buildings and 170 acres, is valued at $800,000. She has served as national leader in Negro associations, was a member of President Hoover's Home Ownership Committee, and in the Florida hurricane of 1928, organized rescue work among Negroes.

In SUMTER, 88 *m.* (169 alt., 11,780 pop.) (*see Sumter*), are the junctions with US 15 (*see Tour 3a*) and US 521 (*see Tour 4*).

Left from Sumter 1.3 *m.*, on W. Liberty St., State 763, to SWAN LAKE GARDEN, developed as the hobby of a Sumter businessman. A remarkable collection of water and bog plants fringe the lake against a background of azaleas, camellias, and other blooming and berried shrubs. Japanese iris have blooms at shoulder height. In spring tall cypress and native pine trees are bright with yellow jessamine, purple wisteria, trumpet vine, and Cherokee roses. Still water reflections, hardly disturbed by the quiet passage of swans, doubles the beauty of the scene.

Section b. SUMTER to COLUMBIA, 45 m. US 76.

Northwest of SUMTER, 0 *m.*, the route crosses the High Hills of Santee. Santee is believed to be a corruption of *santé* (Fr., health) and to have no connection with the Indian name of the Santee River. This narrow ridge parallels the Wateree River for about 40 miles and the beauty of its scenery, its healthfulness, and its fertile soil brought men of discrimination and wealth in the early part of the eighteenth century to take up lands and build homes. But now it is a region of memories; few of the old plantations are cultivated, and clumps of trees mark the sites of stately homes abandoned or destroyed by fire.

The PALMETTO PIGEON PLANT (*open*), at 2 *m.*, specializing in Carneaux pigeons, annually ships 100,000 squabs to many parts of the United States, Canada, and England.

At 3 *m.* is the junction with US 521 (*see Tour 4*).

At 11.9 *m.* is the junction with a dirt road, State 261.

Left on this road, an old stagecoach route, with dense growths that hide most of the homes. Rolling hills are forested with pine, oak, and elm, their branches hung with moss. Two or three stores and a few houses make up the village of WEDGEFIELD, 4.1 *m.*, once the prosperous trading center for surrounding plantations.

At Manchester village site is MELROSE (R), 8.3 *m.*, built *c.*1760 by Captain Matthew Singleton, on the prevailing story-and-a-half plan that evaded the high tax on two-story dwellings. Small narrow windows and low ceiled rooms bear evidence of its age. Timber is hand-hewn, and the wainscoting is made of boards so wide that each forms a separate panel. Doors are hung with hand-wrought hinges, and nails are handmade.

POINSETT STATE PARK (R), 10.8 *m.*, its 1,000 acres ranging from swamp to highland, was named for Joel R. Poinsett, statesman and botanist (*see Tour* 20). Coquina rock, an indigenous shell formation, has been used in the park buildings.

MILFORD (R), 14.9 *m.*, built by Governor John Laurence Manning about 1850, was so costly that it became known as 'Manning's Folly.' Granite used in its construction was brought from Rhode Island to Charleston by boat, thence up the Santee River, and finally by oxcart into the Sand Hills. The thick exterior and interior walls were built of brick pressed and burned on the estate, and covered with white stucco. Even in 1850 the house was heated by a basement furnace, and water was supplied by a reservoir on a hill at the back. Milford's beauty, inside and out, refutes any suggestion of folly on the part of the builder. Greek Revival in design, the house, in spacious oak-shaded grounds, has a portico supported by six columns on granite bases. A thick mahogany entrance door is framed by classic columns. Green shuttered windows extend to the floor. The main hall is separated from a central rotunda by two large doors. Library and dining room have black marble mantels below gilt framed mirrors that extend to the ceiling. In two rounded corners of the dining room are china closets with mahogany doors. Two drawing rooms are separated by folding doors between columns; these rooms have white marble mantels below large mirrors. From the rotunda a staircase with mahogany rails ascends in a sweeping curve. Much of the furniture was selected in Paris, and some in England at a sale of the Duke of Devonshire's estate.

About 300 yards southeast of the mansion is the SPRING HOUSE, copied from part of Trinity Church (*see Columbia*). In 1865 Brigadier General Potter ordered Milford burned after using it as his headquarters. A staff officer who had attended school in Berlin with a member of the Manning family is believed to have delayed the burning until Captain Julius Rhett arrived announcing the end of the war.

Opposite Milford is the junction with a sandy road; L. on this road 1 *m.* to ST. MARK'S CHURCH, a little brick building, Gothic Revival in style, set in a pine thicket. The congregation's first rector was elected in 1766. The present building, designed by Potter, a brother of the Union general, was completed in 1856.

At 11.6 *m.* is the junction with old US 76 (*to be marked State* 261). Here the old highway leads R. to historic Stateburg and environs (*see below*). Left the new road slices through Wateree swamp along a six-mile causeway completed in 1940 at a cost of approximately $75,000. Spanning the swamp 17 feet above ground-level, the high water crossing represents a short-cut on the main route, saving one mile.

At 12.2 *m.* on old US 76 is the junction with a dirt road.

Right on this road 0.7 *m.* to THE RUINS, a handsome two-story ante-bellum house with flanking wings. Its original lines have been altered by later additions. The house was built by John Mayrant and was the birthplace of John Mayrant, Jr., naval lieutenant under John Paul Jones. The Ruins occupies the site of Buena Vista, pre-Revolutionary home of General Thomas Sumter, who narrowly escaped with his life when the house was fired by Tarleton's soldiers. When the property was acquired by the DeVeauxs, charred remains of the manor suggested the present name.

STATEBURG, 12.6 *m*. on old US 76, was founded by General Sumter and vigorously promoted in 1786 as the future State capital. At one time it had stores, a tavern, a post office, an academy, and a circulating library, but it is now only a scattered group of old houses and a church. The stone wall around GREENE SPRING (R) was built at the command of General Nathanael Greene, whose forces, according to Washington Irving, were camped on these 'breezy, healthgiving hills.' The spring is now used by neighborhood Negroes.

The Episcopal CHURCH OF THE HOLY CROSS (R), built in 1850 of *pisé de terre*, is a notable example of Gothic Revival design. Its simple lines, cruciform plan, corner towers, and pointed arches suggest an Old World parish church. Yellow walls and high-pitched red tile roof contrast vividly with the evergreen in the yard.

BOROUGH HOUSE, opposite the church, was built in 1754 on lands granted to William Hilton, and purchased before the Revolution by Thomas Hooper, Esq., brother of William Hooper of North Carolina, Signer of the Declaration of Independence. Set on a rising knoll, 'The Borough' is shaded by huge old trees, among them 500-year-old Spy Oak, from which Tory spies were hanged. To the rear spreads a pre-Revolutionary garden with a variety of rare and exquisite shrubs and flowers. Of buff *pisé de terre*, the structure has a two-story central section with double colonnaded portico, hip roof, and superimposed Ionic colonnades. At each end is a one-story gable wing, and the library is a small separate building with hip roof and Tuscan colonnade. During the Revolution both Generals Greene and Cornwallis used the big house temporarily. Rudely carved on the doors are the letters 'C. A.,' handiwork of the soldiers of the Continental Army. Here were born Lieutenant General Richard Anderson, ranking line-officer from South Carolina in the War between the States, and his brother, Major William Wallace Anderson, ranking South Carolina surgeon. While visiting Major Anderson, Joel Poinsett died here and he and his wife lie buried in the churchyard opposite. During one of his frequent visits Poinsett planted the large camellia japonica at the western side.

In the house are treasured old furnishings, including a sideboard whose doors show the bayonet thrusts of Potter's soldiers. Letters from General Robert E. Lee, General Thomas Sumter, and other famous men are preserved. Among the portraits are *Mary Heron Hooper* (1783), painted by Copley in England; *Captain Benjamin Heron* (1750), a pastel made in Temple Inn, London; *Colonel Patrick Heron* and *Ann Vining* (1711), by Sir Godfrey Kneller, court painter to Charles II and George I. A Bartolozzi engraving of the Lady Cicely Heron, dated 1798, was copied from the Holbein portrait at Windsor Castle; she was the daughter of Sir Thomas More, and wife of Sir Giles Heron, both beheaded by Henry VIII.

Locally known as the Governor Miller home, ELLISON HOUSE (L) was built either by Governor Stephen D. Miller (1787–1838) or an earlier owner. Hand-wrought hinges, hand-made nails, wainscoting of wide single boards, small window panes, and the narrow central hall and plan of the rooms indicate that it was built before the nineteenth century. Miller, governor of South Carolina (1828–30) and proponent of States' rights, served in the State senate 1822–8, and went to the United States Senate in 1831. Resigning in 1833 because of ill health, he later moved to Mississippi. For years this house was the home of the Ellisons, a family of free Negroes who were themselves slave owners. They founded and operated a cotton gin factory, and their hand-made gins were the standard for half a century.

Right from Stateburg on a dirt road 1.9 *m.* to another dirt road; R. 0.4 *m.* to the HIGH HILLS BAPTIST CHURCH (R), second oldest congregation of that denomination in the State, organized 1770. Its first pastor was Dr. Richard Furman, founder of Furman University, now in Greenville.

At 1.9 *m.* is a dirt road; R. here 0.3 *m.* to the GRAVE OF GENERAL THOMAS SUMTER, marked by a simple monument. Sumter (1734–1832), a Virginian, came to South Carolina October 28, 1762, and later settled as a planter on the Santee River. He was a member of the provincial congress, and during the Revolution served the American cause with distinction. When his home was burned by the British, Sumter escaped to North Carolina. Later he organized a band of upper South Carolinians, a motley group of men clad in hunting shirts, deerskin breeches, Indian moccasins, and animal skin caps, whose weapons were anything from pitchforks to hunting knives. Their highly effective guerrilla warfare brought epithets from a harassed Cornwallis and earned Sumter the *nom de guerre* 'Gamecock' of the Revolution.

Near the general's grave is the tiny DELAGE BRICK CHAPEL covered with tile imported from France. Here worshiped General Sumter's daughter-in-law, Countess Natalie DeLage, a Catholic in a foreign Protestant land, an émigrée from the French Revolution, and a protégée of Aaron Burr. She lies buried beneath the floor on which she knelt in prayer. The door has been sealed against the depredations of souvenir hunters. Near the chapel, but practically inaccessible, is HOME HOUSE, built by General Sumter for his son, Colonel Thomas Sumter, Jr., and his French bride, the countess.

West of the High Hills of Santee farm lands sweep down to the wide Wateree swamps, grown over with hardwood trees, and abounding in small game: mink, otter, raccoon, opossum, squirrel, fox, deer, wild turkey, and quail.

A REFORESTATION PLOT of longleaf pines (R), 13.4 *m.*, set out in 1931 as a private experiment, borders the swamp, which is crossed by a succession of bridges. The banks of the Wateree River are generally planted with corn, but sometimes the crop is washed away. Cleared areas along both sides of the river show log and frame hunting lodges. Part of this route was laid out by an Act of July 2, 1766, and the modern highway, concrete-surfaced, parallels the river in easy curves between terraced and rolling farm lands.

The EPWORTH ORPHANAGE FARM, 36.5 *m.*, a tract of 465 acres, is worked by the older boys of the Methodist institution in Columbia. Vegetables and foodstuff for the 300 children are grown here, as well as feed for poultry and stock.

The UNITED STATES VETERANS' ADMINISTRATION FACILITY (R), 40.5 *m.*, locally called the Veterans' Hospital, provides for more than 600 patients; employees number about 380. The plant was erected in 1932 at a cost of $1,300,000 and was greatly enlarged five years later. It serves war veterans of South Carolina and part of North Carolina.

Beyond an avenue of pines are the RUINS OF MILLWOOD (R), 40.7 *m.*, the vine-covered columns of the Hampton house, burned by Sherman's troops. This was the home of Colonel Wade Hampton (1791–1858), a lieutenant in the War of 1812, and a colonel in the Battle of New Orleans in 1814, who was selected by General Jackson to deliver a report of that victory to President Madison. The colonel is said to have ridden the 1,200 miles from New Orleans to Washington in 10 days, using only one horse, and accompanied only by one Negro and a pack horse.

At Millwood the colonel's son, Wade Hampton III (1818–1902), South Carolina's favorite hero, spent much of his boyhood. At 20 he married Margaret Preston, and after her death in 1851 married Mary McDuffie, daughter of Governor George McDuffie. Wealthy, handsome, six feet tall, Hampton was a graduate of the South Carolina College (later University), trained in law, a lover of books and owner of a fine library, and an excellent planter and sportsman. Before the War between the States he served in the State legislature, resigning in 1861. Then, though he doubted the economic soundness of slavery and the expediency (not the constitutionality) of secession, he offered his cotton in Europe for armaments and raised the Hampton Legion of infantry and cavalry, which won distinction on Virginia battlefields. On the death of General J. E. B. Stuart, Hampton was given command of the cavalry, and later became a major general. Transferred to South Carolina in 1865, he was ordered to evacuate Columbia as Sherman marched on the city, February 17. This was the man whom Sherman accused of burning his own city.

Anxious to restore order to the State, Hampton supported President Johnson's plans for reconstruction. He refused to become a candidate for governor, contending that, as a former Confederate officer, his election would be harmful. Vainly hoping to retrieve his personal fortune, he retired to private life after 1868. But following 12 years of political and economic chaos, Hampton was nominated by the Democrats for governor. To defeat the Republican ticket, red shirted Democrats led by General Hampton rode through the State, campaigning every county. By inducing the vote of some Negroes, by frightening others from the polls, by each man's casting as many votes as he dared, they succeeded in electing Hampton by 1,000 votes. Though for four months the election was contested (*see Columbia*), the victory was at last complete.

Re-elected governor in 1878, Hampton resigned to serve in the United States Senate, and for 15 years his name was the symbol of the political regime of his State. Defeated by J. L. M. Irby, a Tillmanite, he was appointed by President Cleveland commissioner of the Pacific railways. His private fortune had never been restored, and upon his return to South Carolina, his circumstances were straitened. In 1899 his Columbia home burned. With his dog, his gun, and his fishing tackle, Hampton moved into an outhouse, remarking that, if he had only saved his tent, he would be all right. But the people of South

Carolina gave him a new home, southeast corner Senate and Barnwell Streets, and here he spent his last years.

At 41.1 *m.* is the junction with State 760.

Right on this road 1.5 *m.* to FORT JACKSON, home post of the Army's Thirtieth and streamlined Eighth Divisions. Known until 1940 as Camp Jackson, the military reservation was established in 1917 to train soldiers during the First World War. It was used in the 1930's as the summer training grounds for National Guard units of the Fourth Corps area, representing six Southern States. Reminiscent of the feverish haste with which the camp was constructed two decades earlier, more than 5,000 workers were employed in the fall of 1940 to rush accommodations for 40,000 officers and enlisted men. The Army made available millions of dollars from the defense appropriations of Congress, the reservation was enlarged by many thousand acres, and almost overnight the Fort became a bustling city, complete in itself, and by population the third largest in the State.

In COLUMBIA, 45 *m.* (312 alt., 51,581 pop.) (*see Columbia*), are the junctions with US 21 (*see Tour 5a*), US 1 (*see Tour 6a*), and State 215 (*see Tour 18*).

Section c.   COLUMBIA to PRINCETON, 91 m.   US 76.

North of COLUMBIA, 0 *m.*, the highway passes between small cottages and banks sodded with Bermuda grass. White mail boxes lean out into the road, and veritable fences of highway markers direct the tourist. Honeysuckle vines cover the roadside bushes and in spring fill the air with fragrance. In the Dutch Fork section windmills stand by farmhouses and sawmills and gins straddle the road, connected by pipe lines overhead. Swiss and German settlers came into this region about 1745, and their customs are still retained to a remarkable degree by their descendants, who tend self-sufficient farms and sell their crops for top prices in Columbia. It is not unusual to see overalled women at work in fields or vegetable patches. Farther west the rolling hills grow steeper, the highways wind, rising and falling, between cotton fields and pine forests.

The route crosses a modern reinforced concrete bridge at 1.8 *m.*, spanning the Columbia Canal and the Broad River. A dam diverts part of the river into the canal. Completed in 1824, it served as a link in the inland waterway system from near Ninety Six to Charleston by way of Columbia. More than 45,000 bales of cotton went through the canal in 1827. For 20 years it was a profitable freight route. Then, in the 1840's with the advent of railroads, its usefulness in shipping declined and eventually ceased. In 1891 the canal was utilized for water power for a Columbia factory, said to be the first in the world completely operated by electricity. Two of the old motors are preserved in the Ford Industrial Museum at Dearborn, Michigan.

Evidence of the fall line is visible in a highway cut at 2.4 *m.;* strata of pebbles are revealed in the red clay. Here University of South Carolina geology classes study the prehistoric shore line.

The STATE REFORMATORY FOR NEGRO BOYS (R), 5.3 *m.*, is noticeable because of its high water tower. On adjoining State lands the

WOMEN'S UNIT OF THE STATE PENITENTIARY (R), 6.2 *m.*, of reinforced concrete and steel with accommodations for 200 inmates, was opened in 1938. The gate to the grounds of the SOUTH CAROLINA INDUSTRIAL SCHOOL FOR GIRLS (R), 7.1 *m.*, marks the third institution. At 9.1 *m.* is the junction with State 60.

Left here 1.4 *m.* to HARBISON AGRICULTURAL AND INDUSTRIAL COLLEGE, a Negro Presbyterian institution that maintains a farm and owns a considerable amount of land.

LAKE MURRAY, 5 *m.*, 84 square miles in area, was formed in 1930 by impounding the waters of the Saluda River. The dam (called the Saluda Dam and also the Dreher Shoals Dam), nearly two miles long and a quarter of a mile wide at the bottom, rises 208 feet above the valley. The highway across its top affords a view of this artificial lake, its expanse so great that sea gulls are attracted to it in search of food. During stormy weather the birds drift about on the surface, apparently quite at home. Left from the height of the dam spreads the panorama of forested Saluda River Valley with the tops of several Columbia buildings just visible in the distance. Nearer are great craterlike pits that supplied earth for the dam's construction. At the base of the huge earthen structure is a hydroelectric plant (*free guide service*). Lake Murray, well stocked with fish, is assuming importance as a summer resort. Fishermen come here from all parts of South Carolina, and other States as well. Regattas and other water contests are held annually and various types of dwellings, from small white cottages to substantial brick buildings, are grouped at intervals along the 500-mile shore line.

South of Lake Murray the route follows State 6.

In LEXINGTON, 11 *m.* (359 alt., 1,152 pop.) (*see Tour 6b*), is a junction with US 1 (*see Tour 6b*).

At 14.2 *m.* on US 76 is the junction with Old Buncombe Road, State 177.

Right here 1.5 *m.* at the top of a hill, to the OLD BOUKNIGHT PLACE (L), built before 1800. Double piazzas cross the front of the house and the large doors opening on to them have side lights. Window shutters are held to the house with iron S's. Walls are paneled, and large hand-carved mantels frame the fireplaces. A closed stairway rises to the one big second-story room. On the march from Columbia in 1865, a detachment of Sherman's Army stayed here.

BALLENTINE, 15.4 *m.* (518 pop.), a favorite starting point for boat trips on the lake, has long been a trading center for Dutch Fork farmers.

The name WHITE ROCK, 16.4 *m.* (461 alt., 138 pop.), was suggested by outcroppings of white flint. The LOWMAN HOME (L), a Lutheran institution for the aged and helpless, is here, and also St. Paul's Lutheran Church. In the churchyard is a monument bearing the names of members whose graves were covered by Lake Murray. About 14 of these monuments are in the vicinity of the lake.

The big lumber mill (R) at CHAPIN, 23 *m.* (503 alt., 429 pop.), when in operation, lays a pall of smoke over the little town. In lumber yards the new yellow boards are stacked squarely in layers, or leaned on edge, tentlike against a pole, for drying.

Along this stretch of road in 1926 the first experiment with cotton fabric in hard surfacing roads was made by the State highway department. Although the open-weave, burlaplike fabric reduced cracking and minimized upkeep of the bituminous surface, the experiment has not been continued.

LITTLE MOUNTAIN, 29 m. (711 alt., 244 pop.), is named for a monadnock (L), the only hill of its size for miles around.

At 34.5 m. is the junction with a dirt road.

Right here 3.4 m. to JOLLY STREET SCHOOLHOUSE (L), a white frame building with metal hip roof. The pine grove directly behind the school is annually the scene of a midsummer political rally when candidates for various State and national offices speak to crowds of thousands, representing most of the counties in this part of the State. Shirt-sleeved politicians perspire before the small microphone that amplifies their promises in a deep-throated bellow. This open-air rally has been a climax of South Carolina's political season since 1832, and aspiring speakers, assured of extra publicity and an audience larger than usual, save potent punches for that day. Between election years, incumbents and guest speakers pinch hit. The Jolly Street meeting lasts all day and is accompanied by a barbecue dinner—one or two tons of it—and a baseball game.

The highway takes a short cut to PROSPERITY, 36 m. (542 alt., 844 pop.), once just around the corner. Originally named 'Frog Level,' it is a friendly little town where the favorite outdoor sport is pitching horseshoes.

In NEWBERRY, 43 m. (502 alt., 7,298 pop.), seat of Newberry County, an electric sign overhead extends a welcome. Business houses of varied architecture crowd along the rather narrow streets; frame buildings, sometimes plain, sometimes opulent with gingerbread, are sandwiched between utilitarian brick structures of a later period or elbowed against modernistic theaters and filling stations. In abrupt contrast is the spaciousness of residential areas, where wide old houses and smaller, newer ones are set back from the streets.

On the public square, facing Caldwell Street, is the old NEWBERRY COUNTY COURTHOUSE, erected in 1850. Of stuccoed brick, the rectangular building has a six-columned portico with pediment. An outside flight of steps from the street to the second floor mars the façade. The two-column side portico, a later addition, has a pediment bearing a bas-relief symbolizing the spirit of the State during Reconstruction; the work of an ardent Southerner, Osborne Wells, who remodeled the building in 1880, it shows an uprooted palmetto tree held in the talons of the United States eagle; perched upon its roots is a gamecock, wings extended as if defiantly crowing, and in the gold dollar that is his right eye, 'a wicked, baleful glare.' Atop the tree an unobtrusive dove bears an olive branch. During the first term in the renovated courthouse, Wells was called before an irate judge who denounced the odd decoration. With more enthusiasm that discretion, the sculptor responded that had he possessed a picture of His Honor he would just as soon have included it, too.

Among Newberry's prominent citizens was John Belton O'Neall (1793–1863), jurist, civic leader, and historian, who became chief justice of the State in 1859. A descendant of Irish Quakers, O'Neall was an honor graduate from South Carolina College (now the University), class of 1812, received his master's degree in 1816, and served as trustee for nearly half a century. Twice elected a legislator from old Newberry District, he was Speaker of the House 1826-8, and a series of promotions in the State militia led to his appointment as major general. His best known published works are *Annals of Newberry, Sketches of the Bench and Bar of South Carolina,* and *Digest of the Negro Law.* An ardent advocate of temperance, he wrote voluminously on that subject.

NEWBERRY COLLEGE, College St., a coeducational institution with an enrollment of 350, was established in 1856, and is maintained by the Lutheran Church. Six red brick hip-roofed buildings form a quadrangle. Keller Hall, the library, with high-pitched roof and bell tower, contains 20,000 volumes.

One of the oldest churches in Newberry is ST. LUKE'S EPISCOPAL, Main and Calhoun Sts., its congregation organized in 1846. The present brick building, erected in 1855, is Gothic Revival in style and covered with stucco weathered to a muddy pink.

In Newberry is the junction with State 22 (*see Tour 8a*).

At 45 *m.* is the junction with US 176 (*see Tour 12b*).

JALAPA, 51 *m.* (38 pop.), takes its name from the Mexican city where many young soldiers from this section fell during General Winfield Scott's campaign in the Mexican War.

GARY, 53.5 *m.* (85 pop.), formerly Gary's Lane, and KINARDS, 56 *m.* (588 alt., 273 pop.), were named for prominent families of the vicinity. Statesmen, military men, jurists, and physicians bore the distinguished Gary name. Descendants of Martin Kinard, wealthy Dutch Fork planter, were business leaders and educators.

Founded in 1920, the STATE TRAINING SCHOOL (R), 64 *m.*, provides care and training for the feeble minded. Enrollment is approximately 700, and within certain limits the school is open to inspection.

CLINTON, 66 *m.* (678 alt., 5,643 pop.), is practically a monument to the zeal of one man, the Reverend William Plumer Jacobs (1842-1917). When Jacobs descended upon the lively railroad settlement in 1865 as first pastor of a Presbyterian congregation of 30, he found 'a mudhole surrounded by barrooms.' Thoughtful proprietors had laid planks up to their doors, and to thirsty patrons access was easy, though more than one had to be plucked from the mud on an unsuccessful exit. Young Jacobs waged a crusade for temperance; organized a Sunday school, a library society, a lyceum course, and from his hand press put out a thin little monthly. In time the mudhole became a respectable square, and the bricks of the last saloon triumphantly crowned the chimney of his house on South Broad Street. The little publication became the medium through which he raised nearly $1,-000,000 for the support of orphan children, and the library society and lyceum paved the way for a high school which in 1900 developed into a college.

A 50¢ donation from an orphan boy and Dr. Jacobs's faith in 'the God of the fatherless,' founded THORNWELL ORPHANAGE, South Broad Street. Opened in 1875, at the death of its founder the institution had assets worth almost $1,000,000, a school providing industrial and technical training for 350 children, and an accredited high school. An assortment of stone and stone-and-wood buildings make up the plant. The arcade of the three-and-a-half-story administration building is supported by two stubby monolithic columns, whipping posts that once stood in front of the Laurens County Courthouse. Octagonal THORNWELL MEMORIAL CHAPEL has a pyramided roof and a belfry.

Jacobs was also founder of PRESBYTERIAN COLLEGE, South Broad St., a coeducational institution with more than 300 students. In the center of the campus is the domed red brick administration building, its plaza met by a double driveway between extensive landscaped lawns. Faculty houses, dormitories, and class buildings fulfill the plans of Charles Leavitt, landscape architect. The library, in William Plumer Jacobs Science Hall, includes a collection of rare Caroliniana. North of the administration building is Leroy Springs Gymnasium with an exceptionally fine swimming pool. Annually in May, when the State Intercollegiate Track Meet is held on the field east of the gymnasium, hundreds of fans gather here. Tennis is especially promoted as part of the athletic program, and State-wide competition is a yearly event on the well kept clay courts; the school's fall 'Tennis Clinic' draws students from schools and colleges of the southeastern States; instruction is given on the courts, in the gymnasium, and in classrooms, with the aid of motion pictures.

At Clinton is a junction with State 56 (*see Tour 17*).

The COUNTRY CLUB (R), 70 *m.*, is maintained by the towns of Clinton and Laurens.

LAURENS, 74 *m.* (589 alt., 5,443 pop.) (*see Tour 10*), is at the junction with US 221 (*see Tour 17*) and US 276 (*see Tour 10*).

At PRINCETON, 91 *m.* (183 pop.) (*see Tour 8a*), is the junction with US 25 (*see Tour 8a*).

✼✼✼

Tour 10

(Brevard, N. C.)—Caesars Head—Travelers Rest—Greenville—Fountain Inn—Laurens; US 276. North Carolina Line to Laurens, 71.1 *m.*

Roadbed concrete-paved between North Carolina Line and Fountain Inn; the remainder with asphalt.
Greenville and Northern R.R. parallels route between a point 7 m. SE. of North Carolina Line and Greenville; Charleston and Western Carolina between Greenville and Laurens.
Hotels and tourist homes in larger towns; few tourist camps.

In and out among the ancient wooded peaks of the Blue Ridge the route passes summer resorts and mill villages before it reaches the lower region of the Piedmont with its vast industrial interests and rolling farmlands.

Numerous little churches are set back from the road in groves of red or white oak. Services are generally held once a month and a minister's circuit includes several churches in the same neighborhood. In the spring, almost every congregation has a 'graveyard cleaning' when men, women, and children come on a weekday to clear the winter's debris from the cemetery, plant flowers, and prop up tombstones. It is an all-day affair, and unhappy memories are diverted by the midday picnic dinner, during which politics, courting, and gossip vie with ghosts of departed friends and family. A typical announcement of such an occasion in 1939 appeared in a local newspaper: 'All persons having dead buried in the Little River Baptist Church cemetery, Long Run, are asked to meet Thursday morning, July 27, to clear off the cemetery. They are requested to bring tools necessary, and a picnic basket. Lunch will be served on the grounds.'

US 276 crosses the NORTH CAROLINA LINE, 0 *m.*, 12 miles southeast of Brevard, North Carolina.

CAESARS HEAD, 2.6 *m.* (3,115 alt., 10 pop.), a resort since antebellum times, was named for a rock that juts impressively from the mountainside 1,200 feet above the Saluda River Valley. The high promontory overlooks The Dismal, the steep valley below, and remotely resembles a head. Three versions of the name are: a fancied likeness to the profile of Julius Caesar, a resemblance to somebody's dog named 'Caesar,' and the corruption of the Indian word for chieftain, 'Sachem.'

At 9.6 *m.* is the junction with State 183.

Right here 2.7 *m.* to a dirt road; R. here 0.7 *m.* to the reservoir of the GREEN-VILLE MUNICIPAL WATERWORKS, completed in 1928. The tract, including the Saluda River headwaters, supplies almost 10,000,000,000 gallons for the reservoir. No filtering or chemical treatment is necessary.

At 14 *m.* on US 276 is the junction with Jones Gap Road, almost impassable now except on foot.

Left here to a mountain area of great scenic beauty. The road was built in ante-bellum days by Solomon Jones, who may have been 'America's first scenic road builder.' Contradicting the theory of Jones's artistic skill is the legend that Susie, a pig, planned the trail. Loose on the mountainside, Susie dashed hither and yon, Jones close behind. Her caprice created the succession of curves and bends now characterizing the road. When Jones died and was buried, his tombstone was carved with, 'He left the world better than he found it.'

In CLEVELAND, 15.5 *m.* (150 pop.), the highway runs between an old gristmill and the one-room store holding the post office. The town is around a railroad station (L), about half a mile away. Many summer cottages hide in the forest-covered coves.

A WAYSIDE PARK (L), 16 *m.*, has picnicking facilities.

MARIETTA, 20 *m.* (300 pop.), is known over the State for gardens from which flowers and shrubs are sold. Among the old dwellings here is CLEVELAND HOUSE, built about 1830–40 by Harvey Cleveland and still owned by his descendants. Approached through an avenue of unusually large holly trees, the white frame house with two-story portico has paired columns and elliptical arches.

Left from Marietta on a paved road 0.6 m. to the SLATER MILL, which manufactures rayon. A stone in front of the mill office building was taken from the plant built in 1790 by Samuel Slater in Rhode Island; this was the first American textile mill.

TRAVELERS REST, 25.4 m. (1,088 alt., 322 pop.), was early an overnight stop for stagecoaches, the last pause for northbound passengers before the steep climb into the Blue Ridge. Community life here centers about a cotton mill and a 15-teacher consolidated school. After the early breakfast hour, overalled workers stream toward the large textile plant, and school busses, rolling down from remote mountain glens, unload their noisy cargoes of children. Some of the mill workers live on small ancestral patches among the hills and daily come to work in the mills.

This little hamlet was catapulted into prominence in 1938 after the publication of Ben Robertson's *Travelers Rest*. The scene is laid in the region, though the name does not specifically apply to this village. Published by the author, it had little sale until South Carolina patriotic societies advertised it by vituperative attack, asserting the account to be libelous of a heroic age. Hard-bitten frontiersmen swore their way through the story, fighting, loving, and drinking vigorously. Among the author's source material were letters now preserved at the University of South Carolina. When the objections reverberated in the press, there was an overnight demand for the book, reviewers took it up, and it was included in an omnibus of contemporary literature.

At Travelers Rest is the junction with US 25 (*see Tour 8a*), which unites with US 276 between this point and Greenville.

'Bloody Bill' Bates, a troublesome Tory, harassed this section during the torrid months before the Battle of Kings Mountain (*see Tour 16*). Among the frontiersmen Bates was referred to as 'the Plundering Scout' because of his thieving proclivities. After the war Bloody Bill was driven into the mountain hiding places, and later, after his arrest for horse stealing, he was shot without trial while a prisoner in the Greenville jail.

At 29.1 m. the route forks, affording an alternate route into Greenville.

Right at the fork to THE ROCK HOUSE (R), 1.5 m., erected early in the nineteenth century for Captain Billy Young, who had been a boy hero of the Revolution. Set back from the road amid trees in an old-fashioned garden, the two-and-a-half-story structure, with gable roof and modillioned cornice, said to have been built by the same masons who constructed Poinsett Bridge (*see Tour 8a*), has 30-inch walls of irregular blocks of stone. The piazza is a later addition. An old walnut secretary in the wide hall was used as a 'post office' when mail was brought by stagecoach. As one of General Marion's band, Young was known as the 'Terror of the Tories,' although only 23 at the close of the war.

GREENVILLE is at 5.8 *m.* on the alternate route. On the main route to Greenville (L) is the junction with a dirt road 29.1 *m.*

Left here 2.9 *m.* to another dirt road; L. 0.9 *m.* to 1,500-acre PARIS MOUNTAIN STATE PARK (L), which includes three lakes and the wooded slopes of Paris Mountain.

In GREENVILLE, 34.7 *m.* (966 alt., 29,154 pop.) (*see Greenville*), are the junctions with US 25 (*see Tour 8a*), US 29 (*see Tour 7*), and State 13 (*see Tour 14*).

At SIMPSONVILLE, 47.7 *m.* (1,400 pop.), is one of the oldest roads in South Carolina. At first an Indian path, it was utilized for stagecoaches between Georgia and North Carolina. Even now the improved route is called the Old Georgia, or Old Pinckneyville Road.

FOUNTAIN INN, 52.6 *m.* (889 alt., 1,264 pop.), took its name from an inn when stagecoaches stopped here overnight on trips between Greenville and Charleston. The inn was named for a fountain in its yard. A local journalist, Robert Quillen, attracted national interest to the town in the 1920's when he erected a MONUMENT TO MOTHER EVE. It is now hidden in the shrubbery of his fenced grove on Main Street; near the monument is the little study in which Quillen daily prepares his widely syndicated column of biting epigrams and familiar essays. Pansy growing, begun here as the hobby of a retired physician, has developed into an extensive business. Here was born Clayton Bates, Negro dancer, who, despite the loss of a leg in early youth, rose to theatrical fame as 'Peg Leg' Bates.

Right from Fountain Inn on a hard-surfaced county road 5.3 *m.* to a dirt road; L. here 0.3 *m.* to FAIRVIEW PRESBYTERIAN CHURCH (R), a white frame building, with a square-columned portico having a window in its pediment. The church, founded in 1786, is in a grove of tall pines near its graveyard, which contains bodies of soldiers who fought in all the wars of this country. Also here is a monument to family physicians and their wives.

The Fairview stock show (*free; early fall*), established in 1886, is held near the church; it attracts large numbers of people. Homemade refreshments are sold and the show is conducted with the decorum of a Sunday school picnic. Awards consist of ribbons and small cash prizes. Each year plans for the show are made with prayer, and the event has never been spoiled by rain or marred by a serious accident.

FORK SHOALS, 8.3 *m.* on the hard-surfaced road (371 pop.), was the scene of the Battle of Great Cane Brake, concluding battle of the Snow Campaign, so called because of the season's severity. A canal around the shoals here was part of the State's ante-bellum inland navigation system.

West of Fork Shoals a dirt road leads to a junction with US 25 (*see Tour 8a*), 13.6 *m.*, about 18 miles south of Greenville.

OWINGS, 58.7 *m.* (807 alt., 400 pop.), and GRAY COURT, 60.6 *m.* (320 pop.), have combined their schools into one institution placed halfway between them. In this vicinity are many kennels where pedigreed dogs are raised.

LAURENS, 71.1 *m.* (589 alt., 5,443 pop.), seat of Laurens County, is in a homogeneous region. Of the 42,094 people in the county only 37 were not native-born in 1930. Planters and tenants, bank presidents and mill operatives, all are close kin; and their families hark back to the days of pre-Revolutionary Scotch-Irish settlement. The home stay-ing proclivities of Laurens people have persisted through Revolutionary skirmishes, when the Tories were easy to find hereabouts; through hostilities of opposing factions in the secession wrangle; through Con-federate excitement, race riots, and wholesale Ku Klux arrests, which included a leading clergyman; through Red Shirt times when the county's vote was eliminated by Republican officials from the Demo-cratic count; and down to the present. The nostalgia of a native son, later an adopted Low Countryman, is evidenced in *The State That Forgot* (1932) by W. W. Ball, editor of the *News and Courier*, Charleston.

When energies have not been burned up in wrangling, they have turned to civic betterment. Here began the educational efforts of Wil Lou Gray, devoted helper of the underprivileged, whose work in the State Department of Education is known in far places.

On court and election days, both of which are socially and politically significant here as elsewhere in South Carolina, the narrow streets are crowded with folk from the farms and villages. Basket lunches for people and bales of hay for mules are jammed into wagons between men and women who would not miss the occasion except through an act of God. Conversation rises and falls, a sea of talk wherein words like waves are indistinguishable. Couples find courting opportunities, mothers discuss teething nostrums, while politicians argue and orate.

Away from the unimpressive little stores the streets become narrow, and pass between houses with wide lawns developed in recent years by garden clubs. Little River meanders through the town, giving oppor-tunity for park and playground development. A railroad almost circles the midsection and here are the smoke-grimed shacks of the poor. On the edge of the business area, Negro shops and cafés extract the few dollars of the field hands on Saturday. The odor of fried fish is irre-sistible to many whose 'Satdy' is a real holiday.

The LAURENS COURTHOUSE, built in 1838 and remodeled in 1911, rises from the town square, and the 'Oyez—Oyez' of the crier is the signal for the crowd to herd into the small building. Of gray stone, the structure has two four-column Corinthian porticos sheltering bal-conies and balustrade; each portico is approached by a Palladian stair-way, overgrown with vines. A low elliptical dome centers the roof.

In the NATIONAL GUARD ARMORY, opposite the courthouse, occurred a nationally discussed riot in 1870 when armed Negroes, led by a 'scalawag,' whose slogan was 'matches are cheap,' set out to burn the town. The townsmen struck back as one man and smothered the riot, unaware of the attention they had aroused.

On the north side of the square stood the little tailor shop of run-away apprentice Andrew Johnson, later Lincoln's successor in the White House. Here between sessions with his needle and tailor's goose, he pored over his books. At times he would help the young ladies of Laurens in their quiltmaking. Some of the coverlets he designed are still valued heirlooms in the family of a girl whom he wooed without success.

On Main Street at the end of Church Street is the CHURCH OF THE EPIPHANY, consecrated in 1850. The characteristic Up Country building is of red brick, the columns and pilasters of brick stuccoed white. The belfry is of wood painted white.

On the eastern edge of the town is the LAURENS GLASS WORKS, established by citizens who use silicates found in the county and other sand from Williamsburg County. On Main and Holmes Streets is the HOLMES PLACE, an octagon-shaped house, built by Doctor Zelotes L. Holmes about 1825. The plan of this house is unusual, with four porches and four rooms on the ground floor. Besides front and rear halls, there is a central hall, running through both stories and lighted by a skylight. The brick structure, covered with buff stucco, has an octagonal hip roof. The windows have stone lintels and sills, and each porch has four octagonal stuccoed brick columns. Doctor Holmes was a zealous clergyman who established churches and schools throughout the county.

At Laurens is the junction with US 76 (*see Tour 9c*) and US 221 (*see Tour 17*).

Tour 11

(Wilmington, N. C.)—Little River—Georgetown—Charleston—Beaufort—(Savannah, Ga.); Intracoastal Waterway. North Carolina Line to Georgia Line, 203 nautical miles.

Railroads: Atlantic Coast Line Railroad and Seaboard Air Line Railway cross the waterway at intervals, both running nearly parallel to the route from Charleston to Savannah.

Information: Charleston Division of the Coast and Geodetic Survey issues latest information on waterway monthly at the U. S. Engineer's Office, Customhouse, Charleston, S. C. *Inside Route Pilot—New York to Key West,* and charts for the course published by the U. S. Coast and Geodetic Survey, can be obtained from Washington and at the Hammond Book Store, 10 Broad St., Charleston, S. C.

Communications: Telephone and telegraph services available at Georgetown, Charleston, and Beaufort; telephone facilities also available at Socastee Bridge, McClellanville, Isle of Palms, Yonges Island, and Martins Point; mail facilities at all the same points except Socastee Bridge.

Supplies: Limited at Little River, Socastee Bridge, McClellanville, Isle of Palms, Yonges Island, Martins Point, and Beaufort. Ample repair facilities, wharves and supplies, at Georgetown and Charleston.

Accommodations: Limited at smaller points, hotels in larger cities; vary with season.

Waterway Dimensions: Little River to Winyah Bay, 8 feet depth, 75 feet bottom width; Winyah Bay to Charleston, 10 feet depth, 90 feet bottom width; Charleston to Beaufort, 7 feet depth, 75 feet bottom width.

The Intracoastal Waterway in South Carolina, roughly paralleling US 17 (*see Tour* 1), is a sheltered route passing through marshes, between high banks, and behind a shining chain of barrier islands. Blue-green salt water alternates with the dark peat-stained waters of lazy, lowland rivers, and in a few places the waterway is yellowed with mud brought down from the Piedmont. Deer slip to the water's edge in the misty early morning, and the mud often shows the tracks of the elusive wild turkey. The sly 'coon steals to the water to wash his food, and silvery, leaping fish splash ripples on the quiet surface.

Section a. NORTH CAROLINA LINE to GEORGETOWN, 55 m. Intracoastal Waterway.

Tall pines line the banks (R) and marsh grass (L) spreads a green blanket that turns to gold in fall. Beyond the flat marshlands the blue sparkle of the ocean is glimpsed between white sand dunes.

The waterway crosses the NORTH CAROLINA LINE, 0 *m.*, about 50 miles south of Wilmington, North Carolina, and sweeps around TILGHMAN'S POINT (L) into LITTLE RIVER. As late as the first quarter of the eighteenth century, pirates cruised in and out of the sheltered inlets. In history and legend, Captain Kidd, Edward Teach— the ruthless 'Blackbeard'—urbane Major Stede Bonnet, and many others are associated with this area. At Tilghman's Point are the remnants of FORT RANDALL, a Confederate battery.

LITTLE RIVER, 3 *m.* (10 alt., 2,219 pop.), is near the mouth of the river for which it was named. This shell of a once prosperous lumbering town is on US 17 (*see Tour 1a*).

A swing-type drawbridge, 80 feet high, crosses Little River, 6 *m.*, and marks the northern end of the cut through one of the region's few highlands. Bedded in the black banks are lines of white sea shells that record shore lines of ancient times. Big white gannets with black tipped wings lumber overhead, and pigs sometimes wander down from hidden farm houses to nuzzle in the mud.

The bascule bridge at 21.5 *m.* (*signals should be given in good time as the bridge opens slowly*) is used by the Atlantic Coast Line R.R. and a county road.

Left on the county road 4 *m.* to MYRTLE BEACH (*see Tour 1a*).

The canal continues through SOCASTEE CREEK and passes under SOCASTEE BRIDGE, 26.5 *m.*, traversed by US 501 (*see Tour 15*). The bridge replaces old Peachtree Ferry, which was formerly two miles north of the span over the Waccamaw River.

The SOCASTEE YACHT BASIN (R), 17 feet deep, can accommodate approximately 100 yachts (*cabs to Myrtle Beach*).

North of ENTERPRISE (L), 31.7 *m.*, the high cut gives way to low marshland beds where waxy waterlilies cover the sloughs along the water's edge. Enterprise, an all but deserted settlement, was an important shipping point for rice and naval stores. Here the black WACCAMAW RIVER (R) twists into the waterway.

Right on Waccamaw River to CONWAY, 13 m. (25 alt., 3,011 pop.) (anchorage facilities; arrangements can be made for deep-sea and river fishing).

Here is the northern end of Waccamaw Neck, a sliver of land between the ocean and Waccamaw River; the southern end is at Georgetown. Some of the earliest and largest plantations in the State line the river banks, and there are glimpses of white plantation houses behind umbrellalike live oaks. Formerly owned by prosperous rice and indigo planters, these estates are now the sunny playgrounds of rich Northerners. From his grandfather, Isaac Emerson, George Vanderbilt inherited the 10,000-acre Arcadia (formerly Prospect Hill); Bernard M. Baruch entertains friends for duck hunting at his Hobcaw Barony; Tom Yawkey, the Fords, and the DuPonts spend many winter days in this picturesque land with its haunting memories of the past.

Rice growing, of major importance in ante-bellum farming, necessitated the flooding of the fields from May to November, and plantation owners went away during this period to escape the miasmic fumes. In her *Chronicles of Chicora Wood*, Elizabeth W. Alston Pringle (*see Tour* 20) wrote of the annual trek:

At the end of May my father's entire household migrated to the sea, which was only four miles to the east of *Chicora* as the crow flies, but only to be reached by going seven miles in a row-boat and four miles by land. The vehicles, cows, furniture, bedding, trunks, provisions were all put into great flats, some sixty by twenty feet, others even larger, at first dawn, and sent ahead. Then the family got into the row-boat and were rowed down the Pee Dee, then through Squirrel Creek, with vines tangled above them and waterlilies and flags and wild roses and scarlet lobelia all along the banks, and every now and then the hands would stop their song a moment to call out: 'Missy, a alligator! . . .' There were six splendid oarsmen, who sang from the moment the boat got underway.

Each plantation had a 'visiting' boat captained by a Negro uniformed in bright livery, and manned by stalwart, black oarsmen. The songs of these boatsmen were generally known, but each group had an individual variation, which is still apparent among the old timers. Many of the songs and a few colloquial terms still live from the rice era. A *ben horsal* is a half moon embankment introduced into South Carolina according to tradition by a Dutchman, Van Hassel; *Joe Fuller*, nobody knows why, is the name for a stump so large that the drain for the rice field had to detour around it.

Only the rotting remains of a large lumber mill and sagging wharf at BUCKSPORT (R), 33.4 *m.*, indicate that large quantities of lumber were once shipped here. Floating camps were anchored in the swamps and squat, dirty tugboats pulled virgin timber to the mill. Streets of cottages radiated into the thick woods, and a community thrived in the shadow of the steamy mill. Bucksport was the last of three lumber camps established by Henry Buck (*see Tour* 20).

Flowing into the waterway, BULL CREEK (R), 35.3 *m.*, adds a red smear to the black waters of the passage. Opposite Bull Creek, LONG-WOOD CREEK (L) empties into the marshes and the tower of an old lumber mill rises behind a grove of live oaks. A vault in the river bank is said to have been used by smugglers and bootleggers. Though these creeks were once used for traffic, they are now as empty as the abandoned rice fields, with their crumbling chimneys that mark the sites of former rice mills.

WACHESAW LANDING (*private*), 37 *m.*, on the site (L) of an ancient Indian settlement, once shipped large quantities of rice and naval stores.

MONTERINO, locally called Mount Rena, the landing for SANDY ISLAND (R), is just south of Wachesaw Landing. Here were established settlements of slaves so that they would be nearer the fields. Often the plantation houses were some miles away. Hagley, True Blue, Brookgreen, and Wachesaw all refer to sections of the island used by plantations of corresponding name. The present-day Sandy Islanders paddle across the river in early morning and late afternoon in home-made boats, going to and from their work at Brookgreen Gardens. After living for years in primitive simplicity, these Negroes now have a school and hospital, provided by a Northern friend. In the more remote areas of the island the shy white egrets still nest, and a sanctuary for these birds has been established here.

BROOKGREEN CREEK, 45 *m.* (*navigable for boats drawing 6 feet*), leads to the landing for BROOKGREEN GARDENS (*see Tour 1a*).

Yellow with mud, the waterway flows past HAGLEY LANDING (L), 51.8 *m.*, of Hagley Plantation. This was formerly the terminus of the old Georgetown ferry, which has been displaced by the completion of the La Fayette Bridge. Jutting out into the stream, rows of piling show where boats once loaded.

The swing-type draw of LA FAYETTE MEMORIAL BRIDGE, 53.4 *m.*, marks the entrance to WINYAH BAY.

GEORGETOWN, 55 *m.* (14 alt., 5,082 pop.) (*see Tour 1a*), is on the southern rim of Winyah Bay.

Section b.   GEORGETOWN to CHARLESTON, 54.5 m.
Intracoastal Waterway.

The sounds and bays here are rimmed with a jungle of scrub cedars, marsh grass, yaupon, and palms.

South of GEORGETOWN, 0 *m.*, the channel sweeps the southern side of Winyah Bay, in sight of plantation houses beyond groves of live oaks, first at MARYVILLE, then MOUNT HOPE, then BELLE ISLE (*see Tour 1b*), which has a notable garden.

Leaving the bay through the seven-mile-long ESTERVILLE-MINIM CANAL, 5.6 *m.*, the waterway passes NORTH ISLAND with its light, SOUTH ISLAND, and CAT ISLAND, all L. At his plantation on North Island, Major Benjamin Huger entertained La Fayette and DeKalb when they landed in America to offer assistance to the Revolutionary cause. Rice birds, once a serious pest, feed unmolested along the banks. Locally called May-birds, because of the time of their arrival, they settled in chattering multitudes on the growing rice. Plantation 'bird-minders,' armed with muskets, tin pans, and rawhide whips, were stationed on the banks to scare the marauders away. Planters generally prohibited the shooting of wild ducks as they devoured the volunteer rice and prevented its seeding. But ducks were a tasty item on the menu, and a few shots from the gun of a field hand would bring down enough for a large dinner.

The waterway leaves the canal for DUCK CREEK, west of LITTLE CROW ISLAND, to flow into BIG DUCK CREEK, 10 *m.*, then into the NORTH SANTEE RIVER, 12 *m.* The confluence of these streams forms NORTH SANTEE BAY.

FAIRFIELD PLANTATION (*see Tour 1b*) is on the south bank where the SOUTH SANTEE RIVER flows into the waterway, 14 *m.* A line of chimneys (L) shows where the slave quarters stood.

ALLIGATOR CREEK, 16.7 *m.*, is at the northern end of the CAPE ROMAINE BIRD SANCTUARY, a 35,000-acre wild-life refuge. Extending through Bulls Island, the sanctuary has both salt and fresh water to attract migratory birds. The great heron, the Louisiana heron, and the black-crowned night heron as well as gulls, plovers, and ducks all live here in the sheltered swamps. The big white egret soars peacefully over the palmettos and live oaks on the mainland. The great blue heron is a dignified fisherman here, though among the natives his long lanky frame gives him the name of 'Po' Joe.' A perennial local question is: 'Did you ever see a fat "Po' Joe" sitting on a dead live oak stump eating green blackberries and taking a fresh salt water bath?' The CAPE ROMAINE LIGHT (L) has been leaning noticeably for 70 years, but it is considered sound and the lenses have been adjusted to the angle.

From Alligator Creek the waterway leads through a number of other small natural passages to McCLELLANVILLE, 22.5 *m.* (600 pop.) (*see Tour 1b*), a post village on TOWN CREEK (*anchorage for small boats*).

Now a blue-green salty stream, the waterway passes through MATTHEWS CUT into HARBOR RIVER, 27.2 *m.*, which empties into BULLS BAY, 30.2 *m.* Oysters from Bulls Bay are famous over South Carolina, and the village of AWENDAW, 33 *m.*, near Awendaw Creek, owes its livelihood to the preparation of oysters for shipping. SEWEE BAY (L) was named for an Indian tribe, and on its shores are numerous mounds of refuse from prehistoric dwellings. After the white men came, the Sewee Indians felt that the settlers were not giving them a fair deal, and they planned to seek the English king and personally lay their grievances before him. Building huge canoes, they sailed into the open sea and were never heard of again, though a pirate, captured soon after the Indians' disappearance, swore that he had seen the canoes far out in the Atlantic. The waterway passes many small islands and oyster beds that swarm with birds. At PRICE'S CREEK, 37.3 *m.*, dikes (R) hold back the salt mud thrown up by the dredges, and protect the oyster beds.

The southern boundary of the Cape Romaine Bird Sanctuary is at CAPERS INLET, 40.6 *m.* Whitecaps break against the sand dunes of CAPERS ISLAND (L). Crossing wide BULL YARD SOUND the waterway reaches DEWEES INLET, 44 *m.*, and goes into SEVEN REACHES and MEETING REACH. In prohibition days GOAT ISLAND (R), covered with palms and thick underbrush, was a popular resort for bootleggers. It now has only one inhabitant. On PORCHER'S BLUFF (R) are huge piles of shells containing pieces of broken pottery left from Sewee Indian days.

Just north of LITTLE GOAT ISLAND (L) is HAMLIN CREEK, 45.7 *m.*

> Right on Hamlin Creek (*navigable for boats drawing 5 feet*) 1.3 *m.* to the ISLE OF PALMS (*see Tour 1b*), a beach resort.

At the southern end of this island a bridge over Breech Inlet connects with SULLIVAN'S ISLAND (R), 49 *m.*, which was named for Captain Florence O'Sullivan, captain of the *Carolina*, first English ship to bring settlers here, 1670, and a member of the provincial parliament in 1672. On Sullivan's Island is FORT MOULTRIE (*see Tour 1b*).

SULLIVAN'S ISLAND NARROWS, the inland passage west of the island, passes into COVE INLET, which is spanned by a swing-type drawbridge 62 feet high (*use northeast opening, other foul and obstructed*).

CHARLESTON HARBOR (*see Charleston*), is about three miles wide where the waterway crosses it. The COOPER RIVER BRIDGE soars on two high spans 150 feet above the water to connect Charleston with the mainland at MOUNT PLEASANT (*see Tour 1b*). CASTLE PINCKNEY (R) was built at the harbor entrance as a fortification and is now a depot for buoy tenders. HOG ISLAND (R), granted to Landgrave Edmund Bellinger in 1694, is only a marshy plat on the surface of the water. Opposite Castle Pinckney and Hog Island is FORT SUMTER (R), deserted and gloomy, its weathered brick walls enclosing only bright-hued oleanders. Named for General Thomas Sumter, the 'Gamecock' of the Revolution, this fort was begun in 1829 but was still unfinished in 1860 when South Carolina seceded. Six days after secession Major Anderson and his Federal garrison from Sullivan's Island occupied the fort; the Secessionists retaliated by seizing the surrounding islands and all United States property in Charleston. The first shots of the war were fired when the steamer, *Star of the West*, bringing troops and provisions to Fort Sumter, was shelled by a Confederate battery on Morris Island across the bay. Three months later

the Confederate commander General Beauregard bombarded the fort
33 hours until it was evacuated. Confederates then occupied and held
it until 1865, despite many desultory Federal attacks and three long
furious bombardments, 1863–4. An ironclad squadron was repulsed;
13-inch mortars used by Federals were found ineffective, as were the
Requa 24-barreled machine guns, said to be the first rapid-fire guns
using metallic cartridges employed in actual combat. When the fortifications here and elsewhere in and around Charleston were evacuated
February 17, 1865, due to Union land successes, there had been 567
days of continuous military operations against them. 'It was, and still
remains,' said a military writer in 1937, 'the longest siege in modern
history.' After the war, Fort Sumter was repaired and garrisoned for
a while by the United States. The 160-foot lighthouse on MORRIS
ISLAND (L), beyond Fort Sumter, was for many years the only light
south of Delaware Capes on the Atlantic Coast. The UNITED STATES
QUARANTINE STATION is on JAMES ISLAND (L).

South Carolina's largest city is CHARLESTON, 54.5 m. (9 alt.,
62,265 pop.) (see Charleston) (municipal yacht basin south of city
opposite waterway's south entrance; nominal docking fee).

Section c. CHARLESTON to GEORGIA STATE LINE, 93.5 m.
Intracoastal Waterway.

As the route proceeds southward, palmettos increase in number and
size, and march along the skyline as if in military formation. Skirting
the southern tip of CHARLESTON, 0 m., the waterway winds northwest up the ASHLEY RIVER in view of THE BATTERY (R), Charleston's fashionable promenade and residential section. ELLIOTT's or WAP-
POO CUT is a narrow passage bulkheaded on both sides with granite.
Vegetation becomes more lush, making it apparent why early planters,
searching for a variety of exports, introduced many tropical plants.
Oranges and olives were successfully grown and exported, though in
small quantities during the early colonial days.

South of Charleston the islands and the border of the mainland are
more populous than they are farther north. Many islands are inhabited
only by Negroes. For years the men of this section have gone to the
creeks and the ocean for oysters, shrimp, crabs, clams, and fish for
their tables and for market. These people produce some truck crops,
and they also serve as guides when the hunting preserves are open
in winter.

Wappoo Cut passes into the upper reaches of the STONO RIVER,
4 m.

> Left on the Stono River 13 m. to FOLLY ISLAND (see Tour 1c), a popular
> seashore resort. Great oaks line this passage and many Negroes in leaky home-
> made boats ply the course searching for sea food. Tall green-topped cane patches
> almost hide the little cabins, and pickaninnies rush out to hail the passing boats.

A Seaboard Air Line drawbridge spanning the waterway, 8.3 m. is
63 feet high. The JOHNS ISLAND BRIDGE, 11 m., is a 60-foot-high

drawbridge connecting the island with the mainland. Numerous small settlements are along the route.

The channel passes another Seaboard Air Line drawbridge, 12.3 *m.*, into CHURCH FLATS, wide marshlands. About a mile eastward two tides meet coming westward up Church Creek and Wadmalaw River, and it is said that in olden days, when travel hereabouts was chiefly by boat, parishioners often came to church on the rising tide and returned on the ebb.

In WADMALAW SOUND the route passes GLOVER PLACE (L) and DIXIE PLANTATION (R), old estates. It was ever the custom for families coming up this crooked passage from Beaufort to Charleston to land at COOK'S KITCHEN, in the marshes here, to prepare their last meal before reaching the city.

From the headwaters of WADMALAW RIVER, 17.4 *m.*, the waterway sweeps past NEW CUT PLANTATION (R), opposite the new settlement of TOWLES, which has a mansard-roofed building stilted on high brick pillars. In WADMALAW SOUND the route goes to YONGES LANDING, 21.3 *m.*, a post settlement (*railroad terminus*). There is a small factory here for shipping oysters, and some truck is grown.

MARTIN'S POINT, 22 *m.*, is a settlement on WADMALAW ISLAND (L). The passage twists through shell banks and marshes to the NORTH EDISTO RIVER, where it is joined by the DAWHO RIVER (R).

Left down the North Edisto 13 *m.* to BOHICKET CREEK; L. here 1.7 *m.* to ROCKVILLE, where sailboat races are annually held the first Tuesday, Wednesday, and Thursday of August, attracting several thousand spectators. Many of the competing boats are locally designed with a tremendous sail spread. Instead of the customary boom of a little brass cannon, the crack of a shotgun in the hands of the local chief-of-police is the signal for the race to start. Across Bohicket Creek, opposite Rockville, are SEABROOK ISLAND and KIAWAH ISLAND.

SLANN HOUSE, an old plantation dwelling, is on SLANN ISLAND (R), as the passage narrows to a small canal bordering (R) WHOOPING ISLAND. A swing-type draw, DAWHO BRIDGE, 30.2 *m.*, joins the mainland with EDISTO ISLAND (L), on which is Edisto State Park (*see Tour 1c*). Built in 1790, PROSPECT HILL, on Edisto Island, was designed by James Hoban, afterward architect of the White House in Washington.

Just east of the bridge the Dawho River sweeps R. and the canal turns L., passing through NORTH CREEK and WATTS CUT to the SOUTH EDISTO RIVER, 33 *m.* The river winds past SAMSON ISLAND (R) and RACCOON ISLAND (L), a hunting preserve belonging to the Dodge family. This section of the waterway is popular with hunters and with fishermen seeking trout and bass.

FENWICK CUT, 39.5 *m.*, leads to ASHEPOO RIVER, 41 *m.* The channel proceeds through an artificial cut to ROCK CREEK, and to the entrance of ST. HELENA SOUND, 44.7 *m.*, one of the broadest estuaries on the lower coast. Its greatest width is 6.5 miles.

Left here for sailors unafraid of approximately 11 miles of open sea rounding HUNTING ISLAND and swinging R. to rejoin the waterway in PORT ROYAL SOUND at the southern tip of St. Helena Island.

The main waterway crosses the sound and proceeds up the COOSAW RIVER with MORGAN ISLAND (L) adjoining COOSAW ISLAND at 47 *m.* The last is inhabited only by Negroes, and has never known an automobile, telephone, or bathtub. During the Indian uprising of 1715 the Coosaw descended on the island and carried off the wife of Captain John Bull, who was away from home. Upon his return he found his wife's slippers, dropped in the woods, but he never saw her again.

Separated from Coosaw Island by a narrow creek is LADIES ISLAND, connected by a bridge with ST. HELENA ISLAND (*see Tour 5C*). Leaving the Coosaw River, 53.4 *m.*, the passage continues through BRICKYARD CREEK to the BEAUFORT RIVER and to BEAUFORT, 60.4 *m.* (21 alt., 2,776 pop.) (*see Beaufort*), the second oldest city in South Carolina (*steamboat connections with Savannah and Charleston; anchorage at city wharves*). Here, on a broad expanse of water, returning oyster boats are seen in the late afternoon, with their wide-spread sunset-dyed sails; and smaller craft with dripping shrimp nets steal in close to the banks. Negroes pole awkward homemade boats along the banks and in and out of the marshy creeks searching for shrimp and crabs for the canneries at Port Royal.

Southeast of Beaufort the waterway continues down the Beaufort River toward Port Royal Sound, between PORT ROYAL ISLAND (R) and LADIES ISLAND (L). On CAT ISLAND (L) was once a nudist colony (*see Tour 5c*).

The three-sided tabby structure seen at 62.5 *m.* is FORT FREDERICK, erected in 1731. The fort has lost its fourth side to the tides.

BATTERY CREEK (L) and ARCHER CREEK (R) empty into the BEAUFORT RIVER, 63.4 *m.*

1. Right on Archer Creek to the BROAD RIVER for an alternate route in very rough weather; L. down Broad River to Port Royal Sound; R. to rejoin the waterway as it enters SKULL CREEK between HILTON HEAD ISLAND (L) and PINCKNEY ISLAND (R) (*take warning: rifle range near by*).

2. Left 1 *m.* inland on Battery Creek to Port Royal (800 pop.) (*see Tour 5c*).

Southeast across Battery Creek is PARRIS ISLAND, United States Marine Post (*see Tour 5c*).

Extending (L) for 6 miles is ST. HELENA ISLAND (*see Tour 5A*). In the early morning Negroes go into the marshes in small boats to gather the marsh grass that grows between the islands for use as provender for their farm animals. On the tip of the island just east of the water tower is FORT FREMONT. BAY POINT is at the extreme southeastern end of these islands.

In PORT ROYAL SOUND, 69.5 *m.* (*see Tour 5c*), the course bears westward. In 1663 the *Adventure* out of Barbados under Captain William Hilton was the first English ship to enter these waters. Three years later Captain Robert Sandford touched here with Doctor Henry

Woodward, an English surgeon. They promised the Indians to come back with more settlers, and Doctor Woodward voluntarily remained as a hostage while an Indian sailed back to England with Sandford. Woodward was captured by Spaniards and taken to the East Indies where he was picked up in 1670 by an English vessel. He returned to Charleston and introduced Madagascar rice to Carolina.

During the War between the States, the Federal Government set up a coaling station in Port Royal Sound, and in 1861 sent a fleet of 16 ships with 12,000 men and 175 cannon under General Thomas W. Sherman and Commander S. F. DuPont. The Confederacy having concentrated all efforts on protecting Charleston, only 41 cannon—19 of them considered effective—were left to guard the two small Confederate strongholds, Fort Walker on Hilton Head and Fort Beauregard on Bay Point. The Confederates were commanded by General Thomas F. Drayton, related to Percival Drayton, commander of the *Pocahontas* in the Federal fleet. The Federal forces landed, took possession of the territory, and occupied the sound for the duration of the war.

Below Port Royal Sound SKULL CREEK, which flows between PINCKNEY ISLAND (R) and HILTON (L), enters the waterway at 73.7 *m.* The name of Skull Creek is supposedly a corruption of 'Skulk,' which was applied to the creek because the Indians would skulk in their canoes along the stream when they attacked white settlers. Hilton Head, the site of a large ante-bellum plantation, is a hunting preserve. The island's only means of communication with the mainland is the bi-weekly Beaufort-Savannah steamer.

Pinckney Island was once the estate of Chief Justice Charles Pinckney, whose second wife was Eliza Lucas (*see Tour 1c*). No trace remains of the plantation and mansion house, and the island is inhabited only by Negroes. It was one of several estates inherited in 1752 by the Chief Justice's eldest son, Charles Cotesworth Pinckney (1746–1825), a signer of the Federal Constitution. Young Pinckney, a graduate of Oxford University and law student under Blackstone, was a captain of the first regiment of militia organized in South Carolina for the Revolutionary army and was made brigadier-general by brevet before the end of the war. He was in command of Fort Johnson (*see Tour 1c*) in 1775, and of Fort Moultrie during the siege of Charleston, having served meantime as aide to Washington. When the city fell in 1780, he was among the officers imprisoned at Snee Farm. Before the Revolution, he had served in the provincial assembly, as State attorney-general, and in the provincial congress. As a delegate to the Constitutional Convention in 1788, he was active in important discussions. In 1804 and 1808 he was a candidate for President, but remained a staunch Federalist and refused to offer as Vice President on the Republican ticket with Jefferson. He declined Washington's appointment to the Supreme Court, and later appointments as Secretary of War and Secretary of State, but in 1796 accepted the post of minister to France. Though his wealth and interests were all in the Low Country and he wished Charleston to remain the capital, he was in 1801 one of the strongest advocates of the founding of a State university in Columbia, and served on its first board of trustees. A staunch member of the Anglican church, he was in favor of its disestablishment as the State church. He was the first president of the Charleston Library Society, first vice president of the South Carolina Society of the Cincinnati and in 1806 became president general of the latter, continuing to serve until his death.

SEABROOK LANDING, 74.6 *m.*, has a plant that ships oysters from the many oyster beds in the vicinity.

Skull Creek joins MACKEY'S CREEK, 77.6 *m.*, and empties into CALIBOGUE SOUND. MAY RIVER enters from the west.

Right on the May to BLUFFTON, 6.2 *m.* (520 pop.) (*see Tour 5A*), a small fishing and bathing resort.

The COOPER RIVER (R), 83.3 *m.*, one of two streams of that name in the State, enters Calibogue Sound between DAUFUSKIE ISLAND (L) and BULL ISLAND (R). At HAGUE POINT, locally called Egg Point, on the northern end of Daufuskie Island, is an unused lighthouse. On the northeast end of the island is BLOODY POINT. In the days of early settlement, frequent attacks by Georgia Indians occurred, during which the natives murdered the settlers and plundered the plantations. On what is said to have been the last foray, the Indians got some whisky and camped for the night on the point, where they carelessly built fires that were observed by the whites. The planters were able to slip up on their foes, cut them off from the canoes, and murder all except one, who escaped by swimming to TYBEE ISLAND (L). Hence the name of the point. The treacherous nature of the strip of beach that juts into the ocean here has caused the drowning of many.

At RAMS HORN CREEK, 86.5 *m.*, the tides from Calibogue Sound and Tybee Roads meet and run with considerable strength. The passage proceeds into NEW RIVER, 88 *m.*, and passes DAUFUSKIE LANDING, a regular stopping point for the Beaufort-Savannah steamer.

WALLS CUT, 90 *m.*, a short narrow passage, connects New River with WRIGHT RIVER, 90.7 *m.* The route continues through FIELDS CUT, 91.5 *m.*, which forms the Georgia boundary at a point about 10 miles southeast of Savannah, Georgia.

Tour 12

(Tryon, N. C.)—Landrum—Spartanburg—Union—Junction with US 76; US 176. North Carolina Line to Junction with US 76; 87.6 *m.*

Roadbed concrete-paved with short sections of asphalt.
Southern Ry. parallels route between North Carolina Line and Spartanburg.
Frequent accommodations; hotels in larger towns.

This route winds across the Piedmont. Turbulent rivers produce electric power for textile mills, and natural beauty has been sometimes sacrificed to industrial development. Farmers stolidly follow their plows on former battlefields where their forefathers fought and died, and in cemeteries along the way veterans of seven wars are buried. Dead towns and forsaken mansions attest the river aristocracy of the nineteenth century that fell with the transfer of freight transportation from river to railroad and improved highways. Great plantations have given way to busy textile mills whose collective pay roll is now a larger source of revenue in South Carolina than agriculture.

Section a. NORTH CAROLINA LINE to JUNCTION WITH STATE 11, 55.7 m. US 176.

The highway traverses a countryside of peach orchards and small towns, fences and roadside barns plastered with tattered circus posters. In March the orchards spread a rosy mantle over the hillsides for miles along the highway, and both spring and fall add their changing colors to the forested hills.

In this section sorghum, a kind of syrup-cane, is often grown in bottomland patches. It has little resemblance to the sugar cane of the Low Country, but looks like a slender and graceful stalk of corn with no ears and a cluster of reddish-brown seed at the top. Just before frost, the cane is cut down and stripped of its leaves, after which the stalks are hauled in wagons to the syrup mill, a small outdoor affair owned by a local farmer who makes syrup for his neighbors 'on the shares.' The mill is simply two steel rollers set in a heavy frame, with a long pole attached as a lever. A mule walks round and round to turn the mill, into which a small boy feeds the cane. The sweetish juice runs off into a tub. Everybody is in a good humor, and jokes are cracked about the mule, who is too old and feeble to do more strenuous work. 'A white mule never does die,' declares the farmer; 'when he gets to be fifty years old he turns into a Methodist preacher.' If the speaker is a Methodist, he substitutes 'Baptist preacher.'

The cane juice is poured into the evaporator, a shallow sheet-iron tank fitted into a homemade rock furnace. A wood fire is kept burning, and the smoke is carried off by a low-built chimney. As the greenish juice boils, it must be constantly skimmed and ladled over shallow partitions toward the far end of the evaporator where it will be drained off as finished syrup. Bees fly about the sticky juice and often fall into the boiling vat. The farmer deplores their loss, but knows they will add a honeylike flavor. When fully cooked the syrup is turned into jugs and pails, two thirds of which go to the grower and one third to the owner of the mill. Clear, amber-colored, and with a rich heavy flavor, sorghum is a staple food of the region. One farmer declared: 'I made a hundred gallons last fall, but the children et it up before Christmas and I had to buy sixty gallons more to last 'em till spring.'

US 176 crosses the NORTH CAROLINA LINE, 0 *m.*, about 2 miles south of Tryon, North Carolina.

On the line is the junction with Blackstock Road.

Left on Blackstock Road 0.6 *m.* to a dirt road; R. 0.1 *m.* to the OLD BLOCK- HOUSE, whose stout timber walls have sheltered Indian traders, soldiers of two wars, renegades, bootleggers, and tenant farmers. Erected as a frontier fort and trading post during the Royal Period, it was later a stopping place for drovers on their way to Charleston markets. In the Indian wars settlers frequently with- stood attacks by barricading themselves in the stronghold; it was used alter- nately by both Tories and Whigs during the Revolution; and in the War be- tween the States 500 deserters took refuge in it.

The building straddles the boundary line between North and South Carolina, and also that of two South Carolina counties, Spartanburg and Greenville. Whether or not this geographic position simplified transactions in illicit whiskies, it is known that former bootlegger occupants enjoyed a particular freedom in the sale of their 'corn likker.'

The ROCK CUT (L) at 1.3 *m.* remains from an early effort to estab- lish transmontane communication by rail.

LANDRUM, 2 *m.* (1,063 alt., 1,212 pop.), a popular summer re- sort until the paved roads opened the way to North Carolina moun- tains, was named for a prominent Baptist minister, the Reverend J. G. Landrum, founder of many churches in the section, and father of a South Carolina historian, the Reverend J. B. O. Landrum.

Right from Landrum on a paved road to GOWANSVILLE, 9 *m.* (1,048 alt., 50 pop.), which is several miles away from its ante-bellum location. The old community was on Blackstock Road. Just after the War between the States, the McMakin family came here as refugees and built the first houses on the present site, hoping to develop a health resort around a mineral spring.

GRAMLING, 11.2 *m.* (856 alt., 150 pop.), shipping point for hun- dreds of carloads of peaches annually, bears the name of the man who, from meager beginnings, developed an enterprise that brought indus- trial importance to his small community. The search for new crops, made necessary by the ravages of the cotton boll weevil, resulted in the discovery that peaches grown here ripened just after those of Georgia and before those of North Carolina, thus reaching an un- crowded market.

At 21.3 *m.* is the junction with a hard-surfaced road.

Right on this road 0.7 *m.* to the large TAYLOR-COLQUITT COMPANY PLANT, which specializes in turning out creosoted poles and crossties for railroad, power, and telephone companies. A village for employees surrounds the plant.

In SPARTANBURG, 25.4 *m.* (875 alt., 28,723 pop.) (*see Spartanburg*), are the junctions with US 29 (*see Tour 7*), US 221 (*see Tour 17*), and State 9 (*see Tour 21b*). State 9 unites southeastward with US 176 for 3.3 miles.

At 27.9 *m.* is the junction with an asphalt road.

Left on this road to the SPARTANBURG COUNTRY CLUB (*greens fee 50¢*), 1.5 *m.* The cotton mill at GLENDALE, 3.4 *m.* (1,250 pop.), developed from a small factory established in 1830 by Dr. A. W. Bivings to card wool and make it into rolls. In 1880 the company was reorganized and the town's first name, Bivingsville, was changed to the present one.

A mill pond here covers the SITE OF WOFFORD'S IRON WORKS, a Revolutionary munitions plant where the horses of Colonel William Washington's troops were shod before the Battle of Cowpens (*see Tour 18*). Built in 1773, the plant, first of its kind in the State, was variously known as Berwick's, Buffington's, and Wofford's. Shortly before the foundry was destroyed by Tories in 1781, a running battle in the vicinity resulted in a draw. The scattered engagement is sometimes referred to as the Second Battle of Cedar Spring, sometimes as the Peach Orchard Fight. Tradition says the two peach trees that grew for many years on the site sprang from the kernels of peaches in the pocket of a fallen British soldier.

At 28.7 *m.* is the southeastern junction with State 9 (*see Tour 21b*).

BOBO HOUSE (L) or Foster's Tavern, 29.1 *m.*, at the intersection of the Georgia and Old Union Roads, was built by Anthony Foster about 1812, when a brick house hereabouts was rare. Under a pedimented entrance portico, added in 1845, is a second floor balcony; at each end of the gable roof are large chimneys. During stagecoach days this was a popular stop, and numerous well-known people slept under its roof. The garden contains the burial plot of the Foster family.

The SOUTH CAROLINA SCHOOL FOR THE DEAF AND BLIND (L), 30 *m.*, is usually called the Cedar Spring School. The large building is of stuccoed brick painted red, its design and balanced composition showing English Renaissance influence. On an arcaded basement is a four-columned Corinthian portico with pediment. Lintels, keystones, and sills of the casement windows are painted white. Balance is achieved in the wings by arcades and balconies. Although the use of painted architectural features cheapens the effect, the building has scale, dignity, and good proportions.

The school has been under supervision of the Walker family of Spartanburg since 1849. When the Word Academy was established here in 1824, Cedar Spring was a popular resort with hotels and sporting facilities of the period. In 1855 the school was reorganized to care for blind children, and two years later was taken over by the State. After the War between the States a building was opened for the education of Negroes, but when radical authorities later decreed that they be quartered and taught with the whites, the superintendent, officers, and teachers resigned, thus closing the school. Upon restoration of white authority, the building was reopened and in 1883 a special department was organized for Negroes.

At 30.4 *m.* is the junction with a dirt road.

> Left on this road 0.6 *m.* to CEDAR SPRING BAPTIST CHURCH (L), a plain white clapboarded building with gable roof. The congregation, organized in 1787, is one of the oldest Baptist groups in the Up Country.

At PAULINE, 35.7 *m.* (39 pop.), named about 1875 for Pauline Lancaster, daughter of the community's postmaster-physician, is a junction with State 56 (*see Tour 17*).

GLENN SPRINGS, 38.7 *m.* (164 pop.), was described in Mills' Atlas of 1825 as the center of population and culture in this part of the State. As early as 1765 settlers noticed that their healthy cattle were particularly fond of the marsh surrounding a deer lick near the springs. Analysis of the waters showed minerals, and their therapeutic qualities were advertised by promoters who mixed the water with mud for baths they said would work miracles. But it was the medicinal effect produced by drinking the water that made the springs notable. In 1838 a company was formed to erect a summer hotel, a group of cottages, and other accommodations, and by the mid-century, when South Carolina had reached a zenith of prosperity, this was a gay resort for eager health seekers from several States, remaining popular to the early 1900's. Many who no longer go to the springs still buy the water in demijohns and feel that no summer can be endured without it.

Southeastward the road traverses rolling country, partly uncultivated and sometimes desolate. Bleak shanties and weather-worn farmhouses, squatting against wasted fields, are the only habitations for many miles. Fertility is being restored to these depleted lands by the State Soil Conservation Service, which demonstrates to farmers such methods of erosion control as terracing, strip cropping, and crop rotation.

The three abandoned gold mines in and near WEST SPRINGS, 43.3 *m.* (30 pop.), were all producers at one time. Their weed-grown shafts stare vacantly at sightseers who visit the spot. Formerly the springs attracted many guests who had great faith in the medicinal properties of the waters.

In the yard of a cottage (L), 47.1 *m.*, is the KU KLUX HOLLY TREE, sometimes called the Confederate Holly. In Reconstruction days three Klansmen, pursued by soldiers with warrants for their arrest, found themselves almost overtaken here at nightfall, shinned up this tree, and hid themselves in its branches. By chance the soldiers camped directly beneath, and the fugitives could hear long discussions of plans for their capture. At daybreak, muscle-cramped and sleepy, but still undetected, they watched the soldiers resume their pursuit.

FAIRFOREST CREEK, 50.5 *m.*, threads its way through an area affectionately called The Forest. People speak of picnicking 'on The Forest' (referring to the creek), or of a man's living 'across The Forest.' Through this leafy strip, opposing Revolutionary forces played a serious game of hide and seek.

The little mill town of BUFFALO, 52.1 *m.* (1,620 pop.), preserves the memory of the wild buffalo that once roamed the country and resorted to licks near by.

After sundown superstitious Negroes lose no time in hurrying past the 'hangin' ground,' 54 *m.*, which is about 100 yards (R) in a clump of pines. The voice of wind brushing through pine needles seems peculiarly mournful here, where the hangman's knot was worn smooth until legislation in 1912 centered the execution of condemned criminals in Columbia, and the electric chair superseded county gallows.

At 55.7 *m.* is the junction with State 11 (*see Tour* 18).

Section b. JUNCTION WITH STATE 11 *to JUNCTION WITH US* 76, 31.9 *m. US* 176.

South of the junction with State 11, 0 *m.*, US 176 runs through a section with old mansions, few of them painted, most of them rundown, and all of them weather-beaten. These big structures, relics of the ante-bellum gentry that established large estates here, exemplify early Up Country architecture at its best. Farm tenants, assigned to the mansions by landlords financially unable to restore them, are surrounded by carved woodwork, wrought iron, and delicately molded plaster ornamentation.

UNION, 0.9 *m.* (578 alt., 7,419 pop.), seat of Union County, is pervaded by a sort of lazy atmosphere that belies the bustling activity of its factories and mills. The plain-faced shops on both sides of the narrow main street draw farmers and mill villagers for trade. The ponderous brick courthouse on the northwest corner of Main and Herndon Streets in addition to its legal functions, serves a typical South Carolina custom as a gathering place for farmers and mill workers when they come to town. In warm weather small groups bask along the knee-high wall that borders the terrace, their lethargy only slightly shaken by the soapbox sermons of local and visiting evangelists—carpenters, mill operatives, and mechanics by trade, but long-winded preachers by avocation. In winter the gatherings move inside the courthouse, where spittoons and benches conveniently scattered through the corridors are dragged closer to steaming radiators, each the center of an open forum on crops, wages, weather, and politics.

Most of the streets in the residential section north and south of Main Street are paved. Mountain Street and North Church Street, the latter winding crookedly across town, are said to follow former Indian trails. Gadberry Street between Main and South Streets, is still known as Poverty Flat; here the rowdiness of pre-dispensary saloons and questionable hotels made it nothing short of scandalous for 'ladies' of the community to be seen on the sidewalks. Pinckney Street, for one block south of Main, is called Wall Street, because of the little row of Negro shops where local darkies who have ventured North occasionally return to display the elegance of their spats, derbies, and Yankee talk.

East of the railroad tracks, Main Street extends into a well-kept residential section, where the privacy of substantial houses and green-banked gardens is intensified by the shadows of oaks and magnolias. The street continues along a railroad cut through two adjoining mill villages into the open countryside.

Union was settled in 1791 around the 'Union' Church, where Episcopalian and Presbyterian congregations worshipped, and was called Unionville. In 1800, it usurped the political prestige of Pinckneyville (*see Tour 21b*) on the Broad River and acquired the district courthouse and jail. Twenty years later the town had 20 houses and 200 citizens. Prior to the War between the States, it prospered as a crossroad where stagecoach and produce wagons met near the Broad and Tiger Rivers. The town saw relatively little military activity during the war, but when Sherman was advancing on Columbia from Savannah, Governor Magrath and other State officials hurried here with valuable papers and records. They were guests of Judge Dawkins whose home was surrounded by sentinels. A constant stream of couriers to and from Broad River brought news of Sherman's movements to the governor and his staff.

Immediately after the war the town became a hotbed of antagonism between Democratic and Radical forces. Negro militiamen were stationed here, and a near riot occurred when Matt Stevens, a one-armed Confederate veteran, was killed by one of them. Klansmen killed several of the militiamen and left a note for the sheriff: 'Once again we have been forced by force to use Force. We want and will have Justice, but this cannot be till a bleeding fight for freedom is fought. Until then the Moloch of Iniquity will have his victims, even as the Michael of Justice must have his martyrs. K.K.K.'

The OLD UNION JAIL, 68 W. Main St., was designed by Robert Mills and built in 1823. This building of hand-hewn granite blocks has a hip roof, four chimneys, and a triple arcade on the front with the arches springing from square monolithic piers. The massive blocks in the arches are characteristic of Mills.

In the World War Memorial Park, Main St. between Herndon and Enterprise Sts., is a MONUMENT TO JOHN PRATT, inventor of a typewriter. Born in Unionville in 1831, Pratt moved to England during the War between the States, and there patented his 'Ptereotype,' December 1, 1866. The machine, its principles of spacing and alignment still employed by manufacturers, sold for about $15 in London. Pratt later sought to patent it in this country, but found that Christopher Latham Sholes, with a machine he called a 'typewriter' had secured a patent two months earlier. Disappointed, Pratt sold out to a New York capitalist for cash and a $2,500 life annuity.

The CARNEGIE PUBLIC LIBRARY, SE. corner of South Mountain St. and South St., contains 7,000 volumes and numerous relics, including the flag of the Pea Ridge Volunteers and a scrap of the banner carried by the 5th Regiment, South Carolina Volunteers. The latter was not surrendered at Appomattox Courthouse, but was cut into pieces the night before the surrender by some men of the regiment, who grimly divided the scraps among themselves.

The remodeled brick and stucco GENERAL WILLIAM WALLACE HOUSE, 97 E. Main St., retains little of its former design except a Palladian doorway and pedimented windows. The front piazza is arcaded, with elliptical wooden arches springing from brick piers. General Wallace was speaker of the 'Wallace House' in 1876-7 (see Columbia). When Jefferson Davis was entertained here various citizens eagerly contributed dishes for the feast.

The red brick CULP HOUSE, 28 N. Mountain St., was built about 1857. The design is a version of the Greek Revival. The front portico has a superimposed colonnade with six white fluted columns in each tier, and a balcony with pierced balustrade. The symmetrical plan shows a practical combination of Georgian and classical influences, while the wide airy balconies are characteristic of Southern plantation architecture. From the front porch Mrs. Ann Hill presented a flag to the Johnson Rifles, Union's first company of Confederate Volunteers. In October 1876, Wade Hampton made an address from the same porch.

A typical Up Country adaptation of Greek Revival design is the MENG HOUSE, 2 Academy St., built by Zacharias Herndon in 1832 and designed by W. W. James. Two and a half stories high, of white frame, the house has three modified-Doric porticos, the entrance portico with flat roof and balustrade, the side porticos with fanlighted pediments. Lumber used in its construction was brought from Columbia or Charleston, as there were no Up Country lumber mills at that time.

HERNDON TERRACE, N. Pinckney St., is on a hill which commands a view of the surrounding country. Development of the terrace and gardens began before the War between the States. The house, Greek Revival in design, with columns on front and side porticos, was built in 1848. High frescoed ceilings and elaborately carved woodwork characterize the interior. Old slave quarters and a kitchen are in the rear yard.

The white frame GOVERNOR JETER HOUSE, 1 Thomas Boulevard, has a gable roof with a bizarre scalloped cornice. Above the living room bay window is a small balcony, while the eave drain has a cap dated 1859 and decorated with stars. Small bells, once used to summon slaves, still hang beneath the eaves, attached to wires that run through the house. There is a carved mantel in the living room, and plaster ceiling molds have egg-and-dart and acanthus leaf designs. Governor Jeter served as chief executive of South Carolina for a short while in 1880.

In Union are junctions with State 11 (see Tour 18), State 215 (see Tour 18), and State 92 (see Tour 17).

Right from Union on N. Pinckney St., unpaved, which becomes Gist Bridge Road and swings R. through what was once one of the most prosperous parts of the State, the upper border of old Goshen Hill Township. In Revolutionary times this area was the scene of much fighting between Whigs and Tories, in which Generals Sumter and Marion participated, particularly the former. General Nathanael Greene and his Continentals were also engaged. Colonel Tarleton and Major Wemyss led the Loyalists.

At 3.2 *m.* is the junction with a dirt road; L. 0.1 *m.* to the unmarked SITE OF BRANDON'S DEFEAT, an encounter between Carolina militia under Colonel Thomas Brandon and a detachment of British regulars and Tories in the fall of 1780. Though the skirmish was of minor significance, Brandon's defeat served to spur the Whigs toward their victories at Kings Mountain and Cowpens. The militia, then under Sumter, received little pay, fought as they wished, became bored with camp life, and between battles usually returned home to plow and plant. It was their efforts, however, that brought American control to South Carolina after the fall of Camden and Charleston.

At 8.8 *m.* on the Gist Bridge Road is the junction with a private road; L. here 0.3 *m.* to the GIST MANSION (*visited by permission*), built in 1832 by William H. Gist, governor of South Carolina (1858–60). Behind the wrought-iron fence surrounding the front yard are the scant remains of the once lovely garden. Ancient magnolia and crape myrtle trees tower above weed-choked rose-bushes and boxwood—still fragrant in their seasons. The house is built of stuccoed brick, buff color, with gable roof, pedimented portico, front and rear piazzas, and two chimneys at each end. The front entrance is framed with side lights, an elliptical fanlight, and three-quarter pilasters, with entablature and soffit panels. The hand-forged iron strap hinges that support shutters and doors are of local workmanship. A brick walk of herringbone pattern leads from the rear to former slave quarters and kitchens. Ornamentation, more refined than is usual in Up Country houses built in this period, shows close adherence to Greek prototypes and reveals highly skilled craftsmanship. Twist molding is found throughout the house on door frames and wainscoting and the broad fireplaces have mantels with moldings, rosettes, pilasters, and entablature. A staircase spirals upward to the second floor; a trap door in the parlor leads to a large cellar.

William H. Gist (1807–74) was born in Maryland, but spent most of his life in South Carolina where he served for many years in the general assembly, and was elected governor in 1858 because of his secession leanings. He was a member of the Secession Convention and the South Carolina Executive Committee of Safety. In 1862, however, he abandoned his political career, and returned to his home where he remained until his death. In keeping with the chivalrous order of the day, Gist once engaged in a duel over a lady; his opponent, Samuel Fair, was killed.

SEDALIA, 12.3 *m.* (75 pop.), at the end of the Gist Bridge Road, was once a crossroads on a stagecoach route and had a Friends' meetinghouse. Though these Quakers were slave owners, the sect disapproved of slavery, and orthodox members moved to the Northwest where slavery had been prohibited by the Ordinance of 1787. Their exodus was hastened by the jeremiads of Zachary Dicks, a Friend who passed through South Carolina between 1800 and 1804 foretelling the dire calamities that would befall slave owners. By 1807 few Quakers were left in the State.

South of Sedalia the route becomes the Sedalia Road.

PADGETT'S CREEK BAPTIST CHURCH (L), 14.6 *m.*, was established November 22, 1784, as Tiger River Church. The present building, of white frame with gable roof and simple pedimented portico is the second. Old church records show earlier congregations forbade marriage on the Sabbath, gave Nathan Langston permission 'to pray in public and to exhort when convenient,' and appointed Frederick Jackson 'to set tunes when called on.'

South of Union the route passes terraced farmlands and the ABRAM McJUNKIN HOUSE, 6.4 *m.*, built about 1795 with the durability of old time workmanship. The Scotch-Irish McJunkins were among the fiercest of the Up Country Whigs during the Revolution. Joseph Mc-

Junkin, brother of Abram, the builder, was a colonel under General Sumter.

At 9 *m.* on US 176 is the junction with a dirt road.

Left here 1 *m.* to a field (R). Across this field are the REMAINS OF OTTERSON FORT, 0.5 *m.*, one of the few remnants of stone forts of the Indian war period. Though much of its material has been used in the construction of neighboring houses, an outline of the post can be traced in the foundation.

The ROBERT BEATY HOUSE (R), 12 *m.*, built in 1845, typifies the desolation that has come to this region. The dingy white two-story frame building stands in grounds where razor backed hogs and scrawny chickens root and scratch among the cockleburs that have choked out the former garden. The unkempt children of sharecroppers sprawl over a portico whose fluted Doric columns and windowed pediment frame a balcony. Makeshift furniture is sparsely placed in the wide hall and the eight high-ceiled rooms, with their broad sash windows and wide fireplaces.

At 15.1 *m.* is the junction with State 7.

Left on this road 1.3 *m.* to the Old Buncombe Road; R. here through an area filled with the ghosts of a vanished prosperity, past homes of former luxury and affluence, now tumbled down among boxwood hedges on land so depleted that broom sedge hardly survives. The invention of the cotton gin stimulated planters to open up the mid-State lands, clear them of woods, and plant thousands of acres to the profitable crop. These planters, from the Low Country and from other States, had their scores of slaves and an unlimited ambition for wealth—but little respect for the earth itself. Profits were made so quickly that there was no transition from pioneer life to one of luxury. Large homes were built immediately, and mahogany furniture, heavy carpets, cutglass, and silver were brought up the rivers from Charleston. Scarborough, the fashionable painter, came up to portray the lace-frilled ladies and gentlemen with their high stocks. Slaves labored in the rich fields, and cotton, ever mounting in value, brought more and more wealth. This river aristocracy did not suffer from swamp fevers; energy abounded as it rarely did on the rice plantations of the coast. Cotton was easily poled down the small streams to Granby below Columbia. Shipping costs were low. But the land was ill cared for, the soil was soon washed away and gullies were cut through the formerly productive acres. With the coming of railroads, this section was left stranded, because it was too expensive to lay tracks across the network of rivers and creeks. The War between the States shortly followed with complete destruction of the labor system. When the shock of conflict had worn away, the mansion owners found themselves surrounded by barren fields and hungry families of Negroes. Most of the fine establishments became a mockery. So little ambition remained that few made an effort to dispose of their possessions. Today, a regal portrait may dominate a room where grain is stored; a harpsichord, with its high keys, stands among scattered corn shucks; and untrimmed boxwood traces the outline of formal gardens where statesmen settled the State's destiny. Bordered by broom sedge, eroded fields, and cutover forest, Old Buncombe Road skirts a wide field, 0.5 *m.*, that was a celebrated race track in the heyday of Up Country cotton prosperity. On eventful days, barrels of spirits were placed at intervals along the road so that parties of sportsmen could be regaled by slaves with long-handled gourds full of the liquor.

A square hole in the ground (L) at 1.8 *m.* and scraps of rotting timber are the REMAINS OF GOSHEN TRADING POST, over whose counters traffic in furs and skins established fortunes before the Revolution. Here, as at countless other 'factories,' Indians hastened the complete expropriation of their country by bartering it, bit by bit, for the attractive products of the encroaching whites.

THE OAKS (L), 5.6 *m.*, a two-and-a-half-story house of unpainted pine, was built about 1839 by James Douglas. Although a late product of the Classical Revival, the treatment has a lightness not usual in that period. Instead of columns rising two stories, the double piazza has small fluted Doric columns that are superimposed, and a pediment containing a fanlight. Both first and second floor piazza entrances have delicately carved wooden keystones. A master craftsman among the slaves superintended details of construction. The interior has an accumulation of heirlooms. Rugs laid by the builder, their patterns still clear and bright, mahogany and rosewood furniture, and old silver remain in everyday use. A Scarborough portrait of Anna Hardy, a member of the family, hangs over the parlor mantel.

The RUINS OF ORANGE HALL (L) are at 6.5 *m.* The brick structure was built about 1797 by John Rogers. The disintegrating effect of time was climaxed in 1929 by a tornado that created the present ruins. Former grandeur is recalled only by broken columns, piles of brick, and a garden fountain carved from stone in the shape of a harp. The house was so named because of the orange designs on posts at the driveway entrance. These posts, carved in 1860 by J. E. Sherman, a Northern stonecutter, are now in Spartanburg.

At 6.7 *m.* is the junction with a dirt road; R. here to MAYBINTON, 2 *m.* (50 pop.), named for Colonel Benjamin Maybin, a pioneer. For many years the settlement was a busy seat of trade and traffic on a stage route between western North Carolina and Charleston. In the immediate neighborhood were numerous plantations whose houses are in various stages of dilapidation or altogether ruined.

On State 7 is OLD ROGERS METHODIST CHURCH (L), 1.9 *m.*, in the mid-nineteenth century one of the wealthiest churches in the Methodist Conference. The structure, now dilapidated, stands among ragged lands.

Residents of WHITMIRE, 17.1 *m.* (424 alt., 2,763 pop.), realize incomes from farm products as well as from cotton mills that operate more than 1,000 looms and 70,000 spindles.

The frame DRUCILLA WHITMIRE MUSEUM was built as a trading post about 1801 by George Frederick Whitmire, ancestor of publisher William Randolph Hearst, who has helped to restore the structure. The Phoebe Hearst garden, around the museum, is a memorial to Hearst's mother, who was one of the founders of the Parent-Teachers Association.

The EPPS HOME, 19.5 *m.* (R), 100 yards from the highway, is an unpainted ante-bellum frame structure with gable ends. The pedimented four-columned portico has square, tapered, unfluted columns of brick and stucco, and a decorated frieze. The rough structural work was performed by slaves, the fine interior plaster work and staircase construction by skilled craftsmen. In the front hall a staircase corkscrews upward through three stories with rail and newel post of mahogany. Another staircase rises from a rear downstairs room to a bedroom. In the parlor, plaster ceiling molding has been skilfully elaborated into acanthus and egg-and-dart designs.

At 31.9 *m.* is the junction with US 76 (*see Tour 9c*) at a point 2 miles north of Newberry (*see Tour 9c*).

Tour 13

(Lumberton, N. C.)—Dillon—Marion—Conway—Myrtle Beach; US
501. North Carolina Line to Myrtle Beach, 79 *m.*

Atlantic Coast Line R.R. parallels route between North Carolina Line and Latta,
also between Aynor and Myrtle Beach.
Roadbed concrete-paved between North Carolina Line and Marion; elsewhere
asphalt-paved.
Tourist accommodations at short intervals; hotels in towns.

This route traverses wide fields of the Pee Dee River basin, where
bright leaf tobacco fills the high barns in season, and where lumbering is still profitable. The use of modern farm machinery, to which
the flat land is well suited, has increased rapidly during recent years.

US 501 crosses the NORTH CAROLINA LINE, 0 *m.,* about 18
miles southwest of Lumberton, North Carolina.

In HAMER, 1.4 *m.* (170 pop.), the stark brick walls of a small yarn
mill contrast sharply with the farm lands and woods around it.

The LITTLE PEE DEE RIVER, 4.2 *m.,* has since Indian times
been famous as a fishing stream.

In DILLON, 6.6 *m.* (119 alt., 2,731 pop.) (*see Tour 21a*), is the
junction with State 9 (*see Tour 21a*).

South of Dillon lies Maple Swamp, overspread by coffee-colored
water on whose surface white lilies bloom in late spring. Peaceful now,
this marshland was once a refuge of Confederate deserters, who saw no
reason to fight for slavery when they owned no slaves themselves.

LATTA, 12.9 *m.* (1,166 pop.), preserves the name of the construction engineer who in 1888 had charge of the Atlantic Coast Line
branch, the Wilson Short Cut, on which the town was laid out. Still a
rural village, it stirs to brisker life in tobacco season and when cotton
comes to town. Gins and warehouses cluster about the edge. On late
fall afternoons, the high piled wagons and trucks roll in from fields
where the cotton has been weighed and hands have been credited with
the day's picking. Overhanging tree limbs catch tufts of cotton as the
vehicles pass under them on their way to the ginneries. Often the
wagons, lined up along the approach to the gin, must wait far into the
night for their turn. Daytimes, the farmers ride out to their wide acres
but the women stay in town to look after their housework and gossip
placidly with neighbors on the front porch.

From Latta's Carnegie Library trucks go out into the county to
distribute books and magazines.

The junction with State 38 (*see Tour 3a*) is in Latta.

South of Latta lie some of the State's best timberlands. Narrow dirt

Sports and Recreation

Photograph by courtesy of Calder W. Seibels

AMBITION ACHIEVED—A WILD TURKEY

RACING AT MYRTLE BEACH

Photograph by Paul M. Pillsbury

KNIGHTS PARADING AT TILTING TOURNAMENT (1940), KINGSTREE

Photograph by courtesy of David K. Summers

Photograph by courtesy of Camden Chamber of Commerce

OFF FOR THE DRAG HUNT

POLO, AIKEN

Photograph by courtesy of Aiken Chamber of Commerce

STATE FIDDLERS' CONTEST WINNERS

Photograph by Louise Jones DuBose

FAMILY REUNION

Photograph by Bill King

FOURTH OF JULY PICNIC, NEAR BEAUFORT

ANDERSON COUNTY FAIR

SAILBOAT RACES, ROCKVILLE

Photograph by Tom Peck; courtesy of The News and Courier

A GOOD CATCH, GEORGETOWN

Photograph by courtesy of South Carolina Magazine

Photograph by United States Forest Service

FISHING IN THE CHAUGA RIVER, OCONEE COUNTY

Photograph by courtesy of S. C. Department of Agriculture
CROWNING THE QUEEN, AZALEA FESTIVAL, CHARLESTON

HOTEL, MYRTLE BEACH

Photograph by courtesy of South Carolina Magazine

roads, deeply rutted, head into the thick woods, where tangled vines barely give room for the logging trucks to pass. Farther in the swamp the roads are raised on double wooden runways, which end at a planked island known as the loading yard. To the top of a tall straight 'rig' tree, stripped of its branches, are attached guy wires and a cable, like streamers from a Maypole; the puffing steam engine, or 'skidder,' furnishes power for the cable, which hauls great logs from the depth of the swamp to the loading yard. The scraping rhythm of a crosscut saw is followed by a warning yell. The tree crashes to the ground—gum, pine, oak, or sycamore—perhaps 75 feet tall and from 50 to 200 years old. After being measured with an 8-foot rod and shorn of its top, the log is fastened to tongs at the end of the cable. The crew calls out that all is ready; the operator of the engine, about 1,000 feet away, answers with a toot of his whistle; the cable stretches taut, and the log creeps to the loading pile near the rig-tree. Here it is sawed into sections, placed on a heavy truck, chained down with others, and started on its journey to the lumber mill. A Negro picks up the cable tongs, hooks them to the traces of his mule, and rides back into the swamp for another log.

About two dozen men, usually Negroes, compose a skidder crew and pull about 3,500 feet of logs a day. At noon the men sit in the hot sun to eat their lunch of corn bread, string beans, and fat back, washed down with buttermilk. Toward night they pile into a truck for the lumber camp a few miles out of the swamp. Whites and Negroes live in separate camps—Negroes in portable shacks with two narrow rooms and a tiny porch, whites in slightly more permanent structures. After a five-day week of hard work, Saturday and Sunday are apt to bring demoralization. Arguments that pass off quietly on work days may burst into fatal stabbings or pistol fights after the men have visited liquor shops in town. Lumber camps are temporary affairs, remaining in one place for a few months to several years.

The little frame building at 14 m. is one of the two Dillon County schools for the Croatans (see Tour 21a).

In the large two-story frame ELLERBE HOUSE (L), 19 m., lived and died William H. Ellerbe, governor of the State 1897-9. A henchman of 'Pitchfork Ben' Tillman (see Tour 8b), Ellerbe was carried to office by the element favoring State liquor dispensaries. His first term was dominated by strenuous effort to enforce the law, but defeat in his second race was imminent until he promised to support a referendum for the law's repeal. His failure to take this stand in the general assembly in 1899 aroused much hard feeling among his constituents, but he died in June before opposition could be successfully organized.

On the marked SITE OF THE BATTLE OF BOWLING GREEN, 20.1 m., General Francis Marion defeated the British Major Gainey, in a quick skirmish, June 8, 1782. A big tree that stood near this point for generations was called the Lone Oak, and was said to be a rendezvous for Tories.

In front of OAK LAWN, 24.3 m., a white, two-story house, there stood until 1935 the Methodist Oak, under whose branches Bishop Asbury first exhorted the people of this community in 1786.

In MARION, 25 *m.* (68 alt., 4,921 pop.) (*see Tour 9a*), is the junction with US 76 (*see Tour 9a*).

Swamps, fertile highlands, and flat, flower-covered savannas alternate along the southeastern route. East of the Little Pee Dee Causeway, 34.6 *m.*, on a swampy island occurred the Battle of the Blue Savanna, August 16, 1780. When they had routed the British Captain Barfield's forces, comfortable and hilarious with food and peach brandy foraged in the vicinity, the ragged half-starved Colonials paused in their pursuit to enjoy the Tory spoils—turkey and pig roasting over campfires and a half-pint of peach brandy each. After a night's rest the patriots set out again to harass the enemy when a group of them stumbled on a dead Britisher. No bullet marks were found, and the Americans were puzzled until a teetotaler among them saw a rattlesnake slithering into the bushes. One soldier took aim to shoot the reptile, another begged for his life, and it was decided to court-martial the snake. Carried back to camp on a horsehair noose, the rattler rested safely while his attorney pled for his life. 'If this creature is a murderer, then so are we all. This snake has killed one British soldier; we have killed many. This is not murder, gentlemen. This is war.' The soldiers cried, 'Not guilty!' and the snake crawled off to his lair.

The LITTLE PEE DEE CAUSEWAY is raised high above the slow-moving dark water as a protection against spring floods which sometimes inundate the section. The bridge at 38 *m.* takes the place of Gallivant's Ferry, which was used until 1892 when a wooden span was built. On the eastern bank beneath cypress trees is the *Ruth,* an old river boat, now a rotting hulk full of yellow primroses. Little here indicates the busy traffic of former times, when side wheelers and schooners plied between settlements to exchange manufactured goods for cotton and lumber products. Cooters, turtles, and alligators are the busiest inhabitants now, as they flop into the water for food or sun themselves on drifting logs. Occasionally a fisherman in his bateau slides out from the overhung banks.

In 1930 the quiet Horry countryside was surprised by an aerial survey. F. A. Melton and William Schriever, Oklahoma geologists, took photographs from the air and proposed the theory that this area, now dotted with lakes, was visited by a meteoric shower some 2,000,000 years ago. The pictures show elliptical scars, with elevated rims, the southeastern end invariably higher. The stellar attack must have veered earthward with a northwest slant, and embedded the meteors below the depression.

AYNOR, 43.6 *m.* (375 pop.), and COOL SPRINGS, 47.3 *m.* (32 pop.), are farm-store settlements, to which customers ride or walk from the interior to hear of the outside world and lay in provisions.

At 55.9 *m.* is the junction with US 701 (*see Tour 20*), which unites with US 501 between this point and CONWAY, 59.5 *m.* (25 alt., 3,011 pop.) (*see Tour 20*).

South of Conway the route traverses an area opened up when the high water bridge at Conway was finished in 1938 and the span over the Intracoastal Waterway was completed a few years before.

East of SOCASTEE, 62.5 *m.*, the highway passes sandy pine groves where dogwood lights up the woods in spring and the scrubby little chigger weed or butterfly plant snuggles down in the hot summer, its deep orange flower resembling in color the 'red bug' or chigger. This innocent milkweed is avoided by many who believe the minute mites have pre-empted the plant as a citadel from which to attack.

At MYRTLE BEACH, 79 *m.* (*see Tour* 1a), is the junction with US 17 (*see Tour* 1a).

Tour 14

Greenville—Clemson College—Madison—(Gainesville, Ga.); State 13. Greenville to Georgia Line, 60.3 *m.*

Roadbed concrete-paved.
Southern Ry. parallels route.
Limited accommodations; hotels in towns.

State 13 slides down to the Saluda River through mill towns, cotton and corn fields, and woodlands. This region was one of the last refuges of the Cherokee, and most of the streams still bear the musical names given by the first Americans. Beyond the Saluda Valley the road traverses high flat lands with the Blue Ridge Mountains visible as hazy, wide scallops on the northwestern horizon.

State 13 branches southwest in GREENVILLE, 0 *m.* (*see Greenville*), from its junctions with US 29 (*see Tour* 7), US 276 (*see Tour* 10), and US 25 (*see Tour* 8a).

At 2.2 *m.* is the junction with an asphalt-paved road.

Right on this road 1 *m.* to PARKER DISTRICT SCHOOL, the chief unit in South Carolina's secondary education project of recent years. Before 1923 there were 14 independent schools in this industrial area, none of them offering more than seventh grade work; at that time not more than 50 pupils from the region attended high school in Greenville. Under the leadership of L. P. Hollis in 1923 the 14 districts were organized into the Parker School District, forming the largest consolidation of schools in the history of South Carolina. Immediately specialists in education were employed as consultants to local teachers for the purpose of substituting for the formal school a new system built on the everyday needs of the people of an industrial community. New buildings embodying the most modern ideas in school design gradually replaced the old structures. The classrooms, supplied with tables and chairs instead of desks, became work shops rather than places for questions and answers. The course of study was built around interests of the various groups and the pupils were given an opportunity to learn through doing. Mimeographed texts developed by teachers and pupils on community problems supplemented formal texts. The school became the educational center of the community, serving the adults as well as the children.

Today, near the high school building is a 'maternity shelter,' where prenatal care and instruction are given. Other innovations are: Hobbyland on Parris Mountain, where pupils go camping as a school project; an annual excursion to Charleston and other interesting places in the State; and science fairs that have brought 26,000 people to the high school gymnasium. A 'schoolmobile'—a truck equipped with refrigerator and stove—is used to give traveling demonstrations in cooking, and a weekly radio broadcast tells of school activities. In the library are books, pictures, stereopticons, and museum specimens. This progressive program has been justified by the results. In 1939 about 1,400 high school pupils were enrolled, against 50 in 1923. More than 5,000 pupils are in the elementary grades.

EASLEY, 13.6 m. (1,000 alt., 4,886 pop.), is a little foothill town brought to life by the railroad as a trading point in the midst of cotton lands. Established as a station in 1874, it remained for 26 years a line of tin-topped stores; then the first of its four mills was built and the village grew at the rate of Jack's beanstalk. Living within a two-mile radius are more than 8,000 people whose dependence is first on the mills and second on farming.

Left from Easley on a dirt road 1 m. to the SITE OF PICKENSVILLE, from 1791 to 1798 the seat of Washington District, which embraced the present counties of Greenville, Anderson, Pickens, and Oconee. Nothing remains of the town except part of the jail dungeon, now surrounded by a quiet pasture.

LIBERTY, 20 m. (1,040 alt., 2,128 pop.), was once called Salubrity because of its situation in the Blue Ridge foothills. Tradition maintains the name was changed in 1776 when worshippers in a brush arbor learned that the Liberty Bell had rung and asserted national independence. Salubrity became Liberty afterward.

In LIBERTY is the junction with US 178 (see Tour 15a).

So named because it was half way between Atlanta and Charlotte, CENTRAL, 27.9 m. (850 alt., 1,440 pop.), was famous as an eating stop for Southern Railway passengers before the days of dining cars. Here is WESLEYAN METHODIST COLLEGE, a coeducational school of junior rank.

In the ROADSIDE MARKET, 31.7 m., conducted by Clemson Agricultural College, cadets sell produce from the school's large experimental farm. Fruits and grapes are displayed with vegetables, dairy products, and honey.

Here is the junction with State 28 (see Tour 19a), which unites with State 13 for 12 miles.

At CLEMSON, 32.1 m. (850 alt., 420 pop.), a village composed mainly of professors and their families, is CLEMSON AGRICULTURAL COLLEGE, a State institution with more than 2,000 students. In winter the streets and highways swarm with gray-clad cadets; hardly have they gone home in summer before young people and old come in from farms all over the State for special courses. The Opportunity School brings them the rudiments of education or the chance to continue neglected schooling. A State Fiddlers' Convention and a Singing Association enliven the warm summer days.

The highway follows the curve of a small valley leading through the village; the rolling 200-acre landscaped lawns of the campus (L), shaded with native trees, is dotted with large red brick buildings designed with military simplicity. Between the trees along curving drives and walks are vistas of the Blue Ridge Mountains. The college property covers about 1,544 acres, with an experimental farm and its greenhouses, cattle barns, poultry plant, veterinary hospital, laboratories for scientific research, and barracks.

Clemson College, a land-grant college, was founded and named in 1889, when Thomas G. Clemson (1807–88), son-in-law of John C. Calhoun, bequeathed the bulk of his estate for 'the establishment of an Agricultural College which will afford useful information to the farmers and mechanics.' The founder, a native of Philadelphia, had been educated at the Royal School of Mines in Paris, studied art under French masters, and worked in the Royal Mint of France. In 1838 he had married Anna Maria Calhoun and settled in this vicinity as a planter. From 1844 to 1852 he served as *chargé d'affaires* in the American legation at Brussels. He had been a promoter of Maryland Agricultural College, served 1860–1 as Superintendent of Agricultural Affairs in the Department of the Interior, and in 1863–5 as Supervisor of Mining and Metal Works in the Trans-Mississippi Departments of the Confederacy.

The college opened in 1893 with 446 students. Though prior to this time sporadic efforts had been made to develop agricultural and mechanical departments in the University of South Carolina, the opening of Clemson College marked the first successful effort to reach the farmers' sons and to teach them scientific farming. The school offers more than 20 vocational courses. A bachelor's degree in science is awarded upon the completion of the four-year courses and graduate degrees are given in civil, electrical, and mechanical engineering.

Among the most important work of the college is operation of the Agricultural Experiment Stations of South Carolina. In addition to the main station at Clemson, there are five substations scattered over the State in areas having diverse soil and agricultural problems. The results of experiments conducted in co-operation with the United States Department of Agriculture are disseminated over the State in bulletins, circulars, and letters. The Agricultural Extension Service of the college supervises the work of county farm agents, and in co-operation with Winthrop College (*see Rock Hill*), of home demonstration agents, thus reaching practically every farm home in the State. Seventeen Negro farm agents are stationed in places where the Negro population is largest, in co-operation with the State college at Orangeburg.

At the intersection with a paved drive encircling the campus is the LIBRARY (L), a red brick building with massive white columns across its portico; it has 23,000 books, 20,000 bound volumes of pamphlets and bulletins, and 35 paintings collected or copied by Clemson in Brussels. W. W. Corcoran, founder of the Corcoran Art Gallery in Washington, had commissioned him to purchase pictures. Clemson believed he had acquired for his own collection two Rubens, a Velasquez, and a Rembrandt, but there is some doubt about their authenticity. One of the Rubens, *A Virgin and Child*, and the Velasquez *Head*, are in the library here—as well as *Peasant's Repast*, by Franz Hals, and *Study of a Head* by Greuze.

BOWMAN FIELD, opposite the library at the foot of a slope, is the parade ground where cadets participate in drills that lead to membership in the Reserve Officers' Training Corps in their junior and senior years. A spur of the drive leads to the brow of the hill and directly to the three-story ADMINISTRATION BUILDING, which contains offices and classrooms, and in its north end Memorial Hall, an auditorium seating about 1,800. Behind the Administration Building is the SITE OF FORT RUTLEDGE, marked with a miniature fort of concrete blocks. The original fortification was erected in July 1776 by General Andrew Williamson, then a colonel, who rallied 1,000 local inhabitants to oppose the Cherokee, whom the British had incited against the settlers. The fort, named for John Rutledge (*see History*), was sometimes called Fort Salvador for Captain Salvador, Williamson's Jewish-English aide, who is said to have been shot and scalped by Cherokee at the Indian village of Esseneca.

South of the Administration Building the encircling drive passes the Chemistry Building (L), the old post office, Riggs Hall—the Engineering Building—and the new TEXTILE BUILDING, an immense brick structure, completed in 1938, in which students do practical work and receive theoretical training. They have the choice of several courses: textile engineering, textile chemistry and dyeing, or weaving and designing.

FORT HILL (R) was the home of John C. Calhoun (*see History*). About 1803 the Reverend James McElhenny, pastor of the Old Stone Church (*see Tour 19a*), built the house and called it Clergy Hall. After his death his plantation was added to the estate of Mrs. Calhoun's father and in 1825 Calhoun brought his family here. The property was renamed Fort Hill to commemorate the post built in 1776. In the grove around the mansion are a varnish tree, given Calhoun by Stephen Decatur after one of his trips to Madagascar, a hemlock presented by Webster, and an arbor vitae by Henry Clay. The cedars were planted by the Calhouns, says tradition, in the belief that they would prevent the rise of miasmas—supposed to carry malaria from the lowlands to the hilltop. The two-story white frame structure has two tall four-column porticos; the south portico, with gently sloping roof, was part of the old house and the pedimented east portico was added when the house was enlarged during Calhoun's ownership. The columns are of stuccoed brick, a common detail in the Up Country; the workmanship is substantial though crude. Clemson decreed in his will that the house and furniture should remain intact and become a second Mount Vernon, but this provision was not carried out. The college and patriotic organizations, however, are refurnishing the house with Calhoun and Clemson pieces or reproductions of them. Among the former is the Constitution sideboard, a massive piece with central broken arch, made of mahogany from officers' cabins of the frigate *Constitution,* famous in the War of I8I2. After the vessel had been condemned in I828, the sideboard was made and presented to Henry Clay. Further destruction of the ship was halted when sentiment was aroused by Oliver Wendell Holmes's poem, 'Old Ironsides.' Clay presented the sideboard to Calhoun after Calhoun's speech defending the Federal Constitution; the piece was inherited by Clemson's granddaughters, moved to New York, sold, and for years lost to view. After persistent search it was found in I938. Clemson's massive bedroom furniture is said to have been designed by Mrs. Calhoun and executed by W. J. Knauff, a Pendleton cabinet-maker.

John C. Calhoun (I782–I850) in his birth and upbringing was a product of the post-Revolutionary back country of South Carolina; by marriage and political career he was allied to the coastal section. His father, Patrick Calhoun, came with other Scotch-Irish traders to the Long Cane region of Abbeville County in I756 (*see Tour* I9*b*). John, Patrick's son by his second wife, Martha Caldwell, was educated at Willington Academy and Yale College, and studied law at Litchfield, Connecticut. He completed his legal training in the Charleston offices of Chancellor Henry W. DeSaussure. Elected to the legislature in I807 and to Congress in I8I0, Calhoun entered on his political career as a member of the nationalist wing of Jefferson's party. He resigned from Congress in I8I7 and served as Secretary of War until I825. In those years he began nursing his ardent and long-lived ambition to reach the Presidency. In I824, and again in I828, he had to content himself with election as Vice President, under John Quincy Adams and Andrew Jackson. Anticipating the fight on slavery, he resigned the vice presidency in I832 and as United States senator bent all his energies to consolidating the South and forcing full recognition of its viewpoint by the North. He served almost continuously in the Senate until I850, except for two years (I843–5) spent at Fort Hill writing a book on government. He came out of his retirement to serve briefly as Secretary of State in I844.

In I8II Calhoun married his youthful cousin, Floride, daughter of John Ewing Colhoun of Berkeley County, who spelled his name with an 'o' instead of an 'a' in the first syllable. Floride was a charming bride, but became an exceedingly high-handed mistress of her domain. Tradition recounts that she sometimes locked up 'every closet, storeroom, and smokehouse on the plantation and drove off with the keys,' so that on one occasion many doors had to be smashed before her husband could give a long-planned dinner to the gentlemen of Pendleton District. She is also credited with adding a room to Fort Hill

whenever she took a notion in Calhoun's absence; but a rapidly increasing family gave her some justification for that.

Calhoun died in Washington and was buried in St. Philip's churchyard in Charleston.

A small marker (R), 34.4 *m.*, recalls SENECA OLD TOWN, which was
destroyed by Williamson in 1776. Bartram, visiting here earlier that
year, recorded that 'The Cherokee town of Sinica is a very respectable
settlement situated on the East Bank of the Keowee River . . . Sinica
is a new town rebuilt since the Indian war . . . the number of inhabitants are now estimated at about five hundred.' Old Seneca, according
to some historians, was established by the Nunda Wadigi (Ind., bright
sun-colored people) tribe of the Iroquois Indians who migrated from
New York into South Carolina about 1630. These Indians are said
to have been nicknamed Sinabars (cinnabar, red paint) by the New
York Dutch. When Williamson attacked the village, the Indians were
led by John Cameron, British agent. The town was completely demolished, stored corn burned, and cornfields and peach orchards were laid
waste.

At 38.3 *m.* is the junction with State 130.

> Right on this road 1 *m.* to NEWRY (1,000 pop.), named for the family seat
> of the Courtenays in Ireland, the settlement having grown up around the planta-
> tion of Captain W. A. Courtenay, mayor of Charleston in the 1880's. Through
> his foresight, *Charleston Year Books* issued during his administration included
> the *Shaftesbury Papers*, which give valuable information concerning early Caro-
> lina. At Newry the bell that formerly rang the curfew for slaves still clangs
> each night.

Cool, clean SENECA, 42.6 *m.* (950 alt., 1,929 pop.), perched on a
high crossroad and looking up to a rugged horizon of blue hills, was
established in 1874, when the railroad arrived. Most of the residents
are employed in one way or another in local print mills. People from
communities around the town also work here, to supplement their farm
incomes. Women help grow the cotton, and then in the mills spin the
fibre into cloth. Children from mountain fastnesses near by are brought
to consolidated schools in busses that cannot travel the steep clay roads
in rainy weather, and thus school terms are often interrupted.

In Seneca lives Professor McDuffie Weems, one of the best known
singing teachers of the shape-note system in the South. Since 1896 he
has pitched these white spirituals here and elsewhere with his tuning
fork and made a living through his work. His pupils, whose main recre-
ations are allied to church life, are chiefly adherents of 'the old time
religion.' In school buildings, country churches, or private homes the
singing schools meet one evening a month or all day on Sunday, with
an elaborate picnic dinner at noon. Week-night pupils pay 10¢ each,
and the classes include all ages of both sexes, some junior leaders being
only four years old. Professor Weems's younger colleagues work in
the mills by day and teach the fa-sol-la classes by night. Some of these
'professors,' as they are always called, have studied formal music but
most of them have learned their art in the family or community. They
compose music and words, play many instruments, and some publish

their own paperbound hymnals. 'They go in more for rhythmics now than in the old days when folks liked melodics better,' remarked Professor Weems as he listened to the almost tuneless thumping of two grand pianos, staccato shrieks of a fiddle, and swingtime harmony of 300 people singing about the New Jerusalem.

At 43.8 *m.* is the western junction with State 28 (*see Tour 19a*).

The road twists in and out among the hills seeking the easiest grade down to the Savannah River Valley.

On the site of an Indian village, WESTMINSTER, 51.5 *m.* (919 alt., 1,774 pop.), is another railroad stop of the 1870's that was later boosted by textile mills utilizing waterpower. Thirsty Georgians, living under local option liquor laws, seek the community as the nearest point with legal sale of intoxicants.

South of MADISON, 57.8 *m.* (80 pop.), the highway falls from the high plateau and crosses the TUGALOO, 60.3 *m.*, headwaters of the Savannah River, and the GEORGIA LINE at a point 51 miles northeast of Gainesville.

⚜⚜⚜⚜⚜⚜⚜⚜⚜⚜⚜⚜⚜⚜⚜⚜⚜⚜⚜⚜⚜⚜⚜⚜⚜⚜⚜⚜⚜⚜⚜⚜⚜⚜⚜⚜⚜⚜

Tour 15

(Brevard, N. C.)—Pickens—Liberty—Anderson—Greenwood—Saluda—Orangeburg—Junction with US 52; US 178, US 78. North Carolina Line to Junction with US 52, 249 *m.*

Roadbed concrete-paved with short sections of asphalt.
Southern Ry. and Piedmont and Northern R.R. parallel route between Anderson and Greenwood.
Tourist accommodations at frequent intervals; hotels in larger towns.

In deep mountain shadows US 178 winds down the foothills through lands that belonged to the Cherokee and follows the lines of old trading paths into the Low Country. Traders and scouts who scorned the safety of older settlements were the first to open up the region. Then came farmers from the Northern colonies and plantation owners from the coast who resorted to the mountains in summer to escape malaria and remained to establish year-round homes.

Section a. NORTH CAROLINA LINE to ANDERSON, 50.7 m.
US 178.

In the early days hunters and cow drivers penetrated the upper part of the State by way of the Keowee Path and came back with glowing accounts of the beauty and luxuriant growth of the 'prairie lands,' of great forests, of vast canebrakes often extending in unbroken lines for many miles, and of enormous herds of buffalo and deer. The buffalo have vanished, few deer remain, and much of the land has been given over to industry and agriculture, but the natural beauty of this section holds even greater attraction for people of today. In summer, families migrate to their mountain cottages or to hotels and inns. Around numerous springs, lakes, and rivers are permanent camps where young people rise at dawn, take part in a variety of sports, follow their counselors into the forests for firsthand study of nature-lore, and roll into their bunks at an early hour.

US 178 crosses the NORTH CAROLINA LINE, 0 *m.*, about 15 miles southwest of Brevard, North Carolina.

At 3 *m.* is the junction with a dirt road.

Left here 0.5 *m.* to ROCKY BOTTOM CAMP for rural boys' and girls' clubs of the State. A path leads from the camp to a lookout tower on the summit of Sassafras Mountain (3,548 alt.), the highest point in South Carolina. On its lower slopes the sassafras tree, ordinarily a shrub, but sometimes reaching a height of 60 feet and a diameter of 24 inches, grows abundantly. The spicy roots of this plant were once esteemed for their supposed medicinal value, and were shipped in quantity to England. Mountain people still declare, 'If you drink sassafras tea during the month of March, you won't need a doctor for the rest of the year.'

At 11.5 *m.* is the junction with a hard-surfaced road.

Left here 2.8 *m.* to another hard-surfaced road; L. 2.6 *m.* to TABLE ROCK STATE PARK (*cabins for rent*). From the entrance the Pinnacle Mountain sky line is visible, showing the flat-topped Table at the rear and the Stool at its right, where Indians said a gigantic chieftain sat to dine more than 3,000 feet above ordinary mortals. A 40-foot dam stems Garrick's Creek and a tributary stream to form the peanut-shaped lake stocked with rainbow trout. Following the creek a footpath winds three miles from the bathhouse area to the top of the Table. Nine hundred feet below is the sparkling blue water of the Greenville reservoir; across the wide valley Caesars Head (*see Tour 10*) stands out boldly.

At the 200-foot elevation the trail joins a wagon road over which patrons of the fashionable old Keith-Sutherland Hotel could take a 75¢ oxcart tour to Governor's Rock; from here the more adventurous walked the rest of the way to the mountain top. The governors of both Carolinas attended the gala opening of the hotel in 1848. For the festivities a cannon was to be dragged by rope to the summit, but a pelting rain halted the proceedings at this rock, and here the celebration was held, doubtless to the relief of South Carolina's Governor David Johnson, who was enormously fat. According to one of many such stories it was on this occasion that the governor of North Carolina made to the governor of South Carolina that deathless remark: 'It's a damned long time between drinks.' The secretary of the Historical Commission of South Carolina has tried to kill the myth, but Hydra-like it crops up at one spot after another.

PICKENS, 20 *m.* (1,050 alt., 1,130 pop.), seat of Pickens County, is the highest incorporated town in South Carolina. Pickens's one railroad extends seven miles southeast to Easley; and the single shuttle train is locally called the 'Pickens Doodle.'

Town and county were named in honor of General Andrew Pickens

(1739–1817) of Revolutionary War fame. Pickens was the son of immigrants whose Huguenot forebears had been driven from France to Ireland by the revocation of the Edict of Nantes. The family moved to South Carolina about 1752 from Pennsylvania where Pickens was born. He married a first cousin of John C. Calhoun and settled in Long Cane Creek section. When pre-Revolutionary skirmishing began in South Carolina, Pickens took part in the fighting at Ninety Six (*see Tour 8a*) in 1775 and afterward helped to negotiate a treaty with the Loyalists. A farmer and justice of the peace at the outbreak of the Revolution, he pledged himself immediately to the cause of the colonies and became, with Sumter in mid-State and Marion in the Low Country, one of the three great Partisan leaders. After the fall of Charleston and Camden he was captured and paroled, but when the British burned his house he gave notice that he was breaking parole, and despite their threats, rejoined the Partisans. General Pickens was elected to the legislature in 1782, and in the same year he raised and commanded a company of 500 men, which in six weeks subdued the warring Cherokee nation. In 1785 at the direction of Congress he effected a treaty with the Indians. Pickens went to Congress in 1793, riding to Washington on a spirited white horse. The general himself was magnificently turned out, and an 'African attendant' in splendid livery followed him.

Hanging in the courthouse office of the Pickens county treasurer is a death certificate, issued by the United States Army, stating that Corporal Jesse B. Gillespie 'died with honor in the service of his country May 18, 1918.' Wounded and left for dead when most of his company was wiped out in the Cantigny drive, Mr. Gillespie recovered in a French hospital. To regain his status as a citizen of the United States, the 'deceased' corporal was required two years later to swear to an affidavit that he was alive. Since 1925 he has served as treasurer of his county.

1. Left from Pickens on State 183 to the junction with a dirt road, 0.9 *m.;* L. here 0.3 *m.* to the POTTERY SHOP, owned by a young man who makes use of a clay deposit on his father's farm. The old wheel on which he shapes jugs and vases, is some little distance from the shop.

2. Right from Pickens on State 183 to the junction with a dirt road 1.5 *m.;* R. here 16 *m.* to the SITE OF FORT PRINCE GEORGE, marked by a large mulberry tree. The fort was built in 1753 by Governor Glen to protect English traders from Spanish and French invasion. This point was the gateway from South Carolina to Cherokee country, and the Cherokee gave 2,000 acres for the fort's erection. Terms were arranged by their chief Attakullakulla (Ind., Little Carpenter). When the French began their war to gain control of the American Colonies, their agents persuaded the Cherokee that Fort Prince George and others like it were not intended for the protection of trade, but as outposts that finally would be used in slaughterous aggression. Old Hop and Attakullakulla tried to counteract these rumors, but a series of tragic misunderstandings in 1756 led to the Cherokee War. Fort Prince George became a focal point in the conflict; the most crucial battles of the war were fought here. After the last engagement victorious troops began a 30-day march through Cherokee country, destroying settlements and cultivated fields. The conquered Cherokee begged for peace. Attakullakulla led a group of chiefs to Charles Town for a

conference with Governor William Bull, and at his plantation, Ashley Hall, they gathered around a fire to smoke the pipes of peace.

Across the Keowee (Ind., Place of Mulberries) River is the SITE OF KEOWEE VILLAGE, a Cherokee settlement which extended for several miles along the valley in scattered homes and farms. Old cannon balls and Indian relics are still plowed up occasionally in the vicinity. From Keowee, legend says Cateechee (or Isa-queena) rode to Ninety Six (*see Tour 8a*).

The village marked the end of the Old Keowee Path, used as early as 1717 for travel between Cherokee lands and the coast. At first just a footpath, it later became the route for pack horse trains and finally a great highway between Charleston and the Up Country. The path traversed the districts of Charles Town, Orangeburg, Edgefield, and Abbeville, passing near the towns of Orangeburg, Ridge Spring, Ninety Six, Coronaca, Cokesbury, and through the headstreams of Savannah River tributaries to Keowee. The building of railroads caused the abandonment of such market thoroughfares.

Here Sir Alexander Cuming (*c.*1690–1775), an erratic Scot, maneuvered single-handed an important treaty that kept the war-minded Cherokee at peace with the colony for 30 years. In 1730 Sir Alexander arrived in Charleston, announcing he had come in accord with his wife's dream that he should bring Christianity to the savage Indian. Pretending great wealth he ran up many bills and left town hurriedly when his creditors decided that even the very rich should eventually pay. Traveling through the back country, he heard worried traders discussing a threatened uprising of the Cherokee. French agents had been inciting the Indians against English traders and settlers. Cuming decided to take over the entire matter, and outlined his scheme. The settlers were horrified—considering the man crazy. So Cuming carried on alone. Arriving at Keowee he strode into the forbidden council chamber of the chiefs and with a flourish laid down several pistols, a gun, and a sword; at the end of a histrionic speech he invited them to drink to the health of their great chief, His Royal Majesty, King George II, of England. The Indians were deeply impressed and agreed to attend a grand meeting of the Cherokee to take place ten days later at Keowee. Cuming made a flying trip to other Cherokee towns, seldom staying longer than necessary to drive home his propaganda with a fiery stump speech; he even crossed the Blue Ridge into the Tennessee River Valley to invite the Over-hill Cherokee. Triumphantly he returned to Keowee, and amid feasting, dancing, and singing, the Indians swore undying love for their 'Great White Chief,' the English king, and loyalty to the people of his colony. The wily Scot, by this time known to his red friends as the 'Great Warrior,' then invited them to send their chiefs to England to sign a treaty with the king. This was going almost too fast, and not until Cuming flattered an impressionable young chief into accepting was he able to round up a delegation of seven. In London the Cherokee were lionized by society, lavishly entertained, and received at court with pomp and ceremony. From marble halls they recrossed the Atlantic to their crude little villages where they strengthened the treaty they had signed with glowing accounts of the sights they had seen and the kindness with which they had been received.

On the banks of the Keowee River, 14 *m.* on State 183, is the SITE OF OLD PICKENS, marked only by an old church and a few buildings. Here a flourishing village, seat of Pickens District, existed from 1828 to 1868 when the District was divided into Pickens and Oconee Counties. The commissioners appointed to select a site for a county seat rode horseback until they came to a spot which they declared more favorably situated than Rome, for 'While Rome was built on seven hills with the Tiber flowing by, Pickens was all hills, with the Keowee flowing by.'

At 22.4 *m.* on State 183 is a hard-surfaced road; R. here 2.1 *m.* to the SITE OF PICKET POST, occupied by a country store. The post was established before the Revolution and was used by pickets to guard against Indians. It is also said to have been used in the War between the States by Confederate pickets, who may have been stationed there to deal with deserters from the Confederate Army. Contrary to popular Southern belief, during the War between the States many small landowners, especially those in the hill country, were indifferent to the Confederate cause. Economically isolated, owning few or no slaves, they had suffered little from the shock of sectional strife, and refused to volunteer their services. When additional forces were desperately needed to replenish Lee's thinning ranks, the backwoods were invaded by enlistment officers. Surly men and boys, unattuned to the patriotic fervor about them, were conscripted; but before their short training period was up, they deserted in large numbers and fled to their homes where densely forested hills and valleys offered natural refuge. Branded as criminals, some turned to outlawry and proceeded to terrorize Up Country towns and villages that the exigencies of war had stripped of normal civic protection. What was true of this section was true of other isolated spots through the South.

At 2.2 m. on the hard-surfaced road is a dirt road; L. on this 1.2 m. to the junction with four dirt roads; L. on the second road from the left 0.5 m. to OCONEE STATION, built in 1760, the last of three guardhouses built by a Colonel Montgomery who commanded English and Scottish troops against the Cherokee in 1762. The walls are of fieldstone and the interior contains brick fireplaces in a large central chimney. The one-foot thick walls are pierced at intervals by musket holes. The building is believed to have been used by Colonel Montgomery to house soldiers until after the Revolution. In the basement are an old loom and spinning wheel, and bullet molds.

Adjoining the guardhouse is the two-story brick RICHARDS HOUSE, with gable roof and large chimneys. A marble stone, set in the brickwork, is incised: 'William Richards, 1805.' Richards was one of the three English brothers who came to the section with Colonel Montgomery and remained to establish their home. At the foot of the hill (L), the grave of his sister is inscribed: 'Margaret Richards who crossed the ocean for love of her brothers.'

TAMASSEE, 6.7 m., one of two industrial schools in the United States owned and run by the D.A.R., was established in 1914 for young people of the Southern mountains. Almost every State in the Union has contributed to the school's support. The name, Tamassee (Ind., sunlight of God), is derived from the legend of a Cherokee fire prophet, who attributed his power of healing to a large ruby. From far and near Indians came to the village with their ailments and wounds. When the prophet died, the hill where he was buried with the stone was called Tamassee. On or near the campus are many interesting places that students gladly show to visitors.

The SITE OF RED HOUSE is marked by two ivy-covered stumps. Here General Andrew Pickens died suddenly in 1817 while seated in a large chair beneath his favorite cedars. Through his declining years, the pioneer was so revered by the Indians, whom he had once fought, that they brought him gifts, and called him Skyagusta (Ind., wizard owl).

On Tamassee Creek, a bronze tablet on a boulder marks the SITE OF THE RING FIGHT, 1799, General Pickens's last victory over the Cherokee. Surrounded by yelling savages, Pickens saved the day by setting fire to the canebrake about them. The joints of burning bamboo exploded with a sound like rifle fire, and, according to legend, caused the Indians to flee from imaginary reinforcements.

In WALHALLA, 26 m. (1,060 alt., 2,388 pop.) (*see Tour 19a*), is the junction with State 28 (*see Tour 19a*).

LIBERTY, 26.9 m. (1,040 alt., 2,128 pop.) (*see Tour 14*), is at the junction with State 13 (*see Tour 14*).

At 46.9 m. is the junction with State 28 (*see Tour 19a*), which unites briefly with US 15.

In ANDERSON, 50.7 m. (754 alt., 14,383 pop.) (*see Anderson*), are junctions with US 29 (*see Tour 7*) and State 28 (*see Tour 19a*).

Section b. *ANDERSON to JUNCTION WITH US* 52, 198.3 *m.*
US 178, US 78.

Roughly paralleling the Georgia Line, US 178 swings coastward
from ANDERSON, 0 *m.* In the Low Country, swamp forests are tinted
with pale pink and green long before spring actually arrives. Later the
perfume of sweet bay blossoms and yellow jessamine fills the air. In
winter the black swamp waters, broken by spectral cypress knees and
overhung with gray draperies of Spanish moss, appear gloomy.

BELTON, 9 *m.* (1,756 pop.), was named for Judge Belton O'Neall,
early railroad magnate, lawyer, and historian. Two cotton mills here
operate a total of more than 68,000 spindles and 1,500 looms.

At 11.9 *m.* is the junction with a dirt road.

Right here 4 *m.* to the SITE OF ORR'S TAVERN at the tiny village of Crayton-
ville. In the early decades of the nineteenth century the tavern was kept by
Mrs. Anna Hanks, a member of whose family was named Nancy. John C.
Calhoun, Nullificationist and Vice President of the United States, was said to
be a frequent guest at the tavern where he was attracted by the comely Nancy.
On this slender basis rose the story that Calhoun was the father of Lincoln.
In his *Paternity of Abraham Lincoln,* William E. Barton disposes of the account
by asserting that the Craytonville Nancy was married to a Mr. South and that
at the time Calhoun was stopping at Orr's Tavern the Nancy Hanks who was
Lincoln's mother was in Kentucky with her lawful husband, Thomas Lincoln.

The curiously double name of HONEA (Ind., path) PATH, 67.6 *m.*
(810 alt., 2,740 pop.), was adopted when as many whites as Indians
frequented this section. Another version is that Honea was the name of
a family who lived here. At Honea Path in the late summer of 1934
occurred a mill riot that grew out of a Nation-wide textile strike. All
South Carolina mills did not close on the zero hour, and 'flying squadrons' of strikers and union sympathizers paid quick visits to mills that
continued to operate. As a rule the squadrons were orderly, engaging
in demonstrations to persuade the mill hands to strike; but minor
injuries to their opponents kept them before the public eye. When
arbitration failed, Governor Ibra C. Blackwood called out the National
Guard. About 700 guardsmen were stationed in the Greenville area,
and 600 citizens were deputized in Anderson to assist in preserving
order. On September 6 a flying squadron visited Honea Path, to be
met by a group of deputies and excited townsmen. Arguments grew
into fist fights and gunplay, in which six strikers were slain and a
seventh mortally wounded. At the same time a man was killed by a
deputy in the Greenville area, and from Greenville and Pickens Counties came requests for the application of martial law. The governor
issued a proclamation against flying squadrons, and the Honea Path
mill, for whose closing seven pickets had died on Thursday, opened
the next Monday, protected by soldiers with machine guns. After the
National Guard had been on duty for about a month, most of the
strikers throughout the region decided to go back to work.

DONALDS, 23.3 *m.* (760 alt., 220 pop.), has an air of serenity, extending principally along its one chief street, where little groups of farmers collect under the shade of tall oaks.

Right from Donalds on State 20 3.6 *m.* to DUE WEST (730 alt., 620 pop.), once an old trading center, Duett's or DeWitt's Corner, and often called The Holy City. It is a traditional jest that here the Sabbath quiet is so cherished that roosters crowing on Sunday are apt to find themselves in a stew on Monday. The history of Due West is interwoven with the history of the Associate Reformed Presbyterian Church, which sponsors Erskine College, of which the Woman's College of Due West and the Erskine Theological Seminary are a part. Erskine, an accredited college with an enrollment of about 375, was founded in 1839. The four-mile branch railroad line now serving Due West lacks a turntable, and the single train backs the distance from Donalds daily except Sunday. The only occasion of a Sunday run was when a desperately ill woman was rushed to the Southern mainline in order to reach a Baltimore hospital as soon as possible.

Near here an important Indian treaty was made, May 20, 1777, when the Cherokee signed away extensive claims in South Carolina following Pickens's invasion of their territory. In the previous year many settlers had fallen victims to marauding bands of Tories and Indians, whose forays were guided by 'passovers' reminiscent of the Jewish hegira from Egypt. Tories erected clothbound poles near their cabins, and the raiders knew by this sign that these homes were to be spared. Throughout the section were small stockades to which others fled when such a raid was expected.

A Wayside Park (R), 30.3 *m.*, is maintained by the South Carolina Forestry Commission.

During the War between the States, Engineer George W. Syfan would puff his little wood-burning engine through this section and anxious families would listen for his whistle—long, loud, and triumphant when news from the front was good.

At 33.3 *m.* is the junction with US 25 (*see Tour 8a*), which unites with US 178 for 8 miles.

In GREENWOOD, 41.3 *m.* (671 alt., 11,020 pop.) (*see Greenwood*), are junctions with State 7 (*see Tour 17*), State 10 (*see Tour 19b*), and US 25 (*see Tour 8a*).

At 46.3 *m.* is the southern junction with US 25 (*see Tour 8b*).

Over the red rolling hills US 178 cuts through fields planted with a variety of crops. Since the early settlement of this section the productive soil has yielded melons, berries, grains, and forage crops.

In SALUDA, 69.3 *m.* (1,381 pop.), seat of Saluda County, is the RED BANK CHURCH, two blocks from the business section. The brush arbor which was the congregation's first home was replaced in 1784 by a log hut, in 1855 by a frame building, and in 1913 by the present brick structure with a tower and white columns.

Saluda County was formed from a part of Edgefield in 1895, and the name Butler proposed in honor of a family long prominent in the section. Benjamin R. Tillman, politically influential at the time and opposed to all that the aristocratic Butler family represented, championed the name Saluda (Ind., river of corn), which was chosen.

In Saluda is the junction with State 43 (*see Tour 19b*).

At BATESBURG, 85.3 *m.* (660 alt., 2,839 pop.), is the junction with US 1 (*see Tour 6b*).

The scrubby woods lining the road on both sides lack the dignity of those southeast of here. Tidy new farm bungalows contrast with the big, rambling houses of another era.

In the early fall the SOUTHERN DAHLIA FARM (R), 120 *m.*, attracts visitors, butterflies, and bumble-bees when its 14 acres burst into bloom, with flowers ranging in color from white to purple and red, and in size from a button to a dinner plate.

NORTH, 121.3 *m.* (755 pop.), is at the junction with State 5 (*see Tour 5A*).

In ORANGEBURG, 139 *m.* (264 alt., 8,776 pop.) (*see Tour 5b*), is the junction with US 21 (*see Tour 5b*).

At 140.3 *m.* is the junction with a dirt road.

Right here 0.5 *m.* to the FEDERAL FISH HATCHERY (*open 8–5 weekdays; Sun. 2–5*). Fed by the waters of the Edisto River, the hatchery is a breeding place for varieties of bass, bream, redbreast, and other fish native to these waters.

Pecan orchards are numerous near BOWMAN, 153.6 *m.* (140 alt., 754 pop.), a small town where speed laws are strictly enforced. The fertile soils of the section support a prosperous rural population, descendants of the Colonial settlers. In another period, the region was given to vast plantations and fine old Colonial homes, remnants of which are still discernible along the route.

At ROSINVILLE, 164.7 *m.*, is the junction with US 15 (*see Tour 3b*).

HARLEYVILLE, 170.1 *m.* (88 alt., 371 pop.), is a small trading center for surrounding farms that produce such a variety of products they are almost entirely self-sustaining.

At 177 *m.* is the junction with US 78 (*see Tour 6b*), which the route follows southeastward.

At 180.8 *m.* is the junction with State 27.

Right here 7.5 *m.* to State 65; R. here 3.3 *m.* to a dirt road; R. here 0.1 *m.* to GIVHANS FERRY STATE PARK (*cabins for rent*), more than 1,000 acres along the high banks of the Edisto River. For 100 years the old ferry for which the park is named was the only means of crossing the river in this vicinity. On the north edge of the park a fence encloses the entrance to the 24-mile Edisto-Goose Creek Tunnel, which conducts the water supply of the city of Charleston.

At the COAST EXPERIMENT STATION (L), 187.3 *m.*, operated by Clemson College, fields of truck crops and grain are planted and cultivated to discover those best suited to the section.

The route presents typical Low Country vistas—old trees with hanging moss, swamp lowlands, and little shanties, and passes SUMMERVILLE, 190.3 *m.* (2,575 pop.) (*see Tour 1c*), at the junction with State 61 (*see Tour 1c*).

At 198.3 *m.* is the junction with US 52 (*see Tour 2b*), about 15 miles north of Charleston (*see Charleston*).

Tour 16

(Gastonia, N. C.)—York—Chester; US 321. North Carolina Line to Chester, 36 *m.*

Carolina and Northwestern Ry. parallels entire route.
Limited accommodations; hotels in Chester.
Roadbed concrete-paved with short sections of asphalt.

US 321 traverses a prosperous farming section in the rolling red hills of the Piedmont. The Scotch-Irish settlers of this region were quick to fight for independence in Revolutionary days; their thrift and dignity are still reflected in substantial houses and well-kept barns. Fields of corn and wheat alternate with peach orchards, and pasturage is abundant. Herds of Guernsey cattle graze along the creeks, or rest in the shade. Cotton mills have grown up in the towns, but have not destroyed the old-time spirit of self-reliance.

US 321 crosses the NORTH CAROLINA LINE, 0 *m.*, about 8 miles south of Gastonia, North Carolina.

Between two mill villages, the business section of CLOVER, 4 *m.* (3,111 pop.), parallels the railroad tracks that run through the center of town. On both sides of the track lie residential sections where houses are set in wide hedge-bordered yards. On the southern edge of town is a baseball diamond and park, the latter used mostly for political rallies.

Right from Clover on State 55 to a dirt road, 3 *m.;* L. here 0.3 *m.* to the THOMAS BROTHERS TURKEY RANCH (*open weekdays*). On land that has been in the Thomas family for five generations, a cluster of low buildings forms a small village from which the turkey population ranges in gobbling droves. The birds are all of one breed, Goldbank Giant Bronze, and the purity of the strain is preserved by careful selection. Poults make their advent into a custombuilt hatchery, and for four weeks are kept in electrically warmed brooders. From sun porches they graduate to the growing range, with its drinking fountains, open feeders, and hundreds of feet of roosts. In the early morning it is a strange sight to see the birds 'taking off'—flying from the three-foot roosts instead of hopping down. During growing season they consume hundreds of tons of a specially prepared mash, and in the fall, their thirstiest season, they drink thousands of gallons of water a day. A tattooed brand beneath the wing, registered all over the country, protects the turkeys from thieves, but there are also guards who watch over them day and night. The birds are sold principally to Eastern markets, from September to June, with heavy sales during Thanksgiving and Christmas holidays. At Easter and the Jewish Passover prices are higher. Baby turkeys and hatching eggs are sold from February to August. During the laying season, from the middle of February until July, eggs must be gathered every day, for despite modern conveniences, the hens refuse to lay in prepared nests. On the wide laying range—moved every three months—the brood hens hide their eggs under leaves and sticks.

Established in 1918 by 9-year-old T. M. Thomas and his 6-year-old brother

Paul, because with their $5 capital they could not afford a calf, the business in 1938 produced 26,000 turkeys and 60,000 eggs. The college-trained Thomases have put their education to use in making extensive and valuable experiments. At 6 *m.* on State 55 is the junction with State 161 and State 216.

1. Left on State 161 0.5 *m.* to BETHANY ASSOCIATE REFORMED PRESBYTERIAN CHURCH, a red brick structure with arcaded entrance portico, mauve and tan windows with circular heads, and a belfry with battlemented parapet. The congregation owes its origin in 1793 to the introduction of hymns into the worship of a Presbyterian church in the vicinity of Kings Mountain. This innovation caused the withdrawal of a number of families, who sent Andrew Ferguson and John Miller to the Associate Reformed Synod of the Carolinas to ask for a minister. To John Miller is ascribed a hearty prayer of battle: 'Good Lord, Our God that art in Heaven, we have great reason to thank Thee for the many battles we have won. There is the great and glorious battle of King's Mountain, where we kilt the great Gineral Ferguson and took his whole army; and the great battle at Ramseur's and Williamson's; and the iver memorable and glorious battle of the Coopens, where we made the proud Gineral Tarleton run doon the road healter-skelter; and Good Lord, if ye had na suffered the cruel Tories to burn Bill Hill's iron works, we would no have asked any mair favors at Thy hands. Amen.' Among the ministers of Bethany were the Reverend William Dixon, dismissed for drunkenness and soon thereafter reinstated; a Reverend Mr. Banks, whose abolition sentiments made him so unpopular that he had to return to the North; and the Reverend R. C. Grier, later president of Erskine College and grandfather of its president by the same name in 1939.

2. Right from State 55 on State 161 to the North Carolina Line, 4 *m.*, about 6 miles south of Kings Mountain, North Carolina.

3. Right from State 55 on State 216 to 4,000-acre KINGS MOUNTAIN NATIONAL MILITARY PARK (*free guide service*), 5 *m.* The tallest monument was erected by the U. S. Government in 1909. Another near by was placed by the Kings Mountain Centennial Association in 1880. Markers include a granite stone where Ferguson is said to have fallen and others which memorialize various leaders and events of the battle. Here on October 7, 1780, was fought the battle that practically broke British control in South Carolina. Colonel Patrick Ferguson, called the best shot in the English army, had taken his place on a ridge of the mountain and announced that 'God Almighty could not drive him from it.' This debonair Scot, courageous and intensely loyal to the king, had spent months in the back country after the British had taken Charleston, organizing Tories and equipping them for battle, some with the breech-loading rifle he had invented. Many former Whigs succumbed to his magnetism and followed him into western North Carolina; but certain frontiersmen or 'over mountain' men farther west would not be charmed. Ferguson sent word to the Patriots under Colonel Isaac Shelby that he would come over, hang the rebels, and ruin their lands. Shelby made no reply, but with Colonels John Sevier, William Campbell, and Benjamin Cleveland, he began bringing up militia from the Carolinas, Georgia, Virginia, and what is now Tennessee and Kentucky, to stop Ferguson before he could join Cornwallis at Charlotte. They expected to overtake him at Gilbert Town (now Rutherfordton), North Carolina, but he had gone before they arrived. The Whigs continued to Cowpens on October 6, regaled themselves with beef from Tory Hanna's stock, and were joined by Colonel James Williams with a detachment of South Carolinians. On surveying their men they discovered that they had little equipment and no provisions. Campbell was elected officer of the day, 900 horsemen were selected, and at 8 P.M. they set out for Kings Mountain, 30 miles away. 'Buford' was the countersign, referring to Tarleton's massacre of Buford's men (*see Tour 21a*) a few weeks before. They rode all night and until 3 the next afternoon, with pauses for reconnoitering. Within a mile of the enemy they were discovered and the fight began.

On the mountain top, almost bald except for a few trees and large boulders, the well-equipped Tories were drawn up for battle. The Whigs were clad in moccasins, coon-skin caps, and hunting shirts, and crudely armed with tomahawks, scalping knives, and long-barreled rifles, but they were hidden in thick woods and managed to surround the enemy. Shelby warned, 'Never shoot until you see an enemy, and never see an enemy without bringing him down.' Fat, unwieldy Cleveland advised, 'When you can do no better, get behind trees or retreat; but I beg of you not to run quite off . . . If any of you are afraid, such have leave to retire, and they are requested to take themselves off.' The British drums beat to arms, Ferguson blew his silver whistle, and ordered a charge. The Whigs fell back before Tory bayonets, but rallied immediately. As they scrambled up the slope, enemy bullets whizzed over their heads. Red-haired Campbell shouted, 'Shoot like hell and fight like devils!' Three times the red coats charged with bayonets and the over-mountain men rallied, first on one side then on another. The drums rattled, Ferguson dashed around on a white horse, his checked hunting coat flowing over his uniform, his sword in his left hand to cut down the white flags his weakening men raised. The Whigs replied with volleys from behind trees or rocks and tore the air with Indian war whoops and the cry of 'Buford's Quarter.' For an hour they fought; then Ferguson, spurring his horse, charged desperately into the Whig line, only to fall from his horse pierced by six or eight balls. He died with his foot still in the stirrup. Immediately the British drums beat a parley; Captain De Peyster, second in command, raised the white flag of surrender. The Whigs fought on a few minutes until their leaders ordered them to stop. The entire British force was killed, wounded, or captured; the Whigs lost 28 killed and 62 wounded. Colonel James Williams fell a few yards from Ferguson. Hurriedly two shallow trenches were dug for the dead; Ferguson, divested of his regimentals, was buried in a raw beef hide. According to tradition, his mistress, Virginia Sal, was buried with him; but another lady-friend, Virginia Paul, rode around the camp nonchalant and scornful. She and the other prisoners were started to American headquarters in North Carolina—a hurried march, as the victors feared an attack by Tarleton. Most of the 700 prisoners escaped, though some of the Tories identified as participating in various murderous raids were court-martialed and executed. A scarcity of provisions, change of allegiance among the prisoners, and the gradual dispersion of the Whigs, who insisted on going back home when the battle was over—all this accounted for the fact that there were only 132 prisoners and hardly more of their captors when the company reached North Carolina.

Back on the mountain the wolves found the shallow pits where the dead lay. 'The vulture and the wolf divided their carcasses among them,' and for many years wolf-hunting was a chief sport thereabout. In 1815 neighborhood folk gathered scattered bones and buried them and Dr. William McLean placed a small boulder to commemorate the battle.

Conservative YORK, 13 *m.* (720 alt., 2,862 pop.), formerly York-ville, is still dominated by the traditions of its Scotch-Irish settlers, and has been little attracted to such modern sources of income as the tourist trade and industry. The town was settled when some Pennsylvanians came here about 1757 and took up land around Fergus Cross, a stagecoach tavern. They planted the elms and oaks that now meet above the streets; their sedate old houses now look out between tall crape myrtles and sweet olives.

Interest in local history is keen, and most of the women are members of the D.A.R. or the U.D.C. The White Rose Club, a civic organization, appropriates the symbol of the English House of York. In community gatherings, Indian fighters, Whig patriots, battling dominies, and the Ku Klux Klan (*see History*) all come alive again.

The first Ku Klux Klan in South Carolina is said to have been organized here in 1868. At first it was largely a social organization, but in 1870, when bearing arms was allowed to Negroes and forbidden to white by carpetbag law, the Klan determined to enforce the supremacy of the whites.

Arrayed in ghostly white robes made from sheets and pillow cases, the Klansmen aimed at playing on the superstitious fears of newly freed Negroes. In time the Klan's activities got beyond the control of the leaders and they urged its disbanding.

Major Lewis Merrill of the United States Army, stationed in York to suppress the Klan, was later accused of receiving $15,700 from the 'radical' State legislature for arresting 195 citizens without warrant, usually on suborned evidence. Dr. Rufus Bratton, a Klansman, escaped from York to Canada, but was kidnapped there by Federal officials; the incident led to diplomatic complications. Dr. Bratton was the prototype of a character in Thomas Dixon's novel, *The Clansman*, which was adapted for the motion picture, *The Birth of a Nation*. Relatives of Thomas Dixon lived here and he visited the community often.

At one time York was an important educational town of the Up Country. Kings Mountain Military Academy, founded in 1855, continued until 1886; in 1894 it was reopened for a short time by Baptists and in 1900, under a new management, was reopened as a boys' preparatory school. The property was bought in 1908 by Episcopalians who established the Church Home Orphanage, which now cares for 125 children.

The Yorkville Female College was opened in 1852 as Bethel Female Institute by Presbyterians and continued until 1875. The walls of its main buildings are now used by the public high school, the interior having been burned. John R. Schorb (1818–1908), a German immigrant who taught music and chemistry in the college until it closed its doors, was a skilled photographer as early as 1853. He had studied under a pupil of Daguerre's; examples of his work are exhibited at the York library.

Sharply contrasted with the mellow background is the Barnett Brothers' Circus, which has made its winter home here since 1929 in a long stone building on W. Madison Street, known as the 'animal house.' Keepers sleep upstairs over the stalls and cages; every Friday, open-house day, they station themselves at strategic points to keep a watchful eye on local visitors, who know the names of each animal, speak to their favorites, and are sometimes tempted to stand too near them. In a vacant lot near by are trailers, allotted permanent parking space, and empty trucks used as work shops, paint shops, wardrobe, and storage rooms. A tent is the mess hall. Some of the employees sleep in the trailers but others board in town; a few own homes here. The welfare of Barnett Brothers' Circus is a matter of civic pride with York, and relations between winter crew and townfolk have a family touch. The man who supervises the painting and refurnishing of trucks and trailers, using gallons of gilt paint each season, in his leisure time does portraits of local children. Town boys beg for the privilege of driving new trucks from the factory to York, which means a trip to Ohio, Kansas, Texas, or possibly to Quebec. The milky-white pet dogs of many of the children here come from the annual litters of somersaulting terriers. Each Christmas the shopping season is opened by a parade in which Santa Claus, escorted by the high-school band, comes swaying down Congress Street on the back of an elephant. Servants and housewives have grown accustomed to false reports that 'the big snake is out,' and the only animal really to escape during a decade of circus residence was Jocko, an ugly baboon that frightened a motorist and a field worker before disappearing altogether.

Almost inevitable was the home-talent circus that sprouted in 1930, with neighborhood kids risking their bones on wires stretched tight between backyard trees; but the result was unexpected. Sponsored and managed by five brothers, the little top's first season attracted only indulgent adults at 5¢ per head. Professionals of the big show encouraged the young plagiarists, however, and extended more than moral support. The management donated a slightly tattered but otherwise excellent tent, whose seating capacity was 300. Taking their cue from the conscientious habits of the elder performers, the youngsters practiced with a seriousness that brought real skill, and their annual extravaganza, combining elements of circus, vaudeville, and minstrel, attracted larger and larger audiences. Their crowning success was achieved when they made an extended and profitable tour of surrounding towns.

In York, Cupid is almost as active as the circus. From Charlotte and other populous North Carolina areas just across the State line couples come to the buff courthouse on Congress Street and vow matrimonial allegiance while the ink dries on their marriage licenses. The county judge of probate does a rushing business in uniting North Carolina lovers who have no patience with their State's requirement that marriage be deferred until three days after application for a license. South Carolina's indulgence to impulsive suitors is matched by its refusal to grant divorce on any grounds.

In York is the junction with State 5 (*see Tour 7A*).

Left from York on State 49 1 *m.* to the CANNON MILL (*open*), which manufactures towels.

In GUTHRIESVILLE, 20 *m.*, is the junction with a dirt road.

Left on this road 2 *m.* to BRATTONSVILLE, where Captain Christian Huck and his plundering Tories and British regulars were defeated by a small band of Whigs about 5 A.M. on July 12, 1780. Aroused from their blankets by the surprise attack, several hundred sleepy-eyed British defended themselves behind two lanes that flanked their camp, surrendering when 40 of their number, including Huck, had been killed. This battle was one of the first victories of American militia over British cavalry. A little house (L), about 100 yards from the monument commemorating this fight, was the scene of an incident still told hereabout. Colonel William Bratton and his wife, Martha, lived there. The colonel was away when the Tories arrived. Mrs. Bratton, refusing to reveal his route and scorning to accept the proposal that she try to sway him to the

Tory cause, was attacked by a Britisher who pinned her head to the porch rail by a reaping hook over her neck. A more considerate Britisher rescued her. The day after the fight the latter was among the captured and Mrs. Bratton interceded for him, thus preventing his execution. Colonel Bratton was an old man at the time, having been a member of Braddock's Company which was defeated in the French and Indian War some 24 years before. The large house right of the monument is a later Bratton house, and was once the home of Dr. Rufus Bratton. A skeleton that he used is still in one of the upper rooms.

One of the two or three country homes in LOWRY'S, 27 *m.*, is the two-story white frame ERWIN HOME (L), which includes two additions to a pre-Revolutionary log house. The mid-section was the first addition and the front part was built in 1800 by J. Lowry, a Presbyterian minister affectionately known as the Old Parson, who used his popularity in drawing hard-bitten sinners to the fold. The two-story portico has superimposed Roman Doric and Ionic columns, and its classic cornice is enriched by dentils and modillions. The interior, crowded with family heirlooms, has three levels on the first floor, because of the distinctly separate buildings. According to local tradition, the shade of Lowry still lingers, and strange noises in the attic are attributed to his nightly perambulations.

CHESTER, 36 *m.* (484 alt., 5,528 pop.) (*see Tour 5a*), is at the junction with US 21 (*see Tour 5a*) and State 9 (*see Tour 21b*).

Tour 17

(Forest City, N. C.)—Spartanburg—Laurens—Greenwood; US 221, State 7. North Carolina State Line to Greenwood, 83 *m.*

Roadbed concrete-paved, with short sections of asphalt.
Route paralleled between North Carolina State Line and Spartanburg by Clinchfield R.R.; between Spartanburg and Greenwood by Charleston and Western Carolina R.R.
Numerous accommodations; hotels in larger towns.

US 221 winds through the Blue Ridge foothills, whose rich variety of plant and animal life has for years attracted naturalists. Violets, Judas trees, azaleas, and rhododendrons cover the slopes in spring; golden hickory and tulip trees, scarlet sourwood and maples give the brightness of an oriental carpet to the autumn woods. Corn patches cling to the hillsides where it is said farm animals are born with legs shorter on one side than the other, so they can plow the steeps without falling off.

Every farmer keeps hogs for the family meat supply, and hog-killing is a process that has changed little since pioneer days. Cold, frosty mornings are 'good hog-killin' weather'—and all the family must help, as well as some of the neighbors. At early dawn, water is heated in a great iron pot out under the trees, or brought to the boiling point in a barrel or gasoline drum by heated stones. Children pick up chips and sticks to keep the fire going. An empty barrel is ready for the scalding, a few low tables, a rope swung from a limb, and plenty of sharp knives.

The hogs in the pen near by begin to scent the excitement, and set up a lively grunting and squealing. They are suspicious of the ears of corn thrown down to keep them quiet. One of the men approaches with a .22 rifle, selects his victim and plants a bullet between the eyes. If the aim is good the hog drops without a sound—but more often the small bullet fails to reach the brain and the hog rushes around wildly squealing. Eight or ten shots may be needed to quiet him—annoying to the farmer, as the flavor of the meat is spoiled by overheating. Sometimes the hog is knocked in the head with an axe instead of being shot.

Once down the animal is stuck in the throat with a long knife and bled. The carcass is immersed in the barrel of boiling water and thoroughly scalded, then laid on a low table and the bristles scraped off. After being washed he is strung up by the hind legs, the belly slit open, and the entrails removed. Children wait eagerly for the bladder, which makes a beautiful balloon when blown up and dried, or a rattle when filled with a handful of peas. The carcass must cool for several hours before being cut up, but 'chitlings' can be started at once. These are the small intestines, scraped clean, turned inside out, and soaked in water for several days. They are then cut in sections, looped in knots, and boiled—after which they may be served as they are or rolled in flour and fried.

If the weather is cold enough, the meat may be cut up the same day, but it is generally allowed to hang over night. The method of cutting is not the orthodox one followed by meat packers. Instead of being split down the middle, the backbone is cut out. Then each side is cut into hams, middlings, and shoulders. Backbones and spare ribs are cooked immediately, and generous portions of 'the fresh' given to neighbors. Nothing is allowed to go to waste—head cheese, liver mush, liver pudding, sausage, and souse meat account for the various odds and ends. Tails and ears, properly fried, are especially valued by Negroes.

The heavily salted meat is packed into boxes or barrels for about two weeks. The middlings, now called bacon, are then washed and salted again—after which they will keep almost indefinitely. Hams and shoulders require further treatment. A mixture of black pepper, brown sugar or sorghum, and corn meal is carefully rubbed over the surface, and the meat is hung up in a cool, dry place. Sometimes soaking in a brine of salt, sugar, and a small amount of saltpetre is substituted. This preliminary cure may be followed by smoking in a tightly closed smokehouse. Hickory chips are used for fuel—or corn cobs, which give a richer flavor. When finished, the meat is sewed up in brown paper or cotton bags as a protection against flies.

Trying out lard is a separate process. The fatty tissues that line the back, along with scraps of fat trimmed from the meat, are put into a huge iron kettle, often outdoors, and cooked for several hours. The resulting lard is preserved in churns and buckets, and will keep through the year for frying or other cooking purposes. The crisp brown 'cracklings' that are left when the lard is tried out are mixed with corn meal batter and made into a delicious bread, which is a favorite accompaniment of collards and hog jowls.

US 221 crosses the NORTH CAROLINA LINE, 0 *m.*, about 16 miles south of Forest City, North Carolina.

At 3 *m.* is the junction with State 11 (*see Tour* 18).

CHESNEE, 5 *m.* (764 pop.), has a print mill and a lumber plant, whose employees largely hail from the surrounding hills. It was named for the Chesney family who had land grants here in 1750 and who remained loyalists through the Revolution. Alexander Chesney's *Journal*, published with copious annotations, gives a stirring account of the war from the point of view of a rampant Tory in a region where 'scarcely a day passed without some skirmishing.'

A large faded white frame hotel supports the claim of CHEROKEE SPRINGS, 15.1 *m.*, that it was a popular Carolina spa in former years. Local residents still fill kegs and demijohns with spring water for their own use while the vacant hotel windows stare down upon them.

South of the springs the route dips to the Pacolet River, then rises to a watershed above Lawson's Fork. Hereabout lived the pioneers, Indian fighters who worked, loved, and drank with gusto, looked to the plow for subsistence, to the rifle for protection. Over these lands hardheaded Whigs and Tories fought tooth and nail, each convinced of the rightness of his cause. Here Bishop Asbury came on the heels of the Revolution to struggle fervently with the sins of his hearers.

In SPARTANBURG, 25.4 *m.* (876 alt., 28,723 pop.) (*see Spartanburg*), are the junctions with US 29 (*see Tour* 7), US 176 (*see Tour* 12*a*), and State 9 (*see Tour* 21*b*).

ROEBUCK, 27.5 *m.* (733 alt., 250 pop.), a little south of the site of the Revolutionary 'Becca,' where the Old Georgia Road and the Old Blackstock Road intersected, was named for Colonel Benjamin Roebuck, commander of the First Spartan Regiment during the last months of the Revolution.

The ancestral home of the Moore family, FREDONIA (R), 29.9 *m.*, occupies lands granted in 1763 to Charles Moore by George III. The present two-story white clapboarded house was built around the pre-Revolutionary log cabin. Moores of Fredonia have been prominent in the State's history. Thomas, son of Charles Moore, graduate of the University of Dublin, Ireland, served in the Revolution and as major general in the War of 1812. He was a member of the State legislature and the United States Congress. In 1832 a Moore led the fight for Nullification in the county. Colonel T. J. Moore, an experimental agriculturist, was a bitter anti-Tillmanite. In the family burying ground is the grave of Kate Moore Barry, sister of Thomas Moore and wife of

Captain Andrew Barry, who lived at neighboring Walnut Grove. It is said that at the news of an impending Tory attack, Mrs. Barry tied her little girl to a bedpost while she rode through the neighborhood to give warning.

MOORE, 31.6 *m.* (743 alt., 60 pop.), and SWITZER, 34.2 *m.* (745 alt., 120 pop.), were named for local families and grew about the railroad stations. Chief excitement is the arrival of the mail, though during peach season shipment of the fruit rouses a spirit of activity.

A Main Street, nearly 70 feet wide in WOODRUFF, 39.7 *m.* (750 alt., 3,175 pop.), is edged by the town's entire business section and shaded by water and willow oaks. Until a few years ago the street was lit by kerosene lamps—a highly unsatisfactory arrangement, for after Saturday night festivities townspeople and country men thought nothing of detaching a lantern to light their way home. The community was variously known as The Hill, Cross Roads, and Woodruff Tavern, until 1876, when it was surveyed and incorporated under its present name.

ENOREE, 47 *m.* (611 alt., 1,500 pop.), was known as Mountain Shoals in the early history of Spartanburg District. After the Riverside Cotton Mill was built, the town was named for the Enoree River near by.

Left from Enoree on State 92 9 *m.* to CROSS ANCHOR and a junction with State 56.

1. Right from Cross Anchor 2.5 *m.* on State 56 to the SITE OF THE BATTLE OF MUSGROVE'S MILL, fought August 19, 1780, and won by the Americans. North Carolinians, Georgians, and South Carolinians, under Colonels Shelby, Clarke, and Williams, rode all night to attack the British post here, only to find that the garrison had received reinforcements. Their horses were too worn for retreat. Desperately the Americans constructed brushwood breastworks, drew the British into combat, depleted their ranks, and quickly retired. Nearing North Carolina they were overtaken by a runner bringing news of Gates's disastrous defeat at Camden, and Colonel Ferguson's advance. Hastily the men dispersed to protect their mountain homes. A few, under Colonel James Williams, herded their 70 British prisoners into North Carolina on a grueling four-day march. A battle marker and a monument to Colonel Samuel Inman, American leader, give details of the skirmish. Musgrove's Mill, scene of John Kennedy's *Horseshoe Robinson,* was owned by Edmund Musgrove, a man of education and comfortable means, who had sons fighting on both sides during the Revolution. Mary Musgrove, the miller's daughter, was the heroine of Kennedy's novel; she was said to have loved an American soldier and upon his death wasted away to such an extent that her body was carried to the grave on a silk handkerchief borne by four young girls. Her grave is pointed out near the Musgrove house. Less romantic but more dependable records indicate that she recovered, married, and raised a family. Her father's will, made after the war, mentions his daughter Mary and her children. Right from Musgrove's Mill on a dirt road 2 *m.* to RIVERSIDE, on a bluff overlooking the river, a summer recreation camp for children and alumni of Thornwell Orphanage.

At 12.3 *m.* on State 56 is the junction with a dirt road; L. here 4.6 *m.* to another dirt road; L. here 0.8 *m.* to DUNCAN'S CREEK PRESBYTERIAN CHURCH (R), a granite structure, erected in 1842 on the site of an earlier church, which was built about 1763 by a group of Scotch-Irish emigrants from Pennsylvania. The church was remodeled in 1927 and its slave gallery removed. Inserts of stone in the side indicate former entrances. In 1788 the large congregation became involved in a schism between adherents of Rouse's and Watts's versions of the Psalms which were sung at services, and a large portion seceded to form a Baptist church. Numerous Revolutionary soldiers are buried in the large graveyard, whose earliest grave is that of Susannah Long, 1776. During the Revolution, Britain's Colonel Tarleton camped on the hill near by and the American leader Logan camped on Duncan's Creek.

At CLINTON, 13 *m.* (678 alt., 5,643 pop.) (*see Tour 9c*), on State 56 is the junction with US 76 (*see Tour 9c*).

2. Left from Cross Anchor on State 56 to the TIGER RIVER, 6 *m.*, which was the scene of much activity before the railroads came, when cotton was poled down its stream to the Broad River, thence to Columbia to be shipped to the port of Charleston. The name comes from a French trader, Tygert, who sired the half-breed children of a Cherokee squaw. The Indians knew the river as 'Arroyes-Creek' or 'Oudalee' the former possibly from *arroyo* (Span., little stream). Juan Pardo, Spanish explorer, is said to have visited these parts about 1567. In the neighborhood east of here was born William Walker (1809–75), the widely known 'Singin' Billy,' whose Baptist ardor inspired him to write and publish many hymns (*see Music*). His setting for 'Amazing Grace' is still used by his musical followers. With meager education but abundant ambition he organized singing classes and taught throughout the southeast as far west as Kentucky, always using the shape-note system that originated among the Greeks and survived through old English forms. At 24 he married Amy Golightly, and they had ten children. During the War between the States, though more than 50 years old he helped nurse the sick and wounded. For many years he had a book store in Spartanburg. He said he preferred 'A.S.H.' (Author Southern Harmony) after his name to 'Pres.' before it, and these three letters are inscribed on his tombstone in Spartanburg.

State 56 continues to a junction with US 176 in PAULINE, 14 *m.* (39 pop.) (*see Tour 12a*).

State 92 continues eastward. At 10.5 *m.* is BELMONT (R), surrounded by cedars and the remnants of an old garden, near the site of Judge John Foucheraud Grimké's summer home, the earlier Belmont. The present two-story house, built in 1840, has the paneled doors, the mantels, and much of the hand-pressed brick of the Grimké house. The interior is finished with lumber cut and dressed on the site.

Judge Grimké (1752–1819), distinguished jurist who first codified the laws of South Carolina, was born in Charleston of Huguenot ancestry. Of his 14 children, two daughters, Sarah (1792–1873) and Angelina (1805–79), made names for themselves as woman suffragists, food faddists, dress reformers, and, chiefly, as abolitionists—bringing down on their heads the social wrath and condemnation of their native city. So extreme were the two sisters in their equalitarian views that they avowed kinship with, and assisted in the education of, two Charleston mulatto boys who had the Grimké name. The elder, Archibald Henry (1849–1930), was appointed minister to San Domingo by President Cleveland; and the younger, Francis James (1850–1936), became a Presbyterian minister in Washington.

The Dillard family, Belmont residents since 1857, has a collection of Indian handiwork and relics of four wars. In the attic, now used as a library, are stored old books and curios. The huge scuppernong vine in the front yard was planted by Mrs. Catherine Dillard in April 1861, on the day the first volunteers left Cross Anchor for the War between the States. Behind the hill is Belmont Cemetery containing graves of early settlers.

At 12 *m.* on State 92 is a dirt road; L. here 1 *m.* to BLACKSTOCK BATTLEFIELD, where, November 20, 1780, Sumter and his men, encamped for the night, were warned by Mrs. Mary Dillard of Tarleton's approach. Forsaking their supper, the men scattered to strategic positions in the old log trading post and barn and under cover of a fence along the road. Tarleton, anticipating no such preparedness, decided to wait for his artillery and other troops; Sumter, however, forced battle. Volunteers sallied forth to draw pursuit from the enemy, and in the four-hour contest the British were routed, leaving 200 killed and wounded. One American was killed and three wounded, including the Game-cock himself. With a severe wound through his breast, General Sumter was carried on a raw cowhide slung between two horses, as the Americans, with their prisoners and captured supplies, departed for North Carolina.

CROSS KEYS HOUSE (L), 14 *m*. on State 92, a square brick building of the Georgian Colonial type, gives its name to the surrounding settlement. This house, begun in 1812 and completed in 1814, and Cross Anchor, which stood several miles away, were planned by two Englishmen, brothers, captain and purser of their own ship. Brick and tile were brought from England, granite was quarried near the site, and lumber brought from Charleston or near-by forests. Though the brothers did not live to see their houses completed, their plans were followed and in the gables of each house plaques bore their in-signia—the captain's anchor and the purser's keys. Cross Anchor was burned several years ago, but Cross Keys is excellently preserved. Beautiful carving decorates its interior in wainscoting, molding, and mantels. Old furniture, china, glass, and silver have been in use for many years. Jewelry and mementos, little old-fashioned toys, and a collection of family daguerreotypes present the tastes and fashions of other generations. A luncheon guest here was Jefferson Davis, who did not disclose his identity until his departure. Two old milestones in front of the house were markers for an early highway system; '12 M.' indicates the distance to Union, '68-C' notes the mileage to Columbia by the Old Buncombe Road.

FOREST HILLS ESTATE, 20.6 *m.*, comprises 500 acres of the lands granted Thomas Fletchall by King George III, in 1772. The present house was built in 1923 on the site of Fletchall's imposing pre-Revolutionary home. In the landscaped grounds are two certified buddings from the Washington elm, which formerly stood in Cambridge, Massachusetts. A wealthy and influential man, Fletchall was colonel of the Upper Saluda Regiment when William Henry Drayton and William Tennant, delegates of the Committee of Safety, tried unsuccessfully to secure his allegiance to the American cause. After the Revolu-tion, confiscation brought the estate into possession of Colonel Thomas Brandon, of the Second Spartan Regiment, one of General Sumter's leaders. It was Sumter's policy to reward his men with such property in lieu of money for their voluntary services, and Brandon acquired thousands of acres in the Up Country. Judge Grimké's plantation, Belmont, and a large part of the present city of Greenville once belonged to him. A mill and a trading post were once at MURPHY'S SHOALS, 21.2 *m.*, on Fair Forest Creek, scene of lively Whig and Tory skirmishes.

In UNION, 25 *m.* (578 alt., 7,419 pop.) (*see Tour 12b*), are the junctions with US 176 (*see Tour 12b*) and State 11 (*see Tour 18*).

Before the railroads came, ORA, 49.5 *m.* (697 alt., 375 pop.), was called Scuffletown. At the post office and cross-roads store, members of the community met to trade, to get the mail, to race their horses, and to indulge in their primary pastime, boxing and wrestling, which occa-sionally terminated in general scuffles and free-for-alls. A railroad sur-veyor, enamored of a local girl, renamed the town for her; the town-ship retains the old name.

Comfortable homes, lawns, and shrubbery, and recreational facilities make WATTS MILL VILLAGE, 55.3 *m.*, one of the attractive mill communities in the State.

In LAURENS, 56.6 *m.* (589 alt., 5,443 pop.) (*see Tour 10*), are the junctions with US 276 (*see Tour 10*) and US 76 (*see Tour 9c*).

In COLD POINT, 64 *m.*, is the junction with State 39.

Left here 9 *m*. to LIBERTY SPRINGS PRESBYTERIAN CHURCH, named for a Revolutionary encampment of Sons of Liberty. The congregation was organized about 1786, and five churches have occupied the site. The present structure, erected in 1857, is typical of Up Country churches built by Scotch-Irish Presbyterians in that period. A white frame structure with octagonal steeple, it has a slave gallery with separate outside entrance.

In the church preceding the present structure, in 1853, Mrs. Louise Bird Cuningham, her daughter, Miss Ann Pamela Cuningham, and five other ladies of the community, organized the Mount Vernon Ladies Association and collected contributions for the purchase of Mount Vernon for the Nation.

A tomb in the churchyard bears an inscription to Captain Zachary Pulliam, 2nd Rifle Regiment, SCV, composed by his fiancée, 'This tribute of affection erected by her to whom he was dearest, and on whose bleeding heart the fair picture of his heavenly excellence will be forever drawn.' Captain Pulliam died at the age of 32 from wounds received in the second battle of Manassas.

Along here wild flowers fringe the highway, delicate Queen Anne's lace and maypop blossoms, flamboyant trumpet vines and butterfly weed, goldenrod and devil's shoestring. Clusters of mail boxes indicate the existence of isolated farmhouses somewhere in the multitudinous dirt roads that crisscross the section. Gradually the land grows less hilly. Through this farming country are outcroppings of the same rock stratum that forms Stone Mountain in Georgia.

Near WATERLOO, 69 *m.*, is the SITE OF ROSEMONT MANOR, in its time the stateliest house in the Up Country. It was built in 1769 by Patrick Cuningham on lands granted him by King George. During the Revolution the family remained loyal, and for a while were exiled to the West Indies, but like many other Tories, finally returned to their homes. Cuningham, and later his son, Robert, were members of the legislature from Laurens County. At Rosemont Ann Pamela Cuningham, an invalid from childhood, worked unceasingly to make Mount Vernon a national shrine. Long a showplace, Rosemont was destroyed by fire in 1931, and its owner, Robert Cuningham, perished in the flames.

At 73 *m*. is a junction with State 7, which the route follows southwestward.

In GREENWOOD, 83 *m*. (671 alt., 11,020 pop.) (*see Greenwood*), are junctions with US 25 (*see Tour 8a*), US 178 (*see Tour 15b*), and State 10 (*see Tour 19b*).

****

Tour 18

Junction with US 221—Gaffney—Union—Monticello—Columbia; State 11, State 215. Junction with US 221 to Columbia, 112.8 *m.*

Concrete-paved with short sections of asphalt.
Southern Ry. parallels route between Jonesville and Carlisle.
Limited accommodations.

This route, leading through the Enoree District of the Sumter National Forest, crosses many streams stained red with the lost soil of upland farms. Deep gullies scar the naked hills, and attest the greed of a generation of cotton planters who cared more for quick wealth than for the preservation of their land. As the topsoil washed away, the top layer of population moved westward to join the 'cotton rush' of the 1830's and 1840's in the Mississippi Delta. The Forestry Service is doing much to reclaim the land, but centuries must lapse before its fertility is altogether restored. Past forlorn plantation houses, dead villages of stillborn hopes, and little towns where optimism has been revived by the establishment of textile mills, the road winds down to the capital of South Carolina in the center of the State.

State 11 branches east from US 221, 0 *m.*, about 3 miles south of the North Carolina Line.

At 0.8 *m.* on State 11 is a junction with a paved road.

Right here 0.1 *m.* to the SITE OF THE BATTLE OF COWPENS (L) commemorated by the tall white shaft of a national monument that rises in a swarded park. The old marker near by was erected in 1856 by the Washington Light Infantry of Charleston, who marched up for the jubilee. This fluted iron shaft topped with a cannon ball and bronze eagle has a base of native stone mortared with sand and shells from under Fort Moultrie. Here, January 17, 1781, Colonel Tarleton was routed when he attacked General Daniel Morgan's troops on the hill and General Andrew Pickens's at the foot of the slope. Pickens's home had just been destroyed by Tory raiders, and irate neighbors who agreed with him that the British could not be trusted had hastily assembled to march with him and join Morgan. Pickens told every third man to fire when the enemy was within 150 yards, the others to wait till the Britishers were closer. Officers in bright regalia were the chosen targets. This victory, following Kings Mountain (*see Tour* 16), marked the decline of British power in South Carolina.

At GAFFNEY, 12 *m.* (779 alt., 6,827 pop.) (*see Tour* 7), is a junction with US 29 (*see Tour* 7).

The scene of John P. Kennedy's historical romance, *Horseshoe Robinson, a Tale of Tory Ascendency in South Carolina,* was laid at DOGWOOD SPRING, 14 *m.* Tradition records that here Colonel William Washington cut off Tarleton's fingers with his sword. A British officer, galloping up, aimed his musket at Washington, but a Negro servant proved quicker and with his shot broke the officer's arm.

At ASBURY, 23 *m.*, a village with a big school, is a junction with a dirt road.

Right here to ASBURY CHAPEL, 2 *m.*, a bare frame structure with many-paned windows typical of the old-time meetinghouse. It was dedicated by Bishop Asbury after the Revolution when he established Methodist congregations in this Presbyterian and Baptist region.

The ADAM GOUDELOCK HOUSE (R), 4.9 *m.*, built before 1834 by General Elijah Dawkins on the site of the home of Adam Goudelock, and soon afterward returned to the original owners, has been in the Goudelock family for five generations. The dwelling has a 'log core,' hand-carved woodwork, and other contemporary characteristics; boxwood hedges in the garden are in fine order. Tradition runs that Miss Sallie Goudelock, lively daughter of the first Adam, once rebuked a parson for preaching against worldly amusements, declaring she could pray as fervently on a dance floor as in private. 'Yes,' commented a spiteful acquaintance, 'I'll warrant Sallie Goudelock prays fervently for partners!'

At 24 *m.* on State 11 is a junction with a dirt road.

Right here 2 *m.* to GRINDAL SHOALS, once a prosperous settlement. Only the old stones of rival grist mills on opposite sides of the Pacolet River remain today. Here Morgan encamped for some time before the Battle of Cowpens; later Tarleton, chasing Morgan, set up his camp here. A noted citizen of old Grindal Shoals was Judge Abram Nott (1768–1830), member of Congress, who moved here from Connecticut and later went to Columbia. His sons were Josiah Clark Nott, M.D. (1804–73), who in 1848 suggested the 'mosquito theory' for the transmission of yellow fever; and Henry Junius Nott (1797–1837), author and a teacher at the University of South Carolina.

In the trough of the Pacolet River, just below a steel bridge, 27 *m.*, salmon once came to spawn. John H. Logan, in his *History of Upper South Carolina*, gives a vivid account of Up Country river fish.

Named for Charles Jones, its first postmaster and school teacher, JONESVILLE, 31 *m.* (1,153 pop.), is grouped around its textile mills. The JONES HOUSE, or Wayside Inn, a red brick residence with hip roof, was once the post office. A blockhouse was built here before the Revolution by John Haile, with an inner wall of brick to serve as protection against Indian attack.

At Jonesville is the junction with State 9 (*see Tour 21b*), which unites eastward with State 11 for 1 mile.

Right from Jonesville on a dirt road to another dirt road, 3.5 *m.*; R. here 2 *m.* to FAIRFOREST CEMETERY (L), which was laid out around a Presbyterian church established in 1771 by Scotch-Irish from Pennsylvania who arrived in 1751 and camped on a hill above a 'fair forest.' Buried in the wall-enclosed plot are members of the Means family, who furnished soldiers for the Revolution and the War of 1812, and a governor for the State. At the outbreak of the Revolution only 10 per cent of these Up Countrymen signed their names with a mark.

At 41.3 *m.* is a junction with US 176 (*see Tour 12a*), which unites with State 11 between this point and UNION, 42.5 *m.* (578 alt., 7,519 pop.) (*see Tour 12b*). Between Union and Columbia the route is State 215.

Along the Roadside

Photograph by Post; courtesy of Farm Security Administration

CABIN HOME, NEAR SUMMERVILLE

LOW COUNTRY TRANSPORTATION

Photograph by Carlisle Roberts

QUAIL HATCHERY, NEAR MURRELL'S INLET

Photograph by Bill King

RICE HARVESTERS, COMBAHEE RIVER PLANTATION

AN OUTDOOR BLACKSMITH

GOOSE CREEK CHURCH (1711-19), NEAR CHARLESTON

A COUNTRY ROAD, ST. HELENA ISLAND

Photograph by Walter Connolly

RUINS OF SHELDON CHURCH (1745-8), NEAR BEAUFORT

Photograph by courtesy of South Carolina State Commission of Forestry

FOREST TREE SEEDLING NURSERY, NEAR GEORGETOWN

HIGHWAY AND RAILROAD BRIDGE, INTRACOASTAL WATERWAY, NEAR MYRTLE BEACH

Photograph by Mabel Montgomery

FISH REARING POOLS, CHATTOOGA TROUT HATCHERY, SUMTER NATIONAL FOREST

PORTABLE SAWMILL

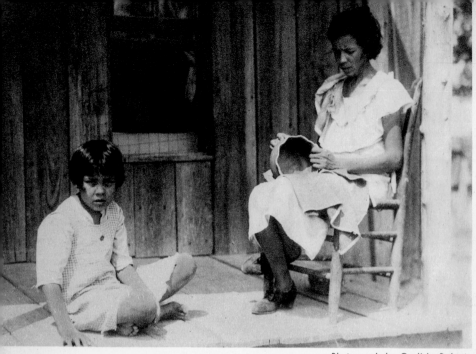

CATAWBA INDIANS MAKING POTTERY ON RESERVATION, NEAR ROCK HILL

CLASS IN OPPORTUNITY SCHOOL, CLEMSON COLLEGE

Adjacent to Union are the MONARCH and OTTARAY MILLS, surrounded by neat villages. The former, manufacturing print cloth and one of the largest textile plants in the State, has erected a $100,000 two-story brick school with a large auditorium, for which the drop curtain was painted by Norman Rockwell. The school is on the site of a tournament field, where the young gallants of ante-bellum Union dashed down the field on their thoroughbreds, while belles of the community, decked in their best, watched from their carriages, each hoping she would be crowned queen.

The character of the land gave name to SANTUCK, 51.7 *m.*, the sandy ridges formerly being called 'sand tucks,' which, according to local jokers, had its origin when a small Negro opined, 'San' tuk all dis country.' The trim little CANE CREEK PRESBYTERIAN CHURCH was built in 1884 with materials from a Quaker meetinghouse erected near by about 1784. When Quaker settlers began migrating to Ohio about 1805, their meetinghouse was bought by a group of people for several sects, but in 1850 the Presbyterians gained full control.

Among red oaks on a hilltop commanding a fine view, HILLSIDE (R), 55.6 *m.*, is a two-story white frame house built in 1832 by James Hill on the estate acquired by his father in 1791. Greek Revival in style, its superimposed slender Greek Doric columns form a portico, with second floor piazza; in the pediment is a semicircular fanlight. The hand-carved mantels have Ionic pilasters and the ceiling of one room is timbered with hand-hewn beams. At the gateway large granite posts ` coarsely chiseled in grapevine pattern by J. E. Sherman in 1861 form an unusual entrance. Except for the cypress shingles, all building materials were produced and finished on the place; even the locks were forged in the plantation blacksmith shop. Hillside slaves had their own chapel, pastor, and cemetery, and their quarters, whitewashed with clay from the gullies, were scattered to prevent epidemics and lessen the danger of insurrections.

Called Fish Dam until 1890, CARLISLE, 56.1 *m.* (382 pop.), was named for the Reverend Coleman Carlisle, a Methodist divine. It is a junction for the Seaboard Air Line and Southern Railway.

> Right from Carlisle on a dirt road 3 *m.* to TUCKERTOWN, whose name was supposedly coined by insurance salesmen for a Negro settlement around the 'big house' built in 1836 by the Reverend George Tucker. A rail fence bounds the property, the two-story frame dwelling itself enclosed by a picket fence; a wide piazza flanks three sides of the house, with hand-hewn exposed ceiling beams. Around the old well the descendants of former slaves still congregate daily. Parson Tucker did not allow his calling to prevent his amassing a small fortune from his stables and race track, of which traces are still visible.

East of Carlisle the highway dips into Broad River Valley. By Broad River Bridge, 58.8 *m.*, is (L) FISH DAM FORD, visible only at low water, a zigzag chain of rocks placed there by Indians for a crossing and a fish trap. Nets were hung below a narrow central opening, and the Cherokee would frighten the fish into them by beating the water upstream. When pursued by white men, the braves would leap nimbly from one hidden rock to another, crossing the river as if by magic. In the nineteenth century the central opening was widened to permit the passage of flatboats carrying cotton to Charleston docks, but otherwise the primitive ford is still in good condition.

On the east side of the bridge a marker designates the SITE OF THE BATTLE OF FISH DAM FORD, in which General Thomas Sumter was severely wounded while turning the tables on Major Wemyss, November 9, 1780. The latter had smugly assured Tarleton that he would return with the 'Gamecock' as his prisoner; instead, Sumter captured Wemyss. In the Britisher's pocket was a list of houses he had burned in Williamsburg County.

At the junction with State 7, 60.2 *m.*, the route turns south, running between rolling hills.

At 66.3 *m.* is the junction with a dirt road.

Right on this road 5 *m.* to PURITY CEMETERY, the wall-enclosed burying ground and former site of a Presbyterian church that began about 1770 as Bull Run, the name being changed to Purity in 1786. Services were held in the eighteenth-century edifice here until it burned in 1904.

At 66.7 *m.* on State 215 is the junction with a dirt road.

Right on this road 4 *m.* to SHELTON, a small settlement around SHIVAR SPRINGS and a bottling plant. Curative powers were claimed for this mineral water long before the present large plant was established for the manufacture of ginger ale and similar products.

Between 72.7 *m.* and Salem Crossroads, 76.4 *m.*, the highway is constructed of cotton fabric, asphalt, sand, and stone. This strip contains six tons of cotton and is one of several experiments in the use of the fiber for road building. Though plantations hereabouts are now divided into small farms, this is still a prosperous area; where the soil is not eroded, the red clay is rich and loamy.

The DAVIS HOUSE (R), 76.4 *m.*, a typical plantation dwelling with two stories and columned piazza, was the home of Dr. James Bolton Davis (1809–55), who retired from the practice of medicine to become a scientific farmer. When the sultan of Turkey requested President Polk to send a Southern planter to Turkey to demonstrate cotton planting in 1846, Davis was selected. He took with him six Negroes. On his return he brought nine Cashmere goats and one pair each of Brahmin cattle and black water buffalo, which were exhibited here and there in the United States and won several medals for Davis and the local sobriquet of 'Goat' Davis.

A preparatory academy was chartered before 1804 at MONTICELLO, 79.2 *m.* (50 pop.), and later named for the Virginia home of Thomas Jefferson, who is said to have given funds to the school. It continued until 1861; its two-story building was burned by Sherman in 1865. A pupil of the Reverend James Rogers, principal in 1804, was William Harper, first student to matriculate at the University of South Carolina in 1805 and later a senator and chancellor. A two-story house (R) was GENERAL KILPATRICK'S HEADQUARTERS after Sherman's memorable visit to Columbia.

At 82.2 *m.* is the junction with a dirt road.

Left 0.6 *m.* to a junction with a main side road; R. here 0.5 *m.* to a junction with another road and L. 0.1 *m.* to ROCK CREEK BAPTIST CHURCH (L), an immense frame structure in a large and crowded cemetery which has served since the early 1800's.

By the same road, in a shady grove on the banks of Little River is BRICK CHURCH (R), 1.2 *m.*, a severely plain edifice in a rock wall enclosed cemetery; it was erected in 1788 by an Associate Reformed Presbyterian congregation organized before the Revolution. After their crops were laid by, the men of the church molded clay for brick, which they baked in the sun. Here in 1803 the Associated Synod of South Carolina (A.R.P.) was organized. In the 1860's, Union soldiers encamped in the church, and on leaving tore up the floor and sleepers to build a bridge over the river, the escaping Confederates having burned their bridge behind them. The Unionists wrote a note on the church door apologizing for their destruction and explaining that only thus could they catch the 'Rebs.' Not until 1891 was the building repaired, the congregation revived, and services resumed. The waiter, tankard, cups, and Irish linen cloths of the communion service belong to the early years.

The CURRY HOUSE (L), 1.1 *m.*, on the main side road, is a large unpainted ante-bellum mansion, with four columns on the front piazza. Where belles and beaux in crinoline and satins rustled through stately rooms, Negroes now fill the old house, stringing their red peppers and rabbit tobacco from one paneled wall to another, and pickaninnies clad in flour sacks slide down the hand-carved banisters.

ST. BARNABAS MISSION, 1.8 *m.* on the same road, was established by the Upper Diocese of the Protestant Episcopal Church of South Carolina. The mission operates a farm and a school for Negroes.

At JENKINSVILLE, 86.7 *m.* (35 pop.), is a junction with a dirt road.

Right here to PARR SHOALS, 2.6 *m.*, the site of Broad River Power Company's 14,900 kw. capacity hydroelectric plant, where the impounded waters of Broad River form the reservoir. Employees' homes are scattered over a landscaped hillside above the lake.

State 215 crosses LITTLE RIVER, 95.5 *m.*, in a sparsely settled region to a dirt road at 97.5 *m.*

Left on this road to CEDAR CREEK METHODIST CHURCH (L), 0.8 *m.*, its congregation organized by Bishop Asbury. Some of the people hereabouts were driven from the Saxe-Gotha community on account of the Weber heresy (*see Tour 5b*).

At EAU CLAIRE, 109.8 *m.* (2,915 pop.) (*see Tour 5a*), is a junction with US 21 (*see Tour 5a*), which unites with State 215 between this point and Columbia.

In COLUMBIA, 112.8 *m.* (312 alt., 51,581 pop.) (*see Columbia*), are junctions with US 1 (*see Tour 6a*) and US 76 (*see Tour 9b*), and US 21 (*see Tour 5a*).

Tour 19

(Highlands, N. C.)—Mountain Rest—Walhalla—Clemson College—
Anderson—Abbeville—(Augusta, Ga.)—Allendale—Yemassee; State
28. North Carolina Line to Yemassee, 247.9 *m.* (includes 14 miles in
Georgia).

Roadbed asphalt-paved with short sections of concrete.
Route paralleled between Walhalla and Anderson by Blue Ridge R.R.; between
McCormick and Yemassee by Charleston and Western Carolina R.R.
Limited accommodations; hotels in Anderson.

In South Carolina's most mountainous territory, State 28 crosses the
North Carolina Line and traverses a resort area replete with Indian
legend and the traditions of pioneer days. Men came in search of precious metals and stayed to realize fortunes in fertile soils, swift rivers,
and vast timberlands. De Soto and his Spaniards explored the region,
and later comers found adventure aplenty in establishing their communities in the remote wilderness. Mountain streams foaming along
rocky beds supply addicts of the rod and reel with some of the finest
trout in America, and flow into rivers that furnish power to large textile plants. Antedating these giants of industry were old gristmills,
whose overshot and undershot waterwheels survive in places as picturesque reminders of the times when every man had to raise his own
grain if he wanted bread.

Section a. NORTH CAROLINA LINE to ANDERSON, 52.1 m.
State 28.

Curling between mountain ridges, State 28 crosses the NORTH
CAROLINA LINE, 0 *m.*, about 15 miles south of Highlands, North
Carolina. Between here and Anderson the highway traverses the west-
ern tip of South Carolina, for 8 miles running through the Mountain
Ranger District of Sumter National Forest.

MOUNTAIN REST, 6 *m.* (29 pop.), is the leading resort in the
Chattooga Ranger District. When stages were the chief means of transportation, the little hilltop town was a regular stop.

At 8 *m.* is the junction with State 107.

Left on this road to OCONEE STATE PARK (*cabins, trailer space, camping
and recreational facilities*), 2.4 *m.*, 165 acres of forest land on a high plateau
between Station Mountain and Stump House Mountain. The natural charm of
the place is enhanced by a man-made lake.
The CHATTOOGA TROUT HATCHERY (*open, picnic area and parking space*),
12.4 *m.* (2,500 alt.), is at the confluence of the Chattooga River and Indian

Camp Creek. Since Indian days fish and game have been plentiful along the creek, which still has the finest trout water in America. From the hatchery, one of the largest in the country devoted exclusively to trout, are annually distributed about 3,000,000 fish to waters of the Carolinas and Georgia.

Like giant fish bowls, 40 circular pools teem with sportive fry that anticipate the daily feeding hour and converge in reckless confusion on the pulverized bits of beef heart thrown to them. Each of the shallow pools, 25 feet across, holds 30,000 fish, whose darting movements can easily be watched through the clear water. The water is continuously circulated, being changed in each pool every 60 seconds. Year-round water temperature varies little, ranging from 48° Fahrenheit in coldest weather to 55° in hot, dry spells. The stone hatchery building contains 72 troughs, accommodating 2,000,000 eggs at a time. From these spawn are hatched three species: the brook or speckled, the rainbow, and the Loch Leven or brown.

A jointed rod, a reel, and artificial flies are helpful in catching mountain trout—but the adroitness of the fisherman is much more important. A light pole cut in the woods, a few small hooks, and a can of angle worms yield excellent results if the fisherman knows how to use them. The secret is to drop the hook in the pool without being seen by the fish. The wary fisherman will wade up stream, or steal silently along the bank, crouching among the bushes. If the trout doesn't bite at once he isn't going to bite—and the fisherman moves on. The streams of this region are constantly being restocked from Government hatcheries; and the State game laws, if enforced, give ample protection from depletion, but wardens are few and complete enforcement has proved impossible. The dynamiting and seining of fish are all too common; one man goes to the head of a trout stream and throws mud in the water, and the trout, who can live only in clear water, rush downstream. There they are dipped up, a bushel at a time, by men with a tow-sack seine. When reproached for this method of fishing, the mountaineer will reply: 'If we don't get 'em, the city fellers will—and the fish just natcherly belong to us.'

At 10.8 *m.* on State 28 is the junction with a dirt road.

Left on this road to abandoned STUMP HOUSE MOUNTAIN TUNNEL, 1.5 *m.*, partly filled with water. The gaping hole, a costly memorial to South Carolina's early progressive spirit, marks the attempt in 1853 to pierce one-and-a-half miles of mountain stone at Rabun Gap, with the purpose of linking the Blue Ridge Railroad, of Knoxville, Tennessee, with the Charleston line, and providing a shipping route from the Mississippi to the Atlantic Seaboard. The project was financed by the State at a loss of $1,000,000. When the work got under way, the now abandoned town of Tunnel Hill had a population of 1,500. For six years workmen slaved at the task of drilling, dynamiting, and boring from opposite ends. The job was about two thirds completed in 1859 when funds gave out. The War between the States, two years later, doomed the enterprise, its failure aiding New Orleans at the expense of Charleston. Two later efforts to complete the project, one in 1876, the other in 1900, were unsuccessful. The attempt was again revived in 1940.

Legend attributes the name of Stump House Mountain to the adventures of Cateechee, an Indian, and her white husband, who temporarily made their home here in a log cabin, built on stumps of the felled trees. As she fled from her angered people with her baby on her back, Cateechee was closely followed by the Indians. Rushing toward the tumbling falls of Oconee Creek, she disappeared over the brink. Believing her dead, the pursuers turned back; but mother and child were safe on a ledge. The falls were named Isaqueena, as this is said to be Cateechee's name in the Creek language. According to some writers, both names mean deer head.

Commanding a lovely vista, YELLOW BRANCH CAMPGROUND (*picnic and camping facilities*), 10.9 *m.,* is maintained by the National Forest Service.

WALHALLA, 16.2 *m.* (1,060 alt., 2,388 pop.), seat of Oconee County, was founded in 1850 by General John A. Wagener of the German Colonization Society of Charleston. The community was named by settlers who enthusiastically declared the site as beautiful as the Valhalla, garden of Norse immortals. The courthouse was transferred from Old Pickens (*see Tour* 15) in 1868, when Pickens District was divided into Oconee and Pickens Counties. That same year the *Keowee Courier*, Walhalla's present weekly newspaper, was moved here from Old Pickens, where it had been established in 1849. Popular as a summer resort, the town has two cotton mills, employing nearly 500 people.

If, as it is said, the Creek brought with them from Mexico the seed of the tomato, Oconee County is probably the first place in the United States to cultivate the plant. Such Mexican Indian names as Tomatley and Tomatola still exist in the section.

Oconee County has most of South Carolina's section of the Blue Ridge Mountains. The Cherokee called them Sahkanaga (Ind., the Great Blue Hills of God), which to the prosaic English became Blue Ridge.

In Walhalla is the junction with State 183 (*see Tour* 15a).

A reform movement was responsible for the name of WEST UNION, 18.1 *m.* (300 pop.). Colonel Joseph Greshim, a Baptist minister of Pickens District, moved here, formed a temperance union, and named it West Union, because of its geographic relation to his former home.

At 23.7 *m.* is the junction with State 13 (*see Tour* 14), which briefly unites with State 28 between this point and the eastern junction with State 13 (*see Tour* 14), 35.8 *m.*

At 36.7 *m.* is the junction with a dirt road.

Right on this road 0.7 *m.* to the OLD STONE CHURCH (R), completed in 1802 for the Hopewell Presbyterian congregation, organized about 1789, which first used a log building. The architect and contractor for the church was John Rusk, father of Thomas Jefferson Rusk (1803–57), soldier, chief justice, and senator of Texas. The field stone building is a well preserved specimen of frontier workmanship, though the interior, which contained walnut pews and pulpit, was destroyed by fire; it is gradually being restored, however. Some of the first Scotch-Irish members of the congregation followed General Pickens into the Revolutionary battles of Ninety Six, Cowpens, and Eutaw Springs. The first pastor was the Reverend Thomas Reese, first South Carolina minister to receive the degree of Doctor of Divinity. Sixty Confederate soldiers are buried in the adjoining graveyard. Other headstones in the quiet enclosure mark the graves of General Pickens and his son, Andrew, who became governor of the State (1816–18); John Miller (*see below*) and members of his family; the Reverend McElhaney, D.D., who built Calhoun's Mansion, Fort Hill; Turner Bynum, Nullificationist, who was killed in a duel by B. F. Perry, Unionist and later governor of South Carolina; Sidney Reese, son of the first pastor, who also lost his life in a duel; Andrew F. Lewis and John Maxwell, signers of the Ordinance of Secession; Colonels F. W. Kilpatrick and J. W. Livingston, and Dr. Oliver M. Doyle, brigade surgeon in the War between the States; and John Milledge Gordon, World War soldier killed in the Argonne.

At the church is the junction with a dirt road; R. on this road to another dirt road, 1 *m.*; L. on this road 0.7 *m.* to a fork.

1. Right from the fork 0.1 *m.* to HOPEWELL (L), sometimes called Cherry Place, home of General Andrew Pickens, on a bluff overlooking the Keowee

River. The house is white frame, two stories, with hip roof and slender columned portico. In 1806 the diary of Edward Hooker, a guest, recorded: 'After breakfast Mrs. Pickens entertained me with a number of turns on her pianoforte accompanied by her voice. It was a species of entertainment that I had little expected to find among the unrefined people of the upper country. Mrs. Pickens informs me there are two pianos besides her own in Pendleton.'

On the grounds of Hopewell stood an oak under which was signed the Treaty of Hopewell, negotiated in 1785 by General Pickens with several Indian tribes. By this treaty the aborigines, who had no understanding of land ownership, surrendered their rights to about one third each of Georgia and Tennessee, North Carolina west of the Blue Ridge, and to the present counties of Oconee, Anderson, Pickens, and Greenville in South Carolina. Representatives of the other areas concerned and some 1,000 Indians, including 37 chiefs, attended the council, which lasted 10 days. One provision of the treaty led to the exchange of Anna Calhoun, a relative of the statesman, who was a prisoner of the Indians. 'Treaty Oak' stood for more than 100 years after it had sheltered the council. After its decay, one sound limb was used by Mrs. Mary Cherry Doyle, owner of the place, for making gavels that were presented to various chapters of the D.A.R.

2. Left from the fork to a narrow woods road, 2 *m.;* R. on this road 0.1 *m.* to the SITE OF HOPEWELL (Keowee) PRESBYTERIAN CHURCH, whose congregation was organized in 1787.

Beyond the site is the GOVERNOR ANDREW PICKENS HOME, 0.8 *m.*, a large white frame house built around and concealing a log structure. The present house, probably erected in 1812, is believed to have been the boyhood home of Governor Francis W. Pickens.

In 1806 PENDLETON, 38.9 *m.* (850 alt., 1,035 pop.), was described as a village 'pleasantly scattered over a cluster of stony little hills.' Planned in 1790 as the seat of old Pendleton District, the town was named for Judge Henry Pendleton of Culpeper, Virginia, who organized the Culpeper Minute Men, one of the South's first Revolutionary companies.

Pendleton was the first South Carolina town settled above Camden, and for years was the center of business, culture, and government in the northwestern part of the State. Its position, at the point where the Cherokee Trading Path into the Low Country crossed the Catawba Path into Virginia, rendered it accessible to traders from both directions, and its climate attracted wealthy coastal planters. The community was noted for fine cabinet and carriage makers; many Charlestonians preferred Pendleton carriages to those made in Europe. Among the prominent craftsmen of this flourishing trade were William Henry Drayton Gaillard, W. F. Knauff, and the Sittons. Another extensive industry was ironworking. Pendleton's reputation for fine livestock dates back to its early raising of Jersey and Devon cattle, and some of the finest race horses in the country.

One of the first newspapers in upper South Carolina, established about 1807, was published here as *Miller's Weekly Messenger*, becoming *The Pendleton Messenger* in 1808. John Miller, its founder, one of the London publishers involved in the renowned *Junius Letters* episode that set the British Government on its ear, migrated to Philadelphia in 1782. Persuaded by eminent Carolina statesmen to move to Charleston, he served for a while as State printer and publisher of the *South*

Carolina Gazette and General Advertiser, came to Pendleton in 1785, and became the first clerk of court for Pendleton District. One of the first agricultural magazines in the South, *The Farmer and Planter,* was also published here.

On the town square stands the PENDLETON FARMERS' SOCIETY HALL (*open*), where this society still meets. Organized in 1815, it was the third of its kind in the United States. Construction of building, originally intended for a courthouse, was begun in 1826. When the county seat was moved from Pendleton that year, the society bought the hall and completed it within a year or two. The rectangular structure, with four-columned pedimented portico on each end, is of brick covered with white plaster, a common method of construction in the Up Country when hand-made bricks and unskilled labor produced crude walls. Windows are recessed in thick walls. The small cannon in front of the building was once the property of Hampton's Red Shirts, and in the hall above is a flag used by the same group.

ST. PAUL'S EPISCOPAL CHURCH, Queen's St., reflects the rising prosperity of the Up Country in the 1820's. The white frame building was built in 1822, with a belfry having an ogee-shaped shingle roof at the center front. A stairway in the vestibule, reached by a side entrance, leads to the slave gallery, which is still intact. Each of the transepts has a pedimented portico. Other exterior features include semicircular headed windows and a modillioned cornice. The bell tower contains an old cracked ship's bell, still used on the Sabbath.

Among those buried in the graveyard are William Henry Trescot (1822–98), historian and U. S. diplomat in China; General Barnard E. Bee (1824–61), who gave to General Jackson the soubriquet 'Stonewall' and who was killed in the Battle of Manassas; the Reverend Jasper Adams (1793–1841), first president of Hobart College, N. Y., later president of the College of Charleston; Mrs. John C. Calhoun (1792–1866) with most of her children; Thomas G. Clemson (1807–88) and his wife, Anna Maria Calhoun Clemson (1817–75) (*see Tour 14*).

Left from Pendleton on a graveled road to a dirt road, 1.7 *m.;* L. on this road 1.8 *m.* to MONT PELIER, also called the Maverick Place. Magnificently situated on a knoll about 100 yards from the road, the large frame two-story white house, built about 1850, with gable roof and the familiar pedimented portico, is typical of Up Country plantation homes. The four large square columns are of pine. An exquisite wrought-iron balcony juts in front of one of the ground-floor windows. The modillioned cornice and moldings were simplified by the relatively unskilled local craftsmen. Here lived Samuel Maverick, whose ignorance of range customs was responsible for the term 'maverick,' as applied to unbranded cattle. Maverick, who moved his law office from South Carolina to Texas, was no cattleman despite a widespread belief to that effect. He accepted 600 head of cattle as an attorney's fee, and from this number hoped to breed a much larger herd. His unbranded yearlings, however, fell into the hands of other cattlemen who promptly placed their brands upon the animals. After ten discouraging years Maverick sold his depleted stock for the amount of the original fee.

At 39.7 *m.* on State 28 is the junction with a dirt road.

Right on this road to a fork, 0.6 *m.*; R. at the fork 0.3 *m.* to WOODBURN, also called the Smythe Place, whose house was built about 1810 by Charles Cotesworth Pinckney, Jr., nephew of the Constitution Signer. The white frame house has a two-story portico with a window in its pediment. In the square columns panels replace the customary fluting. The house contained a basement dining room—an idea probably brought by Pinckney from Charleston. A brick walk under the rear porch is laid in herringbone pattern.

BOSCOBEL, 40.8 *m.*, was the home of Dr. John B. Adger of Charleston after he moved to the Up Country. The white frame house, surrounded by a thick towering grove of bamboo, has square columns in the portico, and French windows opening on the piazza. Opening from the central hall are four rooms on each floor. White fireplaces have freestanding columns. Serving in Smyrna, Dr. Adger was one of the first Presbyterian foreign missionaries; for several years he was a professor at the Columbia Theological Seminary (*see Columbia*) and Adger College, which flourished at Walhalla from 1877 to 1889, was named for him. A large swimming pool and golf course (*nominal fee*) adjoins the house.

In 1838 the Pendleton Manufacturing Company built its plant at LA FRANCE, 41.5 *m.* (1,000 pop.). Production, which still goes on, was not suspended even during the War between the States.

At 48.3 *m.* is the junction with US 178 (*see Tour 15a*) which unites briefly with State 28.

In ANDERSON, 52.1 *m.* (754 alt., 14,383 pop.) (*see Anderson*), are the junctions with US 178 (*see Tour 15a*) and US 29 (*see Tour 7b*).

Section b. ANDERSON to the GEORGIA LINE, 80.9 m. State 28.

South of ANDERSON, 0 *m.*, State 28 traverses overlapping red clay hills and passes many old farmhouses somewhat similar to those seen in Pennsylvania: two stories high, with gables and outside brick chimneys. Often dilapidated, their generous dimensions attest former opulence among Scotch-Irish settlers. More modern dwellings sit in clean, well-cultivated fields used largely for cotton growing. Negro cabins are few, and white men and women are often seen working in the fields.

At 2 *m.* is the junction with State 81 (*see Tour 19A*).

The gray two-and-a-half-story frame NORRIS HOUSE, 7.8 *m.*, surrounds an earlier log house that was built about 1813 by Colonel Robert Norris. It has a portico with square wooden columns, a simple pediment, and a cornice ornamented with large modillions. Inside, low ceiling-beams are exposed, and all timber is dove-tailed and hand hewn. Colonel Robert Norris was one of a group of citizens delegated in 1826 to select a seat for Anderson County. Tradition is that they met at a blacksmith's shop near the center of the new county and opened a keg of whisky to toast the occasion. But they toasted too many times; only Colonel Norris retained the use of his legs and he dutifully planted a flagstaff in front of the shop, declaring that there should be the site of the courthouse. With none to contest his selection, the courthouse was there erected (*see Anderson*).

ANTREVILLE, 16.9 *m.* (107 pop.), formerly Centreville, owes its later name to the handwriting of a postmaster whose 'Ce' was interpreted as 'A.'

Throughout this section the population is largely white, derived from French Huguenots, Scotch-Irish, and Germans who were granted tracts a short while before the Revolution. Refugees from religious persecution, they were ardent supporters of the theme: '. . . resistance to tyrants is obedience to God.' Though with one accord they supported the Protestant Church, many leaders in the region developed divergent opinions as to the exact definition and identity of 'tyrants,' and their political harangues sometimes ended in bloodshed. John C. Calhoun, apostle of States' rights, and James L. Petigru, Union leader of the State, were born within a few miles of each other; George McDuffie, the able 'Orator of Nullification,' within a few miles of Langdon Cheves, Unionist, who was described by Washington Irving as the first orator he had ever heard who satisfied his idea of Demosthenes. The activities of such statesmen in national politics from 1811 to 1850 prompted W. A. Schaper, Northern educator, to comment 'after 1816 South Carolina became the real political leader and example of the South.'

Perched on many small hills, ABBEVILLE, 30.6 *m.* (536 alt., 4,414 pop.), seat of Abbeville County, centers around a large square, from which streets ramble off among ante-bellum houses on wide green lawns. The slender spire of Trinity Church rises high above the business buildings. On the edge of town, particularly westward, are the sections where red roads and asphalt streets thread between small frame houses in the mill village. Named for Abbeville, France, by Huguenot settlers, the town still treasures thick-stemmed grapevines that cling to rotting trellises. They were planted by the French immigrants, who ordered expensive vines from home in the hope of establishing a winemaking industry. They had some success until a State law declared the business illegal.

Abbeville is often referred to as 'The cradle and the grave of the Confederacy,' and the claim as often disputed (*see Tour 6*). Here, it is claimed, the meeting that began the secession movement was held November 22, 1860, on what is now called Secession Hill; and the last Confederate cabinet meeting of President Jefferson Davis was held, on May 2, 1865, in the BURT MANSION. The two-story white frame structure, on the corner of Main and Greenville Sts., was built about 1850. Under the pedimented portico is a small balcony. The corners of the building are accented by pilasters, and the solid square chimneys have paneled sides. The house is almost hidden from the street by magnolias, deodars, and old shrubbery.

Escorted by a detachment of cavalry and accompanied by his wife and children, Davis was hurrying southward, hoping desperately that he would find a haven in Alabama or beyond the Mississippi where he could revive the Confederate cause. In his wake followed officers, soldiers, and Richmond employees of the fallen government, some on horseback, others on foot, stampeded to flight by Federal forces converging toward northwestern Georgia in an attempt to intercept the president. The decisions of the cabinet that late spring afternoon were that Mr. Davis should proceed immediately to Washington, Georgia, where existing conditions would dictate the further route of his retreat; that the wagon train of specie, remnant of the Confederate treasury, which had been hauled south under heavy guard, should be equally divided among officers and men, about $25 for each; and that brigade commanders should be allowed to furlough or discharge any officer or private instantly upon application. In another section of the State General Wade Hampton, taking the stand that his command was purely a State force and therefore exempt from the terms of Lee's surrender, was trying to communicate with Davis relative to offering his military support for a continued campaign from the West. He failed to reach the president, accepted his parole, and took the oath of allegiance to the United States Government. Davis left Abbeville and crossed into Georgia, but with most strategic points in that State already in the possession of the enemy, the weary leader was captured on May 10, the second anniversary of Stonewall Jackson's death, which is still observed in most Southern States as Memorial Day. He was charged with treason, spent two years in prison, and was released on bond May 14, 1867. In December of the following year, the Federal Government entered a *nolle prosequi* in the case.

TRINITY EPISCOPAL CHURCH, Church St., an adaptation in English Gothic, is of stucco-covered brick, weathered to a pinkish hue. A characteristic tall steeple, silhouetted against the sky, towers above ornamental buttresses and battlemented parapet. The deeply recessed front entrance is richly molded and niched. Paths bordered with boxwood lead beneath magnolia trees to an old cemetery in the rear.

Left from Abbeville on State 20 1.2 *m.* to UPPER LONG CANE PRESBYTERIAN CHURCH (R), a worn white frame building with long narrow windows, which in 1813 replaced a log structure built in 1784.

In LONG CANE CEMETERY (L), 1.4 *m.*, are buried veterans of eight foreign wars. One of the markers was erected by the South Carolina Medical Society to Dr. Wesley C. Norwood (1805-84) for his discovery of the sedative, *veratrum veride*. Also buried here is Lieutenant Frederick Salleck, an officer of the Palmetto Regiment, first American contingent to enter Mexico City during the Mexican War; Salleck raised the regiment's flag over the city.

At 32.6 *m.* is the junction with State 7 (*see Tour 19A*) and at 41.7 *m.* with a dirt road.

Right on the dirt road 0.9 *m.* to HOPEWELL PRESBYTERIAN CHURCH (L), whose congregation, first known as Lower Long Cane, was organized about 1760 by Covenanters under the leadership of Patrick Calhoun. The white frame structure, with no steeple, has painted window glass and a pedimented portico with square columns. To the original small church near this site worshippers rode horseback and carried muskets for protection against the Indians. The minister even preached with a gun in his hand and a powder horn suspended from his shoulder. The church lot was donated in 1788 by an Irishman, who stipulated that none of it should be used for a cemetery.

At 47.1 *m.* is the junction with State 82 (*see Tour 19A*).

At 52.4 *m.* is the junction with State 10.

Left on this road to TROY, 4.5 *m.* (219 pop.), once known as Indian Hill, and home of Patrick Noble (1787–1840), who died while serving the State as governor. A graduate of Princeton, Noble became the law partner of John C. Calhoun and was honored by important positions in the State legislature.

In the environs of Troy are many Negroes addicted to eating clay. The variety they seek as a delicacy is distinguishable by its coloring along ditch-banks, but they sometimes find it by crawling on their stomachs and sniffing the earth. The clay is considered best after a rain, when it is soft and moist. In this spongy state it is often rolled into a lump about the size of a small apple and carried to school by Negro children, who munch it as they would candy. Some of the older folk consider it a cure-all for body ailments; others declare 'it jus' na'chully good.' So fixed does the habit become that addicts who have moved to other sections have quantities of the clay shipped to them in shoe, candy, and cigar boxes. 'Dirt eaters' are found in various parts of the State, and residents can point to spots where banks and hillocks have been leveled by these odd appetites. In the lower section of the State large parts of clay chimneys are sometimes devoured. Medical men explain the habit as the result of some dietetic deficiency that the clay supplies.

1. Right from Troy on an old road (*impassable in wet weather*), once an Indian path, 2.7 *m.* to EDEN HALL (L), former home of the country physician, Dr. William Hearst, relative of publisher William Randolph Hearst. The two-story white frame structure has a gable roof and the usual portico, in this case with four square tapered columns of stuccoed brick and sheltering a small balcony supported by brackets. The pediment is decorated with a simple triangular panel.

2. Left from Troy on a dirt road to another dirt road, 0.3 *m.*, which becomes the main side road. Left on this, 0.4 *m.*, to another dirt road; R. here 3.9 *m.* to LOWER LONG CANE CHURCH, which was built by 'Seceders' from traditional Presbyterianism. The rectangular white frame structure has a pedimented portico with four modified Doric columns of red stucco over brick. Two of the four entrances lead to a slave gallery. Beneath the old oak across the road the strait-laced worshippers gathered in 1790 to form the South Carolina-Georgia Presbytery of the Associate Reformed Presbyterian Church. There they held open-air services until their church was built, a plank between this oak and another, whose stump remains a few feet away, served as a pulpit.

At 1.3 *m.* on the main side road is the junction with a red dirt road; R. on this road 1 *m.* to an unpainted frame house (L). A pasture directly behind the house is the SITE OF THE LONG CANE MASSACRE, where approximately 150 settlers, fleeing to Augusta, Georgia, were attacked by Cherokee warriors on February 1, 1760. The Calhouns and their friends, warned in advance, were trying to reach the protective stockade of Fort Moore near Augusta when the Indians struck. William Calhoun cut a horse loose from one of the wagons, helped his wife to mount, and told her to ride for the fort. Clinging low she rode through the yelling horde and escaped into the forest. During the night she stopped at a deserted cabin where her child, a boy who lived to the age of 17, was born. One of two Calhoun children captured by the Indians was never heard of again; the other was returned through treaty negotiations. This and other raids, all occurring within a few weeks, retarded further settlement of the vicinity for a number of years. A granite stone in the pasture here marks the single large grave in which 23 victims of the massacre were buried by survivors.

BRADLEY, 9.7 *m.* on State 10 (135 pop.), was named for the family of Irish Patrick Bradley, ardent supporters of the reform movement, which consolidated at Lower Long Cane Presbyterian Church (*see above*).

'Paddy,' as Bradley was called, a lovable, rakish sort of person, brought from his old home numerous legends that are recounted today by his descendants. One is an odd version of the story of the half-legendary Finn MacCumhail and his mighty opponent Cuchulinn. It relates that Finny McCoul, an Irish giant, lived in fear of another giant, Cucullin, whom he had never seen. Cucullin was so strong he once flattened a thunderbolt with a blow of his fist, and carried it around in his pocket in the shape of a pancake. Finny was working with his relatives on the Giant's Causeway to Scotland when he heard the great Cucullin was coming to challenge his strength. Hurrying home he held frantic consultation with his wife, Oonagh, who took charge of the situation, dressed him in baby clothes, and placed him in a cradle with a bottle of milk in his hands. When Cucullin arrived and asked for Finny McCoul she told him that Finny was away, but that the baby was in the cradle. Seeing a baby of such generous proportions, Cucullin concluded that he had no desire to meet Finny himself.

Right from Bradley on a dirt road to another dirt road, 2.7 *m.;* L. on this road 1.4 *m.* to a third dirt road; R. on this road 1.3 *m.* to GREEN PASTURES, a large cattle ranch, the only one in the State operated on Western principles. It was begun by a Texas ranchman, who was attracted by grazing and climate possibilities. Hereford cattle are raised for the market and are driven over the country roads to Bradley for shipment.

At VERDERY, 14.3 *m.* (150 pop.), on State 10 is the junction with a dirt road; L. on this road, 4 *m.,* to CEDAR SPRINGS COMMUNITY, a former stagecoach junction, where three old pikes came together, from Verdery, Troy, and Abbeville. Here is the weatherboarded tavern where horses were changed and meals served. Beyond a long avenue of cedars is (R) the tall PRESSLY HOUSE (*visited by permission*), built in 1852 by Captain James Frazier. The brick house, stuccoed white, is a fantastic product of the builder's caprice; four tall square columns and pilasters, with V-shaped fluting, run through the three galleries to the roof, forming a portico with piazza and two balconies. The three front rooms on each floor are octagonal and joined by a hallway that encircles the central room. Double entrances and twin stairs that meet on a small landing are other features. Behind the hall is a wing containing the present dining room and kitchen. Despite its nonconformity to tradition, the house presents an imposing façade, southern in feeling.

Left from Cedar Springs 0.2 *m.* on the Bradley Road to the red brick CEDAR SPRINGS A.R.P. CHURCH (R) of a congregation founded in 1779 by Thomas Clark, of Ireland. The rectangular building, with hip roof, stone lintels and sills, was completed in 1850. Among the old graves in the church cemetery are those of Clark, James Frazier, and members of the Hearst family.

At 17.3 *m.* on State 10 is THE PROMISED LAND, a Negro settlement covering several thousand acres. After the War between the States the area was deeded to Negroes by the Federal Government, which slapped together cabins and turned them over to freed slaves. The little frame structures were meant to be only temporary homes, but they are still used by descendants of the group for which they were built.

GREENWOOD, 23 *m.* (*see Greenwood*), is at the junctions with US 25 (*see Tour 8a*), State 7 (*see Tour 17*), and US 178 (*see Tour 15b*).

McCORMICK, 54.4 *m.* (535 alt., 1,304 pop.), seat of McCormick County, was named for Cyrus McCormick, inventor of the reaper, who gave to the town a large part of the land on which it is built.

Gold was first taken in 1852 from the now abandoned DORN'S GOLD MINE, which Dorn discovered while on a fox hunt. His hounds, digging into a burrow, unearthed the vein that in subsequent years produced large quantities of gold. The owner bought more and more slaves with his new wealth, and according to legend would exclaim, 'Here's another nigger!' every time a new blast was set off.

1. Right from McCormick on an eroded dirt road to PETIGRU, 2 *m.*, formerly a small railroad stop named for the ardent Unionist, James L. Petigru (1789–1863), who spent his childhood here. In 1861 there was a popular saying: 'Everybody in South Carolina has seceded except Petigru.' While a young man he moved to Coosawhatchie, where in 1816 he was elected solicitor and married Jane Amelia Postell. Three years later he moved to Charleston and became a law partner of James Hamilton, Jr. From 1822 to 1830 he was attorney general. As a Unionist he opposed Secession to the extent of his power. In Columbia when the first Secession Convention was being held, Petigru was asked by a friend to direct him to the Insane Asylum. He indicated the First Baptist Church, where the ordinance was being considered, and said that it might look like a church but that it was really an asylum filled with 164 maniacs. In spite of his opposition to leaders in South Carolina, he had their loyalty and veneration, and in 1859 was appointed to codify the State laws, serving in this capacity until his death four years later.

In the Petigru community, part of a two-mile avenue of white oaks leads to the SITE OF BADWELL, Petigru's boyhood home and the estate of his grandfather, Pierre Gibert. A few plants, a dilapidated fountain, and part of a sundial mark the garden. A few formerly magnificent oaks survive from the avenue Petigru planted. Each tree was named for a friend and most carefully tended during Petigru's life. The small stone structure here was the dairy house. On its lintel is the inscription, 'J. L. Petigru, 1851.' Though opposed to slavery on economic grounds, Petigru owned slaves; in the graveyard lies one of his servitors, Daddy Tom.

2. Left from McCormick on State 43 to a dirt road, 6 *m.;* R. on this road 0.7 *m.* to LIBERTY HILL, where numerous Indian artifacts have been found. Until the late 1880's there were two notable schools here, one for girls and one for boys. Among students who attended the latter and afterwards became prominent were Brigadier General M. C. Butler, later U. S. senator; Governor J. C. Sheppard; and B. R. Tillman, governor and U. S. senator. A race track, tilting tournaments, and gander pullings offered diversion from classroom work.

At 15 *m.* is the junction with US 25 (*see Tour 8b*).

At 27.3 *m.* is the junction with a dirt road; L. here 0.6 *m.* to FAITH CABIN LIBRARY. This little log cabin, the Lizzie Koon Unit, is the first of the five libraries founded for Negroes on 'faith and a dime' by Willie Lee Buffington, in gratitude to a Negro school teacher. The young white boy, who lived on a small farm in Saluda County about a mile from this place, had been encouraged by a Negro teacher, Eury Simpkins, to go to the Martha Berry School in Rome, Georgia. There he worked in the school library, with 'Uncle Eury' sending advice and money. When he went to work in a textile mill where racial prejudice probably reaches its highest peak, Buffington's gratitude toward the Negro teacher and his determination to help the race did not change. He had just a dime when the idea of establishing libraries came to him. The dime went for stamps, and Buffington wrote to people he did not know but who, he felt, would be interested in his plan. Two months later he received his first response: 1,000 books from the congregation of a Negro minister in New York City. From that beginning have grown the five libraries, at Newberry, Ridge Spring, Belton, Pendleton, and this one at Plum Branch.

At SALUDA, 32 *m.* (1,381 pop.) (*see Tour 15b*), is the junction with US 178 (*see Tour 15b*).

PARKSVILLE, 59.8 *m.* (175 pop.), was named in 1758 for Anthony Park, an Indian trader. West of here swamps afforded refuge in 1876 to criminal Ned Tennent, head of Negro militia stationed in Edgefield, when he fled from a searching party of whites. Radical Governor Chamberlain had disbanded the rifle clubs of the Democrats and armed the Negroes. Though Tennent was caught and executed, the incident precipitated a riot in which several whites were killed and six Negroes lynched.

MODOC, 68.9 *m.* (90 pop.), was named in the early 1870's when the Augusta-Knoxville railroad was laid through this territory and trouble with the Modoc Indians of Oregon occupied national attention. Local landowners were so arbitrary in granting property rights for the new line that officials of the railroad derisively applied the tribal name to their stop.

CLARK'S HILL, 73 *m.* (120 pop.), recalls pre-Revolutionary Blacksmith Clark whose forge and farm were just below the present settlement. Here lived George Tillman, the bushy-haired congressman, brother of 'Pitchfork Ben' (*see Tour 8*). He was a colorful individual and listed among the strong anti-Tillmanites, as the political adversaries of his more famous brother were called.

At the Savannah River the highway crosses the GEORGIA LINE, 80.9 *m.*, 14 miles northwest of Augusta, Georgia, returning to South Carolina at a point southeast of that city.

Section c. GEORGIA LINE to YEMASSEE, 96.9 m. State 28.

Following an old Indian path, State 28 roughly parallels the Savannah River through rich farming sections, extensive timberlands, and rosin-producing pine groves. Along the route small communities serve the surrounding truck farms and plantations. Beginning about the middle of March yellow jessamine, dogwood, wild plum, honeysuckle, and wild wisteria sparkle against cypress, pine, and oak.

At the GEORGIA LINE, 0 *m.*, 4 miles southeast of Augusta, Georgia, is (R) the SITE OF SAND BAR FERRY and two duelling grounds by the bridge. Here South Carolina and Georgia duellists outwitted their respective governments while crossing arms. On the Georgia side was a sand bar from which the ferry took its name, extending about 50 yards from the riverbank, and about 300 yards downstream. Parties from South Carolina would cross the river on the ferry, settle their differences along the bar, and immediately recross to the northern bank where authorities from Georgia had no jurisdiction. On the Carolina side, in a large level field, Georgia duellists would exchange leaden compliments and retire promptly to their own State.

At BEECH ISLAND, 8.3 *m.*, land is mostly owned by independent farmers, direct descendants of the first white settlers. Here are preserved the rural activities found in long-established communities: stag barbecue picnics, from which the womenfolk are barred, and annual May picnics, attended by entire families and ushering in the busy farming period. Beech Highland, as the section was first called, drew its name from the beech trees and the hilly terrain. 'Island' is the corruption of the early name. The Beech Island Agricultural Society, organized in 1846, still operates with great influence on crop production in the section.

Left on a dirt road to the small white BEECH ISLAND PRESBYTERIAN CHURCH, 1.8 *m.*, which antedates the War between the States and was attended by the mother of Woodrow Wilson.

REDCLIFFE, 2.6 *m.*, was built in the early 1850's by J. H. Hammond, U. S. senator (1834–6) and governor of South Carolina (1842–4). Hammond is credited with popularizing the phrase 'Cotton is king.' The house, perched on a red hill for which it was named, is approached by a quarter-mile lane of magnolias. Near the site of an earlier Hammond home, the square two-and-a-half-story structure with stuccoed basement was patterned after other houses of its day.

At 18.3 *m.* on State 28 is the junction with a dirt road.

Right on this road to SILVER BLUFF, 3.3 *m.* In 1540 De Soto and his half-famished army were received by gentle natives whose province of Cofatichiqui was reported extremely populous and fertile. The explorer was welcomed by a gracious 'princess' who presented him with a string of pearls as a token of friendship; he in turn placed upon her finger a ruby-set ring of gold. Although his tired troops begged him to remain and settle in the peaceful region, the Spanish leader was adamant, and moved westward—taking the 'princess' along as captive.

In 1735 George Galphin, a young Irishman, settled upon the site of Cofatichigui and named it Silver Bluff, from the tradition that De Soto and his troops searched there for silver, misled by the glitter of mica in the various strata of the bluff. Galphin built a trading post that became a military garrison during the Revolution. Just above Silver Bluff the Government is installing locks and improving the channel to render the Savannah River more easily navigable to Augusta, Georgia.

In the environs of ELLENTON, 29.9 *m.* (154 alt., 620 pop.), occurred a riot on May 15, 1876, that, nonpolitical in the beginning, assumed major proportions because of the race hatred engendered by the times. It resulted from an attempt to arrest two Negroes who had beaten a white woman. Armed Negroes from miles around appeared in large numbers, and whites from adjacent sections took to their guns. In two days 15 Negroes and two whites were killed before State militia restored peace.

Throughout this pine section, where the turpentine industry is an old one, the valuable sap of countless young pines is bled into small buckets attached to their trunks. Instead of operating their own stills, as in the past, landowners lease turpentine rights to large companies employing scientific methods in drawing and refining the naval stores. The distilling process involves the boiling of eight or ten barrels of gum with water in huge kettles. As the gum heats, the dross is skimmed off. When the mixture reaches the boiling point the top goes on the kettle and a high temperature is maintained. Water is added from time to time, and both water and turpentine issue from the kettle in the form of steam. This is condensed as it passes through coils of pipe immersed in cold water, and finally empties into a barrel in which the turpentine gradually rises to the top. When it hardens, the remaining rosin is not unlike jewels in color and luster—ranging from black through shades of red and yellow to a transparent clarity. Of the 13 grades of rosin the first three are named extra, water-white, and window glass. The remaining ten grades, for no good reason, run to common Christian names, five masculine and five feminine: Mary, Nancy, Kate, Isaac, Harry, George, Frank, Edward, Dolly, and Betsey. Among other things, this product is used for the manufacture of soap, paper, varnish, and linoleum. The turpentine, in addition to its medicinal value, is used in the making of paint and shoe polish. No tree under nine inches in diameter is tapped for rosin, and only one cup is hung to a tree. Once a week, usually from March through October, chipping by a sharp diagonal hack increases the flow. The gum is collected and carried to the distillery once a month.

APPLETON, 57.3 *m.* (259 alt., 167 pop.), is the home of Mrs. Dora Dee Walker, appointed in 1911 one of the first home demonstration agents in the United States, after teaching school for 30 years. Through her efforts, the first pimientos grown in this country were introduced in Barnwell County with seed imported from Spain in 1912. Affectionately known as 'Mother Walker,' she was largely responsible for the State-wide campaign to beautify private and public grounds, parks, and highways.

ALLENDALE, 61.3 *m.* (192 alt., 2,066 pop.), seat of Allendale County, is an old community whose hitching rails have not been surrendered to progress. Here the neighbor spirit is strong, and residents have a special propensity for relaxation. If farming is the bread of Allendale, fishing and hunting is its meat, for every merchant and planter is a sportsman, who takes a pride in his guns and dogs and leaves his business for frequent excursions into the surrounding forests. The section abounds in quail, turkeys, and deer, and comfortable hunting lodges are maintained by wealthy vacationists from the North.

Allendale grew from a settlement about four miles southwest of here. Pioneers of the mid-eighteenth century, pushing their way up from the coast, established large estates in the area. In 1849 the growing community acquired a postmaster, Paul H. Allen, for whom it was named. When, 23 years later, one of the early railroad companies ignored the town by running its line several miles away, enterprising residents purchased three plantations near the tracks and moved the village to them.

The devotion of a country doctor was memorialized by the people of Allendale when white and Negro citizens delayed their Sunday dinners on March 12, 1939, to attend the unveiling of a monument to Dr. F. H. Boyd, who served the town for 40 years.

The enrollment of ALLENDALE COUNTY TRAINING SCHOOL, one of the few accredited Negro schools in lower South Carolina, has increased steadily since the school was opened in 1929. Many teachers of the State attend its summer sessions.

South of Allendale the commonest houses are little cabins of rough unpainted lumber, with wooden shutters instead of glass windows. Their small rooms are overcrowded with large families, most of whose members work in the surrounding watermelon fields. Harvesting begins about the middle of June and lasts four or five weeks, at which time the highways are alive with melon carriers—wagons sturdy and decrepit, trucks large and small. Up to their knees among the vines, Negroes select the ripe melons and place them in long rows, white side up so the wagon driver can see them. Between picking and loading the workers rest and 'pleasure' themselves under shade trees at the edge of the field. Some of the largest melons are thumped to determine their ripeness, then broken against a tree or on the ground. Jubilant black faces disappear behind the jagged hunks, which are soon reduced to thin green rinds.

FAIRFAX, 67.3 *m.* (136 alt., 1,376 pop.), lies along the railroad, with brick warehouses and stores on both sides, and not a single vacant one. It is a fast-growing community, sharing in the prosperity brought by truck farms and livestock to this section, and profits also as a resort for sportsmen. Here the fire alarm is sounded every Saturday to test its efficiency.

At Fairfax is the junction with State 5 (*see Tour 5A*).

Community life at HAMPTON, 76.5 *m.* (105 alt., 811 pop.), seat of Hampton County, centers largely around the courthouse square, a big sandy lot with old oaks and a seldom-used bandstand. Across the street is the Hampton Hotel, a gaunt yellow structure whose porch during court sessions is used more by lolling farmers than by guests. But there is less talk about crops and the weather than about cases up for trial. At mealtimes young forest rangers and booted lumbermen stamp into the dining room and add their opinions to the discussion.

During the decade of Reconstruction, Beaufort, seat of the old district, was overrun with Northern soldiers, carpetbaggers, and scalawags. To escape subsequent indignities, people in the area that is now Hampton County withdrew from the old district and named the new one for General Wade Hampton, who laid the cornerstone for the new courthouse in 1878. On that memorable fall day, Hampton's Red Shirts drilled before their hero in new uniforms—red blouses stitched about the collars, cuffs, and pockets with narrow black braid, with brass buttons down the front—uniforms made especially for the occasion by mothers, wives, and sisters.

At YEMASSEE, 96.9 *m.* (12 alt., 589 pop.), are junctions with US 17 (*see Tour 1c*) and US 21 (*see Tour 5b*).

Tour 19A

Junction with State 28—Starr—Calhoun Falls—Willington—Junction with State 28; 49.8 *m.*, State 81, State 82.

Roadbed concrete- and asphalt-paved; unpaved between Willington and junction with State 28.
Charleston and Western Carolina R.R. parallels route.
No accommodations.

State 81 roughly parallels the Savannah River and leads through little towns that owe their origin to river freight, and more recent communities that sprang up after the coming of railroads. In the nineteenth century the region produced some of the South's leading citizens and saw some of the earliest experiments in education, as well as diversified farming. Indian raids were frequent and the crumbling ruins of old refuges from those attacks remain.

State 81 branches south from State 28 (*see Tour 19b*), 0 *m.*, at a point 2 miles south of Anderson (*see Anderson*).

STARR, 7.8 *m.* (361 pop.), is noted for an eating house, which has never been advertised, but draws patronage from clubs and parties in this State and Georgia. A small white frame edifice near the railroad tracks, called the 'setback house,' was built by a group of enthusiasts as a card-playing room. Between trains, the station agent locks up his office and joins in the game.

South of Starr the route follows State 82.

IVA, 13.8 *m.* (1,273 pop.), is one of many little towns named by officials for pretty girls when the railroads first came through. Established between the Savannah and Rocky Rivers about 1884, the town draws trade from rich farms around it. The chief industry here is the Jackson Mill which manufactures sheeting.

LOWNDESVILLE, 21 *m.* (210 pop.), a village with some fine old houses, was incorporated in 1839, and its growth seemed assured as a depot for shipping cotton to the coast by floating it down the river. But good roads and automobiles ruined the community's prospects. 'Lowndesville fell in the well,' says the local historian, 'and not feet foremost, either.'

CALHOUN FALLS, 31.8 *m.* (1,759 pop.), is named for the Calhoun family whose property holdings extended for many miles along the Savannah River.

Left from Calhoun Falls on State 7, 1.9 *m.*, to a dirt road and L. here 5.4 *m.* to a field (R). Beyond the field, on a small hill, is a low embankment of rocks and vine-grown timber, believed to be the RUINS OF BULL TOWN FORT, birthplace of Langdon Cheves.

Langdon Cheves's father, known as 'Honest Sandy Chivas,' was a cattleman in this section, which is still known as Bull Town. Langdon was born within the little stockade September 17, 1776, during an Indian raid, when the whites were crowded here for protection. In a similar raid three years later, his mother died at the age of 29. Young Cheves came of a family divided in political opinion. His father served as a Tory captain; his Uncle Thomas held the same rank with the Whigs. Taken to Charleston for schooling at an early age, Langdon was tutored by an old Scot, who flogged him for his Up Country twang and tried to supplant it with the broad Scottish pronunciation. He had little other education, but earned an early reputation for brilliance and was admitted to the bar in 1797. After holding many public offices in the city and State, Cheves became an outstanding figure in Washington, where he served as chairman of the Naval Committee, and Speaker of the House. Later he declined an appointment to the Supreme Court to become president of the Bank of the United States. In 1829 he returned to South Carolina, where his favorite pastime was building houses, of which he had six. He died in Columbia June 26, 1857, and was buried in Charleston's Magnolia Cemetery. Opposing Nullification, Cheves devoted his oratorical talents to its defeat.

At 11.5 *m.* is the junction with State 28 (*see Tour* 19*b*), 2 miles south of Abbeville.

In the small village of MT. CARMEL, 40.7 *m.* on State 82, is the junction with a dirt road.

1. Right here 3 *m.* to the SITE OF CHERRY HILL, between Little River and the Savannah River, the former home of George McDuffie (1790–1851). Lawyer, planter, governor, soldier, and senator, McDuffie was called the Orator of Nullification. Born in Georgia, he became a protégé of the Calhouns when he arrived in their Long Cane section with all his possessions tied in a small box. His early friendliness changed to a forbidding bitterness after he had received serious wounds in two duels with Colonel William Cumming. McDuffie had numerous friends, however, and inviting one of them to visit him at Cherry Hill, he wrote, 'I can give you a hearty welcome, cool healthy air, old wine, fresh butter, fat beef and mutton, and have bread made of home-made flour equal to the Richmond family flour.'

2. Left here to the CALHOUN BURIAL GROUND, 5.8 *m.*, on the McGaw place (R), owned by a descendant of the family. The cemetery's tallest monument was erected by John C. Calhoun to his Irish father, his Virginia-born mother, and his sister, Catherine, the first wife of Dr. Waddel (*see below*).

At WILLINGTON, 44.2 *m.* (425 pop.) on State 82, is the junction with a dirt road.

Right here 6 *m.* to the SITE OF VIENNA, one of four little towns on the Savannah River built to encourage shipping to the coast. Petersburg, Southampton, and Lisbon, the latter still a dot on the Georgia map, were the other ambitious but fleeting settlements at the confluence of the Broad River in Georgia, the Savannah, and a South Carolina wagon trail. Here in 1801 Dr. Moses Waddel (1770–1840), later president of the University of Georgia, established his school, a village of little cabins, built by the students themselves of logs from the neighboring woods and chinked with moss or clay that in summer was removed for ventilation. The academy differed from the student cabins only in size, but these rude buildings, during the 15 years of Dr. Waddel's supervision, housed boys who were later to become distinguished leaders of the South: Calhoun, McDuffie, Legare, Petigru, Crawford, Gilmer—governors of South Carolina and Georgia, statesmen, ministers, and lawyers. Dr. Waddel, 'The Carolina Dr. Arnold,' a bushy-browed disciplinarian nearly six feet tall, insisted on thoroughness of study and simplicity of habits. His teaching of the classics was the keystone of the academy and attracted the attention of educators throughout the Nation. Among other unusual methods was his practice of sending the students into the forests for study periods. There the wild woods of the Savannah resounded with echoes of Homer and Virgil, Cicero and Horace. Misdemeanors were not infrequent, and youthful pranksters were arraigned before Monday morning courts where the schoolmaster served as judge, and five members of the student body as jurors. Waddel was a firm believer in the rod, but this form of punishment was less bitter to his charges than the tongue lashings he sometimes administered. Though the school bell had a lusty tone, it was rung only for effect: Dr. Waddel would run out into the academy 'street' and whoop 'Books, books, young men!' and they all would come flocking. The bell and a large slate blackboard, both imported by Waddel from Italy, are preserved in the Willington schoolhouse.

On the riverbank, immediately southeast of the site of Vienna, are the RUINS OF FORT CHARLOTTE, erected by the crown in 1765 at the boundary between the English province and the land of the Cherokee. Before construction began a stockade was built near by and manned with soldiers for the protection of laborers. The frontier fort was among the first seized by American troops at the beginning of the Revolution, a Captain Kirkland taking possession on July 16, 1775.

At 46.9 *m.* on State 82 is the junction with State 821, unpaved.

Right here 1.9 *m.* to BORDEAUX, formerly New Bordeaux, settled in 1764 by 212 Huguenot émigrés who purchased about 30,000 acres in the section, expecting to produce wine and silk. Pierre Gibert and Elias Boutiton, leaders of the group, had suffered severely in France and had been forced to flee to England for safety. Mrs. Gibert remained in France and only by a ruse escaped across the English Channel. Secretly nailed in a hogshead, part of an outgoing cargo, she was saved from death by a stevedore who induced his weary companions not to throw their last heavy barrel into the sea. Gibert, meeting the shipment in England, had a hard time persuading the importers that his wife was concealed in one of their barrels.

In allotting this section to the Huguenots the Royal Government was interested not only in providing for worthy colonists but in establishing a buffer settlement between the warring Cherokee and the Low Country. For a time the Huguenots raised their precious silk and wine, but the two industries were doomed to failure. The Indian and Revolutionary Wars and the introduction of cotton retarded development, and jealous French vintners saw to it that the orders of their American competitors were filled with grapevine shoots of an inferior quality.

At 3.9 *m.,* in the middle of a large field, is a huge granite cross where stood the house of worship for the French Protestant congregation of New Bordeaux, organized in 1764.

At 48.5 *m.* on State 82 is the junction with a dirt road.

Right here 0.1 *m.* to the DE LA HOWE STATE SCHOOL, founded in 1797, a pioneer agricultural school. A series of frame cottage dormitories and brick administrative buildings accommodate 200 indigent South Carolina children and the school staff. Left of the landscaped campus are numerous farm outhouses. The institution was taken over by the State in 1918. Dr. John de la Howe, the founder, a practical, serious, hardworking physician, approved the rugged country life. He provided in his will that the children's beds have mattresses stuffed with beech leaves 'gathered before frost and dried in the shade,' which he declared would make 'as comfortable and far more healthy bedding than feathers, as they will remain good for four or five years and may be easily renewed.' The founder's will makes no mention of his wife, a Charleston woman with whom he had not lived for many years; instead it ordered that his remains be placed 'as near as it can be to the spot where those of the late Miss Rebecca Woodin (De la Howe's housekeeper) are deposited . . . as the last mark and testimony of my friendship and sense which I ever have retained of her merit.'

He further willed that their unmarked graves be surrounded by a brick wall 8 feet high and 8 feet square with a wrought-iron door containing their names and death dates. The door was to be locked and the key thrown into the river near by—all of which was done when the physician died in 1797. The two graves, set deep in the virgin forest of De la Howe's former estate, are reached by a devious dirt road leading from the school (*student guides available*).

At 49.8 *m.* is the junction with State 28 (*see Tour 19b*), 7 miles northwest of McCormick.

✱✱

Tour 20

(Elizabethtown, N. C.)—Green Sea—Conway—Georgetown; US 701. North Carolina Line to Georgetown, 64.5 *m.*

Atlantic Coast Line R.R. roughly parallels route.
Roadbed paved with asphalt between North Carolina Line and Conway; between Conway and Georgetown with concrete.
Tourist accommodations available at short intervals; hotels chiefly in towns.

The upper section along US 701 was for years almost counted out of South Carolina's economic and social reckoning, and rose to importance only when modern roads cut through the swamps to connect farms with established communities. Beyond the Waccamaw and Pee Dee marshlands the road passes ghost towns of the early lumbering era, when South Carolina built ships for national trade, and winds through plantation seats of the rice-made aristocracy.

US 701 crosses the NORTH CAROLINA LINE, 0 *m.*, about 41 miles southwest of Elizabethtown, North Carolina.

GREEN SEA, 6 *m.* (190 pop.), took its name from Green Sea Bay, an impenetrable marshy area near by. In Green Sea is the junction with State 9 (*see Tour 21a*), which unites with US 701 to a point at 8 *m.*

At 24 *m.* is the junction with US 501 (*see Tour 13*), which unites with US 701 between this point and CONWAY, 28 *m.* (25 alt., 3,011 pop.), seat of Horry (O-ree) County, still sometimes called the Independent Republic of Horry. Always with a preponderantly white population, the county is an anomaly in Low Country development. Early settlers came from North Carolina to work in lumbering operations and the naval stores industry. Hemmed in by swamplands, the inhabitants were connected with the outside world only by the rivers down which they shipped their logs and turpentine to the coast. In their remoteness they were forced to subsistence farming, and developed a spirit of independence that is today a powerful factor in their success with new crops. Horry-ites are among the rare folk who deliberately live within their means. A house may be built one room at a time, but the owner-occupants are happily secure because that one room is paid for. Few farms are operated by tenants.

Nowadays Horry is among the most progressive counties in the State, with its fertile fields of tobacco, truck crops, melons, and strawberries. Where oxcarts used to labor through sandbeds and swamplands, trucks and trailers speed over paved roads with produce for eastern markets. Between 1910 and 1930, illiteracy here decreased from 24 to 12 per cent. Eagerness of the citizens to advance is only equaled by determination to pay as they go. With neither a tradition of 'culture' nor a burden of debt, they are able to start square and progress.

Conway is the principal port for Waccamaw traffic, in which lumber still dominates. Between Waccamaw River and Kingston Lake, the little town rises around the city hall. The one- or two-story commercial buildings are similar to those in other small Southern towns except in their display of fishing tackle, hunters' outfits, and beach costumes. Old time fishermen and their bateaux may be hired by visitors, but many are the secret jibes cast at the catalog fisherman who comes from the city with newfangled gadgets to which the Waccamaw fish are not accustomed. Wise-eyed oldsters act as guides to hunters; quail, doves, turkeys, duck, and deer find it hard to escape the folk who know their habits and feeding grounds. With kerosene lamps and boxes of snuff are sold bathing suits of latest style—an innovation inspired by Myrtle Beach and other neighboring resorts.

Though Conway (as Kingston) was established on land granted by George II of England, it was for decades hardly more than a river wharf. In 1801 it became Conwayborough, honoring General Robert Conway to whom the State made a grant overlapping the town site. The suffix was dropped about 1881. The greatest spurt of growth occurred in 1854 when Burroughs and Collins, with headquarters on the river, bought extensive timberlands, built lumber plants, organized a bank, established boat service to Charleston, and built a railroad.

Already the old courthouse, now CONWAY CITY HALL, Main St., had been erected by Russell Warner after designs by Robert Mills. Above a high basement is a simplified Greek Doric portico flanked by twin stairs. The much larger brick courthouse built years later is on the edge of town. By 1858 the KINGSTON PRESBYTERIAN CHURCH had been erected on the banks of Kingston Lake to take the place of a little edifice abandoned in 1795. This second structure, frame with a shingled steeple rising above a portico with four small columns, is still in use. The lake, down a slight incline north of the business section, is Conway's beauty spot, its clear tea-colored waters surrounded by live oaks, hoary with moss; a driveway around its shore is bordered with shrubs, azaleas, and other bright flowering plants.

There are few old mansions here, because development did not begin in earnest until after the plantation era. Some substantial houses with gables, towers, and bay windows hark back to the prosperous nineties, but later residences are of restrained design. Many pieces of excellent furniture adorn these homes, a number having come from a local establishment that makes good reproductions of early pieces. The cabinetmaker who operates the business has a love of his work that turns manual labor into an art.

In Conway is the junction with US 501 (*see Tour* 13).

TODDVILLE, 32.8 *m.* (25 pop.), small country village formerly on the Waccamaw River, was once a busy port for river traffic.

At 33.7 *m.* is the junction with a dirt road.

> Left on this road 2.3 *m.* to the old Conway-Georgetown road; L. here 0.5 *m.* to UPPER MILL, scene of the first Buck lumber camp. In 1830, Henry Buck, for whose shipbuilding family Bucksport, Maine, was named, came here to exploit the extensive forests of yellow pine along the Waccamaw. He built several sailing ships, carried on trade with his New England home, was a slave owner, and successively established three lumber camps on the west bank of the Waccamaw. The unpainted three-story frame BUCK HOUSE has a gable roof and large chimneys at each end. The old outhouses (L) remain and from a clump of trees near by rises the round 40-foot smokestack of the old lumber mill, topped with a fish for a weather vane. Smooth 'Belgian blocks' reinforcing the riverbank in front of the house are believed to have been ballast, unloaded from trade ships when lumber was taken aboard as cargo. About 150 yards west is the slave burial ground, still in use. Several graves are marked by wooden headpieces with slate inserts, inscribed in Spencerian script by a former mistress.
>
> At 3.1 *m.* on the Conway-Georgetown Road is the junction with a dirt road; L. here 0.6 *m.* to BUCKSVILLE, whose chief landmark is the red brick smokestack high above the trees. As late as 1892 there was a thriving settlement here. Soon afterward, with the timber gone, the people moved away. Acquisitive visitors carried off the lumber and bricks of which houses and stores were built. Now there is not even the outline of a street in the groves.
>
> Here the Intracoastal Waterway (*see Tour* 11a) comes in from the east to follow the Waccamaw.

The YAUHANNAH CAUSEWAY AND BRIDGE, 39.5 *m.*, about two miles long, spans the Pee Dee River. A fort and trading post, Euhanie, was established on the riverbanks by pre-Revolutionary traders.

PLANTERSVILLE, 49.4 *m.* (80 pop.), is one of the old summer villages of the pinelands. Slaves built the log houses and after dark it was their duty to light tall bonfires of pine kindling to keep off dampness from the swamps.

> Left from Plantersville 100 yards on a dirt road to PRINCE FREDERICK CHAPEL OF EASE (R), which was a summer seat of worship for rice planters. Of white frame with gable transepts and a small four-columned portico, it became the mother church of this parish. Later Gunn Church (*see below*) was built.
>
> At 1.8 *m.* is the junction with a narrow sandy road; R. here between plantation fences. Gates open into oak-lined avenues that lead to old houses, and to a few more recently built. Most of these are owned by out-of-State sportsmen, who come to South Carolina during the hunting season. Estates face the Pee Dee River, which threads far away (L) among the marshes.
>
> HASTY POINT, 2.1 *m.*, is an old estate, whose name refers to a hurried escape of General Francis Marion from Britishers.
>
> CHICORA WOOD, 3.7 *m.*, is the former home of Robert Francis Withers Allston (1801–64), South Carolina governor, 1856–8. Far back in the oak grove, surrounded by wide lawns close cropped by placid sheep, rises the two-and-a-half-story frame house, glistening white, above its high brick basement. A broad piazza extends around three sides. Chicora reigns peacefully above the red-

flowing Pee Dee. Allston, who died before his house was raided by Union soldiers, was a member of a distinguished family of planters and statesmen. He graduated from West Point in 1817, and returned to assist his widowed mother in managing her properties, becoming an authority on rice culture. Chicora was one of many plantations under his supervision. Before he became governor he had served more than 30 years in the State legislature. His wife was Adele, sister of James L. Petigru (*see Tour 19b*), an ardent but respected Unionist. His daughter, Elizabeth Allston Pringle, described home life here in her *Chronicles of Chicora Wood,* and under the *nom de plume* 'Patience Pennington' recorded in *A Woman Rice Planter* the effort to continue rice planting at Casa Blanca (*see below*) after the War between the States.

Faded pink GUNN CHURCH, 4.6 *m.,* named for its contractor, is of stuccoed brick. Refinement in the rather heavy design was achieved by the use of a fan-lighted entrance, wheel window, and pinnacled belfry in the front tower. It was built in 1859–60 as Prince Frederick Parish Church, to take the place of a structure that was later moved to Plantersville. Records of the parish date back to 1713, before it was separated from Prince George Winyah Parish.

ARUNDEL, 5.2 *m.,* owned by the La Bruce family, is one of the few plantations still owned by the family to whom it was granted. The white frame house has a gable roof and a broad one-story piazza across the front, facing the Pee Dee River. It was built about 1850 on the site of a structure destroyed by fire. Present owners cater to tourists, and the old slave overseer's house, with remodeled interior, is now a guest cabin. The Gothic windows of this and the slave quarters are bordered with hand-carving, and the entrance gate to the plantation was carved with acorns.

The SITE OF WHITE HOUSE or Casa Blanca is at 11.1 *m.* This former home of Joel Robert Poinsett (1779–1851) is now part of a private hunting preserve. A scientist and statesman, Poinsett is recalled by the scarlet poinsettia, which he introduced from Mexico. Many and varied were the plants he brought from his extensive travels, but only a few now remain in the old garden. Of Huguenot forebears who made fortunes in South Carolina, Poinsett at the age of 24 was left fatherless but wealthy. His early military interests, thwarted by his father; his medical training, cut short by tuberculosis; and his cultural aspirations, limited in South Carolina—all had outlet as he visited Europe, Mexico, and South America. Though he was financially independent, he never forgot that his grandfather Pierre had been a silversmith, and throughout his long and varied career he was described as a 'flaming evangel of democracy.' He became the first accredited agent of a foreign government in Chile (1812); a State representative (1816); chairman of the first South Carolina board of public works (1817); United States congressman (1820); minister to Mexico (1825–9); and Secretary of War (1835). He was an intellectual leader in Washington, serving (1841–5) as first president of the National Institute for the Promotion of Science, the forerunner of the Smithsonian Institution. He was consulted by A. J. Downing, pioneer landscape gardener, when the latter was engaged to lay out the grounds of the White House. Among his protégés were Robert Mills, whom President Jackson appointed first Federal architect at Poinsett's suggestion, and John Charles Frémont, for whom he obtained the appointment in Washington that eventually led to his Western career. In Charleston, soon after 1820, Poinsett aided in founding the Academy of Fine Arts, which existed a few years and which later resulted in the establishment of the Gibbes Memorial Art Gallery there. Many roads and bridges in South Carolina were built through Poinsett's efforts, and in his desire to promote his State's welfare, he urged diversification of crops and the raising of cattle and sheep. When fellow statesmen were decrying protective tariffs and promoting the slave trade, he supported manufacturing and deplored slave labor.

On KEITHFIELD PLANTATION, 11.3 *m.,* the story-and-a-half frame house has been renovated with timber from old buildings on the place. The interior walls of the first floor are paneled with polished wood of mellow tones. The old stable and carriage house have been converted into servants' quarters. The naturally beautiful setting of the house, with its grove of live oaks, has been enhanced by formal landscaping. During the azalea season a vista of the brilliantly colored flowers and the smooth lawn sloping down under trees to the clear waters of Black River is seen through the opened gate.

At 56.4 *m.* on US 701 is the junction with State 51, paved.

Right here through an area settled under the leadership of the Reverend William Screven, militant Anti-pedobaptist minister. Dissenters, some of them Scotch-Irish Presbyterians, made their homes here as early as 1710. Their settlement, extending from the Black to the Pee Dee River, was called Winyah. Though still sparsely populated and with few large or interesting houses along the way, it is a rich farming area.

Black Mingo Creek, the Black, Lynches, and Little Pee Dee Rivers, besides numerous lakes, make this region a delight to the fisherman. The waters abound in warmouth, catfish, mollies, and red-breasted bream, and shad come miles up Black River to spawn in early spring. Along the streams are sites long known as seine yards, where shad are hauled in, to bring perhaps $1 for the buck and $1.50 for the roe shad. For the river fish, seining is forbidden. All that is needed is an old-fashioned cane pole, a fish-hook and line, a can of worms, and a shady spot on the bank of the stream or lagoon. In this state of well-being, Izaak Walton's devotees may think the fish only a minor consideration, but when a nibble comes on the line, even the most phlegmatic angler feels a tremor of excitement. If he is wise, he waits till the fish has firmly hooked himself before pulling in his catch. Because it is impossible for the game warden to find all the secluded pools, a primitive and illegal form of making a large haul is sometimes practiced. A bottle filled with lye, its cork slit to allow the seepage of water, causes a scarcely audible explosion, but kills the fish—and also any stock that may subsequently drink the water. Tickling and pegging fish are not only illegal, but unsportsmanlike: tickling consists of hemming game fish into a hole where, escape impossible, they may be pegged with a sharp stick, or taken from the water with the hands.

This area is prized by Northern sportsmen for both its fishing and quail hunting. As many who lease hunting rights do not build lodges, most farmhouses have their quota of hunting-season visitors. Farm incomes are substantially boosted by these paying guests and by the lease of hunting rights, which do not preclude the owner's planting his accustomed crops.

At 21 *m.* is the junction with State 512; L. here 6.3 *m.* to white frame BELIN'S BAPTIST CHURCH (R), built about 1843 by a Huguenot, Clelin Belin (pronounced Blain), as a Presbyterian church. It has a double roof put together with handmade pegs, and carved inscriptions on the cornices. Titles to the property are said to be sealed in the wall behind the columns right of the pulpit.

The SITE OF WILLTOWN is at 7 *m.* on State 512; it was settled in 1750, and by 1800 was the largest town in this section of the State, and the trading post for English boats from Georgetown. At the tavern Aaron Burr sometimes spent the night as he journeyed to the home of his daughter, Theodosia Burr Alston, near Georgetown. Over Black Mingo bridge at Willtown, General Francis Marion threw blankets to silence the hoof-beats of his horses before the advancing enemy. September 19–21, 1780, Marion met and defeated Major Wemyss near here in the Battle of Black Mingo, with fearful cost to both sides. Not far away the Swamp Fox often rested his men between maneuvers at Snow's Island, a spot inaccessible except by boat and never discovered by the British.

Incorporated in 1913 and named for a leading citizen, HEMINGWAY, 26 *m.* on State 51 (351 pop.), was formerly called Lambert. It is the trading center of a fertile area where tobacco is the leading crop, but where as many as 16 vegetables are grown even in the coldest months, and shipped to various points. Illustrative of how well a thrifty man can live on this soil is the record of what a Hemingway attorney has accomplished on the one-acre lot around his home. Besides 180 dahlias, 2,500 gladioli, and specimens of every shrub and flower known to the owner's family, there are 12 grapevines, 6 pecan trees, 4 apple trees and several peach and pear trees. In addition about 300 chicks are annually raised for broilers and the family has all the eggs needed; a cow supplies the home and neighbors with milk, butter, and buttermilk (for family and chicks); in the garden many vegetables are raised and canned; the hog pen has supplied the family's meat for 15 years. The owner has built a scientifically planned house, in which the year-round temperature varies little, for storing meats, potatoes, and canned articles. Behind it is a curing house, where fresh pork is converted into hams, shoulders, and bacon to be hung in the brick house, with about 200 quarts of sausage canned each season, besides that eaten fresh. The family buys few groceries, and could live, if necessary, on what they have grown and stored at home. So well known is this model acre that during the depression, 'do-less' farmers have come here to ask for a 'mess' of the vegetables they had failed to plant.

Though an old established crossroads settlement, JOHNSONVILLE, 31 *m.* (325 pop.), was laid out and sold in town lots not long before the World War. Its nickname is 'Ashboro,' because everything in town except the artesian well is said to have burned at one time or another.

Boasting three tobacco warehouses, PAMLICO, 48 *m.* (467 pop.), a young town, comes to life when the season opens in late summer, and the population is swelled with the influx of tobacco warehousemen, buyers, auctioneers, and their families.

At 66 *m.* is the junction with US 52 (*see Tour 2a*), about 2 miles south of Florence.

From the FOREST TREE SEEDLING NURSERY (R), 58.3 *m.* on US 701, largest under the State Forestry Commission, millions of young trees are annually shipped to organizations and private individuals for reforestation.

In GEORGETOWN, 64.5 *m.* (14 alt., 5,082 pop.) (*see Tour 1a*), are the junctions with US 17 (*see Tour 1a*) and US 521 (*see Tour 4*).

Tour 21

Junction with US 17—Green Sea—Nichols—Dillon—Bennettsville—Chesterfield—Lancaster—Chester—Spartanburg—(Asheville, N. C.); State 9. Junction with US 17 to North Carolina Line, 247.4 *m.*

Roadbed partly concrete-paved; partly asphalt-paved.
Seaboard Air Line Ry. parallels route between Dillon and Clio; Chesterfield and Lancaster R.R. between Kollock and Pageland; Lancaster and Chester R.R. between Lancaster and Chester; Southern Ry. between Lockhart and Spartanburg.
Limited accommodations; hotels in cities.

From tidewater South Carolina, State 9 weaves northwestward through swamplands and arable acres of tobacco, grain, cotton, and vegetables, skirting the North Carolina boundary for most of its course. Farther, it rises and falls like a scenic railway among red Up Country hills, finally to climb the mountains into North Carolina. Variety of life and livelihood marks the long route, crisscrossed by many other highways on which cars and trucks speed north and south.

Section a.   JUNCTION WITH US 17 to LANCASTER, 167.5 m.
State 9.

Through swamps and fertile sedimentary soils the route passes few large towns and no cities in this section. Grinding sounds of sawmills, the odor of rosin, and black clouds from metal smokestacks testify to a vigorous lumber industry.

State 9 branches northwest from US 17 (*see Tour 1a*) at NIXON'S CROSSROADS, 0 *m.*, 18 miles northwest of Myrtle Beach (*see Tour 1a*).

Nixon's Crossroads is a meeting place for farmers and summer visitors as well as tourists who find articles of all sorts for sale, from fresh fish to metropolitan newspapers.

LORIS, 22 *m.* (900 pop.), has of late years emerged as the biggest strawberry market in the State and one of the principal tobacco markets. The berry crop in the spring and the 'weed' in the fall promote year-round activity on the farms, which, with rare exceptions, have no tenantry.

At 27 *m.* is a junction with US 701 (*see Tour 20*), which unites with State 9 between this point and Green Sea, 29 *m.*

At 40 *m.* is a junction with US 76 (*see Tour 9a*), which unites with State 9 between this point and NICHOLS, 42 *m.* (61 alt., 239 pop.). The Nichols community depends on tobacco culture and sells its crop at Mullins (*see Tour 9a*) when warehouses open and buyers come to town.

DILLON, 63 *m.* (119 alt., 2,731 pop.), seat of Dillon County, built up about 1887 when the Atlantic Coast Line Railroad came through, is named for J. W. Dillon, a progressive leader and head of the local railroad movement. Dillon, of an Irish shipping family, selected this section for his home after several voyages to America, and from meager beginning built his fortune and fame, much like an Alger boy. His municipal namesake is a town of wide streets that begin in fields of tobacco, cotton, and wheat, and end at the courthouse, which covers the site of Revolutionary skirmishes. Produce flows in to be shipped to Eastern and Northern markets by rail or truck. A textile mill and other factories have brought industrial interests into this farming area. Older residents remember when the business section was a pond where they caught trout, redbreast, and bream.

In Dillon County live a number of Croatans, a peculiar and primitive people, the majority of whom are found in North Carolina. Their claim of descent from the Lost Colony of Roanoke is generally questioned. Ethnologists assert they are racially a mixture of Indian, pioneer white, and Negro, with possibly a Latin strain from seamen who came in trading vessels. The Croatans vary in color from light blond to dark brown; but Indian features and straight hair predominate, along with traits and customs reputedly Indian, such as walking in single file and maintaining a stolid inarticulateness. Only in recent years have the Croatans been benefited by schools and social agencies which have taken cognizance of their isolation and penetrated their ancient resentment.

At Dillon is the junction with US 501 (*see Tour 13*).

In the rich alluvial lands, stones are such a rarity that the presence of one at LITTLE ROCK, 67.1 *m.* (274 pop.), gave the village its name. A cannon once stood near the rock in the center of town to herald marriages, births, funerals, and holidays, but it was stolen before the War between the States.

At BENNETTSVILLE, 87 *m.* (151 alt., 1,657 pop.) (*see Tour 3a*), is the junction with US 15 (*see Tour 3a*).

At 100.5 *m.* is the junction with US 1 (*see Tour 6a*), which unites with State 9 between this point and CHERAW, 103.4 *m.* (145 alt., 3,575 pop.) (*see Tour 6a*). Here is the junction with US 52 (*see Tour 2a*).

Chesterfield County, of which CHESTERFIELD, 116.4 *m.* (1,030 pop.), is the seat, lies almost entirely in the Sand Hill regions (*see Tour 6a*). It was organized in 1798 and named for Lord Chesterfield. Most of its citizens were Welsh Baptists (*see Tour 3a*) from Delaware, or Scotch-Irish and English from other States. The town was an early center of local government, surrounded by a farm community. From the more fertile lands in the northwest part of the county, bumper cotton crops have continued to modern times. Not even the boll weevil was appreciably able to invade this section, where the crop matures too late for the borer's attack. Most of the southern part of the county is under Federal management. The Sand Hills Development Project in 1935 laid out a program to reforest and reclaim 91,105 acres. This is the largest of three projects in the State developed with the aim of finding out the best uses of the land and applying such discovery.

In one of General Sherman's last raids the courthouse and public buildings were razed. On the grounds of the modern courthouse where Main Street crosses the route a granite marker asserts that the first meeting favoring secession was held here. Abbeville disputes this claim (*see Tour 19b*). Opposite the courthouse is the CRAIG HOUSE, built in 1798 by John Craig, one of the founders of the town. Gray with antiquity, untenanted and unpainted, the house is roofed with the original cypress shingles, which are still held fast by wooden pegs. In olden days this house was famous for hospitality, especially when notables came to town on court days to attend the 'Governor's Review,' and the State executive inspected the militia companies in parade.

CRAIG PARK (R), 116.2 *m.*, is a municipal playground for old and young. An outdoor theater, barbecue hut, community house, and free swimming pool are provided.

Westward the road rises along the upper ridges of the sand hills. Sunburned fields stretch far and wide; north is a fringe of woodland.

Narrow streams slide under the culverts as the road dips and then gradually rises into the Piedmont section.

PAGELAND, 135.9 *m.* (707 pop.), borders the highway, and concerns itself chiefly with textile interests, a lumber mill, and cotton. It was called 'Old Store' until the Cheraw and Lancaster Railroad placed a depot here in 1904 and named the stop for its president, S. H. Page. Today the village is chiefly remembered for the huge country dinners served at one of the hotels. Several kinds of meat, numerous vegetables, three to five drinks, with pie, cake, and other desserts, are laid out on a long table. Salesmen, highway engineers, and many others make it convenient to be near when the big brass bell announces the meal.

At Pageland is the junction with State 151 (*see Tour 3a*).

In the hills of the area are several granite quarries, furnishing building stone or crushed rock for roadbeds, and a few gold mines which are worked spasmodically.

In FIVE FORKS CEMETERY, 139.9 *m.*, lies James H. Miller under a stone engraved, 'Murdered in Retaliation.' Miller, a cavalryman under General Wade Hampton, was executed by a firing squad at the order of General Sherman in 1865. Leaving South Carolina after the burning of Columbia, the Federals swarmed the countryside, foraging for supplies. Hampton's men, too few in number to stage a battle, took pot shots at the Yankees, sometimes with fatal results. Sherman warned the Southern general, according to Congressional war records, that the next raider killed would mean a Confederate prisoner's death. Hampton replied that such an act would be murder. A few days afterwards, Northern raiders under Sergeant Woodford, 46th Ohio Regiment, visited a farm near by, drove off the livestock and kidnapped Dick Sowell, a slave. When they stopped for dinner and Woodford fell asleep, Sowell crushed the sergeant's head with a lightwood knot, rounded up the animals, and returned home. Sherman learned of the occurrence and ordered Confederate prisoners to cast lots for the one to be shot in accordance with his threat. James H. Miller was the victim and fell before the Union firing squad. Sergeant Woodford was buried with a lightwood knot at his head, where it remained until recently.

At 149 *m.* is the junction with a dirt road.

Left here 1.5 *m.* to FORTY ACRE ROCK, a broad stretch of granite, spotted with a thin growth of trees and flowers, and lined with trickling streams. Now a popular resort for picnickers, it is associated with Indian legend and accounts of runaway slaves who hid in House Rock Dungeon, one of two caves beneath the surface. It is said that once a fox ran under the rock and came out five miles away.

At 151.5 *m.* on State 9 is the junction with State 903, unpaved.

Left on State 903 2 *m.* to the junction with a dirt road; L. here 2.1 *m.* to FLAT CREEK BAPTIST CHURCH (R), where a congregation was organized in 1776 by the dream-inspired George Pope of North Carolina. The stone above his grave here tells how he received a vision, ignored it, and was visited by disaster until a second vision persuaded him to evangelize the folk about Lynches River. His grave, marked 'G. P.,' is pierced by a maple tree. His successor was also inspired by a dream.

At 158.2 *m.* on State 9 is the junction with a rocky road.

Right here 4.5 *m.* to the place where on May 29, 1780, Colonel Tarleton massacred Colonel Abraham Buford's Virginia patriots after their surrender. Subsequently the Britisher was known as 'Bloody Tarleton' and the Americans grimly took up the war cry, 'Remember Tarleton—no quarter.' A long stone-enclosed trench holds the American dead.

LANCASTER, 167.5 *m.* (600 alt., 3,545 pop.) (*see Tour* 4), is at the junction with US 521 (*see Tour* 4).

Section b. LANCASTER to NORTH CAROLINA LINE, 79.9 m.
State 9.

From the red soil and the granite boulders, exposed like bones of an emaciated earth, the route west of LANCASTER, 0 *m.*, dips to the Catawba River, red with Piedmont topsoil, but powerful in whirling turbines. Overgrown fields give first-rate pasturage to Holstein and Guernsey cattle. From dawn to dusk the people are busy, going to the fields or hurrying into factories.

At FORT LAWN, 8 *m.* (169 pop.), named for the Fort family, is the junction with State 5 (*see Tour* 7A).

At CHESTER, 29 *m.* (487 alt., 5,528 pop.) (*see Tour* 5a), is the junction with US 21 (*see Tour* 5a) and US 521 (*see Tour* 16).

Left from Chester on State 7 3 *m.* to CHESTER STATE PARK (L). In a setting of forested hills and rolling cleared land, the park area includes a lake, a custodian's house, picnic grounds, hiking trails, and bridle paths.

LOCKHART, 49 *m.* (1,848 pop.), is busy with textile and hydroelectric industries. The 25 acres included in grounds about the homes of mill officials have been effectively landscaped. Remains of an old dam border the mill property.

ROBAT, 51.9 *m.* (55 pop.), formerly Mount Tabor, reversed the spelling of its name to avoid confusion with Mount Tabor, North Carolina.

Right from Robat on a county road to a junction with a dirt road, 1.5 *m.;* R. here 0.5 *m.* to REIDSTOWN, once an important river port and stagecoach stop between Charleston and North Carolina. Here the river makes a half-loop, attaining such depth that the bend is known as the 'bottomless horseshoe.' Tradition asserts that a monster frequently disrupted the normal peace of Reidstown by roaring beneath the water's surface.

At 3 *m.* on the county road is the junction with a dirt road; R. here 1 *m.* to the SITE OF PINCKNEYVILLE, old seat of Pinckney District, established in 1791, whose streets were named to correspond with Charleston's. All that remains of the ambitious community are a brick store and the old TOWN JAIL, with brick walls about 18 inches thick, and a heavy door between two small wooden shuttered windows. Prisoners were confined in the dungeon beneath the floor. Pinckneyville yielded to Union as county seat in 1800, but remained the principal town for another decade.

At KELLY PINCKNEY SCHOOL (R), 59 *m.*, Professor Thaddeus S. C. Lowe dropped from the heavens one April day in 1861 to startle the populace and disprove his theory that the balloon in which he ascended at Cincinnati would be swept westward by high altitude air currents. The scientist's descent, coming when sectional feeling was high, almost proved his undoing. Negro slaves, dismayed by the apparition, fled shrieking from the fields. Grim-faced farmers, grabbing pitchforks and shotguns, went in a body to investigate. Some believed the balloon to be an infernal machine, sent from the North to wreak destruction. Before the professor could declare his innocent intent, the group of excited countryfolk decided he was a spy and prepared to lynch him. But Hezekiah McKissick, a resident of the community, arriving late at the scene, recognized Lowe's Masonic sign of distress, verified the stranger's identity, and whisked him to Union where he was received by local Masons and others. Lowe made the return trip to Cincinnati by train.

At 59.1 *m.* is the junction with a dirt road.

> Right on this road 1.9 *m.* to KELTON (62 pop.), a little village in the Pea Ridge Section that got its name from a bumper pea crop in the severe drought of 1845. In the section's early history an itinerant minister remarked that when he went to Pea Ridge he always expected to be invited to gamble on a horse race or participate in a brawl before leaving. In a Kelton church, when a heated argument once began at morning services, a devout old deacon arose from his seat in the 'amen corner' and announced he was going to do for the church what the devil had never done—leave it.

At 63 *m.* is the junction with State 11 (*see Tour* 18), which unites with State 9 between this point and JONESVILLE, 64.4 *m.* (1,153 pop.) (*see Tour* 18).

At 76.2 *m.* is a junction with US 176 (*see Tour* 12*a*), which unites with State 9 for 3.3 *m.* (*see Tour* 12*a*).

In SPARTANBURG, 79.5 *m.* (875 alt., 28,723 pop.) (*see Spartanburg*), are the junctions with US 29 (*see Tour* 7), US 221 (*see Tour* 17), and US 176 (*see Tour* 12*a*).

BOILING SPRINGS, 85.3 *m.*, was an attraction to visitors as early as 1780. Today the shallows give little indication of ever having 'boiled,' but local historians assert the springs once spouted upward more than four feet, depositing clean white sands on the surrounding banks. A vengeful father whose child almost drowned in the springs tried to stem the flow by choking the holes with large rocks. Early in the twentieth century, pipe lines were run to three near-by houses, and used until installation of more modern waterworks.

At 87.6 *m.* is the junction with a paved road.

> Right here 1.2 *m.* to RAINBOW LAKE, Spartanburg city reservoir, surrounded by a 75-acre park. The hillsides sloping down to the water are terraced with walls of rock.

In the village of NEW PROSPECT, 94.2 *m.* (35 pop.), is a Baptist church (L), which occupies the SITE OF NEW PROSPECT ACADEMY, in 1825 one of the most highly rated schools in the Up Country, but closed in the War between the States.

Along an increasingly hilly route of mountain vistas the highway meanders to Pacolet River and at 99.6 *m.* recrosses the North Carolina Line, about 46 miles southeast of Asheville, North Carolina.

PART IV
Appendices

Chronology

1525	Spaniards from San Domingo, sent out by Lucas Vasquez de Ayllon and others, skirt coast almost as far north as River Jordan (probably Cape Fear River), carrying away 150 natives as slaves. Hilton Head is discovered on St. Helen's Day by Pedro de Quexos, who named it Punta de Santa Elena—by the last two words the adjacent harbor and country were long known.
1526	First settlement is made by Spaniards under Vasquez de Ayllon (abandoned after a few months); probably on Winyah Bay.
1562	French Huguenots under Jean Ribaut unsuccessfully attempt to settle on what is now Parris Island at Santa Elena, or Port Royal.
1566–87	Spaniards settle at Santa Elena (maintained about 20 years).
1629	Territory between 31st and 36th parallels and extending from sea to sea is granted by Charles I to his Attorney General, Sir Robert Heath, and named *Carolana*.
1663	Same territory is granted by Charles II to eight Lords Proprietors, who renamed it *Carolina* (limits extending in 1665 from 29° to 36° 30′). Exploration of the coast, which extends through two years, is begun by order of Lords Proprietors, as aid to future settlements.
1669	John Locke writes Fundamental Constitutions, or 'Grand Model,' for the Proprietors, who adopt it as a feudal system for Carolina.
1670	First permanent settlement, Charles Town, is located on the southern bank of the Ashley River, ten miles from its mouth.
1680	Charles Town is moved from Albemarle Point to Oyster Point, at the confluence of the Ashley and Cooper Rivers. Charles II authorizes transportation for about 45 French Protestant immigrants in H.M.S. *Richmond*.
1685–1700	Rice becomes South Carolina's staple crop, continuing as such until 1850.
1682	Province is divided into three counties: Berkeley, Craven, and Colleton.
1687	Huguenot Church is organized in Charles Town; only one of this creed extant in United States.
1696	An act is passed making all alien inhabitants freemen on petitioning the governor and swearing allegiance to the king, and granting liberty of conscience to all Christians except Papists.
1697	Congregationalists from Massachusetts, with their pastor, the Reverend Joseph Lord, settle at Dorchester, near the head of the Ashley River.
1698	Thomas Welch, South Carolina Indian trader, crosses the Missis-

sippi into the northern part of the present State of Arkansas. Free library is established for province.

1700   Estimated population of province is more than 5,000.

1702   Carolina land and sea forces, under Moore and Daniell, besiege St. Augustine in September, and burn the town but fail to capture fort. Carolinians retire upon arrival of Spanish men-of-war.

1703   Province issues first paper money May 8—£6,000 in bills of credit to pay war expenses.

1706   French-Spanish expedition against Charles Town fails. Church of England becomes the established church. Province is divided into 12 parishes.

1712–13   Colonel John Barnwell, with a force consisting of some South Carolinians and 500 friendly Indians, helps defeat the Tuscarora in North Carolina. Colonel James Moore captures Fort Nahucke, North Carolina, garrisoned by 800 Tuscarora.

1715   The Yamasee War. Four hundred colonists are killed. Indians are defeated and driven out. The territory becomes safe for new settlers.

1718   Governor Robert Johnson and Colonel William Rhett rid the Carolina coast of pirates.

1719   Proprietary government is overthrown by colonists, who set up temporary government, and ask the king to make Carolina a royal province.

1721   Crown appoints Sir Francis Nicholson as provincial governor.

1729   Crown purchases property rights of Proprietors.

1730   Robert Johnson becomes first Royal Governor of South Carolina. Nine townships are laid out to extend settlement and provide better defense for colony. First attempt made to define boundary line between North and South Carolina. (Finally settled in 1815.)

1732   Thomas Whitmarsh founds *South-Carolina Gazette;* first issue January 8.

1735   Friendly Society for the Mutual Insuring of Houses Against Fire is organized. First theater erected in Charles Town; *The Orphan* is presented the following February 12.

1739   Twenty-one whites are killed in Stono slave insurrection; 44 Negroes killed or executed.

1740   Shipbuilding begins at Charles Town and Beaufort. Nearly half of Charles Town is destroyed by fire.

1744   Eliza Lucas, after three years of experiment, brings a good crop of indigo seed to maturity. She distributes seed and persuades a number of her neighbors to join her in raising the plant, thereby beginning its commercial production in South Carolina.

1747   More than 100,000 pounds of indigo exported to England.

1753   Governor Glen secures several thousand acres from the Cherokee on the Keowee River, and erects thereon Fort Prince George.

1755   Governor Glen makes treaty with Old Hop, Cherokee chief, at Saluda Old Town whereby the Cherokee cede the land later included in Ninety Six District (10 of the present counties).

1760   Cherokee War begins, lasting into following year.

1762   St. Cecilia Society is founded as a musical organization. Exists today, however, only as a social organization.

1765   Stamped paper is stored in Fort Johnson by order of Governor Bull.

   Thomas Lynch, John Rutledge, and Christopher Gadsden attend Stamp Act Congress in New York.

1769   An association of 'Regulators,' forms in the inland settlements to suppress horse-stealing, arson, etc., and leads to a law establishing circuit courts of justice throughout the province, instead of in Charles Town alone. Province is divided into districts: Charles Town, Georgetown, Beaufort, Orangeburg, Cheraw, Camden, and Ninety Six, with circuit courts in each.

1773   Cargoes of tea sent to South Carolina are stored, and consignees restrained from offering it for sale.

   Charles Town Chamber of Commerce is organized.

1774-5   Delegates Christopher Gadsden, Thomas Lynch, Henry Middleton, Edward and John Rutledge attend Continental Congress; Middleton serves as president the last six days of the session of 1775.

1775   Estimated population of province 140,000: 60,000 whites; 80,000 Negroes.

   First Provincial Congress meets (January 11), appoints Secret Committee, and seizes public arms and ammunition.

   A Council of Safety is appointed on June 4 to manage all affairs of the colony.

   Royal administration ends September 15, when Governor Campbell dissolves assembly and flees to man-of-war in Charles Town harbor.

   First bloodshed of the Revolution takes place at Ninety Six in September.

1776   Independent government set up, with constitution, March 26, with John Rutledge as president, Henry Laurens as vice president, and William Henry Drayton as chief justice.

   June 28. British fleet of eleven warships under Admiral Parker is repulsed at Charles Town by Colonel William Moultrie from his fort of palmetto logs on Sullivan's Island.

   July 4. Thomas Heyward, Jr., Thomas Lynch, Jr., Arthur Middleton, and Edward Rutledge agree to sign the Declaration of Independence.

1777   May 20. Cherokee nation cede to South Carolina all their land except a small strip in the northwest.

   June 14. General La Fayette and Baron De Kalb land on North Island, Georgetown.

   November 1. Henry Laurens elected president of Continental Congress.

1778 Second State Constitution adopted by general assembly March 19.
It disestablishes the Anglican Church.

1780 British win at old Moncks Corner April 14.
Charles Town surrenders to British May 12, after two-month siege.
Americans win Battles of Hanging Rock July 30 and August 6.
British win Battle of Camden August 15 and 16.
Americans win Battles of Kings Mountain October 7 and Blackstock November 20.

1781 Americans win Battle of Cowpens January 17.
British win at Hobkirk's Hill April 25.
On May 12 Americans capture the British 'Post at Motte's.'
Indecisive Battle of Eutaw Springs occurs September 8.
Several engagements take place at Fort Watson and Wright's Bluff, British posts. Maham log tower, an unusual strategy, employed at the former.

1782 Charles Town is evacuated by British December 14.

1783 Name of Charles Town changed to Charleston August 13.

1786 Legislature provides for removing capital from Charleston to a point near center of State, resulting in the founding of Columbia.

1788 Constitution of the United States is ratified by the State May 23.

1790 Third constitution is adopted by State.
Census gives population as 249,073; whites 140,178, Negroes 108,895.

1800 Population (U. S. Census) 345,591: whites 196,255, Negroes 149,336.
Santee Canal is completed, connecting Charleston with the Santee River system.

1801 South Carolina College is chartered by State, and opens at Columbia in January 1805. Now University of South Carolina.
The legislature pays Miller and Whitney $50,000 to allow South Carolinians to manufacture cotton gins after their patented models for use within the State.

1808 Amendment is adopted to State constitution basing representation on white population and taxable wealth.

1810 Suffrage extended to all white men.
Census gives population as 415,115: whites 214,196, Negroes 200,919.

1811 Free school system instituted, mainly for benefit of indigent children.

1812 State Bank of South Carolina is incorporated.
John C. Calhoun, Langdon Cheves, David R. Williams, and William Lowndes take lead in bringing about the declaration of war with England, Calhoun writing the bill.
Paul Hamilton of South Carolina becomes Secretary of War.

1813 The *Decatur,* a Charleston privateer, commanded by Captain Diron, captures the British ship *Dominicia,* 15 guns and 80 men, and shortly afterwards takes the *London Trader* with a valuable cargo.

1817 President Monroe appoints John C. Calhoun Secretary of War.

1820 Census gives population as 502,741: whites 237,440, Negroes 265,301.

1822 Suppression of slave conspiracy led by Denmark Vesey, a free Negro.

1828 Andrew Jackson, native South Carolinian, is elected President of the United States; John C. Calhoun elected Vice President.

1830 Census gives population as 581,185: whites 257,863, Negroes 323,322.

Public meeting on States' rights held in Columbia September 20. Governor Hamilton advises legislature to pass Nullification Act. Famous States' rights debate takes place in Congress between Robert Y. Hayne and Daniel Webster.

1832 Legislature passes Ordinance of Nullification November 20, forbidding enforcement of Federal tariff act after February 1 of following year. (Ordinance repealed March 11, 1833, after the Clay Compromise.)

1833 The Charleston-Hamburg railroad line of 136 miles completed, at the time the longest steam railroad in the world.

1837 Joel R. Poinsett is appointed Secretary of War by President Van Buren.

1840 Census gives population as 594,398: whites 259,084, Negroes 335,314.

1841 Hugh S. Legare appointed United States Attorney General by President Tyler.

1845 Charter is granted William Gregg's cotton factory and factory village at Graniteville.

1847 Palmetto Regiment, made up of 1,100 volunteers under Colonel Pierce M. Butler, plays conspicuous part in winning Mexican War. Regiment's flag is first to fly over captured Mexico City.

1850 John C. Calhoun dies March 31, and is buried in St. Philip's churchyard, Charleston.

Population (U. S. Census) 668,507.

1852 A State convention declares right of State to secede.

1860 Population (U. S. Census) 703,708.

South Carolina secedes from Union December 20.

1861 Jan. 2. Fort Johnson, Charleston, is occupied by State troops.

Jan. 9. The *Star of the West* retires when fired upon by batteries on Morris Island and Fort Moultrie.

Jan. 11. Governor Pickens demands surrender of Fort Sumter. April 12. War between the States begins; Howitzer batteries on James Island fire on Fort Sumter; Fort Sumter is surrendered by Major Anderson.

1861–5 War between the States (*see Essays, Cities, and Tours for extensive reviews*).

With a voting population of only 47,000, South Carolina furnishes about 60,000 soldiers to Confederate armies.

1865   Jan.–March. Sherman marches across State; burns Columbia.
        April 9. War ends, with surrender of Lee at Appomattox.
        June 30. Benjamin F. Perry is appointed provisional governor by
        President Johnson.
        September. New constitution adopted, James L. Orr is elected
        governor.

1868   Jan. 14. Constitutional convention, made up of 34 whites and 63
        Negroes, meets in Charleston.
        March 17. Draft of new constitution completed.
        Constitution ratified April 14–16.
        June 25. State readmitted to Union; Negroes, carpetbaggers, and
        scalawags begin eight-year rule.

1870   Population, 705,606.

1876   General Wade Hampton elected governor; whites regain control
        of State.

1880   Population, 995,577.
        Cotton mill industry begins rapid expansion. Next three decades
        show increase from 14 mills with less than $3,000,000 capital to
        160 mills with a capital of more than $100,000,000. (*See also
        1938.*)

1886   August 31. Ninety-two persons are killed in earthquake centering
        at Charleston; property loss approximately $8,000,000.

1889   Clemson Agricultural and Mechanical College established; for-
        mally opens in 1893.

1890   Population, 1,151,149.
        The 'Farmers' Movement,' led by Benjamin R. Tillman, triumphs
        in State election. Tillman is elected governor.

1892   General assembly establishes State Dispensary for sale and control
        of liquor.

1893   Hurricane sweeps the State, causing great property damage and
        the loss of 1,000 lives along the coast.

1894   Winthrop College, the State college for women, opens at Rock
        Hill.

1895   South Carolina adopts sixth constitution, providing some limita-
        tions to suffrage and the nominating of State officials by direct
        primary.

1896   First direct primary election in which all State officials and mem-
        bers of Congress are nominated.

1898   South Carolina furnishes for the Spanish-American War, two
        regiments, an independent battalion of infantry, and a body of
        naval reserves; M. C. Butler is commissioned Major General in
        the United States Volunteer Army; Major Micah Jenkins and
        Lieutenant Victor Blue cited for heroism.

1900   Census gives population as 1,340,316: whites 557,807, Negroes
        782,321, others 188.

1901–02 Interstate and West Indian Exposition held at Charleston.

1907   Dispensary law repealed.

1910   Population, 1,515,400.

1913   National Corn Show held in Columbia.

1915   Five-year movement for establishment of social welfare agencies begins: State Board of Charities, later State Board of Public Welfare; Girls' Industrial School; and State Training School for Feeble-minded.

State-wide prohibition law enacted.

1917–18   South Carolina furnishes about 62,000 soldiers for World War. Of this number, about 57,000 serve in the Army, about 5,000 serve in the Navy, and about 300 serve in the Marine Corps. Contributions to benevolent agencies, $3,012,740; purchase of Government securities, $94,211,740. Six of the 78 Congressional Medals are won by South Carolinians. Only New York and Illinois receive a greater number.

Camp Jackson, the National Army camp, is located at Columbia, the National Guard camps at Greenville and Spartanburg, and a navy yard at Charleston.

1920   Census gives population as 1,683,724: whites 818,538, Negroes 884,719, others 467.

1924   The 6-0-1 school law provides more nearly equal educational opportunities for rich and poor school districts.

1929   State Highway Department starts State-wide highway-building program.

1930   Census gives population as 1,738,765: whites 944,040, Negroes 793,681, others 1,044. Whites predominate in population first time since 1810.

Dreher Shoals dam and power house on Saluda River near Columbia are completed; capacity 200,000 h.p.

1934   Prohibition repealed; State regulates sale of liquor.

1936   Constitutional amendment allows participation in national social security program.

1938   A 40-hour law for textile industry is enacted by legislature, but is superseded in a few months by the national 44-hour Fair Labor Standards Act. The 286 mills, operating 5,753,779 spindles and 144,296 looms, have invested capital of $198,987,588.

On September 20, two tornadoes strike Charleston; 29 killed; property damage more than $2,000,000.

1940   Population (U. S. Census) 1,905,815.

In June, Camp Jackson made permanent Army Post, renamed Fort Jackson. Eighth Division and later, Thirtieth Division, stationed here.

On August 12, hurricane lashes coast; Beaufort, Edisto Island, and Charleston hardest hit; about 40 killed; property damage nearly $5,000,000. Damage to crops over State estimated at $5,000,000.

Bibliography

These titles are listed merely as suggestions of additional information for those who wish to know more about South Carolina. In no sense are they a bibliography of sources used in the compilation of the Guide; to give them would require more than another volume. If those who have read our guide are induced to pursue their special interests further by utilizing this list, we feel that we have done them and our State both a service.

GENERAL DESCRIPTION

Ball, William Watts. *The State That Forgot: South Carolina's Surrender to Democracy.* Indianapolis, The Bobbs-Merrill Co., 1932. 307 p.

Mills, Robert. *Statistics of South Carolina.* Charleston, S. C., Hurlbut & Lloyd, 1826. 782 p. A general and particular survey of the natural resources, and of the civil and military history of the State.

———— *Atlas of the State of South Carolina.* Baltimore, Toy, 1825. A new edition of Mills' Atlas has been prepared by Lucy Hampton Bostick and Fant H. Thornley in a volume containing maps of the 28 districts into which the State was divided at that time (1825) and a hand-colored map showing all the districts. Columbia, Bostick and Thornley, 1938.

Williams, George Croft, *Social Problems of South Carolina.* Columbia, S. C., The State Co., 1928. 194 p. A brief but keen analysis of the State's maladjustments.

NATURAL RESOURCES

Bagley, W. S. *South Carolina Clays.* Bull. 708, Washington, Government Printing Office, 1922. 314 p.

Coker, William Chambers, and Henry Roland Totten. *Trees of the Southeastern States.* Chapel Hill, Univ. of N. C. Press, 1934. 399 p.

Gee, Wilson Parham. *South Carolina Botanists.* Columbia, S. C., Univ. Press, 1918. 52 p. Bull. 72, with biography and bibliography.

Holbrook, John Edwards. *Ichthyology of South Carolina.* Charleston, S. C., Russell & Jones, 1860. 205 p., 28 colored plates.

Sloan, Earl. *Catalogue of the Mineral Localities of South Carolina.* Columbia, The State Co., 1908. 505 p., plates, maps.

South Carolina State Board of Agriculture. *Resources, Industries, Institutions, and Population of South Carolina.* Charleston, Walker, Evans & Cogswell, 1883. 726 p., illus.

INDIANS

Adair, James. *History of the American Indians.* London, E. & C. Dilly, 1775. 464 p. Reprint by South Carolina Association of Colonial Dames of America, Johnson City, Tenn., Wautauga Press, 1930. 508 p. A portrayal of the origin, language, manners, religious and civil customs, laws, and government of the Indians of South Carolina.

Green, Edwin Luther. *Indians of South Carolina.* Columbia, S. C., Univ. Press, 1920. 81 p.

Lawson, John. *History of Carolina.* London, T. Warner & Co., 1718. 258 p., map. 'Containing the exact description and natural history of the Country; together with the present state therof, and a journal of a thousand miles travel'd thro' several nations of Indians, with account of their customs, etc.' Reprint: Raleigh, N. C., O. H. Perry & Co., 1860. 390 p.

Mooney, James. *Myths of the Cherokees.* Washington, Government Printing Office, 1897–8. 576 p. 19th annual report Bur. Amer. Ethnol., 56th Cong. 2nd Ses. part 1. House Doc. 539.

HISTORY AND BIOGRAPHY

Bartram, William. *The Travels of William Bartram.* New York, Macy-Masius, 1933. 414 p.

Boddie, William Willis. *History of Williamsburg.* Columbia, The State Co., 1923. The first settlers of this county; its social, economic, and political data.

Carroll, Bartholomew Rivers. *Historical Collections of South Carolina.* New York, Harper, 1836. 2 vol., 1106 p. Embraces reprints of many rare and valuable pamphlets, and other documents relating to the history of the State from its first discovery to its independence in 1776, nature of soil, climate, resources, and social elements.

Gregg, Rev. Alexander. *History of the Old Cheraws.* Columbia, reprinted by The State Co., 1905. 627 p. A history of the Pee Dee section from its earliest settlement through the Revolution; also of the aborigines there; notices of families and sketches of individuals.

Hennig, Helen Kohn, ed. *Columbia, Capital City of South Carolina, 1786–1936.* Columbia, R. L. Bryan Co., 1936. 429 p., illus. A description of the historical and contemporary aspects of Columbia's institutional, economic, social, and cultural life.

Hughson, Shirley Carter. *The Carolina Pirates and Colonial Commerce, 1670–1740.* Baltimore, Johns Hopkins Press, 1874. 134 p. A study in historical and political science.

Houston, David Franklin. *A Critical Study of Nullification in South Carolina.* New York, Longmans, Green & Co., 1896. 169 p.

Jervey, Theodore Dehon. *Robert Y. Hayne and His Times.* New York, Macmillan, 1909. 555 p., illus. Describes the issues of Federal and State relations during the first five decades of the State's constitutional history, and her influence on the Union.

Kennedy, Robert M., and Thomas J. Kirkland. *Historic Camden*. Columbia, The State Co., 1905. 2 vol., 907 p. Historic incidents of the settlement and growth of Camden, also numerous genealogies of old families.

Logan, John H. *History of the Upper Country of South Carolina*. Charleston, Courtney & Co., 1859. 521 p. Covers the early period to the close of the Revolution in the upper part of the State.

McCrady, Edward. Vol. 1. *History of South Carolina under the Proprietary Government*, 1670–1719. New York, Macmillan, 1897. 762 p. Vol. 2. *History of South Carolina under the Royal Government*, 1719–1776. New York, Macmillan, 1899. 847 p. Vol. 3. *History of South Carolina in the Revolution*, 1775–1780. New York, Macmillan, 1901. 899 p. Vol. 4. *History of South Carolina in the Revolution*, 1780–1783. New York, Macmillan, 1902. 787 p.

Mitchell, Broadus. *William Gregg, Factory Master of the Old South*. Chapel Hill, Univ. of N. C. Press, 1928. 331 p. The founder of the cotton mills in the vicinity of Graniteville in the 1840's, pictured as a forerunner of the new industrial era in the South.

Montgomery, Mabel. *Worthwhile South Carolinians*. Columbia, The State Co., 1934. 48 p. Biographical sketches in vivid and simple style adapted to younger children.

Ramsay, David. *History of South Carolina from the First Settlement in 1670 to the year 1808*. Newberry, S. C., W. J. Duffie, 1858. 579 p.

Ravenel, Mrs. Harriett Horry. *Eliza Pinckney*. New York, Scribner's, 1896. 331 p. The story of the pioneer of indigo culture, with side lights on Colonial and Revolutionary problems; depicts the Southern matron of that era.

Rippy, James Fred. *Joel R. Poinsett, Versatile American*. Durham, N. C., Duke Univ. Press, 1935. 257 p.

Simkins, Francis Butler, and Robert Hilliard Woody. *South Carolina During Reconstruction*. Chapel Hill, Univ. of N. C. Press, 1932. 610 p., illus., maps.

Simkins, Francis Butler. *The Tillman Movement in South Carolina*. Durham, N. C., Duke Univ. Press, 1926. 274 p. This movement, sometimes called the 'Farmers' Movement,' instituted a new spirit and leadership.

Simms, William Gilmore. *Life of Francis Marion*. New York, Darby & Jackson, 1858. 347 p. A vivid portrayal of the 'Swamp Fox' and his activities during the Revolution.

Stoney, Samuel Gaillard. *Plantations of the Carolina Low Country*. Charleston, S. C. Published by Carolina Art Association, 1938. Sketch of country and its people from first settlers; architectural trends, with history of buildings by periods; photos, floor plans, and elevations.

Todd, John R., and Francis M. Hutson. *Prince William's Parish and Plantations*. Richmond, Garrett & Massie, 1935. 265 p., illus., maps, diagrams.

Wallace, David Duncan. *History of South Carolina*. New York, American Historical Society, Inc., 1934. 4 vol., illus., maps. A comprehensive account of the State from its earliest times; Vol. 2 gives account of canal building; Vol. 4 is biographical.

———— *Life of Henry Laurens*, with a sketch of the life of Lieutenant Colonel John Laurens. New York, Putnam, 1915. 532 p. The life of this importer and commission merchant portrays the economic and political issues of his era.

Wooten, Bayard, and Samuel G. Stoney. *Charleston; Azaleas and Old Bricks*. Boston, Houghton Mifflin Co., 1937. 147 p., illus., 61 plates. A description of Charleston life, gardens, and architecture.

THE NEGRO

Brawley, Benjamin G. *A Social History of the American Negro*. New York, Macmillan, 1921. 420 p. A history of the Negro problem in the United States.

Doyle, Bertram Wilbur. *The Etiquette of Race Relations in the South*. Chicago, Univ. Chicago, 1937. 249 p. Analysis of formalities and proprieties of relations between the planter, poor white, and Negro of the Old South, and their present Nation-wide acceptance.

Phillips, Ulrich Bonnell. *American Negro Slavery*. New York, Appleton, 1918. 529 p. A survey of the supply, employment, and control of Negro labor as determined by the plantation regime.

Woofter, T. J., Jr. *Black Yeomanry*. New York, Henry Holt, 1930. 291 p. Life as depicted on St. Helena, typical along the Carolina coast.

AGRICULTURE

Derrick, Samuel M. *Farm Tenure in South Carolina*. Columbia, Univ. of S. C. Press. Bull. 89, August 1920. 32 p.

Doar, David. *Rice and Rice Planting in the South Carolina Low Country*. Charleston, The Charleston Museum, 1936. 70 p., plates, maps, diagrams.

Frayser, Mary E. *A Study of Expenditures for Family Living by 46 South Carolina Rural Families*. Clemson College, 1934. Bull. 299.

Heyward, Duncan Clinch. *Seed from Madagascar*. Chapel Hill, Univ. of N. C. Press, 1937. 256 p., illus. Rice culture on the Combahee River as typical of the industry on the coast.

Johnson, Charles S., Edwin R. Embree, and W. W. Alexander. *The Collapse of Cotton Tenancy*. Chapel Hill, Univ. of N. C. Press, 1935. 81 p. Summary of field studies and statistical surveys 1933–5.

State Agricultural & Mechanical Society of South Carolina. *A History of the Society from 1839 to 1845*. Columbia, R. L. Bryan Co., 1916.

INDUSTRY AND LABOR

Jacobs, William Plumer. *Problems of the Cotton Manufacturer in South Carolina*. Clinton, S. C., Jacobs & Co. Press, 1932. 193 p. A portrayal through narrative, photographs, pictographs, and statistic tables.

Kohn, August. *The Cotton Mills of South Carolina*. Charleston, Press of Daggett Printing Co., 1907. 238 p. Republished from the *News and Courier* files. Issued by the S. C. Dept. of Agri., Com., & Immigration.

A special investigation of the history and current operations of the cotton mills of the State.

Potwin, Marjorie Adella. *Cotton Mill People of the Piedmont*. New York, Columbia Univ. Press, 1927. 166 p. A study in social change.

Snowden, Yates. *Notes on Labor Organizations in South Carolina, 1742–1861*. Columbia, Univ. of S. C. Press. Bull. 38, July 1914. 54 p., illus.

TRANSPORTATION

Derrick, Samuel M. *Centennial History of South Carolina Railroad*. Columbia, The State Co., 1930. 335 p., illus., maps.

Phillips, Ulrich Bonnell. *A History of Transportation in the Eastern Cotton Belt to 1860*. New York, Columbia Univ. Press, 1908. 405 p. A review of transportation in relation to economic conditions and problems.

EDUCATION

Gray, W. S., and Wil Lou, and Tilton J. Warren. *The Opportunity Schools of South Carolina*. New York, American Association for Adult Education, 1932. 141 p. An experimental study of adult education conducted by the Department of Education of South Carolina.

Meriwether, Colyer. *History of Higher Education in South Carolina*. Washington, Government Printing Office, 1889. 247 p. Containing a sketch of the free school system.

Thompson, Henry T. *The Foundation of the Public School System of South Carolina*. Columbia, R. L. Bryan Co., 1927. 237 p.

RELIGION

Bernheim, Gotthardt D. *History of the German Settlements and of the Lutheran Church in North and South Carolina*. Philadelphia, Lutheran Book Store, 1872. 557 p. An account of the German, Swiss, and Dutch settlements up to middle of nineteenth century.

Chreitzberg, Abel M. *Early Methodism in the Carolinas*. Nashville, Pub. House M. E. Church, South, 1897. 264 p.

Dalcho, Frederick. *History of the Protestant Episcopal Church of South Carolina*. Charleston, E. Thayer, 1820. 621 p. In which civil affairs are interwoven with church.

Elzas, Barnett A. *The Jews of South Carolina from the Earliest Times to the Present Day*. Philadelphia, Lippincott, 1905. 353 p.

Hirsch, Arthur Henry. *The Huguenots of Colonial South Carolina*. Durham, Duke Univ. Press, 1928. 338 p., maps, plans. The religious, social, and economic contributions of the Huguenots in South Carolina.

Jones, Frank Dudley, and W. H. Mills, eds. *History of the Presbyterian Church in South Carolina since 1850*. Columbia, R. L. Bryan Co., 1926. 1094 p. Emphasizes Presbyterian activities in education, and gives history of churches by Presbyteries.

Lathan, Robert. *History of the Associate Reformed Synod of the South, to which is prefixed a History of the Associate Presbyterian and the Re-formed Presbyterian Churches.* Harrisburg, Pa. Published by the author, 1882. 418 p.

O'Connell, Jeremiah Joseph. *Catholicity in the Carolinas and Georgia; Leaves of Its History,* A.D. 1820–1878. New York, D. & J. Sadlier & Co., 1879. 647 p.

Townsend, Leah. *South Carolina Baptists,* 1670–1805. Florence, S. C., Florence Printing Co., 1935. 391 p. The organization and problems of the Baptists in the State.

FOLKLORE

Hawkins, John. 'Magical Medical Practice in South Carolina.' Popular Science Monthly. Vol. 70, February 1907. pp. 165–74.

Smith, Reed. *Gullah.* Columbia, Univ. of S. C. Press, Bull. 190. 45 p. The dialect of the Negroes of the coast and sea islands; some spirituals.

—— (ed.) *South Carolina Ballads.* Cambridge, Harvard Univ. Press, 1928. 174 p. With a study of the traditional ballad and music of today.

SPORTS

Elliott, William. *Carolina Sports by Land and Water.* Charleston, Burges & James, 1846. 172 p. Incidents of devil fishing, wildcat and bear hunting.

Rutledge, Archibald Hamilton. *Plantation Game Trails.* Boston, Houghton Mifflin Co., 1921. 300 p.

Smith, Harry W. *Life and Sports at Aiken and Those Who Made It.* New York, Derrydale Press, 1935. 237 p., illus. Horse racing, polo, etc.

LITERATURE

Bennett, John. *The Treasure of Peyre Gaillard.* New York, Century Co., 1906. 370 p. An account of the recovery, on a South Carolina plantation, of a treasure which had remained buried and lost in a vast swamp for more than 100 years.

Galsworthy, John. *A Hedonist (in Caravan).* New York, Scribner's, 1925. Contains a description of Magnolia Gardens.

Gonzales, Ambrose. *The Black Border.* Columbia, The State Co., 1922. 348 p. Gullah stories of the Carolina Coast.

Griswold, Francis. *The Tides of Malvern.* New York, W. Morrow & Co., 1930. 333 p. A story of divided family loyalty, with setting near Charleston.

Heyward, DuBose. *Porgy.* Garden City, N. Y., Doubleday, Doran & Co., 1928. 196 p. The Negro beggar of Charleston.

McCants, Elliott Crayton. *White Oak Farm.* New York, Longmans, Green & Co., 1928. 240 p. Plantation life and problems during Reconstruction.

Peterkin, Julia Mood. *Scarlet Sister Mary.* Indianapolis, Bobbs-Merrill Co., 1928. Negro life on isolated plantations.

Robertson, Ben. *Traveler's Rest.* Clemson, S. C. The Cottonfield Publishers, 1938. 268 p. Pioneers in upper Carolina.

Simms, William Gilmore. *The Yemassee*. New York, Harper & Bros., 1835.
454 p. A romance of the early colonists and the Indians.

Timrod, Henry. *Poems*. Richmond, B. F. Johnson, 1901. 194 p. With memoirs and portrait.

Wauchope, George Armstrong. *Writers of South Carolina*. Columbia, The State Co., 1910. 420 p. A critical introduction, biographical sketches, and selections in prose and verse.

ARTS

Prince, Alfred Coxe. *The Arts and Crafts in Philadelphia, Maryland and South Carolina*. Topsfield, Mass., Wayside Press, 1929. Series 1, 323 p. Series 2, 259 p.

Salley, Alexander S., Jr. 'Art in the Province of South Carolina.' Columbia, The State Co., 1935.

Snowden, Yates. 'South Carolina Painters and Pictures.' Columbia, The State Co., 1912.

Whele, Harry B., and Theodore Bolton. *American Miniatures, 1730–1850*. Garden City, N. Y., Doubleday, Page & Co., 1927. 127 p. 173 portraits selected, with descriptive accounts, and biographical dictionary of the artists.

MUSIC

Simons, Mrs. Elizabeth Potter. *Music in Charleston from 1732 to 1919*. Charleston, J. J. Furlong & Son, 1927. 86 p.

Smythe, Augustine T., Herbert Ravenel Sass, and others. *The Carolina Low Country*. New York, Macmillan, 1931. 327 p., illus., by Anna H. Taylor, A. T. S. Stoney, and others. Narrative and descriptive of Charleston plantation life, Negro life, and Negro spirituals with words and music.

ARCHITECTURE

Casey, William. *Charleston Doorways; Entrance Motives from a South Carolina City*. New York, F. R. Whitehead, 1928. 264 p.

Leiding, Harriette Kershaw. *Historic Houses of South Carolina*. Philadelphia, Lippincott, 1921. 318 p., illus. Historic and architectural details of houses.

Rines, Edward Francis. *Old Historic Churches of America—Their Romantic History and Their Traditions*. New York, Macmillan, 1936. 373 p. Churches of South Carolina described, pp. 218–39.

Salley, Alexander S., Jr. *The State Houses of South Carolina, 1751–1936*. Columbia, Cary Printing Co., 1936. 39 p. History, with pictures of each building.

Simons, Albert, and Samuel Lapham, Jr., eds. *Charleston Architects and Charleston Architecture*. New York, Press of the American Institute of Architecture, Inc., 1927. Vol. 1, 200 p.

DRAMA

Willis, Eola. *Charleston Stage in the XVIII Century*. Columbia, The State Co., 1927. 483 p. With social settings of the times.

HANDICRAFTS

Rose, Jennie Haskell. 'Some Charleston Silversmiths and Their Work.' Antiques Magazine. Vol. 13, No. 4. April 1928. pp. 301–7. Illus.

Simons, Albert, and Samuel Lapham. 'Early Iron Work in Charleston.' New York, Roger & Mason Co., Architectural Forum, 1926. April 1. pp. 233–42.

COOKERY

Rhett, Mrs. Blanche, comp., and Lettie Gay, ed. *200 Years of Charleston Cooking*. New York, J. Cape and H. Smith, 1930. 289 p.

GARDENS

Duncan, Francis. 'An Old Time Garden.' Century Magazine, Oct. 1910. pp. 803–11. Description of Middleton Gardens near Charleston.

Hemingway, Laura Cromer. 'The Huntingtons Donate Brookgreen to State.' Columbia, The State, March 21, 1936. Description of gardens and museum near Georgetown.

Shaffer, Edward Terry Hendri. *Carolina Gardens*. New York, Huntington Press, 1937. 289 p. The history, romance, and traditions of many gardens of two States through more than two centuries.

List of Consultants

Anderson, R. L., Department of Architecture, Clemson College
Bass, Robert, Department of English, University of South Carolina
Black, Frank, Statistician, United States Department of Agriculture
Blanding, J. Douglas, Educator, Sumter
Brearley, H. C., formerly of Department of Sociology, Clemson College
Buie, T. S., Regional Director, United States Soil Conservation Department of Agriculture, Spartanburg
Burton, E. Milby, Director, Charleston Museum
Calhoun, F. H. H., Department of Geology, Clemson College
Carlisle, H. B., Lawyer, Spartanburg
Chamberlain, E. B., Scientific Department, Charleston Museum
Coker, W. C., Keenan Professor of Botany, University of North Carolina
Cunningham, J. Whitney, former President, South Carolina Chapter American Institute of Architects
Davis, Henry E., Lawyer, Florence
Derieux, James C., Associate Editor of *The State*, Columbia
Dozier, James C., Adjutant General of South Carolina
Easterby, J. H., Department of History, College of Charleston
Gilchrist, A. D., Architect, Rock Hill
Gray, Wil Lou, Supervisor Adult Schools, South Carolina Department of Education
Green, E. L., Department of Ancient Languages, University of South Carolina
Harley, W. Rhett, South Carolina Commissioner of Labor
Harmon, G. Thomas, Architect, Hartsville
Hennig, Helen Kohn, Author, Columbia
Herbert, W. C., South Carolina Railroad Commissioner
Heyward, Katharine, Department of Art, University of South Carolina
Holmes, A. G., Department of History, Clemson College
Hope, J. H., Superintendent, South Carolina Department of Education
Horton, McDavid, Editor of *The State*, Columbia
Irvin, Willis, Architect, Aiken
Jacobs, William P., Secretary and Treasurer, South Carolina Cotton Manufacturers' Association
Jones, F. Dudley, Past President, South Carolina Historical Society
Jones, J. Roy, South Carolina Commissioner of Agriculture
Lafaye, Robert S., Architect, Columbia
Lapham, Samuel J., former President, South Carolina Chapter American Institute of Architects
Levin, J. D., Architect, Beaufort

487

Lewis, D. L., South Carolina Department of Education

Lucas, Mrs. Cora Cox, former President, South Carolina Federation of Music Clubs

McKissick, J. Rion, President, University of South Carolina

Martin, Dexter, Secretary South Carolina Aeronautic Commission

Meeks, B. S., State Railroad Representative for *The American Guide Series*

Merchant, G. C., United States Weather Bureau

Meriwether, R. L., Head Department of History, University of South Carolina

Milling, Dr. Chapman J., Author and Naturalist, Columbia

Mills, W. H., Department of Rural Sociology, Clemson College

Mitcham, R. W., Architect, Camden

Moise, L. C., Supervisor Music, Public Schools, Sumter

Moore, W. Bedford, Jr., Columbia

Nates, J. W., former South Carolina Commissioner of Labor

Richardson, A. A., South Carolina Game Warden

Salley, A. S., Jr., Secretary South Carolina Historical Commission

Sass, Herbert Ravenel, Author and Naturalist, Charleston

Sears, H. M., Bureau of Forestry Service, United States Department of Agriculture

Smith, H. A., State Forester

Smith, Reed, Author and Authority on folk-lore; Dean of Graduate School, University of South Carolina

Sprunt, Alexander, Jr., Supervisor Southern Sanctuaries, National Audubon Societies, Charleston

Sutherland, J. L., Assistant Supervisor Agriculture, South Carolina Department of Education

Taber, Stephen, State Geologist and Professor of Geology and Mineralogy, University of South Carolina

Wallace, D. D., Historian, Wofford College, Spartanburg

Whitelaw, Robert N. S., Director, Gibbes Art Gallery, Charleston

Williams, G. Croft, Head Department of Sociology, University of South Carolina

Williams, W. P., Architect, Spartanburg

Negro:

Birnie, W. C., Consultant, Sumter

Johnson, C. A., Principal Booker T. Washington High School, Columbia

Reed, O. D., former State Supervisor Vocational Negro Training under FERA, Columbia

Simpson, A. L., President, Allen University, Columbia

Starks, J. J., President, Benedict College, Columbia

1940 *Census Figures*

(The following figures are taken from the preliminary report of the Census Bureau and are subject to revision. Figures for towns and villages not listed were not available in time for publication.)

Abbeville	4,927	Fort Lawn	167	Newberry	7,511
Aiken	5,918	Fort Mill	2,925	Ninety Six	1,435
Allendale	2,215	Fort Motte	1,604	North	732
Anderson	19,414	Fountain Inn	1,346	North Augusta	2,627
Appleton	198			Norway	488
		Gaffney	7,620		
Bamberg	3,004	Georgetown	5,552	Orangeburg	10,510
Barnwell	1,921	Glenn Springs	130		
Batesburg (Lexing-		Gray Court	402	Pageland	989
ton County)	2,929	Greenville	34,743	Pamplico	555
Beaufort	3,163	Greenwood	13,018	Patrick	270
Belton	2,114	Greer	2,935	Pendleton	1,279
Bennettsville	4,863			Pickens	1,636
Bishopville	2,739	Hampton	997	Port Royal	340
Blacksburg	1,916	Hardeeville	611	Prosperity	718
Blackville	1,457	Harleyville	380		
Bluffton	459	Hartsville	5,370	Ridgeland	1,021
Bonneau	351	Hickory Grove	272	Rock Hill	14,868
Bowman	799	Holly Hill	1,067		
Branchville	1,350	Honea Path	2,764	Saluda	1,512
				Seneca	2,156
Calhoun Falls	1,832	Iva	1,254	Sharon	388
Camden	5,734			Simpsonville	1,295
Carlisle	303	Jefferson	546	Smyrna	129
Cayce	1,476	Jonesville	1,182	Spartanburg	32,521
Central	1,496			St. George	1,908
Chapin	311	Kershaw	1,260	St. Matthews	2,193
Charleston	70,869	Kingstree	3,127	St. Stephens	1,179
Cheraw	5,152			Summerton	968
Chester	6,383	Lake City	2,519	Summerville	3,053
Clinton	5,680	Lancaster	4,406	Sumter	16,166
Clover	3,066	Landrum	1,287	Swansea	950
Columbia	60,505	Latta	1,299		
Conway	4,915	Laurens	6,838	Timmonsville	1,976
Cowpens	1,338	Leesville	1,218	Trenton	407
		Lexington	1,033		
Darlington	6,235	Liberty	2,240	Union	8,181
Denmark	2,056	Little Mountain	251		
Dillon	3,857	Loris	1,234	Walhalla	2,797
Donalds	271	Lowry's	315	Walterboro	3,372
				West Columbia	1,744
Easley	5,180	Manning	2,381	Westminster	2,015
Eau Claire	3,499	Marion	5,749	West Union	449
Ebenezer	409	Mayesville	519	White Rock	141
Edgefield	2,116	McBee	587	Whitmire	3,272
Ellenton	532	McCall	2,390	Williamston	2,509
Enoree	3,478	McClellanville	427	Williston	1,107
Estill	1,278	McCormick	1,456	Winnsboro	3,174
		Moncks Corner	1,107	Woodruff	3,478
Fairfax	1,381	Mount Pleasant	2,003		
Florence	16,098	Mullins	4,395	York	3,344
		Myrtle Beach	1,600		

Index

Assistant at desk will please see that map is in back
of book before it is charged out or checked in.